# Lecture Notes
# in Business Information Processing 100

## Series Editors

Wil van der Aalst
*Eindhoven Technical University, The Netherlands*
John Mylopoulos
*University of Trento, Italy*
Michael Rosemann
*Queensland University of Technology, Brisbane, Qld, Australia*
Michael J. Shaw
*University of Illinois, Urbana-Champaign, IL, USA*
Clemens Szyperski
*Microsoft Research, Redmond, WA, USA*

Florian Daniel
Kamel Barkaoui
Schahram Dustdar (Eds.)

# Business Process Management Workshops

BPM 2011 International Workshops
Clermont-Ferrand, France, August 29, 2011
Revised Selected Papers, Part II

 Springer

Volume Editors

Florian Daniel
University of Trento
Povo, Italy
E-mail: daniel@disi.unitn.it

Kamel Barkaoui
CNAM-CEDRIC
Paris, France
E-mail: kamel.barkaoui@cnam.fr

Schahram Dustdar
Vienna University of Technology
Vienna, Austria
E-mail: dustdar@infosys.tuwien.ac.at

ISSN 1865-1348                e-ISSN 1865-1356
ISBN 978-3-642-28114-3      e-ISBN 978-3-642-28115-0
DOI 10.1007/978-3-642-28115-0
Springer Heidelberg Dordrecht London New York

Library of Congress Control Number: 2011945866

ACM Computing Classification (1998): J.1, H.4, D.2, J.3

*Typesetting:* Camera-ready by author, data conversion by Scientific Publishing Services, Chennai, India

Printed on acid-free paper

Springer is part of Springer Science+Business Media (www.springer.com)

# Foreword

These volumes collects the proceedings of the workshops held on August 29, 2011, in conjunction with the 9th International Conference on Business Process Management (BPM 2011), which took place in Clermont-Ferrand, France. The proceedings are so-called post-workshop proceedings, in that the authors were allowed to revise and improve their papers even after the workshops, so as to take into account the feedback obtained from the audience during their presentations.

Due to its interdisciplinary nature, which naturally involves researchers and practitioners alike, the BPM conference has traditionally been perceived as a premium event to co-locate a workshop with – both by academia and by industry. The 2011 edition of the conference was no exception: its call for workshop proposals attracted 17 proposals with topics ranging from (among others) traditional BPM concerns like design and analysis to novel, emerging concerns like social BPM and compliance. Given the high quality of the submissions, selecting candidate workshops and assembling the best mix of workshops was not an easy task. Eventually, the following 12 workshops were selected for co-location with BPM 2011:

- *7th International Workshop on Business Process Design (BPD 2011)* – organized by Marta Indulska, Michael Rosemann, and Michael zur Muehlen.

  BPD 2011 focused on the design, innovation, evaluation, and comparison of process improvement techniques and tools to comprehensively cover process enhancement approaches such as, for example, TRIZ, reference (best practice) models, process innovation, or resource-based approaches to process improvement.

- *7th International Workshop on Business Process Intelligence (BPI 2011)* – organized by Boudewijn van Dongen, Diogo Ferreira, and Barbara Weber.

  BPI 2011 aimed to bring together practitioners and researchers from different communities such as BPM, information systems research, business administration, software engineering, artificial intelligence, process and data mining with the goal to provide a better understanding of techniques and algorithms to support a company's processes at build-time and the way they are handled at run-time.

- *4th International Workshop on Business Process Management and Social Software (BPMS2 2011)* – organized by Selmin Nurcan and Rainer Schmidt.

  The objective of BPMS2 2011 was to explore how social software interacts with business process management, how business process management has to change to comply with weak ties, social production, egalitarianism and mutual service, and how business processes may profit from these principles.

- *Second International Workshop on Cross-Enterprise Collaboration (CEC 2011)* – organized by Daniel Oppenheim, Francisco Curbera, Frank Leymann, Dimka Karastoyanova, Alex Norta, and Lav R. Varshney.

CEC 2011 explored the management, coordination, and optimization of complex end-to-end processes carried out collaboratively by people across enterprise boundaries. The goal of the workshop was to foster research in the emerging area of cross-enterprise collaboration.

– *Second International Workshop on Empirical Research in Business Process Management (ER-BPM 2011)* – organized by Bela Mutschler, Jan Recker, and Roel Wieringa.

ER-BPM 2011 stimulated empirical research aimed at the better understanding of the problems, challenges, and existing solutions in the BPM field. The workshop provided an interdisciplinary forum for both researchers and practitioners.

– *5th International Workshop on Event-Driven Business Process Management (edBPM 2011)* – organized by Nenad Stojanovic, Opher Etzion, Adrian Paschke, and Christian Janiesch.

edBPM 2011 continued its tradition of previous editions in exchanging novel ideas, methods, tools, and solutions for event-driven BPM, with the main goal to connect research and industry in better understanding what can be done from the research point of view and what is the need from the industry/business point of view.

– *First International Workshop on Process Model Collections (PMC 2011)* – organized by Hajo Reijers, Marcello La Rosa, and Remco Dijkman.

PMB 2011 aimed to attract novel research in the area of business process model collections. Among its topics, we find concerns related to process model repositories such as version management, efficient storage, querying, and retrieval of process models.

– *First International Workshop on Process-Aware Logistics Systems (PALS 2011)* – organized by Nejib Ben Hadj-Alouane, Ramzi Hammami, Samir Tata, and Moez Yeddes.

PALS 2011 dealt with problems related to the design and optimization of global logistics systems, from a business process management perspective. It is dedicated to exploring and mastering the tools needed for operating, reconfiguring and, in general, making decisions within logistics-based systems.

– *4th International Workshop on Process-Oriented Information Systems in Healthcare (ProHealth 2011)* – organized by Mor Peleg, Richard Lenz, and Manfred Reichert.

ProHealth 2011 focused on the potential and the limitations of IT support for healthcare processes. The workshop provided a forum wherein challenges, paradigms, and tools for optimized process support in healthcare were debated.

– *Second International Workshop on Reuse in Business Process Management (rBPM 2011)* – organized by Marcelo Fantinato, Maria Beatriz Felgar de Toledo, Itana Maria de Souza Gimenes, Lucinéia Heloisa Thom, and Cirano Iochpe.

rBPM 2011 focused on exploring any type of reuse in the BPM domain at its various levels: the basic service-oriented foundation level; the service composition level; the management and monitoring upper level; and, the quality of service and semantics orthogonal level.

- *Second International Workshop on Traceability and Compliance of Semi-Structured Processes (TC4SP 2011)* – organized by Francisco Curbera, Frank Leymann, Hamid Motahari Nezhad, and Beth Plale.

  TC4SP 2011 focused on processes whose lifecycle is not fully driven by a formal process model and a business process management system (BPMS). These processes do not benefit from the advantages of BPMSs, but have the same need for transparency, monitoring, compliance management, and root cause analysis capabilities as fully structured processes.

- *First International Workshop on Workflow Security Audit and Certification (WfSAC 2011)* – organized by Rafael Accorsi and Wil van der Aalst.

  WfSAC 2011 brought together researchers working on innovative, well-founded methods for workflow security audit and certification and industry applying these methods in practical cases.

With these 12 workshops, the BPM 2011 workshop program was the largest workshop program in the history of the conference. Yet, as the unexpectedly large participation in the workshop day testifies (more than 210 registered attendees for all the workshops together), the selected workshops formed an extraordinary and balanced program of high-quality events. We are confident the reader will enjoy this volume as much as we enjoyed organizing this outstanding program and assembling its proceedings.

Of course, we did not organize everything on our own. Many people of the BPM 2011 Organizing Committee contributed to the success of the workshop program. We would particularly like to thank the General Chairs, Farouk Toumani and Mohand-Said Hacid, for involving us in this unique event, the Organizing Chairs, Michel Schneider and Raoul Medina, for the smooth management of all on-site issues, the workshop organizers for managing their workshops and diligently answering the wealth of emails we sent around, and, finally, the authors for presenting their research and work at the BPM 2011 workshops and actually making all this possible.

September 2011

Florian Daniel
Kamel Barkaoui
Schahram Dustdar

# Preface

The following preface is a collection of the prefaces of the post-workshop proceedings of the individual workshops. The actual workshop papers, grouped by event, form the body of these volumes.

## 7th International Workshop on Business Process Design (BPD 2011)

**Organizers:** Marta Indulska, Michael Rosemann, and Michael zur Muehlen

The 2011 International Workshop on Business Process Design (BPD) was the seventh consecutive workshop in its series, organized in conjunction with the 9th International Conference on Business Process Management, held in Clermont-Ferrand, France, 2011. The workshop was born out of the recognition that designing a process that improves organizational performance is a challenging task that requires a plethora of inputs (for example, organizational strategies, goals, constraints, and IT capabilities, to name a few). This task is the most value-adding step in the process lifecycle, yet it has attracted only limited academic contributions thus far. Accordingly, since the workshop's inception in 2005, the workshop has provided a forum for researchers interested in all aspects of design, innovation, evaluation, and comparison of process improvement techniques and tools.

The BPD 2011 proceedings represent a collection of six excellent research papers that were presented in extended presentation and discussion sessions during the BPM2011 conference. The paper selection was based on a rigorous double-blind process, which resulted in a 32% acceptance rate. As Organizing Chairs of the BPD workshop, we would like to sincerely thank the Program Committee for their thorough reviews of BPD2011 submissions. We would like to extend our thanks to the authors for their presentations, and to all participants of the workshop for their comments on the presented papers. We would also like to thank Hajo Reijers, Eindhoven University of Technology, Germany, for his insightful keynote presentation.

September 2011

Marta Indulska
Michael Rosemann
Michael zur Muehlen

# Program Committee

| | |
|---|---|
| Hyerim Bae | Pusan National University, South Korea |
| Jyoti Bhat | Infosys, India |
| Jan vom Brocke | University of Liechtenstein |
| Jorge Cardoso | SAP Research, Dresden |
| Lilia Gzara | Grenoble Institute of Technology, France |
| Guido Governatori | NICTA, Australia |
| Paul Harmon | BPTrends, USA |
| Mathias Kirchmer | Accenture, USA |
| Thomas Kohlborn | Queensland University of Technology, Australia |
| Axel Korthaus | Victoria University, Australia |
| Agnes Koschmider | University of Karlsruhe, Germany |
| Marcello La Rosa | Queensland University of Technology, Australia |
| Jan Mendling | Vienna University of Economics and Business Administration, Austria |
| Chun Ouyang | Queensland University of Technology, Australia |
| Corina Raduescu | University of Sydney, Australia |
| Jan Recker | Queensland University of Technology, Australia |
| Stefanie Rinderle-Ma | University of Ulm, Germany |
| Shazia Sadiq | The University of Queensland, Australia |
| Stefan Seidel | Liechtenstein University, Liechtenstein |
| Norris Syed Abdullah | The University of Queensland, Australia |
| Andreas Wombacher | University of Twente, The Netherlands |
| Moe Wynn | Queensland University of Technology, Australia |

# 7th International Workshop on Business Process Intelligence (BPI 2011)

**Organizers:** Boudewijn van Dongen, Diogo R. Ferreira, and Barbara Weber

Business process intelligence (BPI) is an area that is quickly gaining interest and importance in industry and research. BPI refers to the application of various measurement and analysis techniques in the area of business process management. In practice, BPI is embodied in tools for managing process execution quality by offering several features such as analysis, prediction, monitoring, control, and optimization.

The goal of this workshop is to promote a better understanding of the techniques and algorithms to support business processes at design-time and the way they are handled at run-time. We aim to bring together practitioners and researchers from different communities, e.g., business process management, information systems, database systems, business administration, software engineering, artificial intelligence, and data mining, who share an interest in the analysis and optimization of business processes and process-aware information systems. The workshop aims at discussing the current state of ongoing research and sharing practical experiences, exchanging ideas, and setting up future research directions that better respond to real needs. In a nutshell, it serves as a forum for shaping the BPI area.

The seventh edition of this workshop attracted 16 international submissions. Each paper was reviewed by at least three members of the Program Committee. From these submissions, the top five were accepted as full papers and, in addition, another five interesting submissions were accepted as short papers for presentation at the workshop.

The papers presented at the workshop provide a mix of novel research ideas, practical applications of BPI, as well as new tool support. Ailenei, Rozinat, Eckert, and van der Aalst are motivated by the need for a systematic comparison of existing process mining tools, and their work presents a list of process mining use cases as a first step toward an evaluation framework. Swinnen, Depair, Jens, and Vanhoef present a case study on the use of process mining together with association rule mining for analyzing deviating cases. Clase and Poels describe a method to merge separate log files coming from different systems. Trkman et al. investigate the relationship between business analytics and supply chain performance. Ferreira and Alves present an approach for finding communities in the social network of process participants by means of clustering. Barba, Weber, and Del Valle introduce an approach for assisting users during process execution through a recommendation system that considers both the control-flow and the resource perspectives. Aiolli, Burratin, and Sperduti propose a metric for the comparison of business process models, which is based on the relations defined for the algorithm. Leyer and Moormann suggest the combination of process mining techniques and statistical methods to evaluate customer integration in service processes. Luengo and Sepúlveda apply clustering for the detection of different versions of a business process. Finally, Damer, Jans, Depaire, and Vanhoof propose a new compliance analysis approach based on clustering the log into homogeneous groups.

For the first time this year, the workshop was accompanied by a challenge, for which researchers and practitioners were asked to apply any BPI technique of their disposal to a real-life dataset of a Dutch academic hospital in order to get insights into the treatment processes of that hospital. We invited a jury to rank the proposals and our sponsors – Pallas Athena and Futura Process Intelligence – provided the prizes for the two best submissions.

The BPI challenge attracted three international submissions which were ranked by a jury consisting of practitioners and researchers, as well as the owner of the dataset. The jury unanimously ranked the submissions, which resulted in Filip Caron and J.C. Bose winning the challenge and receiving an iPad 2 each. These proceedings contain a two-page abstract of the two winning submissions. The jury particularly liked the fact that both authors stepped outside of the BPI domain and included knowledge from the medical domain in order to come to certain conclusions. This clearly showed that real-life analysis cannot be done only from within the academic walls, but that the strong relation between researchers and practitioners is and will stay particularly important in the field of BPI.

These proceedings additionally contain the Process Mining Manifesto, which has been jointly developed by more than 70 scientists, consultants, software vendors, and end-users in the BPI area. As part of this workshop, a meeting of the IEEE task-force was held, during which the content of the Process Mining Manifesto was discussed. This document aims to promote the area of process mining and provides a set of guiding principles and challenges.

As with previous editions of the workshop, we hope that reader will find this selection of papers useful to keep track of the latest advances in the area of BPI, and we look forward to keep bringing new advances in future editions of the BPI workshop.

September 2011

Boudewijn van Dongen
Diogo R. Ferreira
Barbara Weber

# Program Committee

| | |
|---|---|
| Wil van der Aalst | Eindhoven University of Technology, The Netherlands |
| Ana Karla Alves de Medeiros | Capgemini Consulting, The Netherlands |
| Gerardo Canfora | University of Sannio, Italy |
| Malu Castellanos | HP, USA |
| Peter Dadam | University of Ulm, Germany |
| Boudewijn van Dongen | Eindhoven University of Technology, The Netherlands |
| Diogo R. Ferreira | Technical University of Lisbon, Portugal |
| Walid Galoul | Insitut Telecom, France |
| Gianluigi Greco | University of Calabria, Italy |
| Daniela Grigori | University of Versailles, France |
| Antonella Guzzo | University of Calabria, Italy |
| Joachim Herbst | DaimlerChrysler Research and Technology, Germany |
| Chen Li | University of Twente, The Netherlands |
| Jan Mendling | Humbolt University, Germany |
| Jürgen Moormann | Frankfurt School of Finance and Management, Germany |
| Oscar Pastor Lopez | Universidad Politécnica de Valencia, Spain |
| Manfred Reichert | University of Ulm, Germany |
| Anne Rozinat | Fluxicon, The Netherlands |
| Pnina Soffer | Haifa University, Israel |
| Alessandro Sperduti | University of Padua, Italy |
| Barbara Weber | Innsbruck University, Austria |
| Hans Weigand | Infolab, Tilburg University, The Netherlands |
| Ton Weijters | Technical University of Eindhoven, The Netherlands |
| Mathias Weske | Hasso Plattner Institute at University of Potsdam, Germany |

# 4th International Workshop on Business Process Management and Social Software (BPMS2 2011)

**Organizers:** Selmin Nurcan and Rainer Schmidt

Social software[1] is a new paradigm that is spreading quickly in society, organizations, and economics. Social software has created a multitude of success stories such as wikipedia.org and the development of the Linux operating system. Therefore, more and more enterprises regard social software as a means for further improvement of their business processes and business models. For example, they integrate their customers into product development by using blogs to capture ideas for new products and features. Thus, business processes have to be adapted to new communication patterns between customers and the enterprise: for example, the communication with the customer is increasingly a bi-directional communication with the customer and among the customers. Social software also offers new possibilities to enhance business processes by improving the exchange of knowledge and information, to speed up decisions, etc.

Social software is based on four principles: weak ties, social production, egalitarianism, and mutual service provisioning.

- *Weak Ties*[2]: Weak ties are spontaneously established contacts between individuals that create new views and allow combining of competencies. Social software supports the creation of weak ties by supporting the creation of contacts on impulse between non-predetermined individuals.
- *Social Production*[3,4]: Social production is the creation of artifacts, by combining the input from independent contributors without predetermining the way to do this. By this means it is possible to integrate new and innovative contributions not identified or planned in advance. Social mechanisms such as reputation assure quality in social production in an a posteriori approach by enabling a collective evaluation by all participants.
- *Egalitarianism*: Egalitarianism is the attitude of handling individuals equally. Social software highly relies on egalitarianism and therefore strives to give all participants the same rights to contribute. This is done with the intention to encourage a maximum of contributors and to get the best solution fusioning

---

[1] R. Schmidt and S. Nurcan, "BPM and Social Software," Business Process Management Workshops, 2009, pp. 649-658.

[2] M.S. Granovetter, "The Strength of Weak Ties," American Journal of Sociology, vol. 78, 1973, S. 1360.

[3] Y. Benkler, The Wealth of Networks: How Social Production Transforms Markets and Freedom, Yale University Press, 2006.

[4] J. Surowiecki, The Wisdom of Crowds, Anchor, 2005.

a high number of contributions, thus enabling the wisdom of the crowds. Social software realizes egalitarianism by abolishing hierarchical structures, merging the roles of contributors and consumers, and introducing a culture of trust.

- *Mutual Service Provisioning*: Social software abolishes the separation of service provider and consumer by introducing the idea that service provisioning is a mutual process of service exchange. Thus both service provider and consumer (or better prosumer) provide services to one another in order to co-create value. This mutual service provisioning contrasts with the idea of industrial service provisioning, where services are produced in separation from the customer to achieve scaling effects.

To date, the interaction of social software and its underlying paradigms with business processes have not been investigated in depth. Therefore, the objective of the workshop was to explore how social software interacts with business process management, how business process management has to change to comply with weak ties, social production, egalitarianism and mutual service, and how business processes may profit from these principles.

The workshop discussed three topics:

1. New opportunities provided by social software for BPM
2. Engineering next generation of business processes: BPM 2.0?
3. Business process implementation support by social software

Based on the successful BPMS2 2008, BPMS2 2009, BPMS2 2010 workshop, the goal of this workshop was to promote the integration of business process management with social software and to enlarge the community pursuing the theme.

We wish to thank all authors for having shared their work with us, as well as the members of the BPMS2 2011 Program Committee and the workshop organizers of BPM 2011 for their help with the organization of the workshop.


September 2011                                        Selmin Nurcan
                                                     Rainer Schmidt

# Program Committee

| | |
|---|---|
| Ilia Bider | IbisSoft, Sweden |
| Jan Bosch | Intuit, Mountain View, California, USA |
| Dragan Gasevic | Athabasca University, Canada |
| Rania Khalaf | IBM T.J. Watson Research Center, USA |
| Ralf Klamma | RWTH Aachen, Germany |
| Agnes Koschmider | Karlsruhe Institute of Technology, Germany |
| Sai Peck Lee | University of Malaya, Kuala Lumpur, Malaysia |
| Gustaf Neumann | Vienna University of Economics and Business Administration, Austria |
| Selmin Nurcan | University Paris 1 Pantheon Sorbonne, France |
| Andreas Oberweis | Karlsruhe Institute of Technology, Germany |
| Gil Regev | EPFL & Itecor, Switzerland |
| Michael Rosemann | Queensland University of Technology, Australia |
| Rainer Schmidt | University of Applied Sciences, Aalen, Germany |
| Miguel-Ángel Sicilia | University of Alcalá, Madrid, Spain |
| Pnina Soffer | University of Haifa, Israel |
| Markus Strohmaier | Graz University of Technology, Austria |
| Karsten Wendland | University of Applied Sciences, Aalen, Germany |

# Second International Workshop on Cross-Enterprise Collaboration (CEC 2011)

**Organizers:** Alexander H. Norta, Daniel V. Oppenheim, Lav R. Varshney, Francisco Curbera, Dimka Karastoyanova, and Frank Leymann

On August 29, 2011, the Second International Workshop on Cross-Enterprise Collaboration (CEC) was held as part of the 9th International Conference on Business Process Management (BPM 2011) in Clermont-Ferrand, France.

Cross-enterprise collaboration (CEC) occurs when two or more organizations collaborate to realize a common goal. The move of process, work, and operations from an organization-centric environment to a collaborative ecosystem of partners and providers is becoming pervasive because many organizations find they can no longer develop all the required innovation in-house or lack necessary capabilities. Sharing the financial cost and overall risk is another important incentive for collaboration, especially in projects with a high degree of uncertainty that may require frequent change and adaptation.

The workshop focused on how to reconcile the continuum from rather informal to very strongly formalized CEC models in which the collaborating organizations utilize organization-bridging choreographies to connect with partner and/or provider in-house business processes for carrying out sourced transactions to achieve the collaboration's goal. The workshop goal was to provide a venue for academics and practitioners to establish a community for CEC with future expansion potential. Consequently, the workshop identified the state of the art, core research challenges, enterprise-collaboration models, corresponding architectures, frameworks, or methodologies.

The first workshop keynote was presented by Hamid Motahari Nezhad from HP Labs, Palo Alto, who discussed CEC in the context of multi-sourced service engagements and outlined a vision and conceptual architecture for offering the supporting technology for CEC as a service. Then there was a keynote presentation by Alex Kass from Accenture Technology Labs. This talk identified collaboration between people and between systems as two pillars of any CEC and presented a vision for a CEC platform in which technology support for knowledge sharing, process sharing, and data coupling has to be offered. The final part of the keynote talks was from Alex Norta on the completed EU-FP6 CrossWork research project on which a recently published book in the Springer *Information Systems* series was based. In this approach external processes could be defined and utilized by the collaborating organizations and then mapped to individual organizations through a layer of conceptual processes.

The subsequent paper presentations covered the following areas. First, an approach was shown by Christian Pichler et al. for creating conflict-free updates of UN/CEFACT-based cross-organizational modeling consensus. The second presentation by Jorge Roa et al. was about using colored Petri-net notation for designing collaborative business processes. The advantage of this approach is the availability of established formal verification techniques. Finally, a paper by Stefan Mutke et al. about a service-provision framework based on prior analysis and deconstruction of customer requirements focused on how to set up enterprise collaborations from the logistics domain.

September 2011

Alexander H. Norta
Daniel V. Oppenheim
Lav R. Varshney
Francisco Curbera
Dimka Karastoyanova
Frank Leymann

## Program Committee

| | |
|---|---|
| Ram Akella | University of California, Santa Cruz, USA |
| Rama Akkiraju | IBM Research, USA |
| Vasilios Andrikopoulos | Tilburg University, The Netherlands |
| Christoph Dorn | Vienna University of Technology, Austria |
| Marta Indulska | University of Queensland, Australia |
| Alex Kass | Accenture Technology Labs, USA |
| Jim Laredo | IBM Research, USA |
| Grace Lewis | Carnegie Mellon University, USA |
| Heiko Ludwig | IBM Research, USA |
| Daniel Schall | Vienna University of Technology, Austria |
| Jianwen Su | University of California, Santa Barbara, USA |
| Liang Zhang | Fudan University, China |

# Second International Workshop on Empirical Research in Business Process Management (ER-BPM 2011)

**Organizers:** Bela Mutschler, Jan Recker, and Roel Wieringa

In an effort to manage and improve business processes to enable business benefits, *business process management* (BPM) heavily relies on the use of IT-based systems. Past years have seen the emergence of holistic enterprise resource planning systems, automated workflow systems, process design tools, expert systems, virtual collaboration systems and business rule systems as process-aware information systems that enable process change and management and thereby contribute to business value generation.

BPM research has traditionally taken one of two forms. One vein of BPM research has focused on the development and extension of associated tools, methods, standards, and technologies. The other vein of BPM research has been concerned with evaluating the suitability of existing BPM technology, to build informed opinions about qualities and deficiencies of BPM practices and tools.

Over recent years, we have witnessed a growing demand for insights or evaluations of BPM technology based on dedicated empirical research strategies. Such research has only recently gained prominence in the community but is now firmly established as an important strand of research around the use of BPM, as evidenced, for example, by dedicated journal special issues on this topic[5]. The benefits of empirical research include improved problem understanding and improved insight into the performance of techniques in practice. These benefits have been demonstrated in areas like software engineering (e.g., in the context of software development processes or code reviews), information systems (e.g., in the form of theories of acceptance and use of information systems), or, indeed, business (e.g., in studies of organizational performance) for a long time, we believe, and are still under-represented in the academic field of BPM, notwithstanding the efforts made to date.

## The Workshop

The Second International Workshop on Empirical Research in Business Process Management (ER-BPM 2011) set out to be a premier forum for researchers to address the demand for further empirical research, and sought to stimulate

---

[5] Recker, J., Mutschler, B., Wieringa, R.: Empirical Research in Business Process Management: Introduction to the Special Issue. in: *Inf. Syst. E-Business Management*, 9(3), pp. 303-306 (2011).

empirical research that, in turn, can contribute to a better understanding of the problems, challenges, and existing solutions in the BPM field.

In particular, the workshop provides an interdisciplinary forum for both researchers and practitioners to improve the understanding of BPM-specific requirements, methods and theories, tools and techniques. Therefore, the workshop deals with different facets of applying and using BPM methods and technologies and strives to provide new insights into the challenges, applications, and perspectives emerging for BPM technology.

ER-BPM 2011 was the follow-up workshop of a very successful first ER-BPM workshop that took place in Ulm (Germany) in conjunction with BPM 2009. The papers from this workshop appeared as part of a dedicated book series[6], and the best papers were also published as extended articles as part of a journal special issue[1].

## The Papers in a Nutshell

At ER-BPM 2011, we accepted six papers for presentation. These articles provide a snapshot of current examples for how empirical research in BPM can be conducted, and what insights such research can uncover.

The paper by Houy et. al investigates theoretical foundations of empirical BPM research based on conceptual considerations and a review of empirical BPM literature. Their analysis clearly shows that empirical BPM research is only to a certain extent guided by existing theory. Furthermore, it can be seen that the investigated contributions often refer to theories originating from other different fields of research, like economics or sociology.

The paper by Michelberger et. al investigates fundamental issues related to process-oriented information logistics based on two exploratory case studies in the automotive and the clinical domain. Additionally, they present results of an online survey with 219 participants supporting the case study findings. Their research does not only reveal different types of process information, but also allows for the derivation of factors determining its relevance. Understanding such factors, in turn, is a fundamental prerequisite to realize effective process-oriented information logistics.

In the third paper, Luebbe and Weske present a new technique for process co-creation with domain experts called tangible business process modeling. More specifically, they present not only results of a laboratory experiment in which the method is applied, they also illustrate how they used action research in two further studies in which groups modeled BPMN and EPCs using tangible tiles on a table.

Soffer et. al propose to study the process of process modeling based on problem-solving theories. Specifically, their work takes the approach that problems are first

---

[6] Rinderle-Ma, S., Sadiq, S.W., Leymann, F.: Business Process Management Workshops - BPM 2009 International Workshops. in: Lecture Notes in Business Information Processing, 43, Springer, Ulm (2009).

conceptualized as mental models, to which solution methods are applied. The paper then suggests that investigating these two phases can help understand and hence improve the semantic and syntactic quality of process models. Specifically, the paper reports on an empirical study addressing the mental model created during process model development, demonstrating the feasibility of such studies. It then suggests designs for other studies that follow this direction.

The paper by Pinggera et. al introduces the formal concept of a phase diagram through which the modeling process can be analyzed, and a corresponding implementation to study a modeler's sequence of actions. In an experiment building on these assets, they observed a group of modelers engaging in the act of modeling. Collected data are used to demonstrate their approach for analyzing the process of process modeling.

Finally, the paper by Pichler et. al investigates in an experimental setting whether either the imperative or the declarative process modeling approach is superior with respect to process model understanding. Their study finds that imperative process modeling languages appear to be connected with better understanding.

September 2011

Bela Mutschler
Jan Recker
Roel Wieringa

# Program Committee

| | |
|---|---|
| Jorg Becker | European Research Center for Information Systems, Germany |
| Ralph Bobrik | Universität Ulm, Germany |
| Maya Daneva | University of Twente, The Netherlands |
| Peter Fettke | German Research Center for Artificial Intelligence, Germany |
| Wolfram Höpken | University of Applied Sciences Ravensburg-Weingarten, Germany |
| Marta Indulska | University of Queensland, Australia |
| Ralf Laue | University of Leipzig, Germany |
| Stephanie Meerkamm | University of Bayreuth, Germany |
| Jan Mendling | Vienna University of Economics and Business Administration, Austria |
| Bela Mutschler (Co-chair) | University of Applied Sciences Ravensburg-Weingarten, Germany |
| Michael Prilla | Ruhr-Universität Bochum, Germany |
| Jan Recker (Co-chair) | Queensland University of Technology, Australia |
| Manfred Reichert | University of Ulm, Germany |
| Hajo A. Reijers | Eindhoven University of Technology, The Netherlands |
| Stefan Seidal | Universität Liechtenstein, Liechtenstein |
| Roel Wieringa (Co-chair) | University of Twente, The Netherlands |
| Barbara Weber | Innsbruck University, Austria |

# 5th International Workshop on Event-Driven Business Process Management (edBPM 2011)

**Organizers:** Opher Etzion, Adrian Paschke, Christian Janiesch, and Nenad Stojanovic

Event-driven computing is gaining ever-increasing attention from industry and the research community and this workshop shows its importance in the business process management domain. We had more than 15 submissions almost uniformly spread over industry and academic communities. Topics ranged from modeling data-intensive processes to various types of monitoring business processes. Events have become first-class citizens in BPM, enabling novel real-time applications on top of the business process execution. However, there is still much to be done, especially in the context of unified terminology and conceptualization (e.g., what is an event in BPM).

We selected nine papers for presentation although, almost all of the submissions contained very interesting material for this kind of workshop and we would like to thank all authors for their great job.

We also thank to the members of the Program Committee for very constructive reviews, which helped authors improve their work.

September 2011

Opher Etzion  
Adrian Paschke  
Christian Janiesch  
Nenad Stojanovic

## Program Committee

| | |
|---|---|
| Rama Akkiraju | IBM Research, USA |
| Alexandre Alves | Oracle Corp., USA |
| Pedro Bizarro | University of Coimbra, Portugal |
| Schahram Dustdar | Vienna University of Technology, Austria |
| Dimka Karastoyanova | University of Stuttgart, Germany |
| Agnes Koschmider | Karlsruhe Institute of Technology, Germany |
| Jim Laredo | IBM Research, USA |
| Mack Mackenzie | Starview, USA |
| Gregoris Mentzas | National Technical University of Athens, Greece |
| Prabir Nandi | IBM Research, USA |
| Marco Seiriö | RuleCore, Sweden |
| Guy Sharon | IBM Research, USA |
| Ljijana Stojanovic | Karlsruhe Institute of Technology, Germany |
| Jan Vanthienen | Katholieke Universiteit Leuven, Belgium |

# First International Workshop on Process Model Collections (PMC 2011)

**Organizers:** Hajo Reijers, Marcello La Rosa, and Remco Dijkman

Nowadays, as organizations reach higher levels of business process management maturity, they tend to collect large repositories of business process models. It is quite common that such collections of industry-strength business process models include thousands of activities and related business objects such as data, applications, risks, etc. These models are increasingly published over an intranet to a large number of stakeholders with varying skills and responsibilities. In that sense, it may not come as a surprise that many organizations struggle to manage such high volumes of complex process models. The problem is exacerbated by overlapping content across models, poor version management, process models that are used simultaneously for different purposes, the use of different modeling notations such as EPCs, BPMN, etc. In light of these challenges, the aim of the First Workshop on Process Model Collections was to present and discuss novel research in the area of business process model collections.

## Topics and Papers

The workshop attracted 14 paper submissions. Each of these submissions was reviewed by at least three Program Committee members. After receiving the reviews, eight papers were accepted for presentation at the workshop. In addition a keynote speaker was invited.

The papers address various topics in the area of process model collections, in particular:

- Similarity of process models
- Clustering of process models
- Variability management and consolidation of process model collections
- Configurable models as a means to consolidate process model collections
- Process log collections in addition to process model collections
- Novel concepts and technology to share process model collections
- Navigating process model collections
- Relations between process models
- Frameworks to organize process model collections
- Searching process models in a collection

The keynote (1) on "Consolidated Management of Business Process Variants" by Marlon Dumas compares three different approaches for consolidating a collection of similar process models: consolidation based on shared subprocesses, consolidation based on configurable process models, and consolidation based on model synchronization. "Towards Cross-Organizational Process Mining in Collections of Process Models and Their Executions" by Joos Buijs, Boudewijn van Dongen, and Wil van der Aalst (2) presents a means to join process model collections

**Table 1.** Topics of the workshop and related papers

| Topic | 1 | 2 | 3 | 4 | 5 | 6 | 7 | 8 | 9 |
|---|---|---|---|---|---|---|---|---|---|
| Similarity | X |  | X |  |  |  |  |  |  |
| Clustering |  | X |  |  |  |  |  |  |  |
| Consolidation | X |  | X |  |  |  |  |  |  |
| Configurable Models | X |  | X |  |  |  |  |  |  |
| Log Collections |  | X |  |  |  |  |  |  |  |
| Sharing Models |  |  |  | X |  |  |  |  |  |
| Navigation |  |  |  |  |  |  |  |  | X |
| Process Relations |  |  |  |  |  |  |  | X |  |
| Organizing Models |  |  |  |  |  |  | X |  |  |
| Search |  | X |  |  |  |  |  |  |  |

with process log collections. By joining these two, questions can be answered like "Which process model in the collection best reflects the behavior of my organization." "Activity-Oriented Clustering Techniques in Large Process and Compliance Rule Repositories" by Stefanie Rinderle-Ma, Sonja Kabicher, and Thao Ly (3) presents techniques for clustering both process models and rules. Clustering allows more efficient checking of rules on a process model collection. "An Open Process Model Library" by Rami-Habib Eid-Sabbagh, Matthias Kunze, and Mathias Weske (4) presents novel concepts and techniques for sharing process model collections, which it calls "process libraries." "Analyzing Differences Between Business Process Similarity Measures" by Michael Becker and Ralf Laue (5) presents an analysis of 22 different process similarity metrics that have been proposed until now. "Comparing Business Processes to Determine the Feasibility of Configurable Models: A Case Study" by Jan Vogelaar, Eric Verbeek, Borana Luka, and Wil van der Aalst (6) presents an analysis of the extent to which process similarity metrics can be used to determine how process models in a collection can be consolidated by means of configurable process models. "Industry Operations Architecture for Business Process Model Collections" by Jorge Sanz, Ying Tat Leung, Ignacio Terrizzano, Valeria Becker, Susanne Glissmann, Joseph Kramer, and Guang-Jie Ren (7) presents a framework for organizing process model collections. "On Formalizing Inter-process Relationships" by Tri Kurniawan, Aditya Ghose, Lam-Son Lê, and Hoa Khanh Dam (8) discusses and formalizes the different relations that process models in a collection can have with each other. "Navigating in Process Model Collections: A New Approach Inspired by Google Earth" by Markus Hipp, Bela Mutschler, and Manfred Reichert (9) presents a novel way to navigate process model collections. Thus, the papers that are presented at the workshop address the topics outlined above as shown in Table 1.

September 2011

Hajo Reijers
Marcello La Rosa
Remco Dijkman

# Program Committee

| | |
|---|---|
| Wil van der Aalst | Eindhoven University of Technology, The Netherlands |
| Marlon Dumas | University of Tartu, Estonia |
| Luciano García-Bañuelos | University of Tartu, Estonia |
| Paul Johannesson | Royal Institute of Technology, Sweden |
| Jana Koehler | IBM Research, Switzerland |
| Agnes Koschmider | University of Karlsruhe, Germany |
| Akhil Kumar | Penn State University, USA |
| Jochen Küster | IBM Research, Switzerland |
| Jintae Lee | University of Colorado at Boulder, USA |
| Jan Mendling | Humboldt University, Germany |
| Markus Nüttgens | University of Hamburg, Germany |
| Manfred Reichert | University of Ulm, Germany |
| Michael Rosemann | Queensland University of Technology, Australia |
| Shazia Sadiq | University of Queensland, Australia |
| Minseok Song | Ulsan National Institute of Science and Technology, South Korea |
| Hagen Völzer | IBM Research, Switzerland |
| Jianmin Wang | Tsinghua University, China |
| Barbara Weber | University of Innsbruck, Austria |
| Mathias Weske | Hasso Plattner Institut, Germany |
| Petia Wohed | Stockholm University, Sweden |
| George Wyner | Boston University, USA |

# First International Workshop on Process-Aware Logistics Systems (PALS 2011)

**Organizers:** Nejib Ben Hadj-Alouane, Ramzi Hammami, Samir Tata, and Moez Yeddes

The PALS workshop spanned one day and intended to bring together researchers and practitioners from BPM and logistics systems communities to discuss the key issues related to the design and optimization of global logistics systems, from a BPM perspective. It was dedicated to exploring and mastering the tools needed for operating, reconfiguring, and, in general, making decisions within logistics-based systems, in order to provide the customers and system users with the greatest possible value.

Operationally, the PALS workshop was grouped into two topics: BPM in logistics systems and optimization of global logistics systems using BPM.

### BPM in Logistics Systems

The first topic of the workshop included three full papers.

- On the Modeling of Healthcare Workflows Using Recursive ECATNets
- Negotiating Deadline Constraints in Inter-Organizational Logistic Systems: A Healthcare Case Study
- Configurable Process Models for Logistics: Case Study for Customs Clearance Processes

The first paper claims that logistic processes in healthcare systems (or careflows) are highly flexible and extremely dynamic. To deal with theses issues, the authors proposed to take advantage of the description power of recursive ECATNets for realizing flexible workflows in the healthcare domain. The benefit of such modeling is that soundness verification of these workflows can be obtained via model checking techniques.

The second paper argues that current logistics methods are more focused on strategic goals and do not deal with short-term objectives, such as, reactivity and real-time constraints. The authors propose to apply inter-organizational workflows for automating logistic procedures in a collaborative context. As a proof of concept they consider a case study of a healthcare process and focus on the negotiations aspects of temporal constraints in critical situations.

The third paper discusses the main challenges for the use of configurable process models in logistics systems and describes some future work. It proposes to use configurable process models in logistics systems and analyzes and creates a set of process models for customs clearance services for import and export processes and delivers the configurable process model out of these models.

## The Optimization of Global Logistics Systems Using BPM

The second topic of the workshop included five full papers.

- A Formal Framework for Cooperative Logistics Management
- Linear Integer Programming for the Home Healthcare Problem
- Evolutionary Algorithm for Scheduling Production Jobs and Preventive Maintenance Activities
- On the Modeling of Logistics Decisions Impact on Product Greenness: Sensitivity Analysis
- A Mathematical Model for Global Supplier Selection

The first paper discusses transportation sharing and vehicle routing within the context of green cooperative logistics for the purpose of reducing carbon emissions and satisfying product delivery deadlines. The author addresses the use of a symbolic calculus permitting users of a large logistics-sharing system to reason about vehicle routes and delivery demands while being aware of carbon emission reductions. We note that this calculus bares resemblance to declarative workflow languages.

The second paper discusses business processes that address vehicle routing and nurse assignment for the purpose of providing healthcare services, at home, for the elderly, and/or disabled persons. This paper addresses a problem that is increasingly gaining importance in today's modern societies. The paper gives a mathematical model for the process and addresses resource assignment and scheduling issues. The third paper discusses a scheduling problem combining production operations as well as preventive maintenance tasks. The paper provides an evolutionary heuristics for producing schedules that aim to reduce the cost of maintenance while optimizing the completion dates of the production operations.

The fourth paper addresses the problem of providing a model for global supply chains that aims to optimize the environmental impacts of production, within the context of current legislation, while still maximizing profit making. A nice application of the model is provided for the case of a textile manufacturing operation. The paper focuses on issues related to the sensitivity of the results with respect to small changes in the problem parameters.

The last paper in this second workshop topic deals with the problem of supplier selection within the context of global logistics chains. The paper deals with this problem by providing a framework for integrating inventory and transportation activities. A multi-stage process is provided for dealing with the supplier selection problem.

## Concluding Remarks

At the end of the workshop we conducted a brainstorming session inviting PALS participants to identify research issues and ideas which they consider to be at the forefront of attention when considering process-aware logistics systems. The main areas of research that stemmed from this discussion are the following:

- Focusing on suitable business process models integrating activities and resources, suitable for capturing logistics systems and problems
- Identifying appropriate workflow patterns for modeling logistics
- Developing tools for transforming workflow models, semi-automatically, into mathematical models that allow for the application of optimizations techniques

The participants showed considerable enthusiasm related to inciting research in the business process area that has a direct impact on modern industrial environments.

We thank all our authors and participants for their valuable contributions. We are also grateful to our Program Committee members who helped us in evaluating the papers for this workshop. Furthermore, we would like to thank the BPM Workshop Chairs and all the BPM organizers for making this event possible.

September 2011                                                Nejib Ben Hadj-Alouane
Ramzi Hammami
Samir Tata
Moez Yeddes

## Program Committee

# 4th International Workshop on Process-Oriented Information Systems in Healthcare (ProHealth 2011)

**Organizers:** Mor Peleg, Richard Lenz, and Manfred Reichert

Healthcare organizations and providers are facing the challenge of delivering high-quality services to their patients, at affordable costs. A high degree of specialization of medical disciplines, prolonged medical care for the ageing population, increased costs for dealing with chronic diseases, and the need for personalized healthcare are prevalent trends in this information-intensive domain. The emerging situation necessitates a change in the way healthcare is delivered to the patients and healthcare processes are managed.

BPM technology provides a key with which to implement these changes. Though patient-centered process support has become increasingly crucial in healthcare, BPM technology has not yet been broadly used in healthcare environments. This workshop elaborated on both the potential and the limitations of IT support for healthcare processes. It further provided a forum wherein challenges, paradigms, and tools for optimized process support in healthcare could be debated. We wanted to bring together researchers and practitioners from different communities (e.g., BPM, information systems, medical informatics, e-health) who share an interest in both healthcare processes and BPM technologies.

The success of the first three ProHealth Workshops, which were held in conjunction with the 5th, 6th, and 7th International Conferences on Business Process Management (BPM 2007, BPM 2008, and BPM 2009), demonstrated the potential of such an interdisciplinary forum to improve the understanding of domain-specific requirements, methods and theories, tools and techniques, and the gaps between IT support and healthcare processes that are yet to be closed, providing insights into the social and technological challenges, applications, and perspectives emerging for BPM in this context.

Enterprise-wide process-oriented information systems have been demanded by healthcare institutions for over 20 years and terms like "continuity of care" have even been discussed for over 50 years. Yet, healthcare organizations are currently using a plethora of specialized non-standard information systems and continue to focus on the development of systems for specialized departments that frequently only focus on their internal processes. Many of the successful existing information systems focus on non-process-oriented systems, such as imaging, drug order-entry, laboratory test result storage, storage of diagnoses and progress notes in electronic medical records, alerts and reminders, and billing applications.

Information systems and decision-support systems for managing patient care processes, however, are still scarcely developed; most often only by a small number of university-led teams. Such patient care management systems are highly complex and pose many challenges: they require availability of encoded data coming from different sources, flexibility in deviating from the encoded process at the discretion of the physician user, and may involve a team of clinical users that together take care of a patient in a coordinated way.

The recent trend toward healthcare networks and integrated care even increases the need to effectively support interdisciplinary cooperation along with the patient treatment process. Recent studies discussing the preventability of adverse events in medicine recommend the use of information technology, since insufficient communication and missing information turned out to be among the major factors contributing to adverse events. Yet, there is still a discrepancy between the potential and the actual usage of IT in healthcare.

The ProHealth 2011 workshop was held in Clermont-Ferrand, France, in conjunction with the 8th BPM Conference. It focused on IT support of high-quality healthcare processes. It addressed topics including the modeling of healthcare processes, conformance and compliance checks of clinical guidelines, adaptive healthcare processes, and process quality improvement as well as healthcare process security.

The workshop received 14 papers from Germany (7), South Korea (2), Canada (1), UK (1), Italy (1), Spain (1), and a paper with authors from the USA and The Netherlands. Papers had to clearly establish their research contribution as well as their relation to healthcare processes. Eight full papers were selected to be presented in the workshop according to their relevance, quality, and originality.

In his keynote paper "Context, Retrospection, and Prospection in Healthcare Process Definitions," Leon Osterweil from the Department of Computer Science at the University of Massachusetts, Amherst, discussed the execution of precise and complete formal definitions of healthcare processes in the Little-JIL formalism, focusing on how the process definition can be used to provide run-time information to guide process participants. This new focus has made it clear that more thought must be given to how to communicate with participants in order to assure more effective guidance. The work suggests that participants, especially human participants, will require that process-provided guidance be accompanied by context, history, and prospective information if the guidance is to be credible, acceptable, and ultimately useful.

The following three papers focus on conformance and compliance checks of clinical guidelines. The paper entitled "Reusing a Declarative Specification to Check the Conformance of Different CIGs" by Adela Grando, Wil van der Aalst, and Ronny Mans explored formal methods for checking whether computer-interpretable guidelines (CIGs) expressed in formal languages such as PROforma (previous work) and GLIF conform to declarative specifications of constraints that the guideline should obey. They started with a GLIF CIG that was automatically translated into a colored Petri net (CPN) and used CPN model-checking tools to establish conformance to a DECLARE specification of the guideline.

In the paper entitled "Conformance Checking of Executed Clinical Guidelines in Presence of Basic Medical Knowledge" Bottrighi, Chesani, Mello, Montali, Montani, and Terenziani explore the interaction between clinical guideline knowledge and basic medical knowledge from the viewpoint of the adherence of an observed CIG execution trace to both types of knowledge. They propose an approach based on the GLARE language to represent clinical guidelines, and on a homogeneous formalization of both clinical guidelines and basic medical knowledge using event calculus and its Prolog-based implementation REC, focusing on a posteriori conformance evaluation.

In the paper "Compliance-Oriented Process Management Using the Example of Clinical Trials," Jörg Schlundt and Stefan Jablonski provide an overview of compliance management in clinical trials, analyzing current scientific approaches and their shortcomings. To overcome the deficiencies, they present a framework for process-oriented compliance management, in which the extraction and modeling of compliance requirements are done in a process-oriented way. In addition they present a matching operator by which different compliance standards can be made comparable.

The next three papers focus on adaptive healthcare processes from different perspectives. Christoph Neumann, Peter Schwab, Andreas Wahl, and Richard Lenz present the "$\alpha$-Adaptive" approach, which is intended to support runtime adaptability of metadata for document-based decentralized process management. The approach extends the $\alpha$-Flow approach, which uses distributed case files ($\alpha$-Docs) as a coordination platform for ad hoc cooperation among different healthcare organizations. The authors demonstrate how the metadata to annotate $\alpha$-Docs can be extended on demand.

In the paper "Guarded Process Spaces (GPS): A Navigaton System Towards Creation and Dynamic Change of Healthcare Processes from the End-User's Perspective," Claudia Reuter, Peter Dadam, Stephan Rudolph, Wolfgang Deiters, and Simon Trillsch introduce a framework that enables user-defined processes based on a predefined set of possible processes. A guarded process space is to be seen as a roadmap that contains all possible processes. Specifying and modifying clinical pathways can be assisted based on that paradigm, as it is essentially just navigating through that roadmap.

The paper "Enabling YAWL to Handle Dynamic Operating Room Management" by Sebastian Schick, Holger Meyer, Markus Brandt, and Andreas Heuer addresses yet another approach to flexibility. The approach is aimed at achieving flexibility by monitoring data changes and specifying where corresponding process changes should take effect. The last two papers focus on process quality improvement and access control. In the paper "Developing a Process Quality Assessment Questionnaire – A Case Study on Writing Discharge Letters," Robert Heinrich, Barbara Paech, Antje Brandner, Ulrike Kutscha, and Bjoern Bergh propose a systematic approach to creating a questionnaire intended to detect business process quality problems. The approach is based on comprehensive standard catalogs of quality criteria for both processes and data. The case-based reduction of these criteria and the deduction of appropriate questions is exemplified by a case study on writing discharge letters.

The paper "A Personalized Access Control Framework for Workflow-Based Health Care Information" by Nazia Leyla and Wendy McCaull finally addresses the important issue of data security in healthcare. The approach presented in the paper is based on the assumption that patients should decide themselves who is allowed to see which data. The authors explain how such individual constraints can be enforced within the NOVA Workflow Management System.

We would like to thank all authors who submitted a paper to the ProHealth Workshop, including those whose papers were not accepted for presentation. We particularly thank the invited speaker as well as the members of the Program Committee and the reviewers for their efforts in selecting the papers (in αbetical order): Joseph Barjis, Oliver Bott, Adela Grando, Stefan Jablonski, Wendy Mc-Caull, Ronny Mans, Bela Mutschler, Oystein Nytro, Lee Osterweil, Hajo Reijers, Shazia Sadiq, Danielle Sent, Yuval Shahar, Ton Spil, Annette ten Teije, Paolo Terenziani, Lucineia Thom, Dongwen Wang, and Barbara Weber. They helped us to compile a high-quality program for the ProHealth 2011 workshop and contributed to improving the initial submissions by their recommendations to the authors. We would also like to acknowledge the splendid support of the local organization and the BPM 2011 Workshop Chairs.

We hope you will find the papers of the ProHealth 2011 workshop interesting and stimulating.

September 2011

Mor Peleg
Manfred Reichert
Richard Lenz

## Program Committee

| | |
|---|---|
| Joseph Barjis | Delft University of Technology, The Netherlands |
| Oliver Bott | Fachhochschule Hannover, Germany |
| Stefan Jablonski | University of Bayreuth, Germany |
| Adela Grando | University of Edinburgh, United Kingdom |
| Richard Lenz | Friedrich-Alexander University, Erlangen-Nuremberg, Germany |
| Wendy MacCaull | St. Francis Xavier University, Canada |
| Ronny Mans | Eindhoven University of Technology, The Netherlands |
| Silvia Miksch | Vienna University of Technology, Austria |
| Bela Mutschler | University of Applied Sciences Ravensburg-Weingarten, Germany |
| Oystein Nytro | Norwegian University of Science and Technology, Norway |
| Leon Osterweil | University of Massachusetts, USA |
| Mor Peleg | University of Haifa, Israel |
| Manfred Reichert | University of Ulm, Germany |
| Hajo Reijers | Eindhoven University of Technology, The Netherlands |
| Shazia Sadiq | University of Queensland, Australia |
| Danielle Sent | Universiteit van Amsterdam, The Netherlands |

| | |
|---|---|
| Yuval Shahar | Ben-Gurion University of the Negev, Israel |
| Ton Spil | University of Twente, The Netherlands |
| Annette ten Teije | Free University Amsterdam, The Netherlands |
| Paolo Terenziani | Università del Piemonte Orientale, Italy |
| Lucineia Thom | Universidade Federal do Rio Grande do Sul, Brazil |
| Dongwen Wang | University of Rochester, USA |
| Barbara Weber | Innsbruck University, Austria |

# Second International Workshop on Reuse in Business Process Management (rBPM 2011)

**Organizers:** Marcelo Fantinato, Maria Beatriz Felgar de Toledo, Itana Maria de Souza Gimenes, Lucinéia Heloisa Thom, and Cirano Iochpe

The current complexity inherent in the corporative world demands a great dynamism from the IT infrastructure in order to provide technical solutions for conducting business. Business process management (BPM), including its service-oriented foundation, has been providing important technological support to improve organization competitiveness. In order to increase dynamism and competitiveness, BPM can benefit from reuse approaches and techniques at several stages of the business process life cycle.

The Second International Workshop on Reuse in Business Process Management was dedicated to exploring any type of reuse in the BPM domain. Therefore, it was a forum in which to discuss systematic reuse applied to BPM at its various levels:

1. The basic service-oriented foundation level—including issues such as service development, description, publication, discovery and selection
2. The service composition level—encompassing service negotiation and service aggregation
3. The management and monitoring upper level—including business process modeling, execution, monitoring, and contract establishment and enactment
4. The Quality of Service and Semantics orthogonal level

Moreover, the impact of reuse on business- and service-oriented engineering as well as how it can help in the design of more high-quality process models were very important topics to be discussed in this workshop.

Different existing reuse approaches and techniques can be extended to be applied to this fairly new domain, including: software product line or software product families; variability descriptors; design patterns such as feature modeling; aspect orientation; and component-based development. In addition, completely new approaches and techniques can be proposed. Their use must also be discussed, preferably under experimentation as well as results analysis.

We would like to thanks the PNPD and the SticAmSud Programs of the Coordenao de Aperfeioamento de Pessoal de Nivel Superior (CAPES) from the Brazilian government.

September 2011

Marcelo Fantinato
Maria Beatriz Felgar de Toledo
Itana Maria de Souza Gimenes
Lucinéia Heloisa Thom
Cirano Iochpe

# Program Committee

# Second International Workshop on Traceability and Compliance of Semi-Structured Processes (TC4SP 2011)

**Organizers:** Francisco Curbera, Frank Leymann, Hamid Motahari Nezhad, and Beth Plale

Semi-structured processes are those business or scientific processes whose life cycle is not fully driven by a formal process model. Often, an informal description of the process is available in the form of a process graph, flow chart, or an abstract state diagram, but the execution is not completely controlled by a central entity (such as a workflow engine), if at all. Instead, a variety of IT and human-centric mechanisms are used, including email, content management systems, Web-based forms, custom applications, or a combination thereof.

Examples of semi-structured processes are collaborative and case-oriented processes as well as most end-to-end line of business processes in commercial enterprises. Even when there is a formally managed process in place, there are often exceptional situations that fall outside the purview of the workflow engine, making measuring compliance against desired business and regulatory policies difficult. In spite of the widespread adoption of BPM technology, semi-structured processes are commonplace in today's commercial and governmental organizations.

Semi-structured processes do not benefit from most advantages provided by business process management systems (BPMSs). In particular, one major advantage of process management is oversight through the inherent provenance of data and actions. Being able to answer the question "Who did what when and how?" makes processes transparent and reproducible, supports compliance monitoring and root cause analysis, and provides the means for deep mining of activities and information.

The goal of the TC4SPs workshop is to investigate how to extend the oversight, traceability, and compliance management of traditional BPMSs to semi-structured processes through techniques and algorithms to gather, correlate, analyze, and persist provenance data of processes. The workshop aims to bring together practitioners and researchers from different communities – such as business process management, scientific workflow, complex event and compliance monitoring, data and process mining – who share an interest in semi-structured processes. We encourage submissions that report the current state of research in the area and share practical experiences.

## Workshop Program

The program of the 2011 edition of the TC4SP workshop included an invited keynote talk and four papers selected among the submissions to the workshop.

*Keynote,* Social BPM: opening organizational processes to social interactions. Piero Fraternali, Politecnico di Milano.

*Abstract*: The talk overviews the motivations, background disciplines, scientific and technical challenges of social BPM, defined as the emerging effort of bringing together the methodological rigor of structured business process management and the flexibility and communication power of social software. The approach of the BPM4People project (www.bpm4people.org) is illustrated, which exploits model-driven architectures and generative software production to support the rapid prototyping and deployment of BPM solutions integrated with social interaction platforms.

## Accepted Papers

Four submitted contributions were presented during the second edition of the workshop focusing on the topics of compliance, noisy provenance capture, and runtime support for semi-structured process execution.

Building on a review of recent research on the topic of governance, risk, and compliance (GRC) in business process management, Thomas Schäfer, Peter Fettke, and Peter Loos trace the high number of failures in compliance enforcement for business processes to three main complexity drivers: the increased complexity of the regulatory environment, the growing complexity of major business processes in an organization, and the high frequency of change of the processes themselves. The authors identify the need for new tools and a new methodology to deal with GRC requirements in BPM practice. Awareness of the three complexity drives they identify is likely to drive a new focus on the economic aspects of compliance management and its impact on processes and organizations.

The need to manage the risk exposure derived from an organization's business processes is the topic of the paper by Yurdaer Doganata and Francisco Curbera. Building on previously published work on the performance of automated auditing tools, the paper first examines the factors that determine the effectiveness of automated auditing tools, and considers the economic returns that an organization can expect form investments in an automated tool providing a certain amount of risk reduction. The design of an auditing tool providing a target level of risk reduction is addressed in the second part of the paper, which gives criteria for how to select the parameters affecting the tool's performance to reach the desired risk reduction.

Provenance databases capture records of process execution to support compliance checking, historical analysis, ensure repeatability, etc. One of the main challenges when analyzing provenance data is that the provenance captured in most real-world use cases is noisy and incomplete. This challenge motivates the paper by You-Wei Cheah, Beth Plale, Joey Kendall-Morwick, David Leake, and Lavanya Ramakrishnan. They discuss the process of creating a large (10 GB) noisy provenance database based on realistic scientific workflows and exhibiting specific rates of certain failure types, and they analyze its performance characteristics. The data are then used to test two analysis techniques that work on noisy data, one assessing the quality of captured provenance traces, and the other using a case reasoning technique to repair broken provenance.

The paper by Bernardo Oliveira Pinto and António Rito Silva considers the problem of enabling and supporting a more flexible execution paradigm of semi-structured processes. They propose an architecture that combines the prescriptive aspects of activity-centric workflows with the flexibility and guidance provided by a goal-based model. The proposed "blended workflow" architecture allows deviation from prescribed activities through a set of predefined, goal-centric operations, and uses a shared data model to maintain consistency between the activity and goal-based sides of the process. The blended architecture provides a seamless extension of the traditional activity models to support a flexible, ad-hoc execution that is semi-structured in nature.

September 2011                                     Francisco Curbera
                                                      Frank Leymann
                                          Hamid Reza Motahari Nezhad
                                                         Beth Plale

## Program Committee

| | |
|---|---|
| Fabio Casati | University of Trento, Italy |
| Schahram Dustdar | TU Wien, Austria |
| Olaf Hartig | Humboldt University of Berlin, Germany |
| Dimka Karastoyanova | University of Stuttgart, Germany |
| Geetika Lakshmanan | IBM Research, USA |
| Paolo Missier | University of Manchester, UK |
| Sudha Ram | University of Arizona, USA |
| Florian Rosenberg | IBM Research, USA |
| Satya Sahoo | Wright University, USA |
| Heiko Schuldt | University of Basel, Switzerland |
| Mathias Weske | University of Potsdam, Germany |

# First International Workshop on Workflow Security Audit and Certification (WfSAC 2011)

**Organizers:** Rafael Accorsi and Wil van der Aalst

The automation of business processes by means of workflow management systems enables the flexible adjustment of enterprise systems to the current demand, which is highly appreciated at managerial level. Technically, it also provides for a systematic separation of processes and IT-architectures, allowing, for example, the seamless outsourcing of process fragments to a cloud or the selection of different service sets for process execution.

Despite these immediate advantages, enterprises are still reluctant in fully relying on automated workflows. For instance, a recent survey carried out in Germany shows that merely 23% of the enterprises employ workflow management systems, whereas security, privacy, and compliance concerns are the main inhibitors for new deployments [7]. While research, methodologies, and corresponding tool support lying at the intersection of business process management, security and privacy, and (formal) analysis could provide an appropriate basis for tackling these issues, the current state of the art fails to do so [8].

*Certification* to provably attest and control workflow adherence to properties and *auditing* to detect violations happening at runtime are essential instruments to achieve reliably secure process-aware information systems. The WfSAC Workshop series on Workflow Security Audit and Certification brings together researchers and practitioners investigating and applying preventive and detective analyses to check security and compliance requirements for workflow models and the corresponding management systems.

## Scientific Program

The program of WfSAC addresses these topics. WfSAC included two invited speakers, five long papers, and three short papers. The balance of authors from academia and industry shows that the topics addressed at WfSAC are of relevance to both communities, indicating a high potential to transfer research techniques into commercial tools.

***Keynotes:*** The *academic* keynote of Ernesto Damiani (Milan University) presented the current state of the art and challenges on service certification, thereby

---

[7] L. Lowis and R. Accorsi. Finding vulnerabilities in SOA-based business processes. *IEEE Transactions on Service Computing*, 4(3):230–242, August 2011.

[8] Statistisches Bundesamt. *Unternehmen und Arbeitstätten. Nutzung von Informations- und Kommunikationstechnologien in Unternehmen (in German).* Statistisches Bundesamt, 2011.

summarizing the efforts in the EU-funded project ASSERT4SOA. The *industry* invited speech given by Mieke Jans (Hasselt University / Deloitte) addressed the use of process mining [9] in audits. Dr. Jans focused on the current technical limitations and economical inhibitors encountered in the application of process mining techniques in large-scale audits, indicating research topics to improve this situation.

## Long Papers

- K. Haller (Swisscom, Switzerland): *Data-Privacy Assessments for Application Landscapes: A Methodology*
- J. Crampton (Royal Holloway, UK), M. Huth (Imperial College, UK): *On the Modeling and Verification of Security-Aware and Process-Aware Information Systems*
- S. Burri (ETH Zurich, Switzerland), G. Karjoth (IBM Research Zurich, Switzerland): *Flexible Scoping of Authorization Constraints on Workflows with Loops and Parallelism*
- A. Baumgraß et al. (Vienna WU, Austria): *Conformance Checking of RBAC Policies in Process-Aware Information Systems*
- E.P. Santos et al. (Curitiba Catholic University, Brazil): *Modeling Business Rules for Supervisory Control of Process-Aware Information Systems*

## Short Papers

- E. Ramezani et al. (Furtwangen HS, Germany): *Separating Compliance Management and Business Process Management*
- S. Schefer et al. (Vienna WU, Austria): *Checking the Satisfiability of Binding Constraints in a Business Process Context.*
- T. Stocker (Freiburg University, Germany): *Time-Based Trace Clustering for Evolution-aware Security Audits.*

September 2011                                                    Rafael Accorsi
                                                              Wil van der Aalst

---

[9] W. van der Aalst. *Process Mining – Discovery, Conformance and Enhancement of Business Processes.* Springer, 2011.

# Program Committee

The WfSAC organizers would like to thank the PC members for their great job producing detailed reports on the submitted manuscripts.

| | |
|---|---|
| Achim Brucker | SAP Labs, Germany |
| Fabio Casati | Trento University, Italy |
| Jason Crampton | London University, UK |
| Isao Echizen | NII, Japan |
| Aditya Ghose | Wollongong University, Australia |
| Jana Koehler | Lucerne University, Switzerland |
| Niels Lohmann | Rostock University, Germany |
| Heiko Ludwig | IBM Research, USA |
| Alexander Mädche | Mannheim University, Germany |
| Raimundas Matulevicius | Tartu University, Estonia |
| Birgit Pfitzmann | IBM Research, USA |
| Silvio Ranise | FBK, Italy |
| Stefanie Rinderle-Ma | Vienna University, Austria |
| Shazia Sadiq | Queensland University, Australia |
| Pierangela Samarati | Milan University, Italy |
| Christian Schlaeger | Ernst &Young, Germany |
| Steffen Staab | Koblenz University, Germany |
| Thomas Stocker | Freiburg University, Germany |
| Barbara Weber | Innsbruck University, Austria |
| Jan Martijn van der Werf | Eindhoven TU, The Netherlands |
| Nicola Zannone | Eindhoven TU, The Netherlands |

# Table of Contents – Part II

## 1st International Workshop on Process Model Collections (PMC 2011)

# 1st International Workshop on Process-Aware Logistics Systems (PALS 2011)

# 4th International Workshop on Process-Oriented Information Systems in Healthcare (ProHealth 2011)

## 2nd International Workshop on Reuse in Business Process Management (rBPM 2011)

## 2nd International Workshop on Traceability and Compliance of Semi-Structured Processes (TC4SP 2011)

## 1st International Workshop on Workflow Security Audit and Certification (WfSAC 2011)

# Table of Contents – Part I

# 4th International Workshop on Business Process Management and Social Software (BPMS2 2011)

# 2nd International Workshop on Cross Enterprise Collaboration (CEC 2011)

## 2nd International Workshop on Empirical Research in Business Process Management (ER-BPM 2011)

## 5th International Workshop on Event-Driven Business Process Management (edBPM 2011)

# Consolidated Management
## of Business Process Variants

Marlon Dumas

University of Tartu, Estonia
marlon.dumas@ut.ee

In business processes within large organizations, one will often find variations stemming from segmentation along customer types, product lines, business units or geographical regions. For example, a business process for handling claims in an insurance company will vary depending on whether the claim relates to a car accident, a property damage or a personal incident. Also, in an insurance company that operates in several jurisdictions or countries, one is likely to observe variations in the way insurance claims are handled across these political boundaries. Similarly, in company mergers, the merged organization often ends up with multiple models describing "equivalent" processes previously executed separately in each organization prior to their merger.

One way of managing such variations is to treat each process variant as a separate process, and to model and manage each variant separately and independently of one another. Under this approach, the above insurance company would model and manage its car accident claims handling process separately from its property damage claims handling process, without any connection between them. This approach has the risk of leading to redundancies, inconsistencies and inefficiencies due to fragmentation. The other extreme approach is to manage an entire family of process variants together, as if they were variations within a single consolidated process. This approach however has the risk of leading to higher complexity, as the consolidated ("uber") process is hard to understand, implement and evolve. Moreover, organizational pressures may sooner or later cause the consolidated process to diverge into multiple ones if there is no strict framework for managing its evolution.

It remains an open question how to best manage the tradeoff between maintaining families of process variants separately versus maintaining them in a consolidated manner, and how to effectively capture and maintain consolidated business process models.

A range of approaches exist that strike different tradeoffs and can be placed at various points in the spectrum from fragmented to consolidated management of process variants. In this talk, we will review some existing techniques. In particular, the talk will discuss three consolidated process management approaches: consolidation based on "shared subprocesses", consolidation based on "configurable models", and consolidation based on "model synchronization".

F. Daniel et al. (Eds.): BPM 2011 Workshops, Part II, LNBIP 100, p. 1, 2012.
© Springer-Verlag Berlin Heidelberg 2012

# Towards Cross-Organizational Process Mining in Collections of Process Models and Their Executions

J.C.A.M. Buijs, Boudewijn F. van Dongen, and Wil M.P. van der Aalst

Department of Mathematics and Computer Science,
Eindhoven University of Technology
P.O. Box 513, 5600 MB Eindhoven, The Netherlands
{j.c.a.m.buijs,b.f.v.dongen,w.m.p.v.d.aalst}@tue.nl

**Abstract.** Variants of the same process may be encountered in different organizations, e.g., any municipality will have a process to handle building permits. New paradigms such as Software-as-a-Service (SaaS) and Cloud Computing stimulate organizations to share a BPM infrastructure. The shared infrastructure has to support many processes and their variants. Dealing with such large collections of similar process models for multiple organizations is challenging. However, a shared BPM infrastructure also enables *cross-organizational process mining*. Since events are recorded in a unified way, it is possible to cross-correlate process models and the actual observed behavior in different organizations. This paper presents a novel approach to compare collections of process models and their events logs. The approach is used to compare processes in different Dutch municipalities.

**Keywords:** cross-organizational process mining, software-as-a-service, process model collections, configurable process models.

## 1 Introduction

More and more organizations will use a *Shared Business Process Management Infrastructure (SBPMI)*. The interest in Software-as-a-Service (SaaS) and Cloud Computing demonstrate that organizations want to share development and maintenance costs. Examples such as salesforce.com, Google Apps, NetSuite and Microsoft Online Services illustrate this. At the same time, organizations need to continuously improve their processes. Moreover, there is the need to support local variations of the same process. Often there are good reasons for differentiation between processes in different organizations, e.g., size of a municipality or local priorities may influence the way building permits are handled.

Configurable process models [2,6] provide a way to model variability in the processes supported by an SBPMI. Given a shared configurable model, organizations can use different configurations to adapt to local needs. Current infrastructures such as salesforce.com hide these configurable models. Nevertheless, the processes supported by salesforce.com can be configured within predefined boundaries.

Existing research on process model collections, such as the Apromore [8] project, tends to focus on informal process models and does *not* consider the event logs

F. Daniel et al. (Eds.): BPM 2011 Workshops, Part II, LNBIP 100, pp. 2–13, 2012.

**Table 1.** Metrics Example

|          | PM 1 | PM 2 | PM 3 | PM 4 | Average Throughput Time |
|----------|------|------|------|------|-------------------------|
| Log 1    | 1.0  | 0.6  | 0.8  | 0.4  | 10 days                 |
| Log 2    | 0.8  | 0.9  | 0.7  | 0.4  | 40 days                 |
| Log 3    | 0.9  | 0.4  | 0.9  | 0.5  | 22 days                 |
| Log 4    | 0.9  | 0.5  | 0.8  | 0.8  | 16 days                 |
| Complexity | 5  | 20   | 10   | 26   |                         |

of the corresponding processes. However, SBPMIs allow for the recording of event logs in a unified manner across different organizations. Moreover, the process variants/configurations can be compared among one another and can be related to the actual behavior observed in event logs.

Process mining is an emerging discipline providing comprehensive sets of tools to provide fact-based insights and to support process improvements [1]. This new discipline builds on process model-driven approaches and data mining. Thus far the focus of process mining has been on process discovery and conformance checking *within one organization*. SBPMIs, however, enable *cross-organizational process mining*.

The availability of (a) process model collections, (b) organization specific variants, and (c) observed behavior recorded in event logs, generates interesting questions from the organizations' point of view:

1. Which organizations support my "behavior" with better process models?
2. Which organizations have better "behavior" which my process model supports?
3. Which set of organizations can I support with my process model?

Consider for instance Table 1, where the behavior of four organizations, recorded in event logs, is compared to the process models of these organizations. Furthermore, an example quality metric is depicted for each event log ($Log1 - Log4$) and process model ($PM1 - PM4$). This quality metric allows us to reason about "better" models and "better" behavior. Note that the approach is independent of the quality metrics selected. The 'complexity' metric shown in Table 1 indicates how 'complex' a certain process model is. For each recording of a process execution, or event log, the average time required to handle a single case is shown. A third viewpoint that can be taken is that of comparing a process model with recordings of process executions. In Table 1 we show the 'fitness' of an event log on a certain process model. The higher the fitness, the better the process model describes the behavior recorded in the event log. Besides the comparison between event logs and process models as shown in Table 1, other comparisons are also possible. Event logs can also be compared to the behavior of different organizations. In a similar way, the process models of organizations could also be compared. The metrics in Table 1 are only examples. Any metric that measures the quality of process models or event logs can be used. In a similar way, any metric that provides comparisons between business processes and/or event logs can be used.

Table 1 provides insights into the business processes, and their executions, of four organizations. For instance, organization 1 has the simplest process model ('complexity' 5) and handles a case in only 10 days. Furthermore, organization 1 never deviates from the modeled process, as is indicated by a fitness of 1 for event log 1.

Organizations 1 and 3 have the simplest process models, while the fitness of these models compared to the logs of organizations 2 and 4 is relatively high. The more complex process models of organizations 2 and 4 however have a low fitness for all organizations other than themselves. We might be tempted to suggest organization 2 to switch to a simpler process model to reduce the average case handling time. However, we do have to keep in mind that other factors might play a role here. It could be the case that organization 2 implements many checks to ensure a high-quality product while organization 1 performs less rigorous check on the products they deliver. This indicates that we need more than a single metric to be able to correctly advise organizations how they could improve their processes.

In this paper, we propose an approach for cross-organizational process mining. As discussed, this is highly relevant for emerging SBPMIs. Section 2 discusses metrics related to process models, process behavior and comparisons of these. In Section 3, we then show that with only a few metrics one can already provide valuable insights and we conclude the paper in Section 4.

## 2    Analyzing Process Models and Event Logs

In this section we discuss examples for three different types of metrics. We first briefly discuss *process model quality metrics* in Section 2.1, such as process model complexity. Next we mention *behavioral quality metrics* in Section 2.2 which are similar to the 'average throughput time' metric used as an example in Table 1. Finally, we discuss *comparison metrics* that can be of interest when comparing process models, process executions or combinations of these in Section 2.3.

### 2.1   Process Model Quality Metrics

Recently, the topic of process model complexity has attracted the attention of many BPM researchers. Many structural process model complexity metrics exist, ranging from simply counting the elements in the process model to more or less complex formulas to indicate process model complexity [9]. Besides structural metrics there are also quality metrics for behavior allowed by the process model. These metrics include soundness, density, separability, sequentiality, connector mismatch, cyclicity and concurrency [9, Chapter 4]. Furthermore, not all metrics are related to the structure or allowed behavior of the process model. Operational metrics such as resource cost or process model maintenance costs are also used.

In this paper, we use simple metrics which have proven to be good predictors of errors [9]. The general approach however does not depend on the selected metrics.

### 2.2   Performance Indicators (Log Metrics)

An event log records events that are relevant for a particular process. Each event corresponds to an execution of a certain activity for a certain case by a resource (e.g. employee or system) at a certain point in time. By using this information, many different metrics can be calculated. As was illustrated in Table 1, we can calculate the average time required for a case to be processed. This is visualized in Figure 1 using a dotted chart representation of the event log. In a dotted chart each dot represents a single event where the color of the dot indicates which activity was executed. Each row in the chart is a case and the horizontal axis is the time. In this case the dotted chart is sorted on case duration and the time is relative, e.g. x days after the case started. These settings clearly show the distribution of the case durations.

Other good performance indicators include:

1. Arrival rate of new cases over time;
2. Time a case spend waiting versus the time it was actually worked upon;
3. Average number of different activities per case.

Actually, most (key) performance indicators used in business process intelligence suites, for instance related to time, cost or quality, can be used. Think for instance of reaching service level agreements (SLAs), resource utilization or the number of failures.

For the purpose of this paper we simply focus on the average time required for a case to be processed in Section 3. Again, the approach does not depend on the chosen metrics.

### 2.3 Comparison Metrics

Besides metrics related to a single process model or a single event log, there are also comparison metrics. One could for instance do a *Model-Model* comparison to detect whether the process models describe similar behavior [4,5,10].

Another comparison that can be done is a *Log-Log* comparison. The behavior can for instance be used to discover a process model. The resulting process model can then be compared with other records of behavior or with the prescribed process model.

Another comparison that can be done is a *Log-Model* comparison. This type of comparison is often used to test the level of conformance of the process execution with respect to the process model. Most algorithms can also visualize where the process execution deviated from the prescribed process model. An example of such fitness metric is the cost-based fitness metric [3]. This metric calculates the fitness of the process execution with respect to the process model. It does so by assigning costs for skipping or inserting activities in the process model in order to be able to correctly replay the

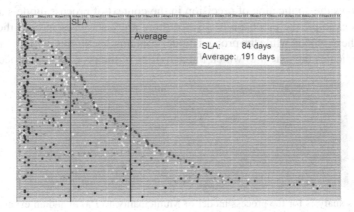

**Fig. 1.** Example of time metrics visualized on a dotted chart

recorded behavior. Part of such a comparison is shown in Figure 2 which shows the different traces found in the event log and where they deviate from the process model. Other metrics that calculate fitness are the token-based fitness metric [1,13], the hidden Markov models' event, trace and model fitness metrics [14], the completeness metric [7] and the continuous parsing measure [15].

A metric related to the fitness metric is behavioral precision [13]. This metric indicates how precisely a process model describes the recorded process executions. A high behavioral precision indicates that the process model does not allow for more behavior than seen in the event log. The 'behavioral appropriateness' metrics [13] keep track of the transitions that are enabled during the replay of the event log on the process model. The more transitions that are enabled at once, the more behavior is allowed and therefore the behavioral appropriateness is reduced. Other behavioral precision metrics are the precision metric of [12] and the $ETC_{precision}$ metric discussed in [11].

When comparing process models and/or behavior, it is very important to take the vocabulary into account. For instance, in the Apromore process repository [8] different process models can describe a similar process while using completely different vocabularies. Even though some techniques exist to (automatically) map activities between process models with different vocabularies [4], this remains a difficult task which is error-prone. Since in a SBPMI environment the process models are configurations, they share a common vocabulary.

Even in a SBPMI environment the variants of a given process model may use different sets of activities. Note that different configurations may result in processes of very different sizes. Because the overlap of vocabulary influences the comparison results of most metrics, the overlap should always be taken into account when interpreting the comparison metrics.

To calculate the overlap of activities we use the *precision* metric. Precision indicates the fraction of correct results in the result set. We define precision as the number of activities in both the process model and the event log divided by the total number of activities in the process model as is formally defined in Equation 1.

$$Precision = \frac{\#True\ Positive}{\#True\ Positive + \#False\ Positive} \tag{1}$$

Figure 3 shows the application of precision in the context of process models and event logs. In this example the precision is $\frac{2}{3}$ since there are 2 activities in both the process model and the event log while the process model contains 3 activities in total. Intuitively, precision indicates the extent to which the activities of the process model occur in the

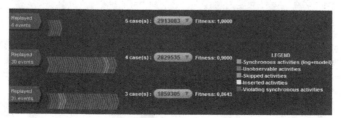

**Fig. 2.** Fitness analysis for the process model of Municipality 1 (*PM1*) and an event log of the same municipality (*Log1*)

event log. A high precision therefore indicates that many of the activities in the process model are also present in the event log. A metric related to precision, recall, indicates which fraction of the events in the event log are also covered by the process model. This is however less important when replaying event logs on process models. If the precision is low, this means that many activities in the process model have no corresponding event in the event log. During fitness calculation these 'free' activities cause a higher fitness than if they were bound to an event in the event log.

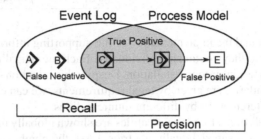

**Fig. 3.** Precision and recall measures for process models describing behavior in event logs

## 3    Cross-Organizational Process Mining in Dutch Municipalities

In the previous section we described which metrics can be used to compare process models and their executions between multiple organizations in a SBPMI environment. In this section we illustrate how to apply a selection of these metrics to several real life examples. To measure the quality of a process model we count the number of tasks and routing elements in the process model. As a quality measure for the behavior we calculate the average flow time of a case. Furthermore, we compare the process model with the recorded behavior using three metrics: precision, cost-based fitness and behavioral appropriateness. These simple metrics allow us to provide answers to questions such as the ones listed in Section 1.

The real life examples come from the CoSeLoG research project[1]. In the CoSeLoG project we investigate how 10 Dutch municipalities execute their processes. Note that municipalities need to support a common set of processes, e.g. requests for passports, handling of taxes and citizen registration. Therefore, different groups of Dutch municipalities are working towards a common SBPMI. For two of the three largest processes in the CoSeLoG project we selected four municipalities that use the same type of information system. This allows us to compare the process executions between these municipalities. Since each municipality starts from the same default process model, the implementation of activities with equal names is the same. In the following we discuss the comparison of these two processes across the municipalities.

### 3.1    Process 1: Building Permits

The first process we investigate is a process that handles building permits. The four municipalities from which we got the data actually collaborated during the definition

---

[1] See http://www.win.tue.nl/coselog

**Table 2.** Process model complexity metrics for process 1

| | Activities | AND | | XOR | |
|---|---|---|---|---|---|
| | | splits | joins | splits | joins |
| PM 1 | 28 | 2 | 3 | 5 | 4 |
| PM 2 | 26 | 1 | 1 | 4 | 4 |
| PM 3 | 24 | 2 | 2 | 4 | 4 |
| PM 4 | 26 | 2 | 2 | 3 | 4 |

**Table 3.** Throughput time metrics for process 1

| | Average Throughput Time | C.V. | SLA |
|---|---|---|---|
| Log 1 | 190d 20h | 0.9489 | 0.2624 |
| Log 2 | 112d 17h | 0.9900 | 0.4470 |
| Log 3 | 267d 04h | 1.6423 | 0.2787 |
| Log 4 | 73d 23h | 0.7215 | 0.8191 |

of the process model and the implementation of the supporting information system. At a certain point in time they continued individually. Each municipality uses a separate instance of the information system installation. Despite this common set-up and the fact that the process boundaries are given by legal requirements, we can clearly see that the system is used in different ways by different municipalities.

The process models of the four municipalities are shown globally in Figure 4. Table 2 displays structural process model quality metrics. First, the number of different activities in the process model is listed. The last four columns show the number of AND and XOR splits and joins. Verification using the Woflan plug-in in ProM shows that each process model is structurally correct. Looking at the metrics in Table 2 we can see that the process models are similar in complexity.

Table 3 shows the average throughput time as a performance indicator for the event logs. The coefficient of variation indicates the variability, i.e. the deviation from the mean. All coefficients of variation are rather large, e.g $M3$ (municipality 3) has a coefficient of variation of more than 1.5. This indicates that all municipalities have cases that take exceptionally long. The process time of municipality 4 is significantly less than for the other municipalities. More detailed analysis of the event log revealed that a lot of the cases where only recorded in the system but no further actions were recorded. The third performance indicator shown in Table 3 is the percentage of cases that is handled within 12 weeks which is a service level requirement set by law. Note that cases can be put on hold when not enough data is present. Furthermore, the municipality can extend the deadline once for each case. This is not taken into account when calculating the metric.

Finally, Table 4 shows the *Log-Model* comparison metrics results. Specifically, Table 4a shows the calculated precision, indicating the amount of overlap in the vocabularies. Table 4b shows the cost-based replay fitness and Table 4c shows the behavioral appropriateness values. Looking at the precision metrics in Table 4a we see a precision of 1.000 on the diagonal. This can easily be explained since the vocabularies of a process model and its event log are equal. From the precision values we can also conclude that *Model2* and *Model3* contain only activities that are also present in *Log1*. This is indicated by the precision values of 1.000 for *Log1* compared with *Model2* and *Model3*. Given that the vocabulary of *Model1* is equal to that of *Log1*, the same observation holds for *Model1* compared to *Model2* and *Model3*. However, *Model1* does contain activities that are not present in *Log2* and *Log3*. This can be observed by the precision values of 0.9286 and 0.8571 when comparing *Log2* and *Log3* with *Model1*. This indicates that *M2* and *M3* execute a subset of the activities of *M1*. Given the fact that all precision values are rather high this indicates that there is a large overlap of activities between municipalities. Therefore we can also take the fitness and behaviorial appropriateness values into account.

If we look at the cost-based replay fitness values in Table 4b, we see that *Model3* has a high fitness for all event logs. We see that the cost-based fitness for *Model3* is highest for *Log1*, with a fitness value of 0.9021. The fitness value when replaying *Log3* on *Model3* is the lowest fitness for *Model3* with 0.8202. The cause for this low fitness can be twofold: first, if some activities in the process model are not mapped to events in the event log, the fitness will go up. Since all activities in *Model3* have a corresponding event in *Log3*, the fitness value will be lower since more activities are taken into account. A second explanation is that the behavior contained in *Log3* is not very structured. This is supported by the low fitness values of *Log3* on the other process models.

Table 4c shows the behavioral appropriateness. Recall that a low behavioral appropriateness indicates that the process model allows for more behavior than what was seen in the event log. We see that *Model1* and *Model2* have a high behavioral appropriateness value of at least 0.9467 for all event logs. When we take a closer look at the process models, as shown in Figure4, we see that *Model1* and *Model2* are very sequential, they don't allow much variation. *Model3* contains three parallel paths and therefore allows for more behavior. The behavioral appropriateness values for *Model3* are still rather high, especially for *Log1* and *Log3*. *Model4* seems to allow even more behavior as is indicated by behavioral appropriateness values as low as 0.7748.

Table 2, Table 3 and Table 4 can be combined into Table 5 to create a table similar to Table 1. The three comparison metrics are combined into a single cell in Table 5. The value in the middle, aligned to the left, is the precision. The value in the top of each cell is the cost-based fitness and the bottom value is the behavioral appropriateness.

Using Table 5 we can answer the following questions from Section 1:

1. *Which organizations support my behavior with better process models?*
   For municipalities 1 and 2 the process model of municipality 3 describes their process behavior rather well while still covering most of the activities. The process model of municipality 3 is equally complex as that of municipalities 1 and 2. Therefore, these municipalities might want to investigate the process model of municipality 3.

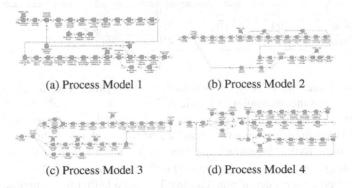

(a) Process Model 1          (b) Process Model 2

(c) Process Model 3          (d) Process Model 4

**Fig. 4.** Process models for process 1

**Table 4.** Process 1 Comparison metrics

|       | PM 1   | PM 2   | PM 3   | PM 4   |
|-------|--------|--------|--------|--------|
| Log 1 | 1.0000 | 1.0000 | 1.0000 | 0.9231 |
| Log 2 | 0.9286 | 1.0000 | 1.0000 | 0.9231 |
| Log 3 | 0.8571 | 0.9231 | 1.0000 | 0.8462 |
| Log 4 | 0.8571 | 0.9231 | 0.9167 | 1.0000 |

(a) Precision

|       | PM 1   | PM 2   | PM 3   | PM 4   |
|-------|--------|--------|--------|--------|
| Log 1 | 0.8268 | 0.7788 | 0.9021 | 0.7232 |
| Log 2 | 0.7611 | 0.8404 | 0.8300 | 0.7398 |
| Log 3 | 0.7048 | 0.7045 | 0.8202 | 0.6920 |
| Log 4 | 0.8288 | 0.7892 | 0.8642 | 0.8636 |

|       | PM 1   | PM 2   | PM 3   | PM 4   |
|-------|--------|--------|--------|--------|
| Log 1 | 0.9487 | 0.9915 | 0.9740 | 0.8735 |
| Log 2 | 0.9662 | 0.9943 | 0.8990 | 0.7968 |
| Log 3 | 0.9799 | 0.9929 | 0.9415 | 0.8882 |
| Log 4 | 0.9718 | 0.9467 | 0.9047 | 0.7748 |

(b) Cost-Based replay fitness          (c) Behavioral Appropriateness

**Table 5.** Combined Metrics for Process 1

|                 | PM 1   | PM 2   | PM 3   | PM 4   | Average Throughput Time | C.V.   | SLA    |
|-----------------|--------|--------|--------|--------|-------------------------|--------|--------|
| Log 1           | 0.8268 | 0.7788 | 0.9021 | 0.7232 |                         |        |        |
|                 | 1.0000 | 1.0000 | 1.0000 | 0.9231 | 190d 20h                | 0.9489 | 0.2624 |
|                 | 0.9487 | 0.9915 | 0.9740 | 0.8735 |                         |        |        |
| Log 2           | 0.7611 | 0.8404 | 0.8300 | 0.7398 |                         |        |        |
|                 | 0.9286 | 1.0000 | 1.0000 | 0.9231 | 112d 17h                | 0.9900 | 0.4470 |
|                 | 0.9662 | 0.9943 | 0.8990 | 0.7968 |                         |        |        |
| Log 3           | 0.7048 | 0.7045 | 0.8202 | 0.6920 |                         |        |        |
|                 | 0.8571 | 0.9231 | 1.0000 | 0.8462 | 267d 04h                | 1.6423 | 0.2787 |
|                 | 0.9799 | 0.9929 | 0.9415 | 0.8882 |                         |        |        |
| Log 4           | 0.8288 | 0.7892 | 0.8642 | 0.8636 |                         |        |        |
|                 | 0.8571 | 0.9231 | 0.9167 | 1.0000 | 73d 23h                 | 0.7215 | 0.8191 |
|                 | 0.9718 | 0.9467 | 0.9047 | 0.7748 |                         |        |        |
| Activities      | 28     | 26     | 24     | 26     |                         |        |        |
| AND split/join  | 2/3    | 1/1    | 2/2    | 2/2    |                         |        |        |
| XOR split/join  | 5/4    | 4/4    | 4/4    | 3/4    |                         |        |        |

2. *Which organizations have better behavior which my process model supports?*
   When we take the viewpoint of municipality 3 then municipalities 1 and 2 show
   behavior supported by their process model. If we look at the average throughput
   time of a case then municipalities 1 and 2 perform much better. So, municipality 3
   might want to look at how municipalities 1 and 2 execute their process.

3. *Which set of organizations can I support with my process model?*
   When the process model of municipality 3 is extended with a couple of activities
   then the processes of municipalities 1 and 2 can also be supported. The process of

municipality 4 could also be supported by this process model but that would require more changes.

## 3.2  Process 2: Housing Tax

Another process investigated in the CoSeLoG project is that of handling citizen complaints on housing tax. Since these complaints arrive in a six week period every year, this is an interesting process to investigate. The four process models are shown globally in Figure 5. Table 6 shows the same metrics as we used for process 1. The three columns on the right provide quality metrics on the event logs. The bottom three rows show quality metrics for the process models. In the center of the table the comparison metrics are shown, on the top of each cell the fitness between the process model and the event log is shown. On the bottom of each cell the behavioral appropriateness is shown. The value in the middle, slightly aligned to the left, indicates the precision of the process model with respect to the event log.

Using the combined metrics of Table 6 we can now again answer a selection of the questions as proposed in Section 1:

1. *Which organizations support my behavior with better process models?*
   The municipalities can be divided in two groups, according to the comparison values. Municipalities 1 and 2 execute similar activities, as can be observed by the high precision values. Municipalities 3 and 4 also form a group, even though the precision values between these municipalities are 0.5000 and 0.4667. The fitness value of replaying event log 4 on process model 3 is rather high. So the process of municipality 4 can be supported by the process model of municipality 3, after adding the missing activities. However, the process model of municipality 3 is more complex than that of municipality 4.
2. *Which organizations have better behavior which my process model supports?*
   The process model of municipality 3 supports the behavior of municipality 4. If we look at the average throughput time of a case then we see that municipality 4 handles a case quicker than municipality 3. Municipality 3 therefore might want to look at the process of municipality 4 to improve the throughput times.
3. *Which set of organizations can I support with my process model?*
   The set of municipalities 1 and 2 can best be supported by the process model of municipality 1. The process model of municipality 1 does need to be extended with 2 activities to fully support the process.

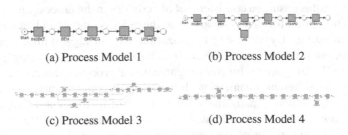

(a) Process Model 1                    (b) Process Model 2

(c) Process Model 3                    (d) Process Model 4

**Fig. 5.** Process models for process 2

**Table 6.** Combined Metrics for Process 2

| | PM 1 | PM 2 | PM 3 | PM 4 | Average Throughput Time | C.V. | SLA |
|---|---|---|---|---|---|---|---|
| **Log 1** | 1.0000<br>1.0000<br>1.0000 | 1.0000<br>0.7143<br>0.6667 | 1.0000<br>0.2857<br>0.2500 | 1.0000<br>0.2667<br>1.0000 | 22d 20h | 3.6007 | 0.9697 |
| **Log 2** | 0.9705<br>1.0000<br>1.0000 | 0.8850<br>1.0000<br>0.8750 | 0.8963<br>0.3571<br>0.3333 | 0.8210<br>0.3333<br>1.0000 | 110d 09h | 1.0206 | 0.9522 |
| **Log 3** | 0.4853<br>0.8000<br>1.0000 | 0.4034<br>0.7143<br>0.8750 | 0.9155<br>1.0000<br>0.9167 | 0.5253<br>0.4667<br>1.0000 | 227d 17h | 0.3813 | 0.7014 |
| **Log 4** | 0.9918<br>0.8000<br>1.0000 | 0.8124<br>0.7143<br>0.6667 | 0.9145<br>0.5000<br>0.9167 | 0.9373<br>1.0000<br>1.0000 | 120d 10h | 0.6614 | 0.9861 |
| **Activities** | 5 | 7 | 14 | 15 | | | |
| **AND split/join** | 0/0 | 0/0 | 0/0 | 0/0 | | | |
| **XOR split/join** | 0/0 | 1/1 | 3/3 | 2/2 | | | |

For municipalities 3 and 4 the process model of municipality 3 seems the best candidate. Given the precision of only 5.000 several activities need to be added to this process model to fully support the process of municipality 4.

# 4   Conclusion

Until now process mining efforts focussed on analyzing a process within a single organization. In this paper, we propose an approach for the comparison of process models and process executions between organizations. Emerging SaaS and Cloud infrastructures stimulate organizations to share a common BPM infrastructure (SBPMI). As a result large collections of process model variants and their execution histories become readily available. One of the challenges for SBPMIs is that they should be able to support different process variations through configuration. By utilizing the possibilities of configurable process models, different variations of a process model can be supported. At the same time this ensures a consistent set of activities in the process model and their executions. This allows for easy comparison of the process models and their executions between organizations. By comparing organizations we can suggest improvements.

Process mining is typically used to gain insights into processes in a single organization. The SBPMI setting allows for cross-organizational process mining, i.e., suggesting improvements for different organizations based on facts/comparisons of process models and event logs across organizations. Three types of metrics can be used: metrics related to process models, metrics related to process executions, and metrics for comparing process models and/or process executions. We presented specific examples for each type of metric. However, the approach is generic and allows the use of any metric.

As an example we used a small set of simple metrics to analyse two sets of process executions across municipalities. We showed that even simple metrics provide valuable insights on how to improve processes.

# References

1. van der Aalst, W.M.P.: Process Mining: Discovery, Conformance and Enhancement of Business Processes, 1st edn. Springer, Heidelberg (2011)
2. van der Aalst, W.M.P., Dumas, M., Gottschalk, F., ter Hofstede, A.H.M., La Rosa, M., Mendling, J.: Preserving Correctness during Business Model Configuration. Formal Aspects of Computing 22(3-4), 459–482 (2010)
3. Adriansyah, A., Sidorova, N., van Dongen, B.F.: Cost-based Fitness in Conformance Checking. In: IEEE 11th International Conference on Application of Concurrency to System Design (ACSD 2011) (2011)
4. Dijkman, R.M., Dumas, M., van Dongen, B.F., Käärik, R., Mendling, J.: Similarity of Business Process Models: Metrics and Evaluation. Information Systems 36(2), 498–516 (2011); Special Issue: Semantic Integration of Data, Multimedia, and Services
5. van Dongen, B.F., Dijkman, R., Mendling, J.: Measuring Similarity between Business Process Models. In: Bellahsène, Z., Léonard, M. (eds.) CAiSE 2008. LNCS, vol. 5074, pp. 450–464. Springer, Heidelberg (2008)
6. Gottschalk, F., Wagemakers, T.A.C., Jansen-Vullers, M.H., van der Aalst, W.M.P., La Rosa, M.: Configurable Process Models: Experiences from a Municipality Case Study. In: van Eck, P., Gordijn, J., Wieringa, R. (eds.) CAiSE 2009. LNCS, vol. 5565, pp. 486–500. Springer, Heidelberg (2009)
7. Greco, G., Guzzo, A., Pontieri, L., Sacca, D.: Discovering Expressive Process Models by Clustering Log Traces. IEEE Transactions on Knowledge and Data Engineering 18, 1010–1027 (2006)
8. La Rosa, M., Reijers, H.A., van der Aalst, W.M.P., Dijkman, R.M., Mendling, J., Dumas, M., García-Bañuelos, L.: APROMORE: An Advanced Process Model Repository. Expert Systems with Applications 38, 7029–7040 (2011)
9. Mendling, J.: Metrics for Process Models: Empirical Foundations of Verification, Error Prediction, and Guidelines for Correctness. LNBIP, vol. 6. Springer, Heidelberg (2008)
10. Mendling, J., Van Der Dongen, W.M.P., Aalst, B.F.: On the Degree of Behavioral Similarity between Business Process Models. In: Geschäftsprozessmanagement mit Ereignisgesteuerten Prozessketten, pp. 39–58 (2007)
11. Muñoz-Gama, J., Carmona, J.: A Fresh Look at Precision in Process Conformance. In: Hull, R., Mendling, J., Tai, S. (eds.) BPM 2010. LNCS, vol. 6336, pp. 211–226. Springer, Heidelberg (2010)
12. Pinter, S.S., Golani, M.: Discovering workflow models from activities' lifespans. Computers in Industry 53(3), 283–296 (2004); Process / Workflow Mining
13. Rozinat, A., van der Aalst, W.M.P.: Conformance Checking of Processes Based on Monitoring Real Behavior. Information Systems 33(1), 64–95 (2008)
14. Rozinat, A., Veloso, M., van der Aalst, W.M.P.: Using hidden Markov models to evaluate the quality of discovered process models. Technical Report BPM Center Report No. BPM-08-10, Eindhoven: BPMcenter.org (2008)
15. Weijters, A.J.M.M., Van Der Aalst, W.M.P., Alves De Medeiros, A.K.: Process Mining with the Heuristics Miner-Algorithm. Technical report, Eindhoven University of Technology (2006)

# Activity-Oriented Clustering Techniques in Large Process and Compliance Rule Repositories

Stefanie Rinderle-Ma[1], Sonja Kabicher[1], and Linh Thao Ly[2]

[1] University of Vienna, Austria
Faculty of Computer Science, Workflow Systems and Technology Group
{stefanie.rinderle-ma,sonja.kabicher}@univie.ac.at
[2] Ulm University, Germany
Institute of Databases and Information Systems
thao.ly@uni-ulm.de

**Abstract.** Organizations often have to deal with large collections of business process models and compliance rules. Particular challenges in this context are compliance checks, consistency checks, and the maintenance of the process and rule repositories. In case that a-priory knowledge about dependencies within the process base and the rule base is not available, compliance checking must be performed by verifying all rules for each process, which turns out to be very costly in a context of large process and rule repositories. In this paper we present activity-oriented clustering techniques for efficient compliance checking which are particularly applicable in process and rule repositories where no a-priori clustering is considered. Further it is shown how the proposed clustering techniques influence the complexity of consistency checks. Finally, qualitative and quantitative aspects of the presented clustering techniques are discussed. The techniques provide a first step to effective and efficient management of large business process and compliance rule repositories.

## 1  Introduction

Recently business process compliance has gained particular interest: enterprises are more and more forced to guarantee that their business processes are executed in accordance with certain compliance rules such as policies, regulations, or guidelines (e.g., Sarbanes-Oxley Act or Six Sigma). Hence several approaches to design, integrate, and verify compliance rules over business processes have been proposed, e.g., [1]. However, none of these approaches paid attention to the existence of large process and rule repositories, even though several case studies show, that the amount of business processes can reach from a small set to hundreds of business processes being subject to several hundred compliance rules [2]. This demands for effective and efficient mechanisms to manage and maintain process models, compliance rules, and their interconnections. Specifically, efficiency is important since verifying compliance of process models with imposed compliance rules as well as consistency checks within the compliance rule base are often complex and expensive. Hence, in this paper we address the

F. Daniel et al. (Eds.): BPM 2011 Workshops, Part II, LNBIP 100, pp. 14–25, 2012.

following research questions:(a)How to determine and manage the interconnections between process models and compliance rules in an effective and efficient manner?, (b)How to accelerate compliance as well as consistency checks?, and (c) How to support the maintenance of compliance rule repositories?

Intuitively, instead of checking compliance of all process models for all compliance rules in the repository, it might be more effective to check only those process models for which the compliance rules are relevant. This *clustering* of compliance rules is already provided by approaches that model compliance rules for business process in a policy-oriented way [3]. The question remains whether we can find a clustering if no a-priori knowledge is available. Furthermore, it is necessary to evaluate the application of clustering techniques for compliance rule and business processes (only apply clustering if beneficiary!).

In this paper we present activity-oriented clustering techniques for compliance rules and process models. These techniques can be applied independently of any a-priori knowledge such as policies associated to compliance rules and independently of any process meta model. We discuss the effectiveness of the different techniques based on performance considerations as well as on their effects on compliance rule consistency and maintenance. Exemplarily, for conflict-freeness of the compliance rule base we introduce a theorem that reduces the number of necessary consistency checks. The techniques are illustrated based on the IT Baseline Security use case as well as evaluated in a quantitative and qualitative way. The presented techniques provide a first step towards effective and efficient management of large business process and compliance rule repositories. Since we cluster compliance rules and process models, in this paper we use the term clustering instead of indexing. However, the clustering techniques could be also combined with further modeling approaches.

## 2  Use Case and Background Information

In this section the use case 'IT baseline security' [4] is presented and serves in the following sections as exemplification of the basic concepts and the techniques presented in this paper. Assume that the organization ORG works with business process models stored in process repository, and a number of compliance rules that affect the execution of the process models and which are stored in a rule repository. In Fig. 4, ORG's business process repository includes six business processes that refer to password protection (P1), screen lock protection (P2), protection against internet services (P3), malware scan of the data base (P4), malware scan of outgoing data (P5), and malware scan of incoming data (P6).

In this paper, we do not restrict our considerations to a certain process meta model or language. Hence, we introduce process models based on the set of activities $N$ and set of edges $E$ they consist of, i.e., a process model $P$ is defined as $P := (N, E)$. To each node $n \in N$ either an activity type $AT$ from the domain of interest $\mathcal{A}$ or a connector type $CT \in \{ANDSplit, ANDJoin, XORSplit, XORJoin\}$ is assigned to[1]. Thus, a node is either an element within the process graph and the

---

[1] CT might be extended by further connector types such as $ORSplit$.

activity type defines which activity is invoked at this point or based on the node and its connector a certain process pattern is defined. Note that in this paper we abstract from data flow issues and leave this to future work.

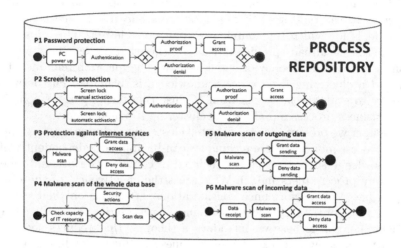

**Fig. 1.** IT Baseline Security: Process Models (in BPMN Notation)

Furthermore, there are eight compliance rules stored in the ORG's compliance rule repository, as illustrated in Fig. 2. Compliance rules are visualized as compliance rule graphs (CRGs) introduced in the SeaFlows approach [5]. Note that we use the SeaFlows formalism in this paper since due to the set-based definition of the CRGs (cf. Def. 1) it can be easily determined whether a compliance rule refers to a process model or not.

**Definition 1 (Compliance Rule Graph (CRG)).** *A compliance rule graph is a 7-tuple $R = (N_A, N_C, E_A, E_C, E_{AC}, nt, p)$ where:*

- *$N_A$ is a set of nodes of the antecedent graph of $R$,*
- *$N_C$ is a set of nodes of the consequence graph of $R$,*
- *$E_A$ is a set of directed edges connecting nodes of $N_A$,*
- *$E_C$ is a set of directed edges connecting nodes of $N_C$,*
- *$E_{AC}$ is a set of directed edges connecting nodes of the antecedent and the consequence graph of $R$,*
- *$nt : N_A \cup N_C \rightarrow \{ANTEOCC, ANTEABS, CONSOCC, CONSABS\}$ is a function assigning a node type to the nodes of $R$, where*
- *$ANTEOCC/ANTEABS$ denotes occurring/absent antecedent nodes in CRG,*
- *$CONSOCC/CONSABS$ denotes occurring/absent consequence nodes in CRG,*
- *$p$ is a function assigning a set of properties (e.g., activity type, data conditions) to each node of $R$.*

Basically, each CRG is built by an antecedent and a consequence pattern where the antecedent pattern might also be empty. Antecedent patterns can be composed from occurrence nodes defining the occurrences of activity executions that activate the compliance rule. Compliance rule R1 (cf. Fig. 2), e.g., is activated by the occurrence of an activity execution associated to the activity type PC Power up. The antecedent pattern may also consist of absence nodes defining the absence of particular activity executions. This allows for refining the occurrence pattern by putting additional conditions on the absence of activity executions (e.g., to express patterns such as "if no malware scan is conducted between data receipt and data access"). According to Def. 1 a compliance rule is activated if either the antecedent is empty or if the antecedent of a compliance rule applies. In both cases, one of the rule's *consequence patterns* must also apply in order to satisfy the rule. Each consequence pattern, in turn, may consists of occurrence as well as absence nodes and corresponding relations. Compliance rule R2 (cf. Fig. 2), e.g., has a consequence absence node in its consequence part demanding for the absence of activity Grant access. The pattern-based design of a compliance rule is visualized as the Fig. 2 shows. Though the compliance rules of our example are quite simple, it has been shown in [5] that more complex compliance rule patterns can be composed easily using the CRG formalism.

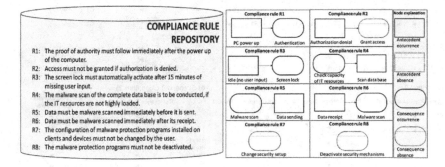

**Fig. 2.** Use Case - compliance rule repository (left)/compliance rule graphs (right)

The formal semantics of a structural compliance rule is based on the corresponding First Order Logic (FOL) formula. The connection between compliance rule (graphs) and process models is accomplished by interpreting the rules over the execution traces that can be produced on a process model. Execution traces are a well-known concept of capturing process instances created, started, and executed over a process model. The benefit of exploiting execution traces is that this information is completely independent of any process meta model.

**Definition 2 (Interpretation of compliance rules).** *Let $\Sigma_P$ be the set of all execution traces of process model $P$ (i.e., all traces $P$ is able to produce). Then, the satisfaction of a compliance rule $c$ over $P$ is defined as:*

$P \models c \leftrightarrow \forall \sigma \in \Sigma_P$ *holds* $\sigma \models c$ *based on the interpretation of the FOL formula of $c$.*

For process P1, e.g., $\Sigma_{P1} = \{$<PC Power up, Authentication, Authorization proof, Grant access>, <PC Power up, Authentication, Authorization denial>$\}$. Obviously, for all $\sigma \in \Sigma_{P1}$: $\sigma \models R1$ holds, i.e., PC Power up is followed by Authentication $\forall \sigma$ in $\Sigma_{P1}$.

## 3  Activity-Oriented Clustering Techniques

In this section we will present activity-oriented clustering techniques for process model and compliance rule repositories. The techniques will be discussed along the effort of creating clusters, the cost reduction for compliance checks and their impact on process model as well as compliance rule maintenance. As a base line for comparison, the effort for compliance checking without applying any clustering and indexing techniques (cf. Fig. 3a) turns out as

$$O(|\mathcal{C}| * |\mathcal{P}| * CE_{max})$$

for set of process models $\mathcal{P}$, set of compliance rules $\mathcal{C}$, maximum compliance checking effort $CE_{max} \forall P \in \mathcal{P}, \forall C \in \mathcal{C}$.

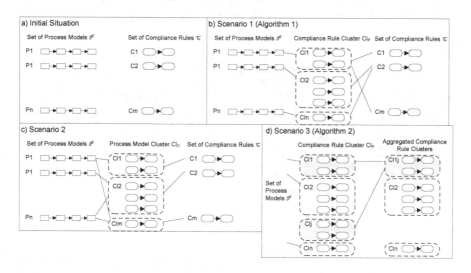

**Fig. 3.** Basic Clustering Scenarios

Without any further knowledge provided by clustering or indexing techniques (semantic or activity-oriented ones), every compliance rule has to be verified for every process model. For the structural compliance rules considered in this paper, all compliance checks can be decided at design time. However, for data-aware [6] or time-aware compliance rules certain compliance checks are to be postponed to runtime [7]. Then clustering techniques become even more favorable, including the information on design and runtime verification.

Depending on the cardinalities of $\mathcal{C}$ and $\mathcal{P}$, the effort of $O(|\mathcal{C}| * |\mathcal{P}| * CE_{max})$ might be not that dramatic. The potential performance bottlenecks more likely arise from the effort of compliance checking $CE_{max}$. For checking compliance verification, most approaches adopt model checking techniques, e.g. based on LTL. These techniques require the transformation of process model and compliance rule into a state-transition system that has to be verified (state explosion problem). Minimizing the number of compliance checks to the absolutely necessary ones is a promising way to keep compliance checking effort under control.

**Scenario 1: Activity-oriented Compliance Rule Clustering** determines all compliance rules that are to be checked for each process model. This clustering could be already given by a semantic clustering based on a policy-oriented modeling of the compliance rules as proposed in [3]. If no semantic clustering is provided, the connection between compliance rule and process model can be determined in an activity-oriented way (at the moment abstracting from other process aspects such as data) as follows: According to Def. 1 a compliance rule is triggered over a process model, if the antecedent pattern of the compliance rule is potentially activated. This holds true if all activities associated with antecedent occurrence nodes of a compliance rule are contained in a process model. In general, this criterion can be used for optimization of compliance checks, e.g., as pre-selection before applying model-checking based techniques. Note that compliance rules that are not associated with any process model are "collected" in complementary cluster $Cl_{comp}$. Based on the set-oriented definition of compliance rules and process models we can define the following function IsTriggered (P,C) for a process model P = (N,E) and compliance rule C=$(N_A,...)$ as follows:

$$IsTriggered : \mathcal{P} \times \mathcal{C} \rightarrow \{0,1\}$$

$$\text{IsTriggered(P,C)} := \begin{cases} 1 & \text{if}(\{n \in N_A \mid nt(n) = ANTEOCC\} = \emptyset) \vee \\ & (\{n \in N_A \mid nt(n) = ANTEOCC\} \subset N) \\ 0 & \text{otherwise} \end{cases}$$

Using function $IsTriggered$ clustering of process models and compliance rules can be easily determined based on Algorithm 1.

---

**Algorithm 1.** Activity-oriented Compliance Rule Clustering

---

**Require:** $\mathcal{P}, \mathcal{C}$
**Ensure:** $Cl_P := \emptyset \, \forall \, P \in \mathcal{P}$, $\text{Cl}_{comp} := \emptyset$
  **for all** $P = (N, E) \in \mathcal{P}$ **do**
    **for all** $C = (N_A, N_C, E_A, E_C, E_{AC}, nt, p) \in \mathcal{C}$ **do**
      **if** $IsTriggered(P,C) = 1$ **then**
        $Cl_P := Cl_P \cup \{C\}$
      **end if**
    **end for**
  **end for**
  **for all** $C \in (\mathcal{C} \setminus \bigcup_P Cl_P)$ **do**
    $Cl_{comp} := Cl_{comp} \cup \{C\}$
  **end for**
  **return** Clustering $Cl_P, Cl_{comp}$

---

Applying Algorithm 1 to our use case results in the clusters depicted in Fig. 4. Note that compliance rules R7 and R8 are contained within every cluster since their antecedent pattern is empty and thus they are activated for every process model. The number of necessary compliance checks is reduced from 48 to 19.

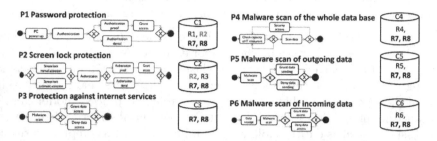

**Fig. 4.** Use Case IT baseline security - activity-oriented compliance rule clustering

The complexity of Algorithm 1 is $O(|\mathcal{P}| * |\mathcal{C}|)$ which has to be considered as initial effort for clustering, i.e., the effort typically occurs once. The effort for compliance checking can be determined as

$$O(\Sigma_P |Cl_P| * CE_{max}) \leq O(|\mathcal{P}| * |\mathcal{C}| * CE_{max})$$

This means that each process model has to be checked for the compliance rules contained within the associated cluster. Based on the "clustering degree" of the clustering the reduction in effort might be significant. In the worst case, no clustering is achieved, i.e., all compliance rules refer to all process models. In this case the effort for compliance checking remains the same as the effort without applying clustering techniques. When comparing effort for compliance checking and effort for building up the clustering we obtain the following conclusion:

$$O(|\mathcal{C}| * |\mathcal{P}|) + O(\Sigma_P |Cl_P| * CE_{max}) \leq O(|\mathcal{C}| * |\mathcal{P}| * CE_{max})$$

The effect of clustering on maintaining compliance rule and process model repositories will be discussed in Section 5.

**Scenario 2: Compliance Checking with Process Model Clustering** can be conducted inversely to Algorithm 1: process models could be clustered for each compliance rule in $\mathcal{C}$ resulting in clusters $Cl_C \ \forall \ C \in \mathcal{C}$. Again the membership within a cluster can be determined by evaluating **Cond** set out in Algorithm 1. The complexity results again in $O(|\mathcal{P}| * |\mathcal{C}|)$. Effort for compliance checking can be determined as $\Sigma_C |Cl_C| \leq |\mathcal{P}| * |\mathcal{C}|$. Due to space limitations we omit further discussion of Scenario 2.

**Scenario 3: Aggregated Rule Clustering** addresses the question whether the results of Algorithm 1 could be still optimized by aggregating clusters. $Cl_{P1}$ and $Cl_{P2}$, e.g., both contain rule R2 (cf. Fig. 4). Hence it could be considered to aggregate those clusters as well as the associated process models. The decision to aggregate can only be answered by evaluating the trade-off between the benefit of reducing the number of clusters and the potential performance penalty

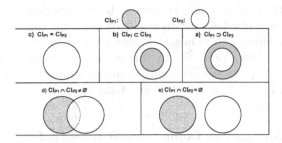

**Fig. 5.** Possible Relations between Compliance Rule Clusters

by increasing the number of unnecessary compliance checks. Figure 5 depicts different relations between two clusters $Cl_{P1}$ and $Cl_{P2}$.

In case a) both clusters are equal, meaning that all of the compliance rules contained within the clusters refer to process models $P_1$ and $P_2$. By merging compliance rule clusters $Cl_{P1}$ and $Cl_{P2}$ into one cluster, the number of clusters is reduced by one and there is no additional effort for any of both process models $P_1$ and $P_2$. Thus in case a) cluster aggregation is advisable. In all other cases, the number of clusters will be also reduced by one, but at the expense of additional (unnecessary) compliance checks: either for $P_1$ against $Cl_{P2}$ (b) or $P_2$ against $Cl_{P1}$ (c) or both (d+e). The maximum number of unnecessary checks will arise in case e. However, to decide on the question whether cluster aggregation is beneficial or not, additional information is needed, e.g., on the similarity of process models. However, we leave these considerations to future work and present Algorithm 2 that aggregates two clusters only if they are equal.

---

**Algorithm 2.** Aggregated Rule Clustering

**Require:** $\mathcal{P}, \mathcal{C}, Cl_P$ (cf. Algorithm 1)
**Ensure:** $\mathcal{P}' = \mathcal{P}, Cl_{P_{i,j}} = \emptyset$
  **for all** $Cl_{P_i}, Cl_{P_j}$ with $Cl_{P_i} = Cl_{P_j}$ **do**
    $Cl_{P_{i,j}} := Cl_{P_i} \cup Cl_{P_j}$
    remove $Cl_{P_i}, Cl_{P_j}$
    $Cl_{P_{i,j}} := \{P_i\} \cup \{P_j\}$
    $\mathcal{P}' := \mathcal{P}' \setminus (\{P_i\} \cup \{P_j\})$
  **end for**
  **return** Clustering $Cl_i, Cl_{P_{i,j}}, \mathcal{P}'$

---

## 4    Clustering Effects on Maintenance Issues

There are several reasons for providing a cluster structure on compliance rules and process models. One reason is maintenance of rule and models. Every time a new compliance rule is added to the rule base, or fragments of compliance rule bases are merged, consistency checks of the resulting base becomes inevitable.

Different approaches for checking knowledge base consistency exist, e.g., [8,9]. Common consistency problems are caused by redundant, conflicting, subsumed, and circular rules. Further there might be knowledge gaps resulting from missing, unreachable or dead-end rules [9]. In this paper, we want to investigate the question: how do the proposed clustering techniques influence the complexity of such consistency checks. As a first step, we claim that compliance rule sets must be *conflict-free*. Formally:

**Definition 3 (Conflict-free Compliance Rule Set).** *Let $C$ be a set of compliance rules that are imposed on a set of process models $\mathcal{P}$. Then we denote $C$ as conflict-free, i.e.,*

$cf(C)=TRUE \Longleftrightarrow \bigwedge FOL_C$ *is satisfiable* $\forall$ $C$ *in* $C$

Assume now that for $C$ with $cf(C)=TRUE$, compliance rule $C_{new}$ is added. Modifying an existing rule C to C' can be treated analogously. Without applying clustering techniques, the effort for checking conflict-freeness of $C \cup \{C_{new}\}$ turns out as $O(|C| * maxSat)$ where $maxSat$ denotes the maximum effort for checking satisfiability of $C_{new}$ and $C \in C$. In addition $C_{new}$ has to be checked for compliance $\forall$ $P \in \mathcal{P}$. Again clustering supports reduction of effort. In case a compliance rule is added, we do not have to check all other compliance rule whether they conflict with the new rule or not, but restrict consistency checks to the clusters $C_{new}$ will be added to:

**Proposition 1 (Conflict Checking for Compliance Clusters).** *Let $C$ be a set of compliance rules that are imposed on a set of process models $\mathcal{P}$ and let $cf(C)=TRUE$. Let further $Cl_P$ be a clustering of $C$ over $\mathcal{P}$. Assume that a new rule $C_n$ is added to $C$ and consequently added to clusters $Cl_{P_1}, \ldots, Cl_{P_k}$, $Cl_{P_i} \in Cl_P, i = 1, \ldots, k.$* [2] *Then:*

$cf(C \cup \{C\})=TRUE \Longleftrightarrow \forall$ $i : cf(Cl_{P_i} \cup \{C\})=TRUE$

*Proof.* "$\Longrightarrow$": $cf(C \cup \{C\})$=TRUE $\Longrightarrow \forall$ $i : cf(Cl_{P_i} \cup \{C\})$=TRUE
    Follows directly from $C = \bigcup_P Cl_P$.
    "$\Longleftarrow$": $\forall$ $i : cf(Cl_{P_i} \cup \{C\})$=TRUE $\Longrightarrow cf(C \cup \{C\})$=TRUE
    Proof by contradiction:
    Contradictory assumption: $\exists$ $i$ with $cf(Cl_{P_i} \cup \{C_n\}) = $ FALSE
    $\overset{Cl_{P_i} \subseteq C}{\Longrightarrow} cf(C \cup \{C_n\}) = $ FALSE
    $\Longrightarrow$ contradiction                                              □

## 5   Discussion

In this section we sketch a simulation approach to quantitatively assess the application of clustering techniques for process models and compliance rule repositories. Further we discuss qualitative aspects in this context.

---

[2] Adding $C_n$ to corresponding clusters results in $O(|\mathcal{P}|)$.

## 5.1   Quantitative Discussion

The quantitative evaluation of applying clustering techniques can be simulated based on the following parameters:

- sizes of compliance rule and process model sets $\mathcal{C}$ and $\mathcal{P}$
- $\Longrightarrow |\mathcal{P}|$ clusters exist after applying clustering
- clustering degree $cd$ with $cd \in [0..1]$

The clustering degree reflects the percentage of compliance rules that are contained within exactly one cluster. Hence, $(1 - c) * |\mathcal{C}|$ compliance rules are contained in several clusters. In worst case, all $(1 - c) * |\mathcal{C}|$ compliance rules are contained within all $|\mathcal{P}|$ clusters, resulting in $(1 - c) * |\mathcal{C}| * |\mathcal{P}|$ (compliance/consistency) checks. Consequently, the overall number of checks results in

$$(1 - c) * |\mathcal{C}| * |\mathcal{P}| + c * |\mathcal{C}| \;=\; |\mathcal{C}| * |\mathcal{P}| \;-\; c * (|\mathcal{C}| * |\mathcal{P}| \;-\; |\mathcal{C}|) := f(c)$$

For $c \in [0..1]$, function $f(c)$ is falling in a linear way between maximum value of $f(0) = |\mathcal{C}| * |\mathcal{P}|$ and a minimum value of $f(1) = |\mathcal{C}|$. For $c = 0$ all compliance rules are contained within all clusters (in fact resulting in no clustering at all) with maximum number of compliance checks $|\mathcal{C}| * |\mathcal{P}|$. If all compliance rules are completely clustered in the sense that every compliance rule is only contained within exactly one cluster, only $|\mathcal{C}|$ compliance checks become necessary. The reduction in this case is $|\mathcal{C}| * |\mathcal{P}| - |\mathcal{C}|$.

In this paper, only a first simple simulation scenario is presented. However, from this starting point, different extensions are possible, e.g., by incorporating probability distributions over the number of compliance rules contained within the different clusters. Further, $f(c)$ only reflects the potential decrease in the number of required checks. A more detailed discussion on decrease efforts will be provided in future work.

## 5.2   Qualitative Discussion

On top of the effort considerations, clustering can be of help for maintaining compliance rule sets. By applying Algorithm 1 (or 2 respectively), the set of compliance rules that do not refer to any process model are filtered out. Reason for such "orphaned" compliance rules might be the continuous evolution of the compliance rule set. The other way round, we can also detect which process models are not subject to any compliance rule. Finally, by aggregating compliance rule clusters as done in Algorithm 2 might yield interesting results, depending on the aggregation strategy. Recall that the presented algorithm only aggregates equal clusters. However, depending on the cluster relation (cf. Fig. 5) other strategies might be pursued. In any case, if clusters can be aggregated for several process models, this might also point to the existences of similar processes or process families. Summarizing, clustering contributes to the quality of compliance rule and process model sets (repositories) in the following ways:

- decreased effort for compliance checks and maintenance
- filtering out orphaned or outdated rules (cf. $Cl_{comp}$ in Alg. 1)

- filtering out process models that are not subject to any compliance rules
- finding process similarities with respect to the imposed compliance rules

## 6   Related Work

For querying large process repositories, query languages on process models have been developed [10,11,12]. BPMN-Q [11], e.g., is a graph-based language for querying process models. A process model will be contained in the result set of a BPMN-Q query if the query graph matches the process graph. In the context of compliance checking, BPMN-Q can be used to query process model repositories for those process models containing activities or structures that are relevant to a compliance rule [13]. Hence, finding associated process models for compliance rules as necessary for clustering can be supported by such query languages, particularly in combination with sophisticated platforms for large process repositories such as APROMORE [14]. Another current stream of research deals with the efficient evaluation of queries on process model repositories. For this, indexing techniques on process models have been developed [15]. As stated above, these indexing techniques can be applied to support the efficient finding of associations between process models and compliance rules. However, approaches for clustering and indexing process models for compliance checking as well as for the compliance rules themselves have not been addressed so far. Our approach can further be combined with approaches to manage compliance rules and their relations to process models such as [3,16]. Further, as the clustering approach does not necessitate a particular compliance checking approach, it can be combined with existing process model verification approaches such as [6,17].

## 7   Summary and Outlook

In this work we presented activity-oriented clustering techniques that particularly support the management of large business process and compliance rule repositories independent of any a-priory knowledge (like policies or process meta models). Summarized in a simplified way, the activity-oriented compliance rule clustering bundles compliance rules for each process model and the aggregated rule clustering technique considers the relations between clusters in order to decide if merging clusters reduces the number and thus the efficiency of compliance checks. Furthermore it was shown how the clustering techniques can accelerate consistency checks by introducing a theorem that reduces checks for conflict-freeness of the overall compliance rule sets to respective checks on the clusters. Finally, aspects of quantitative and qualitative evaluations of applying the clustering techniques were discussed. The techniques were explained by means of the use case IT baseline security. In future work we want to define further techniques for managing large collections of business processes and compliance rules, particularly focusing on e.g. indexing techniques, or clustering according to data flows in business processes. Further, the effects of process model evolution on clustering and indexing will be investigated.

# References

1. Ly, L.T., Rinderle, S., Dadam, P.: Integration and verification of semantic constraints in adaptive process management systems. Data & Knowledge Engineering 64(1), 3–23 (2008)
2. Valkenburg, M.: Van ameyde international case study. Technical report (2010), http://www.bptrends.com
3. Namiri, K.: Model-Driven Management of Internal Controls for Business Process Compliance. PhD thesis, University of Karlsruhe (2008)
4. Federal Agency for Security in IT, G.: It baseline security - catalogues (2006), http://www.bsi.bund.de (in German Language)
5. Ly, L.T., Rinderle-Ma, S., Dadam, P.: Design and Verification of Instantiable Compliance Rule Graphs in Process-Aware Information Systems. In: Pernici, B. (ed.) CAiSE 2010. LNCS, vol. 6051, pp. 9–23. Springer, Heidelberg (2010) 10.1007/978-3-642-13094-6_3
6. Knuplesch, D., Ly, L.T., Rinderle-Ma, S., Pfeifer, H., Dadam, P.: On Enabling Data-Aware Compliance Checking of Business Process Models. In: Parsons, J., Saeki, M., Shoval, P., Woo, C., Wand, Y. (eds.) ER 2010. LNCS, vol. 6412, pp. 332–346. Springer, Heidelberg (2010)
7. Tran, H., Zdun, U., Dustdar, S.: VbTrace: using view-based and model-driven development to support traceability in process-driven SOAs. Software and Systems Modeling 10, 5–29 (2011) 10.1007/s10270-009-0137-0
8. Suwa, M., Scott, A.C., Shortcliffe, E.H.: An approach to verifying completeness and consistency in a Rule-Based expert system. AI Magazine 3(4) (1982)
9. Nguyen, T.A., Perkins, W.A., Laffey, T.J., Pecora, D.: Checking an expert systems knowledge base for consistency and completeness. In: Proc. Int'l Conf. on Artificial intelligence, vol. 1, pp. 375–378 (1985) ACM ID: 1625205
10. Hornung, T., Koschmider, A., Oberweis, A.: A recommender system for business process models. SSRN eLibrary (2007)
11. Awad, A., Sakr, S.: Querying Graph-Based Repositories of Business Process Models. In: Yoshikawa, M., Meng, X., Yumoto, T., Ma, Q., Sun, L., Watanabe, C. (eds.) DASFAA 2010. LNCS, vol. 6193, pp. 33–44. Springer, Heidelberg (2010)
12. Di Francescomarino, C., Tonella, P.: Crosscutting Concern Documentation by Visual Query of Business Processes. In: Ardagna, D., Mecella, M., Yang, J. (eds.) BPM 2008 Workshops. LNBIP, vol. 17, pp. 18–31. Springer, Heidelberg (2009)
13. Awad, A., Decker, G., Weske, M.: Efficient Compliance Checking Using BPMN-Q and Temporal Logic. In: Dumas, M., Reichert, M., Shan, M.-C. (eds.) BPM 2008. LNCS, vol. 5240, pp. 326–341. Springer, Heidelberg (2008)
14. Rosa, M.L., Reijers, H.A., van der Aalst, W.M., Dijkman, R.M., Mendling, J., Dumas, M., García-Bañuelos, L.: APROMORE: an advanced process model repository. Expert Systems with Applications 38(6), 7029–7040 (2011)
15. Jin, T., Wang, J., Wu, N., La Rosa, M., ter Hofstede, A.H.M.: Efficient and Accurate Retrieval of Business Process Models through Indexing. In: Meersman, R., Dillon, T.S., Herrero, P. (eds.) OTM 2010, Part I. LNCS, vol. 6426, pp. 402–409. Springer, Heidelberg (2010)
16. Namiri, K., Stojanovic, N.: Towards a formal framework for business process compliance. In: Multikonferenz Wirtschaftsinformatik, MKWI 2008 (2008)
17. Liu, Y., Müller, S., Xu, K.: A static compliance-checking framework for business process models. IBM Systems Journal 46(2), 335–361 (2007)

# An Open Process Model Library

Rami-Habib Eid-Sabbagh, Matthias Kunze, and Mathias Weske

Hasso Plattner Institute at the University of Potsdam
Prof.-Dr.-Helmert-Str. 2-3
14482 Potsdam, Germany
{rami.eidsabbagh,matthias.kunze,mathias.weske}@hpi.uni-potsdam.de

**Abstract.** Business process elicitation requires high human and financial resources, often only affordable to large organizations. We observed
that many business processes are modeled redundantly consuming a lot
of money and resources. Collecting, sharing, and re-using process models
overcome this problem. Libraries in the real world are a good example
of sharing resources among many members reducing the relative cost of
each item.

In the same way we propose to collect, share, and exchange process
models in a process library. This paper introduces the requirements, design and implementation for a process library with a use case from the
public sector in its initial phase that allows collecting, sharing, and exchanging process models within or across public administrations. Building onto this, we propose challenging research opportunities in the field
of process model libraries.

## 1 Introduction

Business Process Management (BPM) has gained much attention. With technological development and standardization efforts the impact of business processes
has increased. BPM aims at improving an organization's operations and processes,
increasing efficiency and reducing costs [19,31]. Business processes are necessary
to design flexible, robust, and scalable information systems. In this regard, especially elicitation and continuous maintenance of business processes requires much
effort, high human resources, and costs [15,27]. Elicitation of business processes
is often performed redundantly. Collecting, sharing and reusing process models
between isolated large projects is a major benefit, reduces costs and efforts [28].

Most people are familiar with the concept of a library, in which resources and
information of a large variety and in heterogeneous formats, e.g., books, journals,
videos, are shared among many members. Applying the concept of a library to
the process world, hence sharing expertise, business process models and their
artifacts may be a central approach to overcome the effort of redundant process
elicitation, creating synergies within and between organizations. In contrast to
a traditional library the content of a process library shall be provided by the
voluntary contribution of its members. Process libraries are a complementary
approach to process repositories. Whereas a process repository aims at structural

F. Daniel et al. (Eds.): BPM 2011 Workshops, Part II, LNBIP 100, pp. 26–38, 2012.

and behavioral aspects of process models, a library focuses on the metadata and organizational context of the models, thereby addressing a broader variety of users that may not be process model experts.

In an ongoing research project[1], we develop a national process library for German public administrations—across all administrative levels, i.e., federal, state, regional, and municipal. All services that are provided by administration bodies, e.g., to companies, citizens, legal bodies, or within the administration, are supposed to be collected and provided centrally. The public sector serves as a good use case for this setting. It is an entity that consists of legally autonomous organizations with a common goal and a common budget. Back and front office services are often derived from the same legal framework, but still each administration performs its own process elicitation. The taxpayers' money and internal resources are wasted for redundant work.

To share information across organizations and departments, technological and organizational challenges need to be overcome. Technological challenges originate in the heterogeneity of users and input, e.g., modeling notations, meta data, and file formats. The requirements of a process library differ from current approaches of process repositories, cf. [23,34,35]. This paper presents our initial work including the requirements and design of a novel approach to process model collecting, sharing, and re-using, namely process libraries, and illustrates an early prototype of the aforementioned national process library.

The remainder of this work is structured as follows. Section 2 elaborates on the background of this work and the differences between process repositories and libraries, Section 3 defines the requirements of a process library, whereas Section 4 presents the conceptual design and the prototype. Current research challenges for future in this context are given in Section 5, before Section 6 concludes the paper.

## 2 Background

A process library attempts to offer a platform for a large number of users to collect, manage, and share their process models. While such a platform resembles process repositories in some aspects, it also puts specific requirements and constraints on the design of such a system.

As Bernstein states, a *repository* is a "shared data base of information [...] artifacts used by an enterprise" [5] and is considered to be the centerpiece to integrate tools that leverage the stored information. A large body of research discusses specific aspects of process model repositories, e.g., structured query search [1,4] and automatic support for the business process lifecycle [16]. Shahzad et al. [24] and Yan et al. [32] conducted surveys and derived requirements of general process model repositories. In particular, Yan and Grefen [34] define a framework that captures aspects of a business process model repository, i.e., process data, process functions, and process management.

All these approaches have some commonalities in mind. While they accept the fact that many different and no dominant process model language exists [24],

---

[1] Nationale Prozessbibliothek – http://www.prozessbibliothek.de/ (German).

they assume that process meta models are prescriptive for all process models to be stored. This is an important assumption that actually enables advanced features, such as semantic reasoning [16], process lifecycle support [34], compliance checking [2], and similarity search on the process definition level [11,14,33]. Another assumption is that a model is comprised of exactly one representation, e.g., a BPEL file. Whereas many repositories are specific to a certain process format [32], Apromore[2] unifies common business process modeling specifications with a canonical, yet prescriptive, process meta model that captures most aspects of business processes [23].

From our experience, many organizations are faced with conflicting challenges as prescriptive meta models are not applied due to different reasons. Users of process repositories may not understand process model specifications and capture their processes as prose or informal sketches. Hence, a process model is an accumulation of heterogeneous and non-disjoint information. It may be as simple as a textual description of how a service should be carried out by a certain person. This information may be accompanied with several files that depict the process, in formats that are rather unstructured and do not comply with a formal meta model, such as PowerPoint diagrams, or a serialization in any format, e.g., an ARIS file.

(a)                                                    (b)

**Fig. 1.** Examples of process modeling languages *PICTURE* (a) and *Famos* (b)

We encountered many different process modeling languages, common ones, e.g., EPC [12] or BPMN [18], but also proprietary and rather informal notations, e.g., PICTURE [3], cf. Fig. 1(a) and FAMOS, cf. Fig. 1(b). A large share of information is contained in the inscription of modeling elements, while complex control flow structures are not even supported.

This latter issue caters to the third important difference. While process experts are expected to design process models stored in a process model repository, users of a process library are rather unfamiliar with the semantics of formal process model languages and tools. Patig et al. [19] indicate that more than half of all business processes are modeled in non-BPM software, e.g., Power Point. They emphasize the need for human centered languages and tools.

## 3   Requirements of an Open Process Library

In this section, we present the requirements that are needed to cater to the heterogeneity of input files, formats, and users. They were identified in previous research projects and interviews.

---

[2] Advanced Process Model Repository – http://apromore.org

## 3.1  Management of Heterogeneous Data

As the designated users of a process library are unlikely process modeling experts, a wide spectrum of heterogeneity in terms of modeling notations, used terminology, degree of abstraction, and even process model representations are expected.

In contrast to a process repository, a process library shall accept any process model that contributors can provide. By that, no prescriptive meta models or constraints in the formats of stored process model representations can be established. By representations, we refer to any form that can describe a process model, including, but not limited to, text documents, bitmap pictures of process models, diagrams drawn, for example, in Power Point or Visio, as well as proprietary source files. Also, there may exist several representations for the same process model, e.g., a diagram that describes the process on an abstract level, one or more operational guidelines that elaborate on the details thereof, and a set of data models.

To organize process models despite their vast heterogeneity, an elementary set of information that describes a model must be provided, i.e., meta data. This comprises a model title and a short description, information about the origin of the model and information to organize process models. Such information may be provided by users who add or update a process model to the library, it may be provided by tools that support the user, or it may even be extracted from the representations of the process model.

## 3.2  Navigation and Search

Many of the approaches to process model repositories discussed in Section 2 provide taxonomies or ontologies to organize stored process models to make them navigable. Also, recent work on process model indexing [11,14,33] offers means to search for process models according to their structural or behavioral similarity. However, due to the heterogeneity of the provided process model representations, it may not be possible to parse and compare representations. Thus, we need to resort to other means.

All provided data shall be considered for text search. This includes every aspect of meta data stored with the model, as well as information that can be parsed from given process model representations, e.g., text extracted from labels. Dijkman et al. [9] show that text-based indexing and search for process inscriptions already provides good search performance. If a model conforms to an established, open standard and a parser is provided, it should be used to extract information. While this poses interesting challenges, i.e., to combine data of very different quality and precision, it may offer valuable means to find relevant models.

Besides the classification of process models, discussed in Section 3.1, folksonomies provide a user-tailored approach to organizing a set of information items. As users enrich process models with tags, i.e., keywords, they provide an implicit classification of process models. If many users agree on the same tags for a model, they build up a persuasive and unifying organization of process models.

### 3.3   Knowledge Sharing and Information Exchange

As a library's administration office maintains its stock of books, we envision the users of a process library to voluntarily contribute to the stock of process models. To drive contribution, an incentive system is needed to encourage users to share their process models. Koschmider et al. [13] analyzed the impact of social features on business process modeling, which improve the quality of the process models. The authors found out that trust among peers is a significant factor to follow modeling recommendations. Similarly, we expect a community of trusted peers to drive exchange of models and interaction among them, comparable to reading circles in regular libraries.

However, building an incentive system is not in the scope of this paper, but rather technical features that provide easy knowledge sharing and information exchange. This includes simple, intuitive user interfaces that guide users of the library and take from them as much workload as possible. Contributors shall easily add a new process model to the library, upload their representations, and quickly fill in meta data. Waiting times are not acceptable. As we mentioned above, as much information as possible should be extracted from provided data to reduce the workload of completing a model's meta data. Also, it should be easy to download a set of process models as a single file.

In order to sustain contribution, a process library must offer service interfaces that allow its integration into existing infrastructure. Reuse of existing applications, e.g., for process modeling, should be encouraged and users should not be burdened with additional work to add a process model to the library.

A library is an open community to every of its members. However, to access a library's stock, a user has to register first. In the same fashion, exchange of information and sharing of knowledge across organizations in a process library—especially to promote voluntary contribution—requires an access control mechanism that works across organizations. The access control should provide registration and specific rights for reading and writing, groups, and communities. Every registered user should be able to add process models, navigate, and search in the process library, while they may not be allowed to access all models stored.

## 4   Design and Implementation

In this section, we first present the conceptual design of a process library according to the requirements discussed above. In particular the data model addresses the problem of heterogeneous data and process models that do not conform to a prescriptive meta model. Subsequently, we discuss how we implemented the process library in our case study.

### 4.1   Architecture

The conceptual architecture of a process library, illustrated in Fig. 2, comprises a presentation layer, a functional layer, and a database layer. All functionality is provided through a Web user interface. The *search engine* provides all features that are required to capture data for indexing and provide a search user interface. For that reason it has access to all data stored in the process library.

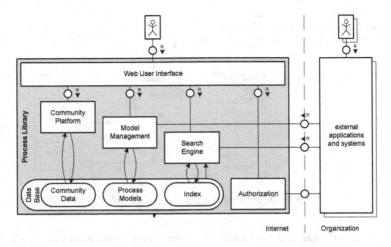

**Fig. 2.** Conceptual Architecture of a Process Library

*Model management* embraces features regarding to stored process models, e.g., inspecting a model, adding, updating, or removing it, uploading representations to a process model, and downloading a collection of process models including their representations. Similar functionality has been proposed for process model repositories, cf. [16,35,22]; Yan and Grefen [34] refer to search and model management, as "process functions".

A process library, however, offers additional features that support building a community and encouraging users to contribute voluntarily. We refer to these social features as *community platform* and envision tools such as wikis, discussion forums, and syndication.

The heterogeneity of provided data from diverse origins imposes that formats of process model representations are not restricted and cannot be known in advance. Therefore, it is unfeasible to offer a generic model editor for the library. Instead, the process library shall expose a set of web services that allow its integration into *external applications and systems*. This way, end users are set with the tools they are used to, instead of being forced to become acquainted with a new one, and still can contribute to the process library. The services require means to search within the library, download a process model, create a new process model, and update an existing one.

Finally, *authorization* identifies users of the library and grants them access to a certain set of process models. Authorization also needs to be integrated with external applications and systems to uniquely and uniformly identify users.

## 4.2 Data Model

We expect a process model to evolve over time, as new volumes of literature replace older ones. Thus, each process model needs to be versioned entirely. We mean the most recent process model version, when referring to a process model, hereafter. Each process model must be self-contained and comprises *meta data*

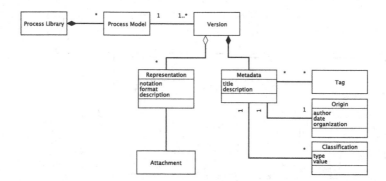

**Fig. 3.** Process Library data model

and potentially several *representations*. These representations are of different formats, i.e., they may be simple bitmap images of a process, structured files, e.g., XML, or proprietary source files. Also, text documents or diagrams in any format shall be accepted. It is of utmost importance to acknowledge any kind of representation that enriches the process model with information.

*Meta data* might be provided by the user explicitly, or may be extracted automatically from a process model's artifacts when adding a process model to the library. Each process model has a name and a textual description. The *origin* of a process model represents the organization that contributed the process; an author and a date of the model's creation are stored for reference purpose. Process models need to be characterized by means of a comprehensive *classification*. This classification is up to the actual use case of the process library. In large companies, it may comprise the departments that are involved in carrying out processes, whether it belongs to primary or supporting processes, legal constraints, etc. The classification of a process model should be extendable to users' desires if applicable.

### 4.3   Implementation of the Case Study

The *classification* of process models complies with a strictly specified regulation framework that defines, for instance, a key that uniquely identifies the service provided through the process, the department that provides the described service, whether the process stays within or crosses administration boundaries, and the receiver of the service (a citizen, a company, other legal bodies). Classification attributes are either optional or mandatory. Additional attributes can be applied to a process and are thus considered process specific.

The national process library[3] is built on top of the open-source web publishing platform Liferay[4]. This platform provides means to easily build a user interface and supply it with specific functional modules. It also provides means for

---

[3] National Process Library – more information available at:
   http://bpt.hpi.uni-potsdam.de/Public/NationalProcessLibrary
[4] Liferay – http://www.liferay.com/

collaboration and community support, i.e., covers the *community platform* and the presentation layer of the aforementioned conceptual architecture, cf. Fig. 2.

The user interface layer of the national process library needs to satisfy certain compliance requirements of the public sector, including full support of outdated Web browsers as well as compatibility with browsers, where JavaScript has been disabled. This has been a major challenge in implementing an intuitive and comfortable user interface.

All functionality comprised by *model management* had to be implemented for the platform, as Liferay did not provide sufficient means to meet the above requirements. To store models, we resorted to a document-oriented database, namely Apache CouchDB[5]—a very flexible database that stores all data in JSON format. A process model, cf. Fig. 3, is stored as a single document in its entirety. For each document a set of binary files can be added as attachment, which is used to store any representations uploaded for a process model. Besides powerful means to create and maintain indexes in a Map-Reduce [7] fashion, the document-oriented, schema-free approach offers benefits to the challenge of heterogeneous process models. It allows adding as many classification attributes as desired and can be easily extended in the future.

For a search engine we resorted to Apache Lucene[6], which is an established search engine implemented in Java. Besides text indexing and search, it supports the use of dictionaries and tokenization. Thus, we built tagging support on Lucene, along with automatic recommendation of keywords and synonyms for certain data.

## 5    Research Challenges

This section introduces challenging research opportunities with regard to the design and development of a process library that caters to the heterogeneity of the users and expected process models.

### 5.1    Process Model Classification

With regard to a library, classification is important for process model integration and retrieval. One typical classification schema for organizations is to differentiate between supporting, management, and core processes on the highest level and between different business functions on lower levels. In many organization processes are organized hierarchically, i.e., components of an abstract process model are refined in a more concrete model with lower abstraction level. Typically, this results in a tree structure that caters to the classification of process models according to their abstraction level.

As a library can be used across organizations and many different users contribute to it, it is virtually unfeasible to establish such a strict organization. Future work shall address the elicitation of implicit categorization schemas, filters, and automatic or semiautomatic classification support for users, who add process models, based on meta data and representations thereof.

---

[5] Apache CouchDB – http://couchdb.apache.org/
[6] Apache Lucene – http://lucene.apache.org/

Information related to a process model, i.e., meta data and representations, may exhibit disparate abstraction levels, which may lead to inconsistent classification. Approaches to business process model abstraction offer means to unify different abstraction levels, based on structural patterns and behavior profiles [20,26,27]. However, in the given setting, representations may not meet requirements, in terms of model structure, meta model compliance, or quality, to apply these approaches.

Future work will investigate new methods to automatically classify process models based on given meta data and other information that, if available, can be extracted from uploaded representations. Solutions need to provide a high degree of flexibility and take into consideration the possible absence of that information. This includes research to define a relation between classification, abstraction levels, and the actual abstraction level of a given process model.

## 5.2   Mining and Searching the Process Library

The success of a process library depends on a good search engine and search functions that allow retrieving the desired process models from the process collection. According to [21] only half of the search results of search engines are relevant to the user. This fact is attributed to short search queries that are incomplete with regard to the user's individual intention. Researching and developing new approaches for mining and searching the process library to improve accuracy and provide desired search results in a short time, will be a major area of work.

Textual search already provides good results according to Dijkman et al. [9]. Based on that, additionally, a combination of data mining and process mining techniques needs to be applied given the heterogeneous process model representations. Identifying similar process models will support the user in their search. In this context effectiveness and accuracy of similarity search approaches will be evaluated [14,33]. However, as explained above, these model representations may not be accessible for each model.

Thus, other information, e.g., meta data, user profiles, and additional unstructured data, should be evaluated to contribute to the accuracy of search results. This poses a major problem as this information may not describe the quality and detail of the process models in their representations. Techniques to extract information from representations, e.g., to identify structural patterns, behavioral aspects, and text inscriptions need to be investigated. Furthermore, search algorithms that observe and learn during the search process will be evaluated to improve the accuracy and relevance of search results.

## 5.3   Filters and Folksonomies

Repetitive meta data labels and textual description, the huge amount of processes, and their representations may lead to many search results. Filtering mechanisms based on the user's intention and their profile needs further attention, e.g., Petschner and Gauch [21] propose an ontology-based, personalized search, which incorporates user profiles. A different approach, using social tagging [10,17,25,30] developed different algorithm to build folksonomies that guide the user to areas of interest and relevance. Trant [29] explores the potential of social tagging to facilitate access to a museum's collection. Following similar ideas and concepts, the potential of tagging in facilitating access to the process library, and improving and filtering search results shall be explored.

### 5.4 Combining Workflow Patterns with Professional Semantics

Identifying process fragments and building blocks for re-use based on meta data and given additional information is a challenging task. Identifying Re-usable process fragments would enhance the sharing of process models through the platform, also possibly increasing the interoperability of processes [6]. Profound research has been done by van der Aalst et al. [8], who described typical workflow patterns on behavioral and structural level. Becker et al. [3] in contrast, derived PICTURE—a process notation from re-occurring building blocks with a simple workflow logic identified in the public sector. By relating professional actions to logical workflow patterns from the data stored in a process library domain based reference patterns shall be identified.

### 5.5 Automated Information Extraction from Heterogeneous Formats

Required meta data and structural and behavioral information of process models, e.g., labels of activities, constraints, roles, shall be extracted from process model representations. On the one hand, this supports a user contributing to the process library; on the other hand, it provides additional information for assuring correct classification of process models, as well as accuracy of the search algorithms and filters.

Being able to extract information from the variety of structured representation formats, e.g., xpdl, pnml, epml, bpmn20.xml, and unstructured information, e.g., txt, ppt, pdf, xls, is a major challenge. To be able to cope with the heterogeneity of these formats, different parsing and optical character recognition (OCR) techniques shall be researched in the future. We will focus our research on performing pattern and character recognition on image files, the main input of a process library. Up to our knowledge, extracting meta data from image files considering the various range of process modeling notations has not been tackled in BPM research yet.

## 6 Conclusion

So far the idea of a process library is new. Most of the existing research deals with process repositories that focus on specific aspects, e.g., automatic support for the business process lifecycle [16], structured query search [1,4] or a unifying process meta model [23].

Motivated by the high effort of process elicitation and redundant work in this context, a new and different concept for collecting, sharing, and reusing process models, a process library, was introduced. The requirements posed to a process library from expected heterogeneous input were described. A conceptual architecture defines the main functions of a process library. We further presented the national process library, as a detailed implementation of the conceptual design. The national process library is still in an early phase, hence no evaluation of the first prototype has been carried out, yet.

Accompanying challenges to be addressed in future research were presented, which address information retrieval from heterogeneous information and its usage to improve search, classification, and model enhancement. Despite all the challenges we are convinced that the approach of sharing process models in a process library will be valuable and offer new interesting insights on the use of BPM.

**Acknowledgments.** The research project "National Process Library" is carried out in cooperation with Humboldt Universität zu Berlin and funded by the Ministry of Interior (BMI), Germany.

# References

1. Awad, A.: Bpmn-q: A language to query business processes. In: EMISA, pp. 115–128 (2007)
2. Awad, A., Decker, G., Weske, M.: Efficient Compliance Checking Using BPMN-Q and Temporal Logic. In: Dumas, M., Reichert, M., Shan, M.-C. (eds.) BPM 2008. LNCS, vol. 5240, pp. 326–341. Springer, Heidelberg (2008)
3. Becker, J., Algermissen, L., Falk, T., Ebrary, I.: Prozessorientierte Verwaltungsmodernisierung: Prozessmanagement im Zeitalter von E-Government und New Public Management. Springer, Heidelberg (2007)
4. Beeri, C., Eyal, A., Kamenkovich, S., Milo, T.: Querying Business Processes. In: VLDB 2006, pp. 343–354. VLDB Endowment (2006)
5. Bernstein, P.A., Dayal, U.: An overview of repository technology. In: VLDB 1994, pp. 705–713. Morgan Kaufmann Publishers Inc. (1994)
6. Chourabi, H., Mellouli, S., Bouslama, F.: Modeling e-Government Business Processes: New Approaches to Transparent and Efficient Performance. Info. Pol. 14, 91–109 (2009)
7. Dean, J., Ghemawat, S.: Mapreduce: Simplified Data Processing on Large Clusters. In: OSDI 2004, pp. 10–10. USENIX Association (2004)
8. van Der Aalst, W., Ter Hofstede, A., Kiepuszewski, B., Barros, A.: Workflow Patterns. Distrib. Parallel Databases 14(1), 5–51 (2003)
9. Dijkman, R., Dumas, M., van Dongen, B., Käärik, R., Mendling, J.: Similarity of Business Process Models: Metrics and Evaluation. Info. Sys. 36(2), 498–516 (2011)
10. Heymann, P., Garcia-Molina, H.: Collaborative Creation of Communal Hierarchical Taxonomies in Social Tagging Systems. Technical Report 2006-10, Stanford InfoLab (2006)
11. Jin, T., Wang, J., Wu, N., La Rosa, M., ter Hofstede, A.H.M.: Efficient and Accurate Retrieval of Business Process Models through Indexing. In: Meersman, R., Dillon, T.S., Herrero, P. (eds.) OTM 2010, Part I. LNCS, vol. 6426, pp. 402–409. Springer, Heidelberg (2010)
12. Keller, G., Nüttgens, M., Scheer, A.W.: Semantische Prozessmodellierung auf der Grundlage "Ereignisgesteuerter Prozessketten (EPK)" (1992)
13. Koschmider, A., Song, M., Reijers, H.A.: Social Software for Modeling Business Processes. In: Ardagna, D., Mecella, M., Yang, J. (eds.) BPM 2008 Workshops. LNBIP, vol. 17, pp. 666–677. Springer, Heidelberg (2009)

14. Kunze, M., Weske, M.: Metric Trees for Efficient Similarity Search in Process Model Repositories. In: IW-PL 2010. Springer, Heidelberg (2010)
15. Luebbe, A., Weske, M.: Designing a Tangible Approach to Business Process Modeling. In: ECDTR (2010)
16. Ma, Z., Wetzstein, B., Anicic, D., Heymans, S.: Semantic Business Process Repository. In: SBPM. CEUR-WS (2007)
17. Mathes, A.: Folksonomies-Cooperative Classification and Communication through Shared Metadata. JCMC 47 (2004)
18. Object Management Group: Business Process Modeling Notation (BPMN) Specification, Version 1.2 (2009)
19. Patig, S., Casanova-Brito, V., Vögeli, B.: IT Requirements of Business Process Management in Practice – An Empirical Study. In: Hull, R., Mendling, J., Tai, S. (eds.) BPM 2010. LNCS, vol. 6336, pp. 13–28. Springer, Heidelberg (2010)
20. Polyvyanyy, A., Smirnov, S., Weske, M.: The Triconnected Abstraction of Process Models. In: Dayal, U., Eder, J., Koehler, J., Reijers, H.A. (eds.) BPM 2009. LNCS, vol. 5701, pp. 229–244. Springer, Heidelberg (2009)
21. Pretschner, A., Gauch, S.: Ontology Based Personalized Search. In: ICTAI 1999, pp. 391–398. IEEE (1999)
22. Rivas, D., Corchuelo, D., Figueroa, C., Corrales, J.: Business Process Repository Based on Control Flow Patterns. In: EATIS 2010. ACM (2010)
23. Rosa, M.L., Reijers, H.A., van der Aalst, W.M., Dijkman, R.M., Mendling, J., Dumas, M., Garcia-Banuelos, L.: Apromore: An Advanced Process Model Repository (2009), http://eprints.qut.edu.au/27448/
24. Shahzad, K., Andersson, B., Bergholtz, M., Edirisuriya, A., Ilayperuma, T., Jayaweera, P., Johannesson, P.: Elicitation of Requirements for a Business Process Model Repository. In: Ardagna, D., Mecella, M., Yang, J. (eds.) BPM 2008 Workshops. LNBIP, vol. 17, pp. 44–55. Springer, Heidelberg (2009)
25. Shepitsen, A., Gemmell, J., Mobasher, B., Burke, R.: Personalized Recommendation in Social Tagging Systems Using Hierarchical Clustering. In: RECSYS 2008, pp. 259–266. ACM (2008)
26. Smirnov, S., Dijkman, R., Mendling, J., Weske, M.: Meronymy-Based Aggregation of Activities in Business Process Models. In: Parsons, J., Saeki, M., Shoval, P., Woo, C., Wand, Y. (eds.) ER 2010. LNCS, vol. 6412, pp. 1–14. Springer, Heidelberg (2010)
27. Smirnov, S., Weidlich, M., Mendling, J.: Business Process Model Abstraction Based on Behavioral Profiles. In: Maglio, P.P., Weske, M., Yang, J., Fantinato, M. (eds.) ICSOC 2010. LNCS, vol. 6470, pp. 1–16. Springer, Heidelberg (2010)
28. Smirnov, S., Weidlich, M., Mendling, J., Weske, M.: Action Patterns in Business Process Models. In: Baresi, L., Chi, C.-H., Suzuki, J. (eds.) ICSOC-ServiceWave 2009. LNCS, vol. 5900, pp. 115–129. Springer, Heidelberg (2009)
29. Trant, J., Project, W.: Exploring the Potential for Social Tagging and Folksonomy in Art Museums: Proof of Concept. New Review of Hypermedia and Multimedia 12(1), 83–105 (2006)
30. Vallet, D., Cantador, I., Jose, J.M.: Exploiting Social Tagging Profiles to Personalize Web Search. In: Andreasen, T., Yager, R.R., Bulskov, H., Christiansen, H., Larsen, H.L. (eds.) FQAS 2009. LNCS, vol. 5822, pp. 629–640. Springer, Heidelberg (2009)

31. Weske, M.: Business Process Management: Concepts, Languages, Architectures. Springer, Heidelberg (2007)
32. Yan, Z., Dijkman, R., Grefen, P.: Business Process Model Repositories - Framework and Survey (2009),
    http://cms.ieis.tue.nl/Beta/Files/WorkingPapers/Beta_wp292.pdf
33. Yan, Z., Dijkman, R., Grefen, P.: Fast Business Process Similarity Search with Feature-Based Similarity Estimation. In: Meersman, R., Dillon, T.S., Herrero, P. (eds.) OTM 2010, Part I. LNCS, vol. 6426, pp. 60–77. Springer, Heidelberg (2010)
34. Yan, Z., Grefen, P.: A Framework for Business Process Model Repositories. In: zur Muehlen, M., Su, J. (eds.) BPM 2010 Workshops. LNBIP, vol. 66, pp. 559–570. Springer, Heidelberg (2011)
35. Ma, Z., Kaczmarek, M., Konstantinov, M., Wieloch, K., Zebrowski, P.: Semantics Utilized for Process Management Within and Between Enterprises - d3.4 Business Process Library Final Prototype. Tech. rep., Information Society Technologies, IST (2008)

# Analysing Differences between Business Process Similarity Measures

Michael Becker[1] and Ralf Laue[2]

[1] Department of Business Information Systems, University of Leipzig, Germany
michael.becker@uni-leipzig.de
[2] Chair of Applied Telematics / e-Business, University of Leipzig, Germany
laue@ebus.informatik.uni-leipzig.de

**Abstract.** Nowadays, it is not uncommon that organisations maintain repositories containing hundreds or thousands of business process models. For the purpose of searching such a repository for models that are similar to a query model, many similarity measures have been suggested in the literature. Other measures have been suggested for different purposes like measuring compliance between a model and a reference model.

As those similarity measures differ in many aspects, it is an interesting question how they rank "similarity" within the same set of process models. In our study, we investigated, how different kinds of changes in a process model influence the values of 22 different similarity measures that have been published in academic literature.

Furthermore, we identified eight properties that a similarity measure should have from a theoretical point of view and analysed how these properties are fulfilled by the different measures. Our results show that there are remarkable differences among existing measures. We give some recommendations which kind of measure is useful for which kind of application.

## 1 Introduction

Business Process Models (BPMs) are nowadays a common approach to analyse existing processes and to create new processes in a structured way. They are used for purposes like supporting the communication in organisations, documentation in projects, and training of employees [1]. This wide area of application has led to the existence of a tremendous amount of BPMs. Large scale enterprises usually own repositories consisting of hundreds or thousands of models [2], usually developed by different persons. To manage these repositories, suitable methods for searching a BPM repository are necessary. A common requirement is to search for BPMs that are similar to a given query model. For this purpose, there is a need of a similarity measure that quantifies the similarity between models.

As the similarity measures that have been suggested in the literature differ in many aspects, it is an interesting question how the different measures rank "similarity" within the same set of BPMs. In our study, we investigated, how different

F. Daniel et al. (Eds.): BPM 2011 Workshops, Part II, LNBIP 100, pp. 39–49, 2012.

kinds of changes in a BPM influence the values of 22 different similarity measures that have been published in academic literature. To our best knowledge, no study has been made so far that compares such a large number of different BPM similarity measures.

After explaining some fundamental preliminaries in Sect. 2, we discuss some properties that a "good" similarity measure should have in Sect. 3. We apply different changes (described in Sect. 4) to an example model and calculate the similarity between the original model and its variants in Sect. 5 together with a discussion about the implications from our results. Finally, Sect. 6 gives a conclusion.

## 2   Approaches for Measuring Process Similarity

When BPMs have to be compared, the first challenge is to identify the activity nodes in one model that correspond to activity nodes in the other model. In particular, if the models have been created in different organisations or if they describe a business process on different levels of detail, this can become a non-trivial task. This first step is, however, not in the focus of our paper. We assume that a mapping between corresponding activity nodes in the BPMs to compare has been established, either by using one of the existing algorithms or based on experts' judgment. The interested reader can find a discussion of different mapping techniques in [3,4,5].

Once a mapping between the activities has been established, several approaches have been suggested for measuring the similarity of BPMs. Rather simple measures are related to the number of activities that two BPMs have in common [6,5] or the percentage of nodes and arcs that can be found in both BPMs [7,8,9,10]. These measures can be considerably improved by considering as well the position that an activity has within a BPM [11].

As in the most common modelling languages, BPMs are modelled as directed attributed graphs, other researchers suggested to use graph-based approaches for comparing BPMs. A graph-based similarity measure is the edit-distance, i.e. the lowest number of elementary operations (like adding or deleting a node) that transfers one model (or graph) into another. Such measures are discussed in [12,13,14,15]. In [16], the use of a graph-edit distance based on high-level operations (containing more than one elementary operation) is discussed. Bae et al. [17] transform BPMs into trees before calculating a graph-based similarity measure between those trees.

Other authors compare the set of all possible traces (or possible sequences of activities) of a BPM [18]. As this set of traces can become very large or even infinite, it has also been suggested to compare process logs, i.e. a finite subset of the set of traces which can be obtained from simulation [19]. Another stream of research investigates relationships between activities in a BPM (like "A is always followed by B") in order to draw conclusions about their similarity [20,21,22,3].

# 3   Desirable Properties of Distance and Similarity Measures

For introducing desirable properties for similarity measures for BPMs (or distance measures that aim to measure dissimilarity), we make use of the research results on properties of similarity measures in general [23,24,25].

Let $\mathbf{M}$ be the set of BPMs. A *distance measure dist* is a function $dist : \mathbf{M} \times \mathbf{M} \to \mathbb{R}^+ \cup \{0\}$. We assume that for comparing a BPM $M_0$ with a BPM $M_1$, a partial function $map$ has been established that maps the nodes in $M_0$ to "corresponding" nodes in $M_1$. $M_0$ is said to be equal to $M_1$ (symbol: $M_0 = M_1$) if the set of nodes of $M_0$ is $n^1, n^2, \dots n^n$ while the set of nodes of $M_1$ is $map(n^1), map(n^2), \dots map(n^n)$, and the set of arcs of $M_1$ is identical to all those arcs $(map(n), map(m))$, where $n$ and $m$ are nodes in $M_0$.

A *similarity measure* is a function $sim : \mathbf{M} \times \mathbf{M} \to [0, 1]$. The formula

$$sim(x, y) = \frac{1}{1 + dist(x, y)} \tag{1}$$

can be used for a transformation between distance (i.e. dissimilarity) and similarity measures.

Santini and Jain [23] point out that a number of dissimilarity measures proposed in the literature assume that those measures are distance measures in a metric space. $(\mathbf{M}, dist)$ becomes a metric space, if the following properties hold:

**Property 1.** $dist(M_0, M_1) \geq 0 \quad \forall M_0, M_1 \in \mathbf{M}$ (non-negativity)
**Property 2.** $dist(M_0, M_1) = dist(M_1, M_0) \quad \forall M_0, M_1 \in \mathbf{M}$ (symmetry)
**Property 3.** $dist(M_0, M_1) = 0 \Leftrightarrow M_0 = M_1$
**Property 4.** $dist(M_0, M_2) \leq dist(M_0, M_1) + dist(M_1, M_2)$ (triangle inequality)

For measuring the "dissimilarity" distance between BPMs, it is reasonable to require Property 1 and Property 2. Property 3 that says that the distance between two models is 0 if and only if the models are identical is too strict for certain application areas. The same set of traces (i.e. the same set of possible executions of activities of a model $M$, denoted as $\Sigma(M)$) can be obtained in different ways. For example, the model shown in Fig. 2(a) (see Sect. 4) has the same set of traces as the model shown in Fig. 2(b). A distance measure that calculates the distance between both models as 0 would correctly describe the fact that both models show exactly the same business process.

A more relaxed requirement is that $dist(M_0, M_1)$ is 0 iff both models have the same set of traces. For our purposes, the sets of traces $\Sigma(M_0)$ and $\Sigma(M_1)$ are considered as being the same (symbol: $\Sigma(M_0) \equiv \Sigma(M_1)$) if $\langle s_1, s_2, \dots \rangle \in \Sigma(M_0)$ implies that $\langle map(s_1), map(s_2), \dots \rangle \in \Sigma(M_1)$ and vice versa, $\langle t_1, t_2, \dots \rangle \in \Sigma(M_1)$ implies that there is a $\langle s_1, s_2, \dots \rangle \in \Sigma(M_0)$ such that $map(s_i) = t_i \; \forall i$. With this interpretation of equality between sets of traces, Property 3 can be substituted by the less strict requirement:

**Property 3a:**
$dist(M_0, M_1) = 0 \Leftrightarrow \Sigma(M_0) \equiv \Sigma(M_1)$.

Property 4, the triangle inequality, is not essential for measuring the dissimilarity (distance) between BPMs (or for (dis)similarity measures in general, see [24]), therefore we will not examine the suggested measures with respect to this property. It is a useful property anyway, because a distance measure that fulfills all four properties given above allows to organize a BPM repository using data structures in which the search for similar models is very fast [26].

From an information-theoretic discussion of the concept of similarity (see [24,25]), one more requirement for a similarity measure can be derived: Such a measure should take into consideration both the commonality between two models as the differences between them (**Property 5**). For example, we would not get a good similarity measure by just counting the number of activities that are shared among two models without relating this number to the overall number of activities in the models: If two models with 20 nodes have 15 node names in common, it would be reasonable to say that they are more similar to each other than two models with 200 nodes from which 15 node names can be found in both models.

As mentioned before, the definition of the function *map* that assigns "corresponding" nodes between two models is outside the main focus of this paper. We just assume that such a mapping has been established. The approaches that calculate *map* automatically start with a function *corr* which quantifies the similarity between single activities. It would be a desirable property of a similarity measure $sim : \mathbf{M} \times \mathbf{M} \to [0, 1]$ if the information gained from the similarity measure *corr* between *activities* would be considered in the calculation of the similarity measure *sim* between the *models as a whole* (**Property 6**). This is illustrated in Fig. 1, showing three sequential models $M_0$, $M_1$ and $M_2$ with four activities and the mappings between them (as dotted arrows). Assume that

$$1 = corr(\text{"confirm draft"}, \text{"confirm draft"})$$
$$> corr(\text{"confirm draft"}, \text{"dismiss draft"})$$

and that

$$1 > corr(\text{"sign draft contract"}, \text{"sign contract"})$$
$$= corr(\text{"sign draft contract"}, \text{"archive draft contract"})$$

(which could be the result *corr* defined as a simple word-by-word comparison). In such a case, it would be desirable that the result that the activities in $M_2$ are more similar to the activities in $M_0$ than those in $M_1$ would not "get lost" when the similarity measure *sim* is calculated, i.e. we would prefer to have $sim(M_0, M_1) < sim(M_0, M_2)$ instead of $sim(M_0, M_1) = sim(M_0, M_2)$.

Furthermore, it is reasonable to require that a distance or similarity measure can be applied for comparing arbitrary BPMs without imposing additional syntax restrictions (such as that the model must not contain loops) (**Property 7**). And last but not least, there is another requirement that is related to the computational complexity of the calculation of a distance or similarity measure. In simple terms, it should be possible to calculate the values of distance / similarity

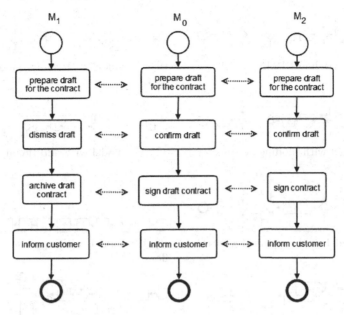

**Fig. 1.** Models with corresponding labels

measures quickly (**Property 8**). Approaches that require the calculation of the whole set of traces of a BPM often do not fulfill this requirement.

## 4   Model Changes

In order to analyse the values of similarity measures, we compute the similarity between some example models. For this purpose, we use BPMN models that can be built from the notational elements start event (exactly one per model), end event (exactly one per model), activity, AND connectors (i.e. split or join gateways in BPMN terminology), XOR connectors and inclusive OR connectors. Almost all similarity measure published in the literature are restricted to this subset of notational elements.

Starting from a moderately sized BPMN model, we apply different change operations as described in [27,28,29] and shown in Fig. 2. For the various similarity measures that have been described in the literature, we compute the similarity between the original model $V_0$ (Fig. 2(a)) and each of its variants $V_1, \ldots V_7$. If the original authors of a measure described it as a distance measure rather than a similarity measure, we use Equation 1 for transforming the distance measure into a similarity measure.

First, we modify the original model $V_0$ of Fig. 2(a) by splitting some XOR connectors into more than one connector (see Fig. 2(b)). Note that $\Sigma(V_1) = \Sigma(V_0)$. Next, we change the types of connectors: In model variant $V_2$ (Fig. 2(c)), all XOR connectors ($\Diamond$) have been replaced by inclusive OR connectors ($\blacklozenge$). In variant $V_3$ (Fig. 2(d)), four additional activities A, B, C and D have been added to the original model.

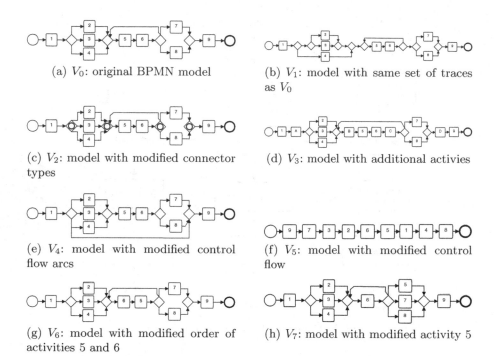

(a) $V_0$: original BPMN model

(b) $V_1$: model with same set of traces as $V_0$

(c) $V_2$: model with modified connector types

(d) $V_3$: model with additional activies

(e) $V_4$: model with modified control flow arcs

(f) $V_5$: model with modified control flow

(g) $V_6$: model with modified order of activities 5 and 6

(h) $V_7$: model with modified activity 5

**Fig. 2.** Initial model $V_0$ and variants $V_1 \ldots V_7$

Model variant $V_4$ (Fig. 2(e)) has exactly the same nodes as $V_0$, but one arc has been added while another one has been deleted. Variant $V_5$ (Fig. 2(f)) does contain the same activities as $V_0$, but no connectors at all. The order of the activities does not correspond to the order in which the activities occur in executions of $V_0$. In model variant $V_6$ (Fig. 2(g)), the order of activities 5 and 6 has been changed. Finally, in model variant $V_7$, (Fig. 2(h)), activity 5 has been moved inside the second conditional control block.

## 5    Results and Discussion

Tab. 1 shows the support of the different measures for the properties discussed in Sect. 3. The results for property 8 are based on a somewhat subjective judgment – measures that require to calculate the set of traces of a BPM were categorised as computationally inefficient. From Tab. 1, we can see that no measure fulfills all desirable properties.

Tab. 2 shows the similarity values we have computed between our example model $V_0$ and its variants $V_1 \ldots V_7$. For measures that can be parametrised by attaching different weights to factors, we used the most reasonable and simple parameters. The table shows that a variety of measures deliver results that do not comply with the intuitive (but rather subjective) understanding of "process model similarity".

**Table 1.** Comparison of similarity measures by adherence to properties in Sect. 3

| | 1 | 2 | 3 | 3a | 5 | 6 | 7 | 8 |
|---|---|---|---|---|---|---|---|---|
| Measures based on the correspondence of nodes and edges (not taking into account the control flow) | | | | | | | | |
| Percentage of Common Activity Names [6] | yes | yes | no | no | yes | yes | yes | yes |
| Label Matching Similarity [3] | yes | no | no | no | yes | yes | yes | yes |
| Similarity of Activity Labels [5] | yes | no | no | no | yes | yes | yes | yes |
| Feature-Based Activity Similarity [11] | yes | yes | no | no | yes | yes | yes | yes |
| Percentage of Common Nodes and Edges [12] | yes | yes | no | no | yes | yes | yes | yes |
| Node- and Link-Based Similarity [10] | yes | yes | no | no | yes | yes | yes | yes |
| Measures based on graph edit distances | | | | | | | | |
| Graph Edit Distance [3] | yes | yes | yes | no | yes | yes | yes | yes |
| Graph Edit Distance [30] | yes | yes | yes | no | no | no | yes | yes |
| Label Similarity and Graph Edit Distance [13] | yes | yes | no | no | yes | yes | yes | yes |
| Label Similarity and Graph Edit Distance [26] | yes | yes | yes | no | no | yes | yes | yes |
| Number of High-Level Change Operations [16] | yes | yes | no | yes | yes | no | n/a | yes |
| Comparing BPMs Represented as Trees [17] | yes | yes | no | no | yes | no | yes | yes |
| Distance Between Reduced Models [7] | yes | no | no | no | yes | no | yes | yes |
| Measures that analyse causal dependencies between activities | | | | | | | | |
| Comparing Dependency Graphs [8,9] | yes | yes | no | no | yes | no | yes | yes |
| Comparing Dependency Graphs [22] | yes | yes | no | no | yes | no | n/a | yes |
| Reference Similarity [21] | yes | yes | no | yes | yes | no | yes | no |
| TAR-Relationship [21] | yes | yes | no | no | yes | no | yes | no |
| Causal Behavioural Profiles [20] | yes | yes | no | no | yes | no | no | yes |
| Causal Footprints [3] | yes | yes | no | no | yes | no | yes | no |
| Set of Traces as n-grams [14] | yes | no | no | no | no | no | yes | no |
| Measures that compare sets of traces or logs | | | | | | | | |
| Longest Common Subsequence of Traces [18] | yes | yes | no | no | yes | no | yes | no |
| Similarity Based on Principal Transition Sequences [31] | yes | yes | no | no | yes | no | yes | yes |
| Similarity Based on Traces [19] | yes | yes | no | no | yes | no | yes | yes |

Similarity measures for BPMs have been proposed for a number of purposes. The purposes named in the literature include:

- finding "related" models in a repository [11]
- finding "similar" models in a repository for the purpose of reuse, preventing duplication and assisting process design [3,26,31,21,22,6]
- minimise the efforts to transform one model into another one with the aim to support dynamic process changes [16,20]
- identifying common or similar models in the context of company mergers [3,21]
- measuring the conformance between a BPM used as system specification and a workflow model that implements the process [20]
- finding models or model parts that should be merged into one integrated model to improve the maintainability of the BPM repository [13]
- discovering services from a description of their behaviour [30,19,14]
- measuring the conformance between a BPM and a reference model [18,20]

**Table 2.** Similarity Measures for our Example Models

| | Similarity between $V_0$ and ... | | | | | | |
|---|---|---|---|---|---|---|---|
| | $V_1$ | $V_2$ | $V_3$ | $V_4$ | $V_5$ | $V_6$ | $V_7$ |
| Measures based on the correspondence of nodes and edges (not taking into account the control flow) | | | | | | | |
| Percentage of Common Activity Names [6] | 1.00 | 1.00 | 0.82 | 1.00 | 1.00 | 1.00 | 1.00 |
| Label Matching Similarity [3] | 1.00 | 1.00 | 0.82 | 1.00 | 1.00 | 1.00 | 1.00 |
| Similarity of Activity Labels [5] | 1.00 | 1.00 | 1.00 | 1.00 | 1.00 | 1.00 | 1.00 |
| Feature-Based Activity Similarity [11] | 1.00 | 1.00 | 0.82 | 1.00 | 1.00 | 1.00 | 1.00 |
| Percentage of Common Nodes and Edges [12] | 1.00 | 1.00 | 0.40 | 0.95 | 0.58 | 0.76 | 0.79 |
| Node- and Link-Based Similarity [10] | 0.55 | 0.60 | 0.49 | 0.59 | 0.61 | 0.60 | 0.55 |
| Measures based on graph edit distances | | | | | | | |
| Graph Edit Distance [3] | 1.00 | 1.00 | 0.63 | 0.97 | 0.73 | 0.86 | 0.12 |
| Graph Edit Distance [30] | 0.05 | 0.04 | 0.20 | 0.33 | 0.03 | 0.33 | 0.17 |
| Label Similarity and Graph Edit Distance [13] | 0.81 | 1.00 | 0.60 | 0.96 | 0.61 | 0.79 | 0.84 |
| Label Similarity and Graph Edit Distance [26] | 0.05 | 0.03 | 0.06 | 0.33 | 0.03 | 0.14 | 0.20 |
| Number of High-Level Change Operations [16] | 1.00 | 0.17 | 0.20 | 0.33 | 0.14 | 0.50 | 0.50 |
| Comparing BPMs Represented as Trees [17] | 1.00 | 1.00 | 0.07 | 0.12 | 0.06 | 0.14 | 0.14 |
| Comparing BPMs Represented as Trees [17] | 1.00 | 0.07 | 1.00 | 1.00 | 0.00 | 0.80 | 0.81 |
| Measures that analyse causal dependencies between activities | | | | | | | |
| Comparing Dependency Graphs [8,9] | 1.00 | 1.00 | 0.04 | 0.33 | 0.06 | 0.09 | 0.10 |
| Comparing Dependency Graphs [22] | 1.00 | 0.93 | 0.54 | 0.90 | 0.51 | 0.98 | 0.83 |
| Reference Similarity [21] | not defined ($V_0$ has a loop!) | | | | | | |
| TAR-Relationship [21] | 1.00 | 0.57 | 0.04 | 0.85 | 0.11 | 0.41 | 0.47 |
| Causal Behavioural Profiles [20] | 1.00 | 0.93 | 0.63 | 0.93 | 0.22 | 0.98 | 0.89 |
| Causal Footprints [3] | 1.00 | 1.00 | 0.45 | 0.80 | 0.59 | 0.97 | 0.84 |
| Set of Traces as n-grams [14] | 1.00 | 0.10 | 0.04 | 0.33 | 0.05 | 0.09 | 0.10 |
| Measures that compare set of traces or logs | | | | | | | |
| Longest Common Subsequence of Traces [18] | 1.00 | 0.86 | 0.79 | 1.00 | 0.43 | 0.93 | 0.90 |
| Similarity Based on Principal Transition Sequences [31] | 1.00 | 0.83 | 0.61 | 0.84 | 0.20 | 0.85 | 0.83 |
| Similarity Based on Traces [19] | 1.00 | 0.90 | 0.33 | 0.83 | 0.22 | 0.72 | 0.65 |

- comparing models that are constructed from the same template in order to manage process variants and to support flexible workflow systems [12,7].

Our observations gives some first insights which measures are more useful than others for a given purpose. These suggestions are based on the results shown in Tab. 2. However, it must be stated that several advantages and disadvantages of the measures can only be evaluated based on specific application areas. For example, it cannot objectively be decided wheter $V_3$ or $V_7$ should be regarded as more similar to $V_0$.

Simple measures that just count the number of common nodes or arcs in the models are useful for finding related models from a repository (and less useful for purposes that make reference to the model behaviour). An interesting use case for such rather simple measures has been suggested by [11]: A search for related models can be used as a first step of a search in a large repository. It helps to filter out unrelated models such that the more precise (but also slower) algorithms can be applied to a small subset of the original search space.

When models are compared with the aim of discovering services or measuring conformance, approaches that consider the actual behaviour of a process execution have to be used. Preference should be given to the methods that exploit relationships between activities (such as [20,21,22]) instead of requiring a calculation of the whole set of traces (as [18]).

The reason is that calculating the whole set of traces of a model can demand large memory and processing resources. It has to be noted that the approach based on causal footprints described in [3] is computationally inefficient as well and cannot be recommended to be used in the context of large BPM repositories.

Processing speed can be less important if only two models have to be compared, for example to measure conformance. In such cases, using approaches that require to calculate the set of traces can be an option.

Some applications require to compare BPMs that have been designed on different levels of granularity. For example, this can be the case if the conformance between a BPM serving as a specification and the actual implementation in a workflow system have to be compared. In such cases, it is recommended to use a measure that finds a similarity even between such models. In particular, the approaches described in [7,20,18,30] support the comparison of models on different abstraction levels.

Although not extensively discussed in our paper, it should be noted that the quality of the mapping between the nodes has a significant contribution to the quality of a similarity measure. In particular, regarding nodes as corresponding to each other only if they have exactly the same label is reasonable only in a few special application areas such as comparing models that have been derived from the same template.

To furthermore enhance the reproducability and significance of our findings, we developed an analysis plugin[1] for the well-known ProM - Framework for Process Mining tool [32]. The plugin takes two arbitrary types of process models as inputs and shows the similarity values for the different approaches presented in this paper. In this paper we only presented a qualitative analysis to show first insights about the various measures. Based on the plugin implementation, several process model repositories will be analysed, e.g. the SAP reference model consisting of more than 600 models [33].

# 6  Conclusion

In our paper, we elaborated a number of desirable properties for BPM similarity measures. We analysed 22 similarity measures that have been described in the literature with respect to those properties. Also, we computed the similarity between example BPMs using the different similarity measures. While the rather small number of example models cannot show the relationships between the measures in a comprehensive manner, some first conclusions can be drawn. The results show that hardly a measure fulfills all desirable properties. Furthermore, it can be seen that different similarity measures rank the similarity

---

[1] Available at https://sourceforge.net/projects/prom-similarity/

between BPMs very differently. We conclude that there is not a single "perfect" similarity measure. Instead, we gave some recommendations for the selection of an appropriate similarity measure for different use cases.

# References

1. Gulla, J.A., Brasethvik, T.: On the challenges of business modeling in large-scale reengineering projects. In: IEEE International Conference on Requirements Engineering, p. 17 (2000)
2. Dumas, M., García-Bañuelos, L., Dijkman, R.: Similarity search of business process models. IEEE Data Engineering Bulletin 32, 23–28 (2009)
3. Dijkman, R., Dumas, M., van Dongen, B., Käärik, R., Mendling, J.: Similarity of business process models: Metrics and evaluation. Inf. Syst. 36, 498–516 (2011)
4. Weidlich, M., Dijkman, R., Mendling, J.: The ICoP Framework: Identification of Correspondences between Process Models. In: Pernici, B. (ed.) CAiSE 2010. LNCS, vol. 6051, pp. 483–498. Springer, Heidelberg (2010)
5. Ehrig, M., Koschmider, A., Oberweis, A.: Measuring similarity between semantic business process models. In: Fourth Asia-Pacific Conference on Comceptual Modelling, vol. 67, pp. 71–80 (2007)
6. Akkiraju, R., Ivan, A.: Discovering Business Process Similarities: An Empirical Study with SAP Best Practice Business Processes. In: Maglio, P.P., Weske, M., Yang, J., Fantinato, M. (eds.) ICSOC 2010. LNCS, vol. 6470, pp. 515–526. Springer, Heidelberg (2010)
7. Lu, R., Sadiq, S.: On managing process variants as an information resource. Technical report, The University of Queensland, School of Information Technology and Electrical Engineering (2006)
8. Bae, J., Liu, L., Caverlee, J., Rouse, W.B.: Process mining, discovery, and integration using distance measures. In: IEEE International Conference on Web Services, pp. 479–488 (2006)
9. Bae, J., Liu, L., Caverlee, J., Zhang, L.J., Bae, H.: Development of distance measures for process mining, discovery and integration. Int. J. Web Service Res. 4, 1–17 (2007)
10. Huang, K., Zhou, Z., Han, Y., Li, G., Wang, J.: An Algorithm for Calculating Process Similarity to Cluster Open-Source Process Designs. In: Jin, H., Pan, Y., Xiao, N., Sun, J. (eds.) GCC 2004. LNCS, vol. 3252, pp. 107–114. Springer, Heidelberg (2004)
11. Yan, Z., Dijkman, R., Grefen, P.: Fast Business Process Similarity Search with Feature-Based Similarity Estimation. In: Meersman, R., Dillon, T.S., Herrero, P. (eds.) OTM 2010, Part I. LNCS, vol. 6426, pp. 60–77. Springer, Heidelberg (2010)
12. Minor, M., Tartakovski, A., Bergmann, R.: Representation and Structure-Based Similarity Assessment for Agile Workflows. In: Weber, R.O., Richter, M.M. (eds.) ICCBR 2007. LNCS (LNAI), vol. 4626, pp. 224–238. Springer, Heidelberg (2007)
13. La Rosa, M., Dumas, M., Uba, R., Dijkman, R.: Merging Business Process Models. In: Meersman, R., Dillon, T.S., Herrero, P. (eds.) OTM 2010, Part I. LNCS, vol. 6426, pp. 96–113. Springer, Heidelberg (2010)
14. Wombacher, A., Rozie, M.: Evaluation of workflow similarity measures in service discovery. In: Service Oriented Electronic Commerce: Proceedings zur Konferenz im Rahmen der Multikonferenz Wirtschaftsinformatik. LNI., GI, vol. 80, pp. 51–71 (2006)

15. Dijkman, R., Dumas, M., García-Bañuelos, L.: Graph Matching Algorithms for Business Process Model Similarity Search. In: Dayal, U., Eder, J., Koehler, J., Reijers, H.A. (eds.) BPM 2009. LNCS, vol. 5701, pp. 48–63. Springer, Heidelberg (2009)
16. Li, C., Reichert, M., Wombacher, A.: On Measuring Process Model Similarity Based on High-Level Change Operations. In: Li, Q., Spaccapietra, S., Yu, E., Olivé, A. (eds.) ER 2008. LNCS, vol. 5231, pp. 248–264. Springer, Heidelberg (2008)
17. Bae, J., Caverlee, J., Liu, L., Yan, H.: Process Mining by Measuring Process Block Similarity. In: Eder, J., Dustdar, S. (eds.) BPM Workshops 2006. LNCS, vol. 4103, pp. 141–152. Springer, Heidelberg (2006)
18. Gerke, K., Cardoso, J., Claus, A.: Measuring the Compliance of Processes with Reference Models. In: Meersman, R., Dillon, T., Herrero, P. (eds.) OTM 2009, Part I. LNCS, vol. 5870, pp. 76–93. Springer, Heidelberg (2009)
19. Alves de Medeiros, A.K., van der Aalst, W.M.P., Weijters, A.J.M.M.: Quantifying process equivalence based on observed behavior. Data Knowl. Eng. 64, 55–74 (2008)
20. Weidlich, M., Mendling, J., Weske, M.: Efficient consistency measurement based on behavioural profiles of process models. IEEE Transactions on Software Engineering 99 (2010)
21. Zha, H., Wang, J., Wen, L., Wang, C., Sun, J.: A workflow net similarity measure based on transition adjacency relations. Comput. Ind. 61, 463–471 (2010)
22. Jung, J.Y., Bae, J., Liu, L.: Hierarchical clustering of business process models. International Journal of Innovative Computing, Information and Control 5, 1–11 (2009)
23. Santini, S., Jain, R.: Similarity measures. IEEE Trans. Pattern Anal. Mach. Intell. 21, 871–883 (1999)
24. Lin, D.: An information-theoretic definition of similarity. In: Proceedings 15th International Conference on Machine Learning, pp. 296–304 (1998)
25. Tversky, A.: Features of similarity. Psychological Review 84, 327–352 (1977)
26. Kunze, M., Weske, M.: Metric trees for efficient similarity search in process model repositories. In: Proceedings of the 1st International Workshop Process in the Large (IW-PL 2010), Hoboken, NJ (September 2010)
27. Dijkman, R.: A classification of differences between similar business processes. In: Proceedings of the 11th IEEE International Enterprise Distributed Object Computing Conference, pp. 37–50. IEEE Computer Society, Washington, DC, USA (2007)
28. Weber, B., Reichert, M., Rinderle-Ma, S.: Change patterns and change support features - enhancing flexibility in process-aware information systems. Data Knowl. Eng. 66, 438–466 (2008)
29. Weidlich, M., Barros, A., Mendling, J., Weske, M.: Vertical Alignment of Process Models – How Can We Get There? In: Halpin, T., Krogstie, J., Nurcan, S., Proper, E., Schmidt, R., Soffer, P., Ukor, R. (eds.) BPMDS 2009 and EMMSAD 2009. LNBIP, vol. 29, pp. 71–84. Springer, Heidelberg (2009)
30. Grigori, D., Corrales, J.C., Bouzeghoub, M., Gater, A.: Ranking BPEL processes for service discovery. IEEE Transactions on Services Computing 3, 178–192 (2010)
31. Wang, J., He, T., Wen, L., Wu, N., ter Hofstede, A.H.M., Su, J.: A Behavioral Similarity Measure between Labeled Petri Nets Based on Principal Transition Sequences. In: Meersman, R., Dillon, T.S., Herrero, P. (eds.) OTM 2010, Part I. LNCS, vol. 6426, pp. 394–401. Springer, Heidelberg (2010)
32. van Dongen, B.F., de Medeiros, A.K.A., Verbeek, H.M.W(E.), Weijters, A.J.M.M.T., van der Aalst, W.M.P.: The ProM Framework: A New Era in Process Mining Tool Support. In: Ciardo, G., Darondeau, P. (eds.) ICATPN 2005. LNCS, vol. 3536, pp. 444–454. Springer, Heidelberg (2005)
33. Curran, T., Keller, G., Ladd, A.: SAP R/3 business blueprint: understanding the business process reference model. Prentice-Hall, Inc., Upper Saddle River (1998)

# Comparing Business Processes to Determine the Feasibility of Configurable Models: A Case Study

J.J.C.L. Vogelaar, H.M.W. Verbeek, B. Luka, and Wil M.P van der Aalst

Technische Universiteit Eindhoven
Department of Mathematics and Computer Science
P.O. Box 513, 5600 MB Eindhoven, The Netherlands
{h.m.w.verbeek,w.m.p.v.d.aalst}@tue.nl

**Abstract.** Organizations are looking for ways to collaborate in the area of process management. Common practice until now is the (partial) standardization of processes. This has the main disadvantage that most organizations are forced to adapt their processes to adhere to the standard. In this paper we analyze and compare the actual processes of ten Dutch municipalities. Configurable process models provide a potential solution for the limitations of classical standardization processes as they contain all the behavior of individual models, while only needing one model. The question rises where the limits are though. It is obvious that one configurable model containing all models that exist is undesirable. But are company-wide configurable models feasible? And how about cross-organizational configurable models, should all partners be considered or just certain ones? In this paper we apply a similarity metric on individual models to determine means of answering questions in this area. This way we propose a new means of determining beforehand whether configurable models are feasible. Using the selected metric we can identify more desirable partners and processes before computing configurable process models.

**Keywords:** process configuration, YAWL, CoSeLoG, model merging.

## 1   Introduction

The results in this paper are based on 80 process models retrieved for 8 different business processes from 10 Dutch municipalities. This was done within the context of the CoSeLoG project [1,5]. This project aims to create a system for handling various types of permits, taxes, certificates, and licenses. Although municipalities are similar in that they have to provide the same set of business processes (services) to their citizens, their process models are typically different. Within the constraints of national laws and regulations, municipalities can differentiate because of differences in size, demographics, problems, and policies. Supported by the system to be developed within CoSeLoG, individual municipalities can make use of the process support services simultaneously, even though their process models differ. To realize this, *configurable process models* are used.

Configurable process models form a relatively young research topic [7,9,10,3]. A configurable process model can be seen as a union of several process models into

F. Daniel et al. (Eds.): BPM 2011 Workshops, Part II, LNBIP 100, pp. 50–61, 2012.

one. While combining different process models, duplication of elements is avoided by matching and merging them together. The elements that occur in only a selection of the individual process models are made configurable. These elements are then able to be set or configured. In effect, such an element can be chosen to be included or excluded. When for all configurable elements such a setting is made, the resulting process model is called a configuration. This configuration could then correspond to one of the individual process models for example.

Configurable process models offer several benefits. One of the benefits is that there is only one process model that needs to be maintained, instead of the several individual ones. This is especially helpful in case a law changes or is introduced, and thus all municipalities have to change their business processes, and hence their process models. In the case of a configurable process model this would only incur a single change. When we lift this idea up to the level of services (like in the CoSeLoG project [1,5]), we also only need to maintain one information system, which can be used by multiple municipalities.

Configurable process models are not always a good solution however. In some cases they will yield better results than in others. Two process models that are quite similar are likely to be better suited for inclusion in a configurable process model than two completely different and independent process models. For this reason, this paper strives to provide answers to the following three questions:

1. *Which business process is the best starting point for developing a configurable process model?* That is, given a municipality and a set of process models for every municipality and every business process, for which business process is the configurable process model (containing all process models for that business process) the less complex?
2. *Which other municipality is the best candidate to develop configurable models with?* That is, given a municipality and a set of process models for every municipality and every business process, for which other municipality are the configurable process models (containing the process models for both municipalities) the less complex?
3. *Which clusters of municipalities would best work together, using a common configurable model?* That is, given a business process and a set of process models for every municipality and every business process, for which clustering of municipalities are the configurable process models (containing all process models for the municipalities in a cluster) the less complex?

The remainder of this paper is structured as follows. Section 2 introduces the 80 process models and background information about these process models. Section 3 makes various comparisons to produce answers to the proposed questions. Finally, Section 4 concludes the paper. For additional details, we refer the interested reader to [13], which is the technical report which underlies this paper.

## 2  YAWL Models

We collected 80 YAWL[8] models in total. These YAWL models were retrieved from the ten municipalities, which are partners in the CoSeLoG project: Bergeijk, Bladel,

Coevorden, Eersel, Emmen, Gemert-Bakel, Hellendoorn, Oirschot, Reusel-de Mierden and Zwolle. In the remainder of this paper we will refer to these municipalities as $Mun_A$ to $Mun_J$ (these are randomly ordered).

For every municipality, we retrieved the YAWL models for the same eight business processes, which are run by any Dutch municipality. Hence, our process model collection is composed of eight sub-collections consisting of ten YAWL models each. The YAWL models were retrieved through interviews by us and validated by the municipalities afterwards.

The eight business processes covered are:

1. The processing of an application for a receipt from the people registration (3 variants):
   (a) When a customer applies through the internet: $GBA_1$.
   (b) When a customer applies in person at the town hall: $GBA_2$.
   (c) When a customer applies through a written letter: $GBA_3$.
2. The method of dealing with the report of a problem in a public area of the municipality: $MOR$.
3. The processing of an application for a building permit (2 parts):
   (a) The preceding process to prepare for the formal procedure: $WABO_1$.
   (b) The formal procedure: $WABO_2$.
4. The processing of an application for social services: $WMO$.
5. The handling of objections raised against the taxation of a house: $WOZ$.

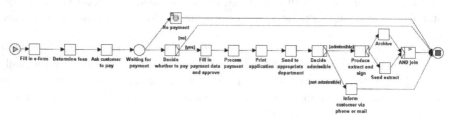

**Fig. 1.** $GBA_1$ YAWL model for $Mun_E$

To give an indication of the variety and similarity between the different YAWL models some examples are shown. Figure 1 shows the $GBA_1$ YAWL model of $Mun_E$, whereas Figure 2 shows the $GBA_1$ YAWL model of $Mun_G$. The YAWL models of these two municipalities are quite similar. Nevertheless, there are some differences. Recall that $GBA_1$ is about the application for a certain document through the internet. The difference between the two municipalities is that $Mun_E$ handles the payment through the internet (so before working on the document), while $Mun_G$ handles it manually after having sent the document. However, the main steps to create the document are the same. This explains why the general flow of both models is about the same, with exception of the payment-centered elements.

People can apply for this document through different means too. Figure 3 shows the $GBA_2$ YAWL model for $Mun_E$. This model seems to contain more tasks than either of the $GBA_1$ models. This makes sense, since more communication takes place during

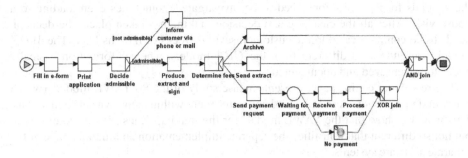

**Fig. 2.** $GBA_1$ YAWL model for $Mun_G$

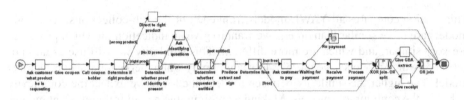

**Fig. 3.** $GBA_2$ YAWL model for $Mun_E$

the application. The employee at the town hall needs to gain the necessary information from the customer. In the internet case, the customer had already entered the information himself in the form, because otherwise the application could not be sent digitally. As the YAWL model still describes a way to produce the same document, it is to be expected that $GBA_2$ models are somewhat similar to $GBA_1$ models. Indeed, the general flow remains approximately the same, although some tasks have been inserted. This is especially the case in the leftmost part of the model, which is the part where in the internet case the customer has already given all information prior to sending the digital form. In the model shown in Figure 3 the employee asks the customer for information in this same area. This extra interaction also means more tasks (and choices) in the YAWL model.

Figure 4 shows the $WOZ$ YAWL model for $Mun_E$, which is clearly different from the three $GBA$ models. The $WOZ$ model shown in Figure 4 is more time-consuming. Customers need to be heard and their objections need to be assessed thoroughly. Next,

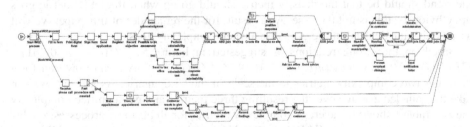

**Fig. 4.** $WOZ$ YAWL model for $Mun_E$

the grounds for the objections need to be investigated, sometimes even leading to a house visit. After all the checking and decision making has taken place, the decision needs to be communicated to the customer, several weeks or months later. The $WOZ$ models are quite a bit different from the $GBA$ models, where information basically needs to be retrieved and documented.

The remainder of this paper presents a case study of the 80 YAWL models (which can found in Appendix A of [13]), and compares them within their own sub-collections. This way, we show that the YAWL models for the municipalities are indeed different, but not so different that it justifies the separate implementation and maintenance of ten separate software systems.

# 3   Comparison

This section compares all YAWL models from each of the sub-collections. As certain models are more similar than others, we want to give an indication on which processes are very similar, and which are more different. This similarity we will use as an indication of which models have more or less complexity when merged into a configurable model. The higher the similarity between models, the lower we expect the complexity to be for the configurable models. Making a configurable model for equivalent models (similarity score 1.0) approximately results in the same model again (additional complexity approx. 0.0), since no new functionality needs to be added to any of the original models.

First, we apply a combination of three known complexity metrics to all YAWL models. Second, we compare the models using a combination of two known similarity metrics. Third and last, we answer the three questions as proposed earlier using these metrics.

## 3.1   Complexity

For every YAWL model, we calculated the CFC [4], density [11], and CC metric [12] (see also [13] for details) to get an indication of its complexity. The complete results can be found in Appendix B of [13]. Figure 5 shows the relation between the CFC metric and the other two complexity metrics. Clearly, these relations are quite strong: The higher the CFC metric, the lower the other two metrics. Although this is to be expected for the CC metric, this is quite unexpected for the density metric. Like the CFC metric, the density metric was assumed to go up when complexity goes up, hence the trend should be that the density metric should go up when the CFC metric goes up. Obviously, this is not the case. As a result, for the remainder of this paper we will assume that the density metric goes down when complexity goes up.

Based on the strong relations as suggested in Figure 5 ($CC(G) = 0.4611 \cdot CFC(G)^{-0.851}$ and $density(G) = 1.1042 \cdot CFC(G)^{-0.791}$) we can now transform the other two complexity metrics to the scale of the CFC metric. As a result, we can take the rounded average over the resulting three metrics and get a unified complexity metric. Table 1 shows the average complexity metrics for all business processes. As this table shows, the processes $WABO_2$ and $WMO$ are the most complex, and $GBA_1$ and $WABO_1$ the least complex.

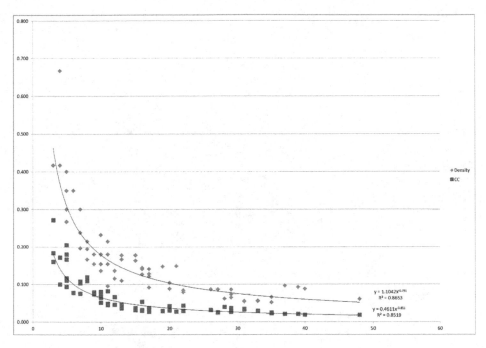

**Fig. 5.** Comparison of the CFC metric with the CC and Density metrics

**Table 1.** Comparison of the business processes on the complexity metrics

|         | $GBA_1$ | $GBA_2$ | $GBA_3$ | $MOR$  | $WABO_1$ | $WABO_2$ | $WMO$  | $WOZ$  |
|---------|---------|---------|---------|--------|----------|----------|--------|--------|
| CFC     | 5.100   | 14.400  | 9.800   | 15.400 | 4.700    | 29.800   | 33.800 | 12.000 |
| Density | 0.383   | 0.165   | 0.170   | 0.159  | 0.305    | 0.061    | 0.080  | 0.132  |
| CC      | 0.147   | 0.038   | 0.088   | 0.035  | 0.119    | 0.034    | 0.024  | 0.064  |
| Unified | 5       | 15      | 9       | 17     | 5        | 30       | 33     | 13     |

## 3.2 Similarity

For every pair of YAWL models from the same sub-collection, we calculated the GED and SPS metric [6] (see also [13] for details) to get an indication of their similarity. The complete results can be found in Appendix C of [13]. Figure 6 shows the relation between the GED and the SPS metric. Although the relation between these metrics $(SPS(G_1, G_2) = 2.0509 \cdot GED(G_1, G_2) - 1.082)$ is a bit less strong as the relation between the complexity metrics, we consider this relation to be strong enough to unify both metrics into a single, unified, metric. This unified similarity metric uses the scale of the SPS metric, as the range of this scale is wider than the scale of the GED metric. Table 2 shows the averages over the values for the different similarity metrics for each of the processes. From this table, we conclude that the $GBA_2$ models are most similar to each other, while the $MOR$ models are least similar.

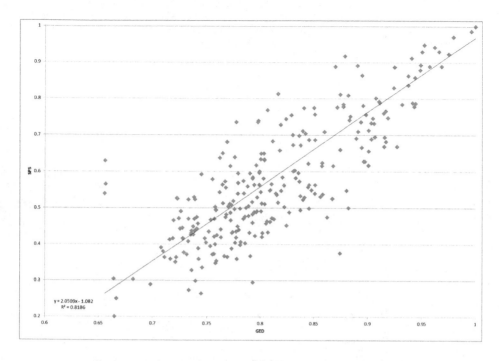

$$y = 2.0509x - 1.082$$
$$R^2 = 0.8186$$

**Fig. 6.** Comparison of the GED metric with the SPS metric

**Table 2.** Average similarity values

|        | $GBA_1$ | $GBA_2$ | $GBA_3$ | $MOR$ | $WABO_1$ | $WABO_2$ | $WMO$ | $WOZ$ |
|--------|-------|-------|-------|-------|--------|--------|-------|-------|
| GED    | 0.829 | 0.916 | 0.828 | 0.797 | 0.871  | 0.891  | 0.830 | 0.820 |
| SPS    | 0.646 | 0.759 | 0.632 | 0.556 | 0.774  | 0.725  | 0.546 | 0.615 |
| Unified | 0.632 | 0.778 | 0.624 | 0.554 | 0.739  | 0.735  | 0.583 | 0.607 |

Recall that a configurable process model "contains" all individual process models. Whenever one wants to use the configurable model as an executable model, it needs to be configured by selecting which parts should be left out. The more divergent the individuals are, the more complex the resulting configurable process model needs to be to accommodate all the individuals. So, the more similar models are, the easier to construct and maintain the configurable model will most likely be.

The similarity value for the $GBA_1$ models for $Mun_A$ and $Mun_H$ equals 1.0. Merging these models into a configurable model, yields an equivalent model, which we find not so interesting. Taking a look at another high similarity value in the table, we construct the configurable $GBA1$ model for $Mun_D$ and $Mun_I$. The complexity metrics for the configurable model yield 7 (CFC), 0.238 (density), 0.091 (CC), and 7 (unified). Similarly we construct a configurable model for the two least similar models: $Mun_G$ and $Mun_F$. The resulting complexity values are 34 (CFC), 0.108 (density), 0.026 (CC),

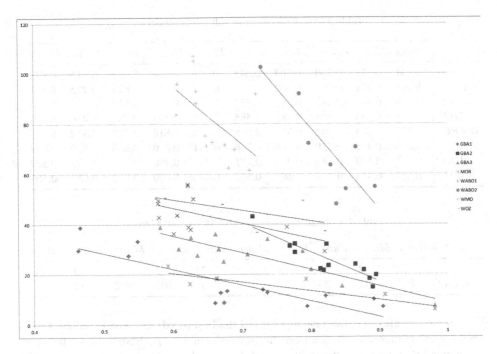

**Fig. 7.** Unified similarity vs. unified complexity for 100 pairs of models

and 28 (unified). These results are in line with our expectations, as the former metrics are all better than the latter.

To confirm these relation between similarity on the one hand and complexity on the other, we have selected 100 pairs of models (each pair from the same sub-collection), have merged every pair, and have computed the complexity metrics of the resulting model. Figure 7 shows the results: When similarity goes down, complexity tends to go up.

Based on the illustrated correlations, we assume that the unified similarity metric gives a good indication for the unified complexity of the resulting configurable model. Therefore, we use this metric to answer the three questions stated in the introduction.

### 3.3 Question 1: Which Business Process Is the Best Starting Point for Developing a Configurable Process Model?

To answer this question we select a specific business process $P$ and compute the average similarity between the YAWL model of process $P$ in a selected municipality and all models of $P$ in other municipalities. Take for example $Mun_D$. For the $GBA_1$ process, the average value for $Mun_D$ (that is, average distance to other municipalities) is $\frac{0.735+0.777+0.670+0.741+0.818+0.430+0.735+0.898+0.526}{9} = 0.703$. Table 3 shows the averages for each municipality and each business process. In this table we can see that for $Mun_D$ the $WABO_2$ process scores highest, followed by $WABO_1$ and $GBA_1$. Note

**Table 3.** Average similarity values per model

|        | $Mun_A$ | $Mun_B$ | $Mun_C$ | $Mun_D$ | $Mun_E$ | $Mun_F$ | $Mun_G$ | $Mun_H$ | $Mun_I$ | $Mun_J$ |
|--------|---------|---------|---------|---------|---------|---------|---------|---------|---------|---------|
| $GBA_1$ | 0.631 | 0.612 | 0.560 | 0.703 | 0.645 | 0.641 | *0.354* | 0.631 | 0.715 | *0.442* |
| $GBA_2$ | **0.766** | **0.821** | 0.667 | 0.602 | 0.807 | **0.771** | 0.751 | **0.821** | 0.725 | **0.821** |
| $GBA_3$ | 0.530 | 0.513 | 0.486 | 0.607 | 0.550 | 0.587 | 0.678 | 0.551 | 0.678 | 0.664 |
| $MOR$ | *0.496* | 0.548 | 0.501 | 0.482 | 0.585 | *0.488* | 0.573 | *0.468* | *0.430* | 0.491 |
| $WABO_1$ | 0.501 | 0.483 | 0.602 | 0.776 | **0.818** | 0.662 | **0.818** | 0.818 | **0.818** | 0.818 |
| $WABO_2$ | 0.646 | *0.419* | **0.730** | **0.800** | 0.746 | 0.741 | 0.800 | 0.800 | 0.750 | 0.644 |
| $WMO$ | 0.621 | 0.539 | 0.543 | *0.426* | *0.491* | 0.503 | 0.496 | 0.625 | 0.615 | 0.522 |
| $WOZ$ | 0.507 | 0.448 | *0.447* | 0.601 | 0.562 | 0.616 | 0.600 | 0.651 | 0.657 | 0.561 |

**Table 4.** Comparing $WABO_2$ and $WMO$ for $Mun_D$

|          | $Mun_A$ | $Mun_B$ | $Mun_C$ | $Mun_E$ | $Mun_F$ | $Mun_G$ | $Mun_H$ | $Mun_I$ | $Mun_J$ | Average |
|----------|---------|---------|---------|---------|---------|---------|---------|---------|---------|---------|
| $WABO_2$ | 92 | 72 | 71 | 51 | 55 | 32 | 32 | 34 | 64 | 56 |
| $WMO$ | 105 | 112 | 84 | 95 | 78 | 85 | 102 | 102 | 82 | 94 |

that for ease of reference, we have highlighted the best (bold) and worst (italics) similarity scores per municipality. So, from the viewpoint of $Mun_D$, these three are the best candidates for making a configurable model. In a similar way we can determine such best candidates for any of the municipalities.

We now construct configurable models for the $WABO_2$ model for $Mun_D$ and each of the other municipalities and take the average complexity metrics for these. We do the same for the $WMO$ model. Table 4 shows the results. Although the complexities of the $WABO_2$ models (30) and the $WMO$ models (33) are quite similar, it is clear that merging the latter yields worse scores on all complexity metrics than merging the former yields. Therefore, we conclude that the better similarity between the $WABO_2$ models resulted in a less-complex configurable model, while the worse similarity between the $MOR$ models resulted in a more-complex configurable model.

From Table 3 we can also conclude that the $GBA_2$, $WABO_1$, and $WABO_2$ processes are, in general, good candidates to start a configurable approach with, as they turn out best for 5, 3, and 2 municipalities.

### 3.4 Question 2: Which Other Municipality Is the Best Candidate to Develop Configurable Models With?

The second question is not so much about which process suits the municipality best, but which other municipality. To compute this, we take the average similarity over all models for every other municipality. Table 5 shows the results for all municipalities. Again, we have highlighted the best match. This table shows that $Mun_H$ and $Mun_I$ are most similar to $Mun_D$. Apparently, these municipalities are best suited to start working with $Mun_D$ on an overall configurable approach.

We calculated the average complexity of the configurable models for $Mun_D$ and $Mun_H$ and for $Mun_D$ and $Mun_A$. Table 6 shows the results. Clearly, the average

**Table 5.** Average similarity values per municipality

| | $Mun_A$ | $Mun_B$ | $Mun_C$ | $Mun_D$ | $Mun_E$ | $Mun_F$ | $Mun_G$ | $Mun_H$ | $Mun_I$ | $Mun_J$ |
|---|---|---|---|---|---|---|---|---|---|---|
| $Mun_A$ | | 0.556 | 0.546 | 0.555 | 0.598 | 0.585 | 0.591 | 0.682 | 0.644 | 0.527 |
| $Mun_B$ | 0.556 | | *0.508* | *0.538* | *0.559* | *0.547* | *0.512* | *0.595* | 0.591 | *0.525* |
| $Mun_C$ | 0.546 | *0.508* | | 0.580 | 0.617 | 0.552 | 0.575 | 0.604 | *0.569* | 0.552 |
| $Mun_D$ | 0.555 | 0.538 | 0.580 | | 0.638 | 0.630 | 0.642 | 0.702 | 0.717 | 0.619 |
| $Mun_E$ | 0.598 | 0.559 | **0.617** | 0.638 | | 0.672 | **0.692** | 0.679 | 0.705 | **0.696** |
| $Mun_F$ | 0.585 | 0.547 | 0.552 | 0.630 | 0.672 | | 0.675 | 0.651 | 0.671 | 0.651 |
| $Mun_G$ | 0.591 | 0.512 | 0.575 | 0.642 | 0.692 | **0.675** | | 0.656 | 0.687 | 0.672 |
| $Mun_H$ | **0.682** | **0.595** | 0.604 | 0.702 | 0.679 | 0.651 | 0.656 | | **0.801** | 0.664 |
| $Mun_I$ | 0.644 | 0.591 | 0.569 | **0.717** | **0.705** | 0.671 | 0.687 | **0.801** | | 0.677 |
| $Mun_J$ | *0.527* | 0.525 | 0.552 | 0.619 | 0.696 | 0.651 | 0.672 | 0.663 | 0.676 | |

**Table 6.** Comparing $Mun_H$ and $Mun_A$ for $Mun_D$

| | $GBA_1$ | $GBA_2$ | $GBA_3$ | $MOR$ | $WABO_1$ | $WABO_2$ | $WMO$ | $WOZ$ | Average |
|---|---|---|---|---|---|---|---|---|---|
| $Mun_H$ | 13 | 29 | 47 | 41 | 12 | 32 | 102 | 26 | 38 |
| $Mun_A$ | 13 | 38 | 34 | 55 | 16 | 92 | 105 | 42 | 49 |

complexity scores when merging $Mun_D$ with $Mun_H$ are better than the scores when merging $Mun_D$ with $Mun_A$. This is in line with our expectations. Also note that only for the $GBA_3$ process a configurable model with $Mun_A$ might be preferred over a configurable model with $Mun_H$.

From Table 5 we can also conclude that $Mun_I$ and $Mun_E$ are preferred partners for configurable models, as $Mun_I$ are the preferred partner for 3 of the municipalities.

### 3.5 Question 3: Which Clusters of Municipalities Would Best Work Together, Using a Common Configurable Model?

The third question is a bit trickier to answer, but this can also be accomplished with the computed metrics. To answer this question, we only need to consider the values in one of the comparison tables (see Appendix C of [13]). We now want to see which clusters of municipalities could best work together in using configurable models. There are different ways to approach this problem. One of the approaches is using the $k$-means clustering algorithm [2]. Applying this algorithm to the mentioned metrics, we obtain the clusters $Mun_B + Mun_D + Mun_E + Mun_F + Mun_I$, $Mun_G + Mun_J$, and $Mun_A + Mun_C + Mun_H$.

Table 7 shows the complexity for all processes, where cluster $k$ is the cluster as selected by the $k$-means clustering technique and cluster 1 up to 10 are 10 randomly selected clusters per process (see Appendix E of [13] for the cluster details). This table clearly shows that the clusters as obtained by the $k$-means clustering technique are quite good. Only in the case of the $GBA_3$ and $WABO_1$ processes, we found a better clustering, and in case of the latter process the gain is only marginal.

**Table 7.** Comparing clusters on CC

| Cluster | $GBA_1$ | $GBA_2$ | $GBA_3$ | $MOR$ | $WABO_1$ | $WABO_2$ | $WMO$ | $WOZ$ |
|---|---|---|---|---|---|---|---|---|
| k | 15 | 25 | 48 | 50 | 19 | 76 | 101 | 59 |
| 1 | 15 | 29 | 54 | 75 | 26 | 92 | 117 | 75 |
| 2 | 28 | 32 | 47 | 67 | 21 | 95 | 116 | 74 |
| 3 | 23 | 33 | 52 | 73 | 27 | 88 | 115 | 88 |
| 4 | 26 | 32 | 45 | 81 | 24 | 87 | 103 | 76 |
| 5 | 27 | 32 | 49 | 69 | 18 | 84 | 130 | 85 |
| 6 | 26 | 30 | 46 | 77 | 27 | 100 | 113 | 80 |
| 7 | 26 | 34 | 48 | 66 | 27 | 90 | 121 | 82 |
| 8 | 24 | 33 | 50 | 71 | 22 | 92 | 107 | 82 |
| 9 | 25 | 32 | 45 | 77 | 24 | 92 | 128 | 80 |
| 10 | 27 | 31 | 51 | 76 | 26 | 77 | 133 | 77 |
| Average | 24 | 31 | 49 | 71 | 24 | 88 | 117 | 78 |

# 4  Conclusion

First of all, in this paper we have shown that similarity can be used to predict the complexity of a configurable model. In principle, the more similar two process models are, the less complex the resulting configurable model will be.

We have used the control-flow complexity (CFC) metric from [4], the density metric from [11], and the cross-connectivity (CC) metric from [12] as complexity metrics. We have shown that these three metrics are quite related to each other. For example, when the CFC metric goes up, the density and CC go down. Based on this, we have been able to unify these metrics into a single complexity metric that uses the same scale as the CFC metric.

The complexity of the 80 YAWL models used in this paper ranged from simple ($GBA_1$ and $WABO_1$ processes, unified complexity approx. 5) to complex ($WABO_2$ and $WMO$ processes, unified complexity approx. 30). The complexity of the configurable models we obtained were typically quite higher (up to approx. 450). This shows that complexity can get quickly out of control, and that we needs some way to predict the complexity of a configurable model beforehand.

To predict the complexity of a configurable model, we have used the GED metric and the SPS metric as defined in [6]. Based on the combined similarity of two process models a prediction can be made for the complexity of the resulting configurable model. By choosing to merge only similar process models, the complexity of the resulting configurable model is kept at bay.

We have shown that the CFC and unified metric of the configurable model are positively correlated with the similarity of its constituting process models, and that the density and CC metric are negatively correlated. The behavior of the density metric came as a surprise to us. The rationale behind this metric clearly states that a density and the likelihood of errors are positively correlated. As such, we expected a positive correlation between the density and the complexity. However, throughout our set of models we observed the trend that less-similar models yield less-dense configurable models, whereas the other complexity metrics behave as expected. As a result, we concluded that the density is negatively correlated with the complexity of models.

# References

1. van der Aalst, W.M.P.: Configurable Services in the Cloud: Supporting Variability While Enabling Cross-Organizational Process Mining. In: Meersman, R., Dillon, T.S., Herrero, P. (eds.) OTM 2010, Part I. LNCS, vol. 6426, pp. 8–25. Springer, Heidelberg (2010)
2. van der Aalst, W.M.P.: Process Mining: Discovery, Conformance and Enhancement of Business Processes. Springer, Heidelberg (2011)
3. van der Aalst, W.M.P., Dumas, M., Gottschalk, F., ter Hofstede, A.H.M., La Rosa, M., Mendling, J.: Preserving Correctness During Business Process Model Configuration. Formal Aspects of Computing 22, 459–482 (2010)
4. Cardoso, J.: How to Measure the Control-flow Complexity of Web Processes and Workflows (2005)
5. CoSeLoG. Configurable Services for Local Governments (CoSeLoG) Project Home Page, http://www.win.tue.nl/coselog
6. Dijkman, R.M., Dumas, M., van Dongen, B.F., Käärik, R., Mendling, J.: Similarity of Business Process Models: Metrics and Evaluation. Information Systems 36(2), 498–516 (2011)
7. Gottschalk, F.: Configurable Process Models. PhD thesis, Eindhoven University of Technology, The Netherlands (December 2009)
8. Hofstede, A., van der Aalst, W.M.P., Adams, M., Russell, N.: Modern Business Process Automation: YAWL and its Support Environment. Springer, Heidelberg (2009)
9. La Rosa, M.: Managing Variability in Process-Aware Information Systems. PhD thesis, Queensland University of Technology, Brisbane, Australia (April 2009)
10. La Rosa, M., Dumas, M., ter Hofstede, A.H.M., Mendling, J.: Configurable Multi-perspective Business Process Models. Information Systems 36(2), 313–340 (2011)
11. Mendling, J.: Testing Density as a Complexity Metric for EPCs. In: German EPC Workshop on Density of Process Models (2006)
12. Vanderfeesten, I.T.P., Reijers, H.A., Mendling, J., van der Aalst, W.M.P., Cardoso, J.: On a Quest for Good Process Models: The Cross-Connectivity Metric. In: Bellahsène, Z., Léonard, M. (eds.) CAiSE 2008. LNCS, vol. 5074, pp. 480–494. Springer, Heidelberg (2008)
13. Vogelaar, J.J.C.L., Verbeek, H.M.W., Luka, B., van der Aalst, W.M.P.: Comparing Business Processes to Determine the Feasibility of Configurable Models: A Case Study. BPM Center Report BPM-11-17, BPMcenter.org (2011)

# Industry Operations Architecture for Business Process Model Collections

Jorge L.C. Sanz, Ying Leung, Ignacio Terrizzano, Valeria Becker,
Susanne Glissmann, Joseph Kramer, and Guang-Jie Ren

IBM Research, 650 Harry Road, San Jose, California

**Abstract.** The absence of a holistic industry-centric architecture for processes is an important BPM shortfall that impacts model collections. This paper introduces a *Componentized Industry Business Architecture* as a vehicle to address this gap and to make processes better integrated with other critical dimensions in organizational design. This architecture provides the foundation for a taxonomy of processes and enables process models to be created or potentially rationalized against a comprehensive framework.

Process theory and industrial organization show that processes have different structure and dynamics. However, most processes used in workflows and case management have a similar 'factory' nature, i.e., production processes in the enterprise. The Componentized Industry Business Architecture shows that not all processes that matter follow this type of behavior. *Oversight Processes* constitute an important example and will be studied in depth.

**Keywords:** Business Process Collections, Industry Operations Architecture, Process Taxonomy, Business Process Management, Process Architecture.

## 1    Introduction

The goal of creating and governing collections of business process models in different industries is central to the success of the life-cycle addressed by Business Process Management (BPM). The broad application of process modeling has stimulated contemporary organizations to create many process models in support of their operations [1], [2]. In fact, a single line-of-business in a large enterprise typically has several hundred key processes. With such large collections of process models, an issue is how to sensibly deal with them, in particular when considering that models should be consulted, updated, and re-used over long periods of time by various stakeholders [3]. Other challenges for process model collections stem from broader issues with BPM [4].

In an extensive and seminal investigation, [5] proposed to *"reduce the confusion"* (sic) by distinguishing between three meanings of process, namely, (1) a logic that explains a causal relationship between independent and dependent variables, (2) a category of concepts of variables that refers to actions of individuals or organizations, and (3) a sequence of events that describes how things change over time. In fact, Van de Ven's work went beyond merely defining a process and addressed one of the most complex processes in organizations, i.e., the strategy process. The depth of Van de

F. Daniel et al. (Eds.): BPM 2011 Workshops, Part II, LNBIP 100, pp. 62–74, 2012.
© Springer-Verlag Berlin Heidelberg 2012

Ven's classification reveals the foundations underlying most business process definitions in BPM. In spite of having been published almost two decades ago, this work from well-known social science researchers has gone unnoticed in most of the BPM review literature and books.

Even though workflow and process modeling have been used extensively over the past 30 years, surprisingly little is known about the act of modeling and which factors contribute to a "good" process model in terms of human understandability [6]. To guarantee a certain degree of design quality of the model artifact in a wider sense, several authors propose guidelines for the act of modeling [1], [7] but yet with little impact on modeling practice. Also, typical information technology issues arise [3], [8], [9], [10], [11] in managing large collections of processes.

This paper introduces a componentized architecture of business operations[1] based on two important dimensions in organization design: competences and resource hierarchies. This concept realizes the principle of resource aggregation, complexity reduction and related work from different organizational research schools, thus yielding a *componentized* or *modularized approach to industry operations*. This comprehensive architecture helps organize processes in model collections by adding key aspects of organizational design that matter to the semantics of behavior models and covering family of operations beyond those addressed by conventional BPM work. In fact, new *subjects* of operations modeling are introduced in Section 2.2 through the notion of *ensembles of entity instances*. This family builds beyond "factory" processes that have been the main focus of BPM and Case Management. The dynamics of these *subjects* represents a family of enterprise operations called *Oversight Processes*. *Oversight processes* constitute an outstanding example of the comprehensive process taxonomy introduced in this Section.

As one of the goals of this paper is the construction of a model, i.e. the Componentized Business Architecture, we follow the approach of design science as described in [12], [13]. The approach is composed of two activities: creating and evaluating an artifact. In this paper, we propose the model of a Componentized Business Architecture as the artifact. The model contributes to business processes modeling and classification by providing a taxonomy of process founded on business research grounds.

## 2     Process Architecture and Taxonomy for Model Collections: Behavior in the Wider Context of Organizational Design

Process model collections require an adequate architecture that explains the structure of processes and a related taxonomy that helps categorize process models according to what an enterprise is and expects to accomplish with these models. A framework for processes (i.e., an architecture and related taxonomy) should shed light on what operations process models intend to represent and how these representations relate to industries and organizations.

---

[1] In this paper, the term "business operations" is used as a synonym of organization, i.e., a line-of-business or the entire enterprise. It encompasses for-profit, non-profit and government. Thus, "Industry Operations" means enterprises from the same industry segment.

Processes are about the behavior of an organization. This behavior is inseparable from the rest of the constituent elements and attributes of the organization, its goals, capabilities, outcomes (i.e., products, services and related value-propositions), industry segment position, skills and resources in general [14]. Section 2.1 introduces the concept of *Componentized Industry Business Architecture* to model the business from a broader perspective angle than processes. The Componentized Industry Business Architecture is holistic in the sense that it helps fit behavioral models within the broader scope of organizational design and does so by also modularizing business operations. This architecture approach is related to the classical notion of business architecture but it has several distinctive features as will be seen later in this Section.

An important example of the way the taxonomy derived from Componentized Industry Business Architecture widens the perspective on processes is illustrated by *Oversight Processes*. This family of processes goes beyond "factory" models (i.e., *workflows*) and is investigated in depth in Section 2.2. The relationship between *behavior* and *entity* is an important foundational dimension of oversight processes. In fact, this relationship builds on a more general liaison between process and *subject* cultivated for a long time in both social and information sciences. The linkages between behavioral and entity models developed mostly at the realm of the European schools constitute a body of essential, practical and inspirational outcomes [4] surprisingly unnoticed in most of the BPM literature.

## 2.1   Componentized Industry Business Architecture

Defining the boundaries of a process and the main stages that define its progression are key activities in modeling. There are many techniques documented in the BPM literature that tackle these objectives, involving a wide variety of methods [15] and standards [16], such as those based on goals [17], functional and activity-centric [18], Role-Activity Diagrams [19], communication-based [20], workflow-centric [21], based on Petri Nets [22], case-based [21], Event Process Chains [22], and so on. Telling from the difficulty to harvest and reuse found in the existing art of process model collections, it would be reasonable to argue that modeling methods have not been very successful in capturing *semantics of business operations*. These semantics should not be understood only as *clarity* or *understandability* but also as a *language of business design* that goes beyond the description of behavior.

On the other hand, designing business operations holistically is a complex problem and thus, it benefits from a modular architecture. Modularization is a good approach to tackle complex problems [25]. The basic goal of *decomposability* and *near-decomposability* is to *manage complexity* of a system by reducing the number of distinct elements and grouping them into a smaller number of subsystems. Business applications of some componentization ideas have been found in the financial services industry in [26]. Hundreds of engagements and field practice have shown the value of practical ideas to make business architecture an actionable concept in support of the convergence of strategy, operations and information technology [27].

On the other hand, several schools of thought working on theories of the firm state that *resources come in bundles* and argue that resource endowment and continued development of idiosyncratic capabilities by an organization build the foundations of competitive differentiation and sustained performance. It is enough for the purpose of this Section to stress that none of the strategy management schools, particularly the so-called *"resource-based view"*, have proposed any design principle for aggregation of resources for modeling enterprises or industries. In this sense, the paper goes a long way by making some foundations of the theory of the firm into a reusable body of work. As an important byproduct, the *componentization* proposed and its underlying architectural elements provide an important taxonomy to address process model collections within an ambitious and broad economy of scale and reuse.

In order to discuss the design principle, it is necessary to understand that the concept of resource used in organizational design is not limited to physical assets or people. Enterprises are endowed with and also generate a variety of resources that form a hierarchy in terms of the degree of elaboration or entanglement required. By simplifying the resource hierarchy, following [28] and other colleagues from the competence-based theory of firms, it is possible to define the hierarchy as shown in Figure 1. The distinction across these levels is relevant to demonstrate that important activities in an enterprise involve more elaborated constructs than the typical "resource" concept used in BPM and Case Management. The highest levels in this hierarchy, i.e., capabilities and skills, may be found troublesome by computer scientists and information engineers probably more accustomed to the *input-output* mechanism of production processes by which resources are inputs consumed by tasks to produce outputs. *Information,* viewed as a resource in the hierarchy of Figure 1, should be regarded specifically as an *asset*. The interested reader is referred to the extensive and rich literature spanning three decades of research work on capabilities, resource-view and competence-view of the firm for a deeper dive into these concepts [29], [30], [31], among many others.

In fact, the resource hierarchy goes further up from the *capability level* shown in Figure 1 to include also the concept of *competence* and often *core-competence* as well. The notion of *competence* is also used in this design principle to segment the entire enterprise resources into disjoint families. Each competence clusters all significant resources necessary for those specific enterprise activities in direct support of the life-cycle of the competence. Obviously, there are a number of competences and some of them vary across industries. For example, *Upstream* is a competence of a typical oil and gas industry; *Water Procurement* is a competence in the water segment of the utilities industry; *Health Care* and *Environment* are competences in the city

**Fig. 1.** Elements of the Resource Hierarchy involved in the architecture

government segment of the public industry; *Customer Service* is a typical competence where services matter and thus, it takes place in a variety of industry segments such as banking and telecommunications; and so on.

The other aspect of the modularization is based on a typology of the enterprise activities in which resources are also used. This dimension leads to a partition of resources into four levels, as seen in Figure 2. These levels correspond to four broad categories of activities involved in creating outcomes such as those arising in *vision and strategy, learning and innovation, oversight and management,* and *production and maintenance* operations. This hierarchical arrangement builds upon the work of Chandler [32], [33] among several others.

The combination of both aspects above yields a partition of the resource space that is the foundation of the modularization sought. The two dimensional arrangement of this modularization is shown in the layout of Figure 3. A refinement of the main modules may be needed for more detailed description and can be obtained by further partitioning those resources and activities that are needed to produce the different outcomes corresponding to the intersection of each column (i.e., competence) with each row (i.e., a level of hierarchy from Figure 2). In this figure, there are two such partitions shown with four components each, where Component X and Component Y have been highlighted for illustrative purposes.

By using the design principles above, a Componentized Business Architecture has been built for many industry segments, including banking, insurance, oil, chemicals, pharmaceutical, retail, consumer package, telecommunications, different government sectors, health care, automotive, industrial electronics, energy, water, heavy equipment manufacturing, avionics, transportation, to name a few important ones. Typical scenarios in practice have yielded industry architectures having anywhere between 80 and 150 business components [27]. In some cases, the underlying structure has been simplified a bit further by collapsing the middle two layers of the hierarchy of Figure 2 into a single one. As an example, a much simplified architecture for the City Government industry segment is shown in Figure 4, which follows the jargon

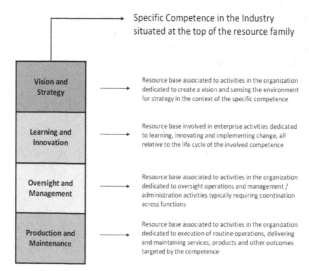

**Fig. 2.** Aggregation of resources for a given competence into hierarchical levels

introduced in [26]. In this case, there are 11 competences while the oversight and learning layers have been integrated into one, called "control" (the Government industry tends to have more oversight operations than learning or innovation activities). The complete model based on this architecture has over 150 business components representing the wide gamut of operations that City Governments may have.

A feature-by-design of the Componentized Business Architecture is that enterprise activities encapsulated by a component are characterized by having the same level of responsibility or accountability (in the sense of the hierarchy shown in Figure 2) and being dedicated to the same specific competence in the enterprise. *Outcomes* from a component explain the reason for the resources to be bundled, i.e., to support the creation of entangled and specific value-propositions in the component. These value-propositions justify the existence of the business component as a true aggregate, albeit virtual, and not only as an architecture artifact.

The Componentized Business Architecture includes more detail than descriptions of industry / cross-industry competences and business components. Each business component contains the specific resources bundled, including capabilities, skills, roles in the organization, assets, physical resources and performance measures. Furthermore, every business component contains individual *activities* (i.e., the behavioral side of the architecture) using resources in the component and supporting their evolution. Typical industry architectures include in the order of 10 to 20 activities per business component.

On the other hand, the dependencies across business components are what make the architecture of the business being modeled come together in one place. While specialization of the operations encapsulated in a component and localization of the resources that support the corresponding activities guarantee a weak coupling, interaction across components do exist. This subject bears an intimate connection to the study of organizations as governance and thus, it goes beyond the goal of this paper. These forms of collaboration should not be confused with *end-to-end processes* that compose behavior from different components in supporting certain critical capabilities. There is no analogy intended or recommended with respect to the conventional notion of "service orientation" from computer science.

The Componentized Business Architecture principles discussed above can be applied to finer-grain organization design such as Line-of-Business (LOBs) or departmental units. In principle, the same concepts can be recursively used to go into more detail from the enterprise or industry level. For example, the business operations encapsulated in one component can also be modularized. To this end, the hierarchy of resources should be repeated within the scope of the business component or LOB. Likewise, competences should also be contextualized to fit the organization domain being modeled.

This has been done in real practice for different business components and entire LOBs such as Finance and Accounting, Human Resources, Information Technology department, and so on. The number of business components, competences and activities is similar in these finer-grain architectures. This means that collecting the content from 10 typical LOBs in an industry, a total of approximately 1,000 business components and 10,000 activities is produced.

The architectural elements and their relationships provide a modularized framework for integrating process models with other enterprise modeling domains. The derived taxonomy for process classification is a helpful guidance to structure and organize process models.

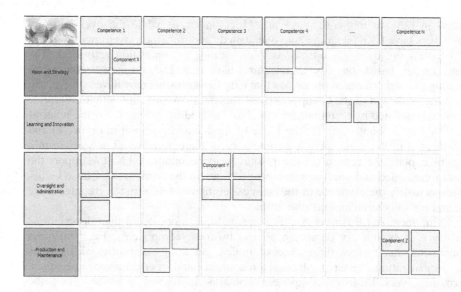

**Fig. 3.** Componentized Industry Business Architecture – A simplified view with a few competences and components highlighted

| | City Strategy & Governance | Public Safety | Transportation | Citizen Health | Energy & Water | Environmental Sustainability | Urban Planning & Building Management | Economic Development | Social Services | Education, Culture & Recreation | Municipal Administration |
|---|---|---|---|---|---|---|---|---|---|---|---|
| Direct | City Vision and Strategy | Public Safety Strategy | City Transportation Strategy | Citizen Health Strategy | City Utilities Strategy | Eco-City Strategy | Urban Planning Strategy | City Economic Policies | Social Services Strategy | Education and Culture Policies | Government-wide Administration Strategy |
| Control | City Performance Management | Crime, Fire and Emergency Management | Transportation Service Management | Health Service Management | Utilities Service Management | Sustainability Programs Management | Development and Permit Management | Economic Programs Management | Social Programs Management | Education and Culture Programs Management | Administration Services Management |
| Execute | City Governance Operations | Public Safety Operations | Transportation Infrastructure Operations | Health Service Operations | Utilities Infrastructure Operations | Sustainability Programs Delivery | Land and Buildings Operations | Economic Development Operations | Social Services Delivery | Education and Culture Operations | Administration Services Delivery |

**Fig. 4.** A simplified view of Componentized Business Architecture for the City Government Industry. The middle two layers of the hierarchy of Figure 3 have been collapsed into a single one due to the nature of this industry segment

Processes can be overlaid against an extensive model of industry operations that represents all known forms of business operations [2].

---

[2] This framework goes deeper than known propositions such as the Process Classification Framework (PCF) (see www.apqc.org).

## 2.2    Modeling beyond Factory Processes

The modeling of processes in BPM has been greatly influenced by information engineering and computer science concepts. In particular, a model hinges around a number of entities whose behaviors are described. Each entity represents an abstraction as "a class of things" that will find many specific *instances* in the real-world. The same pattern of behavior is expected in the organization when dealing with each occurrence of these instances. Typical examples are *purchase orders, customer complaints, payment requests, account opening*, and so on. Thus, efforts invested in modeling and optimizing operations pay back as a consequence of the resulting processes being used over and over again. The repetitious and predicted behavior of the enterprise operations targeted by the modeling effort is the origin of the term "factory". In [18], these processes are called "production processes". Harrison-Broninski correctly argues that case handling is not less factory-oriented than system-centric processes (i.e., workflows). All processes commonly modeled in the literature as workflows and cases are of this nature and consequently, their main goal is efficiency, i.e., time and cost reduction.

While "the factory" is a critical part of an organization, by no means is it the only form of operation that matters and thus, other forms of behavior are necessary beyond production processes. In summary, the variety of real-life processes in organizations calls for a close reexamination of modeling, particularly in the light of the assumptions made by many computer scientists that implicitly circumscribe the real-world being modeled to a fraction of the world that organizations face. The purpose of this section is to dive deeper into the structure of a family of processes corresponding to the *Oversight* level introduced in Section 2.1. These processes are very important in enterprises and their modeling is also interesting as a research topic.

Specifically, the "*subjects*" in the model come in the form of *ensembles of entity instances* but they may not be adequately modeled by the dynamics of entity types in the traditional information engineering sense. An example of this new category the *pipeline of drug compounds* managed in a typical pharmaceutical industry company. This pipeline is uninteresting from the information-centric perspective of "instance" because the *pipeline* is *unique*, i.e., there is a single "*thing*" or "*subject*" in a company called *pipeline*. Another such operation is packaging and shipping orders for clients in the distribution industry. Decision-making in these operations belongs to a sphere of behavior conceptually distinct from those activities found in any individual order being processed. The *ensemble of orders* reflects the need for specialized behavior in the organization whose modeling is also critical. Like in the case of *pipeline* there is a single "*thing*" in the enterprise called *the ensemble of all customer orders*. Oversight processes are critical because, among other reasons, decision-making necessary to successfully progress each individual instance of an entity requires the ability to manage properties of the corresponding ensemble.

In the business literature, it is common to find oversight processes loosely referred to as *management processes* [3]. These processes are definitely not new in enterprises

---

[3] Ould's "management processes" [35] are *oversight processes*. The taxonomy in this Section is rooted into broader organizational design concerns driven by industry business architecture principles. Furthermore, *oversight* is a much preferred term because "management" is a heavily overloaded word.

but they are rarely discussed by computer scientists, BPM designers, or information systems practitioners (see [34] and the work done on the analysis and application of Viable Systems Model [35] as exceptions).

Oversight processes have a different structure from that of factory operations and thus, their modeling is substantially more subtle. A fundamental characteristic in the dynamics of an oversight process is that the development of the underlying entity does not imply a progression from "birth to death". For example, the pipeline never dies or ceases to exist and in fact, related organizational behavior aims to make the pipeline stay away from any chance of being exhausted.

## 2.3   Processes Taxonomy in the Context of Industry Architecture

The process taxonomy introduced in this paper derives directly from the proposed Componentized Business Architecture for an industry or Line-of-Business (LOB). In particular, processes dealing with oversight are an entirely new class of process so far ignored in BPM. Any decision making in a flow is a candidate of fitting within activities in the oversight class. This is by itself, a fundamental aspect of the taxonomy, i.e., including organizational phenomena as organizations actually operate. Every process in an enterprise should then ideally fall either within one of the following categories or be constructed from scratch to fit one of these categories as a best-practice or guidance:

- Process is entirely contained within one of the 1,000 or so highest-level activities of the architecture
- Process spans more than one of such activities in a single business component of the architecture
- Process requires different activities or behavior therein from two or more business components

The three options above are, by design, a complete description of the potential cases a process may fit in. As an example, Figure 5 shows a process being composed of activities from different components, at different competences and resource levels. These scenarios describe the "happy path", i.e., processes designed from scratch. Dealing with legacy processes requires a more involved reconciliation mechanism and its refactoring may be an extremely difficult problem [36]. This reconciliation makes the componentized industry business architecture become a front-end for process knowledge organization. In some cases, this reconciliation may require reengineering of some processes before they can be made part of a reusable base. Many practical cases have been worked out. For example, Figure 6 shows a snap-shot and a summary of a study for the Insurance Industry. On the other hand, other industry processes from PCF have been reconciled with the Componentized Business Architecture of the corresponding industry. These subjects will not be addressed in this paper due to space constrains.

Another critical topic to bear in mind in process model collections is that certain industries have gone through attempts of creating taxonomies or have such taxonomies already. Some industries have a rich experience accumulated through several years of inter-company collaboration and work in this direction. The hurdle is that these efforts hinge on purely functional principles, i.e., taxonomies based on decompositions whose rationale is difficult to explain.

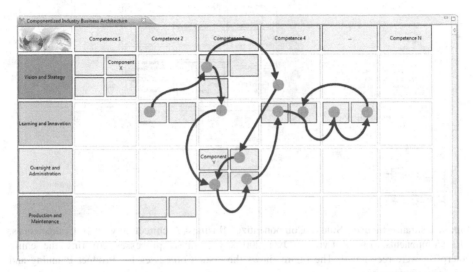

**Fig. 5.** A process combining resources and behavior from different components in an industry business architecture. Green dots indicate behavior contained in an activity of the corresponding business component. Arrows indicate partial order.

A well-designed architecture framework helps establish modeling best-practices instead of leaving them up to individual process designers. The latter leads inevitably to idiosyncratic process decompositions, performance metrics rediscovered under new language, new capabilities outside of the as-is architecture or beyond the organizational strategy to create them, and other "favorite" approaches to the classification and modeling of processes. Thus, not much reuse or improvements of existing content may be expected once process design has been fundamentally flawed by being disconnected from all concerns beyond a specific project. As the proposed architecture in this paper is not just behavioral but also contains intentional aspects of the organization as well as capabilities, skills, performance metrics, roles and resources at a minimum, then process architecture becomes linked to those aspects that help reconstruct semantics and register intent in a model of behavior.

Taxonomies such as the Extended Telecom Operations Map (eTOM) in the telecommunications industry, SCOR in the supply-chain LOB, Process Classification Framework and related industry-specific extensions bring their own challenges as they are not based on any known architecture principle. Furthermore, they do not provide any design guideline to dive into levels below the entire enterprise. In spite of that, these frameworks provide very valuable glossary and decompositions that inform

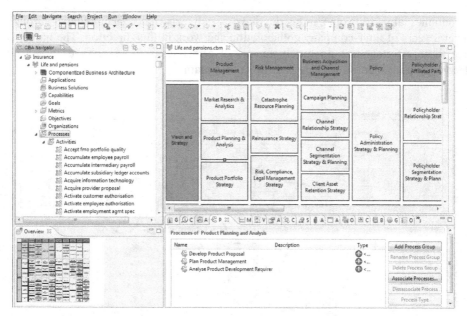

**Fig. 6.** Insurance Industry Study: Componentized Business Architecture with 10 Competences, 110 Components, 730 Activities. Over 200 key business processes covering the entire enterprise were reconciled. The figure shows three such processes for Product Planning and Analysis component.

the componentized business architecture for the same industries. In closing this Section, it is worth remarking that the main concepts presented above have been taken to a substantial level of formalization in most of their salient aspects.

# 3    Conclusions

This paper presented an architecture and taxonomy that anchor process model collections in the wider context of organizational design. This context is important in a number of ways. First, it provides a framework for approaching process modeling within the adequate context of activities, competences, resources, information and performance indicators with which an organization operates. The content available from such broader models is much more than a "glossary" or "business language": it follows a formal business architecture-based view of the organization. On the other hand, the liaison between behavioral modeling and the rest of the architecture of the organization is essential because the intentional, performative, functional and resource dimensions bound and guide the modeling of behavior. In short, process models do not live in isolation and the Componentized Industry Business Architecture provides an ambitious mechanism to accomplish the needed integration across different modeling domains. An important illustration of the value of this context is that large families of operations missing in the context of conventional BPM matter to the correct categorization of behavioral models. This point has been illustrated through oversight processes.

# References

1. Becker, J., Rosemann, M., von Uthmann, C.: Guidelines of Business Process Modeling. In: van der Aalst, W.M.P., Desel, J., Oberweis, A. (eds.) Business Process Management. LNCS, vol. 1806, pp. 30–49. Springer, Heidelberg (2000)
2. Reijers, H.A., Mans, R.S., van der Toorn, R.A.: Improved Model Management with Aggregated Business Process Models. Data & Knowledge Engineering 68(2), 221–243 (2009)
3. La Rosa, M., Dumas, M., ter Hofstede, A.H.M., Mendling, J.: Configurable Multi-Perspective Business Process Models. Information Systems 36(2), 313–340 (2011)
4. Sanz, J.L.C.: Entity-Centric Operations Modeling for Business Process Management. Part 1: An Interdisciplinary Review of the State-of-the-Art. IBM Technical Report (2011)
5. Van de Ven, A., Poole, M.: Explaining Development and Change in Organizations. Academy of Management Review 20(3), 510–540 (1995)
6. Mendling, J., Reijers, H.A., Cardoso, J.: What Makes Process Models Understandable? In: Alonso, G., Dadam, P., Rosemann, M. (eds.) BPM 2007. LNCS, vol. 4714, pp. 48–63. Springer, Heidelberg (2007)
7. Mendling, J., Reijers, H.A., van der Aalst, W.M.P.: Seven Process Modeling Guidelines. Information and Software Technology (2009)
8. Dijkman, R., Dumas, M., García-Bañuelos, L.: Graph Matching Algorithms for Business Process Model Similarity Search. In: Dayal, U., Eder, J., Koehler, J., Reijers, H.A. (eds.) BPM 2009. LNCS, vol. 5701, pp. 48–63. Springer, Heidelberg (2009)
9. Dumas, M., García-Banuelos, L., Dijkman, R.: Similarity Search of Business Process Models. Technical Report
10. Van Dongen, B.F., Dijkman, R.M., Mendling, J.: Measuring Similarity between Business Process Models. In: Bellahsène, Z., Léonard, M. (eds.) CAiSE 2008. LNCS, vol. 5074, pp. 450–464. Springer, Heidelberg (2008)
11. Yan, Z., Dijkman, R., Grefen, P.: Fast Business Process Similarity Search with Feature-Based Similarity Estimation. Eindhoven University of Technology (2010)
12. Hevner, A., March, S., Park, J., Ram, S.: Design Science in Information Systems Research. MIS Quarterly 28, 75–105 (2004)
13. Peffers, K., Tuunanen, T., Rothenberger, M., Chatterjee, S.: A Design Science Research Methodology for Information Systems Research. Journal of Management Information Systems 24, 45–77 (2007)
14. Leung, Y., Bockstedt, J.: Structural Analysis of a Business Enterprise. Service Science 3(1), 169–188 (2009)
15. Recker, J., Rosemann, M., Indulska, M., Green, P.: Business Process Modeling: A Comparative Analysis. Journal of the Association for Information Systems 10(4), 333–363 (2009)
16. Ko, R., Lee, S., Lee, E.: Business Process Management (BPM) Standards: A Survey. Business Process Management Journal 15(5), 744–791 (2009)
17. Kavakli, V., Loucopoulos, P.: Goal-driven Business Process Analysis Application in Electricity Deregulation. Information Systems 24(3), 187–207 (1999)
18. Sharp, A., McDermott, P.: Workflow Modeling: Tools for Process Improvements and Application Development, 1st edn. Artech House (2001)
19. Ould, M.: Business Processes – Modelling and Analysis for Re-engineering and Improvement. Wiley (1995)
20. Harrison-Broninski, K.: Human Interactions - The Heart and Soul of Business Process Management. Meghan-Kiffer Press (2005)

21. Van der Aalst, W., Hofstede, A., Kiepuszewski, B., Barros, A.P.: Workflow Patterns. Journal of Parallel and Distributed Data Bases 14, 5–51 (2003a)
22. van der Aalst, W.M.P., ter Hofstede, A.H.M., Weske, M.: Business Process Management: A Survey. In: van der Aalst, W.M.P., ter Hofstede, A.H.M., Weske, M. (eds.) BPM 2003. LNCS, vol. 2678, pp. 1–12. Springer, Heidelberg (2003b)
23. De Man, H.: Case Management: A Review of Modeling Approaches. BPTrends (2009)
24. Van der Aalst, W.: Formalization and Verification of Event-Driven Process Chains. In: Backhouse, R., Baetenm, J.C. (eds.) Computing Science Report 98/01. University of Technology, Eindhoven (1998)
25. Simon, H., Ando, A.: Aggregation of Variables in Dynamic Systems. Econometrica 29(2) (1961)
26. CBM. Component Business Modeling: Making Specialization Real. Institute for Business Value, IBM Corporation (2005)
27. Harishankar, R., Holley, K., High, R., Sanz, J., Giesen, E., Daley, K., Ibrahim, M., Vaidya, S., Antoun, S., Botros, A., Hamid, T.: Actionable Business Architecture: IBM's Approach. IBM (2010)
28. Heene, A., Martens, R., Sanchez, R. (eds.): Competence Perspectives on Learning and Dynamic Capabilities. Elsevier (2008)
29. Barney, J.: Integrating Organizational Behavior and Strategy Formulation Research: A Resource-based Analysis. In: Shrivastava, P., Huff, A., Dutton, J. (eds.) Advances in Strategic Management, vol. 8, pp. 39–62 (1992)
30. Helfat, C., Finkelstein, S., Mitchell, W., Peteraf, M., Singh, H., Teece, D., Winter, S.: Dynamic Capabilities. Blackwell (2007)
31. Teece, D.: Dynamic Capabilities and Strategic Management. Oxford (2009)
32. Chandler, A.: Scale and Scope: The Dynamics of Industrial Capitalism. Harvard Press, Cambridge (1990)
33. Brumagim, A.: A Hierarchy of Corporate Resources. In: Shrivastava, P., Huff, A., Dutton, J. (eds.) Advances in Strategic Management, Part A, Resource-based View of the Firm, vol. 10. JAI Press (1994)
34. Ould, M.: Business Processes: Modelling and Analysis for Re-Engneering and Improvement. Wiley (2005)
35. Snowdon, B., Kawalek, P.: Active meta-process models: a conceptual exposition. Information and Software Technology 45(15,1), 1021–1029 (2003)
36. Weber, B., Reichert, M., Mendling, J., Reijers, H.A.: Refactoring large process model repositories. Computers in Industry 62(5), 467–486 (2011)

# On Formalizing Inter-process Relationships

Tri A. Kurniawan*, Aditya K. Ghose, Lam-Son Lê, and Hoa Khanh Dam

Decision Systems Lab., School of Computer Science and Software Engineering,
University of Wollongong, NSW 2522, Australia
{tak976,aditya,lle,hoa}@uow.edu.au

**Abstract.** Most medium to large organizations support large collections
of process designs, often stored in business process repositories. These
processes are often inter-dependent. Managing such large collections of
processes is not a trivial task. We argue that formalizing and establishing inter-process relationships play a critical role in that task leading to
a machinery approach in the process repository management. We consider and propose three kinds of such relationships, namely *part-whole*,
*inter-operation* and *generalization-specialization*, including their formal
definitions, permitting us to develop a machinery approach. Analysis
of the relationships relies on the semantically effects annotated process
model in BPMN. This paper presents a rigorous approach to assist the
designer to establish inter-process relationships in a process repository.

**Keywords:** business process, semantic effect annotation, process relationship.

## 1 Introduction

Most medium to large organizations support large collections of process designs
modeled through many business process modeling languages such as Business
Process Model and Notation (BPMN)[1], often stored in *business process repositories*. These are typically characterized by the following features. *First*, the
number, scale and complexity of the processes are large, i.e. consisting hundreds
or even thousands of business process models. For example, the SAP R/3 reference model contains 600+ process models and Suncorp's repository contains
6,000+ process models [4]. *Second*, most of these processes are inter-dependent
(both in terms of design and execution). Some evidences of such dependency
have been discussed in [2]. We can also found some dependencies among processes as shown in the MIT Process Handbook[2] [9], Map of Medicine[3] and the
published literature (see, for example, the clinical process repository described
in [1]). *Third*, changes to any one process are likely to impact several other processes. Approaches to analyze the impact of process changes, depending upon

---

* On leave from a lecturership at University of Brawijaya, East Java, Indonesia.
[1] BPMN homepage http://www.bpmn.org/
[2] MIT Process Handbook homepage http://process.mit.edu/
[3] Map of Medicine homepage http://www.mapofmedicine.com/

F. Daniel et al. (Eds.): BPM 2011 Workshops, Part II, LNBIP 100, pp. 75–86, 2012.
© Springer-Verlag Berlin Heidelberg 2012

type of process dependency, have been described in [2]. Finally, some process designs exist to realize component functionalities of other process designs.

Dealing with such complex process repositories is not a trivial task. Due to this complexity, many issues come up along each process's life-cycle such as managing process variants [5], maintaining relationship consistency among interdependent processes due to any process change drivers [10](problem in process optimization, for example, introduced in [8]), performing process impact analysis [2] if changes applied to any process, finding a particular process in which the other processes depend on or extracting the structure of a process repository. We argue that formalizing and establishing process relationships play a critical role for building a machinery approach in the process repository management.

This paper makes three key contributions. *First*, we propose a taxonomy of inter-process relationships and provide formal definitions for each of them. We leverage semantically annotated process models, in the sense of [6] (or more loosely [13]). This allows us to perform deeper semantic analysis in establishing and checking these relationships than would be possible with simple (un-annotated) process models. *Second*, as the application of establishing such relationships, we outline a procedure for resolving relationship violations, in instance of one relationship type (similar procedures can be defined for other relationship types in our taxonomy, but are omitted due to space constraints). *Third*, for further such application, we show that the relationship types lead to partial orders, permitting us to structure the process repository in terms of *process lattices*. The process lattice view permits a range of formal analysis to support the identification and maintenance of inter-process relationships in a process repository including advanced process queries. We plan to further elaborate the aforementioned applications of process relationships establishment for our future work. In this paper, we only focus on presenting a novel approach for formally establishing relationships between processes modeled in BPMN. Relationship analysis will be performed based on the semantically effects annotated process model [6,7].

The remainder of the paper is organized as follows. Section 2 introduces semantic effect annotations for business process models as the basis for further formal definitions. Section 3 describes and formalizes all relationships between process models. Section 4 briefly surveys the related work. Finally, Section 5 draws some conclusions and outlines our future work.

## 2    Preliminaries

Koliadis and Ghose [7] discussed the concept of semantic effects. An effect annotation relates a specific result or outcome to an activity on a business process model. An activity represents the work performed within a business process. Activities are either atomic (called as *task* i.e. they are at the lowest level of detail presented in the diagram and can not be further broken down) or compound (called as *sub-process* i.e. they are decomposable to see another level of process below) [14]. In an annotated BPMN model, every activity has been annotated with its (immediate) effects. For a complete process, we also define a cumulative effect annotation which is obtained from accumulating the immediate effects of all annotated activities based on all alternative paths (due to XOR gateways) to reach an activity being observed.

We shall leverage the ProcessSEER [6] approach to semantic effect annotation. This framework permits us to determine, at design time, the answer to the following question that can be posed for any point in the process design: what would the effects of the process be if it were to execute up to this point? The answer is necessarily non-deterministic, since a process might have taken one of many possible alternative paths through a process design to get to that point. The non-determinism also arises from the fact that the effects of certain process steps might undo the effects of prior steps - the inconsistencies that result in the snapshot of the domain that we seek to maintain might be resolved in multiple alternative ways (a large body of work in the reasoning about action community addresses this problem). The answer to the question is therefore provided via a set of effect scenarios, any one of which might eventuate in a process instance. The approach simplifies the activity of semantic effect annotation by only requiring that activities (populating a capability library) be annotated with context-independent immediate effects. The tool then contextualizes these effects by propagating them through a process model (specified in BPMN in the current instance) to determine the cumulative effect scenarios at the end of each activity. It uses formal machinery (theorem-provers) to compute cumulative effects, but provides an analyst-friendly Controlled Natural Language (CNL) interface, coupled with a domain ontology, that permits the immediate effects of activities to be specified in natural language (but with a restricted set of sentence formats). The use of CNL permits us to translate these natural language specifications into underlying formal representation, which in turn makes the use of theorem-provers possible. In addition, the tool also makes provision for local (activity-specific) non-functional annotations to be propagated through a process design, so that we are able to determine the cumulative non-functional scenarios for each activity in a process design as well.

## 3  Inter-process Relationships

There are three main concepts to be described. *First*, the taxonomy of inter-process relationships will be identified and formalized. *Second*, we discuss partly (only takes part-whole relationship) the idea of resolving inconsistencies in inter-process relationships due to any changes on a particular process. *Third*, the idea of leveraging lattice theory in constructing process lattices based upon process relationships will be formalized. The last two concepts are derived from taking the advantages of formalizing inter-process relationships.

### 3.1  Relationships Taxonomy

We now propose a taxonomy of relationships that can be established between different processes which are classified into two categories: *functional dependencies* and *consistency links*. A functional dependency exists between a pair of processes when one process depends on the other for realizing some of its functionalities. In other words, a process will not be able to achieve its goals without the support given by the others. In contrast, a consistency link exists between a pair of processes when both of them have intersecting parts represent the same functionality, i.e. the outcomes (e.g. effects) of these parts are exactly the same. They are functionally independent, i.e. one process is not supported by the other.

In such categories, we now define the three different types of relationship that can exist between processes, namely *part-whole*, *inter-operation*, and *generalization-specialization*. The first two fall in the functional dependencies category whereas the third is regarded as a consistency link. We formally define each of these relationship types using the semantic effect analysis on process models. We use $acc(P)$ to denote the cumulative end effects of process $P$; $CE(P, t_i)$ to describe cumulative effect at the point of activity $t_i$ within process $P$; and $es_j$ to denote an effect scenario $j$-th. It is noted that each of $acc(P)$ or $CE(P, t_i)$ is a set of effect scenarios. Each effect scenario is represented as a set of clauses and will be viewed, implicitly, as their conjunction.

**Part-whole**

Part-whole relationship exists between two processes when one process is required by the other process to fulfill some of its functionalities. More specifically, there must be an activity in the "whole" process representing the functionalities of the "part" process. The "part" process is also commonly referred to as a sub-process within the "whole" process. Intuitively, there is an insertion of the functionalities of the "part" into the "whole". We first define the insertion of a process in another process.

**Definition 1.** *The insertion of process $P2$ in process $P1$ at activity $t$, $P1 \uparrow^t P2$, is a process design obtained by viewing $P2$ as the sub-process expansion of activity $t$ in $P1$.*

Literally, the insertion of $P2$ at an activity $t$ in $P1$ simply involves connecting the path entering $t$ with the starting event of $P2$ and connecting the path leaving $t$ with the end event of $P2$. Semantic effects can be applied to in this situation as follows. Let $T1 = \{t_{11}, t_{12}, \ldots, t_{1i}\}$ and $T2 = \{t_{21}, t_{22}, \ldots, t_{2j}\}$ be the set of consecutive activities of process models $P1$ and $P2$ respectively. Let $CE(P1, t_{1s})$ be the cumulative effects of process model $P1$ at the point of activity $t_{1s}$ where $1 \leq s \leq i$. Cumulative effects computation involves a left-to-right pass of evaluating the activities within a process until the defined point of activity $t_{1s}$. Then, $CE(P1 \uparrow^{t_{1s}} P2, t_{1s})$ would be computed by replacing activity $t_{1s} \in T1$ with a set of activities within $P2$ through the following procedures: (1) accumulate the effects from activity $t_{11}$ until activities $t_{1s-1}$ within $P1$, where $t_{1s-1}$ denotes all activities immediately precede activity $t_{1s}$, might be in parallel; (2) continue the effects accumulation involving all activities within $P2$ through passing from the most left activity $t_{21}$ to the most right one $t_{2j}$; (3) continue the accumulation through $t_{1s+1}$ until $t_{1i}$ within $P1$, where $t_{1s+1}$ denotes all activities immediately succeed activity $t_{1s}$.

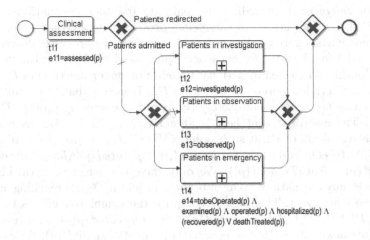

**Fig. 1.** BPMN model of *Management of patients on arrival* process, also showing the immediate effects $e_i$ of each activity $t_i$

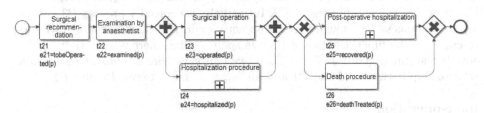

**Fig. 2.** BPMN model of *Patients in emergency* process. This is the sub-process expansion of the process in Fig. 1, also containing the immediate effects $e_i$ of each activity $t_i$

Using the definition of process insertion, we formally define the part-whole relationship as Definition 2.

**Definition 2.** *Given process models $P1$ and $P2$, $P2$ is a direct part of $P1$ iff there exists an activity $t$ in $P1$ such that $CE(P1,t) = CE(P1 \uparrow^t P2, t)$. If there is no insertion point at any activity $t$ in $P1$, then $P2$ is an indirect part of $P1$ iff $\forall es_i \in acc(P2), \exists es_j \in CE(P1,t)$ for any activity $t$ in $P1$ such that $es_j \models es_i$.*

Let us consider an example of part-whole process relationship adopted from [1]. We transformed it, from originally represented in EPC, into BPMN. Fig. 1 (called $P1$) depicts the *Management of patients on arrival* process in the Neurosurgical Ward of Parma Hospital. As can be seen, the neurosurgeron makes a preliminary assessment of the patient's clinical condition and relies on such assessment result to recommend one of the following actions: keeping patients in observation (sub-process *Patients in observation*), patients in further investigation (sub-process *Patients in investigation*), patients in emergency (sub-process

*Patients in emergency*), or redirecting patients to other destinations. Fig. 2 (called *P2*) shows the *Patients in emergency* process in detail. Based on our definition, there exists a part-whole relationship between the processes described in Figures 2 and 1 in which the former is the "part" and the latter is the "whole". Such relationship is reflected by activity *Patients in emergency* $(t_{14})$ in *P1* which is the abstract activity representing process *P2*. It means that the result of executing activity $t_{14}$ in *P1* is completely the result of executing process *P2*, and vise versa. The insertion point here is at activity $t_{14}$ in *P1*. Let us compute the cumulative effects of *P1* at such point, $CE(P1, t_{14}) = \{es_{14}\}$ where $es_{14} = assessed(p) \wedge tobeOperated(p) \wedge examined(p) \wedge operated(p) \wedge hospitalized(p) \wedge (recovered(p) \vee deathTreated(p))$. We only have one effect scenario i.e. $es_{14}$ since there is only one path (no pair of branching-joining XOR) reaching activity $t_{14}$ from the start event. Then, let us compute the cumulative effects by insertion, $CE(P1 \uparrow^{t_{14}} P2, t_{14}) = assessed(p) \wedge tobeOperated(p) \wedge examined(p) \wedge operated(p) \wedge hospitalized(p) \wedge (recovered(p) \vee deathTreated(p))$. We can infer that *P2* is a part of *P1*, since $CE(P1, t_{14}) = CE(P1 \uparrow^{t_{14}} P2, t_{14})$.

We also consider another setting where there exists a process *P3*, e.g. a detailed process (not described in the diagram) of activity *Surgical operation* in Fig. 2, which is a sub-process of *P2*. Intuitively, we consider process *P3* also be a part of process *P1* though there is no activity in *P1* which is completely represented by the functionalities of *P3*. On such setting, there is an activity in *P1* entails the functionalities of *P3*. Then, we can say there is a *direct* part-whole relationship between *P2* and *P1* and an *indirect* one between *P3* and *P1*.

### Inter-operation

Inter-operation relationship exists between two processes when there is at least one message exchanged between them and there is no cumulative effects contradiction between tasks involved in exchanging messages. We formalize the definition of inter-operation relationship as Definition 3.

**Definition 3.** *Given process models P1 and P2, inter-operation relationship exists between these processes including activities $t_i$ and $t_j$ iff the following holds:*

- $\exists t_i$ *in P1* $\exists t_j$ *in P2 such that* $t_i \rightharpoonup t_j$ *denotes* $t_i$ *sends a message to* $t_j$*, or in the reverse direction* $t_j \rightharpoonup t_i$*;*
- *Let* $E_i = \{es_{i1}, es_{i2}, \ldots, es_{im}\}$ *be cumulative effects of process P1 at task* $t_i$ *i.e.* $CE(P1, t_i)$*, and* $E_j = \{es_{j1}, es_{j2}, \ldots, es_{jn}\}$ *be cumulative effects of process P2 at task* $t_j$ *i.e.* $CE(P2, t_j)$*. Then, there is no contradiction between* $E_i$ *and* $E_j$ *for all* $es_{ip} \in E_i$ *and* $es_{jq} \in E_j$ *s.t.* $es_{ip} \cup es_{jq} \vdash \bot$ *does not hold, where* $1 \le p \le m$ *and* $1 \le q \le n$*.*

We say there exists a **direct inter-operation** between processes *P1* and *P2* due to messange exchanged between them. However, we also consider another process *P3* which has a direct inter-operation relationship with process *P2*. Intuitively, process *P3* also has an inter-operation relationship with process *P1* through process *P2*. We say process *P3* is in an **indirect inter-operation** relationship

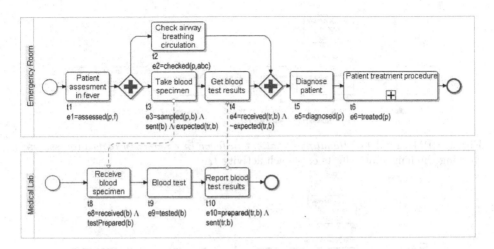

**Fig. 3.** BPMN model of inter-operation processes of *Handling of patient in fever in emergency room*, also containing the immediate effects $e_i$ of each activity $t_i$

with process $P1$ iff there exists another process $P2$ such that $P3$ be in direct inter-operation with $P2$ as well as $P2$ be in direct inter-operation with $P1$. Effects contradiction exists if the expected effects differ from the given effects. If it is the case, we do not consider such relationship as inter-operation though there is a message exchanged between a pair of processes.

Fig. 3 represents an example of inter-operation between processes of *Handling of patient in fever in emergency room*. On this setting, there exist messages sent from task *Take blood specimen* $t_3$ in *Emergency Room* process (called $P1$) to task *Receive blood specimen* $t_8$ in *Medical Lab* process (called $P2$), and from task *Report blood test results* $t_{10}$ in $P2$ to task *Get blood test results* $t_4$ in $P1$ in order to fulfill the functionalities of such processes. Semantically, we can compute $CE(P1, t_3) = \{es_{13}\}$ where $es_{13} = assessed(p, f) \wedge sampled(p, b) \wedge sent(b) \wedge expected(tr, b)$. Similarly, $CE(P2, t_8) = \{es_{28}\}$ where $es_{28} = received(b) \wedge testPrepared(b)$. We can observe that there is no contradiction between $es_{13}$ and $es_{28}$. Dually, we can also compute $CE(P2, t_{10}) = \{es_{210}\}$ where $es_{210} = received(b) \wedge testPrepared(b) \wedge tested(b) \wedge prepared(tr, b) \wedge sent(tr, b)$. And, $CE(P1, t_4) = \{es_{14}\}$ where $es_{14} = assessed(p, f) \wedge sampled(p, b) \wedge sent(b) \wedge received(tr, b) \wedge \neg expected(tr, b)$. Again, it is obvious that there is no contradiction between $es_{210}$ and $es_{14}$. We may consider effect contradiction in the following illustration. For example, see Fig. 3, if we include $labeled(b)$ as the expected effect in immediate effect $e8$ and $\neg labeled(b)$ as the given effect in immediate effect $e3$, then we fall into this contradiction since at $t_8$ we expect that the blood specimen has been labeled at the point of $t_3$.

## Generalization-specialization

Generalization-specialization relationship exists between two processes when one process becomes the functional extension of the other. More specifically, the

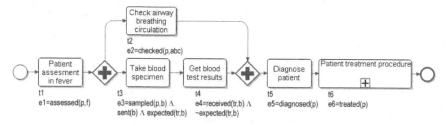

**Fig. 4.** BPMN model of *Handling of patient in fever in emergency room* process, also showing the immediate effects $e_i$ of each activity $t_i$

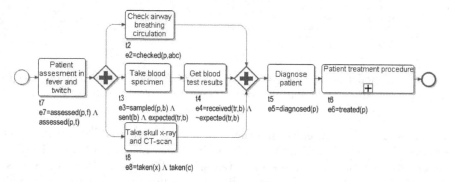

**Fig. 5.** BPMN model of *Handling of patient in fever and twitch in emergency room* process, also containing the immediate effects $e_i$ of each activity $t_i$

*specialized* process has the same functionalities as in the *generalized* one and also extends it with some additional functionalities. Our interpretation of such relationship was inspired by the notion of subtyping that was first made popular in programming language theory and later extended to conceptual modeling. We do not directly link this interpretation to the definition of object-oriented inheritance or subclass, which is in fact a mechanism to achieve subtyping. In essence, we may not apply a pairwise comparison of tasks to the two process models in question. Instead, we compare their cumulative effects to see if the *specialized* process can safely be used in a context where the *generalized* one is expected, as described below. To the best of our knowledge, this interpretation is close to the *projection inheritance* defined in [12].

Using semantic effect analysis, the functionalities are represented as immediate effects (of individual activity) and cumulative effects (of the whole process). One way to extend the functionalities is adding some additional activities such that the intended cumulative effects of the process are consequently extended. Another way involves enriching the immediate effects of the existing activities. In this case, the number of activities remain the same for both processes but the capabilities of the *specialized* is extended. Noted, the *specialized* process inherits all functionalities of the *generalized* process, as formally defined in Definition 4.

**Definition 4.** *Given process models $P1$ and $P2$, $P2$ is a specialization of $P1$ iff $\forall es_i \in acc(P1)$, $\exists es_j \in acc(P2)$ such that $es_j \models es_i$; and $\forall es_j \in acc(P2)$, $\exists es_i \in acc(P1)$ such that $es_i \models es_j$.*

Figures 4 and 5 show an example of two processes describing how a patient in fever should be handled in an emergency room. As can be seen, the process described in Fig. 5 (called $P2$) has exactly the same functionalities as the one in Fig. 4 (called $P1$). The former however has some specific functionalities on tasks *Patient assessment in fever and twitch*, which is the extension of task *Patient assessment in fever*, and *Take skull x-ray and CT-scan*, which is the additional task. Both tasks together extend the functionalities of process in Fig. 4.

Furthermore, we can semantically observe such relationship overs Definition 4. Let us compute the cumulative effects of $P1$, $acc(P1) = \{es_1\}$ where $es_1 = assessed(p,f) \wedge checked(p,abc) \wedge sampled(p,b) \wedge sent(b) \wedge received(tr,b) \wedge \neg expected(tr,b) \wedge diagnosed(p) \wedge treated(p)$. Noted, we only have one effect scenario i.e. $es_1$ since there is only one path (no pair of branching-joining XOR) reaching the end event from the start event in $P1$. Dually, we can accumulate the effects of $P2$, $acc(P2) = \{es_2\}$ where $es_2 = assessed(p,f) \wedge assessed(p,t) \wedge checked(p,abc) \wedge sampled(p,b) \wedge sent(b) \wedge received(tr,b) \wedge \neg expected(tr,b) \wedge taken(x) \wedge taken(c) \wedge diagnosed(p) \wedge treated(p)$. It is evident that $e_7 \models e_1$ such that $es_2 \models es_1$. Obviously, we can also observe that $es_1 \models es_2$.

## 3.2   Process Changes

Now, let us discuss the first benefit of formalizing inter-process relationship in process changes. We consider three ways to look at relationship violations due to process changes between a pair of processes $P1$ and $P2$: (i) identify changes in $P1$ that can trigger violations and resolve them; (ii) identify changes in $P2$ that can trigger violations and resolve them; and (iii) identify resolutions to solve a given violated relationship of a pair of process with unknown changes trigger. Due to space constraint, we only describe the part-whole relationship. As in Definitions 1 and 2, let $P1$ be the whole process and $P2$ be the part one, and let $t_i$ be a sub-process in $P1$ represents $P2$ with the corresponding immediate effects $e_{t_i}$ such that the condition $COND$ is satisfied i.e. $CE(P1,t_i) = CE(P1 \uparrow^{t_i} P2, t_i)$.

*First*, the possible change introduced in $P1$ that can cause violations is changing on $t_i$, i.e. either by: (i) changing $e_{t_i}$ to be $e'_{t_i}$ s.t. $e_{t_i} \neq e'_{t_i}$, or (ii) dropping $t_i$. For the first case, we need to change $P2$ to be $P2'$ by either adding or deleting some activities such that: (a) $COND$ is satisfied with $e'_{t_i}$; and (b) there exists no $P2''$ s.t. $COND$ is satisfied with $e'_{t_i}$. In contrast, we no longer need to maintain the relationship for the second case. Noted, changing $P1$ excluding $t_i$ will not cause any violation. *Second*, any changes in $P2$ which affect the $acc(P2)$ will cause an violation. Resolving such an violation, we need to replace $e_{t_i}$ with $e'_{t_i}$ such that: (a) $COND$ is satisfied with $e'_{t_i}$; and (b) there exists no $e''_{t_i}$ s.t. $COND$ is satisfied with $e''_{t_i}$ and $e_{t_i}\Delta e''_{t_i} \subset e_{t_i}\Delta e'_{t_i}$. There would be a complex case due to a fact that $t_i$ might be being utilized in many other processes. Consequently, if we change $e_{t_i}$, we must propagate this change to the others as well. However, note that changing $e_{t_i}$ will change the cumulative effects of the process being evaluated. Other scenario would be possible such that we can avoid change propagation in a massive manner, i.e. establishing a new task with $e'_{t_i}$ s.t. $COND$ is satisfied. *Third*, any given violated part-whole with unknown changes trigger can be resolved by using the aforementioned approaches after identifying a candidate of $t_i$ which is approached by the closest $COND$ to be satisfied.

## 3.3 Process Lattices

Let us leverage the lattice theory in constructing process lattices as the further benefit of formalizing inter-process relationship. We will show that the relationship types lead to partial orders which is the basis for constructing process lattices from a large collection of processes. We can then define *least upper bound* (lub) and *greatest lower bound* (glb), as described below, for each qualified type. The process lattice view permits us to perform formal analysis to support the identification and maintenance of inter-dependent processes in process repository, such as: (1) lub queries can tell us what the most specific generalization of a set of processes might be; (2) helps localizing change between glb and lub. If the glb and lub of a set of processes are not impacted, then change does not propagate past them; (3) we want to reason with the transitive closure, but explicitly representing it is expensive.

**Definition 5.** *[3] Let $P$ be a set. A partial order on $P$ is a binary relation $\leq$ on $P$ such that, for all $x, y, z \in P$ : (i) $x \leq x$, (ii) $x \leq y$ and $y \leq x$ imply $x = y$, (iii) $x \leq y$ and $y \leq z$ imply $x \leq z$.*

These conditions are referred to, respectively, as reflexivity, antisymmetry and transitivity. A set $P$ equipped with an order relation $\leq$ is said to be an ordered set (or partially ordered set, called poset) [3]. A lattice is a poset in which any two elements have a unique supremum (the least upper bound *lub*; called their *join*) and an infimum (the greatest lower bound *glb*; called their *meet*). If $a \leq c$, $b \leq c$ in a partially ordered set $P = (X; \leq)$, we say that $c$ is an upper bound of $a$ and $b$. If $d \leq a$, $d \leq b$ we say $d$ is a lower bound of $a$ and $b$. We say an upper bound $c$ of $a$ and $b$ is the lub if $c \leq c'$ for every upper bound $c'$ of $a$ and $b$. It is denoted $a \vee b$ and called the join of $a$ and $b$. The glb is defined similarly and denoted $a \wedge b$ and called the meet of $a$ and $b$.

Based on the given properties of a poset, we propose Theorems 1, 2, and 3 for the process relationship types to identify whether or not each type is a poset. Then, we may define a lattice for a relationship type if it qualifies a poset.

**Theorem 1.** *Part-whole is a reflexive, transitive and antisymmetric relationship.*

*Proof.* Let process $P2$ be a part of process $P1$ and their corresponding cumulative effects be $acc(P2)$ and $acc(P1)$ respectively. Let process $P3$, with cumulative effects $acc(P3)$, be a part of process $P2$. Based on Definitions 1 and 2, we have $acc(P1) = acc(P1 \uparrow^t P2)$ and $acc(P2) = acc(P2 \uparrow^t P3)$. Therefore,

$\forall es_k \in acc(P3)$, $\exists es_j \in acc(P1)$ such that $es_j \models es_k$. So part-whole is *transitive*. As for *reflexivity*, $\forall es_i \in acc(P1)$, $\exists es_j \in acc(P1)$ such that $es_j \models es_i$ whereas $i = j$. Finally, it is *antisymmetric* similar with the reflexivity proof.

**Theorem 2.** *Generalization-specialization is a reflexive, transitive and anti-symmetric relationship.*

*Proof.* Let process $P2$ be a specialization of process $P1$ and their corresponding cumulative effects be $acc(P2)$ and $acc(P1)$ respectively. Let process $P3$, with cumulative effects $acc(P3)$, be a specialization of process $P2$. It is obviously *reflexive* because $\forall es_i \in acc(P1)$, $\exists es_j \in acc(P1)$ such that $es_j \models es_i$; and $\forall es_j \in acc(P1)$, $\exists es_i \in acc(P1)$ such that $es_i \models es_j$ whereas $i = j$. Similarly, we can analyze the rest processes. It is *transitive* since $\forall es_i \in acc(P1)$, $\exists es_j \in acc(P2)$ such that $es_j \models es_i$; and $\forall es_j \in acc(P2)$, $\exists es_i \in acc(P1)$ such that $es_i \models es_j$; furthermore $\forall es_j \in acc(P2)$, $\exists es_k \in acc(P3)$ such that $es_k \models es_j$; and $\forall es_k \in acc(P3)$, $\exists es_j \in acc(P2)$ such that $es_j \models es_k$. Then, we can summarize as follows: $es_k \models es_j \wedge es_j \models es_i \Rightarrow es_k \models es_i$; and $es_i \models es_j \wedge es_j \models es_k \Rightarrow es_i \models es_k$. It is *antisymmetric*. If $P2$ is specialization of $P1$ and $P1$ is specialization of $P2$, then $P1 = P2$. Since, $\forall es_i \in acc(P1)$, $\exists es_j \in acc(P2)$ such that $es_j \models es_i$; and $\forall es_j \in acc(P2)$, $\exists es_i \in acc(P1)$ such that $es_i \models es_j$; moreover $\forall es_j \in acc(P2)$, $\exists es_i \in acc(P1)$ such that $es_i \models es_j$; and $\forall es_i \in acc(P1)$, $\exists es_j \in acc(P2)$ such that $es_j \models es_i$. We can summarize as follows: $es_j \models es_i \wedge es_i \models es_j \Rightarrow es_j = es_i$.

**Theorem 3.** *Inter-operation is a non-reflexive, transitive and antisymmetric relationship.*

*Proof.* Let processes $P1$ and $P2$ have messages exchanged between them. So do processes $P2$ and $P3$. It is *non-reflexive* since there is no message sent to and received from the same process. It is *transitive*, i.e. $P1$ and $P3$ are in indirect inter-operation relationship through $P2$. It is *antisymmetric*, but it is not necessarily both processes are the same.

Theorems 1, 2 and 3 imply that part-whole and generalization-specialization qualify posets, thus they are considered in constructing process lattices.

## 4   Related Work

Malone et.al. [9] establish part-use and generalization-specialization to classify processes in the repository. van der Aalst [11] describes message sequence charts to specify the interaction between organizations. Dai et.al. [2] propose a lightweight query-based analysis for process impact analysis based upon process dependencies. van der Aalst and Basten [12] propose inheritance-preserving transformation rules to restrict changes in workflow process definitions. They introduce protocol and projection inheritances. Koliadis and Ghose [7] introduce an inter-operation business process in compliance checking. Different to the others, we specifically propose a framework for formalizing and establishing inter-process relationships based on the semantically effects annotated model. However, we found similar ideas with the aforementioned researches i.e. part-whole in [9], generalization-specialization in [9,12] and inter-operation in [7,11].

## 5  Conclusion and Future Work

We have proposed a rigorous framework for establishing relationships between process models shedding light on further processing on process ecosystems (e.g. re-establishing equilibrium of a process ecosystem such that all inter-process relationship constraints are satisfied). Future works include: i) implementing this approach into a semi-automated system that assists the designer in establishing relationships between process models; ii) maintaining process relationships against changes made to any process model within an ecosystem; and iii) developing a machinery approach for querying processes based on process lattices.

## References

1. Bevilacqua, M., Ciarapica, F.E., Giacchetta, G.: Business Process Re-engineering in Healthcare Management: A Case Study. BPM Journal 17(1), 42–66 (2011)
2. Dai, W., Covvey, D., Alencar, P., Cowan, D.: Lightweight Query-based Analysis of Workflow Process Dependencies. Journal of Syst. and Soft. 82(6), 915–931 (2009)
3. Davey, B.A., Priestley, H.A.: Introduction to Lattices and Order. Cambridge University Press (1990)
4. Ekanayake, C.C., La Rosa, M., ter Hofstede, A.H.M., Fauvet, M.-C.: Fragment-based Version Management for Repositories of Business Process Models. QUT Digital Repository (2011), http://eprints.qut.edu.au/
5. Hallerbach, A., Bauer, T., Reichert, M.: Managing Process Variants in the Process Life Cycle. In: ICEIS 2008, Barcelona, pp. 154–161 (2008)
6. Hinge, K., Ghose, A., Koliadis, G.: Process SEER: A Tool for Semantic Effect Annotation of Business Process Models. In: IEEE EDOC 2009, pp. 54–63 (2009)
7. Koliadis, G., Ghose, A.: Verifying Semantic Business Process Models in Inter-operation. In: IEEE SCC, pp. 731–738 (2007)
8. Kurniawan, T.A., Ghose, A.K., Lê, L.-S.: A Framework for Optimizing Inter-operating Business Process Portfolio. In: Proc. of the 19th International Conference on Information Systems Development, ISD-2010 (2010)
9. Malone, T.W., Crowston, K., Herman, G.A.: Organizing Business Knowledge: The MIT Process Handbook. The MIT Press (2003)
10. van der Aalst, W.M.P., Jablonski, S.: Dealing with Workflow Change: Identification of Issues and Solutions. Int. Journal of CSSE 15(5), 267–276 (2000)
11. van der Aalst, W.M.P.: Interorganizational Workflows: An Approach Based on Message Sequence Charts and Petri Nets. Systems Analysis-Modelling-Simulation 34(3), 335–367 (1999)
12. van der Aalst, W.M.P., Basten, T.: Inheritance of Workflows: An Approach to Tackling Problems Related to Change. Theo. Comp. Sci. 270(1-2), 125–203 (2002)
13. Weber, I., Hoffman, J., Mendling, J.: Semantic Business Process Validation. In: Proc. of the 3rd Int. Workshop on Semantic Business Process Management (2008)
14. White, S.A., Miers, D.: BPMN: Modeling and Reference Guide (2008)

# Navigating in Process Model Collections:
# A New Approach Inspired by Google Earth[*]

Markus Hipp[1], Bela Mutschler[2], and Manfred Reichert[3]

[1] Group Research & Advanced Engineering, Daimler AG, Germany
markus.hipp@daimler.com
[2] University of Applied Sciences Ravensburg-Weingarten, Germany
bela.mutschler@hs-weingarten.de
[3] Institute of Databases and Information Systems, University of Ulm, Germany
manfred.reichert@uni-ulm.de

**Abstract.** In complex business environments, business processes (e.g., engineering processes in the automobile industry) may comprise hundreds up to thousands of process steps. Though typically captured in a process model (or a collection of process models), these processes are presented to process participants in a rather static manner, e.g., as simple drawings. However, to effectively support process enactment and to link processes with relevant information, enterprises crave for new ways of visualizing processes and for interacting with them. In particular, process models must be provided in an interactive, more dynamic manner, i.e., they must be both "experiencable" and user-adequate from the perspective of the user. In this paper, we introduce a new process navigation concept for querying process model collections. Specifically, we pick up an existing navigation concept for complex information spaces, namely Google Earth, and apply it to business processes. Thereby, we distinguish between geographical and semantic zoom functions, introduce different process views and filter mechanisms, and discuss options to manually configure needed process visualizations.

**Keywords:** process navigation, visualization and interaction.

## 1 Motivation

In complex environments business processes (e.g., engineering processes for electric/electronic components in a car) may comprise hundreds up to thousands of process steps, each of them being associated with process relevant information such as engineering documents, contact information, or tool instructions. In existing process repositories models are typically visualized in a static and thus not very helpful manner [1,2,3]. In this context van Wijk confirms that visualizing large data sets often leads to large and static "images" with much detail [4]. Static visualization, in turn, results in a significant information overload, rather

---

[*] This research has been done in the niPRO project funded by the German Federal Ministry of Education and Research (BMBF) under grant number 17102X10.

F. Daniel et al. (Eds.): BPM 2011 Workshops, Part II, LNBIP 100, pp. 87–98, 2012.

disturbing than supporting the user. As different process participants have different perspectives on a business process and related process information, a more flexible visualization of process models and navigation within business process collections become necessary. For example, a business manager is mainly interested in an overview of a process in order to evaluate its process progress, whereas a knowledge-worker needs more detailed information about the process step he is currently involved in. In a case study [5] we showed that no comprehensive approach fulfilling this requirement is currently available. Only specific aspects are addressed in literature so far.

PROVIADO [6], for example, tackles the challenge of flexible process visualization but focuses on the technical viewpoint, i.e., the user viewpoint has not been considered. Interesting concepts have been introduced in the area of user interface design, e.g., zoomable user interfaces (ZUIs) [7]. Smirnov et al. [8] state that *abstraction* has proven to be an effective means to present readable, high-level views of business process models.

Picking up the demand to adopt the user perspective when navigating in process models or process model collections [9,10], we introduce an advanced *navigation concept* allowing users to dynamically adapt the visualization of processes depending on their personal needs. Figure 1 illustrates our understanding of process navigation. The process user starts with a default visualization of a business process (Visualization 1), e.g., depicting the entire process with detailed process information. The user may then change the visualization by interacting with the process(es). *Process interaction* is defined as an activity that transforms one process visualization into another based on user-triggered operations. For example, a user may adjust the zoom level, and the process visualization then changes accordingly. Process navigation comprises a sequence of process interactions and allows the process participant to navigate from a default visualization (Visualization 1) to a more specific one (Visualization 4).

This work was done in the context of the niPRO project, which applies semantic technology to integrate information associated with business processes in personalized *process information portals*. As examples of structured process information consider graphical business process models or data from enterprise information systems such as ERP or CRM systems. Examples of unstructured process information include all kinds of office documents or e-mails, including mainly plain text. The overall goal is to provide knowledge-workers and decision-makers with the needed process information depending on their preferences and current work context.

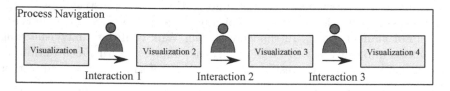

**Fig. 1.** Process Navigation: A sequence of process interactions

This paper is organized as follows: Section 2 presents a navigation example of a complex electric/electronic development process from the automotive domain and summarizes requirements we previously identified on process navigation. Our navigation concept is introduced in Section 3. Section 4 discusses related work and Section 5 concludes with a summary and outlook.

# 2  Process Navigation: Example and Requirements

## 2.1  Practical Example

We first present a real-world case from the automotive domain to illustrate the need for an intuitive process navigation concept. In this case, all relevant processes are documented in forms of process diagrams captured in PDF documents. Furthermore, they are categorized into process areas. Each process area is depicted as image map to users. Altogether, the entire "process world" (or process model collection) comprises various models with different levels of information (cf. Fig. 2).

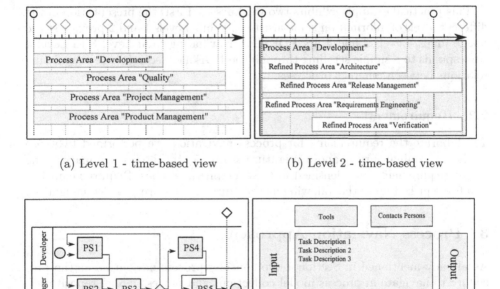

(a) Level 1 - time-based view      (b) Level 2 - time-based view

(c) Level 3 - logic-based view      (d) Level 4 - turtle-view

**Fig. 2.** Real-world example from the automotive industry

Level 1 (cf. Fig. 2(a)) shows the entire process world, i.e., process areas. As displaying single business processes would be too complex at this point, only process areas are depicted. The respective view is time-based, i.e., the length of the rectangles corresponds to the duration of process areas. Level 1 provides the start point for the user. Based on it, he or she may select the process area including the needed process step or process information. By choosing the process area "Development", for example, the user gets a more detailed, but still time-based view of this process area on Level 2 (cf.Fig. 2(b)). The lots of single processes can be displayed at Level 3 (cf. Fig. 2(c)). In our example, the process "Requirements Engineering" is depicted in terms of a process diagram, in which single process steps (PS1...PS5) are connected to indicate causal relations. Further, roles are introduced on this level and are displayed as swim lanes. As opposed to Levels 1 and 2, the view on Level 3 is logic-based, e.g., it allows modelling feedback loops (e.g., to jump back from PS3 to PS1) if a certain condition is not met. Each process step is further refined on Level 4. It provides a "turtle-view" and neither has time nor logic restrictions. A turtle only contains information of a single process step in terms of task descriptions and additional information, e.g., on tools or contact persons. The turtle-view is the most detailed visualization and thus represents an important destination when searching for process information.

This practical example exhibits two weaknesses. First, the presentation of the different levels of information is inconsistent. While Levels 1 and 2 provide static image maps, Levels 3 and 4 are PDF files. Navigating from Level 3 to Level 4 corresponds to a simple scrolling through the PDF file. Second there are missing relations between different processes.

## 2.2   Requirements

To elaborate the requirements for process navigation, we performed two case studies, an online survey, and a literature study [5,11]. Table 1 summarizes the major requirements, we identified in these empirical studies. Requirements 1, 4 and 6 are picked up in the following as they directly concern process navigation.

## 3   Process Navigation Approach

As already mentioned in Section 1, we consider process navigation as the procedure to navigate in process model collections and process model repositories. Process navigation is triggered by a user and comprises a sequence of user interactions.

In this section we present our process navigation approach inspired by Google Earth. Generally, process models and process model collections constitute complex information spaces. Google Earth, in turn, provides a navigation concept for one of the most complex existing information spaces, namely the global geographical information space. Of course, there exist significant differences between process models and global geographical information. Hence, we consider

**Table 1.** Derived requirements from our empirical studies

| Nr. Name | CS1 | CS2 | OS | Lit |
|---|---|---|---|---|
| #1 A graphical visualization of the entire business process is needed | x | x | x | x |
| #2 Enterprise-wide processes being easily accessible in every department are required | x | x | x | |
| #3 Continuously provide information on the process progress | x | | | x |
| #4 An adequate visualization of process information is required | x | x | x | |
| #5 Process information must be explicitly linkable to single process steps | x | | | |
| #6 Information on contact persons should be adequately visualized | | x | | x |
| #7 Process steps must be linked with associated roles | | x | | |
| #8 Process information must be provided on the user's role | x | x | x | x |

CS1: Case Study 1; CS2: Case Study 2; OS: Online Survey; Lit: Literature

the Google Earth navigation approach just as the starting point for our ideas and we are working on necessary extensions and adaptations.

## 3.1 Google Earth

Google Earth[1] is a virtual globe, map and geographical information system. It displays satellite images of varying resolution of the earth's surface, allowing users to browse items like cities and houses looking perpendicularly down or at an oblique angle [12]. Google Earth allows users to search for addresses of certain countries, to enter coordinates, or to simply use the mouse to browse to a particular location. The user is able to zoom, to pan, and to rotate the maps. The level of detail of the displayed information is automatically adjusted to the geographic zoom level. Further, users can switch between different views of the map, e.g., map-view, satellite-view and terrain-view.

## 3.2 Adopting Google Earth for Process Navigation

We now take the Google Earth navigation concept and adopt it to our scenario from Section 2. Table 2 shows the four different levels of the previously described process world from Section 2. Our goal is to map these levels to Google Earth.

**Table 2.** Mapping of terms

| Zoom-Level | Business Processes | Google Earth |
|---|---|---|
| Level 1 | Process World | Globe |
| Level 2 | Process Area | Continent |
| Level 3 | Process | Country |
| Level 4 | Process Step | City |

---

[1] earth.google.com

As can be seen in Figure 3(a), Level 1 of our scenario corresponds to the entire globe in Google Earth. Process areas, in turn, can be considered as continents (cf. Fig. 3(b)). Note, that both the globe and the continents are depicted from the same view (i.e., the satellite view). On Level 3 (cf. Fig. 3(c)), Google Earth switches to another view, namely a map-oriented view. On this level Google Earth shows single countries. Picking up again our scenario, a single country corresponds to a single process. Finally, single process steps (Level 4) correspond to single cities in Figure 3(d). The view has changed again, now to a terrain view in Google Earth.

Obviously, Google Earth can be applied to our real-world scenario and to its different levels of information detail and views.

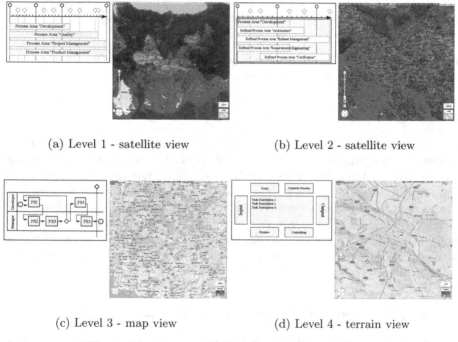

(a) Level 1 - satellite view          (b) Level 2 - satellite view

(c) Level 3 - map view          (d) Level 4 - terrain view

**Fig. 3.** Mapping navigation concept to Google Earth

However, in the presented example, process navigation still remains restricted. The process user, for example, cannot manipulate the hard-wired zoom levels and views. Level 3, for instance, is always depicted as a logic-based view. Indeed, the user can adjust the level of information detail (i.e., one dimension, the dimension X in Fig. 4(a)), but the view is then automatically selected.

The Google Earth concept, in turn, supports two navigation dimensions to overcome these restrictions. The first dimension is the *level of zoom* (X) (i.e., the information detail). The second dimension subsumes different *views* (Y). We can depict these two dimensions as a matrix (cf. Fig.4(b)). As we can identify four different information levels and three different views in our real-world scenario

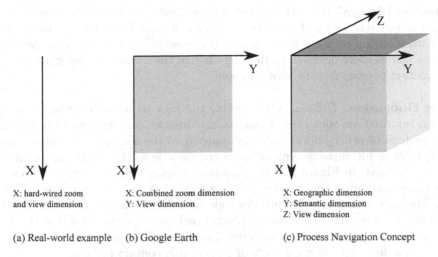

(a) Real-world example    (b) Google Earth                (c) Process Navigation Concept

**Fig. 4.** The enhancement of navigation dimensions

(cf. Section 2), a corresponding Google Earth navigation can be depicted as $4 \times 3$ matrix. Thus, twelve different visualizations are possible compared to the four visualizations of our original example (cf. Fig 2).

Even the Google Earth navigation concept (with its two dimensions) is not able to completely meet all the requirements described in Section 2. For example, consider a manager who wants to see detailed information about the progress of a specific process, but who must also have an overview over all other processes at the same time. Picking up the Google Earth metaphor, this scenario can be described be as follows: The user wants to see selected cities of countries, but also wants to see the whole globe at the same time. The Google Earth navigation concept cannot solve this problem. The user can either zoom in (i.e., he may see single cities, but then looses the overview on the globe at the same time), or he can zoom out (so that he sees the globe, but single cities are not shown).

We address this issue by picking up techniques from the area of user interface design. Reiterer and Buering [7], for example, investigate respective techniques and distinguish between *geographic* and *semantic* zoom. In the following, we enhance the Google Earth navigation concept by introducing these additional dimensions. In total, this leads to three navigation dimensions: the geographic dimension (X), the semantic dimension (Y), and the view dimension (Z) (cf. Fig4(c)).

### 3.3 Process Navigation Dimensions

We now describe the three mentioned dimensions in detail.

**Geographic Dimension.** The geographic dimension allows for a visual zooming without changing the level of information detail. Think of a magnifier while reading a newspaper. To set different zooming levels, scales can be used. In the area of user interface design, Wijk et al.[4] already introduced a similar technique.

**Semantic Dimension.** In the semantic dimension, process information is displayed in different levels of detail. On a high semantic level, for example, only the names of process steps are depicted. If the semantic level of the respective process step is more detailed, further details like the duration, responsible roles and contact persons may be shown as well.

**View Dimension.** Different views enable the user to select different types of process information, such as time aspects, documents, contact persons or logical relationships to other information. As opposed to the semantic dimension, the detail level of information remains on a constant level, i.e., only the point of view is changed. In Figure 2, three dimensions have already been introduced. The time-based view (cf. Fig.3(a)) emphasises time aspects and uses a time line. The logic-based view accentuates logic relations between process steps (cf. fig. 3(c)). Finally, the turtle-view represents task descriptions (cf. Fif 3(d)). An additional (i.e., fourth) view is introduced in Figure 5. Here the focus is on the information flow, i.e., on documents or responsible contact persons.

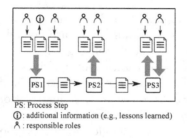

PS: Process Step
ⓘ: additional information (e.g., lessons learned)
⅄ : responsible roles

**Fig. 5.** A view emphasising the information flow between different process steps

With these three navigation dimensions, the user is able to navigate in and across complex business processes.

Generally, a completely unrestricted navigation within and across process models is not always useful as some visualizations do not make sense. As example consider the following scenario in which the geographic zoom is on an abstract level, i.e., the whole process world (the entire globe) is visible. At the same time the semantic zoom corresponds to a very detailed level, i.e., process information is displayed to each process step (information to all cities around the world are shown). As result we would obtain the visualization of the process world with a multitude of detailed process information, overlapping with each other, due to limited screen size.

Figure 6 shows a schematic navigation element supporting these three dimensions. For the geographic dimension (G), a slider control (well known from Google Earth) can be used. To adjust the semantic dimension (S), we use check boxes. A check box gives the user the possibility to select or deselect single levels of information. Finally, as only one view (V) can be depicted at the same time, we use radio buttons to select the respective view.

**Fig. 6.** Three zooming options. (**G**eographic, **S**emantic, **V**iews).

## 3.4 Filter Mechanism

As aforementioned, the freedom to arbitrarily navigate within three navigation dimensions is not always meaningful for the user. Hence, we introduce additional filter mechanisms enabling more sophisticated navigation possibilities. To illustrate our filter mechanism, we pick up our scenario again. Showing process steps (semantic dimension) of the whole process world (geographic dimension) does not make sense unless we use appropriate filter attributes to reduce the amount of displayed information. In general, every process information represents an attribute that can be potentially used to generate filters. Respective filters allow reducing the information displayed in the context of a particular process visualization based on certain rules. These rules, in turn, may refer to a number of filter attributes. For example, one possible filter attribute could be the duration of process steps or the responsible role. For example, the following inquiries are possible:

- Show all process steps associated with the role "Quality Manager".
- Show all process areas with the roles "Quality Manager" and "Software Developer" being involved.

In the following we present an example to illustrate how our process navigation concept works in conjunction with the introduced filter mechanism. Table 3 shows the different views and levels we use in this example.

**Table 3.** Caption for our example

| Level | Semantic Zoom | View |
|-------|---------------|------|
| 1 | Process World | time-based |
| 2 | Process Area | logic-based |
| 3 | Process | turtle-view |
| 4 | Process Step | informationflow |

Navigation starts with a view of the entire process world (cf. Fig. 7(a)), similar to the PDF document. However, it includes additional information. The geographic level corresponds to Level 1, i.e., the entire process from its start until its end is shown (from a time-based view). Semantically, only information on the level of processes is depicted (semantic zoom level 3).

A user having role "E/E (electric/electronic) developer" is only interested in processes, he is involved in. For this purpose, he can use our filter mechanism by setting up attribute role to "E/E developer" (cf. Fig. 7(b)). At the same time he may select semantic level 4 to display all process steps in addition to the processes he is involved in (semantic level 3). As the user is interested in a specific process step in process B, he applies the geographical zoom to process B (cf. Fig. 7(c)) in order to get a better overview on it. Note, that all interactions are user-driven.

Finally, assume that the user is less interested in time aspects, but in what he has to do next, when finishing the current process step. Therefore, he switches to the logic-based view as depicted in Figure 7(d). Here, he can identify successors of the current process step he has worked on.

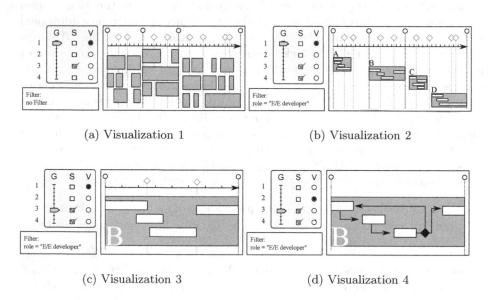

(a) Visualization 1            (b) Visualization 2

(c) Visualization 3            (d) Visualization 4

**Fig. 7.** Example of navigating in three dimensions including the use of filters

The example demonstrates that the combination of our navigation concept with the sketched filter mechanisms supports the user in finding needed information in large process model repositories.

## 4    Related Work

Related work mainly stems from two areas: (1) business process visualization and navigation & (2) zoomable user interfaces.

Vajna [13] introduces a system, which enables the modelling and evaluation of any kind of process or project as well as the dynamic navigation through it. The behaviour of this system is described as "navigation", because it always leaves the control and the decision for the user, as opposed to "process control", where processes are fixed and thus controlled automatically. Bobrik et al. [6] criticise that existing BPM tools lack the flexibility of presenting personalized process views to users. As different users have distinguished perspectives on business processes and related data, in large organizations this flexibility becomes crucial. In response, a view concept is suggested that enables advanced support for process visualization with focus on reducing the complexity of business processes. Schoenhage et al. [14] investigate business visualization in 3D. They pick up a 2D visualization of a business process as a starting point, for which they subsequently provide a 3D visualization. With this approach, data visualization in multiple dimensions (e.g., past, present and simulated data) becomes possible.

In the area of zooming techniques van Wijk and Nuij [4] state that large 2D information spaces such as maps, images or abstract visualizations require views at various levels of detail. They further state that users often switch between these different views and discuss how a smooth migration from one view to another can be realized. For this purpose, they introduce a metric on the effect of simultaneous zooming and panning.

With JAZZ [15] and Pad++ [16], Bederson show how zooming techniques can be used as a foundation for intuitive user interfaces. More general zooming techniques are presented by Reiterer et al. [7]. Zooming facilitates data presentation on limited screen real-estate by allowing the users to alter the scale of the viewpoint such that it shows decreasing fraction of the information space with an increasing magnification. As additional technique, *panning* is introduced, i.e, the moving in constant scale. Such user interface concepts are implemented in *Squidy*, a zoomable design environment for natural user interfaces [17], in *ZEUS*, a zoomable explorative user interface for searching and object presentation [18], and in *ZOIL*, a cross-platform user interface paradigm for personal information management [19]. Dieberger and Frank [20] propose a conceptional user interface metaphor for complex information spaces based on the structure of a city, as people are used to navigate within cities to reach particular destinations.

## 5    Summary and Outlook

In this paper we suggest a new process navigation approach for large process model collections and process models. Specifically, we pick up an existing navigation concept for complex information spaces, namely Google Earth, and apply it to business processes. We introduce geographic and semantic zoom functions and describe different process views and sophisticated filter mechanisms. The presented process navigation ideas, though not fully implemented yet, allow users to better navigate through complex process model collections. Future work will address the further specification and formalization of the presented ideas and their evaluation in case studies and user experiments.

## References

1. Rosa, M.L., Reijers, H.A., van der Aalst, W.M.P., Dijkman, R.M., Mendling, J., Dumas, M., García-Bañuelos, L.: Apromore: An advanced process model repository. Expert Syst. Appl., 7029–7040 (2011)
2. Weber, B., Reichert, M., Mendling, J., Reijers, H.A.: Refactoring large process model repositories. Computers in Industry, 467–486 (2011)

3. Fauvet, M.C., La Rosa, M., Sadegh, M., Alshareef, A., Dijkman, R.M., García-Bañuelos, L., Reijers, H.A., van der Aalst, W.M.P., Dumas, M., Mendling, J.: Managing Process Model Collections with AProMoRe. In: Maglio, P.P., Weske, M., Yang, J., Fantinato, M. (eds.) ICSOC 2010. LNCS, vol. 6470, pp. 699–701. Springer, Heidelberg (2010)
4. van Wijk, J.J., Nuij, W.A.A.: Smooth and efficient zooming and panning. In: IEEE Symposium on Information Visualization, pp. 15–23. IEEE Computer Society (2003)
5. Hipp, M., Mutschler, B., Reichert, M.: On the context-aware, personalized delivery of process information: Viewpoints, problems, and requirements. In: Proc. of the ARES 2011 (2011) (accepted for publication)
6. Bobrik, R., Reichert, M., Bauer, T.: View-Based Process Visualization. In: Alonso, G., Dadam, P., Rosemann, M. (eds.) BPM 2007. LNCS, vol. 4714, pp. 88–95. Springer, Heidelberg (2007)
7. Reiterer, H., Büring, T.: Zooming techniques. In: Encyclopedia of Database Systems, pp. 3684–3689. Springer, US (2009)
8. Smirnov, S., Reijers, H.A., Weske, M.: A Semantic Approach for Business Process Model Abstraction. In: Mouratidis, H., Rolland, C. (eds.) CAiSE 2011. LNCS, vol. 6741, pp. 497–511. Springer, Heidelberg (2011)
9. Reijers, H.A., Freytag, T., Mendling, J., Eckleder, A.: Syntax highlighting in business process models. Decision Support Systems, 339–349 (2011)
10. Reijers, H.A., Mendling, J., Dijkman, R.M.: Human and automatic modularizations of process models to enhance their comprehension. Inf. Syst., 881–897 (2011)
11. Michelberger, B., Mutschler, B., Reichert, M.: On Handling Process Information: Results from Case Studies and a Survey. In: 2nd International Workshop on Empirical Research in Business Process Management, ER-BPM 2011 (2011)
12. Rayle, R.: Google Earth: A platform for open data. Solstice: Electronic Journal of Geography and Mathematics (2010)
13. Vajna, S., Freisleben, D.: Project navigation - modelling, improving and review of engineering processes. In: Proc. of 2002 ASME, Design Engineering Technical Conferences, DETC 2002/DAC34132 h, pp. 919–925 (2002)
14. Schönhage, B., van Ballegooij, A., Eliëns, A.: 3D gadgets for business process visualization. In: Spencer, S.N. (ed.) Proc. of the 5th Symposium on the Virtual Reality Modeling Language (WEB3D-VRML- 2000), pp. 131–138 (2000)
15. Bederson, B.B., Meyer, J., Good, L.: Jazz: an extensible zoomable user interface graphics toolkit in java. In: ACM Symposium on User Interface Software and Technology, pp. 171–180 (2000)
16. Bederson, B.B., Hollan, J.D.: Pad++: A zooming graphical interface for exploring alternate interface physics. In: ACM Symposium on User Interface Software and Technology, pp. 17–26 (1994)
17. König, W.A., Rädle, R., Reiterer, H.: Squidy: a zoomable design environment for natural user interfaces. In: Olsen Jr., D.R., Arthur, R.B., Hinckley, K., Morris, M.R., Hudson, S.E., Greenberg, S. (eds.) CHI Extended Abstracts, pp. 4561–4566 (2009)
18. Gundelsweiler, F., Memmel, T., Reiterer, H.: ZEUS – Zoomable Explorative User Interface for Searching and Object Presentation. In: Smith, M.J., Salvendy, G. (eds.) HCII 2007, Part I. LNCS, vol. 4557, pp. 288–297. Springer, Heidelberg (2007)
19. Jetter, H.C., König, W.A., Gerken, J., Reiterer, H.: ZOIL - a cross-platform user interface paradigm for personal information management. In: CHI 2008 Workshop - The Disappearing Desktop: Personal Information Management (2008)
20. Dieberger, A., Frank, A.U.: A city metaphor to support navigation in complex information spaces. J. Vis. Lang. Comput., 597–622 (1998)

# On the Modeling of Healthcare Workflows Using Recursive ECATNets

Amel Ben Dhieb[1] and Kamel Barkaoui[2]

[1] LSTS Enit, Tunis, Tunisia
dhiebamel@gmail.com
[2] Cedric-Cnam Paris, France
kamel.barkaoui@cnam.fr

**Abstract.** Healthcare enterprises involve complex processes involving clinical and administrative tasks that are supported by a variety of information and logistics systems. Although the workflow technology was introduced in various industries two decades ago, the use of Workflow Management Systems (WfMSs) is rather recent in the healthcare domain. This is due, in particular, by the fact that healthcare processes (or careflows) are highly flexible and extremely dynamic [1]. In this paper, we show how we can take advantage of description power of Recursive ECATNets for realizing flexible workflows in the healthcare domain.

**Keywords:** Workflow management technology, healthcare processes, flexibility patterns, flexible workflows, logistic hospitals, Recursive ECATNet.

## 1 Introduction

The recent push for healthcare reform has lead healthcare organizations to re-engineer their processes in order to deliver high quality care while at the same time reducing costs. These process re-engineering should be accompanied with a logistic application to limit the costs attached to the management of their drugs stocks, their flows of products and materials, their flows of information and personnel leading to improve the effectiveness of the processes.

The logistic view on health service organizations is recently applied. It comprises the design, planning, implementation and control of coordination mechanisms between patient flows, personal, diagnostic and therapeutic activities and drugs distribution [2]. Although the workflow technology was introduced in various industries two decades ago, the use of Workflow Management Systems (WfMSs) is rather recent in the healthcare domain. This is due, in particular, by the fact that healthcare processes (or careflows) are highly flexible and extremely dynamic [1]. In this paper, we show how we can take advantage of description power of Recursive ECATNets (RECATNets for short) [10] for realizing flexible workflows in the healthcare domain while supporting the efficient logistic and for specifying exceptional behaviors of processes by offering practical mechanisms, direct and intuitive support of dynamic creation and suppression of processes.

F. Daniel et al. (Eds.): BPM 2011 Workshops, Part II, LNBIP 100, pp. 99–107, 2012.

The paper is organized as follows. In section 2, we describe the main flexibility patterns in WfMSs. In section 3, we talk about the using of Petri net in logistics. We recall in section 4 the semantics of the RECATNets model, and we illustrate in section 5 its appropriateness in healthcare domain through a simple but significant careflow example. The section 6 concludes this paper.

## 2 Workflow Flexibility Patterns

Workflow models such as they are conceived by the classic WfMSs are a description of a process of ideal work represented generally in a rigid way [3], [4]. The automation of processes is based on a very structured description. Such representations are not well suitable for the reality to organizations where processes are often led to deviate from their initial plan. This is the case in healthcare organizations.

The need of flexibility during process execution i.e. the ability of workflow to adapt its behavior as response to exceptional situations or to the change of constraints and opportunities introduced by the use of new technologies, the needs of the market or the new laws [5] or the logistic application demand becomes critical.

In hospitals, healthcare processes must be able to deal with changes in the operational environment by opening alternate execution paths which may not have been foreseen at design-time and not explicitly catered for by the process modeling [1]. Indeed changes in healthcare treatments, drugs, and protocols may invalidate running instances by requiring reparative or new actions. For example, a care pathway for a patient with a disease condition may need to be changed since new drugs are available. Moreover, these processes are distributed since they involve during a given period multiple healthcare units.

So that the need of a flexible workflow system and the definition of logical principles and detailed workflow descriptions for the different hospital goods (staff, consumer goods, sterile supplies, food, beds, medicine, samples and blood products, waste management, etc.) seems to be crucial to reduce idle time, optimize the technological and human resources use and to handle with the dynamics arising naturally from a working group and the continuous change of the work environment in hospitals. This lead to recognize some flexibility patterns describing the flexibility of business process in healthcare domain [1].

Since the middle of the 90s, multiple approaches were proposed with the aim of treating the problem of the flexibility in the WfMSs [6], [7], [8]. There are basically three types of flexibility patterns:

(1) **Flexibility by adjustment:** it allows the restructuring of the workflow model or an instance or a set of workflow instances. This restructuring may occur before or during the process execution without being anticipated in the design phase.

(2) **Flexibility by partial specification:** is the ability to deliberately under-specify parts of a process model at design-time in anticipation of the fact that the required execution details will become known some future time [1]. This kind of flexibility does not require changing the definition of the process, but rather calls to complete this definition during the execution process. The model is not changed. Approaches that adopt this kind of flexibility assume that all or most

of the deviations that may occur during the workflow execution process are already known (as they may occur and how to deal it).

(3) **Flexibility by design:** it is the ability to incorporate alternative execution paths to the process definition during the design phase. Flexibility by design stems from the inherent power of the description specification language used to describe the process. Therefore there is no partial specification of the process definition or dynamics change of the process structure (in an instance or model).

The description of the parallel execution of tasks, the choice (to give the user the ability to choose an execution path among several alternatives), the ability to run a set of tasks sequentially in any order are considered also as a support flexibility. Indeed, for the same process definition, it can be several different execution paths.

## 3  Using Recursive Petri Nets in Logistics

Logistics is concerned in movement and storage of materials and people. The domain of logistics activities is providing the customers of the system with the right product, in the right place, at the right time.

Recently, logistics has become an important issue in many organizations. To improve their logistic functions, these organizations should control logistic activities. In the case of hospitals, logistic activities are concerned in room schedule, planning and control, in drugs transport, inventory, storage and distribution and in patients transportation management. The management of the logistic systems including hospitals is based on the modeling and the analysis of complex processes which must be usually run at the same time concurrently.

So, whereas modeling concurrent activities is rather straightforward with Petri nets, the management of dynamic objects is limited. Indeed, due to the static structure of the PN, there is no way to keep trace of synchronization between two dynamically created processes. Moreover, the classic Petri net (Place/transition) model is unsuitable to represent complex data structures, to deal with true concurrency semantics, temporal dependencies and dynamic reconfiguration capabilities. Indeed, all these features are preponderant in the logistic context of hospitals. To deal with such features, some extensions of the basic Petri Net model such as Recursive Petri Nets (RPNs) [9] have been introduced to model systems with dynamic structure offering an ability to model complex mechanisms of discrete event systems (DES) like interrupts, fault-tolerance, remote procedure calls and environment-driven behaviors. Also, in RPNs, threads which play the token game of a Petri net can be dynamically created and concurrently executed.

## 4  Recursive ECATNets

The Recursive ECATNets (RECATNets) model [10] is defined on the basis of a sound combination of algebraic PetriNets formalism with the Recursive PetriNets (RPNs) [9]. We remind that algebraic PetriNet combine the expressive power of Petri nets with abstract data types. The places in an RECATNet are associated to a sort and are marked with multisets of algebraic terms. The RECATNets inherit all concepts of the classical PetriNets formalism except that their transitions are partitioned into two types:

-    *elementary transitions* (represented by a simple rectangle. See Fig. 1 (a)).
-    *abstract transitions* (represented by a double border rectangle. See Fig. 1 (b)).

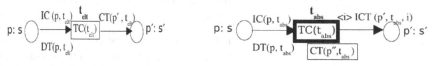

(a)    A generic elementary transition             (b) A generic abstract transition

**Fig 1.** Transition Types

In a RECATNet, an arc from an input place p to a transition t (elementary or abstract) is labeled by two algebraic expressions: IC(p, t) and DT(p, t). The expression IC(p, t) specifies the partial condition on the marking of the input place p for the enabling of t. It takes one of the following forms (see Table 1). The expression DT(p, t) specifies the multi-set of tokens to be removed from the marking of the input place p when the transition t is fired. Also, each transition t may be labeled by a Boolean expression TC(t) which specifies an additional enabling condition on the values taken by local variables of t (i.e. variables related to all the input places of t). When the expression TC(t) is omitted, the default value is the term True.

**Table 1.** The different forms of the expression *IC(p, t)* for a given transition *t*

| IC(p, t) | Enabling condition |
|---|---|
| $\alpha^0$ | The marking of the place p must be equal to $\alpha$ (e.g. $IC(p, t) = \varnothing^0$ means the marking of p must be empty). |
| $\alpha+$ | The marking of the place p must include $\alpha$ (e.g. $IC(p, t) = \varnothing^+$ means condition is always satisfied). |
| $\alpha-$ | The marking of the place p must not include $\alpha$, with $\alpha \neq \varnothing$. |
| $\alpha1 \wedge \alpha2$ | Conditions $\alpha1$ and $\alpha2$ are both true. |
| $\alpha1 \vee \alpha2$ | $\alpha1$ or $\alpha2$ is true. |

An interesting feature of RECATNets is that there is a clear distinction between the firing condition of a given transition *t* and the tokens which may be destroyed during the firing action of *t* (respectively specified via the expression *IC(p, t)* and *DT(p, t)*). A transition *t* is fireable when several conditions are satisfied simultaneously: (1) Every *IC(p, t)* is satisfied for each input place *p* of *t*. (2) The transition condition *TC(t)* is true. Moreover, a RECATNet generates during its execution a dynamical tree of threads (denoting the fatherhood relation and describing the inter-thread calls) where each of these threads has its own execution context. All threads of such a tree can be executed simultaneously. A step of a RECATNet is thus a step of one of its threads. When a thread fires an elementary transition $t_{elt}$, the tokens $DT(p, t_{elt})$ are removed from each input place *p* of $t_{elt}$ and simultaneously the tokens $CT(p', t_{elt})$ are added to each output place *p'* of $t_{elt}$ (in the same manner as transitions of classical ECATNets).

When a thread fires an abstract transition $t_{abs}$, it consumes the multi-set of tokens $DT(p, t_{abs})$ from each input place $p$ of the transition $t_{abs}$ and simultaneously it creates a new thread (called its child) launched with an initial state being the starting marking associated to this abstract transition.

Naturally, when an elementary or an abstract transition is fired, appropriate instantiations of the variables appearing in the expressions $IC$, $DT$ and $CT$, take place. A family $\gamma$ of Boolean terms is associated to a RECATNet in order to describe the termination states of the threads. These termination states, called *final markings*, are specified by conditions on the marking of the RECATNet places. A family of such final markings is indexed by a finite set whose items are called *termination indices*. Therefore, when a thread reaches a final marking $\gamma_i$ (with $i \in I$), it terminates, aborts its whole descent of threads and creates the multi-set of tokens $ICT(p', t_{abs}, i)$ in the output place $p'$ of the abstract transition $t_{abs}$ which gave birth to it (in its father thread). Such an event is called a *cut step* and denoted $\tau_i$ (with $i \in I$). An arc from an abstract transition $t_{abs}$ to its output place $p'$, labeled by an expression $<i> ICT(p', t_{abs}, i)$, means that the tokens $ICT(p', t_{abs}, i)$ are produced in the place $p'$ if the marking $\gamma_i$ is reached in the terminating thread (where $i$ is the index of this termination). Therefore, the production of tokens in the output place of an abstract transition is delayed until the child thread, generated by the firing of this transition, reaches a final marking. Note that if a cut step occurs in the root of the tree of threads, it leads to the empty tree, denoted by $\perp$, from which neither transition nor cut step can occur.

Formally, a RECATNet is a high level net $\varepsilon$ = (Spec, P, T, sort, Cap, IC, DT, CT, TC, I, Y, ICT) where:

- Spec = $(\Sigma, E)$ is an algebraic specification of an abstract data type given by the user (E its set of equations and $\Sigma$ its set of operations and sorts). $T_{\Sigma,E}(X)$ denotes the $\Sigma$-algebra of the equivalence classes of the $\Sigma$-terms with variables in X, modulo the equations E. CATdas(E,X) is the structure of equivalence classes formed from multi-sets of the terms$T_{\Sigma,E}(X)$ modulo the associative, commutative and identity axioms for the operator $\oplus$ (with the empty multi-set as the identity element). The operations $\subset$, - represent, respectively, the multi-set inclusion and the multi-set difference.
- $P$ is a finite set of places.
- $T$ is a finite set of transitions partitioned into abstract and elementary ones.
- $sort : P \rightarrow S$ *(with S the set of sorts of Spec).*
- $Cap : P \rightarrow CATdas(E, \varnothing) \cup \{\infty\}$, *(Capacity).*
- $IC : P \times T \rightarrow CATdas(E,X)^*$, *(Input Condition) where* $CATdas(E,X)^* =$ $\{\alpha^+ | \alpha \in CATdas(E,X)\} \cup \{\alpha | \alpha \in CATdas(E,X)\} \cup \{\alpha^0 | \alpha \in CATdas(E,X)\} \cup$ $\{\alpha_1 \wedge \alpha_2 | \forall i\, \alpha_i \in CATdas(E,X)^*\} \cup \{\alpha_1 \vee \alpha_2 | \forall i\, \alpha_i \in CATdas(E,X)^*\}$
- $DT : P \times T \rightarrow CATdas(E,X)$, *(Destroyed Tokens),*
- $CT : P \times T \rightarrow CATdas(E,X)$, *(Created Tokens),*
- $TC : T \rightarrow CATdas(E,X)_{bool}$ , *(Transition Condition),*
- I is a finite set of indices.
- $\gamma$ is a family, indexed by I, of Boolean terms defined in order to describe the termination conditions (i.e. final markings) of threads,
- ICT: P x Tabs x I $\rightarrow$ CATdas(E,X) *(Indexed Created Tokens).*

The global state of a RECATNet is described by a dynamical tree of threads called an extended *marking* where each thread is associated to an *ordinary marking* describing its internal context. The places of a thread are marked by multi-sets of algebraic terms.

**Definition 1 (Extended marking).** *An extended marking of a RECATNet RN = (Spec, P, T, sort, Cap, IC, DT, CT, TC, I, γ, ICT) is a labeled rooted tree denoted Tr = <V, M, E, A> such that:*

- *V is the set of nodes (i.e. threads)*
- *M is a Mapping V → CATdas(E,∅) associating an ordinary marking with each node of the tree, such that*
  $\forall v \in V, \forall p \in P, M(v)(p) \leq Cap(p)$
- *E ⊆ V × V is the set of edges,*
- *A is a mapping E → Tabs associating an abstract transition with each edge.*

$M(v)$ denotes the marking of a thread $v$ in an extended marking $Tr$ and $M(v)(p)$ denotes the marking of a place $p$ in a thread $v$. A marked RECATNet $(RN, T\, r0)$ is a RECATNet $RN$ associated to an initial extended marking $Tr0$. For each node $v \in V$, $Succ(v)$ denotes the set of its direct and indirect successors including $v$ ($v \in V$, $Succ(v)$ = {$\forall v' \in V$ / $(v, v') \in E^*$} where $E^*$ is the reflexive and transitive closure of $E$). Moreover, when a node $v$ is not the root thread of an extended marking $Tr$, we denote by $pred(v)$ its unique predecessor in $Tr$ (i.e. its father thread). An *elementary step* in a marked RECATNet can be a firing of a transition or a cut step occurrence (denoted $\tau_i$ with $i \in I$).

**Definition 2.** *An elementary transition $t_{elt}$ is enabled in a thread $v$ of an extended marking Tr (with Tr ≠ ⊥) iff: (1) Every IC(p, $t_{elt}$) is satisfied for each input place p of the transition $t_{elt}$. (2) The transition condition TC($t_{elt}$) is true.*

*The firing of an elementary transition telt in a thread v of Tr = <V, M, E, A> leads to an extended marking Tr' = <V 'v, $t_{elt}$, A'> (denoted Tr ────▶ Tr') such that:*

- $V' = V, E' = E,$
- $\forall e \in E', A'(e) = A(e),$
- $\forall v' \in V' \setminus \{v\}, M'(v') = M(v'),$
- $\forall p \in P, M'(v)(p) = M(v)(p)\quad DT(p, t_{elt}) \oplus CT(p, t_{elt}).$

**Definition 3.** *An abstract transition $t_{abs}$ is enabled in a thread v of an extended marking Tr (with Tr ≠⊥) iff:*

*(1) Every IC (p, $t_{abs}$) is satisfied for each input place p of the transition tabs.*

*(2) The transition condition TC ($t_{abs}$) is true. The firing of an abstract transition $t_{abs}$ in a thread v of Tr = <V, M, E, A> leads to an extended marking Tr' = <V 'v, $t_{abs}$ A'> (denoted Tr ────▶ Tr') such that:*

- *Let v' be a fresh identifier in the tree Tr',*
- $V' = V \setminus \{v\}, E' = E \cup \{(v, v')\}$
- $\forall e \in E', A'(e) = A(e), A'((v, v')) = t_{abs},$
- $\forall v'' \in V' \setminus \{v\}, M'(v'') = M(v'')$

$- \forall p \in P, M'(v)(p) = M(v)(p) - DT(p, t_{abs})$

$- \forall p \in P, M'(v')(p) = CT(p, _{tabs})$

**Definition 4.** *A cut step $\tau_i$ is enabled in a thread v of an extended marking Tr (with Tr $\neq \perp$) iff M (v) satisfies the condition of the final marking $\gamma_{iv, \tau_i}$ occurrence of a cut step $\tau_i$ in a thread v of Tr = <V, M, E, A> leads to an extended marking Tr' = <V', M', E', A'> (denoted Tr ———▶ Tr') such that:*

- *If v is the root thread of the tree Tr, then Tr' = $\perp$), otherwise:*
- $V' = V \setminus Succ(v'), E' = E \cap (V' \times V')$
- $\forall e \in E', A'(e) = A(e)$
- $\forall v' \in V' \setminus \{pred(v)\}, M'(v') = M(v')$
- $\forall p \in P, M'(pred(v))(p) = M(pred(v))(p) \oplus ICT(p, A(pred(v), v), i).$

## 5   A Simple Healthcare Process Workflow Modeling Using R-ECATNets

In this first application of our approach for modelling a simple healthcare process workflow based on RECATNets, we limit us to flexibility by design. The process illustrated below contains two types of tasks: basic tasks (represented by elementary transitions) and complex tasks (represented by abstract transitions). We choose this example to illustrate the ability of RECATNets to capture patterns involving multiple instances and cancellation patterns, in a concise way. The execution of a complex task generates dynamically a new (lower-level) plan of actions for the workflow process (See Fig 2).

The initial state of this net is a tree containing a single thread with a token *(N, codeP, listDrugs, initialised)* in the place *PatientConsultation*. This token represents the waiting of patient treatment (corresponds, respectively, to the number of the consultation, the patient code, the list of requested drugs and the initial state of the treatment).

The workflow process starts by the firing of the transition *"StartProcess"* (i.e. a doctor examines the patient in outpatient department). Then, the abstract task *"StartTreatment"* initialises the treatment handling subprocess by creating dynamically a new thread in the tree of threads of the RECATNet with the associated starting marking. The abstract task *"VerifEmptyRoomAndDrug"* checks the availability of an empty room and the availability of the drugs needed for the patient treatment. For that, the task invokes two services in parallel, *Check drugs* and *Verify Empty room*.

In fact, the firing of the corresponding abstract transition creates a new child thread with the associated starting marking. When the service *Check Drugs* is invoked, the task *"ReceiveListRequest"* looks for the name of hospital pharmacy provider offering each requested drug (i.e. elements of the list *L*).

It produces the multiset of couples *(PharmacyPr, Rq)* which correspond, respectively, to the name of the pharmacy provider and the associated requested drug *(PharmacyPr=FindIn(Rq,ListPharmacyProvider)* with the function *FindIn* returns the first provider from the constant *ListPharmacyProvider* associated to the drug *Rq)*. Next the abstract task *"SendRequest"* initialises (at each firing) a new instance of the service *Research in stock Pharmacy providers*.

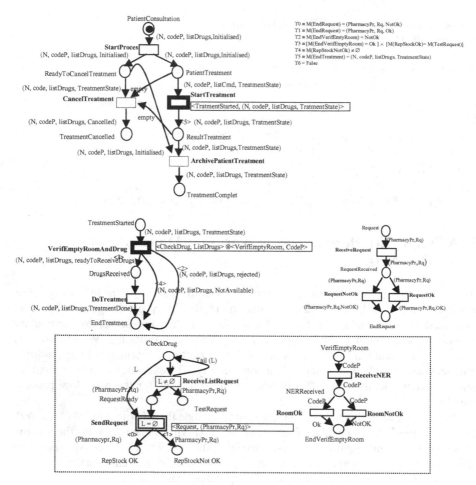

**Fig 2.** A Simple healthcare Process workflow example

The number of running instances of the invoked service is not known at design time. It depends, in fact, on the number of requested drugs. The synchronization of the created instances is specified via the termination states $\Upsilon$. The completion of one instance (i.e. thread) is indicated by a token in *EndRequest* (a termination state reached (see $\Upsilon_0$ or $\Upsilon_1$)).

Another cut step is enabled. This is in the following cases: (1) if one of the requested drug components is not available ($\Upsilon_4$ reached), (2) if we didn't find an empty room ($\Upsilon_2$ reached), or (3) if the empty room and availability of all requested drugs are both OK ($\Upsilon_3$ reached). When a cut step is executed, the corresponding level of action plan terminates and all the threads generated by it are aborted.

During the processing of the treatment, the doctor has the possibility to cancel the treatment (i.e. the task *"CancelTreatment"* is executed) as long as the corresponding treatment is not completed.

When the transition "CancelTreatment" is fired, the thread generated by the transition *"StartTreatment"* is aborted and a token (N, codeP, listDrugs, Cancelled) is produced in the output place of *"CancelTreatment"*. The workflow process terminates by producing a token in one of its final places: (1) a token (N, codeP, listDrugs, Cancelled) is produced in the place *TreatmentCancelled* if the treatment is cancelled by the doctor or (2) a token is produced in the place *TreatmentCompleted* if the treatment is completed (In this case, the value of the produced token depends on the result given by the two services Check drugs and Validity of an empty room).

## 6 Conclusion

The goal of this paper is to show the ability of using Recursive ECATNets for modeling flexible healthcare workflow processes. The benefit of such modeling is that soundness verification [12] of these workflows can be obtained via model checking technique. In future work, we intend to asses the practice of our approach through real case studies and by integrating into the proposed formalism time constraints [11] and shared resources [12].

## References

1. Reijers, H.A., Russell, N., van der Geer, S., Krekels, G.A.M.: Workflow for Healthcare: A Methodology for Realizing Flexible Medical Treatment Processes. In: Rinderle-Ma, S., Sadiq, S., Leymann, F. (eds.) BPM 2009. LNBIP, vol. 43, pp. 593–604. Springer, Heidelberg (2010)
2. Maruster, L., Jorna, R.: From data to knowledge: a method for modeling hospital logistic processes. IEEE Transactions on Information Technology in Biomedicine 9, 248–255 (2005)
3. Halliday, J.J., Shrivastava, S.K., Wheater, S.M.: Flexible workflow management in the openflow system. In: 4th International Enterprise Distributed Object Computing Conference (EDOC 2001), pp. 82–92. IEEE Computer Society (2001)
4. Schonenberg, H., Mans, R., Russell, N., Mulyar, N., Van der Aalst, W.M.P.: Towards a taxonomy of process flexibility. In: CAiSE Forum, pp. 81–84 (2008)
5. Hagen, C., Alonso, G.: Flexible exception handling in the opera process support system. In: International Conference on Distributed Computing Systems, p. 526 (1998)
6. Ellis, C.A., Keddara, K.: A Workflow Change Is a Workflow. In: van der Aalst, W.M.P., Desel, J., Oberweis, A. (eds.) Business Process Management. LNCS, vol. 1806, pp. 201–217. Springer, Heidelberg (2000)
7. Casati, F., Ceri, S., Pernici, B., Pozzi, G.: Workflow evolution. Data Knowl. Eng. 24(3), 211–238 (1998)
8. Siebert, R.: An open architecture for adaptive workflow management systems. J. Integr. Des. Process Sci. 3(3), 29–41 (1999)
9. Haddad, S., Poitrenaud, D.: Recursive Petri nets: Theory and Application to Discrete Event Systems. Acta Informatica 40(7-8), 463–508 (2007)
10. Barkaoui, K., Hicheur, A.: Towards Analysis of Flexible and Collaborative Workflow Using Recursive ECATNets. In: ter Hofstede, A.H.M., Benatallah, B., Paik, H.-Y. (eds.) BPM Workshops 2007. LNCS, vol. 4928, pp. 232–244. Springer, Heidelberg (2008)
11. Barkaoui, K., Boucheneb, H., Hicheur, A.: Modelling and Analysis of Time-Constrained Flexible Workflows with Time Recursive ECATNets. In: Bruni, R., Wolf, K. (eds.) WS-FM 2008. LNCS, vol. 5387, pp. 19–36. Springer, Heidelberg (2009)
12. Barkaoui, K., Ben Ayed, R.: Uniform Verification of Workflow Soundness. Transactions of the Institute of Measurement and Control Journal 31, 1–16 (2010)

# Negotiating Deadline Constraints in Inter-organizational Logistic Systems: A Healthcare Case Study

Mouna Makni[1,2], Nejib Ben Hadj-Alouane[2], Samir Tata[1], and Moez Yeddes[3]

[1] Institut TELECOM, TELECOM SudParis, UMR CNRS Samovar, France
{Mouna.Makni,Samir.Tata}@it-sudparis.eu
[2] National Engineering School of Tunis, OASIS Laboratory, Tunisia
nejib_bha@yahoo.com
[3] National School of Computer Sciences, CRISTAL Laboratory, Tunisia
yeddes@yahoo.fr

**Abstract.** Current logistics methods are more focused on strategic goals and do not deal with short term objectives, such as, reactivity and real-time constraints. Automated logistics management systems tend to facilitate information sharing between companies, in order to support cooperative strategies, improve productivity, control service quality and reduce administrative costs. In this paper, we discuss the application of Inter-Organizational Workflows (IOW) for automating logistic procedures in a collaborative context. A case study of healthcare process is presented, and focuses on the negotiations aspects of temporal constraints in critical situations. We show how our proposed temporal extension of the CoopFlow approach, brings advantages to automating logistics operational procedures, by providing real-time data knowledge and decision routing for the case of emergency healthcare.

**Keywords:** Inter-Organizational Workflows, Logistics, Deadline constraints, Negotiation.

## 1 Introduction

The necessity of automated logistics management is becoming crucial, in various sectors and situations. It deals with challenging operational level problems, which include scheduling, planning and managing constraints (shared resources, deadlines, etc.). Traditionally, logistics systems are important for industries to optimize their existing processes (production, distribution, etc.) and to improve their efficiency. It has been considered as a necessary cost for organizations. But nowadays, with the wide adoption of new information technologies and within the actual economic context, it represents a possible source of competitive advantage.

Because the cost of logistics can not be fine turned to the maximum without controlling business processes, improving these processes becomes a priority for all types of businesses. Automation represents a powerful solution to this issue. In fact, well-defined processes allow managers to better understand current enterprise business and determine inefficiencies and possible improvement.

F. Daniel et al. (Eds.): BPM 2011 Workshops, Part II, LNBIP 100, pp. 108–118, 2012.

Repetitive workers activities, especially logistics tasks, can be automated and replaced by monitoring and control activities. Thus, companies are able to reduce operations costs, achieve better use of resources, increase reactivity, and, thus, promote overall service quality.

But in many cases, the problem is totally distributed. In fact, nowadays we are facing a transformation of businesses in order to cope with the ever increasing economic pressure. Companies are forming strategic associations [1], between entities over different geographical locations, to improve response time and enhance overall competitiveness. In some sectors, the nature of the services involves the implication of entities which are geographically distributed. Setting up such temporary alliances implies the use of a global logistics management solution, which is becoming the core of global competitive business.

Logistics problems, however, are becoming more complex, since they are being considered, more and more, in conjunction with short-term dynamic situations and processes. A dynamic reactive process should have the capability to enable changes, at any given time, with low latency and overhead. Hence, so-called real-time [2,3] and collaborative logistics [4,5] are considered when timing constraints (deadlines) are specified and operations need to be performed by the specified deadlines. In some cases, missed deadlines lead to penalties, and even when they do not prevent achieving the system goals, they typically reduce the service utility especially in critical situations.

Our previous work concerns short-term cooperation within the context of virtual enterprises [6,7], which allows dynamic interconnection of a set of partners with complementary skills according to their needs. Our main purpose is to provide a solution to negotiate and match, not only the semantic conformance of the partners (i.e., the partners which execute complementary tasks can properly interconnect within an IOW) but essentially the timing constraints consistency (i.e., the partners should provide the required service within the specified response times). We also deal with industrial privacy preservation issue, because there are serious consequences for companies fully exposing their business knowledge, in the context of occasional collaborations.

This paper presents the application of our framework in the logistics management field. Our ambition is to provide an IOW based collaborative model, increased with time constraints, for modeling and solving logistics problems. We concentrate on an important issue in a cooperation context which is choosing the best service provider in an emergency case. We principally focus on the time constraints, because we believe that negotiating reasonable temporal constraints, is an important step in any system, and often represents a selection criteria for the collaborative partner choice. We give an illustrative case study to point on this issue. The proposed model capture the negotiation logistics aspects within the context of IOW concepts. Furthermore, it should support the existing logistic solutions, which have reached their limits in a collaborative context. In fact, automated tools can be provided for transforming a workflow pattern in a particular logistic solution, to be solved.

This paper is organized as follows. Section 2 presents a brief description of the temporal extension of the Coopflow approach. Section 3 presents our vision of the collaborative logistics in the healthcare field, based on IOW concepts. Section 4 illustrate an example scenario and our proof of concept implementation for automating the temporal constraints conformance process.

## 2   CoopFlow Temporal Extension

Within the context of short-term collaboration, the authors have developed the CoopFlow approach, which allows the dynamic interconnection of a set of partners with complementary skills, while maintaining their privacy assurances [8,9,10]. CoopFlow consists of three major steps:

(1) workflows abstraction and advertisement,
(2) workflows matching, and
(3) workflows interconnection and cooperation.

In the first step of CoopFlow, each partner has to advertise its offered activities, using a common registry. In order to preserve the industrial secret, prior to the advertisement, companies must reduce their workflow inter-visibility. Therefore, the abstraction process [11,12] consists of hiding, from the private workflow, internal activities which are not involved for collaboration needs. The resulting public workflow exposes only cooperative activities.

The matching process [13,14], in the second step of CoopFlow, consists of comparing the advertised abstractions (i. e. the business behavior of the candidates). It takes into account the description of the control flow, the data flow, and the business semantics of cooperative activities. If the matching result is positive, the workflows are then interconnected.

The third step of the approach consists of the use and application of the inter-enterprises workflow cooperation platform (deployment, execution, management, etc), which allows different Workflow Management Systems (WfMS) to interconnect their workflows for cooperation.

In [6,7], we have addressed the problem of incorporating and verifying the conformance of deadlines on time constraints within the context of Inter-Organizational Workflows. Even when the complementarity of business behavior is validated, missing deadlines may lead to a global execution failure. Based on the existing CoopFlow approach, we proposed a temporal extension using Time Petri Nets models and tools [31]. The verification process can be executed while maintaining the core advantage of CoopFlow, i.e., that each partner can keep the critical parts of its business process private.

In the temporal extension of CoopFlow, the matching process (the second step) is split in two separate phases:

(2a) Semantic matching, and
(2b) Temporal constraints conformance

If the business behavior complementarity of the involved parties is validated as defined in CoopFlow, an analysis is executed to validate whether temporal behavior is also coherent. Following the semantic conformance, and if it is successful, we have added the temporal verification process as follows:

- deadline computation and local validation,
- deadline advertisement, and
- deadline conformance validation.

Given its temporal private workflow (i. e., its internal workflow containing temporal information about activities), a partner should specify a deadline constraint to limit, for a potential candidate, the elapsed time from the instant a service request is sent and its delivery time. The defined deadline should be validated locally in order to suit the internal execution of the workflow. Besides, the partner need to translate such an informal requirement into the temporal model proposed [6] and publish it to the potential candidates as part as the business behavior, in the constrained temporal public workflow generated. This is illustrated in Fig. 1.

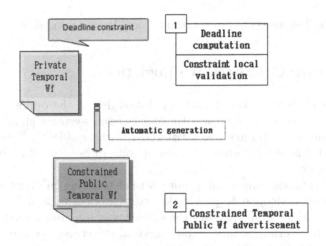

**Fig. 1.** Deadline constraint computation and advertisement

We have also described how eventual candidates execute temporal reasoning and verification [7]. Our idea is based on the propagation of local time constraints to the shared view, which enables partners to capture timing requirements and to check their consistency on their side, and thus the temporal conformance can be achieved while preserving the partner's privacy.

Fig. 2 illustrates a matching process according to the temporal extension of CoopFlow and the workflow versions required for each step (public workflow, private temporal workflow, etc.). In this example, Partner 1 advertise a temporal constraint which should be verified by Partner 2, if the semantic matching is successful.

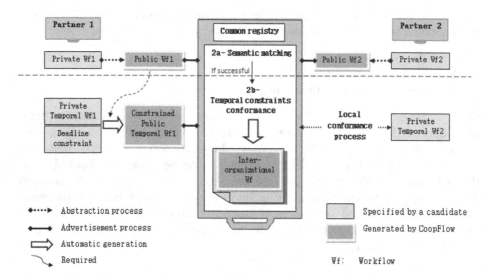

**Fig. 2.** The matching process in the CoopFlow temporal extension

# 3    Healthcare Collaborative Logistics

Cities are nowadays attracting larger population due to the opportunities that they present. Therefore, public institutions logistics systems should be more efficient in order to guarantee the satisfaction of the residents. Especially, the healthcare sector is of increasing government concern because of its importance and critical nature.

Healthcare organizations require more careful planning in order to improve overall quality of service, i.e, to provide low costs services with limited resources to more people. Since in many cases the efficiency of dynamic coordination can save lives, both government and private medical structures need an innovative strategy to be able to provide new logistics concepts.

Due to the emergence of new information technologies in the healthcare sector [15,16], innovative solutions gradually appear in some disciplines, incurring value-added procedures: personal digital assistants [17], electronic patient records [18], etc.

Logistics include a large part of the business activities. In the context of healthcare logistics, many needs are already satisfied by existing systems such as patient scheduling [19]. The inefficiencies essentially appear in a collaboration context, as the information systems involved are isolated and heterogenous and can not deliver the required information at the right time. It is necessary to develop a collaborative healthcare model in order to address these challenges (data exchange and routing, decision making, quality management, etc) and support flexible services integration, with temporal constraints specification.

New automation strategies are needed in the healthcare organizations, for offering valuable healthcare services and efficient logistics systems. In this context, process modeling [20,21] and coordination models have already been proposed using different concepts: multi-agents platforms [22], cloud services [23], etc.

We point that some logistics problems in the entire healthcare solution should be coordinated and controlled using IOW concepts. The emergence of IOW concepts gave already an important contribution to medical structures [24,25]. Furthermore, it can enhance the collaboration between different parties by providing solutions to some collaborative logistics issues, with real-time constraints in critical situations. This is motivated by the fact that the flexibility of the healthcare solution and the management of real-time constraints is essential to avoid overheads, that make the patient's life goes under a great risk.

Our purpose is to propose workflow patterns added with temporal aspects, which can serve as a basis for modeling and solving logistical problems, in a collaborative context. This solution should supply the existing logistic solutions. In fact, automated tools can automatically transform a workflow patterns, to be solved within existing logistic solutions. We focus on a major issue in a cooperation context, which is the ability to negotiate with partners for choosing the best provider, according to time constraints.

# 4    Example Scenario: Ambulance Service

To illustrate the advantages of building a collaborative logistics management platform based on IOW, we present the *Ambulance service* example. This scenario, in the healthcare field, show the importance of automatically selecting an adequate service provider and negotiating deadline constraints between distributed medical processes.

In case of emergency calls, ambulance agencies have to support patients, and arrange their transportation to an adequate medical institution. To be efficient, they should engage in collaborative procedures within the healthcare community in order to select the adequate pre-hospitalization treatment and destination emergency service. Typical examples are road accidents or a situation in which a person is experiencing a heart attack.

Emergency transport involves various logistics problems from the patient call until its discharge to the emergency service. For example, assigning ambulances for patient transportation represents a scheduling problem which is already addressed in the literature [26]. The cooperation brings further issues, such as selecting the adequate clinic or hospital. Ambulance agencies often hold a list of medical structures. Typically, the nearest emergency service is always assigned to take care of the patient.

As we consider an emergency case, we propose that the selection criteria becomes the time within which the patient could receive the necessary treatment and hospitalization. This solution has the advantage to reduce hospital overcrowding [27] and to provide a valuable service to the patient.

This negotiation between ambulance agencies and medical institutions can be viewed as parts of a global cooperative healthcare model that involve these organizations. Thus, we propose the application of the temporal extension of the CoopFlow approach in order to handle the service selection activity with regards to the deadline specified. We assume that ambulances are provided with operational mobile facilities (wireless communication, GPS, smartphones, etc.) to have permanent access to medical systems (from anywhere at anytime) [28].

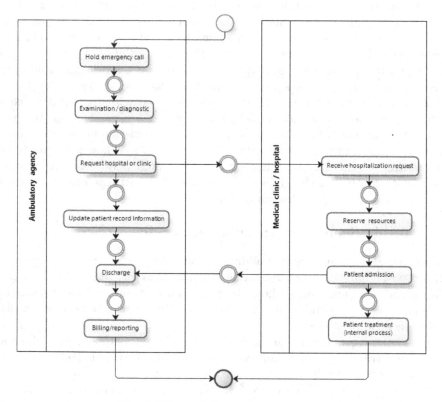

**Fig. 3.** The ambulance service scenario

Fig. 3 illustrates a simplified cooperation workflow between the ambulance agency and the medical institution (hospital or clinic). It focuses on the request/response data exchange between the two partners and do not deals with the internal logistics procedures of each partner.

The CoopFlow approach presents a solution for the collaborative issue between these organizations. The ambulance staff, following a patient examination, should send a hospitalization request, containing semantic information (patients status and needs, location, etc.) and temporal constraints (maximum allowed time for patient care). These data will be advertised to the common registry according to the CoopFlow approach, in order to select the appropriate emergency center. The Fig. 4 presents our proof of concept for automating the temporal conformance process in CoopFlow. We used the TINA toolbox [29] and LPT

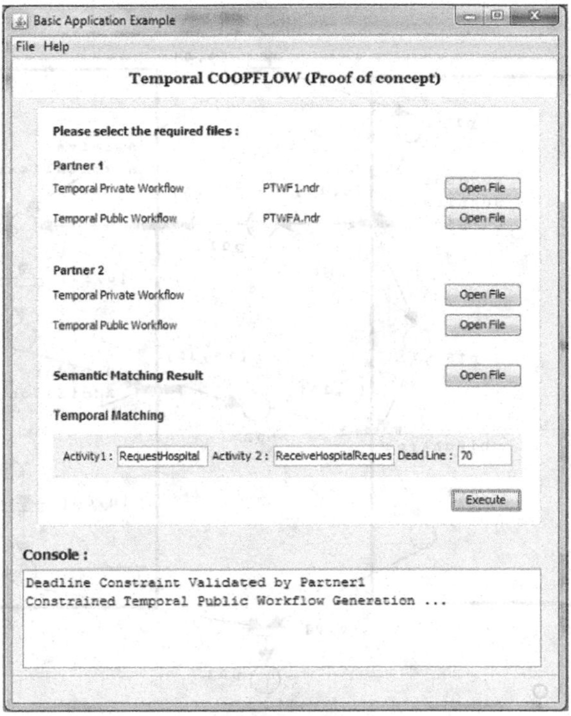

**Fig. 4.** The temporal conformance process automation

tool [30] for workflow modeling and verification using Time Peti Nets tools and model checking algorithms.

This application automatically generates the constrained temporal public workflow of the ambulance agency, illustrated in Fig. 5, and which contains semantic (abstracted workflow) and temporal information (deadline constraint) for requesting hospital or clinic service. The filled transitions refer to the co-operative activities of the agency business process. The local validation process

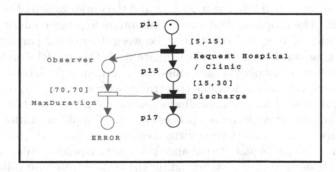

**Fig. 5.** Constrained Temporal Public Workflow Automatic generation

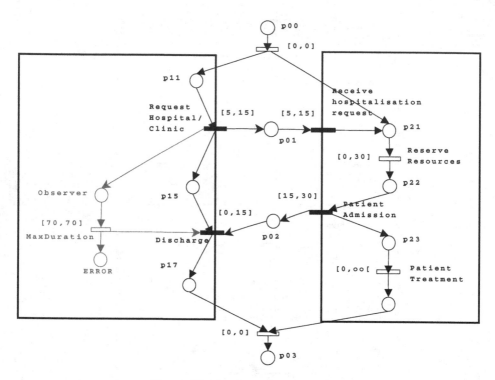

**Fig. 6.** The local verification process

described in [7] is also automated, and in our example, is executed on the generated workflow presented in Fig. 6. The above workflow is constructed by the interconnection of constrained temporal public workflow of the ambulance agency, with the temporal private workflow of the available candidates.

## 5   Conclusions

In this paper, we present an application of our temporal extension of the CoopFlow approach, in order to facilitate the modeling and the optimization of cooperative logistics issues. The proposed model of collaborative logistics enables the automatic negotiation of temporal constraints between distributed partners in critical situations, as considered in the healthcare field. Our model should provide different interfaces to handle various temporal constraints. We have already addressed the specification of a deadline constraint between a request/response activities. Our future work aims at providing a generalized framework by integrating the temporal constraint conformance process into the CoopFlow platform, for the automatic construction of short-term virtual enterprises. Moreover, a negotiation protocol needs to be put in place to enhance the selection process. We also want to enhance our previous work [7], by extending the request/response collaboration pattern used.

# References

1. Kötting, B., Maurer, F.: A Concept for Supporting the Formation of Virtual Corporations through Negotiation. In: Proceedings of 8th IEEE International Workshops on Enabling Technologies: Infrastructure for Collaborative Enterprises, WET ICE 1999, Stanford, CA, USA, pp. 40–47 (1999)
2. Du, Y., Jiang, C.J., Zhou, M.C.: Modeling and Analysis of Real-Time Cooperative Systems Using Petri Nets. IEEE Transactions on Systems, Man, and Cybernetics, Part A, 643–654 (2007)
3. Lee, H.C., Kim, S.D., Hong-Jin, K.: Enhanced Customer Service in On-line and Real Time Logistics Management Environment. In: Proceedings of the 3rd International Conference on Convergence and Hybrid Information Technology, vol. 1, pp. 763–768 (2008)
4. Lyons, J., Ritter, J., Thomas, K., Militello, L., Vincent, P.: Collaborative Logistics: Developing a Framework to Evaluate Socio-Technical Issues in Logistic-Based Networks. In: Symposium on Collaborative Technologies and Systems (2006)
5. Modrak, V.: On the Conceptual Development of Virtual Corporations and Logistics. In: International Symposium on Logistics and Industrial Informatics (2007)
6. Makni, M., Ben Hadj-Alouane, N., Yeddes, M., Tata, S.: Modeling Time Constraints in Inter-Organizational Workflows. In: 12th International Conference on Enterprise Information Systems (ICEIS), vol. (3), pp. 221–229 (2010)
7. Makni, M., Tata, S., Yeddes, M., Ben Hadj-Alouane, N.: Satisfaction and Coherence of Deadline Constraints in Inter-Organizational Workflows. In: Meersman, R., Dillon, T.S., Herrero, P. (eds.) OTM 2010, Part I. LNCS, vol. 6426, pp. 523–539. Springer, Heidelberg (2010)
8. Chebbi, I., Tata, S.: CoopFlow: A Framework for Inter-organizational Workflow Cooperation. In: Meersman, R. (ed.) OTM 2005, Part I. LNCS, vol. 3760, pp. 112–129. Springer, Heidelberg (2005)
9. Chebbi, I., Dustdar, S., Tata, S.: The View-Based Approach to Dynamic Inter-Organizational Workflow Cooperation. Data & Knowledge Engineering 56(2), 139–173 (2006)
10. Tata, S., Klai, K., Ould Ahmed M'Bareck, N.: CoopFlow: A Bottom-Up Approach to Workflow Cooperation for Short-Term Virtual Enterprises. IEEE Transactions on Services Computing, 214–228 (2008)
11. Chebbi, I., Tata, S.: Workflow Abstraction for Privacy Preservation. In: Weske, M., Hacid, M.-S., Godart, C. (eds.) WISE Workshops 2007. LNCS, vol. 4832, pp. 166–177. Springer, Heidelberg (2007)
12. Klai, K., Tata, S., Desel, J.: Symbolic Abstraction and Deadlock-Freeness Verification of Inter-enterprise Processes. In: Dayal, U., Eder, J., Koehler, J., Reijers, H.A. (eds.) BPM 2009. LNCS, vol. 5701, pp. 294–309. Springer, Heidelberg (2009)
13. Klai, K., Tata, S., Chebbi, I.: An Observation-based Algorithm for Workflow Matching. In: Proceeding of MSVVEIS, pp. 193–197 (2006)
14. Klai, K., M'bareck, N.O.A., Tata, S.: Behavioral Technique for Workflow Abstraction and Matching. In: Dustdar, S., Fiadeiro, J.L., Sheth, A.P. (eds.) BPM 2006. LNCS, vol. 4102, pp. 477–483. Springer, Heidelberg (2006)
15. Ahmed, A., Mirza, E., Ehsan, N., Awan, S.A., Ishaque, A.: Information Technology: A Means of Quality in Healthcare. In: 3rd IEEE International Conference on Computer Science and Information Technology (ICCSIT), pp. 26–30 (2010)
16. Lenz, R., Reichert, M.: IT Support for Healthcare Processes - Premises, Challenges, Perspectives. Data & Knowledge Engineering 61(1), 39–58 (2007)

17. Ammenwerth, E., Buchauer, A., Bludau, B., Haux, R.: Mobile Information and Communication Tools in the Hospital. International Journal of Medical Informatics 57(1), 21–40 (2000)
18. Hoher, M., Muller, A., Reinshagen, M., Bauer, S., Kestler, H.A.: A Stepwise Approach Towards a Hospital-Wide Electronic Patient Record Archiving System. Computers in Cardiology, 287–290 (2000)
19. Daknou, A., Zgaya, H., Hammadi, S., Hubert, H.: A Dynamic Patient Scheduling at The Emergency Department in Hospitals. In: IEEE Workshop on Health Care Management (WHCM), pp. 1–6 (2010)
20. Ma, L., Gong, Y., Wang, L., Li, D.: Process Management of Large-Scale Medical Facilities Supported by Information Technology. In: International Conference on Logistics Systems and Intelligent Management, pp. 1169–1172 (2010)
21. Ahsan, K., Shah, H., Kingston, P.: Healthcare Modelling through Enterprise Architecture: A Hospital Case. In: Proceedings of ITNG, pp. 460–465 (2010)
22. Aguilera, A., Herrera, E., Subero, A.: Medical Coordination Work Based in Agents. Biomedical Engineering, 122–126 (2008)
23. Chang, H.H., Chou, P.B., Ramakrishnan, S.: An Ecosystem Approach for Healthcare Services Cloud. In: IEEE International Conference on e-Business Engineering, Macau, China, pp. 608–612 (2009)
24. Dwivedi, A., Bali, R.K., James, A.E., Naguib, R.N.G.: Workflow Management Systems: the Healthcare Technology of the Future? In: 23rd Annual International Conference of the IEEE - Engineering in Medicine and Biology Society (EMBS), Istanbul, Turkey, pp. 3887–3890 (2001)
25. Anzböck, R., Dustdar, S.: Interorganizational Workflow in the Medical Imaging Domain. In: Proceedings of the 5th International Conference on Enterprise Information Systems (ICEIS). Kluwer Academic Publishers, Angers (2003)
26. Andersson, T., Petersson, S., Värbrand, P.: Calculating the Preparedness for an Efficient Ambulance Health Care. In: 7th International IEEE Conference on Intelligent Transportation Systems, p. 785 (2004)
27. Hagtvedt, R., Ferguson, M., Griffin, P., Jones, G.T., Keskinocak, P.: Cooperative Strategies to Reduce Ambulance Diversion. In: Proceedings of the Winter Simulation Conference (WSC), pp. 1861–1874 (2009)
28. Mandellos, G.J., Lymperopoulos, D.K., Koukias, M.N., Tzes, A., Lazarou, N., Vagianos, C.: A Novel Mobile Telemedicine System for Ambulance Transport. Design and Evaluation. In: Proceedings of the 26th Annual International Conference of the IEEE Engineering in Medecine and Biology Society, San Francisco, CA, USA, pp. 1–5 (2004)
29. TINA TIme petri Net Analyzer, http://homepages.laas.fr/bernard/tina/
30. LPT: Little Parametric Tool, http://www.lirmm.fr/~godary/SOFT/Software_en.html
31. Pezze, M., Young, M.: Time Petri Nets: A Primer Introduction. Tutorial Presented at the Multi-Workshop on Formal Methods in Performance Evaluation and Applications, Zaragoza, Spain, pp. 41–46 (1999)

# Configurable Process Models for Logistics Case Study for Customs Clearance Processes[*]

Wassim Derguech, Feng Gao, and Sami Bhiri

National University of Ireland, Galway
Digital Enterprise Research Institute
`firstname.lastname@deri.org`
`www.deri.org`

**Abstract.** Configuration based modelling is one of the reuse oriented modelling techniques that allows for exploiting proven best practices in business processes management. This paper is a case study of the use of configurable process models in logistics. It analysis and creates a set of process models for customs clearance services for import and export processes and delivers the configurable process model out of these models. The paper discusses main challenges for the use of configurable process models in such domain and draws some future work.

**Keywords:** business process modeling, reuse, merging, configuration, logistics.

## 1 Introduction

A logistics service provider is a third party supplier that does all or part of the enterprises logistics functions. Such providers can offer services for transportation, warehousing, distribution, financial services... In our work we are focusing on logistics in custom clearance and more specifically in import and export processes.

Several processes in customs clearance are driven by legislation. Indeed import and export processes are extensively regulated. Regulations in this area, are defining the most important steps, where each customs service in various seaports around the world are having enough freedom to adapt their processes to local needs and preferences, e.g, depending on the goods being imported/exported.

We consider Blue Company, a fictitious company, that offers logistics services for import and export services within several seaports worldwide. Each new customer (i.e., seaport) for this company comes with his current process models describing how the actual work is running. Blue Company is not going to discard that model and proceed with a new one, but rather would integrated it into its behavioural knowledge. By behavioural knowledge we mean the knowledge needed to achieve a certain goal, in this case it refers to the process models

---

[*] This work is funded by the Lion II project supported by Science Foundation Ireland under grant number SFI/08/CE/I1380 Lion-2.

F. Daniel et al. (Eds.): BPM 2011 Workshops, Part II, LNBIP 100, pp. 119–130, 2012.

that describe process steps for import/export customs clearance. However after acquiring several seaports, Blue Company finds itself in a need to manage the various process models that in essence achieve the same goal. Our work here consists of providing Blue Company a way of managing its behavioural knowledge base by using configurable process models.

Configurable process models are introduced to deal with the variability issue of process models like those executed by custom services. Indeed, configurable process models can be constructed by integrating a set of process models. In order to adapt this integrated model to a particular situation, a configuration and individualization steps allow an organisation to derive process models that satisfy its particular needs. We refer the reader to [1,2,3] for details about configuration and individualization.

In our particular context, Blue Company, would use configurable process models both for import and export procedures. These configurable models are created via the integration of several process models from several standardized best practices in various seaports around the world. These configurable models allow Blue Company to derive a particular process model that satisfies the need of a specific seaport (i.e., via configuration and individualization). The configuration step consists of disabling or enabling un/necessary process parts of the configurable process model. In this context the main challenge concerns the creation of the configurable process models which is discussed in this paper.

This paper is a case study for the use of configurable process models in logistics and particularly in import and export customs clearance. Its contributions are (i) the demonstration of the practical usefulness of configurable process models in logistics, (ii) the release of real world business process models expressed in EPC which can be used as a test bed for several research works and (iii) the empirical validation of the merging algorithm introduced in [4].

To illustrate the concept of configurable process models (see Section 2.1 for a background introduction), we have analyzed and defined a set of process models from real word custom clearance services related to import and export processes (see Section 3). These models have been presented using EPC (see Section 3.1). Configurable process models have been automatically generated using our merging algorithm introduced in [4] and briefly presented in Section 3.2. The paper is analyzing some related work in Section 4 where we discuss several proposed solutions for dealing with variability in process models. Finally, Section 5 concludes the paper and discusses our future work.

## 2   Background

This section introduces two main concepts for the rest of the paper. The first one is the configuration-based modelling which is a reuse oriented modelling technique that has been subject of several studies [1,2] and has been adopted for real world cases in municipalities in the Netherlands [5]. The second one is C-EPC which is an extended version of EPC used for modelling configurable process models.

## 2.1    Configuration-Based Modelling

The idea of using configurable models for managing models variability has been widely experienced in the field of business process modelling [3]. Configurable process models can be constructed via the aggregation of several *variants* of a process model [3]. Figure 1[1] depicts, in the left-hand side, two variants of the same business process. These two variants reflect two common practices (i.e., Task A and B), however after this, each variant ends with a different task (i.e., C or D). This difference introduces the choice between the task C or D that represents a variability which is mainly, for example, depending on the cost, the quality of service or the user preference.

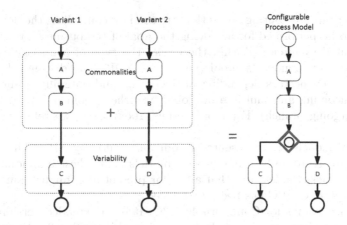

**Fig. 1.** Configurable Business Process Model (adapted from [6])

The right-hand side of Fig.1 shows the configurable process model which is a merger between the two process variants. The variation point is represented by a configurable gateway: an inclusive split gateway marked with a thick red border. Unlike a "normal" BPMN gateway, it does not represent a choice or a parallel split, instead, it represents a design choice that will need to be made by an analyst to adapt the configurable process model to a particular requirement. In this example the configurable gateway captures the fact that one needs to choose whether to select one path (i.e., task C) or the other ( i.e., task D), or possibly both [6].

In this case, the modelling phase consists of enabling or disabling different branches of the configurable process model.

Next we will introduce C-EPC which is one of the proposed modelling notation for configurable process models. C-EPC will be used in the rest of the paper to illustrate our running use case example.

---

[1] Figure following the BPMN notation: www.bpmn.org

## 2.2 Configurable Event-Driven Process Chains

Several modelling languages have been proposed to represent business process models (e.g., Event-driven Process Chain (EPC), UML Activity Diagrams and Business Process Model and Notation (BPMN)). In this paper we will adopt EPC [7]. EPC represents process models by means of nodes and links between them. There are three main nodes in EPC which are activities, events and connectors.

An activity is a task that has to be accomplished within a process, it is represented by a rectangle with rounded edges. Event nodes are used for presenting preconditions that need to be satisfied to perform a particular function, they are represented by hexagons. We refer to Fig. 2 for a visual representation of these nodes. Indeed Fig.2 depicts three of EPC models that are used for our case study.

Connectors are the routing nodes that are used for controlling the flow of tasks that need to be performed for achieving the goal of the business process. They are represented by circles. Within the circle, the type of connector is defined through the corresponding symbol (i.e., ∧, ∨, XOR). We distinguish between join and split connectors depending on incoming and outgoing branches (i.e., split: one incoming and multiple outgoing branches / join: multiple incoming and one outgoing branch). For more details about EPC, we refers the reader to [7].

Individual models are represented in our case study by EPC. The object of our work is to create configurable process models out of these individual process models. EPC lacks the features that allow for presenting configuration facilities. For this purpose, C-EPC has been introduced.

C-EPC [3,8] stands for Configurable EPC. It is an extended version of EPC where some *connectors* can be marked as configurable (see Fig.3). A configurable connector can be configured by reducing its incoming branches (in the case of a join) or its outgoing branches (in the case of a split) [9]. The result will be a regular connector with a reduced number of incoming or outgoing branches. In addition, the type of a configurable OR can be restricted to a regular XOR or AND. After being configured, a C-EPC needs to be individualized by removing those branches that have been excluded for each configurable connector.

Next, we will illustrate our running example using EPC for the individual process models and C-EPC for the configurable process model.

## 3    Creating Configurable Process Models for Customs Clearance Processes

The use of configurable process models provides its high benefits of model reuse when they are applied in an area where business processes are highly standardized, have small variations and are executed frequently [5]. For this purpose we chose to apply this kind of modelling in customs clearance procedures. Indeed, import and export customs clearance processes are highly frequent and standardized. This section starts by introducing the individual process models that we have manually created using EPC notation (i.e., in Section 3.1). Then it explains how we create configurable process models out of them (i.e., in Section 3.2). Finally it discusses main observations related to this case study (i.e., in Section 3.3).

## 3.1   Building the Individual Models

The aim of this study is to show how we can apply configuration based modelling in the area of logistics and specifically in customs clearance processes. Recall, in our work we consider EPC as a modelling notation. Hence, we need to have a set of business process variants of the same logistics process. For this purpose we searched over the web for available customs clearance business processes. All of the available models were either described using simple text or flowcharts using different notations. The first step then of our work consisted of transforming all the available process descriptions into EPC. Next, we will introduce three process models for import customs clearance.

For presentation purposes, in this paper we will present only three import customs clearance processes. Fig. 2 depicts these models. They describe guidance on the basic regulatory requirements that all importers must consider when they plan to import goods. The import customs clearance involves various steps from submission of import documents until recommendation of the release of the imported goods.

The first model[2] in Fig. 2 (i.e., EPC1) describes the import process at Sihanoukville seaport in Cambodia. Originally, it was presented using a non standard flowchart describing steps that need to be taken followed by a detailed textual description. The model depicted here (i.e., Fig.2.EPC1) is a process model mentioning that upon the registration of a custom declaration and submission of import documentations, documents are checked then payment of duties and taxes is performed. After that, if a physical inspection of the goods is required then a detailed examination is done otherwise goods are released. In case of a physical inspection is required, if there are any problems then goods are detained for investigation and the import process is declined, otherwise goods are released.

The second model[3] in Fig. 2 (i.e., EPC2) describes the import process adopted by TRADE-VAN[4] which is a company that offers several eGovernment and logistics services worldwide and essentially in Taiwan. Originally, it was presented using a figure that describes messages exchanged between the shipping company, port authority, container freight station and the importer. The model depicted here (i.e., Fig.2.EPC2) is the simplest model. It is a sequential model that we

---

[2] This model is available at
   http://aseanict.com/bizcenter/0/Import-Cargo-Processing/1329/11992 as accessed on 01-06-2011.
[3] This model is available at http://www.itradevan.com/Custom.jsp as accessed on 01-06-2011.
[4] http://www.itradevan.com

consider as reference model for TRADE-VAN as it operated within several customers (i.e., several seaports). The process starts by the arrival of a ship to the port that triggers the registration of a custom declaration and submission of import documentations. Once documents are checked and duties and taxes are payed, the goods are released and a release notification is sent.

The third model[5] in Fig. 2 (i.e., EPC3) describes the import process at Davao City in Philippines. Originally, it was presented using a figure with a flowchart and accompanied by a text description. The model depicted here (i.e., Fig.2.EPC3) is a process model mentioning that upon the registration of a custom declaration and submission of import documentations, documents are checked and payment of duties and taxes is performed. After checking the content of the cargo a decision about physical inspection is made. If the cargo goes through a priority channel, then it is directly released without inspection, otherwise a physical inspection is required. In this case, depending on several conditions such as the nature or the provenance of the goods a red or green check is performed. A red check goes through a detailed examination of goods and an X-ray scan however a green check needs only an X-ray scan. If there are no problems then goods are released.

## 3.2   From Individual Models to a Configurable Model

In our case study, creating a configurable process model consists of merging the previously introduced individual models into a single model that allows for configuration facilities. Manual creation of configurable process models is tedious, time-consuming and error-prone task. La Rosa et al. [9] mention that it took a team of five analysts and 130 man-hour to merge 25% of an end-to-end process model. In a previous work [4], we proposed a merging algorithm that allows for creating a configurable business process model from a collection of process variants. The proposed algorithm respects the following requirements:

1. The merged model should allow for the behaviour of all the original models. Traditionally, this operation is manually made by business analysts which comes with the risk that some aspects of the original models are accidentally neglected [10]. With the automation support for merging process variants, this risk can be minimized considerably.
2. Each element of the merged process model should be easily traced back to its original model [9]. A business analyst needs to understand what do the process variants share, what are their differences, etc. This can be made possible if he can trace back from which variant does an element originate.
3. Business analysts should be able to derive one of the input models from the merged process model [9]. Indeed, merging business process variants does not necessarily lead to the creation of a configurable process model. This requirement asks that the resulting merged model should provide configuration facilities in order to customize it and derive one of the input models.

---

[5] This model is available at http://kjri-davao.com/?page=news&siteLanguage= English&address_link=127&cat=Economics as accessed on 01-06-2011.

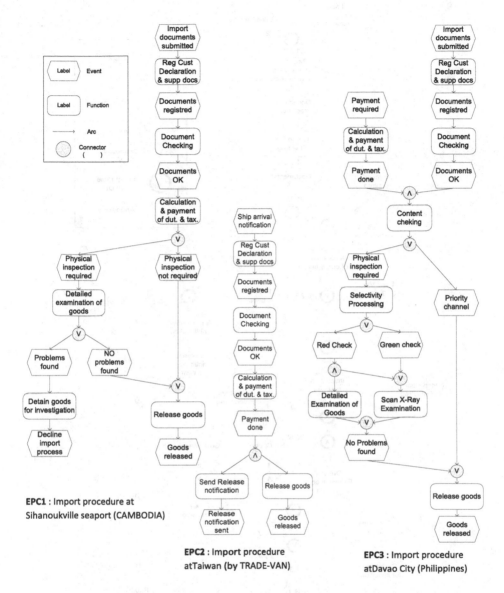

**Fig. 2.** Three individual business process models for import procedure

A tool support for merging business process models in order to deliver a configurable process model was developed and tested over process models from the current case study. Merging the individual models introduced in Section 3.1 results in the configurable process models depicted in Fig. 3.

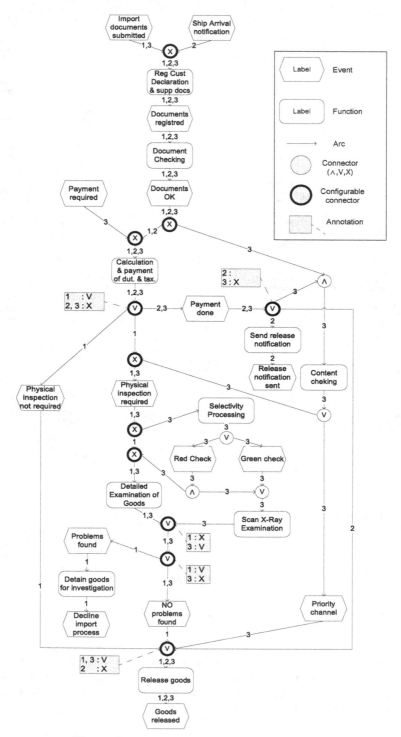

**Fig. 3.** Configurable model for import procedure

## 3.3  Observations

While doing this case study, several remarks are worth to be mentioned. Hence, we are discussing here most important issues related to the creation of configurable process models.

First of all, one should note that the creation of configurable process models for import and export customs clearance procedures was possible due to the high similarity in the structures of the initial process models. Actually, as it was mentioned before, customs procedures are highly standard and frequent processes. The main steps are common, easy to determine, and sequential in nature. We can notice that an import process can be seen as a sequence of the following tasks: document receiving, taxation, cargo examination and release/withdraw. Variability in such models is due to some ordering preferences of tasks or detailed process parts (e.g., cargo examination). Similarly, the export customs clearance process can be seen as a sequence of these tasks: Export cargo moves into the warehouse, document receiving, cargo examination and release/loading to ship.

Even though the creation of the configurable process models was automated by a merging tool, it still remain several challenges. The first challenges came from the creation of the initial models. Indeed, deriving EPC models from various notations and text descriptions was not straightforward step. It comes with the risk to neglect some process tasks or events, however this is not so deceiving as the aim of this study is rather to show the feasibility of the configuration based modelling rather than creating concrete and complete EPC models. The second challenge in this work is matching identical tasks among process variants. We deliberately use in this work the same labels for referring to the same tasks in each variant in order to overcome this challenge. Therefore, overcoming this challenge is part of our future work. The third challenge concerns the tasks order in the initial process models, it was sometimes difficult to decide whether tasks should be executed in a certain order or if the order does not matter such as the case of the task "Calculation and payment of duties and taxes" of our use case example.

In order to derive one of the input models from the configurable process model, one can parse all the configurable connectors and enable only branches (i.e., arcs) that are annotated with the process identifier that corresponds to the process model that he wants to derive. For example to derive the model depicted in Fig.2.EPC1, the process modeller can enable all the arcs that are annotated by "1" and disable others (i.e., annotated by "2" or "3") of the configurable process model of the Fig 3. Additionally, he can set the types of the configurable connectors by selecting one fom those indicated in the annotations.

## 4  Related Work

Several approaches have been proposed for defining and managing business process variants. In this section we state four current approaches dealing with process variability.

The first approach is the most intuitive solution to variability management. It consists of managing a repository of process variants. Each process variant is stored as an individual entity in the repository. Users have to formulate a query according to their requirements and the system should provide the most suitable model. This approach has been explored by [11,12,13] where it is revealed that it needs a rich formal model for describing business process. In our work, we do not use individual models because the main problems of that solution are resource allocation and inconsistency. Indeed, (i) storing each variant individually leads to duplicated data storage for common parts of the process models and (ii) in case of new regulations enforcement, all process variants have to be updated which is resource consuming and error prone task. In addition, variation points are not explicitly handled as shown in [11], configuration-based modeling relies on querying the process models repository based on structural aspects of the to-be process. Therefore the business user has to know what are the possible process structures he is allowed to ask for.

The second approach as it is presented in [14,15], overcomes the problems of resource allocation and inconsistency. This solution considers a "basic process model" that represents common parts of all process models and variability is handled as a global property containing a set of operations (e.g., add, delete, modify, move operation). In fact, each variant is then generated via applying these operations on the basic model. However, the business user's control becomes limited to a set of operations generating rules which fire when they comply with all the business requirements. These rules capture only non functional aspects (i.e., quality aspects like cost and performance) leaving out details about structural and functional aspects of the variants.

The third approach studied in [16], exploits a hierarchical representation of the process into sub processes. The top level sub process encompasses the core activities and their associated variability, which is annotated by specific stereotypes, while the lower level sub processes express all details related to higher level activities and variabilities residing in them. However, the concept of hierarchical representation is supported more for hiding complexity than for managing variability.

The use of configurable process models has been studied intensively and highlighted the benefits of reuse in business process modelling [17,18,19,3]. Additionnaly, Gottschalk et al. studied the use of configurable process models in municipalities in [5]. This also proved that the suggested technique is suitable for highly standardized and frequent processes.

All these previous works were mainly dealing with process variability. To the best of our knowledge, there is no previous work that was discussing or studying this particular issue in case of logistics systems. However, Gottschalk et al. [5] did a case study for the use of configurable process models in administration and particularly in municipalities processes. Both administration and logistics processes are highly standardized, have small variations and are executed frequently which made the use of configurable process models beneficial.

Additionally, we have analyzed a set of related works where authors proposed algorithms for merging business process models. Actually, Gerth et al.

[20] propose a formalism for the detection and resolution of version conflicts. It is implemented as a tool support for model merging in IBM WebSphere Business Modeler [21]. The merge procedure defined here is not intended to be fully automated, it is rather developed for reducing the number of false-positive differences and conflicts in models management. Gottschalk et al. [10] define an approach exclusively intended for merging EPC models. The object in their approach is not to create a configurable EPC, there are no configurable connectors introduced which would allow for extracting one of the original models. La Rosa et al. [9] propose a technique that allows for the three requirements presented in Section 3.2. All these techniques either fail in fulfilling the pre-mentioned requirements or they allow only for merging pairs of process models. However our proposed approach allows for merging a set process variants in once.

## 5    Conclusion and Future Work

The object of this paper is to study a use case of the configurable process models in logistics. It takes as example import and export customs clearance processes and delivers their corresponding configurable process models. Initial models were obtained from real world processes available on the Web.

The paper discussed the use of configurable process models only in import and export process in custom clearance. We have selected few process models with minor variations for this study. These processes are of number of 10 of each procedure (i.e., 10 for import and 10 for export), they are available for any requester and they will be publicly available after few checks. However, there exist other models for more specific cases for example when considering the nature of imported/exported goods. Actually, there are models for managing cargo charges containing food or drug. There are also other available models for office regulations or inspections that can be subject of further case studies and that we plan to consider in our future work.

Most important and first of all, one should notice that it was possible to define initial models as they are publicly available even though they are not using any standard notation. The creation of configurable process models was automatically done by a merging tool that implements the approach previously introduced in [4] under the constraint of using identical tasks labels in the process variants. As part of our future work, we plan to break this assumption. In fact, the labels of functions and events have a specific meaning which needs to be interpreted in order to understand the process. Two different labels might mean the same and have as a result the same semantic during the process execution. In addition if two labels are the same then the meaning might be different depending on the context.

## References

1. Gottschalk, F.: Configurable Process Models. PhD thesis, Eindhoven University of Technology, Eindhoven, Netherlands (December 2009)
2. La Rosa, M.: Managing Variability in Process-Aware Information Systems. PhD thesis, Queensland University of Technology, Brisbane, Australia (April 2009)

3. Rosemann, M., van der Aalst, W.M.P.: A configurable reference modelling language. Inf. Syst. 32(1), 1–23 (2007)
4. Derguech, W., Bhiri, S.: Merging Business Process Variants. In: Abramowicz, W. (ed.) BIS 2011. LNBIP, vol. 87, pp. 86–97. Springer, Heidelberg (2011)
5. Gottschalk, F., Wagemakers, T.A.C., Jansen-Vullers, M.H., van der Aalst, W.M.P., La Rosa, M.: Configurable Process Models: Experiences from a Municipality Case Study. In: van Eck, P., Gordijn, J., Wieringa, R. (eds.) CAiSE 2009. LNCS, vol. 5565, pp. 486–500. Springer, Heidelberg (2009)
6. La Rosa, M., Dumas, M.: Configurable Process Models: How To Adopt Standard Practices In Your How Way? BPTrends Newsletter (November 2008)
7. Mendling, J., Nüttgens, M.: EPC Syntax Validation with XML Schema Languages. In: EPK (2003)
8. Weber, B., Mendling, J., Reichert, M.: Flexibility in Process-Aware Information Systems (ProFlex) Workshop Report. In: WETICE. IEEE CS (2006)
9. La Rosa, M., Dumas, M., Uba, R., Dijkman, R.: Merging Business Process Models. In: Meersman, R., Dillon, T.S., Herrero, P. (eds.) OTM 2010, Part I. LNCS, vol. 6426, pp. 96–113. Springer, Heidelberg (2010)
10. Gottschalk, F., van der Aalst, W.M.P., Jansen-Vullers, M.H.: Merging Event-Driven Process Chains. In: Meersman, R., Tari, Z. (eds.) OTM 2008, Part I. LNCS, vol. 5331, pp. 418–426. Springer, Heidelberg (2008)
11. Lu, R., Sadiq, S.: On the Discovery of Preferred Work Practice Through Business Process Variants. In: Parent, C., Schewe, K.-D., Storey, V.C., Thalheim, B. (eds.) ER 2007. LNCS, vol. 4801, pp. 165–180. Springer, Heidelberg (2007)
12. Markovic, I., Pereira, A.C.: Towards a Formal Framework for Reuse in Business Process Modeling. In: ter Hofstede, A.H.M., Benatallah, B., Paik, H.-Y. (eds.) BPM Workshops 2007. LNCS, vol. 4928, pp. 484–495. Springer, Heidelberg (2008)
13. Vulcu, G., Derguech, W., Bhiri, S.: Business Process Model Discovery Using Semantics. In: zur Muehlen, M., Su, J. (eds.) BPM 2010 Workshops LNBIP, vol. 66, pp. 326–337. Springer, Heidelberg (2011)
14. Hallerbach, A., Bauer, T., Reichert, M.: Context-based Configuration of Process Variants. In: TCoB (2008)
15. Hallerbach, A., Bauer, T., Reichert, M.: Managing Process Variants in the Process Life Cycle. In: Cordeiro, J., Filipe, J. (eds.) ICEIS, vol. (3-2) (2008)
16. Razavian, M., Khosravi, R.: Modeling Variability in Business Process Models Using UML. In: ITNG. IEEE Computer Society (2008)
17. Dreiling, A., Rosemann, M., van der Aalst, W.M.P., Sadiq, W., Khan, S.: Model-driven process configuration of enterprise systems. In: Wirtschaftsinformatik. Physica-Verlag (2005)
18. Lapouchnian, A., Yu, Y., Mylopoulos, J.: Requirements-Driven Design and Configuration Management of Business Processes. In: Alonso, G., Dadam, P., Rosemann, M. (eds.) BPM 2007. LNCS, vol. 4714, pp. 246–261. Springer, Heidelberg (2007)
19. La Rosa, M., Lux, J., Seidel, S., Dumas, M., ter Hofstede, A.H.M.: Questionnaire-driven Configuration of Reference Process Models. In: Krogstie, J., Opdahl, A.L., Sindre, G. (eds.) CAiSE 2007 and WES 2007. LNCS, vol. 4495, pp. 424–438. Springer, Heidelberg (2007)
20. Gerth, C., Luckey, M., Küster, J.M., Engels, G.: Detection of semantically equivalent fragments for business process model change management. In: SCC (2010)
21. Küster, J.M., Gerth, C., Förster, A., Engels, G.: A Tool for Process Merging in Business-Driven Development. In: CAiSE Forum, vol. 344, CEUR-WS.org (2008)

# A Formal Framework for Cooperative Logistics Management

Ichiro Satoh

National Institute of Informatics
2-1-2 Hitotsubashi, Chiyoda-ku, Tokyo 101-8430, Japan
ichiro@nii.ac.jp

**Abstract.** This paper presents a process calculus for specifying and reasoning about earth-friendly logistics management systems. It is necessary to reduce fossil fuel consumption and carbon dioxide emissions resulting from transport on account of environmental protection. Cooperative logistics enables multiple shippers to share trucks. It has been one of the most effective and popular solutions to this problem, but it makes it be complicated to implement in a logistics management system. We propose a language for specifying the routes of trucks and an order relation between the requirements of routes and the possible routes of trucks. The former is formulated as process calculus and the latter selects suitable trucks according to their routes. Our language and selection mechanism were implemented on a PaaS-based cloud computing infrastructure.

## 1 Introduction

Transportation accounts for about 23-% of energy-related carbon dioxide ($CO_2$) emissions[4]. IEA has expected, given the current trends, energy demand and $CO_2$ emissions in transport nearly 80-% higher by 2050 without any improvements in efficiency. Trucks, which play an essential role as carriers in modern logistics services, emit huge quantities of carbon dioxide ($CO_2$) into the atmosphere.

To reduce fossil-fuel consumption and $CO_2$ emissions from transport, we need to enhance the efficiency of trucks. Cooperative logistics has been expected to be a key solution to improving truck-load ratios and reducing the number of trucks. to reduce the consumption of fossil-fuel and $CO_2$ emissions from transport. In fact, several industries, e.g., food and automobile manufacturers, in addition to the dairy industry, have attempted to use cooperative logistics. However, most attempts at cooperative logistics have fallen through because of management problems with logistics operators and customers. Cooperative logistics provides more than one truck whose routes may differ. However, individual customers have their own requirements, but all these requirements cannot be satisfied in cooperative logistics. The customers are confronted by another problem: they need to design truck routes and select suitable trucks with routes that will satisfy their requirements.

Existing cooperative logistics has a serious problem with its business processes. Most cooperative logistics management has tended to depend on humans, e.g., logistics managers at suppliers and truck drivers. This may be rational in small scale cooperative logistics consisting of two or three suppliers, but it seriously affects scalability. We

F. Daniel et al. (Eds.): BPM 2011 Workshops, Part II, LNBIP 100, pp. 131–142, 2012.

need a systematic and scalable approach toward managing cooperative logistics. We propose a management approach toward managing cooperative logistics. The approach is unique to other existing methodologies because it specifies truck routes like programs and select a suitable route from several available routes by using a technique used for to verify software. Note that graph search algorithms, including traveling salesman problems, are not available in cooperative logistics, because such algorithms may be useful to generate routes that can satisfy particular constraints, e.g., shortest distance, but the selection of trucks in cooperative logistics need to find suitable trucks whose routes are already assigned.

The basic idea behind the framework is to treat cooperative logistics as programs. Each truck corresponds to a program execution and select truck routes that can satisfy the requirements of shippers by using software verification. It describes each truck route in a language formulated as a process calculus. We have also provided a selection engine for truck routes. It is constructed based on our algebraic relation to determine whether a truck can visit various points, e.g., farmers and manufacturers, along its route to collect or deliver items. The relation enables collection/delivery points to select trucks according to their routes because the routes they take is critical in determining their efficiency. The framework is based on an early version of the framework presented in this paper [10]. The previous framework aimed at managing a typical cooperative logistics, called *milk-run*, which is discussed in the next section. It also assumed that it was executed on a high performance server. This paper presents another selection mechanism designed to be executed on cloud computing, in particular PaaS, because the framework should support many carriers and customers. It partially uses a heuristic approach in selecting efficient routes. to reduce $CO_2$ emission from trucks.

## 2    Example Scenario

Before presenting our approach, we will describe an example scenario, called a *milk-run*, which is one of the most typical and popular in cooperative logistics. It refers to a means of transportation in which a single truck cycles around multiple suppliers to collect or deliver freight. It is derived from the milk-runs carried out by farmers who collect milk from dairy cows spread out over pastures (Fig. 1). We have here supposed that five factories send their products to one processing plant every weekday. Using the milk-run approach, one truck calls at each of the suppliers on a daily basis before delivering the collected milk to the customer's plant. Cooperative logistics, including the milk-run approach, effectively reduces the amount of $CO_2$ emitted by trucks.

Although collecting milk from farmers may be simple, real logistics tends to be complicated. For example, factories or warehouses not only deliver items but also collect items from other factories or warehouses. We assumed that these factories had for dependencies: i) Factory A manufactures products and ships to factories B and C. ii) Factory B manufactures products and ships to factory D. iii) Factory C manufactures products and ships to factory D. iv) Factory D manufactures products and ships to factory E.

We here assumed that a truck has sufficient carrying capacity. It starts at factory A and may visit factory A again. Figure 2 shows four trucks carrying out milk-runs along

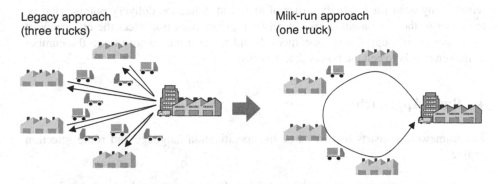

**Fig. 1.** Legacy approach and milk-run approach

different routes. The first, second, and third trucks can satisfy the above requirements but the fourth cannot. The third is less efficient than the first and second on their rounds. Customers and suppliers have to decide which truck and which route will best satisfy their requirements, and this decision is not an easy one. The framework proposed in this paper aims at solving such problems in selecting trucks.

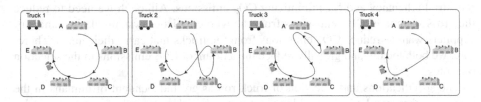

**Fig. 2.** Four trucks for cooperative logistics

## 3   Requirements

Before explaining the framework, we will describe our assumptions and requirements. Trucks may be shared by multiple suppliers and customers, so that they collect products at one or more source points and deliver the products at one or more destination points on their way. The trucks need to visit the source points before they visit the destination points. The framework therefore needs to specify the order in which trucks call at various points. Each of trunks' routes may differ, their points, i.e., suppliers and customers, need to select appropriate trucks according to their routes.[1].

The routes taken by trucks may also affect product quality. For example, foods should be transported by the shortest route possible to maintain their freshness, and perishable foodstuffs should be picked up later than preservable foodstuffs and taken to food processor or consumers. Some products may be collected/delivered at points by trucks

---

[1] The routes of most trucks except for home or office delivery services tend to be regular and static, although they may be changed weekly or monthly.

without any need for a specific order of arrival at collection/delivery points. That is, the order of the movement of trucks between points does not affect the efficiency of their operations. Suppliers or customers should select trucks according to the number of movements between the points that they visit.

## 4    Basic Approach

The framework consists of two parts: the specification language and route selection engine.

- The language is aimed at only specifying the routes of trucks formulated as an extended process calculus with the expressiveness of truck routes between collection/delivery points.
- The engine is constructed based on an algebraic order relation over the terms of the language. The relation is defined based on the notion of bisimulation and compares possible truck routes and the routes required by its specifications. This allows us to accurately determine whether the former satisfies the latter.

The selection of the routes of trucks for cooperative logistics operations is critical for industrial efficiency and for minimizing $CO_2$ emissions. Although we need to reduce the gross volume of $CO_2$ emissions from the whole logistics system, all customers or suppliers want to reduce $CO_2$ emissions from the trucks that carry their items. Therefore, we both locally and globally reduce the amount of $CO_2$ emissions in the selection of routes.

The specifications and selection of truck routes are independent of humans in the sense that they can be processed by computers. Note that the order relation is not intended to generate the most efficient route, because truck routes tend to be designed according to external factors. Thus, the computational complexity for this relation is not large. Some readers may think that simple executable languages, such as Lisp and Prolog, should be used to specify routes, but it is difficult to verify whether or not routes written in such languages will satisfy the requirements of customers and suppliers because these languages have many primitives that are not used in describing routes. We will explain why the framework is constructed as a process calculus-based approach, because itinerary plans, which transporters are obligated to make for their trucks, can be treated as sequences of destinations that the trucks visit like expressions of process calculi. Therefore, we can easily transform itinerary plans for trucks into process calculus-based specifications in comparison with other approaches, i.e., logic-based and graph-based specifications.

## 5    Specification Language for Cooperative-Logistics Routes

This section defines a language for specifying and reasoning about truck routes. The language consists of two classes. The first is designed to specify truck routes and the second is designed to specify the routes required by products or customers. The latter is defined as a subset of the former. The operators used in the language are inherited from notations in existing process calculi, e.g., CCS [6] and CSP [3].[2]

**Definition 1.**   The set $\mathcal{E}$ of expressions of the language, ranged over by $E, E_1, E_2, \ldots$ is defined recursively by the following abstract syntax:

$$E ::= 0 \mid \ell \mid E_1 ; E_2 \mid E_1 + E_2$$
$$\mid E_1 \# E_2 \mid E_1 \% E_2 \mid E_1 \& E_2 \mid E^\star$$

where $\mathcal{L}$ is the set of location names ranged over by $\ell, \ell_1, \ell_2, \ldots$, and where points correspond to the locations of suppliers and customers. We often omit 0. We describe a subset language of $\mathcal{E}$ as $\mathcal{S}$, when eliminating $E_1 \# E_2$, $E_1 \% E_2$, $E_1 \& E_2$, and $E^\star$ from $\mathcal{E}$. Let $S, S_1, S_2, \ldots$ be elements of $\mathcal{S}$.                                                 $\square$

This framework assumes that each truck has its own route written in $\mathcal{S}$ and that its driver visits points along the route, i.e., intuitively, the meaning of the terms is as follows:

**Termination:** 0 represents a terminated route.
**Destination:** $\ell$ represents that a truck moves to a point called $\ell$.
**Sequential movement:** $E_1 ; E_2$ denotes the sequential composition of two routes $E_1$
    and $E_2$. If the route of $E_1$ terminates, then the route of $E_2$ follows that of $E_1$.
**External selection:** $E_1 + E_2$ represents the route of a truck according to either $E_1$ or
    $E_2$, where the selection is done by the truck.
**Internal selection:** $E_1 \# E_2$ means that a truck itself can go through either $E_1$ or $E_2$.
**Commutability:** $E_1 \% E_2$ means that a truck can follow either $E_1$ before $E_2$ or $E_2$
    before $E_1$ on its route.
**Interruption:** $E_1 \& E_2$ means that two routes, $E_1$ and $E_2$, may be executed asyn-
    chronously.
**Closure:** $E^\star$ is a transitive closure of $E$ and means that a truck may move along $E$ an
    arbitrary number of times.

where in $E_1 + E_2$ the truck can select the $E_1$ (or $E_2$) route when the $E_1$ route is available. For example, if the $E_1$ route is available and the $E_2$ route is congested, the truck goes through the $E_1$ route. $E_1 \# E_2$ means that a truck can go through either $E_1$ or $E_2$. $E_1 \% E_2$, $E_1 \& E_2$, and $E^\star$ are used to specify possible routes. For example, $E_1 \# E_2$ permits the truck to go through one of the $E_1$ or $E_2$ routes. $E^\star$ specifies that the truck follows the $E$ route more than zero times like the notion of Kleene closure. The operator is used to specify that the requirement of a truck's route permits the truck to visit specified destinations if the truck wants to do this. The language does not needs recursive or loop notations, because each truck does not continue to run for 24 hours everyday.

We introduces the notion of sort on $\mathcal{S}$. $\mathcal{L}(S)$ is defined as $\mathcal{L}(0) = \phi$, $\mathcal{L}(\ell) = \{\ell\}$, $\mathcal{L}(S_1 ; S_2) = \mathcal{L}(S_1)$ where $S_1$ is not 0, $\mathcal{L}(S_1 + S_2) = \mathcal{L}(S_1) \cup \mathcal{L}(S_2)$. When in $S_1 + S_2$ $\mathcal{L}(S_1) \cap \mathcal{L}(S_2)$ is not empty, $S_1 + S_2$ is called as non-deterministic selection. Hereafter, we assume $S$ does have any non-deterministic selections.

Like other process calculi, e.g., CCS [6], the semantics of the language are defined by the following labeled transition rules:

---

[2] The operators except for the $\%$ operator have similar semantics to corresponding operators in
   CCS and CSP. The $\%$ operator can be encoded by a combination of CCS's or CSP's operators.

**Definition 2.** The language is a labeled transition system whose transition $\longrightarrow$ is defined by two kinds of axioms or induction rules as given below:

$$\frac{\quad-\quad}{\ell \xrightarrow{\ell} 0} \qquad \frac{E_1 \xrightarrow{\ell} E_1'}{E_1 ; E_2 \xrightarrow{\ell} E_1' ; E_2} \qquad \frac{E_1 \xrightarrow{\ell} E_1'}{E_1 + E_2 \xrightarrow{\ell} E_1'} \qquad \frac{E_2 \xrightarrow{\ell} E_2'}{E_1 + E_2 \xrightarrow{\ell} E_2'}$$

$$\frac{E_1 \xrightarrow{\ell} E_1'}{E_1 \, \& \, E_2 \xrightarrow{\ell} E_1' \, \& \, E_2} \qquad \frac{E_2 \xrightarrow{\ell} E_2'}{E_1 \, \& \, E_2 \xrightarrow{\ell} E_1 \, \& \, E_2'}$$

$$\frac{-}{E_1 \# E_2 \dashrightarrow E_1} \quad \frac{-}{E_1 \# E_2 \dashrightarrow E_2} \quad \frac{-}{E_1 \, \% \, E_2 \dashrightarrow E_1 ; E_2} \quad \frac{-}{E_1 \, \% \, E_2 \dashrightarrow E_2 ; E_1}$$

$$\frac{E_1 \dashrightarrow E_1'}{E_1 ; E_2 \dashrightarrow E_1' ; E_2} \quad \frac{E_1 \dashrightarrow E_1'}{E_1 + E_2 \dashrightarrow E_1'} \quad \frac{E_2 \dashrightarrow E_2'}{E_1 + E_2 \dashrightarrow E_2'}$$

$$\frac{E_1 \dashrightarrow E_1'}{E_1 \, \& \, E_2 \dashrightarrow E_1' \, \& \, E_2} \quad \frac{E_2 \dashrightarrow E_2'}{E_1 \, \& \, E_2 \dashrightarrow E_1 \, \& \, E_2'}$$

where $0 ; E$, $E \, \& \, 0$, and $0 \, \& \, E$ are treated to be syntactically equal to $E$ and $E^*$ is recursively defined as $0 \# (E ; E^*)$. We often abbreviate $E_0 \dashrightarrow E_1 \dashrightarrow \cdots \dashrightarrow E_{n-1} \dashrightarrow E_n$ to $E_0 (\dashrightarrow)^n E_n$. $\qquad\square$

In Definition 2, we introduce two kinds of transitions: $\ell$-transition (notated as $\xrightarrow{\ell}$) and $\tau$-transition (notated as $\dashrightarrow$), because they can reduce the number of backtrace operations in analyzing our algebraic order between two expressions in comparison with a transition system with a single kind of labels. The former transition defines the semantics of a trucks movement. For example $E \xrightarrow{\ell} E'$ means that the truck moves to a point named $\ell$ and then behaves as $E'$. Also, if there are two possible transitions $E \xrightarrow{\ell_1} E_1$ and $E \xrightarrow{\ell_2} E_2$ for a truck, the processing by the truck chooses one of the destinations, $\ell_1$ or $\ell_2$. The latter transition corresponds to a non-deterministic choice of a truck's routes.

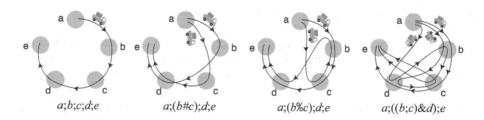

$a;b;c;d;e \qquad a;(b\#c);d;e \qquad a;(b\%c);d;e \qquad a;((b;c)\&d);e$

**Fig. 3.** Examples of specification

We show several basic examples of the language as shown in Fig. 3.[3]

---

[3] There examples intend to be common in our previous framework [10] to prove that the expressiveness of the current language support that of the previous one.

- Route specification, $a \, ; \, b \, ; \, c \, ; \, d$, in $\mathcal{S}$ is interpreted as follows:

$$a \, ; \, b \, ; \, c \, ; \, d \xrightarrow{a} b \, ; \, c \, ; \, d$$
$$\xrightarrow{b} c \, ; \, d$$
$$\xrightarrow{c} d$$
$$\xrightarrow{d}$$

The first diagram in Fig. 3 illustrates the above derivation.
- Next, we show an example of a specification in $\mathcal{E}$. This is a route requirement.

$$a \, ; \, (b \, \# \, c) \, ; \, d \, ; \, e \xrightarrow{a} (b \, \# \, c) \, ; \, d \, ; \, e$$
$$\dashrightarrow b \, ; \, d \, ; \, e \quad \text{or} \quad c \, ; \, d \, ; \, e$$

where # corresponds to a combination of two required routes so that trucks are required to follow both routes as shown in the third diagram in Fig. 3. That is, a truck needs to call at point $a$ and then at either $b$ or $c$. Next, it calls at $d$ and then $e$.
- We show another route requirement specification, $a \, ; \, (b \, \% \, c) \, ; \, d \, ; \, e$, in $\mathcal{E}$. It has two derivations as follows:

$$a \, ; \, (b \, \% \, c) \, ; \, d \, ; \, e \xrightarrow{a} (b \, \% \, c) \, ; \, d \, ; \, e$$
$$\dashrightarrow b \, ; \, c \, ; \, d \, ; \, e \quad \text{or} \quad c \, ; \, b \, ; \, d \, ; \, e$$

where % means that trucks can take either one of the two routes before they take the other. The second diagram in Fig. 3 shows possible routes that could satisfy this requirement specification.
- $a \, ; \, ((b \, ; \, c) \, \& \, d) \, ; \, e$ in $\mathcal{E}$ is an example of & .

$$a \, ; \, ((b \, ; \, c) \, \& \, d) \, ; \, e \xrightarrow{a} ((b \, ; \, c) \, \& \, d) \, ; \, e$$
$$\xrightarrow{b} (c \, \& \, d) \, ; \, e$$
$$\xrightarrow{c} d \, ; \, e$$
$$\xrightarrow{d} e$$

where & corresponds to asynchronous reduction. Thus, this permits a truck to move to $d$ while moving along $c \, ; \, b$. As shown in the fourth diagram in Fig. 3, the following two derivations are possible in addition to the above derivation.

$$a \, ; \, ((b \, ; \, c) \, \& \, d) \, ; \, e \xrightarrow{a} ((b \, ; \, c) \, \& \, d) \, ; \, e$$
$$\xrightarrow{b} (c \, \& \, d) \, ; \, e$$
$$\xrightarrow{d} c \, ; \, e$$
$$\xrightarrow{c} e$$

or

$$a \, ; \, ((b \, ; \, c) \, \& \, d) \, ; \, e \xrightarrow{a} ((b \, ; \, c) \, \& \, d) \, ; \, e$$
$$\xrightarrow{d} (b \, ; \, c) \, ; \, e$$
$$\xrightarrow{b} c \, ; \, e$$
$$\xrightarrow{c} e$$

- The first requirement presented in the previous section is described as specification $(a \; ; (b \, \% \, c)) \, \& \, d^* \, \& \, e^*$. We show one of the possible derivations from the specification as follows:

$$(a \; ; (b \, \% \, c)) \, \& \, d^* \, \& \, e^* \xrightarrow{a} (b \, \% \, c)) \, \& \, d^* \, \& \, e^*$$
$$\xrightarrow{b} c \, \& \, d^* \, \& \, e^*$$

We can also have another derivation from the specification as follows:

$$(a \; ; (b \, \% \, c)) \, \& \, d^* \, \& \, e^* \xrightarrow{a} (b \, \% \, c)) \, \& \, d^* \, \& \, e^*$$
$$\xrightarrow{c} b \, \& \, d^* \, \& \, e^*$$

where $E \, \& \, d^*$ means that the truck can visit $d$ more than zero times while it moves along $E$.

$$(a \; ; (b \, \% \, c)) \, \& \, d^* \, \& \, e^*$$
$$\overset{\text{def}}{=} (a \; ; (b \, \% \, c)) \, \& \, (0 \, \# \, d \; ; \; d^*) \, \& \, e^*$$
$$\dashrightarrow (a \; ; (b \, \% \, c)) \, \& \, (d \; ; \; d^*) \, \& \, e^*$$
$$\xrightarrow{d} (a \; ; (b \, \% \, c)) \, \& \, d^* \, \& \, e^*$$

# 6   Order Relation for Route Selection

This section defines an order relation for selecting trucks according to their routes based on the concept of bisimulation [6]. The relation is suitable for selecting a truck for a cooperative logistics operation with a route that satisfies the requirements of suppliers and customers.

**Definition 3.**   A binary relation $\mathcal{R}^n$ ($\mathcal{R} \subseteq (\mathcal{E} \times \mathcal{S}) \times \mathcal{N}$) is an *n-route* prebisimulation, where $\mathcal{N}$ is the set of natural numbers, if whenever $(E, S) \in \mathcal{R}^k$ where $k \geq 0$, then, the following holds for all $\ell \in \mathcal{L}$ or $\tau$.

*i)* if $E \xrightarrow{\ell} E'$ then there is an $S'$ such that $S \xrightarrow{\ell} S'$ and $(E', S') \in \mathcal{R}^{k-1}$

*ii)* There is an $E'$ such that $E \, (\dashrightarrow)^* \, E'$ and $(E', S) \in \mathcal{R}^k$

*iii)* if $S \xrightarrow{\ell} S'$ then there exist $E', E''$ such that $E \, (\dashrightarrow)^* E' \xrightarrow{\ell} E''$ and $(E'', S') \in \mathcal{R}^{k-1}$

where $E \sqsupseteq_n S$ if there exist some $n$-route prebisimulations such that $(E, S) \in \mathcal{R}^n$. We call the $\sqsupseteq_n$ *n-route* order. We often abbreviate $\sqsupseteq_n$ to $\sqsupseteq$ where $n$ is infinite.   □

The informal meaning of $E \sqsupseteq_n S$ is that $S$ is included in one of the permissible routes specified in $E$ and $n$ corresponds to the number of movements of a truck that can satisfy $E$. Since the language supports an external selection operator, i.e., $+$, like other process calculi, our truck selection cannot be defined as simple algebraic relations, e.g., trace-based semantics. We show several basic properties of the order relation below. Let us look at some basic examples.

- $(a \, \% \, b) \, ; \, c \sqsupseteq_3 a \, ; \, b \, ; \, c$
  where the left-hand-side requires a truck to carry products to $a$, and $b$ in an indefinite order and then return to point $c$; the right-hand-side requires a truck to carry products to three points, $a$, $b$, and $c$, sequentially. When the right-hand-side is changed to $b \, ; \, a \, ; \, c$, the relation is still preserved, but when the right-hand-side becomes $c \, ; \, a \, ; \, b$ or $a \, ; \, c \, ; \, b$, the relation is not preserved.
- $(a \, ; \, b \, ; \, c) \, \# \, (a \, ; \, c \, ; \, b \, ; \, c) \sqsupseteq_3 a \, ; \, b \, ; \, c$
  where the left-hand-side means that a truck follows one of either $a \, ; \, b \, ; \, c$ or $b \, ; \, c \, ; \, a$. When the right-hand-side becomes $a \, ; \, c \, ; \, b \, ; \, c$, the relation is not preserved, because $\sqsupseteq_3$ means that the truck can visit its destinations at most three times. Nevertheless, $\sqsupseteq_4$ is preserved with $a \, ; \, c \, ; \, b \, ; \, c$ at its right-hand-side.
- $((a \, ; \, b \, ; \, c) \, \& \, d^*) \, ; \, d \sqsupseteq_6 a \, ; \, d \, ; \, b \, ; \, d \, ; \, c \, ; \, d$
  where the left-hand-side allows a truck to drop in at point $d$ an arbitrary number of times on route $a \, ; \, b \, ; \, c$ and then finish its movement at point $d$. The right-hand-side is a star-shaped route between three destinations, $a$, $b$, $c$, and point $d$ satisfies the left-hand-side. When the right-hand-side becomes $a \, ; \, b \, ; \, d \, ; \, c \, ; \, d, a \, ; \, d \, ; \, b \, ; \, c \, ; \, d$, or $a \, ; \, b \, ; \, c \, ; \, d$, the relation is preserved, but $a \, ; \, b \, ; \, c \, ; \, d$ is the most efficient route.

# 7  Early Experience

This section describes a prototype implementation of our framework. The experiment was constructed as a distributed logistics management system consisting of six supplier points in addition to a customer point with a route-selection server. Figure 4 shows the basic structure of the system. The server was responsible for receiving route requirements from suppliers and customers through a network and selecting suitable trucks with routes that satisfied these requirements.

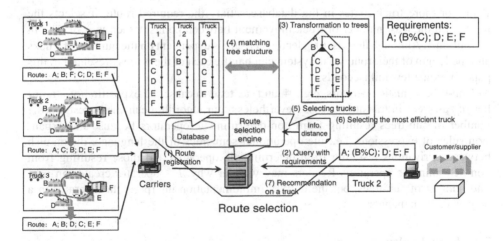

**Fig. 4.** Basic structure of logistics management system

## 7.1    Route Selection Algorithm

Here, let us explain the selection algorithm used for the current implementation, which we tried to make as faithful to Definition 3 as possible. To enable the algorithm to be executed on cloud computing, it maintains information in a key-value store or blob-store, which Google App Engine and Microsoft Azure supports. For example, it maintains its own repository containing the routes of trucks in a key-value store. To reduce the cost of the selection algorithm, the possible routes written in $\mathcal{E}$ are transformed into tree structures before they are stored in the database. These are called `transition trees` or `derivation trees` in the literature on process calculi [6].

Each tree is derived from a route in $\mathcal{E}$ according to Definition 2 and consists of arcs corresponding to $\ell$-transitions or $\tau$-transitions in the route. When a route selection server receives a required route from suppliers or customers, it extracts the required route written in $\mathcal{S}$ and then transforms the route into a transition tree. It next determines whether or not the trees derived from the routes stored in the database system can satisfy the tree derived from the required route by matching the two trees according to the definition of the order relation ($\sqsupseteq_n \subseteq \mathcal{E} \times \mathcal{S}$) as in the following.

(1) If each node in one of the two trees has arcs corresponding to $\ell$-transitions, then the corresponding node in the other tree can have the same arcs, and the sub-nodes derived through the matching arcs of the two trees can still satisfy either (1) or (2).
(2) If each node in the tree derived from the required route has one or more arcs corresponding to $\tau$-transitions, then at least one of the nodes derived through the arcs and the corresponding node in the tree derived from the truck's route can still satisfy (1) or (2).
(3) If neither (1) nor (2) is satisfied, the route selection server backtracks from the current nodes in the two trees and tries to apply (1) or (2) to their two backtracked nodes.

If one or more truck routes in the database satisfy the required route, it selects the truck with the least number of truck movement between points, which is $n$ of $\sqsupseteq_n$ in Definition 3. Although the cost of selecting a route is dependent on the number of trucks and the length of their routes, the system can handle each of the routes presented in this paper within a few milliseconds.

Non-deterministic operators, e.g., # and %, tend to cause the exposition of a number of sub-trees in transition trees. Nevertheless, our algorithm can easily restrain the number of sub-trees resulting from non-deterministic operators because the expansion rules of expressions, i.e., the operational semantics of the language, distinguish between derivations resulting from deterministic operators and those resulting from non-deterministic operators. Readers may wonder why $E^*$ operator creates an infinite number of sub-trees, but the current implementation interprets the operator in a lazy evaluation manner.

## 7.2    Early Implementation

We have implemented the framework on a PaaS cloud computing infrastructure, called Google' App Engine. Trucks' routes are maintained in a key-value store, called Bigtable, provided by the infrastructure [2]. When our system receives a truck route from a truck operator, it transforms the required route into a tree structure and stores the structure into the Bigtable database. When it receives a request with a required route, our route selector engine transforms the required route into a tree structure and matches between the structure and the structures corresponding to trucks' routes. This means truck operators and suppliers do not need any special equipment to use the logistics management system. This is important because in cooperative logistics, most suppliers are small to medium enterprises that do not want to have to invest in additional equipment for cooperative logistics.

## 8 Related Work

There have been many attempts to use process calculi, e.g., as formal methods for processes in various business enterprise processes. Several researchers have used process calculi, e.g., $\pi$-calculus, as business-process modeling languages, such as BPEL, [12,5,8,11]. $\pi$-calculus has been used as a formal language for software composition and Web service compositions, e.g., Orc [7] and SCC [1]. Process calculi are theoretically sound and support bisimulation analysis and model checking. They are also gaining increasing acceptance as a support tool in industry. However, there have been no process-calculus-based formal methods for logistics, particularly to improve the transport efficiency of trucks. The author of this paper presented a formal method of using mobile agents in network management systems [9]. However, this method was only aimed at mobile agents and assumed the notion of two-layer mobile agents. We proposed an early version of the framework presented in this paper [10], but the previous paper addressed theoretical definition of the language. This paper describes an implementation of the calculus on the cloud computing infrastructure.

## 9 Conclusion

This paper presented a formal method for improving transport efficiency, using the example of cooperative logistics, to reduce the environmental impacts of transport operations. The method was formulated based on a process calculus-based language and an order relation over two terms corresponding to truck routes and the required routes in the language. The language can specify truck routes for milk-run operations and the required routes for shipping. The relation can be used to accurately determine whether a truck route satisfies the requirements of customers and suppliers. A prototype implementation system based on the framework was constructed on a cloud computing infrastructure. As mentioned previously, the goal of the proposed framework is to establish both a theoretical and practical foundation for earth-friendly logistics.

**Acknowledgments.** This research was supported in part by a grant from the Promotion program for Reducing global Environmental loaD through ICT innovation (PREDICT) made by the Ministry of Internal Affairs and Communications in Japan.

# References

1. Boreale, M., Bruni, R., Caires, L., De Nicola, R., Lanese, I., Loreti, M., Martins, F., Montanari, U., Ravara, A., Sangiorgi, D., Vasconcelos, V., Zavattaro, G.: SCC: A Service Centered Calculus. In: Bravetti, M., Núñez, M., Tennenholtz, M. (eds.) WS-FM 2006. LNCS, vol. 4184, pp. 38–57. Springer, Heidelberg (2006)
2. Chang, F., Dean, J., Ghemawat, S., Hsieh, W.C., Wallach, D.A., Burrows, M., Chandra, T., Fikes, A., Gruber, R.: Bigtable: A Distributed Storage System for Structured Data. In: Proceedings of 7th Symposium on Operating Systems Design and Implementation (OSDI 2006), pp. 205–218. USENIX Association (2006)
3. Hoare, C.A.R.: Communicating Sequential Processes. Prentice Hall (1985)
4. International Energy Agency, Transport Energy and CO2 (Moving Toward Sustainability, IEA (2009)
5. Mazzara, M., Lucchi, R.: A pi-calculus based semantics for WS-BPEL. Journal of Logic and Algebraic Programming 70(1), 96–118 (2006)
6. Milner, R.: Communication and Concurrency. Prentice Hall (1989)
7. Misra, J., Cook, W.R.: Computation orchestration: A basis for wide-area computing. Journal of Software and Systems Modeling (2006); (A preliminary version of this paper appeared in the Lecture Notes for NATO summer school August 2004)
8. Puhlmann, F., Weske, M.: Using the $\pi$-Calculus for Formalizing Workflow Patterns. In: van der Aalst, W.M.P., Benatallah, B., Casati, F., Curbera, F. (eds.) BPM 2005. LNCS, vol. 3649, pp. 153–168. Springer, Heidelberg (2005)
9. Satoh, I.: Building and Selecting Mobile Agents for Network Management. Journal of Network and Systems Management 14(1), 147–169 (2006)
10. Satoh, I.: A Specification Framework for Earth-Friendly Logistics. In: Suzuki, K., Higashino, T., Yasumoto, K., El-Fakih, K. (eds.) FORTE 2008. LNCS, vol. 5048, pp. 251–266. Springer, Heidelberg (2008)
11. Smith, H.: Business Process Management-The Third Wave: Business Process Modeling Language (BPML) and Its Pi-Calculus Foundations. Information and Software Technology 45(15), 1065–1069 (2003)
12. Xu, K., Liu, Y., Zhu, J., Wu, C.: Pi-Calculus Based Bi-transformation of State-Driven Model and Flow-Driven Model. International Journal of Business Process Integration and Management (2006)

# Linear Integer Programming for the Home Health Care Problem

Sarra Trabelsi, Rim Larbi, and Atidel Hadj Alouane

OASIS Laboratory, National Engineering School of Tunis,
BP 37, Le Belvédère 1002 Tunis, Tunisia
{sarra.trab,larbi_rim}@yahoo.fr, atidel.hadj@enit.rnu.tn

**Abstract.** Home health care is a growing medical service. It includes medical, paramedical and social services delivered to patients at their own homes. The main benefits of home health care are the significant decrease in the hospitalization and the cost reduction in the entire health system. However, this service is not an easy task because it combines the vehicle routing problem and the nurse assignment problem.

In this paper we propose a linear integer scheduling model developed to provide staff short term planning in home care. In particular, the model deals with the problem of deciding (a) which patients should be assigned to each nurse and (b) when to execute the service during the planning horizon, in order to satisfy the time windows constraints for each patient.

**Keywords:** Home health care, linear programming, time windows.

## 1 Introduction

Home health care service consists in visiting and offering medical, paramedical and social services to patients at their homes. Such structures have been created fifty years ago in order to solve the problem of cluttering in the hospitals and to reduce health care costs. The home health care service represents an economic and social stake. It decreases the hospitalization rate and reduces costs, while improving the patient quality of life [1].

Minimizing the costs in the home health care consists in minimizing the staffing costs, the medicines acquisition costs and the transportation costs. Therefore, an accurate resource planning is crucial to guarantee a service quality for both patients and care providers. As a consequence, plans should enhance the quality of care by reducing the waiting time and satisfying personal preferences of patients, such as the affinity with certain care providers, time windows for the visits, etc. They must also guarantee a service quality towards the care providers through a fair distribution of workloads and the satisfaction of their personal preferences (e.g. non-working periods, time windows, etc.).

There are many articles devoted to the home health care problem. Cheng and Rich formulate the problem as a vehicle routing problem with time windows and multiple depots [2]. They propose a combined mixed-integer program (MIP)

F. Daniel et al. (Eds.): BPM 2011 Workshops, Part II, LNBIP 100, pp. 143–151, 2012.

and a heuristic approach to minimize salary costs. In [3] the authors introduce a scheduling problem for a variety of home care providers which is modeled as a set partitioning problem and solved using repeated matching algorithms. In [4] a hybrid method is presented. It combines linear programming, constraint programming and heuristics minimizing transportation costs and maximizing satisfaction of patients and care providers. In [5] a decision support system based on simple scheduling heuristics is proposed. Mathematical models based on integer linear programming techniques are developed in [6] and [7]. In this paper, we propose to study the home health care problem where patients can request one or more nurses at the same visit considering time window constraints. The objective of balancing workload for this case has not been studied.

This paper is organized as follows: In Section 2 we describe the problem. In Section 3, we present the solution approach in formulating our problem as a linear integer program. Numerical results are then presented in section 4. Finally some concluding remarks are given in section 5.

## 2    Problem Description

Nowadays, more patients receive their medical treatments at home. For each one, a care plan which states the type of services that should be performed and the corresponding duration. Planners in home health care services must then establish a daily visit plan which specifies when each visit should be made and which nurse should be assigned to it. Our work is a combination of assignments and routing problem, the quality of the planning is measured by balancing the workload among all the nurses to ensure a better quality of care. For this it is assumed from the beginning that the human and material resources are still available it is for this reason we have not integrated cost optimization in the model may .

We consider that the duration of each visit is given and that a visit must be made during a pre-specified time window. A visit is also described by the type of required skills. Evidently, a nurse ensuring the task will have to fulfil the required skills. We also consider that some visits might require more than one nurse, due to, for example, the need for different skills.

We are interested in task assignment for full-time nurses, during on working period (e.g. a day). Each nurse has its own individual schedule. We suppose that nurses start and return to the hospital.

When solving the problem, we assume that all patients are visited, and we do not allow a routes' duration to exceed a maximal working time. We also consider that each route does not include two successive visits exceeding a certain maximal distance.

Our purpose is to provide a decision support tool for constructing nurses' schedule in a home health care system. The objective is then to find the best schedule that balances the workload amongst nurses. Here, the workload is the sum of the total travel times and duration of visits to patients.

Below, we present the notations which will be used throughout the article.

- N : number of nurses $(i = 1...N)$;
- P : number of patients $(j = 0...P$ with $j = 0$ represents the hospital);
- $st_j$ : start time visit's time window of patient $j$;
- $et_j$ : end time visit's time window of patient $j$;
- $D_j$ : duration of the visit of patient $j$;
- $nb_j$ : number of nurses needed for patient $j$;
- $dist_{jk}$ : distance between patients $j$ and $k$;
- $max\_time$ : maximal working time of all nurses;
- $skill_{ij}$ : is equal to 1 if nurse $i$ possesses the skills required by patient $j$, 0 otherwise;
- $dist\_max$ : maximal distance between two successive visits;
- $H$ : a sufficiently large positive constant.

## 3  A Linear Integer Programming for the Home Health Care Problem

In this section, we will present a linear integer program for the home health care problem. We recall that types of skills requested by each patient and the duration of each visit are supposed to be known and deterministic. We consider in this work a daily scheduling problem.

To model the problem, we define two decision variables as follows :

- $y_{ijk} = \begin{cases} 1, \text{ if nurse i visits patient k after patient j}; \\ 0, \text{ otherwise}. \end{cases}$
- $Arrive_{ij}$ : the arrival date of nurse $i$ to patient $j$.

We define also :

- $Load_i$ : the work load of nurse $i$,
- $Z_{max}$ : the maximum work load $(Z_{max} = \max_i Load_i)$,
- $Z_{min}$ : the minimum work load $(Z_{min} = \min_i Load_i)$,
- $Start_i$ : the start time of nurse $i$,
- $End_i$ : the end time of nurse $i$.

The problem can then be formulated as the following linear integer programming model:

$$\min(Z_{max} - Z_{min})$$
$$s.c.$$
$$Z_{max} \geq Load_i; \forall i \tag{1}$$
$$Z_{min} \leq Load_i; \forall i \tag{2}$$
$$Load_i = End_i - Start_i; \forall i \tag{3}$$
$$Start_i = \min_{j \neq 0}(Arrive_{ij} + (1 - y_{i0j})H - \sum_u dist_{0j}.y_{i0u}); \forall i \tag{4}$$

$$End_i = \max_{j \neq 0}(Arrive_{ij} + (y_{ij0} - 1)H + D_j + \sum_{u \neq j} dist_{j0}.y_{iuj}); \forall i \tag{5}$$

$$\sum_i \sum_{j \neq k} y_{ijk}.skill_{ij} = nb_k; \forall k \tag{6}$$

$$\sum_i \sum_{k \neq j} y_{ijk}.skill_{ij} = nb_j; \forall j \tag{7}$$

$$\sum_{k \neq 0} y_{i0k} = 1; \forall i \tag{8}$$

$$\sum_{j \neq 0} y_{ij0} = 1; \forall i \tag{9}$$

$$Arrive_{ik} \geq Arrive_{ij} + D_j + dist_{jk} + (y_{ijk} - 1)H; \forall i, \forall j, \forall k \neq \{0, j\} \tag{10}$$

$$st_j \leq Arrive_{ij}; \forall i, \forall j \tag{11}$$

$$Arrive_{ij} + D_j \leq etj; \forall i, \forall j \neq 0 \tag{12}$$

$$Arrive_{ij} + D_j + dist_{j0} \leq max\_time; \forall i, \forall j \neq 0 \tag{13}$$

$$\sum_i \sum_{j \neq h} y_{ijh} \times i = \sum_i \sum_{k \neq h} y_{ihk} \times i; \forall h \tag{14}$$

$$Arrive_{ij} = Arrive_{uj}; \forall i, \forall u \neq i, \forall j \neq 0 : nb_j \geq 2 \tag{15}$$

$$Arrive_{ik} - Arrive_{ij} - D_j + (y_{ijk} - 1)H \leq Dist\_max; \forall i, \forall j, \forall k \neq \{0, j\} \tag{16}$$

$$y_{ijk} \in 0, 1; \forall i, \forall j, \forall k \tag{17}$$

$$Arrive_{ij} \geq 0; \forall i, \forall j \tag{18}$$

$$Load_i, Start_i, End_i, Z_{max}, Z_{min} \geq 0; \forall i \tag{19}$$

The objective function is to balance the workload of the nurses. The constraints (1) and (2) calculate the maximal and the minimal load of nurses. Constraint (3) specifies the load of each nurse. Beginning and ending time of work of each nurse are fixed by constraints (4) and (5). Constraints (6) and (7) ensure that all the patients receive the requested number of nurses having the required skills. Constraints (8) and (9) guarantee that each nurse starts and returns to the hospital. We remind that $j = 0$ represents the hospital. Constraints (10) calculate the arrival date of the nurse $i$ to patient $k$ after visiting patient $j$. The arrival date takes into account the travel time between two patients visited consecutively and the duration of the visit. Constraints (11) and (12) impose that each service is completed within a time window that may correspond to the availability of patients at home. Constraints (13) impose a maximum time on total working hours for each nurse. Constraint (14) ensures that each tour is coherent; i.e. realized by the same nurse. Constraint (15) makes sure that nurses arrive at the same time when a patient requests two or more nurses for the same visit. Constraint (16) guarantees that a maximal travel time $Dist\_max$ between two patients visited consecutively is not exceeded. Constraint (17) is the binary restrictions on the decision variable $y_{ijk}$. Finally, constraints (18) and (19) ensure that variables $Arrive_{ij}$, $Load_i$, $Start_i$, $End_i$, $Z_{max}$ and $Z_{min}$ are non-negative.

## 4    Numerical Results

In this section, we present the results obtained after solving the linear integer program described above. The scheduling model was solved using OPL Studio version 6, ILOG Cplex version 12 and tested on random instances. We conducted all the tests on an Intel Pentium M with 2.20 GHZ CPU. First, we present the results obtained for an example of 3 nurses and 7 patients. Second, we test the mathematical model for different instances.

### 4.1    Results for a Case Study

In order to illustrate the results of our model, we solve the linear integer program for 3 nurses and 7 patients. We consider that the maximal travel time authorized is equal to $Dist\_max = 540$. Time window constraints $(st_j, et_j)$, duration of visits $(D_j)$ and the requested number of nurses $(NB_j)$ of each patient $j$ are presented in table 1. Table 2 illustrates travel times between each pair of patients and each patient and the hospital. We remind that the hospital is represented as a fictitious patient (Patient 0). Table 3 illustrates which nurses possess the skills required by each patient $(skill_{ij})$.

**Table 1.** Data related to patients

| Patient | $st_j$ | $et_j$ | $D_j$ | $NB_j$ |
|---------|--------|--------|-------|--------|
| 1 | 60 | 120 | 30 | 1 |
| 2 | 300 | 480 | 55 | 1 |
| 3 | 240 | 300 | 20 | 1 |
| 4 | 180 | 300 | 30 | 2 |
| 5 | 35 | 120 | 25 | 2 |
| 6 | 30 | 240 | 35 | 1 |
| 7 | 60 | 240 | 20 | 1 |

Table 4 illustrates the results obtained for our example. The solver calculates a planning for the 3 nurses in 1 secondes with an optimum objective value of 0 which means that the three nurses have the same workload . We can observe that patients 4 and 5 receive nurses at the same time because the number of nurses requested by these patients is equal to 2.

### 4.2    General Results

We test the model for different problem sizes: from 4 to 15 patients for 2, 3 and 4 nurses. We present in this paper only the results obtained for 7, 10 and 15 patients and 2, 3 and 4 nurses. For each instance, we solve the model by considering two cases :

**Table 2.** Travel times

| 0 | 1 | 2 | 3 | 4 | 5 | 6 | 7 |
|---|---|---|---|---|---|---|---|
| 0 | 0 | 30 | 15 | 35 | 22 | 35 | 18 | 45 |
| 1 | 30 | 0 | 20 | 20 | 13 | 19 | 24 | 22 |
| 2 | 15 | 20 | 0 | 10 | 45 | 25 | 36 | 19 |
| 3 | 35 | 20 | 10 | 0 | 12 | 45 | 22 | 34 |
| 4 | 22 | 13 | 45 | 12 | 0 | 20 | 15 | 18 |
| 5 | 35 | 19 | 25 | 45 | 20 | 0 | 45 | 25 |
| 6 | 18 | 24 | 36 | 22 | 15 | 45 | 0 | 20 |
| 7 | 45 | 22 | 19 | 34 | 18 | 25 | 20 | 0 |

**Table 3.** $skill_{ij}$

| | 1 | 2 | 3 |
|---|---|---|---|
| 1 | 1 | 1 | 1 |
| 2 | 1 | 0 | 1 |
| 3 | 0 | 1 | 1 |
| 4 | 1 | 1 | 1 |
| 5 | 1 | 1 | 1 |
| 6 | 0 | 1 | 1 |
| 7 | 1 | 1 | 0 |

**Table 4.** Results for the case study

| Nurse | Patient | Arrival time |
|---|---|---|
| 1 | Patient 0 | 08h00 |
| | Patient 5 | 08h35 |
| | Patient 1 | 09h30 |
| | Patient 4 | 11h00 |
| | Patient 0 | 11h52 |
| 2 | Patient 0 | 08h00 |
| | Patient 5 | 08h35 |
| | Patient 7 | 10h00 |
| | Patient 6 | 11h00 |
| | Patient 0 | 11h52 |
| 3 | Patient 0 | 10h38 |
| | Patient 4 | 11h00 |
| | Patient 3 | 12h30 |
| | Patient 2 | 13h20 |
| | Patient 0 | 14h30 |

– Each patient requests only one nurse (i.e. $nb_j = 1$);
– Patient request one or more nurse (i.e. $nb_j \geq 1$).

For each case, we solve 3 randomly generated sets of instances. Tables 5, 6, 7 present the mean value obtained for the two cases. We obtain optimal planning providing task assignment within a computation time of few seconds or minutes. In all cases, we have respected the working hours of nurses and ensured the skills needed for each patient while balancing workload amongst nurses. We consider a maximal execution time of one hour, i.e. we stop the solver when it exceeds this time.

**Table 5.** Results for N=2

| N | P | $nb_j$ | Exec. Times (s) | Objective value | Optimum |
|---|---|---|---|---|---|
| 2 | 7 | 1 | 1 | 0 | × |
| 2 | 7 | ≥ 1 | 1 | 48 | × |
| 2 | 10 | 1 | 1 | 5 | × |
| 2 | 10 | ≥ 1 | 1 | 35 | × |
| 2 | 15 | 1 | 840 | 0 | × |
| 2 | 15 | ≥ 1 | 210 | 0 | × |

**Table 6.** Results for N=3

| N | P | $nb_j$ | Exec. Times (s) | Objective value | Optimum |
|---|---|---|---|---|---|
| 3 | 7 | 1 | 6 | 19 | × |
| 3 | 7 | ≥ 1 | 2 | 0 | × |
| 3 | 10 | 1 | 19 | 0 | × |
| 3 | 10 | ≥ 1 | 19 | 18 | × |
| 3 | 15 | 1 | 360 | 0 | × |
| 3 | 15 | ≥ 1 | 1595 | 222 | × |

**Table 7.** Results for N=4

| N | P | $NB_j$ | Exec. Times (s) | Objective value | Optimum |
|---|---|---|---|---|---|
| 4 | 7 | 1 | 60 | 52 | × |
| 4 | 7 | ≥ 1 | 60 | 127 | × |
| 4 | 10 | 1 | 1908 | 2 | × |
| 4 | 10 | ≥ 1 | 1080 | 0 | × |
| 4 | 15 | 1 | 240 | 0 | × |
| 4 | 15 | ≥ 1 | 420 | 90 | × |

In the case of 7 patients, we notice that the computation time varies from 1s to 60s for $N=2, 3$ and 4. We obtained the optimal solution for all instances. The value of the objective function is better when each patient requires only one nurse per visit. In the case of 10 patients, we also obtain the optimal solution. The computation time varies between 1s and 35s for $N = 2$ and $N=3$. However, for $N = 4$ it exceeds 31 minutes. Finally for $P = 15$, our optimal solution is given for $N = 2$, 3 and 4 with an execution time varying between 3 and 26 minutes.

## 5  Discussion

The home health care area is increasing rapidly in size which raises the need for decision support tools to provide adequate planning and improve the quality of service provided to patients. The short term planning process in such an area requires to consider a large number of constraints and objectives, regarding both the efficiency of the system and the quality of care. For this reason, a mathematical support tool for home health care providers was developed. Our objective is to balance workload amongst nurses while respecting time windows constraints of patients, qualifications of nurses and the number of nurses requested for each visit.

Additional testing of our model is in progress. Evidently, enhancement must be made in terms of execution time. Improvements for this model could be achieved by considering a weekly planning. Future developments could address the creation of a model for the short term planning of materials in home health care providers, parallel to the human resources considered in this paper, we can also considering the problem from a yield management view point, we can add a constraint that sets a minimum income for a nurse, so we will have a reasonable travel time compared to the duration of treatment that are the source of income.

The current study opens up several perspectives. In this work, duration of visits and travel times are considered deterministic. Indeed,the problem is more complicated if we consider non-deterministic durations and/or travel times. One idea to handle this type of uncertainty is to start with a deterministic setting and make necessary updates of the nurses's schedule whenever necessary.This will require on-line information exchange between the decision maker and the nurses as the schedule is being executed. Another direction would be to automatize the planning and update processes by embedding the optimization model into a workflow model that handles the entire problem of home hare care from the reception of patients' demands until the completion of home care activities.

## References

1. Chahed, S., Matta, A., Sahin, E., Dallery, Y.: Operations management related activities in home health care structures. In: Proceedings of INCOM Conference (Information Control Problems in Manufacturing), Saint-Etienne, France, vol. 3, pp. 641–646 (2006)
2. Cheng, E., Rich, J.L.: A home care routing and scheduling problem. Technical Report, TR98-04, Department of Computational And Applied Mathematics, Rice University (1998)
3. Eveborn, P., Flisberg, P., Ronnqvist, M.: LAPS CARE-an operational system for staff planning of home care. European Journal of Operational Research 171, 962–976 (2006)

4. Bertels, S., Fahle, T.: A hybrid setup for a hybrid scenario: combining heuristics for the home health care problem. Computers & Operations Research 33, 2866–2890 (2006)
5. Begur, S.V., Miller, D.M., Weaver, J.R.: An integrated spatial Decision Support System for scheduling and routing home health care nurses. Technical report, Institute of operations research and the management science (1997)
6. Borsani, V., Matta, A., Beschi, G., Sommaruga, F.: A Home Care Scheduling Model For Human Resources. In: International Conference on Service Systems and Service Management, pp. 449–454 (2006)
7. Ben Babouch, R., Fakhfakh, M., Guninet, A., Hajri-Gabouj, S.: Planification de la tournée des infirmiers dans une structure de soins à domicile. Technical report, INSA Lyon (2009)

# Evolutionary Algorithm for Scheduling Production Jobs and Preventive Maintenance Activities

Maher Rebai[1,*], Imed Kacem[2], and Kondo H. Adjallah[3]

[1] University of technology of Troyes, 12 rue Marie Curie, 10010 Troyes, France
maher.rebai@utt.fr
[2] University Paul Verlaine Metz, Ile du Saulcy 57000, Metz, France
kacem@univ-metz.fr
[3] Ecole Nationale d'Ingénieurs de Metz, 1 route d'Ars Laquenexy, Metz, France
adjallah@enim.fr
http://www.univ-metz.fr

**Abstract.** We propose in this article an evolutionary algorithm for the problem of scheduling $N$ production jobs on $M$ parallel machines. Each machine should be blocked once during the planning horizon for reasons of preventive maintenance. In our study, the maintenance tasks should continuously be performed because the maintenance resources are not sufficient. We aim to find a schedule composed of the production jobs and the maintenance tasks with a minimal preventive maintenance cost and total sum of production job's weighted completion times.

Computational experiments are performed on randomly generated instances. The results show that the evolutionary algorithm is able to produce appropriate solutions for the problem.

**Keywords:** Maintenance, Scheduling, Evolutionary algorithm.

## 1 Introduction

The preventive maintenance operations are necessary in most manufacturing and industries shops in order to keep processing equipments in well working conditions. In practice, each preventive maintenance task should be characterized by two deadlines: an optimistic deadline and a pessimistic deadline. The optimistic deadline is the first best execution time for the preventive maintenance task that allows a minimal preventive maintenance cost. The pessimistic deadline constitutes the last best execution time for the preventive maintenance task allowing a minimal preventive maintenance cost. More precisely, each instant between the optimistic deadline and the pessimistic deadline of a preventive maintenance task may be considered as a good execution time for the preventive maintenance task that allows a minimal preventive maintenance cost. In contrast, when the preventive maintenance task is performed after the pessimistic deadline or before the optimistic deadline, the preventive maintenance cost increases. In general,

---

* Corresponding author.

F. Daniel et al. (Eds.): BPM 2011 Workshops, Part II, LNBIP 100, pp. 152–161, 2012.

the two deadlines of a preventive maintenance task are determined in advance using the failure distribution low of the machine.

In numerous manufacturing and industries situations, the maintenance resource is very expensive. Consequently, it is not possible to find more than one unit of maintenance resource in the shop. In such a situation, when several preventive maintenance deadlines arrive, just one machine is taken for preventive maintenance. The remaining machines continue to work until the maintenance resource will be free again. Indeed, when a preventive maintenance task is performed after its pessimistic deadline, two important facts may frequently occur: The first one is related to the damages that may affect the machine's components while the second fact is related to the defect products'rate that may quickly rise. These facts increase considerably the preventive maintenance cost. The total damage cost of the maintained machines may be minimized if we determine a maintenance plan for which we define for each maintenance task its own execution time.

Because many preventive maintenance plans may be established, many machines availabilities' plans may exist. Each one has its own impact on the global solution of scheduling the maintenance tasks and the production jobs. Hence, it is recommended to jointly scheduling the maintenance activities and the production jobs in order to optimize the global solution of the problem. In the literature, few researchers were interested in the problem of jointly scheduling jobs and maintenance activities. Lee et al.[9] treated two cases for this problem. In the first case, they considered sufficient maintenance resources. In the second case, the maintenance resources are not sufficient so that just one machine may be maintained at a time. Both cases are shown NP-hard and solved by a branch and bound algorithm based on column generation approach. Results show that the branch and bound algorithm is capable to solve optimally medium sized problems within a reasonable computational time. Graves et al [5] solved the problem of scheduling a set of jobs on a single machine using a dynamic programming approach. The machine should be maintained in certain intervals and when a job is not completely handled before the machine is turned off for maintenance, a set up time is needed before restart the treatment. The authors optimize two criteria: the total weighted jobs completion times and the maximum delay. Aghezzaf et al [1] are interested with the batch production type problem. Random failures may affect the production system and at each maintenance intervention the production system is turned off. In their study, they aim to determine a plan for which the cost of production and maintenance is minimized. The problem was solved using a linear programming approach.

In this study, our objective consists in finding a schedule with the $N$ production jobs and $M$ maintenance tasks for which the sum of the weighted completion times of the production jobs and the preventive maintenance tasks' cost are minimized. The preventive maintenance cost is equal to the total early-tardy cost of the preventive maintenance tasks. The tardy cost corresponds to the damage cost caused by a tardy execution of a preventive maintenance activity. In the same way, the early cost is the consequence of an early execution of a preventive maintenance task. Economically, the early cost corresponds to the part of the equipment that is not efficiently used by advancing the preventive maintenance from its optimistic deadline. The remainder of this paper is organized as follows: A description of the problem and necessary notations are presented in Section 2. In Section 3, we describe the proposed evolutionary algorithm. In Section 4, we describe a lower bound for the problem. In Section 5, computational results will be discussed. Finally we conclude by summarizing the main proposals presented in this paper.

## 2    Problem Description and Notations

The considered problem consists in scheduling a set of $N$ production jobs on $M$ parallel machines. Each machine should be taken once during the planning horizon for a preventive maintenance activity. A production job $i$ is characterized by a processing time $p_i^p$ and a weight $w_i^p$. To each machine $j$ corresponds a preventive maintenance task $j$ having a processing time $p_j^m$, a tardy weight $w_j^m$, an early weight $h_j^m$, an optimistic deadline $d_{j1}$, a pessimistic deadline $d_{j2}$, greater or equal to $d_{j1}$ and a minimal preventive maintenance cost $C_{j0}^m$. The preventive maintenance plan should start at time zero. The running of the preventive maintenance tasks on the machines should be continuous during the planning horizon because there is a lack in maintenance resources. When a preventive maintenance task $j$ is performed between the optimistic deadline $d_{j1}$ and the pessimistic deadline $d_{j2}$, the preventive maintenance cost associated to the task is minimal and it is equal to $C_{j0}^m$. Otherwise, when the preventive maintenance task $j$ is executed before its optimistic deadline $d_{j1}$, the preventive maintenance cost increases. It will be equal to $h_j^m(d_{j1} - t_j) + C_{j0}^m$ where $t_j$ is the starting time of task $j$. Similarly, when the preventive maintenance task $j$ is executed after its pessimistic deadline $d_{j2}$, the preventive maintenance cost increases and will be equal to $w_j^m(t_j - d_{j2}) + C_{j0}^m$. We aim in this paper to provide a schedule composed of the $N$ production jobs and the $M$ preventive maintenance tasks for which the preventive maintenance cost and the total weighted completion times of the $N$ production jobs are minimized.

## 3    The Evolutionary Algorithm

Evolutionary algorithms are probabilistic and heuristic algorithms that can be applied to several combinatorial problems. They can provide good solutions for hard and complex problems in a reasonable time. In this section, we describe the main elements of our evolutionary algorithm: the initial population, the crossover operator, the mutation procedure and the replacement strategy. For more details, the reader is invited to consult Rebai [14].

### 3.1    The Initial Population

The initial population of an evolutionary algorithm is a set of $N_p$ initial solutions for the problem that are called individuals or chromosomes. Each individual or chromosome is represented by a table of size of $M+N$ genes. The first $M$

genes of the chromosome constitute the sequence of the preventive maintenance tasks. The remaining $N$ genes represent the machines on which the $N$ production jobs should be performed. In general, the chromosomes of a population are randomly generated. Sometimes they are determined by specific rules. In our implementation we have generated an initial population of size of $150$ chromosomes $(Np=100)$. Each chromosome is randomly generated. The produced chromosome is translated into a solution for the problem as follows: We first determine the availabilities of the machine by the first $M$ genes of the chromosome. After that, we test if the first production job of the $WSPT$ sequence $(job\ 1)$ may be assigned before the maintenance task of the machine determined by the gene in the rank $M+1$ of the chromosome. If it is possible, we assign it. If it is not possible we assign it on the same machine after the maintenance task. We repeat the procedure until assigning the last production job $N$ of the $WSPT$ sequence.

## 3.2    The Crossover Operation

In the crossover operation, two parents should be selected from the population of the current generation in order to produce at least one child. In our genetic algorithm, two children are generated at each crossover operation. We note that only 90% of the best chromosomes participate in the crossover operation. The principle of parent's selection is as follows: First, the $1^{st}$ parent and the $66^{th}$ parent are selected. After that, the second and the $67^{th}$ parent, etc... until the $65^{th}$ parent and the $134^{th}$ parent . After the selection of each two parents, we randomly generate two integers $k_1$ and $k_2$ respectively from the uniform $[1,\ M]$ and $[M+1,\ M+N]$. The first child noted $C_1$ inherits the subsequence $[1,\dots,k_1]$ of its genes from the first parent. The remaining empty maintenance genes $[k_1+1, \dots, M]$ are determined according to their order of appearance in the first $M$ genes of the second parent. $C_1$ also inherits the subsequence $[M+1,\dots, k_2]$ of its genes from the first parent and its remaining empty production genes $[k_2,\dots,M+N]$ from the second parent. The second child noted $C_2$ inherits the subsequence $[1,\dots,\ k]$ of its genes from the second parent. The remaining empty maintenance genes $[k+1, \dots, M]$ are determined according their order of appearance in the first $M$ genes of the first parent. $C_2$ also inherits the subsequence $[M+1,\dots, k_2]$ of its genes from the second parent and its remaining empty production genes $[k_2,\dots,M+N]$ from the first parent.

## 3.3    The Mutation Operation

The mutation operation is a randomly selection of a set of chromosomes from the population where each chromosome undergo a slight modification. The main purpose of the slight modification is to introduce more diversity to the population. In our algorithm, we apply the mutation on ten individuals randomly chosen from the population. The slight modification consists in permutating two maintenance genes and two production genes randomly selected.

## 3.4  The Replacement Strategy

In a genetic algorithm, the number of new solutions increases from a generation to another. A replacement strategy that consists in replacing the individuals (solutions) in the population with worst fitness by the new children with better evaluations is necessary to avoid the amplification of the population size. In our implementation, we have taken at each generation all the best *150* chromosomes.

# 4  Lower Bound for the Problem

To evaluate the performance of the proposed evolutionary algorithm, we propose a lower bound for the problem. The main principle of the proposed lower bound is to decompose the problem into two sub-problems. The first sub-problem deals with the minimization of the maintenance cost. The second sub-problem deals with the minimization of the sum of weighted completion time of the jobs and the maintenance tasks that should be scheduled on the machines available all the time. Indeed, if we optimally solve the first sub-problem and computing a lower bound for second sub-problem from which we subtract the maximum value of the weighted sum of the maintenance tasks' completion times we can obtain a lower bound for our problem. For more details, the reader is invited to consult Rebai [14].

**Definition 1.** *Let consider $P_1$ the problem of minimizing the sum of weighted early tardy maintenance tasks on a single machine and $S_1$ be the optimal solution of $P_1$.*

**Definition 2.** *Let consider $P_2$ the problem of scheduling $N$ jobs on $M$ parallel machines. Each job $i$ ($i = 1 \ldots N$) has a processing time $p_i^p$ and a weight $w_i^p$ while each machine $j$ is not available during the time period $[T_{j1}T_{j2}]$ for the reason of preventive maintenance.*

**Definition 3.** *Let $P_3$ denotes the problem of scheduling $N+M$ tasks on $M$ parallel machines available all the time. The $N$ tasks correspond to the $N$ production jobs of $P_1$ while the $M$ tasks $(N+1,\ldots,N+M)$ are the maintenance tasks with processing times equal to the unavailability periods of the machines $(p_{N+j}^m = T_{j2} - T_{j1})$ and with weights $w_{N+j}^m$ ($j=1,\ldots,M$) to be determined. Let $W$ be the weights vector of the new $M$ jobs ($W = (w_{N+1}^m, \ldots, w_{N+M}^m)$).*

**Definition 4.** *Let consider $P_4$ the problem of maximizing the sum of weighted completion time of the maintenance tasks on a single machine and $S_2$ be the optimal solution of $P_4$ obtained by applying the WLPT (Weighted Largest Processing Time) rule on the maintenance tasks after computing $W$. We note $C_i^{P_4}$ the completion time of the maintenance task $i$ in the optimal solution of $P_4$. We also note $T_{j2}^{opt}$ the completion time of the maintenance task $j$ in $P$.*

**Lemma 1.** *If $\gamma(P_3(W))$ be a lower bound for the problem $P_3$ ($P_m||\sum w_i C_i$), therefore the following expression is a lower bound for $P$:*

$$LB(W) = \gamma(P_3(W)) - S_2 + S_1$$

## 4.1  Optimal Solution of $P_1 : 1|d_{j1}d_{j2}| \sum h_i E_i + w_i T_i$

To solve optimally $1|d_{j1}d_{j2}| \sum h_i E_i + w_i T_i$ problem, we have used the branch-and-bound algorithm (B&B) proposed by Rebai et al [13]. In the initial phase of this B&B algorithm, the initial solution is determined using an iterated local search algorithm. In the branching phase, two strategies are adopted: the depth first strategy with a backward sequencing and the forward sequencing branching rule. In the bounding phase, two lower bounds are used. The first lower bound is inspired from the lower bound proposed by Li [10]. The second lower bound is computed by the sum of $M$ costs assigned to the $M$ maintenance tasks. The objective of the assignment problem is to minimize the total cost assignment.

## 4.2  Lower Bound for $P_3 : P_m, h_{j1}|| \sum w_i C_i$

Many lower bounds exist in the literature for $P_3$. We will use in this study the lower bound proposed by Eastman et al. [3] that is computed by the following expression: $\gamma(P_3(W)) = \frac{1}{M}(\sum_{i=1}^{N} w_i^p C_i^p(WSPT) + \sum_{j=1}^{M} w_{N+j}^m C_{N+j}^m(WSPT)) + \frac{M-1}{2M}(\sum_{i=1}^{N} w_i^p p_i^p(P_2) + \sum_{j=1}^{M} w_{N+j}^m p_{N+j}^m(P_2))$ where $C_i^p(WSPT)$ is the completion time of the job $j$ in the $WSPT$ sequence and $C_j^m(WSPT)$ is the completion time of the maintenance task $j$ in the same $WSPT$ sequence.

In our implementation, we have used a multiplier adjustment method, introduced in Potts and Van Wassenhove [12], to compute the best value of $W$ allowing a good quality of the lower bound for $P_3$. The procedure is as follows:

We first insert the maintenance tasks between the production jobs in order to determine interesting values for the Lagrangian multipliers vector $W$ which maximize $\gamma(P_3(W))$. According to the lower bound formula, the weights of the maintenance tasks should satisfy for each maintenance task $i$ the conditions of the $WSPT$ order of the sequence composed of the $M + N$ tasks. In other words, the ratio $\frac{p_i^m}{w_i^m}$ of a maintenance tasks $i$ should not exceed the ratio $\frac{p_k^p}{w_k^p}$ of the first job $k$ after the maintenance task $i$ and should not be less than the ratio $\frac{p_{k'}^p}{w_{k'}^p}$ of the first job that precedes the maintenance task $i$.

By these restrictions, we can define the Dual Lagrangian problem as follows:

$$MaxZ = \frac{1}{M} \sum_{i=1}^{M} w_i^m C_j^m(WSPT) + \frac{M-1}{2M} \sum_{i=1}^{M} w_i^m p_j^m$$

*Subject to*

$$w_i^m \geq \frac{p_i^m w_k^p}{p_k^p} \qquad \forall i = 1 \dots M \qquad (1)$$

$$w_i^m \leq \frac{p_i^m w_{k'}^p}{p_{k'}^p} \qquad \forall i = 1 \dots M \qquad (2)$$

$$w_i^m \geq 0 \qquad \forall i = 1 \dots M \qquad (3)$$

$C_i^m$ corresponds to the completion time of the maintenance task $i$ in the $WSPT$ sequence. By solve optimally this model, we can obtain the Lagrangian multipliers vector $W$. After that, we compute the $\gamma(P_3(W))$ value from which we subtract $\sum_{j=1}^{M} w_j^m C_j^{P_4}$ and we add to it the optimal solution of $P_1$ in order to obtain the lower bound value of our problem.

# 5   Computational Results

Our evolutionary algorithm is tested on many instances. Each one is generated as follows: we first identify the number of production jobs $N$ $\in \{100, 200, 300, 400, 500\}$ and the number of machines $M \in \{5, 10, 15\}$ that corresponds to the number of maintenance tasks. For each production job $i$, we generate its processing time $p_i^p$ from a uniform distribution $[1,\ldots,50]$ and its weight $w_i^p$ from a uniform distribution $[1,\ldots,10]$. For each maintenance task $j$, we determine, according the range factor $R$ and the tardiness factor $T$, the optimistic deadlines $d_{i1}$ from the uniform distribution $[d_{min},\ldots,d_{min}$ $+ P_{mean}]$, where $d_{min} = max\{0, x(T - \frac{R}{2})\}$ and $P_{mean}^m = \frac{\sum_{i=1}^{M} p_i^m}{M}$, the pessimistic deadlines $d_{i2}$ from the uniform distribution $[d_{i1},\ldots,d_{i1} + P_{mean}]$ and the processing time from $[0.5P_{mean}^p,\ldots,2P_{mean}^p]$ where $P_{mean}^p$ corresponds to the mean of the job's processing times. The tardiness and the earliness penalties $w_j^m$ and $h_j^m$ of the maintenance tasks are tested on two intervals: In a first time, they are generated from the uniform distribution low of $[1,\ldots,10]$ interval. In a second time, they are generated from $[1,\ldots,30]$ interval. We note that the tardy factor $T \in \{0.2, 0.4, 0.6, 0.8\}$ and the range factor $R \in \{0.1, 0.2, 0.3, 0.4, 0.5, 0.6, 0.7, 0.8\}$. 5 instances have been generated for each combination of $N$, $M$, $T$ and $R$. The algorithms were coded in the $C$ language and implemented on a Pentium IV-500 personal computer using concert technology technique with Cplex 10.1 to solve the Dual Lagrangian model of the proposed lower bound.

## 5.1   Computational Results When $w_j^m, h_j^m \in [1,\ldots,10]$

The first column of table 1 represents the production job number $N$. The second, the third and the fourth columns represents the mean percentage gap value

**Table 1.** (%)Mean gaps value between the evolutionary algorithm solution and the lower bound

| N /M | 5 | 10 | 15 |
|------|------|-------|-------|
| 100 | 5,21 | 12,51 | 21,14 |
| 200 | 3,33 | 5,45 | 10,12 |
| 300 | 2,55 | 4,2 | 6,05 |
| 400 | 2,02 | 3,02 | 4,8 |
| 500 | 1,72 | 1,96 | 3,99 |

between the evolutionary algorithm solution and the lower bound respectively for M = 5, M = 10 and M = 15. According to this table, we observe that the mean gap value between the evolutionary algorithm and the lower bound is globally acceptable. It seems relatively important for the instances of size of 100. The weakness of the lower bound value for these instances may be the main cause of the increase of the gap. Indeed, we look from the table that when the number of production jobs increases, the mean percentage gap value between the evolutionary algorithm solution and the lower bound decreases. The second remark from the same table is that the mean percentage gap value between the evolutionary algorithm solution and the lower bound increases when the number of machines increases. However it remains well acceptable.

**Table 2.** Computational time in average

| N /M | 5 | 10 | 15 |
|------|------|------|------|
| 100 | 0,82 (s) | 1,56 (s) | 2,97 (s) |
| 200 | 1,69 (s) | 3,89 (s) | 5,31 (s) |
| 300 | 3,38 (s) | 5,84 (s) | 8,19 (s) |
| 400 | 4,25 (s) | 7,82 (s) | 10,61 (s) |
| 500 | 5,32 (s) | 9,33 (s) | 13,25 (s) |

The first column of Table 1 represents the production job number $N$. The second, the third and the fourth columns represent the average of time spent to obtain a solution by the evolutionary algorithm respectively for M = 5, M = 10 and M = 15. According to Table 2, we observe that for all generated instances, the mean computational time is not important relatively to the size of instances and to the problem complexity. Hence, we can confirm that the proposed genetic algorithm is efficient in terms of solution quality and computational time.

## 5.2   Computational Results When $w_j^m, h_j^m \in [1, \ldots, 30]$

The following two tables represent respectively the average mean spent computational time to obtain a solution by the evolutionary algorithm and the mean percentage gaps value between the evolutionary algorithm solution and the lower bound.

**Table 3.** Computational time in average

| N /M | 5 | 10 | 15 |
|------|------|------|------|
| 100 | 0,58(s) | 1,56(s) | 3,07(s) |
| 200 | 1,7(s) | 4(s) | 5,61(s) |
| 300 | 3,47(s) | 5,88(s) | 8,57(s) |
| 400 | 4,3(s) | 7,46(s) | 10,58(s) |
| 500 | 5,42(s) | 9,17(s) | 14,06(s) |

**Table 4.** (%)Mean gaps value between the evolutionary algorithm solution and the lower bound

| N /M | 5 | 10 | 15 |
|------|------|-------|-------|
| 100 | 6,84 | 13,87 | 35,16 |
| 200 | 3,29 | 9,46 | 16,7 |
| 300 | 1,99 | 5,94 | 10,58 |
| 400 | 1,82 | 3,62 | 7,92 |
| 500 | 1,29 | 3,91 | 5,97 |

By comparing tables 2 and 3, we can observe that the change of the penalties interval doses not affect the computational time for obtaining a solution. However, we observe a slight increase in terms of average mean gap value between the evolutionary algorithm and the lower bound.

# 6    Conclusion

In this paper we have proposed an evolutionary algorithm for the problem of scheduling $N$ production jobs on $M$ parallel machines where each machine should be maintained once during the planning horizon. We have simultaneously minimized the total sum of the production job's weighted completion times and the preventive maintenance cost. Computational results show that the evolutionary algorithm produce excellent solutions for the problem in terms of the computational time and the gap value between the evolutionary algorithm solution and the lower bound.

Other comparisons and experimental results are available in Rebai [14].

**Acknowledgements.** This work has been funded by the Champagne Ardenne Regional Council (France).

# References

1. Aghezzaf, E.H., Jamali, M.A., Ait-Kadi, D.: An integrated production and preventive maintenance planning model. European Journal of Operational Research 181, 679–685 (2007)
2. Aghezzaf, E.H., Najid, N.M.: Integrated production planning and preventive maintenance in deteriorating production systems. Information Sciences 178, 3382–3392 (2008)
3. Eastman, W.L., Even, S., Isaacs, I.M.: Bounds for optimal scheduling of n jobs on m processors. Management science 11, 268–279 (1964)
4. Mellouli, R., Cherif, S., Chou, C., Kacem, I.: Identical parallel-machine scheduling under availability constraints to minimize the sum of completion times. European Journal of Operational Research 197, 1150–1167 (2009)
5. Graves, H.G., Lee, C.-Y.: Scheduling Maintenance and Semiresumable Jobs on a Single Machine. Naval Research Logistics 46, 845–863 (1999)

6. Kacem, I., Chu, C., Souissi, A.: Single-machine scheduling with an availability constraint to minimize the weighted sum of the completion times. Computers & Operations Research 35, 827–844 (2008)

7. Kubiak, W., Blazewicz, J., Formanowicz, P., Breit, J., Schmidt, G.: Two-machine flow shops with limited machine availability. European Journal of Operational Research 136, 528–540 (2002)

8. Lee, C.-Y.: Minimising the makespan in the two machine scheduling scheduling problem with an availability constraint. Operational Research Letters 20, 129–139 (2000)

9. Lee, C.-Y., Chen, Z.-L.: Scheduling Jobs and Maintenance Activities on Parallel Machines. Naval Research Logistics 47, 145–165 (2000)

10. Li, G.: Single machine earliness and tardiness scheduling. European Journal of Operational Research 26, 546–558 (1997)

11. Liaw, C.-F.: A branch and bound algorithm for the single machine earliness and tardiness scheduling problem. Computers & Operations Research 26, 679–693 (1999)

12. Potts, C.N., van Wassenhove, L.N.: A Branch and Bound Algorithm for the Total Weighted Tardiness Problem. Operations Research 33(2), 363–377 (1985)

13. Rebai, M., Kacem, I., Adjallah, K.H.: Earliness tardiness minimization on a single machine to schedule preventive maintenance tasks: metaheuristic and exact methods. Journal of Intelligent Manufacturing (2010), doi:10.1007/s10845-010-0425-0

14. Rebai, M.: Ordonnancement des taches de production et de maintenance preventive sur machines paralleles. PhD Thesis of Troyes University of Technology 2011, Troyes, France July 1 (2011)

15. Sourd, F., Keded-Sidhoum, S., Rio Solis, Y.: Lower bounds for the earliness-tardiness scheduling problem on parallel machines with distinct due dates. European Journal of Operational Research 189, 1305–1319 (2008)

16. Smith, W.E.: Various optimizers for single-stage production. Naval Research Logistics Quarterly 3, 59–66 (1956)

# On the Modeling of Logistic Decisions Impacts on Product Greenness: Sensitivity Analysis

Imen Nouira[1,2], Yannick Frein[1], and Atidel B. Hadj-Alouane[2]

[1] Grenoble-INP / UJF-Grenoble 1 / CNRS, G-SCOP UMR5272 Grenoble, F-38031, France
yannick.frein@g-scop.inpg.fr, imen.nouira@g-scop.inpg.fr
[2] Laboratoire OASIS, ENI Tunis BP 37, LE BELVEDERE 1002 Tunis
atidel.hadj@enit.rnu.tn

**Abstract.** In this paper we present a mathematical model that illustrates the impact of supply chain activities on the environmental quality of manufactured products while maximizing the profits of the company under a set of constraints such as those related to the environmental legislation. We present the application of the model to a textile example and we focus on the sensitivity analysis.

**Keywords:** environmental quality, market segmentation, environmental constraints, mixed linear program.

## 1 Introduction

During the last two decades, industrial markets have changed due to several reasons. Globalization leads to opened markets providing more choice to customers. Nowadays, customers are now able to compare prices, and more importantly, they require finding products that meet their different needs (Xu *et al.*, 2007)). Customer requirements and evaluation criteria are constantly changing. Obviously, the quality and the price are major elements in choosing a product but a new value which is the product greenness becomes one of the main criteria that guide customers in their purchases. Green product development, which addresses environmental issues, is receiving significant attention from consumers. With the emergence of green issues, the market is being divided into two segments: ordinary customers and green customers (Chen, 2001). Ordinary customers purchase any kind of products, i.e. regardless of their greenness level. However, green customers only purchase products with a certain greenness level. Thus, the demand of a product depends on its greenness level. The same observation can be made for the selling price. Generally, the greener is the product the higher is its price. Firms must jointly address both the ordinary and green segments. Green product development is also stimulated by various forms of environmental standards imposed by governments around the world, which have become increasingly more stringent in the past thirty years.

There are many works that consider the environmental regulations in the management of supply chains. The literature is also abundant with eco-design works. But few studies simultaneously address supply chain optimization and product development

F. Daniel et al. (Eds.): BPM 2011 Workshops, Part II, LNBIP 100, pp. 162–176, 2012.
© Springer-Verlag Berlin Heidelberg 2012

issues under environmental constraints. In the present work, we propose to analyze this problem through mathematical optimization. The mathematical model, described below, as well as some preliminary results, will be presented in the International Congress of Industrial engineering (CIGI 2011). In this paper, we focus on the model's sensitivity analysis.

The remainder of this paper is organized as follows: in the first section we present the studied problem and the proposed mathematical model. Section 2 is devoted to the model's sensitivity analysis, and we finish the paper we some concluding remarks.

## 2    Problem Definition

We assume that a final product can be produced using more than one operating procedure (Letmathe and Balakrishnan, 2005); each procedure may consume a different amount of resources, and results in different production yields and emission outputs. Based on the emission outputs of the operating procedures, different varieties of one final product with different greenness levels can be produced.

We consider that a product is characterized by two attributes: traditional and environmental. The environmental attribute of a product is represented by the amount of different emissions created from its production process and the rate of green components used in terms of the total composition. The company needs to find the optimal combination of environmental and traditional attributes in order to maximize the firm's profit and satisfy the customers. Consumers may have heterogeneous preferences over these attributes. Our model allows for defining two varieties of a final product. One variety is offered to traditional customers and a green variety for the green customers.

From the legislation side, we consider three different types of policies.

- Flexible policies: legislations based on the 'Polluter-pays principle'. Where the polluter should bear penalties and taxes that are based on the output amount, and/or emission allowances that can be traded between firms. These legislations provide a firm with flexibility.
- Strict policies: thresholds values (upper limits) that can't be violated.
- Another type of regulations that impose recycling/remanufacturing rates.

Our model mainly incorporates the following issues:

- Among different potential operating procedures, one must be chosen for each variety (green or traditional) of the finished product.
- Each operating procedure is characterized by a given rate of emissions.
- The emissions amount (of the used operating procedure) and the rate of the green used components are used to characterize the product variety (green or traditional).
- The product greenness is represented by two attributes: the first is related, as we noted earlier, to emissions and the second one is related to the rate of green components used compared to the total composition of the product. The two attributes are scaled to 1. The total greenness of a product is the sum

of the two attributes (so the total greenness is scaled to 2). If the product greenness is equal to 0, this corresponds to the lowest greenness level. In this case the product doesn't contain green components and the used procedure is the most polluting among the potential ones. The higher is the greenness level the more ecological is the product.

-       The market is shared between green and ordinary customers. Customers in the green segment purchase products with a certain greenness level. They express a higher willingness-to-pay a green premium on an ecological product (Mahenc, 2008; Chen, 2001). Ordinary customers are only interested in the product price.

-       In order to increase its profit, the company should offer a product for each market segment.

-       Emission thresholds that cannot be exceeded on some emissions.

-       Taxes (penalties) based on the amount of output on some emissions.

-       Trading of output allowances for some emissions, with differences in transaction costs for purchasing and selling these allowances

## 3       Mathematical Formulation

### 3.1     Parameters

$F$: number of operating procedures

$M$: total number of emissions

$N$: number of emissions subject to emission taxes and/or threshold values ($N \leq M$),

$R$: total number of components required per a final product

$\mu_r$: represents the importance of the component $r$ in terms of its environmental impact. The sum $\sum_{r=1}^{R} \mu_r$ is equal to 1. For example if the greenness of a final product depends on the amount of green component compared to the total composition of the product, then $\mu_r$ represents the ratio: number of required component $r$ / total number of required components. If the greenness of a final product is highly related to one component which has a dangerous impact on environment (such as mercury in batteries), then $\mu_r$ will be more important for this component ($\sim 1$) than for others. For some final products, $\mu_r$ may represent the weight percentage, etc.

$Q_{m:}$ unit penalty for emission m (m=1, . . ., N),

$Q^{+}_{m:}$ unit purchase price for traded emission m (m=N+1, . . .,M),

$Q^{-}_{m:}$ unit selling price ($Q^{-}_{m} \leq Q^{+}_{m}$) for traded emission m (m=N+1, . . .,M),

$E^{T}_{m}$ : allowance units for traded emission m (m=N+1, . . .,M),

$E_{m:}$ maximum allowed of emission m (for relevant m, m=1, . . .,N) (overall emission limit),

$\varepsilon_{mf}$: amount of emission m (m=1, . . .,M) per unit of product produced using operating procedure f (f=1, . . .,F),

$\varepsilon_{max}$: maximum amount of emission per unit of product produced using the most polluant operating procedure,

$C_f$: unit production cost using the operating procedure f,

$k_f$: fixed cost of operating procedure f. This cost may include the purchasing machine cost, the training costs, etc.,

$P_r^T$ : unit purchase price for traditional component r

$P_r^G$: unit purchase price for green component r

$\delta_r$ : amount of component r required per a unit of final product (according to the bill of materials)

$S_1$: unit selling price of product if its greenness belongs to the interval $[0,\alpha_1]$

$S_2$: unit selling price of product if its greenness belongs to the interval $[\alpha_1,\alpha_2]$

$S_3$ : unit selling price of product if its greenness belongs to the interval $[\alpha_2, 2]$

$D^O_1$: demand of ordinary segment if the product greenness belongs to the interval $[0,\alpha_1]$

$D^O_2$: demand of ordinary segment if the product greenness belongs to the interval $[\alpha_1,\alpha_2]$

$D^O_3$: demand of ordinary segment if the product greenness belongs to the interval $[\alpha_2, 2]$

$D^g_1$: demand of green segment if the product greenness belongs to the interval $[0,\alpha_1]$

$D^g_2$: demand of green segment if the product greenness belongs to the interval $[\alpha_1, \alpha_2 ]$

$D^g_3$: demand of green segment if the product greenness belongs to the interval $[\alpha_2, 2]$.

Depending on the product greenness, we can deduce the price of ordinary product ($S^O$ ) and the price of green product ($S^g$). These prices can be equal to $S_1$, $S_2$ or $S_3$.

Depending on the product greenness, we can also deduce the ordinary and green demand (respectively $D^O$ and $D^g$).

## 3.2    Decision Variables

$z_f^g$: 1 if operating procedure f (f=1, . . . .,F) is used to produce green product, 0 otherwise.

$z_f^o$: 1 if operating procedure f (f=1, . . . .,F) is used to produce ordinary product, 0 otherwise.

$x_f^o$ : production quantity of ordinary product using operating procedure f (f=1, . . .,F),

$x_f^g$ : production quantity of green product using operating procedure f (f=1, . . . .,F),

$v_r^o$ : 1 if the component r (r=1, . . . .,R) used for ordinary product is green, 0 if it is traditional.

$v_r^g$: 1 if the component r (r=1, . . . .,R) used for green product is green, 0 if it is traditional.

The model determines mainly the operating procedures used (through binary variables $z_f^g$ and $z_f^o$), the nature of used component (green or ordinary) through binary variables ($v_r^o$ and $v_r^g$) and produced quantities ($x^o$ and $x^g$).

Depending on the values of variables $z_f^g$, $z_f^o$, $v_r^o$ and $v_r^g$ we can determine the greenness of products offered for green and ordinary market ($a^o$, $a^g$, $b^g$, $b^o$). The value of the following variables can also be determined

1. $a^o$: rate of green components compared to the total composition of the ordinary product (greenness attribute related to the product composition)
2. $a^g$ : rate of green components compared to the total composition of the green product (greenness attribute related to the product composition)

$b^g$: total amount of emission per unit of a green product (greenness attribute related to the emission of operating procedure used for green product)

$b^o$: total amount of emission per unit of an ordinary product (greenness attribute related to the emission of operating procedure used for ordinary product)

$e_m$: amount of emission $m$ ($m=1, \ldots, M$),

$e_m^+$: allowance units purchased for emission $m$ ($m=N+1, \ldots, M$),

$e_m^-$: allowance units sold for emission $m$ ($m = N +1 \ldots M$),

$\theta_r^o$ : total amount of « traditional » component $r$ ($r = 1 \ldots R$) required for ordinary products ($\theta_r^o = \sum_{f=1}^{F} x_f^o (1 - v_r^o) \delta_r$)

$\theta_r^g$ : total amount of « traditional » component $r$ ($r = 1 \ldots R$) required for green products ($\theta_r^g = \sum_{f=1}^{F} x_f^g (1 - v_r^g) \delta_r$)

$\beta_r^o$ : total amount of « green » component $r$ ($r = 1 \ldots R$) required for ordinary products ($\beta_r^o = \sum_{f=1}^{F} x_f^o v_r^o \delta_r$)

$\beta_r^g$ : total amount of « green » component $r$ ($r = 1 \ldots R$) required for green ucts ($\beta_r^g = \sum_{f=1}^{F} x_f^g v_r^g \delta_r$)

$\sigma_f := 1$ if operating procedure $f$ ($f=1, \ldots, F$) is chosen; 0 otherwise.

### 3.3    Objective Function

The objective is to maximize profit, which is calculated as the total revenue obtained by product sales and the sale of tradable emission allowances, less the total cost (of components purchase, fixed costs of operating procedures, production costs, etc.), emission penalties that are payable, and purchase cost of tradable emission allowances. This may be expressed as follows:

$$
\text{Max } \left( S^g \sum_{f=1}^{F} x_f^g + S^o \sum_{f=1}^{F} x_f^o - \sum_{f=1}^{F} C_f(x_f^o + x_f^g) - \sum_{r=1}^{R} (\theta_r^o P_r^T + \beta_r^o P_r^G) - \sum_{r=1}^{R} (\theta_r^g P_r^T \right.
$$

$$
+ \beta_r^g P_r^G) - \sum_{f=1}^{F} k_f \sigma_f - \sum_{m=1}^{N} Q_m e_m + \sum_{m=N+1}^{M} Q_m^- e_m^-
$$

$$
\left. - \sum_{m=N+1}^{M} Q_m^+ e_m^+ \right)
$$

We consider that a variety of final product (green/ordinary) must be produced only by one operating procedure (constraints (1) and (2)). This means that the total amount of final product offered to green market must be produced by the same operating procedure (same for the ordinary products).

$$\sum_{f=1}^{F} z_f^o = 1 \tag{1}$$

$$\sum_{f=1}^{F} z_f^g = 1 \tag{2}$$

Next, we identify the total amount of each emission resulting from the production of all products.

$$e_m = \left( \sum_{f=1}^{F} \varepsilon_{mf} (x_f^g + x_f^o) \right) \quad \text{for relevant m} \tag{3}$$

The threshold may be an upper bound on the total quantity of an emission. It may often be defined as the average emission per time unit, e.g., per week, month, or year. The constraint may be expressed as follows:

$$e_m \leq E_m \qquad \text{for m = 1...N} \tag{4}$$

As noted earlier, some of the emissions may have output allowances (usually allocated by the environmental regulatory authority of the country in which the firm operates) that can be traded with other firms. As mentioned in the introductory statement, members of the EU have committed to establish a scheme for greenhouse gas emission allowance trading within the community (Council Directive 96/61/EC). Emission trading in the EU has started since 2005 with the trading of carbon dioxide.

Purchase costs will typically be higher than selling prices due to differences in transaction costs for selling and purchasing these allowances. We therefore use two variables $e_m^-$ and $e_m^+$, to represent the amount of emission allowances sold and purchased, respectively.

$$e_m + e_m^- - e_m^+ = E_m^T \qquad \text{for m = N+1...M} \tag{5}$$

As noted earlier, the product greenness of each variety may be expressed with two attributes: the total emission amount of operating procedure (per a unit final product) and the amount of green components used (per a unit final product).

The following constraints express the greenness attributes of ordinary product ($a^o$ related to the amount of green components and $b^o$ related to amount of emissions) and the greenness attributes of green product ( $a^g$ and $b^g$).

$$a^o = \sum_{r=1}^{R} v_r^o \mu_r \tag{6}$$

$$b^o = \frac{\varepsilon_{max} - \varepsilon_o}{\varepsilon_{max}} \qquad \varepsilon_o = \sum_{f=1}^{F} \sum_{m=1}^{M} \varepsilon_{mf} z_f^o \tag{7}$$

$$a^g = \sum_{r=1}^{R} v_r^g \mu_r \tag{8}$$

$$b^g = \frac{\varepsilon_{max} - \varepsilon_g}{\varepsilon_{max}} \qquad \varepsilon_g = \sum_{f=1}^{F} \sum_{m=1}^{M} \varepsilon_{mf} z_f^g \tag{9}$$

As we noted earlier, the greenness of a product impacts its price and its demand. In our model we suppose that if the greenness of ordinary product is in the interval [0, $\alpha_1$[, its selling price is not high and the demand of ordinary market is maximum. This product is not interesting for green customers because of the weakness of its greenness level (the green demand for this product is null:$D_1^g = 0$).

If the greenness is in the interval [$\alpha_2$, $_2$], the product offers a high environmental quality. Giving its high selling price this product is offered only for green market ($D_3^o = 0$).

The following constraints (10), (11), (12) and (13) are logical constraints which express the relationship between greenness, selling price and demand. These constraints must be linearized.

$$\text{If} \quad 0 \leq (a^o + b^o) < \alpha_1 \quad \text{then} \quad D^o = D_1^o \quad \text{and} \quad S^o = S_1 \tag{10}$$

$$\text{If} \quad \alpha_1 \leq (a^o + b^o) < \alpha_2 \quad \text{then} \quad D^o = D_2^o \quad \text{and} \quad S^o = S_2 \tag{11}$$

$$\text{If} \, \alpha_1 \leq (a^g + b^g) < \alpha_2 \, \text{then} \, D^g = D_2^g \, \text{and} \, S^g = S^o = S_2 \tag{12}$$

$$\text{If} \quad \alpha_2 \leq (a^g + b^g) \leq 2 \quad \text{then} \quad D^g = D_3^g \quad \text{and} \quad S^g = S_3 \tag{13}$$

The company must decide which variety to offer for each market segment.

Once the demand for each product has been expressed, the production of that product is limited by its demand.

$$\sum_{f=1}^{F} x_f^g \leq D^g \tag{14}$$

$$\sum_{f=1}^{F} x_f^o \leq D^o \tag{15}$$

All the following constraints concern the relationship between continuous and binary variables.

$$\frac{1}{M} z_f^g \leq x_f^g \leq M z_f^g \qquad \text{(M is a sufficiently large constant)}$$
$$\frac{1}{M} z_f^o \leq x_f^o \leq M z_f^o$$
$$\theta_r^o \leq M(1 - v_r^o)$$
$$\sum_{f=1}^{F} x_f^o \delta_r - v_r^o M \leq \theta_r^o \leq \sum_{f=1}^{F} x_f^o \delta_r$$
$$\theta_r^g \leq M(1 - v_r^g)$$
$$\sum_{f=1}^{F} x_f^g \delta_r - v_r^g M \leq \theta_r^g \leq \sum_{f=1}^{F} x_f^g \delta_r$$
$$\beta_r^o \leq M v_r^o$$
$$\sum_{f=1}^{F} x_f^o \delta_r - (1 - v_r^o)M \leq \beta_r^o \leq \sum_{f=1}^{F} x_f^o \delta_r$$
$$\beta_r^g \leq M v_r^g$$
$$\sum_{f=1}^{F} x_f^g \delta_r - (1 - v_r^g)M \leq \beta_r^g \leq \sum_{f=1}^{F} x_f^g \delta_r$$
$$z_f^o \leq \sigma_f \leq z_f^o + z_f^g$$
$$z_f^g \leq \sigma_f$$

Finally, we have the non-negativity constraints, represented as

$$e_m, e_m^-, e_m^+, \quad a^o, b^o, a^g, b^o, x_f^g, x_f^o \geq 0$$
$$z_f^o, z_f^g \in \{0, 1\}$$
$$\sigma_f \in \{0, 1\}$$
$$v_r^o, v_r^g \in \{0, 1\}$$

Next we present the equations related to the linearization of the model.

$\rho^o$ et $\omega^o$ two binary variables
$$D^o = \rho^o D_1^o + \omega^o D_2^o$$
$$S^o = \rho^o S_1^o + \omega^o S$$
$$\frac{1}{M}\rho^o - M\omega^o \leq \alpha_1 - (a^o + b^o)$$
$$\frac{1}{M}\omega^o - M\rho^o \leq (a^o + b^o) - \alpha_1$$
$$\rho^o + \omega^o = 1$$

$\rho^g$ et $\omega^g$ two binary variables
$$D^g = \rho^g D_2^g + \omega^g D_3^g$$
$$S^g = \rho^g S + \omega^g S_1^g$$
$$\frac{1}{M}\rho^g - M\omega^g \leq \alpha_2 - (a^g + b^g)$$
$$\frac{1}{M}\omega^g - M\rho^g \leq (a^g + b^g) - \alpha_2$$
$$\rho^g + \omega^g = 1$$

# 4    Model Application

In this section, we discuss a numerical example from the textile sector to illustrate our model. The textile industry uses vast amounts of water, energy and chemicals. Dyes and auxiliary chemicals used in textile mills have hard environmental influences. Textile processing generates many waste streams, including water-based effluent as well as air emissions, solid wastes, and hazardous wastes. Textile manufacturing is one of the largest producers of wastewater. It is also a chemically intensive industry and therefore the wastewater from textile processing contains processing bath residues from preparation, dyeing, finishing, slashing and other operations. These residues can cause damage to the environment.

Governments have begun to target the textile industry to clean up the wastewater that is being discharged from the textile mills and to apply operating procedures that prevent pollution. In this sector, we can distinguish between classical operating procedures which usually generate a higher level of pollution and sustainable (ecological, clean or green) procedures that generate a lower level of pollution. Some of the well known sustainable procedures that are applied in the textile industry are those based on enzymes and membranes.

In our example, we consider four potential operating procedures represented in table 1. As we noted earlier, each procedure is characterized by emission amount. We conduct a sensitivity analysis which first focuses on the impact of emission threshold values (maximum allowable levels) then on the impact of trading transaction costs (price of buying/selling allowances).

## 4.1    Data

Parameters are extracted from the literature (Radulescu *et al.*, 2009) which is based on real-world data from the textile sector in Spain. Some parameters and emission levels are inspired from public web sites. We present here the most significant data. For more details the reader is referred to (Radulescu *et al.*, 2009).

The following table presents four potential operating procedure and resume the emission amount yielded by each procedure ($\varepsilon_{mf}$ : amount of emission $m$ per unit of product produced using operating procedure $f$).

**Table 1.** Emission outputs of potential operating procedures

| Pollutants<br><br>Procedures | CCO–Cr | CBO5 | Biodegradable detergent |
|---|---|---|---|
| Procedure 1 | 2.0 | 1.3 | 0.11 |
| Procedure 2 | 1.6 | 1.1 | 0.11 |
| Procedure 3 | 1.0 | 0.6 | 0.09 |
| Procedure 4 | 0.4 | 0.3 | 0.1 |
| Max allowable level for each Pollutants | 500 | 350 | 25 |

The last operating procedure (Procedure 4) is considered as the most clean in textile sector. This procedure is based on enzymes and membranes. Procedure 4 is based on classical technologies and is the most pollutant of the potential procedures.

The last row of Table 1 presents the maximum allowable emission levels for the considered pollutants ($E_m$).

**Table 2.** Other data

| | |
|---|---|
| Selling prices S1, S2, S3 | 120, 130, 150 |
| Ordinary market demand $D^O_1, D^O_2, D^O_3$ | 200, 170, 0 |
| Green market demand $D^g_1, D^g_2, D^g_3$ | 0, 100, 150 |
| $\alpha_1, \alpha_2$ | 0.5,  1 |

## 4.2    Impact of Threshold Values (Maximum Emission Allowable Levels)

In this section we try to evaluate the impact of the threshold value (of the first emission type E1: CCO–Cr) on:

- The product greenness (products offered to ordinary and green market).
- The total amount of emissions yielded by the production activity (E1+E2+E3).

From the results shown on Table 3, we can observe the following:

- If the threshold value is between 2300 and 3500, the company decides to use the most ecological operating procedure (F4) for the product offered to the green market. Hence, this product has a high greenness level ($a^g+b^g=1.1$). To satisfy the ordinary market, a product with a lower greenness level is produced using the procedure F3.

  Reducing the threshold for emission 1 (see $2^{nd}$ & $3^{rd}$ rows: from 2200 to 1100) impacts positively the greenness of the product offered to the ordinary market. In fact, in order to reduce the total emission amount and to comply with emission regulations, the company has to enhance the operating procedure used to produce the product offered to ordinary customers. In this case

**Table 3.** Impact of emission threshold value

| Threshold value for emission E1 | Total emission amount | Greenness of the product offered to green market | Greenness of the product offered to ordinary market | Operating procedure chosen for ordinary market | Operating procedure chosen for green market |
|---|---|---|---|---|---|
| 3500 – 2300 With step = 200 | 4075 | $a^o=0$ $b^o=0.501466$ | $a^g=0.34$ $b^g=0.768328$ | F3 | F4 |
| 2200 – 1200 With step = 200 | 2528 | $a^o=0$ $b^o=0.768328$ | $a^g=0.34$ $b^g=0.768328$ | F4 | F4 |
| 1100 | 2172.5 | $a^o=0$ $b^o=0.768328$ | $a^g=0.34$ $b^g=0.768328$ | F4 | F4 |
| 1000 | 1975 | $a^o=0$ $b^o=0.768328$ | $a^g=0$ $b^g=0.768328$ | F4 | F4 |
| 800 | 1580 | $a^o=0$ $b^o=0.768328$ | $a^g=0$ $b^g=0.768328$ | F4 | F4 |
| 600 | 1185 | $a^o=0$ $b^o=0.768328$ | No product for green market | F4 | No product for green market |
| 500 | 975 | $a^o=0$ $b^o=0.768328$ | No product for green market | F4 | No product for green market |
| 400 | 790 | $a^o=0$ $b^o=0.768328$ | No product for green market | F4 | No product for green market |
| 300 | 650 | $a^o=0$ $b^o=0.768328$ | No product for green market | F4 | No product for green market |
| 200 | 345 | $a^o=0$ $b^o=0.768328$ | No product for green market | F4 | No product for green market |
| 100 | 197.5 | $a^o=0$ $b^o=0.768328$ | No product for green market | F4 | No product for green market |

the tightening of the emission threshold implies the enhancement of the greenness of the ordinary product. But in other cases, we can observe that tightening environmental threshold can cause the decrease of the product greenness level. In fact when threshold level is less than 1100 (see rows 4 and 5 of Table 3) the greenness level of the green product decreases. Finally when the threshold value is less than 600, the company can no more satisfy the two market segments. It is no longer possible to offer a product for green customers.

- In this example, reducing the threshold for emission E1 causes the total emission amount to decrease.

From this example, it seems that tightening the emission threshold leads to a decrease in total emission. In some cases the consequence would be the enhancement of product greenness. But very strict threshold levels may cause the deterioration of the product greenness.

### 4.3    Impact of Allowance Trading Cost (Maximum Emission Allowable Levels)

As noted earlier, some of the emissions may have output allowances (usually allocated by the environmental regulatory authority of the country in which the firm operates) that can be traded with other firms. In this section, we focus on the impact of the allowance purchasing costs of the emissions E3 on:

- The product greenness
- The total amount of emissions yield by the production activity (E1+E2+E3).

The results of this sensitivity analysis are shown in Figures 1 and 2, where Figure 1 illustrates the greenness of products offered to the green and ordinary markets, and Figure 2 shows the total amount of emissions, each as function of allowances purchasing cost. From these results, we observe the following:

- From Figure 2, we observe that increasing the allowances purchasing costs causes the decrease of amount of purchased allowances and the increase of total emissions. This result seems to be counter-intuitive. In fact, one can expect that the increase of the allowances purchasing, and hence the decrease in the amount of pollutants allowances should result in a decrease in total emission.

  In fact when allowance purchasing cost is less than 40 euros, the most ecological procedure (F4) is used to produce green product. But this operating procedure F4which has the less total emission amount (E1+E2+E3) yield more amount of emission E3 compared with the procedure F2. The increasing of the allowance purchasing cost of emission E3 allowance, make the company choose the procedure F3. In this case the company pollutes more and pays more penalties for emissions E1 and E2 in order to avoid the high cost of allowances purchasing.

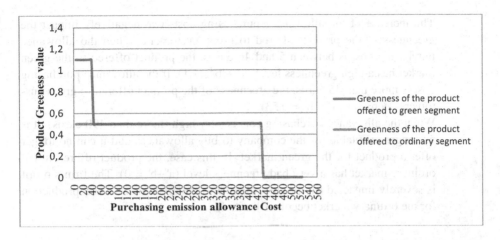

**Fig. 1.** Greenness as a function of allowance purchasing price

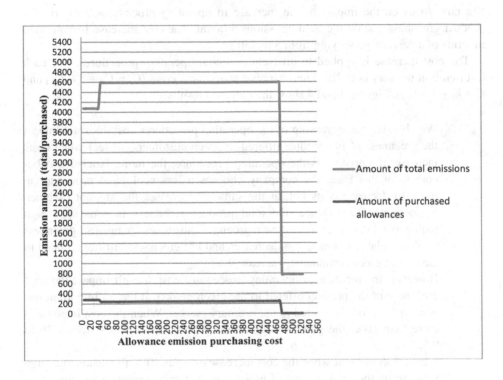

**Fig. 2.** Emissions amount as a function of allowances purchasing cost

- The increase of the allowances purchasing costs can negatively impact the greenness of the product offered to green customers. When the allowance purchasing cost is between 5 and 46 euros, the product offered to the green market has a high greenness level ($a^g + b^g =1.1$). If the allowance purchasing cost is more than 45 euros, the greenness of the product offered to green customers decreases ($a^g + b^g = 0.53$).
- When the allowance purchasing cots is very high (more than 490 euros), it is no longer profitable for the company to buy allowances and it can no longer offer a product for the green market. In this case, the product offered to the ordinary market has a very bad greenness level ($a^o+b^o = 0$). The firm's profit is severely impacted (no product offered to the green market and production for the ordinary market becomes limited).

## 4.4    Impact of Operating Procedures Cost

We now focus on the impact of the increase in operating procedures costs on the product greenness and on the total emissions amount. The cost increase is expressed in terms of a percentage varying from 5 to 150%.

The cost increase is applied to different potential operating procedures. For each test iteration we vary both fixed and variable procedures costs ($C_f = C_f + 5\% \ C_{f-1}$ and $k_f = k_f + 5\% \ k_{f-1}$). Figures 3 and 4 show the obtained results.

- We observe that increasing of the operating procedures cost does not impact the greenness of the product offered to green customers. In fact when costs increase, the greener is the operating procedure, the more expensive it becomes. In this case, the company chooses a less ecological procedure in order to decrease costs but, at the same, it increases the amount of green components used. Hence, the total product greenness is constantly high (equal to 1.1) but the value of each greenness attributes change ($a^g$: greenness attribute related to emissions decreases and $b^g$ : greenness attribute related to the rate of green components increases).
- However, the increase of operating procedures cost doesn't impact the total greenness of the product offered to the green market. It has an important impact on the product offered to the ordinary market. When the cost increase is more than 40%, the greenness of ordinary product decreases from 0.76 to 0.5.
- Figure 4 shows that when the cost increase exceeds 40%, this leads to a large increase on the total amount of emissions. In fact, when the cost increase is between 5% and 35 %, the company chooses the most ecological procedure (of the potential procedures: F4) but when the procedures cost increase is beyond 40%, the company chooses a less ecological procedure (F3).

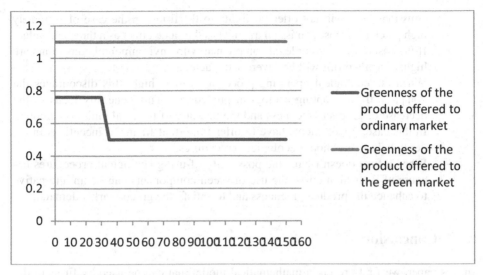

**Fig. 3.** Greenness as a function of operating procedures cost increase

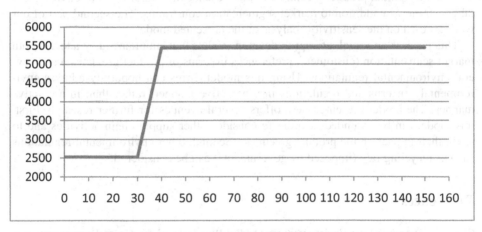

**Fig. 4.** Total emissions amount as a function of operating procedures cost increase

## 4.5    Conclusions

Several interesting observations may be derived from the results of this sensitivity analysis, as listed below:

- Tightening the threshold value for a specific emission will not necessarily lead to the enhancement of product greenness or to the decrease of total emissions amount. Very strict environmental laws may cause the decrease of product greenness and the increase of the total amount of emissions.
- The influence of emission trading depends on the transaction costs of the trading and the amount of basic allowances for the emission. If purchasing costs are high (which implies that buying allowances is very expensive), trading

emissions laws will not offer flexibility to the firms. In the case of extremely high purchasing costs, emission trading has the same effect as a threshold value.

- If the costs of achieving legal compliance with environmental constraints are high, a firm's profit will be severely impacted.
- When the ecological operating procedure cost is high, this discourages the company from adopting ecological procedures. This generally leads to the decrease of product greenness and the increase of the total emission amount. In this case, governments have to offer important financial incentives in order to help firms choose ecological procedures.
- When a firm doesn't have the possibility of using ecological procedures because of their high costs, the use of green components can be an alternative to enhance the product greenness and to satisfy the green market demand.

## 5    Conclusion

In this paper, we first present a mathematical model that can be used by firms to determine the optimal product greenness in the presence of several types of environmental constraints, in addition to market segmentation constraints. The second part of our work focused on the sensitivity analysis of the presented model.

This paper is an initial attempt to develop models that simultaneously address both market segmentation (customer's preferences in terms of product greenness) and several environmental regulations. Using this model, firms can hopefully address environmental concerns and regulations in a proactive manner, rather than in a reactive manner. The model presented here offers several avenues for further research. First, this model can be extended in order to consider other supply chain activities and to study their impact on the product greenness. Second, other environmental regulations such as recycling rate (imposed by governments) can be considered.

## References

Chen, C.: Design for the Environment: A Quality-Based Model for Green Product Development. Management Science 47(2) (2001)

Letmathe, P., Balakrishnan, N.: Environmental considerations on the optimal product mix. European Journal of Operational Research 167, 398–412 (2005)

Mahenc, P.: Signaling the environmental performance of polluting products to green consumers. Int. J. Ind. Organ. 26, 59–68 (2008)

Nouira, I., Frein, Y., Alouane, A.H.: Impact de décisions logistiques sur la qualité environnementale des produits. International Congress of industrial engineering (2011)

Radulescu, M., Radulescu, S., Radulescu, C.Z.: Sustainable production technologies which take into account environmental constraints. European Journal of Operational Research 193, 730–740 (2009)

Xu, X., Fang, S.L., Gu, X.J.: Mass customization and variety. Computer Integrated Manufacturing Systems 13(7), 1330–1335 (2007)

# A Mathematical Model for the Global Supplier Selection

Ramzi Hammami

Toulouse Business School, 20, bd Lascrosses - BP 7010 - 31068 Toulouse - France
`r.hammami@esc-toulouse.fr`

**Abstract.** In this paper, we focus on the supplier selection in a global context. The main features that characterize the global supplier selection are first identified. They mainly include the necessity of integrating inventory and transportation issues and considering several buyers' sites. We then propose a two-phase global supplier selection approach: a first pre-selection phase with a scoring method and a final selection phase using a mathematical optimization model. Finally, we perform computational experiments in order to illustrate the consistency of the model.

**Keywords:** Supplier selection, global purchasing, Low-cost suppliers, Optimization models.

## 1    Introduction

In this paper, we focus on the supplier selection (SS) process. A synthesis of the purchasing literature reveals that the main SS decisions are: which suppliers to select? and what quantities of each product to order from each supplier in each period? In the last decades, the SS problem has acquired an increasingly pronounced international dimension. Indeed, with globalization and fierce international competition, many companies are nowadays implemented worldwide, especially in low-cost countries, and have a large international network of suppliers. This is accentuated by the increase of outsourcing all over the world. Hayes et al. (2005) and Wadhwa and Ravindran (2007), among many other authors, point out that firms are increasingly outsourcing raw materials and component parts. The SS in an international environment has various characteristics which are discussed below:

- The SS decision is correlated with some major logistics issues within a company such as inventory (inventory level, cost, and capacity in buyers' sites) and transportation (transportation mode selection, delivery frequency, etc.). In the international context where suppliers and buyers are geographically dispersed, such interrelation is much more profound than for the traditional SS problem and thus cannot be ignored. To illustrate this proposal, we give the example of the French multinational company Valeo (automotive sector) in which we have acquired a professional experience. When Valeo delocalized its harnesses manufacturing activities to North Africa (Tunisia), it adopted a new purchasing strategy which consists in replacing (for its

F. Daniel et al. (Eds.): BPM 2011 Workshops, Part II, LNBIP 100, pp. 177–186, 2012.

Tunisian delocalized sites) some European suppliers by local (Tunisian) suppliers. Such a decision was mainly motivated by the fact that these suppliers were able to ensure daily deliveries of small quantities by truck (just to fulfill the needs of one day of production). This led to reducing the inventory level and the inventory costs. Note that both seaway and roadway transportation modes were used to import products from European suppliers which requires weekly deliveries. As a result, relatively high inventories used to be kept.

- In the international context, a company has always several sites worldwide and is concerned with purchasing raw materials and components for all these sites. Moreover, the purchasing decisions for these different buyers' sites are highly correlated and cannot be decomposed; such a correlation is manifested in the supplier management cost, the supplier production capacity, etc. Hence, we should consider a multi-buyer situation when we deal with the international SS problem.

In the international context, each of the above factors is relevant. In addition, they are highly correlated and, consequently, must be simultaneously considered. Thus, selecting suppliers in an international context is a complex problem that involves different interrelated decisions and specific criteria and constraints. The area of international SS has attracted much interest in the last years, especially from practitioners and managers of multinational companies. Therefore, there is a need to develop specific decision aid tools for this problem.

In this work, we develop a mixed integer programming model for the supplier selection problem in the global context. The remainder of the paper is organized as follows. A description of the proposed model is given in section 2. In section 3, we develop the mathematical formulation. We dedicate section 4 to the computational experiments. We finally conclude with an outlook on future research directions.

## 2    Model Description

We use the mathematical modeling since it is the better method that takes into account the correlation between the SS decisions and the transportation and inventory decisions which are of major importance in the global context. It also allows for considering the different parameters and constraints of the problem. We choose the minimization of the total cost as the objective of the proposed model. Nevertheless, this does not mean that the qualitative criteria are ignored. Indeed, they are considered in a pre-selection stage to rank suppliers and to identify the set of potential suppliers. We also include, among the model constraints, the so-called minimum qualitative performance constraint which allows for considering the performance of potential suppliers according to the qualitative criteria. Such performances can be obtained using a scoring method in the pre-selection stage. The proposed SS approach is described below:

1. Pre-selection stage. At this stage, the considered suppliers are ranked according to different qualitative criteria. We suggest using the Analytical Hierarchical Process (AHP) to perform this step. Using pairwise comparison, this accurate multi-criteria

scoring method has been widely applied for the SS problem (Ghodsypour and O'Brien, 1998, Wang et al., 2004, Narasimhan et al., 2006, Xia and Wu, 2007, etc.). It involves a multi-disciplinary team and allows for determining the score of each supplier according to the criteria being considered. Here, a first elimination of weak suppliers can be made based on their scores. The suppliers who pass this first stage (depends on whether an elimination rule is applied or not) are considered as potential suppliers and are introduced in the mathematical model (final stage) with their associated scores.

2. Final selection stage. It consists in using an optimization model for the SS. The objective of the model is the minimization of the total cost. Here, the total cost includes the pertinent costs that are incurred by the purchasing process in a global context. Basically, these costs are: the purchasing cost, the transportation cost, the inventory cost and the management cost. In the mathematical model, the scores of suppliers obtained at the first stage are not used as coefficients of an objective function as was made in most published works (Ghodsypour and O'Brien, 1998, Benyoucef et al., 2003, Wang et al., 2004, Xia and Wu, 2007, Sanayei et al., 2008, Kokangul and Susuz, 2009, etc.), but rather as coefficients of a model constraint. This constraint guarantees that the set of selected suppliers satisfies a minimum performance level regarding the qualitative criteria. By doing so and since the AHP is used to obtain the scores, we take into account the multi-criteria and the multi-actor aspects of the SS problem.

In order to be adapted to the global context, the proposed mathematical model takes into account the relevant issues related to inventory and transportation management in addition to the traditional decisions of supplier selection and order quantity allocation. Indeed, we include the decision of transportation modes selection (which connect suppliers' sites to buyers' sites) while characterizing each transportation mode by a delivery frequency and a transportation capacity. We also consider the inventory levels that are incurred in the buyers' sites while including the constraints of inventory capacity. Clearly, different buyers' sites are considered in the model. The model is developed as a multi-period model.

## 3    Model Formulation

Now, we focus on the mathematical formulation of the proposed SS model. We assume that the pre-selection has been accomplished and that the potential suppliers as well as their final scores have been obtained. The different sets of products, potential suppliers, buyers' sites, available transportation modes, and time periods are respectively denoted by R, I, J, K, and T. Clearly, since we deal with a strategic planning level, the products may be grouped into families of products. The length of a planning period can be taken as one year.

The following notation is used for the different parameters of the model:

$D_{rj}^t$: demand of product $r$ by buyer site $j$ in period $t$. The total demand of product $r$ (by all buyers' sites) in period $t$ is denoted by $D_r^t$.

$S_{ri}^t$: capacity of supplier $i$ in period $t$ regarding product $r$. We consider a time-dependent supplier capacity in order to take into account some relevant real situations such as the variation of the supplier production capacity over time periods and the fact that some suppliers may require an integration time to be available (due to quality problems, absence of certification, etc.).

$V_r$: unit volume of product $r$.

$H_j^t$: average inventory capacity in site $j$ in period $t$ (expressed as a volume).

$M^k$: unit capacity of transportation mode $k$ (expressed as a volume). For instance, if $k$ corresponds to road transportation (by trucks), the unit capacity can be considered as the capacity of one container (the load of the truck).

$F_{ij}^{kt}$: delivery frequency from supplier $i$ to site $j$ in period $t$ using the transportation mode $k$. It is expressed as the number of deliveries (shipments) over a period. We assume that, for given $i, j, t,$ and $k$, the same quantity of products is transported at each delivery. This assumption is applied by many companies in the automotive industry.

It is important to note that both $M^k$ and $F_{ij}^{kt}$ do not depend on the product. Thus, we take into account the fact that different products that are delivered from a given supplier to a given buyer in a given period and with a given transportation mode can be grouped together.

$U_{ri}^t$: qualitative score of supplier $i$ in period $t$ regarding product $r$ (obtained in the first pre-selection stage). It depends on the product since the performance of a supplier may change from one product to another. It is also time-dependent in order to take into account the possible improvement or degradation of supplier performance over the planning periods.

$\underline{U}_r^t$: minimum acceptable qualitative score for the selected suppliers regarding product $r$ in period $t$. The sum of all suppliers' scores weighted by their respective supplied quantities must not be smaller than the minimum acceptable qualitative score.

We consider the following decision variables:

$q_{rij}^{kt}$: quantity of product $r$ purchased by buyer site $j$ from supplier $i$ in period $t$ and transported by the transportation mode $k$.

$q_{rij}^t$: quantity of product $r$ purchased by buyer site $j$ from supplier $i$ in period $t$.

$y_i^t$: equals 1 if the supplier $i$ is chosen in period $t$, 0 otherwise.

$y_i$: equals 1 if the supplier $i$ is chosen at least once, 0 otherwise.

$n_{ij}^{kt}$: number of transportation units of transportation mode $k$ (e.g., number of containers) used at each delivery from supplier $i$ to site $j$ in period $t$. We recall that the same quantity of products is transported at each delivery from supplier $i$ to site $j$ in period $t$ using the transportation mode $k$. The integer variable $n_{ij}^{kt}$ takes the null value if and only if the transportation mode $k$ is not used between $i$ and $j$ in period $t$.

Finally, we use the following notation for the different cost factors:

$P_{ri}^t$: unit purchasing cost of product $r$ from supplier $i$ in period $t$.

$G_i$: fixed cost of managing supplier $i$. It is incurred once the supplier is selected even for only one period. For low-cost suppliers, this cost may include training costs, auditing costs, integration costs, etc. Such costs can be substantial as experienced by many delocalized multinational companies.

$C_{ij}^{kt}$: unit transportation cost from supplier $i$ to buyer site $j$ in period $t$ using the transportation mode $k$. This cost corresponds to the use of one transportation unit of the transportation mode $k$ (e.g., one container). The total transportation cost from supplier $i$ to buyer site $j$ in period $t$ using the transportation mode $k$ is then given by $C_{ij}^{kt} F_{ij}^{kt} n_{ij}^{kt}$. This way of modeling transportation costs is more realistic than if they are incorporated in the purchasing cost or considered as a linear function of the transported quantity of products. It also takes into account the economies of scales that can be made if different products are grouped together. In addition, it is relatively easier to estimate the real values of transportation costs in this case. It is possible that a transportation unit is used while not being fully loaded. As for real situations, the full cost is charged.

$B_{rj}^t$: unit inventory holding cost of product $r$ in site $j$ over period $t$. We assume that no inventory is kept at the end of each planning period (this is a logic assumption especially when the length of the period is taken as one year). The average inventory of a given product that is incurred during a period depends on the purchased quantity and the delivery frequency. Indeed, for each delivery, the imported quantity of a given product is $\frac{q_{rij}^{kt}}{F_{ij}^{kt}}$. Thus, the average inventory that is incurred between two consecutive deliveries is $\frac{q_{rij}^{kt}}{2(F_{ij}^{kt})^2}$. Consequently, the average inventory level over the whole period is given by $\frac{q_{rij}^{kt}}{2F_{ij}^{kt}}$. Hence, the total inventory cost of product $r$ in site $j$ in period $t$ is given by $B_{rj}^t \left( \sum_{i \in I} \sum_{k \in K} \frac{q_{rij}^{kt}}{2F_{ij}^{kt}} \right)$.

The objective function of the proposed model consists in minimizing the total cost over the whole planning horizon. This cost is the sum of the purchasing cost, the inventory cost, the transportation cost and the supplier management cost. The objective function is then given by (1).

$$
Min \quad
\begin{aligned}
&\sum_{t \in T} \sum_{i \in I} \sum_{r \in R} P_{ri}^t \left( \sum_{j \in J} q_{rij}^t \right) \\
&+ \sum_{t \in T} \sum_{j \in J} \sum_{r \in R} B_{rj}^t \left( \sum_{i \in I} \sum_{k \in K} \frac{q_{rij}^{kt}}{2F_{ij}^{kt}} \right) \\
&+ \sum_{t \in T} \sum_{j \in J} \sum_{i \in I} \sum_{k \in K} C_{ij}^{kt} F_{ij}^{kt} n_{ij}^{kt} \\
&+ \sum_{i \in I} G_i y_i
\end{aligned}
\tag{1}
$$

The model constraints are listed below. Constraint (2) guarantees the satisfaction of buyers' demands in each period. The suppliers' capacities are expressed by constraint (3). Constraint (4) is relative to the buyers' inventory capacity and imposes that the total average inventory level (for all products) that is incurred in a given buyer site over a given period does not exceed the available inventory capacity. Constraint (5) is concerned with the determination of the amount of transportation units (per delivery) that is required from a given supplier to a given site in a given period. This amount depends on the volume of the delivered quantity (at each delivery), $\sum_{r \in R} V_r \frac{q_{rij}^{kt}}{F_{ij}^{kt}}$, and the unit transportation capacity (in term of volume) of the involved transportation mode, $M^k$. The minimum qualitative performance level of selected suppliers is given by constraint (6) where the score of a supplier regarding a given product in a given period is weighted by the quantity purchased from this supplier. Finally, constraints (7), (8), (9), and (10) are relative to the logical relationships between the different decision variables.

$$\sum_{i \in I} q_{rij}^t = D_{rj}^t \qquad r \in R, j \in J, t \in T \tag{2}$$

$$\sum_{j \in J} q_{rij}^t \leq S_{ri}^t \qquad r \in R, i \in I, t \in T \tag{3}$$

$$\sum_{i \in I} \sum_{k \in K} \sum_{r \in R} V_r \frac{q_{rij}^{kt}}{2F_{ij}^{kt}} \leq H_j^t \qquad j \subset J, t \subset T \tag{4}$$

$$n_{ij}^{kt} - 1 < \frac{\sum_{r \in R} V_r q_{rij}^{kt}}{M^k F_{ij}^{kt}} \leq n_{ij}^{kt} \qquad i \in I, j \in J, k \in K, t \in T \tag{5}$$

$$\sum_{i \in I} \left( \sum_{j \in J} q_{rij}^t \right) U_{ri}^t \geq \underline{U^t}_r D_r^t \quad r \in R, t \in T \tag{6}$$

$$\sum_{k \in K} q_{rij}^{ki} = q_{rij}^t \qquad r \in R, i \in I, j \in J, t \in T \tag{7}$$

$$\frac{1}{\left(\sum_{r \in R} D_r^t\right)} y_i^t < \sum_{r \in R} \sum_{j \in J} q_{rij}^t < \left(\sum_{r \in R} D_r^t\right) y_i^t \qquad i \subset I, t \subset T \tag{8}$$

$$y_i \leq \sum_{t \in T} y_i^t \leq |T| y_i \qquad i \in I \tag{9}$$

$$q_{rij}^{kt} \in IR^+, n_{ij}^{kt} \in IN^+, y_i^t \text{ and } y_i \in \{0, 1\} \qquad r \in R, i \in I, j \in J, k \in K, t \in T \tag{10}$$

## 4    Computational Experiments

Now, we turn to the computational experiments on the proposed mathematical model. We consider a case study that is constructed based on our experience with the automotive industry. It is about a French multinational company that manufactures automotive wiring harnesses and that is concerned with the provisioning of two of its sites (buyers' sites) with electrical wires. The first buyer site is located in France (origin site, $j1$) and the second is located in Tunisia (delocalized site, $j2$). We consider two types of wires: *r1* and *r2*. Both are delivered in spools of around 0.03 m³ volume. Here, we assume that the inventory capacity allocated to the considered products in sites *j1* and *j2* is around 40 m³and 60 m³, respectively.

There are four potential suppliers that can be divided into two groups: European suppliers (*i1*, *i2*, and *i3*) and one low-cost Tunisian supplier (*i4*). The management costs of the suppliers are 10000, 8000, 8000, and 60000, respectively. The products are delivered from a given supplier to a given buyer by roadway only or by seaway and roadway according to the geographical locations of the involved sites. For both cases, the company has the choice to use containers of 20 or 40 feet. Hence, we consider four transportation modes denoted by *k1*, *k2*, *k3*, and *k4* for respectively road transportation with 20 feet container, road transportation with 40 feet container, maritime transportation with 20 feet container, and maritime transportation with 40 feet container. Here, maritime transportation refers to the transportation by seaway and roadway. The planning horizon is assumed to be three years with each year (*t*) representing a period. The values that we consider for the other parameters of the model are given in the Tables below.

**Table 1.** Demand (spools/year, ∀t )

| $D_{rj}^t$ | *j1* | *j2* |
|------------|-------|-------|
| *r1* | 20000 | 80000 |
| *r2* | 30000 | 70000 |

**Table 2.** Purchasing cost (∀t)

| $P_{ri}^t$ | *i1* | *i2* | *i3* | *i4* |
|------------|------|------|------|------|
| *r1* | 36 | 37 | 38 | 30 |
| *r2* | 15 | 16 | 16 | 12 |

**Table 3.** Holding cost (∀t)

| $B_{rj}^t$ | *j1* | *j2* |
|------------|------|------|
| *r1* | 4 | 3.5 |
| *r2* | 2 | 1.5 |

**Table 4.** Suppliers' capacities

| $s_{ri}^t$ | *i1* | *i2* | *i3* | *i4* |
|------------|-----------|-----------|-----------|--------------------------------------|
| *r1* | 100000 (∀*t*) | 100000 (∀*t*) | 100000 (∀*t*) | 40000 (*t1*), 70000 (*t2*), 100000 (*t3*) |
| *r2* | 100000 (∀*t*) | 100000 (∀*t*) | 100000 (∀*t*) | 50000 (*t1*), 100000 (*t2*), 100000 (*t3*) |

**Table 5.** Unit transportation cost (for the shipment of one container, $\forall t$)

| $C_{ij}^{kt}$ | $k1$ | $k2$ | $k3$ | $k4$ |
|---|---|---|---|---|
| $i1 \rightarrow j1$, $i2 \rightarrow j1$ | 230 | 400 | 140 | 250 |
| $i3 \rightarrow j1$ | 230 | 400 | | |
| $i1 \rightarrow j2$, $i2 \rightarrow j2$, $i3 \rightarrow j2$ | | | 655 | 1250 |
| $i4 \rightarrow j1$ | | | 655 | 1250 |
| $i4 \rightarrow j2$ | 200 | 380 | | |

**Table 6.** Qualitative score ($\forall t$)

| $U_{ri}^{t}$ | $i1$ | $i2$ | $i3$ | $i4$ |
|---|---|---|---|---|
| $r1$ | 1.7 | 1.9 | 2 | 1.2 |
| $r2$ | 1.7 | 1.9 | 2 | 1.2 |

**Table 7.** Delivery frequency (number of shipments per period t, $\forall t$)

| $F_{ij}^{kt}$ | $k1$ | $k2$ | $k3$ | $k4$ |
|---|---|---|---|---|
| $i1 \rightarrow j1$, $i2 \rightarrow j1$ | 150 | 150 | 100 | 100 |
| $i3 \rightarrow j1$ | 200 | 200 | | |
| $i1 \rightarrow j2$, $i2 \rightarrow j2$, $i3 \rightarrow j2$ | | | 50 | 50 |
| $i4 \rightarrow j1$ | | | 50 | 50 |
| $i4 \rightarrow j2$ | 150 | 150 | | |

## 5     Model Illustration

In order to illustrate the feasibility and the consistency of the model, we give and discuss the model solution that corresponds to the case study described above with a minimum acceptable qualitative score, $\underline{U}_r^t$, fixed to 1.6 for each product $r$ and period $t$. In order to solve the model, we used the commercial software Cplex 11.0 coupled with C++. The obtained value of the objective function is 15173.2 x 10³. The results regarding the variables $q_{rij}^t$ and $n_{ij}^{kt}$ are summarized in the table below where only the non-zero values are presented. The values of the other variables can be easily deduced.

The model selects three suppliers for each product: $i2$, $i3$, and $i4$. The supplier $i2$ is only selected at the first time period, and is subsequently replaced by $i3$ and $i4$. The selection of supplier $i3$ which has the highest qualitative score, but also the highest selling price, is mainly justified by the necessity of satisfying the constraint of minimum acceptable qualitative score. The delocalized site $j2$ is partially delivered by the

**Table 8.** Model solution

| | | $q_{rij}^t$ | | $n_{ij}^{kt}$ | | | |
|---|---|---|---|---|---|---|---|
| | | r1 | r2 | k1 | k2 | k3 | k4 |
| i1 | j1 | - | - | - | - | - | - |
| | j2 | - | - | - | - | - | - |
| i2 | j1 | 20000 (t1) | 30000 (t1) | - | - | 1 (t1) | - |
| | j2 | 40000 (t1) | - | - | - | 1 (t1) | - |
| i3 | j1 | 20000 (t2), 20000 (t3) | 30000 (t2), 30000 (t3) | 1 (t2), 1 (t3) | - | - | - |
| | j2 | 30000 (t2), 30000 (t3) | 23750 (t1), 20000 (t2) 20000 (t3) | - | - | 1 (t1), 1 (t2) 1 (t3) | - |
| i4 | j1 | - | - | - | - | - | - |
| | j2 | 40000 (t1), 50000 (t2) 50000 (t3) | 46250 (t1), 50000 (t2) 50000 (t3) | 1 (t1), 1 (t2), 1 (t3) | - | - | - |

low-cost supplier i4. In practice, the company X has adopted a similar strategy. Indeed, it has partially or totally replaced some European suppliers of its delocalized sites by local low-cost suppliers. The supplier i4 does not supply the origin site j1.

The model chooses the maritime transportation mode from supplier i2 to site j1 instead of road transportation. Indeed, although more inventory costs are incurred in this case (due to smaller delivery frequency and then higher inventory level), the maritime transportation is still more profitable given its low transportation cost. For both selected transportation modes k1 and k3 (which use a 20 feet container), only one container is used for each delivery ($n_{ij}^{kt} = 1$). Given that the cost of one 40 feet container is lower than the cost of two 20 feet containers, it can be easily demonstrated that, for any optimal solution, at maximum only one unit of transportation modes k1 and k3 can be used from a given origin to a given destination in a given period ($n_{ij}^{kt} \leq 1$ for k1 and k3). Depending on the required transportation capacity, the model first determines the adequate amount of 40 feet containers to be used; and if the transportation capacity that is still required is smaller than the capacity of a 20 feet container, one 20 feet container will then be added. In our case, none of the transported quantities of products exceeds the capacity of a 20 feet container. Hence, the model does not use 40 feet containers but only use one 20 feet container.

Beyond the model instance corresponding to the above case study, we solved different instances with different number of suppliers (from 2 to 10), buyers' sites (from 2 to 6), products (from 2 to 4), and transportation modes (from 2 to 4) in order to evaluate the computational performance of the model. We found that computation time is less than 6 min for all tested instances.

# 6    Conclusion

This paper focuses on the selection of suppliers in a global context. The main aspects that characterize the global supplier selection problem were first identified. These aspects are: the emergence of transportation and inventory issues, the necessity of considering multiple buyers' sites and different time periods with dynamic parameters. Then, we developed a two-phase global supplier selection approach that takes into account the major global features identified in this paper. The first phase of pre-selection uses a scoring method while the second phase of final selection is based on a mathematical optimization model. The proposed mathematical model is multi-product, multi-buyer and multi-period. We finally performed computational experiments based on a case study from the automotive industry in order to illustrate the feasibility and the consistency of the model.

The global purchasing is also characterized by many sources of uncertainties (price, supplier capacity, lead-times, etc.). For instance, it is interesting to think about how the model reacts when one (or more) supplier fails. Moreover, it is common that suppliers offer price discounts. In the future, it might be interesting to consider these aspects in our supplier selection approach and to analyze their impacts on model decisions.

# References

Benyoucef, L., Ding, H., Xie, X.: Supplier selection problem: selection criteria and methods. INRIA, Rapport de recherche no. 4726 (2003)

Ghodsypour, S.H., O'Brien, C.: A decision support system for supplier selection using an integrated analytic hierarchy process and linear programming. International Journal of Production Economics, 56–57, 199–212 (1998)

Hayes, R., Pisano, G., Upton, D., Wheelwright, S.: Operations, strategy, and technology. Wiley, NewYork (2005)

Kokangul, A., Susuz, Z.: Integrated analytical hierarch process and mathematical programming to supplier selection problem with quantity discount. Applied Mathematical Modelling 33, 1417–1429 (2009)

Narasimhan, R., Talluri, S., Mahapatra, S.K.: Multiproduct, Multicriteria Model for Supplier Selection with Product Life-Cycle Considerations. Decision Sciences 37, 577–603 (2006)

Sanayei, A., Mousavi, S.F., Abdi, M.R., Mohaghar, A.: An integrated group decision-making process for supplier selection and order allocation using multi-attribute utility theory and linear programming. Journal of the Franklin Institute 345, 731–747 (2008)

Wadhwa, V., Ravindran, A.R.: Vendor selection in outsourcing. Computers & Operations Research 34, 3725–3737 (2007)

Wang, G., Huang, S.H., Dismukes, J.P.: Product-driven supply chain selection using integrated multi-criteria decision-making methodology. International Journal of Production Economics 91, 1–15 (2004)

Xia, W., Wu, Z.: Supplier selection with multiple criteria in volume discount environments. Omega 35, 494–504 (2007)

# Context, Retrospection, and Prospection in Healthcare Process Definitions

## (An Invited Presentation at ProHealth 2011)

Leon J. Osterweil

Laboratory for Advanced Software Engineering Research (LASER),
Department of Computer Science, University of Massachusetts, Amherst, MA 01002  USA
ljo@cs.umass.edu

**Abstract.** Carefully defined processes can be effective tools for guiding and coordinating the actions of healthcare professionals. In past work our group has focused on defining such processes precisely and completely in order to support largely static analyses that demonstrate the absence from the processes of defects and vulnerabilities. Now increasingly our group's focus has been turning to the execution of these processes, using them to provide run-time information to guide process participants. This new focus has made it clear that more thought must be given to how to communicate with participants in order to assure more effective guidance. Our work is suggesting that participants, especially human participants, will require that process-provided guidance be accompanied by context, history, and prospective information if the guidance is to be credible, acceptable, and ultimately useful. A process definition that merely provides needed inputs and resources, and informs a participant that it is time to perform a specified activity is likely to be received with skepticism and to be the target of searching follow-up questioning. Process participants are likely to require answers to questions such as, "why am I being asked to do this?", "who else is doing what at this point?", "what past events have gotten us to the point where we need to do this?", "why am I being asked to do this again when I have already done it before?", and "if I do this, what other activities and resources are going to be required next?". The need for a process definition to be able to support the provision of answers to such questions relies upon the process definition's access to the process execution's current state, its past history, and its future execution possibilities. Providing such access poses difficult and important problems for the developers of process definition languages and formalisms. This talk identifies some of these problems, suggests possible approaches to them, and underlying challenges in solving them.

F. Daniel et al. (Eds.): BPM 2011 Workshops, Part II, LNBIP 100, p. 187, 2012.
© Springer-Verlag Berlin Heidelberg 2012

# Reusing a Declarative Specification to Check the Conformance of Different CIGs

M.A. Grando[1], Wil M.P. van der Aalst[2], and Ronny S. Mans[2]

[1] Division Biomedical Informatics, University of California San Diego, USA
mgrando@ucsd.edu
[2] Department of Information Systems, Eindhoven University of Technology,
P.O. Box 513, NL-5600 MB, Eindhoven, The Netherlands
{w.m.p.v.d.aalst,r.s.mans}@tue.nl

**Abstract.** Several Computer Interpretable Guidelines (CIGs) languages
have been proposed by the health community. Even though these CIG languages share common ideas each language has to be provided with his own
mechanism of verification. In an earlier work we have shown that a DE-
CLARE model can be used for checking the conformance of a PRO*forma*
CIG. In this paper, we show that the same model can also be used for
checking the conformance of a similar CIG expressed in the GLIF language. Besides, as the GLIF model has been expressed in terms of a
Coloured Petri Net (CPN), we also elaborate on the experiences obtained
when applying the model checking techniques supported by CPN tools.

**Keywords:** clinical guidelines, conformance checking, Petri Nets.

## 1  Introduction

Checking the compliance of a medical application to policies and guidelines [1],
the level of adherence of clinicians with respect to the intentions of guideline
authors [2] and critiquing systems by comparing actions performed by the physicians with predefined set of actions [3] are important problems. All these problems share in common that they require the use of verification techniques.

The spectrum of verification techniques used so far is broad, mainly based on:
algorithms [1,2], conformance checking [4,5], model checking [3,6,7] and theorem
proving [8]. But in the mentioned works the proposed verification techniques have
been designed having in mind a specific CIG language and are most probably
not easily reusable for checking properties in CIGs defined in languages different
from the one that inspired the methodology development.

Here we consider the problem of checking the compliance of policies and guidelines which could help to reduce medical errors by detecting inconsistencies, errors of interpretation or incompleteness of an application with respect to the
recommendations on which it is based. We continue the research presented in
[5] based on *a semantic-based approach that is fully independent of the language
used for the specification of the CIG*. By a combination of ontology matching and

F. Daniel et al. (Eds.): BPM 2011 Workshops, Part II, LNBIP 100, pp. 188–199, 2012.
© Springer-Verlag Berlin Heidelberg 2012

process mining the same set of declarative specifications of medical recommendations can be checked in an arbitrary CIG, providing a generic and reusable verification methodology. Given the diversity of languages available for the specification of CIGs [9] an ontology-based approach as the one we proposed here and in [5] is very promising. An additional advantage of our approach is that while the mentioned verification methodologies require the user to know temporal logic, our approach allows the user to specify constraints using a graphical notation that hides its equivalent semantic in temporal logic. The main drawback of semantic conformance checking approaches is that for each CIG to be checked an ontology matching between the terms used in the CIG and the concepts used in the verification tool has to be provided, and this can not be automatically performed and will not necessarily always be achievable.

In Mor Peleg et al. comparative study of languages for CIGs [9] the developers of Asbru, GLIF, GUIDE, EON and PRO*forma* languages were asked to specify CIGs for a set of recommendations inspired by the chronic cough guideline [10] for immunocompetent adult patients. The recommendations on which the study [9] was based, and the repository of the resulting CIGs, is available at the Open Clinical repository (http://www.openclinical.org). In [5] we explained that the mentioned medical recommendations, which were expressed in natural language, could be disambiguated and formalized in a declarative language called DECLARE [11]. In [5] we explained a methodology to check the conformance of the DECLARE recommendations over the PRO*forma* guideline from the Open Clinical repository. While semantic conformance checking does not guarantee correctness for all possible scenarios, it is clear that if more histories of executions are collected, the level of confidence and representativeness of the analysis increases. The main advantage of this approach is that it only requires the process history and therefore it can be applied over any CIG, independently of the language used for its implementation.

The aim of this work was to provide a proof of concept that the same DECLARE model proposed in [5] to check the conformance of the PRO*forma* CIG could be reused to check the conformance of other CIG from the same Open Clinical repository. For the best of our knowledge reusing the same specification for checking multiple CIGs defined in different languages have not been explored before. This study involved finding a suitable ontology mapping between the terms used for the DECLARE model and the terms used in the selected CIG. For this purpose we contacted the developers of the CIGs contained in the repository. The developers of the GLIF CIG provided us with an equivalent mapping of the CIG into a Petri Net (PN), which is not available in the Open Clinical Repository. We have transformed the provided PN into a Coloured Petri Net (CPN). CPNs are an extension of PNs where the tokens (flow of execution in the PN) are associated colors (types) defined by the user. We chose to perform our study over the GLIF CIG because it gave us the additional opportunity to explore the use of the model checking techniques supported by CPN tools, a well known tool for modeling and analyzing CPNs (www.cpntools.org). While languages like PRO*forma*, GLARE, GLIF and GUIDE have been mapped into

PNs, to the best of our knowledge the model checking mechanisms provided by the PN formalism have not been used for the verification of CIGs.

In Section 2 we start explaining the medical recommendations on which our example is based: recommendations taken from the chronic cough guideline [10] for immunocompetent adult patients which were selected by Mor Peleg et al. for performing the comparative study summarized in [9]. In Section 3 and 5 we explain respectively how to perform model checking and semantic conformance checking over the GLIF CPN. As for performing semantic conformance checking both DECLARE and the process mining tool ProM are used, they are both introduced in Section 4. Finally we provide the conclusions of our work.

## 2   Chronic Cough Guideline Recommendations

The analysis and interpretation of natural language medical recommendations is manually done, it requires in most of the cases the expertise of clinicians, as it is non-error free due to incompleteness or ambiguity of the natural language guideline's description. In this section we explain our disambiguation of one of the natural language medical recommendations from the chronic cough guideline [10]. This analysis was already explained in [5].

According to [10] if a patient has a cough which last at least 3 weeks the cough is considered chronic. The chronic cough guideline distinguishes 2 different patient classes for which different diagnostic treatments are prescribed in order to discover the most likely cause of cough and treat it. Here we only consider the case of immunocompetent adult patients.

For this study we have considered the following medical recommendation from the chronic cough guideline for immunocompetent adult patients:

R1)  "chest radiographs should be ordered before any therapy is prescribed in nearly all patients with chronic cough. Chest radiographs do not have to be routinely obtained before beginning treatment for presumed PNDS [post nasal drip syndrome] in young nonsmoker, or in pregnant women, or before observing the result of discontinuation of an ACEI [angiotensin-converting enzyme inhibitor]."

R2)  "When the chest X-ray is normal, PNDS, Asthma, and GERD [Gastroesophageal reflux disease] are the likely causes of chronic cough."

Given the scope of the paper, we refer the reader to [5] for our interpretation of the recommendation R2. Here we restrict yourselves to explaining our interpretation of recommendation R1):

R1)(a) **Pregnant patient or young non smoker with presumed PNDS:** in the case of pregnant women there is medical evidence of grade II-2 that the *x-ray exposes the embryo to radiation.* Evidence of grade II-2 is obtained from well-designed cohort or case-control analytic studies, preferably from more than one center or research group. Medical evidence of grade II-2 is ranked below the evidence of type I (obtained from at least one randomized controlled trial), and below the evidence of type II (obtained from well-designed controlled non-randomized trials). This recommendation is *critical* and provided with a high medical evidence, therefore it is also *mandatory* and it should be satisfied in every CIG that models the chronic cough guideline from [10].

In the case of young non smoker with presumed PNDS there is medical evidence of grade II-2 that the probability of PNDS/Asthma/GERD is higher than the average population, therefore it is more *cost-effective* and less time consuming to skip *Chest X-ray*. This recommendation is *not critical* but provided with a high medical evidence and therefore should be *mandatorily enforced*.

R1) (b) **Patients for whom recommendation R1)(a) does not apply (not pregnant and not young non smokers with presumed PNDS):** therefore for this class of patients obtaining a *Chest X-ray* is strongly recommended based on evidence of grade II-2, promoting the values of maximizing *likelihood of diagnosis* and maximizing *cost-effectiveness* because the X-ray may contain results that can aid in making a correct diagnosis. This recommendation is *not critical* but is provided with a high medical evidence and therefore should be *mandatorily enforced*.

## 3  Model Checking Techniques for Coloured Petri Nets

The developers of the chronic cough GLIF CIG from the Open Clinical repository provided us with a PN model of the CIG specified in the Protege tool (http://protege.stanford.edu). We have extended the provided PN into a CPN by adding types (colors) and adding conditions to the arcs connecting places and transitions. The resulting CPN can be enacted in CPN tools (http://cpntools.org). Figure 1 depicts a part of the resulting CPN.

For the GLIF CIG we have tested the model checker provided by CPN tools. While languages as GLIF, PRO*forma* and GUIDE have been provided with mappings into variants of PNs, to the best of our knowledge none of them have taken advantage of the model checking features provided by PN based tools like the CPN tools.

**Fig. 1.** Screen shot of the part of GLIF specification in CPN tools where recommendation recommendation R1) (a) iii can be checked

Below we explain a generic methodology to apply model checking over CPN specifications of CIGs:

1) Generate state-space graph from the CPN: once the medical guideline has been transformed into an equivalent CPN, tools like CPN tools can be used for model checking. In CPN tools properties can be checked only if it is possible to generate the graph of all possible combinations of transitions in the used CPN.

According to the chronic cough guideline six different cases or patient medical conditions were significant: (1) if the cough is persistent, (2) if the patient is pregnant, (3) if the patient is a young adult, (4) if the patient is a smoker, (5) if PNDS is presumed, (6) if the result of the X-ray is normal.

In the GLIF CPN the flow of execution was given by a unique token of type patient, described as the following tuple:

$< (coughStart, coughEnd), age, (immStart, immEnd), (aceiStart, aceiEnd),$
$pndsCertainty, pregnancyDueDate, (smokingStart, smokingEnd), now >$ where:

- $coughStart, coughEnd, immStart, immEnd, aceiStart, aceiEnd,$
  $pregnancyDueDate, smokingStart, smokingEnd, now$ are of type date
- $age$ and $pndsCertainty$ are integers.

Therefore: (1) if the difference between $now$ and $coughStart$ is greater that 21 day and there is no $coughEnd$ then the cough is persistent, (2) if the $pregnancyDueDate$ is a date after now then the patient is pregnant, (3) if the patient's $age$ is greater than 18 and less than 35 then the patient is a young adult, (4) if the $smokingEnd$ has not been fixed then the patient is a smoker, (5) if the $pndsCertainty$ is greater than 6 then PNDS is presumed.

In order to enact the provided GLIF CPN we needed to initialize it with tokens (patient cases).

The *first option* was to extend the GLIF CPN with random distribution functions which would generate the initial tokens that represent random patient cases. However, a problem which emerges when using random distribution functions is that the resulting CPN becomes non-deterministic because for each state space calculation different random numbers are used for various transitions. This has as result that it is virtually impossible to generate the same state space twice. Consequently, model checking is not possible.

The *second option* was to provide an algorithm which would iteratively enact the CPN from its initial state until some final state, using for each iteration a randomly generated initial token that represents a patient case. In this way we could generate in each iteration a deterministic CPN from which a state space graph could be computed and saved. Each state-space graph contained for the considered patient case all the possible care paths arising from all the possible decision outcomes for each decision point in the GLIF CPN. This is the reason why this methodology is exhaustive and therefore can be considered a type of model checking technique.

2) Verify the chronic cough medical recommendations in the GLIF CPN: CPN tools provides a library which implements a model checker based on a type of CTL temporal logic called ASK-CTL. This logic is an extension of CTL

which is a branching time logic. In order to be able to model data and time, CPN tools is integrated with a functional programming language called Standard Meta Language (SML). SML functions can used in CPN tools to prove medical recommendations by traversing the state-space graph obtained from the GLIF CPN.

We have chosen to specify each recommendation for the chronic cough guideline from Section 2 as a call to SML functions which traverse the sate-space graph generated from the GLIF CPN. For instance in the case of the recommendation R1) (a) iii, it has to be checked on the section of the GLIF CPN shown in Figure 1. This recommendation is verified by checking the following: if the patient has cough and the result of the Xray is normal then every time the transition $Xray$ is enacted transition $Initialization$ has to be enacted. The transition $Initialization$ does not have to be enacted straight after the transition $Xray$ and the transition $Xray$ can be enacted multiple times before the transition $Initialization$ gets enacted. In Figure 2 we present the specification of the recommendation R1) (a) iii in CPN tools. The verification of this recommendation returns true if the following is satisfied: 1) the source nodes of the transitions $Xray$ and $Initialization$ are reachable in the corresponding state space graph, and 2) the patient still shows symptoms of cough, which is equivalent to check that the token that activates the transition $Xray$ has value $CoughEnd = (0,0)$. The GLIF CPN does not provide any equivalent concept to the condition $normalXray$ therefore this conditions could not be checked.

For each of the chronic cough recommendations explained in Section 2 it was possible to define a function which equivalently checks whether the property is satisfied in the state-space graph generated from the GLIF CPN. While the functions were defined in terms of the GLIF ontology, they could potentially be parameterized in order to prove the same properties in another CPN which also models the chronic cough guideline.

For instance in the case of the recommendation R1) (a) iii, it could be parameterized by replacing:

1) the strings "$New\_Page'Xray$    1", "$New\_Page'Initialization$    1" and "$New\_Page'Seq\_or\_Anyorder$    1" corresponding to the labels of the transitions $Xray$, $Initialization$ and $Seq\_or\_Anyorder$ for variables of type string; and 2) the label of the place $p10$, which is the source node of transition $Seq\_or\_Anyorder$, for a variable denoting a place.

```
CPN Tools (Version 2.9.14, November 2010)
   Label : val node1= hd (SearchArcs( EntireGraph, fn n=>(st_TI(ArcToTI(n))="New_Page'Xray 1" ),
           NoLimit, fn n=> SourceNode(n), [] , op ::));
           val node2= hd (SearchArcs( EntireGraph, fn n=>(st_TI(ArcToTI(n))="New_Page'Initialization 1" ),
           NoLimit, fn n=> SourceNode(n), [] , op ::));
           val node3= hd (SearchArcs( EntireGraph, fn n=>(st_TI(ArcToTI(n))="New_Page'Seq_or_Anyorder 1" ),
           NoLimit, fn n=> SourceNode(n), [] , op ::));
           val cough= (#2(#2(hd(Mark.New_Page'p10 1 node3))) = (0,0) );
           val conditionalresponse= Reachable(node1, node2) andalso cough;
```

**Fig. 2.** Specification of the recommendation R1) (a) iii in CPN tools

Each of the defined functions was checked for each of the state-space graphs generated in 2) from the GLIF CPN. With this methodology we could prove that the GLIF guideline fully satisfies the mandatory recommendations RG1), RG2), R1) and R2)i, and that the GLIF CPN partially satisfies the optional property R2)ii.

## 4   Constraint-Based Specification: DECLARE and ProM

DECLARE (www.win.tue.nl/declare/) is a flexible and extendible constraint-based workflow management system that provides multiple declarative languages (DecSerFlow, ConDec, etc.) [11]. Unlike workflow-based languages, like PRO*forma* and GLIF, declarative languages specify *what* tasks should be performed without determining *how* to perform them. PRO*forma* and GLIF are specification methods for structured representation of guideline where processes are organized in terms of: actions, branches, decision points, synchronization steps, etc. With DECLARE instead it is possible to specify unstructured medical recommendations by means of dependencies or constraints between tasks. Dependencies between tasks can be seen as general rules that the user should comply with during a process execution. Any task in the model can be enacted by the user if and only if none of the specified constraints is violated. If an execution trace does not violate a DECLARE specification it is allowed. For a more extensive analysis of the benefits of specifying CIGs using declarative approaches we refer the reader to [12].

DECLARE uses a graphical notation and semantics based on Linear Temporal Logic (LTL). In DECLARE constraints can be *mandatory* or *optional*. Graphically, mandatory constraints are depicted as solid lines and optional constraint as dashed lines. While the considered recommendations from the chronic cough guideline have not been assigned a level of support, DECLARE allows to attach to constraints a level of support from 1 to 10. *Data attributes* can be specified and associated to relevant tasks. While executing a task, its data attributes can be read or written, as specified for that task at design-time. Constraints can be *conditional*, such that if the condition associated to the constraint is true the constraint should be satisfied. The condition can be defined in terms of data attributes. For example an X-ray should be performed only if the patient is not pregnant. Graphically we represent conditions between brackets. By associating to the DECLARE constraints different levels of support and ranges of numeric conditions it is possible to provide flexible constraint specifications. For example, while the prescription of treatment "A" is mandatory for patients with systolic blood pressure between 130 and 140, it can still be recommended (optional DE-CLARE specification with high level of support) for patients with systolic blood pressure greater than 141 but not exceeding 145.

Whereas declarative languages like DECLARE aim to provide flexibility, the goal of *process mining* [13] is to use information stored in information systems. The idea of process mining is to discover, monitor and improve real processes (i.e., not assumed processes) by extracting knowledge from event logs readily available in todays information systems. The first type of process mining is discovery. A discovery technique takes an event log and produces a model without using any a-priori information (e.g. the genetic miner). The second type of process mining is conformance. Here, an existing process model is compared with an event log of the same process. Conformance checking can be used to check if reality, as recorded in the log, conforms to the model and vice versa.

Obviously, process mining is very useful in the healthcare context as processes are not enforced by systems but emerge through human behavior. In the remainder of the paper, we show some initial applications of DECLARE and the process mining tool ProM (www.processmining.org) in this domain.

## 5    Semantic Conformance Checking of the CIG Guideline

In this section we focus on the semantic conformance checking of the CIG. In [5] we showed how to define a DECLARE model to specify the chronic cough medical recommendations explained in Section 2. The obtained DECLARE model was used to check the conformance of the constraints over the PRO*forma* CIG from the Open Clinical Repository. Here we only explain how to model in DE-CLARE the recommendation R1) (a)iii. The corresponding DECLARE model is shown in Figure 3. For the explanation of the other medical recommendations we refer the reader to [5]:

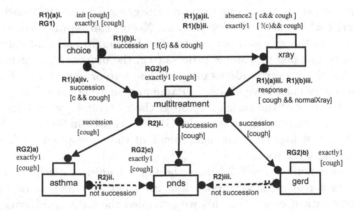

**Fig. 3.** DECLARE model for the considered recommendations from the chronic cough guideline

Recommendation R1) (a)iii: start the treatment for PNDS/Asthma/GERD if after the *X-ray* the patient has persistent cough and the result of the *X-ray* is normal (*cough && normalXray*) (conditional response relation between tasks *xray* and *multitreatment*);

The DECLARE model from Section 5 was used in [5] for checking the conformance of the chronic cough recommendations over a PRO*forma* CIG. The purpose of this study was to analyze how difficult would be to provide an ontology mapping between the terms used in the DECLARE model and the terms

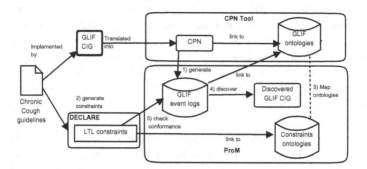

**Fig. 4.** Methodology proposed here: 1) Generate logs by enacting the CPN in CPN tools, 2) Generate LTL constraints from the DECLARE model, 3) Map ontologies, 4) Discover the model mined from the event logs using ProM, 5) Check conformance using ProM

used in the GLIF CIG from the Open Clinical repository. Our ultimate goal was to reuse the same DECLARE model to check the conformance of the GLIF CIG.

Below we explain in detail the steps of the semantic model checking methodology that has been applied (depicted in Figure 4): 1) Generate semantically annotated event logs from the CIG: the execution history (event logs) of a CIG is independent of the language used for the specification of the CIG. An event log contains the executions of one or more processes. To construct such log it is required that each event in the log (e.g. an X-ray) can be mapped to a single case or process instance (e.g. a patient treated for cough) and that each process instance can be mapped to a single process (e.g. the process for treating chronical cough). Similarly, every process instance has zero or more tasks. Every task or audit trail entry must have at least a name and an event type. The event type determines the state of the tasks. Although the methodology explained here is generic, we decided to explain it with the GLIF CIG used in Section 3. We chose to obtain the event logs from the enactment of the corresponding GLIF CPN representation in CPN tools.

Unfortunately none of the CIG from the Open Clinical repository have been used so far in a real medical application. So event logs had to be generated with fictitious patient cases. For this we extended the CPN specification of the GLIF CIG as explained in [14]. With the introduced extensions it was possible to choose the starting transition of the CPN and to select those transitions whose enactment was recorded in the generated event logs. Therefore we chose from the 26 transitions provided in the GLIF CPN only 7 transitions to be ontologically mapped into tasks from the DECLARE specification. For instance we chose the transitions *Evaluate asthma* and *Set PNDS evaluated* from the CPN because they could be mapped into the semantically equivalent tasks *asthma*, *pnds* from the DECLARE model from Section 5. Those transitions that were not selected were those that had no counterpart in the DECLARE model for various reasons. For example, they were generated by the algorithm used to map the GLIF guideline into an equivalent CPN (like the transition *Seq_or_any_order* used in the CPN for simulating scheduling constraints), or they were used to manipulate clinical data (for instance the transition *get_patient_cough_related_data* in the CP). None of those transitions have a counterpart in a declarative formalism like DECLARE that allows to abstract from most of these implementation details. Therefore even if we have modeled all the transitions with no counterpart in the DECLARE model the results presented here would not have changed.

The event logs had to be generated considering random patient cases. But for each of the patient cases more than one process instance could be generated, depending on the flexibility of the decision points provided in the GLIF CIG. For instance in the GLIF CIG, the clinician can chose to carry on the multitreatment for asthma, GERD and PNDS in any of the 6 sequential combinations. For instance, it is possible to test for asthma, then for GERD and then for PNDS. Next to that clinician can also decide not to carry on any test.

By using the CPN Tools import plug-in provided by the ProM$_{import}$ framework (www.prom.win.tue.nl/tools/promimport/) we could automatically convert the event logs generated from the extended CPN into a format that can be interpreted by ProM. So semantic model checking as explained in [5] can be used to check the conformance of the medical recommendations expressed in the DECLARE tool in the CIG:

2) Generate LTL properties from the DECLARE model: the DECLARE tool automatically generates the LTL properties from the constraint model of the medical recommendations explained in Section 5. From the generated LTL properties two ontologies were obtained: a) a data ontology obtained from the DECLARE data perspective and b) an ontology of activities obtained the from the DECLARE tasks. The top rectangle in Figure 5 shows the graphical representation of the ontology of activities, where for instance the DECLARE activities *asthma* and *gerd* are depicted.

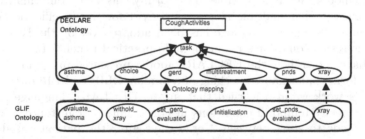

**Fig. 5.** Ontology matching between DECLARE and GLIF activities

3) Map the DECLARE ontology with the GLIF ontology: we performed the ontology mapping shown in Figure 6 between the concepts used in the GLIF CPN and the concepts from the DECLARE ontologies (generated in 2) ). For instance the GLIF task *evaluate_asthma* maps into the DECLARE concept *asthma*.

4) Discover the GLIF model from the semantically annotated event logs. Figure 6 shows the GLIF process mined from the generated event logs using the ProM framework.

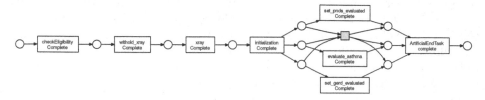

**Fig. 6.** GLIF CPN discovered by the ProM framework. The grey rectangle represents a hidden transition which allows for executing the "set pnds evaluated", "set gerd evaluated", and "evaluate asthma" transitions in any order or not at all.

5) Perform semantic conformance checking of the discovered GLIF model: with the semantic LTL checker plug-in provided by the PROM tool we could check the conformance of the recommendations specified in the DECLARE model (Section 5) in the discovered CPN.

With this methodology we obtained the same results proved in Section 3 with model checking.

# 6   Conclusions

The use of specification languages as DECLARE opens the possibility that medical recommendations become available as formal models defined in terms of standard medical ontologies like the Unified Medical Language System (http://www.nlm.nih.gov/research/umls/). Furthermore if the developers of a CIG, independently of the specification language, can provide a mapping between the terminology used in the CIG and the concepts used to specify the DECLARE model then it is possible to uniformly check the conformance of the CIG. Considering that multiple languages coexist for the specification of CIG and no common standard language has been adopted yet by the Health community, this result could have a considerable practical benefit. To support our claim we have shown how the DECLARE model presented in section 5 can be used to perform conformance checking of a similar GLIF and PRO*forma* CIG.

From this work we also learned that in the DECLARE language it is not possible to specify temporal conditions in constraints. For instance, a medical encounter needs to start between 2 or 3 days after the patient asked for an appointment and the duration of the medical encounter should not last more than 15 minutes. Therefore as future work we plan to extend DECLARE with more expressive ways to specify temporal restrictions.

Besides from the experience we gained in Sections 3 and 5 from model checking and conformance checking the GLIF CPN it seems that:

1) CPN model checking can easily lead to an explosion of the state space graph and the impossibility to perform any analysis.

2) Both techniques provide equivalent mechanisms to define the ontology mapping between the CIG's terms and the DECLARE model.

3) When using the semantic conformance checker it is possible to: differentiate between *mandatory* and *optional* constraints and choose significant transitions while ignoring others (by using event filtering in ProM). None of the mentioned features are provided by the model checker supported by CPN tools.

# References

1. Quaglini, S., Stefanelli, M., Lanzola, G., Caporusso, V., Panzarasa, S.: Flexible guideline-based patient careflow systems. Journal AIME 22, 65–80 (2001)
2. Advani, A., Shahar, Y., Musen, M.A.: Medical Quality Assessment by Scoring Adherence to Guideline Intentions. In: AMIA 2001 (2001)
3. Groot, P., Hommersom, A., Lucas, P.J.F., Robbert-Jan, M., ten Teije, A., Harmelen, F.V.: Using model checking for critiquing based on clinical guidelines. Journal AIME 46, 19–36 (2009)
4. Bottrighi, A., Chesani, F., Mello, P., Molino, G., Montali, M., Montani, S., Storari, S., Terenziani, P., Torchio, M.: A Hybrid Approach to Clinical Guideline and to Basic Medical Knowledge Conformance. In: Combi, C., Shahar, Y., Abu-Hanna, A. (eds.) AIME 2009. LNCS, vol. 5651, pp. 91–95. Springer, Heidelberg (2009)
5. Grando, M.A., Schonenberg, M.H., van der Aalst, W.: Semantic Process Mining for the verification of medical recommendations. In: Int. Conf. of Health Informatics 2011, Rome, pp. 5–16 (2011)
6. Bäumler, S., Balser, M., Dunets, A., Reif, W., Schmitt, J.: Verification of Medical Guidelines by Model Checking – A Case Study. In: Valmari, A. (ed.) SPIN 2006. LNCS, vol. 3925, pp. 219–233. Springer, Heidelberg (2006)
7. Giordano, L., Terenziani, P., Bottrighi, A., Montani, S., Donzella, L.: Model checking for clinical guidelines: an agent-based approach. In: AMIA, pp. 289–293 (2006)
8. Marcos, M., Balser, M., ten Teije, A., van Harmelen, F., Duelli, C.: Experiences in the Formalisation and Verification of Medical Protocols. In: Dojat, M., Keravnou, E.T., Barahona, P. (eds.) AIME 2003. LNCS (LNAI), vol. 2780, pp. 132–141. Springer, Heidelberg (2003)
9. Peleg, M., Tu, S.W., Bury, J., Ciccarese, P., Fox, J., et al.: Comparing Computer-Interpretable Guideline Models: A Case-Study Approach. JAMIA 10(1), 55–68 (2003)
10. Irwin, R.S., Boulet, L.S., Cloutier, M.M., et al.: Managing Cough as a Defense Mechanism and as a Symptom, A Consensus Panel Report of the American College of Chest Physicians. Chest 114(2), 133–181 (1998)
11. van der Aalst, W.M.P., Pesic, M., Schonenberg, H.: Declarative Workflows: Balancing Between Flexibility and Support. Computer Science - Research and Development 23(2), 99–113 (2009)
12. Mulyar, N., Pesic, M., van der Aalst, W.M.P., Peleg, M.: Towards Flexibility in Clinical Guideline Modelling Languages. In: 1st International Workshop on Process-oriented Information Systems in Healthcare, pp. 24–29 (2007)
13. van der Aalst, W.M.P.: Process Mining: Discovery. Conformance and Enhancement of Business Processes. Springer, Heidelberg (2011)
14. Alves De Medeiros, A.K., Günther, C.W.: Process Mining: Using CPN Tools to Create Test Logs for Mining Algorithms. In: Proc. of the Sixth Workshop and Tutorial on Practical Use of CPNs and the CPN Tools, pp. 177–190 (2005)

# Conformance Checking of Executed Clinical Guidelines in Presence of Basic Medical Knowledge

Alessio Bottrighi[1], Federico Chesani[2], Paola Mello[2], Marco Montali[3], Stefania Montani[1], and Paolo Terenziani[1]

[1] DI, Univ. del Piemonte Orientale, via Bellini 25/g, 15100 - Alessandria, Italy
{alessio.bottrighi,terenz,stefania}@mfn.unipm.it
[2] DEIS - Univ. di Bologna, viale Risorgimento 2, 40136 - Bologna, Italy
{federico.chesani,paola.mello}@unibo.it
[3] KRDB Research Centre, Free University of Bozen-Bolzano, Italy
montali@inf.unibz.it

**Abstract.** Clinical Guidelines (CGs) capture medical evidence, but are not meant to deal with single patients' peculiarities and specific context limitations and/or constraints. In practice, the physician has to exploit basic medical knowledge (BMK) in order to adapt the general CG to the specific case at hand. The interplay between CG knowledge and BMK can be very complex. In this paper, we explore such interaction from the viewpoint of the *conformance* problem, intended as the adherence of an observed CG execution trace to both types of knowledge. We propose an approach based on the GLARE language to represent CGs, and on an homogeneous formalization of both CGs and BMK using Event Calculus (EC) and its Prolog-based implementation $\mathcal{REC}$, focusing on "a posteriori" conformance evaluation.

**Keywords:** Clinical Guidelines, Conformance, Event Calculus, Integration with Basic Medical Kwnoledge.

## 1 Introduction

Clinical Guidelines (CGs) are, in the definition of the MeSH dictionary, "work consisting of a set of directions or principles to assist the health care practitioners with patient care decisions about appropriate diagnostic, therapeutic, or other clinical procedures for specific clinical circumstances". One of the main goals of CGs is to capture medical evidence and to put it into practice. However, from one side, evidence is essentially a form of statistical knowledge, and is used to capture the generalities of classes of patients, rather than the peculiarities of a specific patient. From the other side, demanding to expert committees the elicitation of all possible executions of a CG on any possible specific patient in any possible clinical condition is an infeasible task. Thus, several conditions are usually implicitly assumed by experts building a CG:

F. Daniel et al. (Eds.): BPM 2011 Workshops, Part II, LNBIP 100, pp. 200–211, 2012.

(*i*) *ideal patients*, i.e., patients that have "just the single" disease considered in the CG (thus excluding the concurrent application of more than one CG), and are "statistically relevant" (they model the typical patient affected by the given disease), not presenting rare peculiarities/side-effects;

(*ii*) *ideal physicians* executing the CG, i.e., physicians whose basic medical knowledge always allow them to properly apply the CGs to specific patients;

(*iii*) *ideal context* of execution, so that all necessary resources are available.

On the other hand, when a specific physician applies a given CG to a specific patient, the patient and/or the context may not be "ideal". For instance, some laboratory instrument (recommended by the CG) may be missing, and/or the patient may show specific conditions not foreseen in the general CG. As a consequence, the physician has to exploit her/his general knowledge (Basic Medical Knowledge, BMK from now on) in order to adapt the general CG to the specific case at hand. The interplay between these two types of knowledge can be very complex: e.g., actions recommended by a CG could be prohibited by the BMK, or a CG could force some actions despite the BMK discouraging them.

The issue of studying the interplay between the knowledge in CGs and BMK is a fundamental one, to promote the practical applicability of CGs themselves. However, it is relatively new in the literature, and has not yet been deeply investigated. In the last two decades most approaches have focused either on CGs or BMK in isolation, without taking into account how they mutually affect each other. In particular, a plethora of languages and projects has been developed to create domain-independent computer-assisted tools for managing, acquiring, representing and executing CGs [8,13], paying particular attention to the *procedural and control-flow dimension*.

This observation points out another challenging and relatively unexplored issue: while current approaches capture CGs with a workflow-like modeling style, both CGs and the BMK contain a mix of procedural and declarative knowledge. Procedural knowledge comes into play when there is a set of well-accepted, predefined *sequences of operations* that must be followed by the involved stakeholders. Contrariwise, declarative knowledge typically captures *constraints* and *properties* that must be satisfied during the execution, without explicitly fixing how the stakeholders must behave in order to satisfy them.

In this paper, we explore how CGs workflow-based approaches can be extended to take into account also the BMK, providing a uniform underlying logic-based formalization that is able to accommodate both procedural and declarative knowledge. We explore the interaction between CGs and BMK from the viewpoint of the *conformance* problem, intended as the adherence of an observed CG execution trace to both types of knowledge.

From a formal viewpoint, there are many different definitions of conformance. Procedural approaches typically consider a CG execution trace conformant if it contains all and only the actions envisaged by the specification, in the right order. More flexible declarative solutions usually adopt a constraint based approach, where a trace is considered conformant if it satisfies all the imposed constraints. A central issue is that a CG execution trace could seem conformant to the CG and not conformant to the BMK, or vice-versa. Actually, both the CG knowledge and the BMK can be defeated, and it is the physician's responsibility to assess if a trace can be deemed as conformant or not. Hence, our aim is to support the physician in the conformance evaluation task, providing her the most information possible, and consequently easing the evaluation process.

The automatic tool we propose in this paper is based on GLARE [14] to represent CGs, and relies on an homogeneous formalization of both CGs and BMK using Event Calculus (EC) and its Prolog-based implementation $\mathcal{REC}$. In particular, we use the EC to represent procedural aspects of CG, while we exploit Prolog clauses to represent the BMK in terms of logic rules. Note that, even if in the paper we focus on CGs, GLARE is able to manage protocols and since our approch is general, it can be applied to protocols in the same way.

The paper is organized as follows: in Section 2 we motivate our work showing the interaction between CG and BMK; in Section 3 we define a model of action, which accommodates the interaction with the BMK; in Sections 4 and 5, we formalize CG and BMK using the EC, and describe how we tackle the conformance problem. Section 6 concludes the paper and discusses related work.

## 2   CG and BMK Complement Each Other

A CG is defined assuming some ideal conditions, that could not hold when applying the CG in the real medical practice. Hence, a CG cannot be interpreted as a protocol which has to be applied tout cour, and the actions prescribed by CGs cannot be interpreted as "must do" actions. The intended semantics of CGs is much more complex, and cannot be analysed in isolation w.r.t. the BMK. Informally speaking, given a patient $X$ to which a CG $\mathcal{G}$ has to be applied in a context $\mathcal{C}$, $\mathcal{G}$ has to be interpreted as a set of *default prescriptions*: whenever $X$ and $\mathcal{C}$ *fit* with $\mathcal{G}$'s prescriptions, they must be executed. However, $X$ (or $\mathcal{C}$) may have peculiar features, which are not explicitly covered by $\mathcal{G}$. In such a case, the BMK must be considered to identify the correct actions. The interplay between CGs and the BMK can be very complex, as shown by the following examples.

*Example 1. CG: Patients suffering from bacterial pneumonia caused by agents sensible to penicillin and to macrolid, allergic to penicillin, must be treated with macrolid.*
*BMK: Don't administer drugs to an allergic patient.*

In Ex. 1, two alternative treatments (penicillin or macrolid) are envisaged by the CG, but one of them is excluded, given the underlying BMK, because of allergy to penicillin. Here the BMK reinforces the CG and helps to discriminate among different alternatives. In other cases, the BMK may apparently contradict the CG. However, there is no general rule in case of "apparent contradiction": in some cases the BMK recommendations "win" over CG ones, or vice versa.

*Example 2. CG: Patient with acute myocardial infarction presenting with acute pulmonary edema; before performing coronary angiography it is mandatory to treat the acute heart failure.*

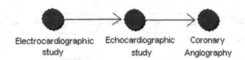

Electrocardiographic     Echocardiographic     Coronary
study                              study              Angiography

**Fig. 1.** Part of the CG for acute myocardial infarction represented in GLARE

*BMK: The execution of any CG may be suspended, if a problem threatening the patient's life suddenly arise. Such a problem has to be treated first.*

*Example 3. CG: In a patient affected by unstable angina and advanced predia-lytic renal failure, coronary angiography remains mandatory, even if the contrast media administration may cause a further final deterioration of the renal functions, leading the patient to dialysis.*

In Example 2 the execution of a CG is suspended, due to the presence of a problem threatening the patient's life. The "contradiction" (logical inconsistency) between CG's recommendations and BMK is only apparent. It arises just in cases one interpret CG's recommendations as must do, while, as a matter of fact, they may be emended by BMK. In Example 3 instead a treatment is performed even if it may be dangerous for the patient. In some sense, not only some CG's prescriptions are "defeasible", since they may be overridden by BMK, but the same also holds for part of BMK.

When considering the conformance of an execution log w.r.t. a specific CG, additional actions not foreseen by such CG might be an issue. This could happen as a consequence of some particular routine, like in Example 4.

*Example 4. Calcemia and glycemia are routinely performed in all patients admitted to the internal medicine ward of Italian hospitals, regardless of the disease.*

Examples 1–4 clearly show that CGs cannot be simply interpreted as a strict, normative procedures. The context of execution and the BMK complement the prescriptions in the CGs, bridging (at least in part) the gap between the "ideal" and the "real" application cases.

Let us now better specify the Example 2, in the context of a CG for the acute myocardial infarction. The following refinement shows that both declarative and procedural knowledge usually come into play.

*Example 5. CG (excerpt):* **Actions (Electrocardiographic study), (Echocardio-graphic study), and (Coronary Angiography)** *should be executed in sequential order.* *BMK: (1) Threats to patient's life must be addressed immediately; (2) an acute heart failure is a life threat; (3) an immediate response for acute heart failure could be a* **(Diuretic Therapy).**

In Example 5, the knowledge of the CG is defined in terms of a procedural specification of the actions to be performed (see Fig. 1); the BMK knowledge instead is given partly in terms of desired properties and definitions (sentences (1) and (2)), and partly in terms of procedural recommendations (Sentence (3) could be read as "in case of an acute heart failure apply Diuretic Therapy").

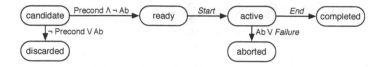

**Fig. 2.** The model for the execution of an action, as a transition system

Summing up, two different types of knowledge must be taken into account: the knowledge deriving from a CG, and BMK that integrates the former one. Such information is often expressed using a mixed declarative/procedural style. In this hybrid situation the property of conformance, intended as the adherence of a trace to CGs and BMK, becomes more and more important, and yet difficult to be captured.

## 3    The Continuos Interplay between CG and BMK

The interaction between clinical knowledge in the CG and BMK takes place during the execution of CGs. To support such an interaction, we have defined a model of the execution of actions in the CG (see Fig. 2).

At a given point in the execution of a CG on a specific patient, the control relations in the CG indicate that a given action is the next action to be executed (or, in case of parallel execution, that a set of actions is expected). At that point, we say that the action is the *candidate* (for execution) action. To be executed, a candidate action must satisfy its *preconditions*, which are a part of the description of the action itself ("precond." in Fig. 2). Preconditions specify the applicability conditions of the action, and have to be evaluated on the basis of the currently available patients data and execution context. Even in case preconditions are satisfied, the action cannot be executed if some *abnormality* ("ab" for short) situation shows up. Abnormalities arise whenever the assumptions on CG execution (*ideal* patient and context, as described in Section 1), do not hold. If the situation is not abnormal and preconditions hold, the action is *ready* to be executed. Otherwise, it becomes *discarded*. When a *ready* action is *started*, it becomes *active*. Two cases are possible then: either the active action is *ended*, leading to a *completed* action; or an *abnormality/failure* shows up during execution, so that the action is *aborted*. *Failures* denote the uncorrect completion (or no completion at all) of an action, due to human and/or technical problems arising during its execution.

It is worth stressing that the points of interactions between CG execution and BMK are explicitly modeled by the *abnormality* arcs shown in Fig. 2. The rationale is the following: whenever, during the execution of the CG, the patient/context are not *ideal* (i.e., they do not fit the assumptions made during the definition of the CG), physicians have to integrate the CG knowledge with their own abilities and expertise. In particular, they must continuously evaluate *preconditions* and *abnormality/failure* situations, then deciding how to act. Observe that the *preconditions* are specified in the CG model, the *failure* situations

**Table 1.** The EC ontology

| | |
|---|---|
| $happens\_at(Ev, T)$ | Event $Ev$ happens at time $T$ |
| $holds\_at(F, T)$ | Fluent $F$ holds at time $T$ |
| $holds\_for(F, [T_1, T_2])$ | Fluent $F$ holds along a time interval $[T_1, T_2]$ |
| $initially(F)$ | Fluent $F$ holds from the initial time |
| $initiates(Ev, F, T)$ | Event $Ev$ initiates fluent $F$ at time $T$ |
| $terminates(Ev, F, T)$ | Event $Ev$ terminates fluent $F$ at time $T$ |
| $mvi(F, T_i, T_f)$ | $(T_i, T_f]$ is a *maximal validity interval* for $F$ |

depend from a specific execution, and the *abnormality* situations are typically handled by the BMK. Further constraints are imposed by the BMK depending on the current context and patient's status; from the operational point of view, such constraints might forbid or require the execution of specific actions.

# 4 Formalisation of the CG and BMK Using the EC

In this section we show how, in spite of their different role and knowledge representation languages, both CG and BMK can be formalized by an uniform logic framework based on the EC.

## 4.1 Introduction to the Event Calculus

The Event Calculus was proposed by Kowalski and Sergot [11] as a logic programming framework for representing and reasoning about time, events and their effects [11]. Basic concepts are that of *event*, happening at a point in time, and *fluent*, a dynamic property holding during time intervals. Fluents are initiated/terminated by events. Given an event narrative (a set of events), the EC theory and domain-specific axioms together ("EC axioms") define which fluents hold at each time. There are many different formulations of these axioms [5]. One possibility is given by the following axioms $ec_1$, $ec_2$ ($P$ stands for *Fluent*, $E$ for *Event*, and $T$ represents time instants):

$$holds\_at(P, T) \leftarrow initiates(E, P, T_{Start})$$
$$\land T_{Start} < T \land \neg clipped(T_{Start}, P, T). \qquad (ec_1)$$

$$clipped(T_1, P, T_3) \leftarrow terminates(E, P, T_2)$$
$$\land T_1 < T_2 \land T_2 < T_3. \qquad (ec_2)$$

$$initiates(E, P, T) \leftarrow happens\_at(E, T) \land holds\_at(P_1, T)$$
$$\land ... \land holds\_at(P_M, T). \qquad (ec_3)$$

$$terminates(E, P, T) \leftarrow happens\_at(E, T) \land holds\_at(P_1, T)$$
$$\land ... \land holds\_at(P_N, T). \qquad (ec_4)$$

Axioms ($ec_3$, $ec_4$) are schemas for defining the domain-specific axioms: a certain fluent $P$ is initiated/terminated at time $T$ if an event $E$ happened at the same time, while some other fluents $P_i$ hold. The expression $happens\_at(E, T) \wedge$ $holds\_at(P_1, T) \wedge ... \wedge holds\_at(P_N, T)$ represents the *context* which causes $E$ to initiate $P$. In general, the context can be any conjunction of literals. To say that a fluent holds at the beginning of time we can use the shorthand $initially(P)$. Note that, to maintain the reasoning consistent w.r.t. the time instants, it is usually assumed that a fluent initiated at time $T$ holds from time $T$ onward; a fluent terminated at time $T$ instead still holds at time $T$, but it does not hold later than $T$. I.e., the interval time on which a fluent holds is open on the left and closed on the right. The EC formalization above is called *simple* EC and uses the Horn fragment of first order logic, augmented with negation as failure.

An EC *theory* is a knowledge base $\mathcal{KB}$ composed by a set of clauses (*initiates*, *terminates*, ...) that relate events and fluents. The set of all EC predicates that will be used throughout the paper is listed in Table 1.

## 4.2    Significative Events within a CG Execution

The first step to model the CG/BMK is to identify the significant events that happen in the system. Such events must be *observable*, in the sense that a system supporting the execution of a CG should be able to properly log them. Indeed GLARE[14], when supporting the execution of a CG, logs many events related to CG, as well as to the patient status and many other health-related aspects.

Among these events, we distinguish between two different types. The first type is related to the execution of actions, in particular to represent the *start/end* of an action's execution, as well as its *discard/abort*. Such events represent the state transitions presented in Fig. 2, with a slight difference. In Fig. 2 when an action is in the *candidate* status, if the preconditions hold and the current context/situation is not abnormal, then such activity becomes ready and it is executed (hence becoming *active*). This process mirrors the typical behavior of a human professional that, having the goal of executing an action, checks for the preconditions and abnormal situations, and then proceeds with the action. However, it is not reasonable to assume that the log of the CG execution will contain this kind of information: almost all the existing CG support systems log only the fact that an action has been executed. Precondition/abnormalities checks are taken for granted since the action has been executed.

The second type of events represents any other type of information that is not strictly related to the execution of an action. In this category falls events like "a patient had a heart failure at time 9" or "at time 16 the patient had a temperature of 39.7 degrees". A brief summary of the events we assume to be observable (logged) during the CG execution is given in Table 2.

## 4.3    The Action Execution Model in EC

In our modeling of the execution model discussed in Section 3 we use a special fluent, namely *status(A, S)*, for representing the fact that action $A$ is in status $S$. Also, we assume that an action is already in the state *candidate* (the elicitation of candidate actions will be detailed in Section 4.4). In such state, our model

**Table 2.** Observable events

| | |
|---|---|
| $exec(event(start, A))$ | The execution of action $A$ has been started |
| $exec(event(end, A))$ | The execution of action $A$ has been ended |
| $exec(event(discard, A))$ | The candidate action $A$ has been discarded by the operator |
| $exec(event(abort(R), A))$ | During its execution, $A$ has been aborted for reason $R$ |
| $heart\_failure$ | The patient has a heart stroke |
| $temperature(36.5)$ | The patient's temperature has been measured to be 36.5° |

foresees two possible events. The first event is the start one, which triggers the transition from *candidate* to *active*, as specified by Axioms $ax_1$ (the candidate status is terminated) and $ax_2$ (the *active* status initiates).

$$terminates(exec(event(start, A)), status(A, candidate), T). \qquad (ax_1)$$

$$initiates(exec(event(start, A)), status(A, active), T) \leftarrow$$
$$holds\_at(status(A, candidate), T). \qquad (ax_2)$$

Note that the termination of the *active* status is not subject to any particular condition. Instead, for initiating the new status *active*, Axiom $ax_2$ explicitly requires that the action $A$ is currently *candidate*.

The second possible event is a *discard*, meaning that the operator has decided to discard a candidate action. Axioms $ax_3$ and $ax_4$ capture the transition form the state *active* to the state *discard*.

$$terminates(exec(event(discard, A)), status(A, candidate), T). \qquad (ax_3)$$

$$initiates(exec(event(discard, A)), status(A, discarded), T) \leftarrow$$
$$holds\_at(status(A, candidate), T). \qquad (ax_4)$$

The formalization of the state transitions from *active* towards *completed*/*aborted* (as consequence of events *end*/*abort*) are similar to Axioms $ax_1$–$ax_4$; we do not report the corresponding axioms for lack of space.

## 4.4   Formalization of a Clinical Guideline Using EC

The procedural knowledge defined within a CG takes often the form of a structured workflow, with simple blocks representing the actions to be executed, and control-blocks such as parallel execution, and/or splits, etc. Our formalization of this workflow part is a variant of [6].Differently from [6], we focus on the elicitation of candidate actions (by raising up the proper fluent). When an action is completed correctly, other action(s) become candidates, depending on what is specified by the workflow. But also in case an action is discarded or aborted, the following actions (as specified by the CG workflow) become candidates, anyway.

The rationale behind this choice is grounded on a practical observation about how the health operators apply the workflow part of a CG. It can happen that some actions are discarded or interrupted (aborted) for many possible reasons, and yet the execution of the CG is brought forward. To support such cases, the workflow part of a CG must be "robust": it should support the operators in executing the whole CG, even if some actions have been discarded/aborted. To represent the candidate action(s) as prescribed by the CG, we use a fluent *nextCGCandidate*, that is continuously updated to represent the next action to be executed, according to the CG. Note also that the action itself is put on state *candidate*, and from that moment on it is treated as specified in Section 4.3.

### 4.5    Formalization of the Basic Medical Knowledge in EC

The EC is a framework based on first-order logic axioms. Although many implementations are available, we are currently using $\mathcal{REC}^1$ [4], a pure Prolog implementation of the EC, built on top of a Prolog interpreter written in Java. Using Prolog and EC for representing the BMK has been a quite natural choice.Note that the definition of BMK cannot be exhaustive (i.e. it is not possible to acquire all basic medical knowledge for all medical problems). Actually, portions of the whole BMK will be captured depending on the specific medical problem (i.e., depending on the CG at hand). For example, the following knowledge base represent the fact that a heart failure is a life threat, and that a diuretic therapy is a possible treatment for it. Moreover, the knowledge base specifies also that an event representing a life threat initiates an abnormality status, that is terminated by starting any treatment for the particular life threat.

$life\_threat(heart\_failure).$          $treatment(heart\_failure, diuretic).$
$initiates(exec(E), abnormality(E), \_) \leftarrow life\_threat(E).$
$terminates(exec(event(start, A)), abnormality(E), \_) \leftarrow treatment(E, A).$

## 5    Conformance Evaluation of an Execution Log

We aim to evaluate when the execution of a CG might not be completely conformant to the CG specification. With no claim of being exhaustive, we propose some possible interesting cases. The first case happens when the CG suggests a candidate action, but the operator starts executing a different action. Axiom $ax_5$ captures this situation, by raising a special fluent *status(cg,nc)*, indicating the possible non-conformance.

$$initiates(exec(event(start, A)), status(cg, nc), T) \leftarrow$$
$$holds\_at(status(nextCGcandidate, B), T), A \neq B.$$    $(ax_5)$

A second case is when an action has been started, but either the preconditions did not hold, or there was an abnormal situation (Axioms $ax_6$ and $ax_7$):

$$initiates(exec(event(start, A)), status(cg, nc), T) \leftarrow$$
$$holds\_at(status(A, candidate), T), \neg preconditions(A, T).$$    $(ax_6)$

---

[1] http://www.inf.unibz.it/~montali/tools.html#jREC

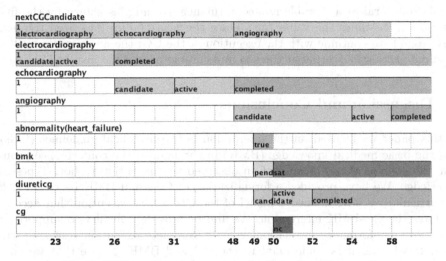

**Fig. 3.** EC-based conformance evaluation of a CG execution

$$initiates(exec(event(start, A)), status(cg, nc), T) \leftarrow$$
$$holds\_at(status(A, candidate), T), holds\_at(abnormality(\_), T). \qquad (ax_7)$$

where *preconditions* is a Prolog predicate, and *abnormality* is a special fluent signaling the abnormal situation. A third, possible non-conforming situation might arise when a candidate action has been discarded, although there was no apparent reason. Such situation is captured by Axiom $ax_8$:

$$initiates(exec(event(discard, A)), status(cg, nc), T) \leftarrow$$
$$holds\_at(status(A, candidate), T), \qquad (ax_8)$$
$$preconditions(A, T), \neg holds\_at(abnormality(\_), T).$$

## 5.1   A Simple Example

Let us consider the CG fragment shown in Fig. 1. Fig. 3 shows the EC-based conformance evaluation for a simple log. Initially, the candidate action is electrocardiography, that is started at time instant 23, and ends 26 (the corresponding fluent switches from candidate to active and then completed). Following the CG, the next suggested action is echocardiography, that becomes *candidate* at time as soon as the previous action is completed (time 26). The echocardiography is started at time 31 and is terminated at time 48. The next action foreseen by the CG is an angiography, that becomes candidate at time instant 48. However, at time 49 the patient has an heart failure. Such event generates an abnormal situation (signaled by the *abnormality* fluent) which triggers the BMK, activating its rules. In fact, in our example the BMK specifies that in case of heart failure, such life threat must be treated immediately, and that a possible treatment is a diuretic therapy. Thus, the action diuretic becomes candidate, and is then executed.However, from the CG viewpoint, the diuretic therapy was not expected at all, and it raises a possible non-conformance warning, as shown by the fluent *cg*, that assumes the value "nc". Once the heart failure has been treated, it is possible to continue with the execution of the CG: the angiography, still a candidate action, is started at time 54 and completed at time instant 58.

# 6    Discussion and Conclusions

In this paper we focused on the interaction between clinical guidelines (CGs) and the basic medical knowledge (BMK) in the light of the conformance problem, intended as the adherence of an observed CG execution to both types of knowledge. We have provided a formalization of CGs and BMK based on EC; in particular we have defined a model of the CG action execution that accommodates the CG-BMK interaction. We aim to provide a facility to support "a posteriori" conformance evaluation: given a complete execution trace, we can evaluate whether it is conformant to the CG and BMK. Notice that we only focus on non-conformance detection, without judging whether the operatum of the physician has been correct or not. Beside supporting quality evaluation processes, our approach can be adopted for educational purposes: given a medical problem, students are called to identify the proper actions to be applied; these can be automatically compared with the ones recommended by CG+BMK.

To the best of our knowledge, many proposals (see e.g. [8,13,7,3]) have considered the BMK only as a source of definitions of clinical terms and abstractions. Instead, the BMK has been exploited in the Protocure and Protocure II EU projects, where CGs are modelled via Asbru, and the BMK is given as a set of LTL formulas. The theorem prover KIV is used to perform quality checks [10] and to check CG properties, while the "a posteriori" conformance is not addressed. Asbru semantic, based on an action model [2], shares some similarities with our semantic, but it does not consider the BMK. Another proposal that takes into account different kind of medical information is Medintel [3]: different medical information sources (e.g., guidelines, reference texts, scientific literature) are used to improve decision support and the quality of care provided by general practitioners, which can be undermined when available information is not used.

Proposals for "a posteriori" conformance have been presented in [9] and [12], respectively focusing on CGs and business processes. Both the approaches focus on the verification of the control-flow, without taking into account parameters and data associated to the actions. Moreover, Asbru provides an a-posteriori critiquing module[1] based on action intentions (i.e. goals): every actions have a set of intentions and the critiquing module checks whether the execution log coveres them. Note that in Asbru critiquing approach the BMK has not been considered.

For the sake of brevity, in this paper we have not taken into account temporal constraints in the CGs. In the future, we aim to extend our approach for run-time compliance verification. In this respect, note that $\mathcal{REC}$ has been specifically developed for run-time reasoning over execution traces, making it possible to naturally extend the approach presented in this paper to the run-time setting. In our opinion, this will provide a significant advancement w.r.t. the other approaches to CG execution, towards integrating into the CG execution engine also the recommendations given by the BMK.

**Acknowledgments.** This work has been partially supported by the Health Sciences and Technologies - Interdepartmental Center for Industrial Research (HST-ICIR) - University of Bologna, by the DEIS Depict Project, and by the EU Project FP7-ICT ACSI (257593).

# References

1. Advani, A., Lo, K., Shahar, Y.: Intention-based critiquing of guideline-oriented medical care: The asgaard project at stanford. In: Proc. AMIA Annual Symposium, pp. 483–487 (1998)
2. Balser, M., Duelli, C., Reif, W.: Formal semantics of asbru-an overview. In: Proceedings of IDPT 2002 (2002)
3. Brandhorst, C.J., Sent, D., Stegwee, R.A., van Dijk, B.M.A.G.: Medintel: Decision support for general practitioners: A case study. In: Adlassnig, K.-P., Blobel, B., Mantas, J., Masic, I. (eds.) Proceedings of MIE 2009, pp. 688–692 (2009)
4. Chesani, F., Mello, P., Montali, M., Torroni, P.: A Logic-Based, Reactive Calculus of Events. Fundamenta Informaticae 105(1-2), 135–161 (2010)
5. Chittaro, L., Montanari, A.: Temporal representation and reasoning in artificial intelligence: Issues and approaches. AMAI 28(1-4), 47–106 (2000)
6. Cicekli, N.K., Cicekli, I.: Formalizing the specification and execution of workflows using the event calculus. Information Sciences 176(15), 2227–2267 (2006)
7. De Clercq, P.A., Blom, J.A., Hasman, A., Korsten, H.H.M.: Gaston: an architecture for the acquisition and execution of clinical guideline-application tasks. Med. Inform Internet Med. 24(4), 247–264 (2000)
8. Fridsma, D.B., (Guest ed.): Special issue on workflow management and clinical guidelines. JAMIA 22(1), 1–80 (2001)
9. Groot, P., Hommersom, A., Lucas, P.J.F., Merk, R.-J., ten Teije, A., van Harmelen, F., Serban, R.: Using model checking for critiquing based on clinical guidelines. Artificial Intelligence in Medicine 46(1), 19–36 (2009)
10. Hommersom, A., Groot, P., Lucas, P.J.F., Balser, M., Schmitt, J.: Verification of medical guidelines using background knowledge in task networks. IEEE Trans. Knowl. Data Eng. 19(6), 832–846 (2007)
11. Kowalski, R.A., Sergot, M.: A logic-based calculus of events. New Generation Computing 4(1), 67–95 (1986)
12. Rozinat, A., van der Aalst, W.M.P.: Conformance Testing: Measuring the Fit and Appropriateness of Event Logs and Process Models. In: Bussler, C.J., Haller, A. (eds.) BPM 2005. LNCS, vol. 3812, pp. 163–176. Springer, Heidelberg (2006)
13. Ten Teije, A., Miksch, S., Lucas, P. (eds.): Computer-based Medical Guidelines and Protocols: A Primer and Current Trends. Studies in Health Technology and Informatics, vol. 139. IOS Press, Amsterdam (2008)
14. Terenziani, P., Montani, S., Bottrighi, A., Molino, G., Torchio, M.: Applying Artificial Intelligence to Clinical Guidelines: the GLARE Approach. In: Teije, et al. (eds.) [13], vol. 139, pp. 273–282 (July 2008)

# Compliance Oriented Process Management Using the Example of Clinical Trials

Jörg Schlundt[1] and Stefan Jablonski[2]

[1] PRODATO Integration Technology GmbH
Hauptstraße 40, 91054 Erlangen, Germany
Joerg.Schlundt@prodato.de
[2] Chair for Databases and Information Systems, University of Bayreuth
Universitaetsstrasse 30, 95447 Bayreuth, Germany
Stefan.Jablonski@uni-bayreuth.de

**Abstract.** Compliance management is a key factor for clinical trials. This paper overviews the current situation of compliance management in clinical trials. The shortcomings of the as-is situation are analyzed as well as the current scientific approaches. To overcome the deficiencies, a framework for process oriented compliance management is presented. The extraction and modeling of compliance requirements in a process oriented way is explained. In addition a matching operator is presented, showing how different compliance standards can be made comparable.

**Keywords:** Compliance management, Standard Operating Procedures, Process Modeling, Clinical Trials.

## 1 Introduction

Managing compliance is a major cost factor in clinical trials [3]. Usually, compliance to regulations is implemented in organizations using procedures, policies and controls [23], in case of clinical trials with standard operation procedures. Standard operating procedures (SOPs) are defined as detailed, written instructions to achieve uniformity of the performance of a specific function [5]. SOPs document certain business processes to make sure they fulfill compliance requirements. Often these SOPs are based on different international, national and regional regulations. As a result SOPs tend to be complex and challenging to staff which has to work with them [3]. Verifying compliance either from an organizational or a regulatory view is a laborious manual process for specialists and hence very cost intensive [4]. Regardless, there is not much tool support to overcome these problems and support compliance management in clinical trials. In this paper we give a process oriented approach on how compliance management in clinical trials can be supported in three different areas: analysis of compliance requirements, design of SOPs, and actual work processes.

This paper is structured as follows. In section 2 an overview on compliance management in clinical trial is given. The drawbacks of today's solution are presented and grouped into three problem areas. Related work is discussed in section 3. Section

F. Daniel et al. (Eds.): BPM 2011 Workshops, Part II, LNBIP 100, pp. 212–224, 2012.

4 contains our process oriented approach to support compliance management. A short overview of aspect oriented process modeling is given in Section 4.1. Based on this general method, the overall approach for process oriented compliance management is explained (section 4.2). It is shown how our approach can overcome the drawbacks of the three problem areas. In section 4.3 we show how requirements of compliance regulations can be extracted and modeled via processes (later referred to as "Standard Processes"). With the introduction of a matching operator (section 4.4), we demonstrate how different compliance regulations can be compared. In section 5, our findings are discussed and the future prospects of our approach of process oriented compliance management are pointed out.

# 2    Compliance Management in Clinical Trials Today

To grasp the as-is situation of compliance management in clinical trials, we analyzed the literature, the current situation at the Coordinating Centers for Clinical Trials (KKS Network) and a major phase of three trials from a big pharmaceutical company. The KKS Network is a platform initiated by the BMBF and offers a wide range of scientific services to scientists in university hospitals for clinical research [6]. A major area of the KKS Network is the development and maintenance of Standard Operating Procedures (SOPs) for all KKS Centers in Germany. The KKS Approach to achieve compliance is the wide spread centered document approach. In our experience SOPs are documents which contain information about business processes and compliance requirements in natural language. The KKS network has about 20 SOPs covering different processes areas like "Adverse Event Reporting" or "Data Management". We found a similar approach in the commercial clinical research. Pharmaceutical companies and contract research organizations implemented the SOP centered approach to achieve compliance, too [7]. During our analysis we found several drawbacks in compliance management systems in academic and industrial sponsored clinical research. They are grouped into three problem areas: compliance regulation standards, standard operating procedures, and actual work processes

## 2.1    Compliance Regulation Standards

Compliance requirements for clinical trials are documented in natural language. Often one trial takes place in several countries and many countries have different compliance requirements. Although there are international guidelines like ICH-GCP [5] that aims to harmonize the different national regulations, there are still many differences between the individual national compliance requirements (cf. Figure 1).

The example in Figure 1 shows two citations from two different regulations. The "ICH-GCP" (Good Clinical Practice) is an international standard issued by the International Conference on Harmonization of Technical Requirements for Registration of Pharmaceuticals for Human Use (ICH). The "GCP-Verordnung" is a national regulation from Germany [24]. Both citations refer to the cancellation of a clinical trial and the reporting rules for investigators. In ICH-GCP the investigator informs the institution where the clinical trial takes place. The institution or the investigator informs another control body, the Institutional Review Board/ Independent Ethics Committee (IRB/IEC). The national regulation "GCP-Verordnung" prescribes to inform the national agency within fifteen days. Without going into much detail, it is clear that there are differences between the two regulations.

---

**ICH-GCP 4.12.2**

*If the sponsor terminates or suspends a trial (see 5.21), the investigator should promptly inform the institution where applicable and the investigator/institution should promptly inform the IRB/IEC and provide the IRB/IEC a detailed written explanation of the termination or suspension.*

**GCP – Verordnung §12(2)**

*(2) The investigator informs the responsible authority about the end of the clinical trial within 90 days. In case the clinical trial was suspended or terminated by the sponsor, the responsible authorities are informed within 15 days with the specification of the reason for the termination or suspension.*

---

**Fig. 1.** Excerpts from ICH-GCP and GCP-Verordnung

There are sporadic analyses which compare the requirements of difference compliance standards [8]; but there is no systematic approach available neither in literature nor in practice. Since requirements are documented in natural language, they are hard to compare and it is not easy to design SOPs that fulfill all requirements of all the different countries a trial is involved with. SOP design is therefore cumbersome and an expert job [4].

## 2.2    Standard Operating Procedures

The implementation of compliance requirements via SOPs has several disadvantages. References to regulations are included in these descriptions but cumbersome to use, especially if more than one compliance standard has to be referenced. Very often it is not clear what compliance requirement is fulfilled by the SOP. On the one hand side SOPs transcribe compliance requirements into organizational procedures. On the other hand side organizational specific policies are included into a SOP. There is no clear separation between these two concepts. The example in Figure 2 is an extract from a KKS-SOP and demonstrates the issues mentioned above

---

*The legal background for the handling of adverse events can be found*

*- AMG nach dem 14. Gesetz zur Änderung des AMG, § 42(3)*

*- GCP-V §12 (4-7), §13 (1-7)*

*- AMG-Anzeigeverordnung, AMG-V*

*[...]*

*3.4 Notification of SAEs*

*3.4.1 Notification by investigator*

*In case the KKS is according to the to trial protocol the institution to be informed, the investigator informs the KKS about the SAE. Definition, form and appropriate time limit for the notification, have to be defined in the trial protocol.*

---

**Fig. 2.** Excerpt from KKS SOP

The first passage shows how compliance standards and SOPs are linked together. There is a reference to the regulation the SOP relates to. It is not clear which requirements of the regulation are met in detail. The second passage (after the brackets) shows a process description. Organizational specific policies are described here. Mostly, SOPs are documented in a pure textual way. Based on our experience participating in the KKS Network, flow diagrams are not very common for these process descriptions. In the textual part of the SOPS tasks, task order, documents, document flows, timelines and decisions with alternative processing options are mixed. In a textual form SOPs lack clarity and structure.

## 2.3    Actual Work Processes

The third problem area regards the actual work processes in clinical trials. As actual work processes we refer to the execution of the defined business processes; in this case SOPs are representing them. SOPs are not yet well integrated in the daily work processes. Most of the time SOPs are available for clinical trial staff in form of paper documents [9]. It is not possible to link them to IT applications. IT applications are widespread in clinical trials and used for various tasks. Data is processed in Clinical Data Management Systems, trials are organized and managed with the help of Clinical Trial Management Systems and adverse events are reported by adverse event reporting systems. Even though SOPs are an integral part of every clinical trial and contain vital information about business processes and compliance requirements, they are not considered to be a part of the usual IT infrastructure [10]. It seems that neither from the SOP point of view nor from the IT application an attempt to integrate both worlds exists. Without this integration it is hard to support compliance conform process execution. Today compliance violations of work processes are mostly identified a posteriori via audits. These audits of the actual work processes are work-intensive because of the missing link between work processes and SOPs.

## 3    Related Work

There are special tools to deal with SOPs. The application "SOP-Creater" was developed by the Institute of medical informatics, statistics and epidemiology university of Leipzig [11]. It is based on a content management system and was designed to process, release and distribute SOPS. Another solution for SOPs is SOPmanage™ von ADS-Limathon Limited [12]. Like the "SOP-Creater" this software supports the creation and distribution of SOPs. Both software examples support basic operations for SOP management, similar to a document management system. The approaches just handle the technical management of SOPs; they do not solve the problems mentioned above, for example the integration of different compliance standards.

Other approaches in the scientific literature don't refer to SOPs directly, but to compliance management in general. Process modeling languages and rules modeling languages (business rules) are candidates for the documentation of organizational policies and procedures [13]. A business rule describes conditions for business processes [14]. Business rules are supposed to control and influence business processes. The Simple Rule Markup Language (SRML) is an example for such an approach [15]. The advantage of a business rule approach is that compliance requirements can be documented in a structured, reusable way. Rules could be used for the actual execution of processes by a rule engine. Still, a rule based approach does not support the comparison of different compliance standards.

There are several papers which address some of the problems mentioned above. In [13] processes and compliance, requirements are modeled via ontologies. This approach supports the structured documentation of compliance standards. It could be used to support a compliance conform design of processes. However, the comparison of different regulations standards is not intended and an execution support of processes is not supported. The gap between designed processes and actual work processes is still existent.

Processes are modeled based on the Resource Description Frameworks (RDF) in [4]. With a query language different processes can be compared. The authors suggest that compliance standards could be modeled in RDF and linked to process descriptions. Based on the query language it can be identified that changes in the modeled processes could lead to compliance violence. It is not envisaged to compare different compliance standards and to support the execution of the modeled processes conform to the regulations.

In [13] the modeling of compliance requirements and processes is separated as well. Compliance requirements are represented via control objects, which represented certain business rules. Based on the control objects in processes a measurement ("compliance distance") can be defined, that indicates how much a process deviates from a compliance standard. Again, the concept does not include the comparison of different compliance standards. The integration into a runtime environment to support the process execution is mentioned but not explained how this could be done.

In [16] a concept is shown, how assessments of organizational processes against a given process standard (SPICE) are simplified. Here, organizational processes are modeled in a process tool and mapped to concepts of the process (compliance) standards. The concept enables the check of processes against given compliance standards and links the two areas compliance standards and processes together. A process execution approach is showed in a subsequent publication [17]. But again, it is not possible to compare different compliance standards with this approach and the compliance standards are not documented in a structured way.

# 4     Process Oriented Compliance Management

This section presents an approach that tackles the deficits of SOPs in all three identified problem areas. To begin with, we give a quick overview on perspective oriented modeling that forms the basis for our approach. Although we introduce the overall framework, only the problem area "compliance standards" is detailed in this paper.

## 4.1     Perspective Oriented Modeling

In perspective oriented modeling, processes are described from different viewpoints [18]. Usually, there are five different perspectives to model processes: function, data, control, application, and organization perspective. The functional perspective describes process steps and hierarchical relationship between processes. Input and output for process steps are modeled by the data perspective. The organizational perspective identifies who is responsible for certain process steps. With the application oriented perspective it is possible to model tools and software applications necessary for process execution. All process elements can be linked together via a dataflow or the control flow. The control flow describes the execution order of the single process steps. The dataflow depict the flow of the data elements within a process. The perspective oriented modeling method was chosen for our approach because it has shown its adaptability and extensibility in various application areas. It was used for clinical treatment processes, scientific processes and software processes [19], [20] [21]. Through adaptability and extensibility the approach can be adapted to the specific requirements of our application field.

## 4.2    Overview on Process Oriented Compliance Management

The framework of our approach consists of three basic concepts (Figure 3), similar to [25]: process standard, process plan, and process instance. A "process standard" is a process model that represents the requirements from a compliance standard. For each compliance standard (e.g. ICH-GCP, GCP-Verordnung) a process standard is designed. The requirements from the regulations are structured by the different process perspective (data, process, organization, application and control flow). The correlations of the different compliance standards can then be defined on basis of these process standards. For this reason we define a "process matching operator". The process matching operator enables users to define the correlations (similarities and differences) between process standards. With the concepts of process standards and the process matching operator it is possible to document the compliance requirement in a structured way and compare the different regulations. Based on process standards a "process plan" (e.g. SOPs) for a new clinical trial can be developed. Existing parts

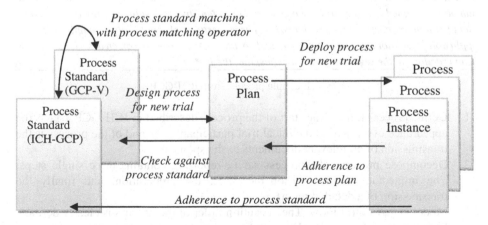

**Fig. 3.** Framework overview

of a process standard can be used or newly developed processes can be taken. Process plans must relate to process standards: either because of the usage of existing process components or because of an explicit relationship that is modeled between them. Thus process plans can be checked for compliance adherence against the process standards.

Process plans can be deployed and instantiated in a process execution environment ("process instance"). Within the execution environment, clinical trial personnel is guided to carry out process instances in accordance to the given process plans. Deviations of process plans are possible but have to be documented for later investigations and auditing. It is possible to analyze the adherence of process instances to process plans, as well as to process standards through the linkage.

## 4.3    Modeling Process Standards

Two main problems were identified in the realm of compliance standards: first, these standards were described rather informally; secondly, there are different standards that have to be applied. To solve these problems we choose a two steps approach: first, compliance requirements are extracted and are incorporated into a process model. Second, relationships between different compliance standards are modeled and made comparable through a matching operator.

Understanding and capturing of business processes is often referred to as process discovery [22]. It is a critical step in process management that is often executed insufficiently. We used the following method based in our process modeling experience to extract the compliance requirement and to model the standard processes. (1) Define process limit; (2) Decompose process; (3) Model Data/Control Flow; (4) Add additional perspectives. An example from ICH-GCP will illustrate the method (Figure 4).

---

*ICH-GCP 4.11 Safey Reporting (Investigator)*

*All serious adverse events (SAEs) should be reported immediately to the sponsor except for those SAEs that the protocol or other document (e.g., Investigator's Brochure) identifies as not needing immediate reporting. The immediate reports should be followed promptly by detailed, written reports. The immediate and follow-up reports should identify subjects by unique code numbers assigned to the trial subjects rather than by the subjects' names, personal identification numbers, and/or addresses. The investigator should also comply with the applicable regulatory requirement(s) related to the reporting of unexpected serious adverse drug reactions to the regulatory authority(ies) and the IRB/IEC.*

---

**Fig. 4.** Example process from ICH-GCP

1.  Define process limits: The start of the process described in ICH-GCP 4.11 is the appearance of an SAE of a clinical trial participant. The end of the process is the transmission of all relevant documents to the sponsor.
2.  Decompose process: The process safety reporting contains three single steps: The immediate notification of the SAE, the preparation, and finally the transmission of a detailed report.
3.  Model Data/Control Flow: The execution order of the process is clearly defined. Firstly notice about the SAE has to be given. After that a detailed report has to

be prepared and then sent to the sponsor. The necessary documents (data flow) for the processes can also be derived from the regulation.

4.  Add organizational perspective: The responsible role for each process step must be added. In this case the investigator role is required.

All four steps together add up to the key process depicted in Figure 5. We used the iPM process modeling tool from [25] to model the processes.

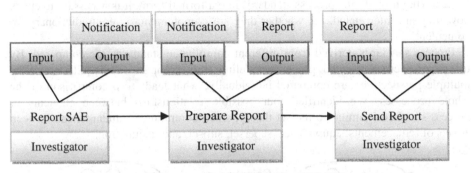

**Fig. 5.** Example process model for ICH-GCP

Figure 5 shows the three process steps (Report SAE, Prepare Report, Send Report). The role investigator is attached to each process step. Additionally, each process step has input and output interfaces for data/documents (here: notification, report). For each element of the process model, it is possible to link to the corresponding part in the regulation. For example, the document notification could link to Chapter 8.3.17 from ICH-GCP which describes notification of SAEs in more detail. This link connects together regulation and process elements in a standardized way and helps to fulfill the complete requirements of the regulation.

We analyzed ICH-GCP and GCP-Verordnung and obtained a large number of processes. To achieve a higher comprehensibility, processes are organized according to a 3-layered schema (Figure 6). The first layer describes the main phases of a clinical trial (design, setup, conduct, and analysis). Each key process (second layer) is assigned to one trial phase. The key processes are detailed on the process layer (third layer). Finally, 18 key processes with ca. 70 processes were identified for the ICH-GCP. The GCP-Verordnung resulted in 11 key processes with 35 processes.

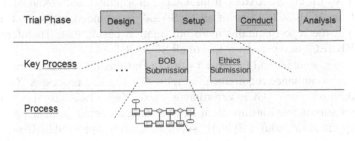

**Fig. 6.** Process layers

A process standards represents the compliance requirements from a regulation in a process based way. Thus the requirements are documented in a structured, re-useable and better understandable way. Thus the first critical issue is coped with: compliance standards are represented in a formal and unique way.

## 4.4    Process Matching

After having brought the process standards into a formal form, it is necessary to check how they are interrelated, i.e. whether they are complementary, contradictionary, or coincident.

Process standards derived from different compliance standards are compared. By using perspective oriented process modeling, this comparison is quite easy: the multiple perspectives are compared individually, what leads to a comparison of the whole processes. We identified four possible relationships between elements of process standards, similar to the set theory, since compliance standards, can be seen as sets of requirements: equivalence, superset, subset, and disjunction,

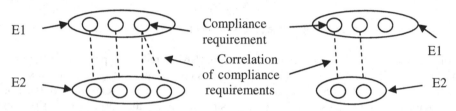

**Fig. 7.** Equivalence relationship            **Fig. 8.** Superset relationship

Two modeling elements (E1 and E2) have an **equivalence relationship** if they have identical compliance requirements (Figure 7). Figure 7 shows two abstract modeling elements E1 and E2. Both elements have compliance requirements that can be correlated. Since all requirements are correlated both elements have an equivalence relationship. An example for such a relationship is the role "Ethikkommission" from the GCP-Verordnung and "Independent ethics committee" from ICH-GCP.

A modeling element E1 has a **superset relationship** to modeling element E2, if all requirements of element E2 are met by E1; besides, E1 has additional requirements which are not met by E2 (Figure 8). An example for such a relationship are the data elements "List of all SUSARs" from GCP-Verordnung and "Annual reports to IRB/IEC" from ICH-GCP. "List of all SUSARs" is included in "Annual reports to IRB/IEC", but the report contains more information beside that. Therefore "Annual reports to IRB/IEC" is superset to "List of all SUSARs".

Modeling elements E1 and E2 have a **subset relationship** if both elements have an intersection of compliance requirements (Figure 9). The key processes "Get approval from Ethikkommission" (GCP-Verordnung) and "Get IEC/IRB-Approval" (ICH-GCP) have a subset relationship. Both key processes contain similar processes like "Submit Application" and "Submit application for approval". However, both processes comprise processes that are not comprised by the other one.

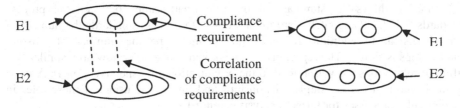

**Fig. 9.** Subset relationship                    **Fig. 10.** Disjunction relationship

Two modeling elements E1 and E2 have **a disjunction relationship** if both elements have no correlation in any compliance requirement (Figure 10). The ICH-GCP regulation defines a role "Contract Research Organisation". This role is not included in the GCP-Verordnung. Therefore the role "Contract Research Organization" has a disjunction relationship to all the roles of GCP-Verordnung.

The above defined four relationships are used to document the correlation of elements from different process standards. Figure 11 shows an implementation of this documentation. Process models that have to be compared are analyzed. In this figure the roles of two compliance standards, ICH-GCP and GOP-Verordnung have to be compared. Existent roles for both process standards are listed (e.g. Sponsor, Investigator). A process analyst can draw arrows between the roles to express their relationship. An arrow with two heads stands for an equivalence relationship (e.g. Sponsor). A dotted arrow with just one head stands for a superset relationship (e.g. Sponsor-Investigator is a superset of Prüfarzt).

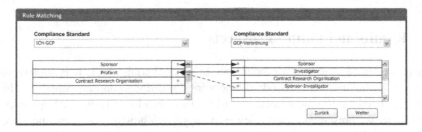

**Fig. 11.** Modeling of matching between roles

The example from above shows a matching between roles. In addition, we identified matchings betweens data/documents processes and control flows. It is needless to say that the documentation/modeling of the relationships has to be done manually by a domain expert. However, through perspective oriented process modeling, these experts are well guided through this analysis. All correlations are stored in the meta data of the process models. Our tool also supports reports of this analysis.

| Overview Roles | | | | | | | |
|---|---|---|---|---|---|---|---|
| Process Standard | | Matching Process Standard | | Equivalence | Superset | Subset | Disjunction |
| Name | Number of Roles | Name | Number of Roles | | | | |
| ICH-GCP | 12 | GCP-Verordnung | 4 | 3 | 1 | 2 | 6 |

**Fig. 12.** Role relationships between ICH-GCP and GCP Verordnung

Figure 12 shows the summary of the role relationships between the process standards ICH-GCP and GCP-Verordnung. For both process standards the number of roles is listed. In addition, for each relationship type the number of existing relationships is shown. The report gives a quick and coarse overview how similar two different regulations are with regard to the organizational perspective (roles). A more detailed report shows the single relationships and link to the usage of these roles in the particular processes for further analysis (Figure 13).

| Roles Detailed | | | | | | | | |
|---|---|---|---|---|---|---|---|---|
| Process Standard | | | | Matching Process Standard | | | Relationship | |
| Name | Role | Usage | Matching existend | Name | Role | Usage | Relationship | |
| ICH-GCP | Sponsor | Link | Yes | GCP-Verordnung | Sponsor | Link | Equivalence |
| ICH-GCP | CRO | | No | na | na | na | Disjunction |

**Fig. 13.** Roles and their matching to other process standards

For two process standards all roles and their relationships can be shown in detail. Via a link, the usage of the roles in process standard can be shown for further analysis. Similar to that, process standards can be compared for the other process element types (processes, data/documents etc.), too. With the modeled process standards, the compliance requirements are structured in understandable and reusable way, separated from the actual organization specific requirements in SOPs. Even non-experts in clinical trial compliance are able to grasp the key compliance requirements for the different trial processes. For experts the link to the actual compliance documents is helpful.

# 5    Results and Future Prospects

Compliance management is a crucial part in clinical trials. Still, it is mostly paper based (e.g. Regulations and Standard Operating Procedures) and a manual job. In the highly regulated environment in clinical trials, there is a lot of room for improvement. In this paper we presented an overview of an approach how to overcome the issues in the three problem areas: compliance regulation standards, standard operating procedures and actual work processes. For the problem area "compliance regulation standards" the approach was explained in more detailed. It was shown how the requirements from regulations can be extracted and documented into process models (process standards). Arranged into process layers, the requirements are represented in a visual and application oriented way, so that the overall complexity of the regulation standards is reduced. Additionally, it was shown how the requirements of different compliance standards can be correlated. Based on these correlations a comparison of different compliance standards is possible. Especially in the fields of clinical trial, where every trial has to deal with manifold national and international regulations, this is a major improvement. We have proved our concept in a prototype implementation. The results are promising. It is now feasible for clinical personal to compare different regulations without having a deep knowledge about the compliance regulations. The real benefit of the correlations between process standards shows in the design of new processes (process plans). Here a process modeler can design a process plan based on a process standard. Via checks it can be assured that a process plan implements the requirements of regulations. Since the correlations of process standards are documented, they can be used to automatically check a process plan against different process standards. We will present this concept in a subsequent publication.

# References

1. Food and Drug Administration: Critical Path Opportunity Report,
   http://www.fda.gov/oc/initiatives/criticalpath/
   (retrieving date January 10, 2011)
2. El Kharbili, M., Stein, S., Markovic, I., Pulvermüller, E.: Towards a Framework for Semantic Business Process Compliance Management. In: Proceedings of GRCIS (2008)
3. Krockenberger, K., Knaup, P., Bez, K., Gleiter, C.H.: The necessity of an electronic SOP retrieval system. Stud. Health Technol. Inform. 116, 1000–1003 (2005)
4. Soto, M., Münch, J.: Using Model Comparison to maintain model-to standard compliance. In: Proceedings of the 2008 Intl. Workshop on Comparison and Versioning of Software Models (2008)
5. ICH: Guideline for Good Clinical Practice,
   http://www.ema.europa.eu/pdfs/human/ich/013595en.pdf
   (retrieving date January 10, 2011)
6. Koordinierungszentren für Klinische Studien, http://www.kks-netzwerk.de
7. Schnurr, B., Chase, D., Gierend, M., Rettig, S.: Qualitätssicherung in der klinischenForschung. Pharm. Ind. 66(9), 1086–1089 (2004)
8. Burke, J.D.: ICH-GCP & FDA Regulations Differences,
   http://louisville.edu/advising/humansubjects/
   ICH%20GCP%20-%20FDA%20Regulations%20Differences_4-20-09.ppt
9. Krockenberger, K., Luntz, S.P., Knaup, P.: Usage and usability of standard operating procedures (SOPs) among the coordination centers for clinical trials (KKS). Methods Inf. Med. 47(6), 505–510 (2008)
10. Ramos, L.: eClinical Trial Software and Vendor Landscape (2006),
    http://www.forrester.com/Events/Content/0,5180,-1325,00.ppt
    (retrieving date January 16, 2011)
11. Ontologies in Medicine – SOP Creator, http://www.onto-med.de/Archiv/
    ontomed2002/en/publicationsflyer/sopcreator.pdf (retrieving date January 19, 2011)
12. Limathon – SOPmanage,
    http://www.limathon.com/ADSL_SOP/SOPmanage_nhs_cpa.HTM
    (retrieving date January 19, 2011)
13. Schmidt, R., Bartsch, C., Oberhauser, R.: Modeling Control Objectives for Business Process Compliance, Ontology-based representation of compliance requirements for service processes. In: Proc. of Semantic Business Process and Product Lifecycle Management, SBPM (2007)
14. Business Rules Group: Defining business rules – what are they really,
    http://www.businessrulesgroup.org/first_paper/br01c0.htm
    (retrieving date February 3, 2011)
15. Simple Rule Markup Language, http://xml.coverpages.org/srml.html
    (retrieving date January 30, 2011)

16. Jablonski, S., Faerber, M.: Integrated Management of Company Processes and Standard Processes: A Platform to Prepare and Perform Quality Management Appraisals. In: ICSE Workshops on Software Quality, WoSQ 2007 (2007)
17. Jablonski, S., Faerber, M., Jochaud, F., Götz, M., Igler, M.: Enabling Flexible Execution of Business Processes. In: Meersman, R., Herrero, P. (eds.) OTM-WS 2008. LNCS, vol. 5333, pp. 10–11. Springer, Heidelberg (2008)
18. Jablonski, S., Bussler, C.: Workflow Management: Modeling Concepts, Architecture and Implementation. Itp New Media (1996)
19. Jablonski, S., Faerber, M., Kastner, N., Metzger, A.: IPM4QM – Eine integrierte Modellierung von Unternehmensprozessen und Anforderungen aus SPICE. In: Proceedings of the SQS Software & Systems Quality Conferences 2007, Düsseldorf, Germany (April 2007)
20. Faerber, M., Meerkamm, S., Schneider, T., Jablonski, S.: Qualitative Prozessanalyse klinischer Prozesse - Vorgehen und Erfahrungen. Arthritis + rheuma, Jahrgang, 29 (2009)
21. Jablonski, S., Volz, B., Rehman, M.A.: A Conceptual Modeling and Execution Framework for Process Based Scientific Applications. In: Proceedings on CyberInfrastructure: Information Management in eScience (2007)
22. Verner, L.: The Challenge of Process Discovery, http://www.bptrends.com/deliver_file.cfm?fileType=publication&fileName=05-04%20WPprocessDiscovery%20-%20Verner%201.pdf (retrieving date February 2, 2011)
23. Wecker, G., van Laak, H.: Compliance in der Unternehmenspraxis – Grundlagen, Organsiation und Umsetzung. Gabler (2008)
24. GCP-Verordnung, http://www.gesetze-im-internet.de/gcp-v/BJNR208100004.html
25. Faerber, M.: Prozessorientiertes Qualitätsmanagement - Ein Konzept zur Implementierung. Gabler (2010)

# Alpha-Adaptive: Evolutionary Workflow Metadata in Distributed Document-Oriented Process Management

Christoph P. Neumann, Peter K. Schwab, Andreas M. Wahl, and Richard Lenz

Friedrich-Alexander University,
Erlangen-Nuremberg, Germany
{christoph.neumann,richard.lenz}@cs.fau.de

**Abstract.** The $\alpha$-Flow project enables process support in heterogeneous and inter-institutional scenarios in healthcare. $\alpha$-Flow provides a distributed case file and represents workflow schemas as documents which are shared coequally to content documents. The activity progress and data flow is controlled by process-related metadata. A use case will motivate user-defined and demand-driven status attributes that are not known at design-time. $\alpha$-Adaptive demonstrates how to apply the EAV data design approach and prototype-based programming concepts in order to provide an adaptive-evolutionary status attribute model for document-oriented processes.

**Topics:** Process-oriented system architectures in healthcare, facilitating knowledge-acquisition of healthcare processes, deferred systems design, case handling.

## 1 Introduction and Objectives

Medical treatment of patients is increasingly evolving from a series of isolated episodes towards a continuous process, incorporating multiple organizationally independent institutions and different healthcare professions. One characteristic of this process is that both the order of treatment steps and the amount of involved parties are usually not known in advance as they are largely dependent on the preceding course of the treatment. Evolutionary workflow approaches are required that enable cooperation and coordination among the participants. It is essential to deal with the semantic and technical heterogeneity of the systems at the participating sites because different information systems and internal workflows are used.

In the case handling paradigm [1], the flow of a patient between healthcare professionals is considered as a workflow—with activities that include all kinds of diagnostic or therapeutic treatments. The workflow is considered as a case, and workflow management in healthcare is to handle these cases.

## 2 Background

Case handling is a new paradigm for process support. Unlike workflow management it is aimed at supporting a team of cooperating process participants in their decisions rather than predefining process steps. The core features that are defined by the case

F. Daniel et al. (Eds.): BPM 2011 Workshops, Part II, LNBIP 100, pp. 225–236, 2012.
© Springer-Verlag Berlin Heidelberg 2012

handling paradigm [1] are: (a) provide all information available, i.e. present the case as a whole rather than showing bits and pieces, (b) decide about activities on the basis of the information available rather than the activities already executed, (c) separate work distribution from authorization and allow for additional types of roles, not just the execute role, and (d) allow workers to view and add/modify data before or after the corresponding activities have been executed. Yet, on the framework level, contemporary case handling focuses on hospital (single institution) scenarios and technologically on a centralized case handling system.

$\alpha$-**Flow Conception:** The $\alpha$-Flow approach, as it is described in [2] and [3], aims to provide case handling in distributed environments and emphasizes on document-oriented systems integration. $\alpha$-Flow is considered as an implementation of distributed document-oriented process management (dDPM). The document-oriented integration style supporting inter-institutional environments was motivated in a-Flow predecessor DEUS [4]. Basically, the traditional paper based interaction paradigm, that uses signed forms for communication, is imitated and extended to exploit the potential of electronic communication. The $\alpha$-Doc is our notion of a distributed case file that contains all case related information to be shared among multiple participants.

An $\alpha$-Doc is decomposed in $\alpha$-Cards that are units of organizational accountability and of validation as well as subject to atomic synchronization actions. Each $\alpha$-Doc represents an entire case which we also name an $\alpha$-Episode. There is a one-to-one relation between $\alpha$-Doc and $\alpha$-Episode: The term $\alpha$-Doc emphasizes on the artifact dimension, whereas the term $\alpha$-Episode emphasizes on the implicit workflow dimension with tasks which are the treatment steps. Each task is planned by creating an $\alpha$-Card descriptor, and it is fulfilled by providing its result report. The treatment process and its state will progress with the creation or change of $\alpha$-Cards, which we elaborated in [5].

$\alpha$-**Flow Artifact Context of Adornments:** For $\alpha$-Adaptive, the focus lies on the structure of an $\alpha$-Card that is outlined in Fig. 1. An $\alpha$-*Card* consists of a descriptor and a payload. The $\alpha$-*Card descriptor* consists of several $\alpha$-*Adornments*. The general term "adornment" is borrowed from the Unified Modeling Language: an adornment adds to the meaning and/or semantics of the element to which it pertains and has a textual or graphical representation. In $\alpha$-Flow, adornments are process-relevant status attributes and represent certain aspects of an $\alpha$-Card's life-cycle and process state. Adornments either classify $\alpha$-Cards passively or an adornment status change can actively act as an event trigger that implies process change.

The basic $\alpha$-*Adornment model* for $\alpha$-Cards has been discussed in [2] and consists basically of adornments for: contributor and object under consideration (OC), validity and visibility, version and variant, fundamental semantic payload type, syntactic payload type and domain-specific semantic payload type. The *payload* of an $\alpha$-Card contains an arbitrary electronic medical document, contributed by a process participant.

One exemplary adornment usage is given from [2]: visibility and validity. An $\alpha$-Card represents an open task if there is only the descriptor but no payload. It represents a fulfilled task if there is a payload with visibility set to "public" and validity set to "valid". $\alpha$-Cards with a contributed payload but still with its visibility or validity adornments set to incipient states (e.g. "private" or "invalid") represent work in progress. To share

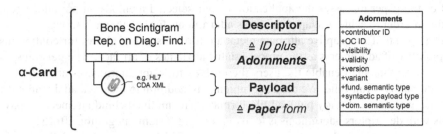

**Fig. 1.** Artifact structure: an $\alpha$-Card with its descriptor & payload

preliminary information, that is not yet validated by a human signature, is common in healthcare, especially for reports on diagnostic findings.

**$\alpha$-Flow Operative Outline:** The "$\alpha$" in all our terms implicates "active", in analogy to the underlying concept of active documents with active properties [6], and "$\alpha$-Doc" essentially means "active document". The idea is to technically form the collective case dossier into a single self-managing file unit, that can be handled as passive files like a PDF or Word file, containing both the case data and the dDPM enactment engine. One appeal of such a solution is as follows: If we provide a technical platform for such eccentric artifacts as our active documents for dDPM purposes, each human actor becomes participant by handing him or her a copy of the $\alpha$-Doc—which is basically the same interaction as making them participants by handing over referral vouchers.

From an operative embedding perspective, the $\alpha$-Flow approach minimizes the initial work for establishing an information exchange between different process participants. From a technological perspective, no pre-installed system components are required to interact with an $\alpha$-Doc. Thus, the $\alpha$-Doc is an instantly available tool that needs no administration.

An $\alpha$-Doc provides a functional fusion of a shared work list editor with instant messaging with version control with access restrictions. Furthermore, the $\alpha$-Doc embeds an $\alpha$-Props subsystem [7] which is a rule engine that guards the adornment changes and executes active properties as the kernel of the active document. Workflow benefits are process planning, process history, and participant management as well as template creation for process structure and process-required roles. An $\alpha$-Doc supports all core features (a) to (d) of case handling. Further details about the $\alpha$-Flow mechanics must be skipped at this point.

## 3    Motivation and Objectives

This paper focuses only on the $\alpha$-Flow adornment model. It does not provide in-depth explanations for the over-arching artifact structures. It will not be necessary to know the overall $\alpha$-Flow operative embedding in order to understand the $\alpha$-Adaptive concerns. The first part of the paper provides a use case which is result of our studies and motivates user-defined adornments by example. The method section then outlines two general state of the art methods to achieve run-time adaptability in information systems. The last part of the paper discusses the application of our selected methods on our adornment model in order to achieve adaptive process adornments for healthcare artifacts.

The appeal of an adaptive attribute metadata model is that it allows for continuous adaptability of adornments as the process status attributes of artifacts. The general system architecture shall enable the users themselves to adapt adornments according to their demands at run-time. We need adornments, in addition to the payload documents, because we allow arbitrary payload file formats. The motive behind augmenting payloads with descriptors/adornments is to avoid upfront system integration efforts.

Status attributes for the artifacts are necessary such that actions can be defined upon their status change and automated by an active property. The users ultimately decide if the efforts to maintain a specific status attribute gains any benefit for cooperation. The use case scenario will motivate domain-specific status attributes whose exact specification cannot or should not be fixed at the design-time of a distributed process infrastructure because they ultimately are subject to semantic consensus finding between actors, institutions and domains.

# 4  Use Case Scenario

This section provides an example for user-defined status attributes and their utilization during treatment episodes. The use case description is independent of our framework—it is based on paper-based working practice in healthcare. This section extends our former description of breast cancer treatment [5].

**Condition Indicator:** The exemplary classifier *condition indicator* can be of use in situations where patients are under periodic medical examination. Consensus finding must happen outside our system (the process platform can only foster it by supporting ad-hoc definitions of adornments as well as changes to the value range by the actors at any time). For the sake of our example, the process participants already have a consensus and we assume that they agreed upon a value range of *normal*, *guarded*, and *serious* for the condition levels. Such status can be attributed to any report and indicates the patient condition at the corresponding time and in regard to the diagnostic context.

After the primary therapy [5], i.e. removal of the tumor, the post-operative care and the adjuvant therapy run in parallel for the first six months. The adjuvant therapy (with chemo therapy, radio therapy and hormonal therapy) is not described in this paper as aggravation is mainly discovered during post-operative care. Post-operative care will continue for about five years. In contrast to primary therapy, the treatments during post-operative care are ambulant. The following use case illustrates how aggravation of a patient's condition spontaneously changes the course of treatment by requiring participation of additional healthcare professionals.

If no health problems arise, the post-operative care will follow a common schema (Fig. 2): Every three months the patient must undergo a clinical examination at her gynecologist ($Gyn^A$). Semi-annually she is referred to a radiologist ($Rad^A$) for a mammography ($RV_M$). Initially, $Gyn^A$ supplies a detailed anamnesis documentation to briefly summarize the preceding treatment. After each examination the radiologist creates a report about the diagnostic findings and makes it available to $Gyn^A$ again.

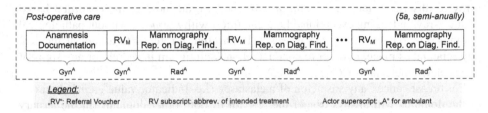

**Fig. 2.** Breast cancer: post-operative care episode; no unclear symptoms

Because this is a periodic monitoring the doctors want to indicate normal and exceptional conditions. Anytime during the five years of post-operative care there is the possibility that the patient reports unclear symptoms or her gynecologist makes a suspicious finding that indicates metastases. Thus, the *condition indicator* is designated as a diagnostic report status attribute.

**An Incidence Occurs:** If, for example, the patient at some point complains about pain in her upper abdomen and/or a yellowish pigmentation of her skin, the gynecologist must find the reason for these symptoms as they may be caused by liver metastases. Fig. 3 illustrates the modified episode. The gynecologist sets the *condition indicator* of an exceptionally created anamnesis report to *guarded* and refers the patient to an internist ($Int^A$) for an upper abdomen sonography ($RV_{AS}$).

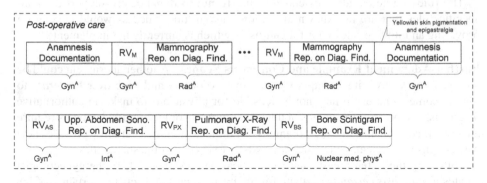

**Fig. 3.** Breast cancer: post-operative care episode; classification of unclear symptoms

The internist might conclude in his report on diagnostic findings that the occurred symptoms are caused by a gallstone. In this case, the *condition indicator* of the sonography would also be set to *guarded* because the participants' consensus is that higher escalations are reserved for metastases. Of course, the patient is treated by the internist against gallstone but this forms another treatment episode.

For another patient, the initial suspicion could be strengthened by the upper abdomen sonography and liver metastases are now indicated. Consequently, the internist sets the *condition indicator* of his report to *serious*. The gynecologist will then instruct further examinations for potential lung or bone metastases: he refers the patient to a radiologist ($Rad^A$) for a pulmonary x-ray to check for lung metastases ($RV_{PX}$). A report on the x-ray results is written. The *condition indicator* would indicate the condition based on the x-ray, indicating exceptional lung condition with *normal* ("without pathological findings") to *serious* ("lung metastases"). In parallel, a referral to a nuclear medical physician takes place, in order to conduct a bone scintigram in search for any signs of bone-related metastases ($RV_{BS}$).

For breast cancer, any suspicion of metastases (i.e. indicator value *guarded*) in one of the domains will always trigger the referral to both other domains (in the ternary set of liver, lung, and bones). Any affirmed suspicion (i.e. indicator value *serious*) will trigger a vital treatment. Treating the metastases will form an episode itself, besides the modified post-operative care. It will require a breast cancer center, an oncologist, and further surgical or chemo-therapeutic measures.

**Benefits and Future Work:** As far as described above, the user-defined attributes only record process-relevant states of the underlying reports. It would be possible to use the indicators as triggers for coordination actions.

Within the scenario, a modification of the *condition indicator* adornment into a *serious* state could trigger special notifications, e.g. notify epidemiological cancer registries which form a hierarchical national organization in Germany and complement the German cancer treatment centers. It would even be possible to offer users some means to define process templates for an escalation process plan. In case of a notable condition indication, the embedded rule engine, $\alpha$-Props as mentioned above, could automatically extend the episode's process structure with the process steps from the escalation plan.

The rule engine could be extended in the future to dynamically support domain-specific rules that are not known at $\alpha$-Flow design-time. Success would depend on providing an intuitive rule editor for end-users which is currently not implemented.

**Further Adornment Example and Consensus Scopes:** Another adornment could be *diagnosis certainty* with exemplary levels from *absolute* and *high* over *moderate* to *low*. In some situations it may not be feasible for physicians to make an authoritative diagnosis. Cooperative treatments of unclear symptoms or multimorbid patients require an intensified exchange of expert opinions. To indicate a limited certainty provides new participants with orientation while they gain an overview of the shared files.

Following the initial breast cancer classification episode (cf. [5]), the gynecologist creates a *diagnosis certainty* attribute for his initial report and sets the certainty of his own report to *low*. The radiologist later on provides a report on mammography and sets the certainty to *moderate* or *high*, according to the BI-RADS[1] indicator of the mammography. Finally in this specific episode, the pathologist contributes his diagnosis based on the biopsy with an authoritative certainty, so he sets the indicator to *absolute*.

Even if it seems possible to specify such adornments at design-time, there will always exist various conceptions of indicators both in name and value range. We propose that consensus finding can either be done ad-hoc during an episode or it can be provided by an institutional standard or a domain standard. An example for an indicator that is standardized for a domain is the BI-RADS score factor for mammographies as mentioned above. It would be perfectly conceivable, if users decide that they want the BI-RADS

---

[1] Breast Imaging – Reporting and Data System.

value directly available as a status attribute for mammography reports in breast cancer episodes. The document-oriented process platform should allow for different consensus scopes and distinguish episode-, institution-, or domain-specific indicators.

# 5   Methods and State of the Art

One of the basic aspects for evolutionary systems is deferred design [8], i.e. to defer decisions from design-time to run-time. In order to achieve continuous adaptability [9], we need to be able to provide user-defined attributes at run-time. Thus, we need concepts to change behavior of program objects in regard to computing and persistence. Common methods are prototype-based programming and the EAV data design approach. In $\alpha$-Adaptive we apply these concepts in order to find out how far they fit our purpose.

**Prototype-Based Programming:**   In class-based programming abstract classes are used to describe the common properties and behavior of concrete objects [10]. These objects are created by instantiation of the classes. In order to get an object with different properties or behavior a separate class has to be modeled. So the semantic decisions for the object are defined during the conceptual design of a system. This restrains the flexibility in the application core, because revising semantic decisions cannot be performed at run-time.

In prototype-based languages there are no classes but only objects. Abstract classes are substituted by *prototype objects*. A new object is created by copying an existing prototype object, which is also called *cloning* with the prototype as a *clone base*. This process supports the concept of inheritance in form of a dangling reference to the clone base: Every time a prototype is modified, all its derived clones are automatically updated. Both the prototype and its clones can be modified at run-time in schema and in value. Prototype changes are propagated to clones but if clones deviate from their parent their specific value remains. Thus, a mechanism is required to determine the difference in structure and in values between a prototype and one of its clones. By avoiding the use of abstract classes, the semantic decisions for the objects in such languages can be deferred from design-time to run-time.

**Entity-Attribute-Value Data Model:**   We must allow persisting data that was not known at design-time or deploy-time. Thus, the same flexibility that prototypes provide for the application core is also needed for persistence. Traditional database schema design freezes semantic decisions at design-time just like classes in programming do. It is not feasible to perform database schema alterations at run-time because schema-derived data access layers in dependent application systems would be disrupted. An update will also always affect all tuples, thus, historic tuples end up with many null values.

Entity-Attribute-Value (EAV) schema design [11] is a generalization of row modeling. EAV is based on association lists that originated in artificial intelligence. In contrast to the traditional schema design, the EAV design proposes a generic table with three columns: 1) the ID of an entity, 2) the name or identifier of an associated attribute, and 3) the corresponding attribute value for the entity. Thus, semantic decisions for an object are decoupled from altering the database schema because an arbitrary number of attribute-value pairs can be added at run-time.

## 6   The α-Adaptive Approach

The α-Adaptive approach focuses on the design of an evolutionary α-Adornment model to manage arbitrary α-Card status attributes. In a first step, we will demonstrate how we apply EAV in order to arrange an adaptive attribute schema. Subsequently, we extend traditional EAV for dDPM purposes and apply concepts of prototype-based programming to provide an attribute template that serves as a clone base for α-Card descriptors.

**Creation of an Adaptive α-Adornment Schema:**  The first step towards an adaptive-evolutionary metadata model is to arrange an adaptive schema for the α-Adornments. The transformation of a static schema into an EAV schema is illustrated by the Entity/Relationship diagrams in Fig. 4. The statical design on the left does not support the extension of the α-Card descriptor with domain-specific adornments at run-time. The basic transformation into an EAV design results in an descriptor that contains no more fixed attributes, but a list of attribute-value pairs representing the α-Adornments.

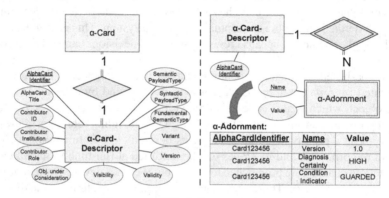

**Fig. 4.** From static E/R design to adaptive EAV design

The first EAV extension concerns user-centric data types. In the original EAV, the physical data type of the attributes is a generic data type like String. There is no data type information included and data type transformations are commissioned to the application. Yet, adornments are user-centric and we require a slender type set from which a user might select a type for his or her adornment. Most data type sets in computer science are system-centric, e. g. primitive types in programming languages[2] or the ones in XML schema as a platform neutral superset. These data types are only comprehensible for programmers and are not adequate to fulfill an end-user's plain idea of data types. As a standard for user-centric types, we use the *Requirements Interchange Format*[3] (ReqIF) as a reference because requirements management is highly user-centric and ReqIF provides a slender type set. Thus, the data types implemented for α-Adaptive are: *String*, *Integer* (e.g. BI-RADS), *Timestamp* (e.g. due dates), *Enumeration* (e.g. our

---

[2] For example, in C++ a programmer in order to create an arbitrary integer variable must choose between types {short int, int, long int} crossed with {signed, unsigned} semantics.

[3] http://www.omg.org/spec/ReqIF/1.0.1/11-04-02.pdf

indicators) and *TextBlock* (e.g. Post-it notes). We extend the EAV schema by adding an additional attribute to store the user-centric data type restriction.

The second EAV extension concerns the consensus scopes, as we motivated them during the use case section. We again extend the EAV-entity schema with an attribute that specifies the consensus scope for each adornment. Currently, four scopes are implemented: users can choose between values *episode-specific*, *institution-specific* and *domain-specific* – the value *generic* is reserved and indicates $\alpha$-Adornments that are used to grant the $\alpha$-Flow platform functionality.

A third extension to the EAV schema is the instance attribute. $\alpha$-Card descriptors with adaptive adornment sets solve only the first half of the $\alpha$-Adaptive requirements. As discussed in the methods section, we need descriptors to provide prototype-oriented semantics, i.e. one $\alpha$-Card descriptor becomes the template for others. Thus, the instance attribute is necessary as a flag and will be explained in the next section.

In conclusion, we can fulfill our data persistence requirements by adapting the traditional EAV approach. All our extensions to the basic EAV design are of general interest, in the context of attribute annotations of process artifacts in dDPM. The result is an attribute schema that is able to persist $\alpha$-Adornments that can be adapted at run-time. The E/R diagram in Fig. 5 illustrates the resulting EAV:dDPM schema.

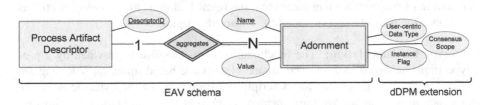

**Fig. 5.** The EAV:dDPM schema

**Administration of the Adaptive $\alpha$-Adornment Schema:** Up to now, it would be possible to manage every single $\alpha$-Card descriptor as a unique EAV-based object. Yet, the definition of adornments (at least within the episode if not within institutions or domains) is subject to a shared consensus of the episode's participants. Thus, we need a shared prototype within the $\alpha$-Doc that serves as a template for all its descriptors. An individual descriptor will normally use only a subset of the prototyped adornments, e.g. BI-RADS will only be used for mammography reports and *diagnosis certainty* will not be used for reports on therapeutic measures.

To fulfill these requirements, the $\alpha$-Adornment model is managed within an episode in form of the so called *Adornment Prototype Artifact* (APA). The APA enables a shared administration of the adornments and serves as a prototype for all $\alpha$-Card descriptors that are generated by cloning the APA within one $\alpha$-Doc. Each descriptor is allowed to use only a subset of the APA-defined adornments. To provide subset semantics, the $\alpha$-Adaptive approach distinguishes between the adornment schema and the adornment instances of an $\alpha$-Card descriptor. Figure 6 illustrates the correlation between the APA as a prototype in contrast to the $\alpha$-Adornment schema and $\alpha$-Adornment instances of each derived $\alpha$-Card descriptor.

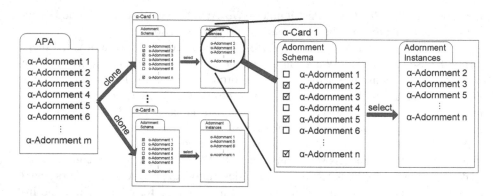

**Fig. 6.** Clone and Select: correlation between the APA prototype and the individual $\alpha$-Cards' adornment-schema & -instances

The adornment schema of an $\alpha$-Card descriptor contains all adornments that were inherited from the APA. The adornment instances, however, are the subset of adornments from the schema that the user actually selects to use for the individual $\alpha$-Card. Thus, the *instance flag* was implemented for adornments as part of the EAV:dDPM schema. The setting of this *instance flag* means that the related adornment has been selected as an instance member of the corresponding $\alpha$-Card descriptor.

**Prototype Implementation:** The functionality of $\alpha$-Adaptive is provided by a prototype implementation in Java. The related classes are based upon the E/R diagram of Fig. 5. For cloning new $\alpha$-Card descriptors a deep copy of the dynamic APA object structure is required. We implemented general-purpose deep cloning in Java by temporarily serializing the APA into a memory buffer and deserializing it. The values cloned from the APA provide default values for the descriptors.

Changes to the APA are propagated to the existing $\alpha$-Card descriptors without overwriting individual adornment values in the descriptors as in prototype-based inheritance. For APA update propagation, every APA modification requires a delta check: The difference quantity between the set of $\alpha$-Adornments in the APA and every $\alpha$-Card descriptor within the $\alpha$-Doc is determined and the descriptors are adapted to the APA's model without affecting the adornments that are part of the intersection between APA and $\alpha$-Card descriptor. Changes like renaming adornments, switching consensus scope, changing default values, or changing Enumeration-based value ranges are transparently allowed and propagated, without disrupting existing descriptors. The prototype contains an embedded editor for visualization and editing of adornments: There are different screens for the APA, the Adornment schema and the Adornment instances of an $\alpha$-Card descriptor.

## 7   Related Work

Content-oriented workflows (e.g. "object-aware" [12], "artifact-centric" [13], or "data-driven" [14] approaches) provide process execution based on data dependencies. The main characteristic in content-orientation is to separate the data structure from the process structure, and to support formal bindings between data state and process enactment, thus it contrasts to activity-orientation with its focus on control flow. Case handling is orthogonal to both. We consider $\alpha$-Flow as a content-oriented workflow approach for case handling in distributed inter-institutional environments.

**Adaptiveness in Activity-Oriented Approaches:** A modern approach to activity-oriented workflows is Proclets[4] by van der Aalst et al. [15,16]. Proclets are interacting processes that exchange messages, named *performatives*, via *channels*. The Proclets approach proposes a shift in focus from control flow to communication in order to reduce control flow complexity. The approach is similar to conversation and choreography diagrams in the BPMN[5] 2.0 standard. Neither Proclets nor BPMN support adaptive change of their data flow objects or message structures.

In contrast, workflow adaption is discussed for ADEPT$_{flex}$ [17] by Reichert and Dadam. ADEPT$_{flex}$ is based on block-structured process description. Change operations in ADEPT$_{flex}$ consider only the control flow. Data flow, as an addendum to the control flow, is addressed for checking correctness of control flow change operations, which is possible because the exchange of data between tasks is based on global variables. Data elements are derived from input/output parameters of tasks. Users can extend the data structure not directly but by inserting new tasks with according parameters or by replacing tasks. This raises a variety of challenging issues with respect to dynamic parameter mapping and leaves significant complexity to the user.

**Adaptiveness in Content-Oriented Approaches:** Content-oriented approaches commonly rely on fixed content schemas and status triggers to drive workflow automation. They do not consider run-time adoption of content schema, life-cycle configuration, or artifact status attributes. A state-of-the-art approach to content-oriented workflows is PHILharmonicFlows [18] by Künzle and Reichert. In PHILharmonicFlows data is managed based on object types. At run-time, the number of object instances and links may vary but the types and their structure is statically defined at workflow design-time. An adaptive artifact attribute model, as we propose in $\alpha$-Adaptive, allows demand-driven data extensions to evolve the process status description at run-time by the human actors.

**Acknowledgements.** The first author wants to thank Dr. med. Helmut Neumann who as a gynecologist explained breast cancer treatment to me and Rita M. Neumann who survived breast cancer and familiarized me with the patient perspective.

# References

1. van der Aalst, W.M.P., Weske, M., Grünbauer, D.: Case handling: a new paradigm for business process support. Data & Knowledge Engineering 53(2), 129–162 (2005)
2. Neumann, C.P., Lenz, R.: Alpha-Flow: A Document-based Approach to Inter-Institutional Process Support in Healthcare. In: Proc. of the 3rd Int'l Workshop on Process-oriented Information Systems in Healthcare (ProHealth 2009), Ulm, Germany (September 2009)

---

[4] From an implementation perspective, Proclets had been based on Petri nets and later on YAWL.

[5] Business Process Model and Notation. Int'l standard by the Object Management Group.

3. Neumann, C.P., Lenz, R.: The alpha-Flow Approach to Inter-Institutional Process Support in Healthcare. Int'l. Journal of Knowledge-Based Organizations 2(3) (2012) (accepted for publication)
4. Neumann, C.P., Rampp, F., Daum, M., Lenz, R.: A Mediated Publish-Subscribe System for Inter-Institutional Process Support in Healthcare. In: Proc. of the 3rd ACM Int'l. Conf. on Distributed Event-Based Systems (DEBS 2009), Nashville, TN, USA (July 2009)
5. Neumann, C.P., Lenz, R.: The alpha-Flow Use-Case of Breast Cancer Treatment – Modeling Inter-Institutional Healthcare Workflows by Active Documents. In: Proc. of the 8th Int'l. Workshop on Agent-based Computing for Enterprise Collaboration (ACEC), Larissa, Greece (June 2010)
6. LaMarca, A., Edwards, W.K., Dourish, P., Lamping, J., Smith, I., Thornton, J.: Taking the work out of workflow: mechanisms for document-centered collaboration. In: 6th European Conf. on Computer Supported Cooperative Work, pp. 1–20. Kluwer Academic Publishers, Norwell (1999)
7. Todorova, A., Neumann, C.P.: Alpha-Props: A Rule-Based Approach to 'Active Properties' for Document-Oriented Process Support in Inter-Institutional Environments. In: Porada, L. (ed.) Lecture Notes in Informatics (LNI) Seminars 10, Gesellschaft für Informatik e.V (GI) (March 2011)
8. Patel, N.V.: Adaptive Evolutionary Information Systems. Idea Group Inc. (2002)
9. Lenz, R.: Information Systems in Healthcare – State and Steps towards Sustainability. In: IMIA Yearbook 2009 – Yearbook of Medical Informatics as a supplement of Methods of Information in Medicine, pp. 63–70 (2009)
10. Borning, A.H.: Classes versus prototypes in object-oriented languages. In: Proc. of 1986 ACM Fall Joint Computer Conference, pp. 36–40. IEEE Computer Society Press (1986)
11. Nadkarni, P.M.: Data extraction and ad hoc query of an entity-attribute-value database. Journal of the American Medical Informatics Association 5(6), 511 (1998)
12. Künzle, V., Reichert, M.: Towards Object-Aware Process Management Systems: Issues, Challenges, Benefits. In: Halpin, T., Krogstie, J., Nurcan, S., Proper, E., Schmidt, R., Soffer, P., Ukor, R. (eds.) Enterprise, Business-Process and Information Systems Modeling. LNBIP, vol. 29, pp. 197–210. Springer, Heidelberg (2009)
13. Cohn, D., Hull, R.: Business Artifacts: A Data-centric Approach to Modeling Business Operations and Processes. In: Bulletin of the IEEE Computer Society Technical Committee on Data Engineering (September 2009)
14. Müller, D., Reichert, M., Herbst, J.: Data-Driven Modeling and Coordination of Large Process Structures. In: Meersman, R. (ed.) OTM 2007, Part I. LNCS, vol. 4803, pp. 131–149. Springer, Heidelberg (2007)
15. van Der Aalst, W.M.P., Barthelmess, P., Eliis, C.A., Wainer, J.: Proclets: A framework for lightweight interacting workflow processes. Int'l. Journal of Cooperative Information Systems 10(4), 443–482 (2001)
16. Mans, R.S., Russell, N.C., van der Aalst, W.M.P., Bakker, P.J.M., Moleman, A.J., Jaspers, M.W.M.: Proclets in healthcare. Journal of Biomedical Informatics 43(4), 632–649 (2010)
17. Reichert, M., Dadam, P.: ADEPTflex – supporting dynamic changes of workflows without losing control. Journal of Intelligent Information Systems 10(2), 93–129 (1998)
18. Künzle, V., Reichert, M.: PHILharmonicFlows: towards a framework for object-aware process management. Journal of Software Maintenance and Evolution: Research and Practice 23(4), 205–244 (2011)

# Guarded Process Spaces (GPS): A Navigation System towards Creation and Dynamic Change of Healthcare Processes from the End-User's Perspective

Claudia Reuter[1], Peter Dadam[2], Stephan Rudolph[3],
Wolfgang Deiters[3], and Simon Trillsch[4]

[1] Zühlke Management Consultants AG, Wiesenstr. 10a,
8952 Schlieren, Switzerland
claudia.reuter@zuehlke.com
[2] Ulm University, Albert-Einstein-Allee 11, 89081 Ulm, Germany
peter.dadam@uni-ulm.de
[3] Fraunhofer Institute for Software and Systems Engineering, Emil-Figge-Str. 91,
44227 Dortmund, Germany
{stephan.rudolph,wolfgang.deiters}@isst.fraunhofer.de
[4] University Hospital of Giessen and Marburg, Baldingerstr., 35033 Marburg, Germany
trillsch@students.uni-marburg.de

**Abstract.** Efficient process management becomes increasingly crucial for hospitals to survive on a competitive market. Process management in this domain must comply with individual conditions of patients and quickly react to changing requirements and organizational parameters. With Guarded Process Spaces (GPS) we developed a formally based concept that makes it possible to enable end-users to create and flexibly change processes themselves. Our approach makes use of existing BPM technology while abstracting from technical interfaces and system-specific modeling paradigms. In this way, it provides the basis to gain user acceptance and to achieve technological independence.

**Keywords:** Healthcare process, clinical pathway, process flexibility, domain specific languages.

## 1 Motivation

Today, healthcare providers are facing the challenge of delivering high-quality services while coping with increasing costs due to demographic change and medical progress. In response to this, hospitals start with the introduction and deployment of standard processes (so called "clinical pathways") to organize the treatment of patients according to a common set of symptoms, a diagnosis, or a therapy. In principle, modern BPMSs (Business Process Management Systems) could help to support clinical pathways in practice and to reduce administrative workload by instantiating pathway templates for patients, documenting and monitoring their progress, and

F. Daniel et al. (Eds.): BPM 2011 Workshops, Part II, LNBIP 100, pp. 237–248, 2012.

managing work lists for doctors and nurses. However, in spite of their potential benefit, BPMSs are barely in use in healthcare environments until now.

Originally, BPMSs have been developed to support production processes in industry. In such settings processes typically shall be executed exactly as preplanned to ensure that the goals in terms of quality and cost are met for all the products. In clinical pathways, however, the focus must be put on the patient as individual being. Therefore, in order to support clinical pathways using BPMSs one must be able to solve the conflict between standardization of treatment processes on the one hand and flexible deviation from standards due to case-based considerations on the other hand.

The fact that healthcare processes pose challenges to traditional BPMSs is not new to the scientific community; frequently, they even serve as motivation for researchers to investigate new approaches [1, 2]. In fact, flexibility and adaptivity during process execution are broadly addressed in BPMS related research in the meanwhile [3]. Therefore, in the near future, we can expect that BPMSs come onto the market, which allow for more process flexibility at runtime. However, supporting flexibility at the BPM system level and making this feature usable by end-users are two different stories. A direct interaction with a BPMS, e. g., to insert or to postpone a task requires profound technical skills, which the medical staff is not able and not willing to acquire. This means, one must find a solution, which enables end-users to flexibly adjust clinical pathways according to the individual demands of a patient, but does not force them to acquire deep system near skills in order to perform this task.

In context of the SPOT project (Service-based and Process-oriented Orchestration Technology)[1] we developed a concept and a prototype demonstrating that such kind of system can be realized. The concept is based on the notion of "Guarded Process Spaces" (GPS). The analogy to GPS navigation devices is intentional, because like such devices, which can answer the question "Which roads are available to me now?", Guarded Process Spaces provide maps of possible directions a process can take and guide the user's decision making as to which paths they can follow to reach a valid goal.

In this paper, we will focus on the benefit of GPS from the end-user's perspective. After a discussion of related work in chapter 2, we will introduce a novel navigation paradigm towards process modeling, which is realized based on GPS in section 3. In chapter 4 we will explain the technical implementation of GPS by way of a practical example from the healthcare domain. After that, we will discuss requirements on BPMSs in terms of process flexibility and show how these demands can be fulfilled by GPS in combination with existing approaches from chapter 2. Finally, we will give a short summary and an outlook on our future work.

## 2     Related Work

Process modeling languages used by process experts are usually too complicated for end-users to model processes themselves. Therefore, domain specific languages

---

[1]  See http://www.spot.fraunhofer.de

(DSL) are developed to facilitate process modeling for end-users in their application domain, like, e. g., public administration [4], workflow-based web applications [5], integrated care [6], or medical guidelines [7]. Another example is the feature modeling approach for modeling variability in product families [8], which has already been applied to process management as well [9]. However, the provision of DSLs alone is not sufficient without ensuring that the technical process templates which are derived from such DSLs can be correctly executed by a BPMS. This means, that DSLs without a proper and suitable formal basis are not very helpful to achieve this goal. Due to the lack of formality of DSLs, they are often transformed into formal languages, like e. g. Petri Nets [10], to perform correctness checks. However, this doesn't prevent the creation of erroneous process templates, which have to be corrected afterwards which, in turn, delays the whole development process, decreases user acceptance, and is certainly not acceptable in case of ad-hoc changes. Instead, one has to provide a modeling environment which guides the user in such a way that "technical" modeling errors (like deadlocks, incorrect or incomplete data flows, etc.) are excluded as far as possible; and the same must hold for ad-hoc deviations at runtime. The "correctness by construction" approach developed in the ADEPT project [11-12] proved to be the best suited one for that purpose and, therefore, was very influential for the development of respective concepts in GPS.

Assumed, we have a DSL with an adequate formal basis, the question remains how to offer the required flexibility to an end-user (e.g., a physician) such that she herself is able to adjust a clinical pathway according to the individual demands of her patient.

In recent years, the scientific community has made great technical advances especially with regard to dynamic process management. [13], e.g., deals with shifting existing tasks within a process instance under correctness constraints. Other authors suggest maintaining the standard way of proceeding together with its variations within the same process template [14-16]. Using respective workflow patterns, placeholder activities (like, e.g., Proclets [17]) or variation points, it is possible to indicate the positions, where alternative routes may be chosen or even created at runtime. The advantage of these approaches is that end-users don't have to comprehend the process template and the usage of change operations to deviate from the standard proceeding. The disadvantage is that such approaches require that the positions where alternative routes may be chosen have to be fixed in advance, which does not reflect the reality in healthcare. E. g., certain conditions, such as infections, can occur at any point in time. Therefore, these simple solutions are falling short of covering these demands. End-users must be able to flexibly change the process structure at runtime.

In [11-12] it is illustrated how an end-user interface to perform an ad-hoc change could be implemented using the application programming interface of the ADEPT2 system. In this example the user wants to insert a new task into the process. After having selected the desired task, the system shows him a simplified process graph within which he can select a process step. This selection informs the system that the new task shall become executable *after* this task. Then the system allows him to choose another process step, *before* which the new task must be completed. Based on this information the system determines where and how the new task is inserted (as serial or parallel step) and performs the necessary transformations of the process graph. Although this approach does not require system-near knowledge to perform such a task, it confronts the user with a different and rather "technical view" of the clinical pathway compared to the GPS approach for process modeling. The goal of GPS is to apply the same user-oriented metaphors for ad-hoc deviations as in case of process modeling.

## 3    Guarded Process Spaces: Applying the Navigation Paradigm to Process Modeling

Our investigations during the SPOT project were driven by the following objectives: Firstly, it must be possible for end-users to design process templates from their business point of view and to automatically execute them using a chosen BPM system. Secondly, end-users must be enabled to change processes both at modeling time and at runtime on a case by case basis.

As already mentioned, we apply a navigation paradigm to process modeling which we call *Guarded Process Spaces* (GPS). Due to lack of space, we cannot describe this approach in detail in this paper. Instead, we will introduce GPS informally and point out their usage by the clinical staff. A detailed and formal description can be found in [18, 19] (where GPS correspond to so called "SPF-type graphs"). From a user's point of view a GPS acts like a navigation system, which uses a given set of streets to offer routes and alternative routes from the current location to the desired destination. At technical level a GPS consists of a set of nodes and has a tree-like structure. The nodes represent navigation points, which are used to implement rules on the selection of process activities. The root of the GPS represents the starting point, from where "travels" can be planned. Like a navigation system, the Guarded Process Space indicates all potential traveling options. By selecting an option, a user is travelling to the next navigation point within the coordinate network; there, further traveling options are available. With every step that a user takes, the amount of traveling options to approach the final destination decreases. The selected route from the starting point to the destination defines an executable clinical pathway.

We illustrate process modeling from the user's perspective by means of a practical example. During their inpatient stay, some patients experience shortness of breath, the reason for which can be a bacterial pneumonia or a left heart failure. The clinical staff shall develop clinical pathways that coordinate the diagnostics of one of these diseases as well as both of them together. Fig. 1 illustrates how this is done. According to the GPS, the pathway for all clinical diagnostics is divided into different categories, such as "Radiology" or "Laboratory". These categories represent the navigation points within the GPS and may contain further specialized navigation points. E. g., the navigation point "Radiology" comprises a chest X-ray examination and encapsulates further radiological activities within navigation point "Additional radiology". Now, the modeler team can decide whether or not additional examinations should be scheduled within the clinical pathway by default.

The pathway modeler team navigates through the GPS in order to develop a clinical pathway for the diagnostics of bacterial pneumonia. All tasks they select will be included in the pathway. After having made all these choices, the clinical pathway is determined and an executable process template can be generated. As we will see later, this does not mean that the resulting clinical pathway is now completely inflexible.

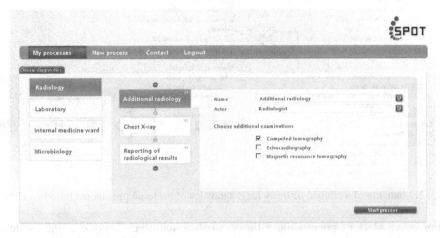

**Fig. 1.** Modeling clinical pathways from the end-users' perspective

If needed, the end-user (e.g., the ward physician) can repeat tasks or can "reactivate" deselected tasks in the context of ad-hoc deviations at runtime to adjust the clinical pathway to the individual needs of a specific patient.) By performing process modeling this way, the end-users can mentally completely stay in their "world" and just select the tasks to be performed. All the other aspects like setting up the resulting control flow, the data flow, deadlock avoidance, and other things are handled at GPS system level and do not bother him. In addition, the GPS also "knows" which tasks depend on each other or, just the opposite, exclude each other. This means that certain kinds of mistakes are automatically avoided.

## 4    Implementation of Guarded Process Spaces

Fig. 2 illustrates how the support for this navigation and decision process is implemented at the technical level. The graph on the left side corresponds to the GPS and the graph on the right side represents the currently developed clinical pathway. The nodes in the GPS graph represent either tasks or logical operators like, e.g., AND, XOR, OR, and OPT (for optional). In Fig. 2, the root node "Clinical diagnostics" is connected with an AND-operator, i. e., all child nodes have to be selected. According to the OPT-operator at "Additional radiology", it is possible to choose an arbitrary number of child nodes or none at all.

Since AND-operators don't leave many options, a big part of the clinical pathway can be automatically derived from the GPS in this case. E. g., a chest X-ray always includes some laboratory examinations and reporting to the ward physician. With regard to the possible variations "Additional radiology" and "Additional laboratory" the modeler have to decide which ones (if any) shall occur in the clinical pathway.

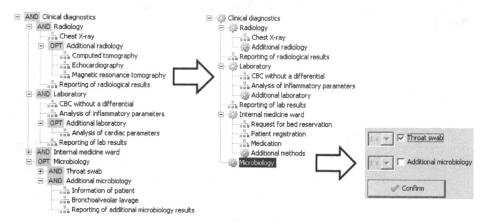

**Fig. 2.** Modeling of a clinical pathway for diagnostics of bacterial pneumonia based on GPS

For diagnostics of pneumonia a throat swab is required. Therefore, the modeler team selects "Throat swab" from the navigation point "Microbiology". After that, the clinical pathway for bacterial pneumonia is complete. In order to obtain the pathway for diagnostics of left heart failure, the modelers must only take a slightly different route with respect to some navigation points.

As indicated above, the GPS can also contain constraints determining the execution order of process activities within the clinical pathway. Constraints are defined as edges connecting GPS nodes on a horizontal axis. E. g., it can be expressed, that the activity "Reporting of radiological results" must not be scheduled as long as "Chest X-ray" and optionally "Additional radiology" are not finished. One could also state that some nodes may require or exclude other nodes. In addition, one can specify constraints for node cardinalities. A node cardinality defines the maximum number of times that a clinical pathway may contain a set of process activities. This feature can be used to model cyclic treatments. In [18, 19] formal correctness criteria are defined to ensure that constraints cannot contradict each other and are in conformance with the GPS structure and its logical operators. Due to flexibility options, kind and amount of data objects the system has to deal with at runtime may vary. This means, the application components that implement process activities must cope with variable data input and output. In [19], an interface specification of process activities is defined, which among others specifies both mandatory and optional data input and output. Moreover, it is described how data dependencies can be considered at GPS level. Further aspects, like e. g. data storage and versioning, must be handled at technical level and are out of scope of the GPS approach.

In general, the more process knowledge a GPS captures, the easier the creation of clinical pathways and – finally – executable process templates becomes for the clinical staff. To make the creation of clinical pathways by end-users as easy as described above, the GPS graph must comprise all potential tasks, choices, and relevant constraints of the considered application area. The range of applicability, the acceptance of the GPS based modeling environment, and the resulting executable clinical pathways depend on the degree to which this graph covers the application area. The clinical staff can (and must) help to develop the initial hierarchical structure of a GPS and to identify relevant process activities. The implementation of the GPS itself, the implementation of activities by executable application components, user interfaces, and task-specific control and data flow aspects will require IT-specialists. To decrease the complexity of this task one can take a stepwise refinement approach by first modeling the GPS graph rather coarsely and re-examine it with end-users using the modeling environment. Then one refines one or several nodes and checks it again, etc.

## 5     Enabling Process Change from the End-User's Perspective

With GPS, end-users are now in the position to create various clinical pathways using the offered navigation paradigm. However, in healthcare it is often not possible to plan the complete treatment process in advance. Instead, the treatment process develops depending on further insights gained during the execution of the process. Under certain circumstances, it may even become necessary to abandon the original plan, to return to a specific point, and to choose a different option. Therefore, in this chapter we describe healthcare-specific requirements on process flexibility and discuss how they can be addressed using GPS in combination with existing BPMSs.

**Flexible Extension of Pathway Instances.** Although, the modelers of clinical pathways determine medical treatment to a large extent, some decisions can only be made by the doctor in charge of the patient. With regard to our pathway example, each patient who is suspected to suffer from bacterial pneumonia will undergo a throat swab. After that, the further proceeding depends on whether the finding is positive or negative. Assuming, the finding is positive, then the GPS specifies the available options; i. e., to carry out a bronchoalveolar lavage (cf. Fig. 2). When selecting this choice, the GPS may enforce an application constraint, e.g., that a bronchoalveolar lavage is only possible if the patient has been transferred to the isolation ward first in order to prevent the spreading of the disease. If this case is not rare to occur, the pathway modelers will have anticipated this additional examination along with the associated tasks and may offer it in terms of conditional branches, placeholder activities or variation points.

**Minor Deviations from Clinical Pathways.** Clinical pathways specify the standard way of proceeding. Accordingly, the pathway for diagnostics of bacterial pneumonia only schedules a chest X-ray in the course of radiological examinations. However, in certain cases, it can become necessary to perform additional procedures. For example, the ward physician examines the chest X-ray and the lab results of her patient. As it is not possible to confirm the diagnosis on the basis of these findings, she decides on scheduling a computed tomography. This examination is not part of the clinical pathway by default. Therefore, in the context of radiology a deviation from the pathway occurs. After changing the configuration of the navigation point "Additional radiology", the new task is added to the work list of the responsible radiologist. Fig. 3 indicates how end-users can handle minor deviations from clinical pathways using the GPS approach.

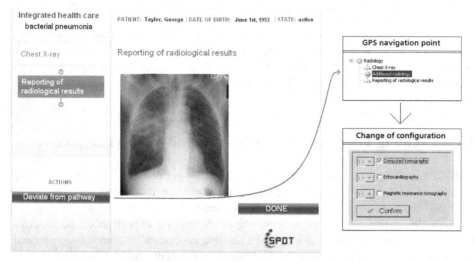

**Fig. 3.** Ad-hoc change of pathway instances from the end-user's perspective

First, one has to signal the need for deviation from the process standard by clicking the button "deviate from pathway" within the user interface. Then, the end-user can choose additional radiological examinations, which are available in the context of the navigation node "Additional radiology" of the GPS. By selecting one or more examinations, the end-user changes the pathway schedule in an ad-hoc manner. Provided that the position where such a deviation may happen is known in advance, it is sufficient to use conditional branches, placeholder activities, or variation points in order to technically realize this ad-hoc change. Frequently, it is not so clear at which point of time a variance arises, however. Regarding the GPS, it is not important when the physician decides to deviate from the pathway. The GPS may define constraints that determine the position where a computed tomography should be performed at best. However, if the execution flow has already passed this position, the examination may be scheduled at the next possible place.

**Complex Deviations from Clinical Pathways.** The detection of second diagnoses or complications may result in more complex deviations from clinical pathways. E. g., a physician chose the pathway for diagnostics of bacterial pneumonia for her patient. During the treatment she discovers symptoms that indicate a left heart failure. She decides to modify the process in a way that it also covers the procedures for this second diagnosis. So, changes can not only occur at isolated spots, but may affect several regions of a process. In our example the doctor would have to insert the activities "Analysis of cardiac parameters" within "Laboratory" and "Echocardiography" within "Additional radiology". Such complex deviations may significantly increase the effort of physicians to perform the change of the pathway and thus raise the probability of errors. Therefore, if the pathway modelers have anticipated such a situation, they could have provided *process variants*, which encapsulate all the changes that have to be made to perform a pathway modification of this kind. In this way, it is even feasible to specify standard ways of proceedings in case of deviations from clinical pathways [19].

Since process variants automate the execution of change operations, it must be ensured that they are in conformance with the medical treatment and the procedures, which have been undertaken so far. As a GPS already determines all the routes that processes may take, possible variations, and relations between certain activities, it can also be used to verify that changes in the context of a process variant do not contradict previous treatment.

## 6     From GPS-Based Clinical Pathways to Executable Processes

The clinical pathway conforms to the tree-like structure of the GPS graph, but contains only those process activities, which have been selected for the pathway under consideration (cf. Fig. 2). To obtain independence from a specific BPMS, the GPS graph as well as this "clinical pathway graph" serve as a neutral representation which is mapped to process templates of the chosen BPMS to achieve executable processes. To support the full spectrum of possibilities as well as to make this mapping simple, the ideal target BPMS should support the full spectrum of ad-hoc deviations as provided by ADEPT2 [1, 11-12], for example, late binding of dynamically composed complex activities like those described in [15] or as provided by YAWL's proclet approach [17], as well as process variants like those described in [16].

Among these desirable BPMS features, the requirement for the full spectrum of supported ad-hoc deviations is the most relevant one. If this feature is present, concepts like late binding and process variants can be handled by the mapping layer which acts as a broker between the GPS runtime for the "clinical pathway graph" and the underlying BPMS. If this feature is missing or available only in a rather limited fashion then the mapping will result in complex process graphs, because now the most relevant choices and variants have to be incorporated in the process graph from the very beginning. Besides complexity aspects, incorporation of all choices and variants does not only contradict the concept of clinical pathways that must define standards of medical treatment instead of all possible variations; it also cannot provide the full spectrum of flexibility, which is needed in the clinical domain, as we will show in fig. 4.

Among the available BPMS ADEPT2 [1, 11-12] resp. its commercial version, the AristaFlow® BPM Suite[2] was closest to the "ideal" BPMS sketched above. It, therefore, was selected as the target BPMS for the proof of concept prototype. In [19] one can find the formally defined transformation rules according to which the compilation to GPS-based clinical pathways to the ADEPT2 process model takes

---

[2]  See http://www.AristaFlow.com

place. Fig. 4 shows in which way the process activities within the context of "Radiology" (cf. Fig. 2) can be mapped to executable ADEPT2 process templates. As radiology comprises both default and optional activities, there are two mapping alternatives in ADEPT2: Either conditional branches are used or the additional activities can be inserted into the process instance on demand.

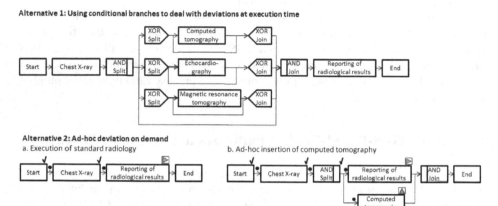

**Fig. 4.** Mapping the "clinical pathway graph" to ADEPT2 process templates

According to the constraints of the GPS, the reporting activity should follow the examinations, whereby the chest X-ray has to be performed first. As several or none of the additional examinations can be selected, in alternative 1 we have to insert a complex construct consisting of a parallel as well as three conditional branches. In alternative 2, we only schedule the default activities and perform ad-hoc insertions on demand depending on the current state of the execution. In Fig. 4.a, the reporting activity has already started as a deviation occurs. Thus, it is not possible to insert the computed tomography directly after the chest X-ray, anymore. Instead, it can be added in parallel to the running activity as illustrated in Fig. 4.b. This example shows that the mapping between pathway graph and process template is much simpler and more flexibly than realizing complex workflow patterns. Furthermore, one can clearly distinguish the process standard from its variations. Consequently, BPMSs providing comprehensive support for ad-hoc changes at the API level like, e.g., ADEPT2, are ideal candidates for this approach. As indicated above, other BPMSs can be supported as well, but one is faced with limited flexibility and with more complex implementations of the mapping and runtime layer to compensate the missing functionality.

# 7     Summary

In spite of their potential benefits, BPMSs are not broadly used in healthcare settings yet. In order to be accepted by end-users, the technology has to fulfill the following requirements: Clinical staff must be enabled to model executable process templates by themselves. Moreover, end-users must have the possibility to flexibly adapt running process instances according to the individual demands of their patient. With Guarded Process Spaces (GPS), we presented an approach which uses a "navigation paradigm" to guide end-users in modeling clinical pathways as well as to assist them to perform ad-hoc deviations at runtime for a patient with specific needs. We showed how this approach supports users to select the necessary tasks in the right order and how tasks can be automatically inserted when required in the given context. We also gave some insights how this guidance is reflected in the underlying implementation. The approach is based on a sound formal concept which could only be sketched here due to lack of space, however. A comprehensive description can be found in [19]. Another goal of the SPOT project was to base creation and change of clinical pathways on a system-neutral, conceptional layer, which is independent from specific process modeling languages and BPMSs. We provide mapping functions to transform clinical pathways derived from GPS into executable process templates of the chosen target engine and verified this approach by a proof of concept implementation using ADEPT2. In this way, the user interfaces for process modeling and adaptation can remain the same, even if the underlying BPM-technology changes.

In the context of the current project "eBusiness Platform for Healthcare"[3], we are planning to use the GPS approach to develop medical processes crossing the border of individual healthcare provider institutions. By doing so, GPS are leveraging execution of integrated workflows based on collective knowledge and in spite of heterogeneous system environments.

**Acknowledgements.** We want to thank the AristaFlow team, especially Kevin Göser, for the support during the development of the proof of concept prototype.

# References

1. Reichert, M., Dadam, P.: ADEPT$_{flex}$ – Supporting Dynamic Changes of Workflows Without Losing Control. Journal of Intelligent Information Systems 10, 93–128 (1998)
2. Dadam, P., Reichert, M., Kuhn, K.: Clinical Workflows - The Killer Application for Process-oriented Information Systems? In: Proc. Int'l Conf. on Business Information Systems, BIS 2000, 4th Int'l Conf., Poznan, Poland, pp. 36–59. Springer, Heidelberg (2000)
3. Weber, B., Sadiq, S., Reichert, M.: Beyond Rigidity - Dynamic Process Lifecycle Support - A Survey on Dynamic Changes in Process-aware Information Systems. Computer Science - Research & Development, special issue on "Flexible Process-aware Information Systems" 23(2), 47–66 (2009)
4. Becker, J., Pfeiffer, D., Räckers, M.: Domain Specific Process Modelling in Public Administrations – The PICTURE-Approach. In: Wimmer, M.A., Scholl, J., Grönlund, Å. (eds.) EGOV. LNCS, vol. 4656, pp. 68–79. Springer, Heidelberg (2007)
5. Freudenstein, P., Buck, J., Nussbaumer, M., Gaedke, M.: Model-driven Construction of Workflow-based Web Applications with Domain-specific Languages. In: Proc. of the 3rd Int'l. Workshop on Model-driven Web Engineering (MDWE 2007), Como, Italy (2007)

---

[3] see http://www.ebpg-nrw.de/

6. Neuhaus, J., Houta, S., Reuter, C.: Ansätze bei der Umsetzung von Behandlungsplanpfaden – Flexibilisierungskonzepte am Beispiel der Behandlung von Wirbelsäulenerkrankungen. In: Hellmann, W., Eble, S. (eds.) Ambulante und Sektoren übergreifende Behandlungspfade, Medizinisch Wissenschaftliche Verlagsgesellschaft Berlin, pp. 79–97 (2010)
7. De Clercq, P., Kaiser, K., Hasman, A.: Computer-interpretable Guideline Formalisms. In: Ten Teije, A., et al. (eds.) Computer-based Medical Guidelines and Protocols: A Primer and Current Trends, pp. 22–43. IOS Press (2008)
8. Kant, K., Cohen, S., Hess, J., Nowak, W., Peterson, S.: Feature-oriented domain analysis (FODA) feasibility study. Technical report CMU/SEI-90-TR-21, Software Engineering Institute, Carnegie Mellon University, Pittsburgh, USA (1990)
9. Puhlmann, F., Schnieders, A., Weiland, J., Weske, M.: Variability Mechniasms for Process Models. PESOA-Report TR 17/2005, Process Family Engineering in Service-Oriented Applications, PESOA (2005)
10. Beccuti, M., Bottrighi, A., Franceschinis, G., Montani, S., Terenziani, P.: Modeling Clinical Guidelines through Petri Nets. In: Combi, C., Shahar, Y., Abu-Hanna, A. (eds.) AIME 2009. LNCS, vol. 5651, pp. 61–70. Springer, Heidelberg (2009)
11. Dadam, P., Reichert, M.: The ADEPT Project: A Decade of Research and Development for Robust and Flexible Process Support. Computer Science - Research & Development, special issue on "Flexible Process-aware Information Systems" 23(2), 81–98 (2009)
12. Reichert, M., Dadam, P.: Enabling Adaptive Processes with ADEPT2. In: Cardoso, J., van der Aalst, W.M.P. (eds.) Handbook of Research in Business Process Modeling. Information Science Reference (an imprint of IGI Global), pp. 173–203 (2009)
13. Igler, M., Moura, P., Faerber, M., Zeising, M., Jablonski, S.: Modeling and planning collaboration using organizational constraints. In: Proc. Collaborative Computing: Networking, Applications and Worksharing (CollaborateCom 2010), Chicago, Illinois (October 2010)
14. Russell, N., ter Hofstede, A.H.M., van der Aalst, W.M.P., Mulyar, N.: Workflow Control-Flow Patterns: A Revised View. BPM Center Report BPM-06-29, BPMcenter.org (2006)
15. Sadiq, S., Sadiq, W., Orlowska, M.: Pockets of Flexibility in Workflow Specification. In: Kunii, H.S., Jajodia, S., Sølvberg, A. (eds.) ER 2001. LNCS, vol. 2224, pp. 513–526. Springer, Heidelberg (2001)
16. Hallerbach, A., Bauer, T., Reichert, M.: Configuration and Management of Process Variants. In: vom Brocke, J., Rosemann, M. (eds.) Handbook of Business Process Management (2009)
17. Mans, R.S., Russell, N.C., van der Aalst, W.M.P., Moleman, A.J., Bakker, P.J.M.: Proclets in Healthcare. BPM Center Report BPM-09-05, BPMcenter.org (2009)
18. Reuter, C.: Composition of Semantic Process Fragments to Domain-Related Process Families. In: van Bommel, P., Hoppenbrouwers, S., Overbeek, S., Proper, E., Barjis, J. (eds.) PoEM 2010. LNBIP, vol. 68, pp. 61–75. Springer, Heidelberg (2010)
19. Reuter, C.: Modellierung und dynamische Adaption klinischer Pfade auf Basis Semantischer Prozessfragmente (SPF). PhD thesis, Technical University of Dortmund, Germany, Computer Science Faculty (2011)

# Enabling YAWL to Handle Dynamic Operating Room Management

Sebastian Schick, Holger Meyer, Markus Bandt, and Andreas Heuer

Database Research Group
University of Rostock
Germany
{schick,hme,mb,heuer}@informatik.uni-rostock.de

**Abstract.** Clinical workflows are known to be often complex and have to be handled very flexible due to the patients individual anamnesis and state of health. Certain situations require urgent changes of the previously planned process at run time. Some choices to be made in this context depend very much on the data from clinical backend systems. Thus, data and processes cannot be treated independently of each other.

We present an approach for flexible, data centric workflows. It extends the control-flow perspective of a workflow management system with new concepts for handling process adaption at run-time. The approach combines the method of late modeling with declarative concepts and underspecification. Due to constraints on data from clinical backend systems, process adjustment is triggered at certain points of the process and is then performed at runtime.

**Keywords:** Workflow, Flexibility, Healthcare, Perioperative Process, YAWL, Flexible Workflow Modeling.

## 1 Introduction

In medical and especially in clinical enviroments the demands not only on increased quality of service but also on better cost efficiency for treatment and care grows constantly. That's why resident doctors and hospitals are obliged to optimize the patient treatment cycle in any possible way. In general a process aware workflow perspective provides opportunities to improve quality of service as well as cost efficiency and thus is progressively acknowledged and embraced by the medical community.

The modelling of patient treatment processes is quite challenging though. Work in this domain is known to be complex and highly flexible. Independant ways to work combined with the different skill levels of the staff are hard to quantify and therefore related workflows have to reflect the differences between these approaches at model level. Beyond that, the patients distinct anamnesis, state of health and aetiopathology are decisive for the course of action. These aspects generally are recorded as structured data which can be properly interpreted in corresponding processes at instance level.

F. Daniel et al. (Eds.): BPM 2011 Workshops, Part II, LNBIP 100, pp. 249–260, 2012.
© Springer-Verlag Berlin Heidelberg 2012

A process oriented data model and an adequate communication protocol within medical environments is the HL7 (Health Level Seven) and CDA (Clinical document architecture) standards. For example HL7 defines structured messages for each high level event and each major task connected with patient treatment and provides a basic structure for clinical documents as well. HL7 compliant integration of data in clinical workflows is appropriate for proactive data provision and thus can enhance medical decision support.

Using an example from the perioperative process we introduce an approach to dynamically adapt the control flow of a process at instance level with respect to (HL7) data from clinical back-end systems. According to the taxonomy from [1] this technique can be classified as *late modeling* combined with declarative elements and under-specification.

The paper is organized as follows. In Sect. 2 we introduce the perioperative process and provide a motivating example together with requirements for flexibility in this domain. Then we discuss related work. In Sect. 3, we present a method for dynamic specification of the perioperative process as well as for the related composition of flexible process parts. Section 4 describes the transformation of our intermediate format into the YAWL process language. In Sec. 5 we illustrate our approach by an example.

## 2   Flexibility in the Perioperative Process

### 2.1   The Perikles Project

In the context the PERIKLES[1] project, we analyzed perioperative processes concerning the demands of flexibility and the data flow ([2,3]). As part of the results of PERIKLES the YAWL engine got extended in several ways. A resource data model has been developed and a corresponding planning service has been implemented as well as a scheduling service for these resources ([4]) and a framework for improved, transactional access to external data sources.

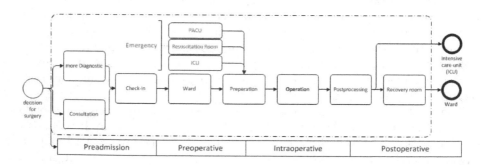

**Fig. 1.** Generalized perioperative process (adapted from [5])

[1] The PERIKLES project (http://www.perikles.org/) is partially funded by the German Federal Ministry of Education and Research under contract 01IS09009B.

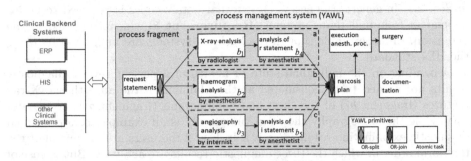

**Fig. 2.** Example fragment of the anaesthesia workflow

In PERIKLES we extended this scope by the preadmissional timespan like shown in Fig. 1. However, in this paper we concentrate on the processes on the day right before the surgical treatment of a patient and the day of the surgery itself. This includes the preoperative preparation notably the examination of the patient by an anaesthetist, the preparation of the patient at the preoperative day and the medication, the transfer to OR area and the anaesthetic preparation and treatment at the day of the surgery. For simplicity we consider the surgical treatment as an atomic task. The postoperative period includes the completion of the narcosis and immediate postoperative care at the Post Anaesthesia Care Unit (PACU) or at the Intensive Care Unit (ICU). The process shown in Fig. 1 illustrates a patient centered perspective. There is also the need of documentation which includes all diagnostic data, every planned (prescribed) action and every executed action in the perioperative process.

## 2.2 Requirements on Flexibility and Data Access

Among other things the results of the requirements analysis in the context of PERIKLES showed that several recurring classes of flexibility structures can be found in these processes.

These are namely *partial order* (some tasks have to be executed in a specified order while other tasks can be executed before or after any given task in the sequence – **Requirement 1**), *optional tasks* (**Requirement 2**), *repetitive execution of complex sub-processes* (**Requirement 3**) and *alternative tasks* (**Requirement 4**). In [6] we described the corresponding processes as well as the identified structures more detailed and presented an implementation approach using the workflow management system (WFMS) YAWL. Due to space limitations in this paper we will provide just one example which includes several of the mentioned structures.

In Fig. 2 a fragment of the perioperative process is shown as it was implemented according to guidelines we provided in [6]. The process fragment in the gray box is implemented in YAWL [7]. The clinical backend systems provide diagnostic findings which are accessible e.g. via HL7 compliant interfaces and can be integrated into the workflow net using the data access extension mentioned in Sec. 2.1. In general the access on external data sources is required to be independent from underlying systems (**Requirement 5**) which is ensured by the extension. In our example though the backend systems are integrated by using the HL7 standard.

Depending on the individual state of health of a patient several diagnostic results are needed to be considered at the planning of the anaesthesia. X-ray pictures (fragment $b_1$) of the chest and haemograms (fragment $b_2$) are mandatory while the angiography shown in the picture is an example for an optional diagnostic examination result (*Req. 2*). In Fig. 2 the users are in control of the temporal order in which the three diagnostic results are analyzed. But in case of X-ray and angiography (fragment $b_3$) the specialists have to make a statement about the results first before the results are enabled to the anaesthetist so there is partial order of execution necessary (*Req. 1*).

After the diagnostic results and statements are analyzed (fragments $b_4$,$b_5$) the anaesthesia can be planned. On the day of surgery the planned anaesthesia is usually put into effect. After the surgical procedure the whole process has to be documented by the participating users.

This example shows one possible implementation of the workflow which is quickly build, stable and especially easy to maintain as long as the number of parallel paths is low. Though there may be a complete blood count (not shown in the picture) needed instead of a haemogram (which is a subset of tests included in the complete blood count) so there may be alternative paths of execution involved (*Req. 4*). Nevertheless, the corresponding task is meant to handle both diagnostic results since they are of the same type. Furthermore, it could be necessary to check all daily blood count results from the patient over the past week (*Req. 3*) which is in Fig. 2 represented by just one task. So this is a rather pragmatic approach which comes with the trade-off that the implementation is not quite as exact and as flexible as the real process in the hospital is.

## 2.3   State of the Art

Several work has been done in the area of supporting healthcare processes using workflow management systems. Of these, few especially were concerned with the perioperative process. Related work can be found in the general area of flexible business process management systems [8,9,10,11]. Few papers explore flexibility in workflows for healthcare, e.g. [12,13,14].

Reijers et al. [12] identifies several flexibility patterns but concentrates on the outpatient management in a Dutch hospital. Furthermore, how current workflow system would support such patterns is also part of the analysis.

Müller, Greiner, and Rahm [13] present a system called *AgentWork* providing support for automated workflow adaption. To cope with exceptions during workflow execution an ECA rule approach based on temporal logic was introduced. The event monitoring is described using ActiveTFL (Active Temporal Frame Logic) which is mapped to database triggers. *AgentWork* is highly related to the underling process management system ADEPT [10] which offer a rich set of change operations supporting dynamic structural adaptations ([1]). However, the trigger mechanism allows only monitoring state transitions. But we need at certain times the exact state of data sources. Additionally, the change of process instances according to the principle of ADEPT is very expensive. Frequent changes in the process model, which may need to be verified by the users, is not acceptable for our application.

Hallerbach et al. [15] configure process models extending the process modeling language. Configuration elements within the modeling language are used to configure the process model. The Provop approach supports flexibility during execution by switching between different process variants. As this method is very costly, our approach compose the required model at runtime.

Pockets of flexibility [11] uses the concept of *open instances*. Within the process model pockets of flexibility were defined within a core process. A pocket is a special build activity which composes activities depending on different constructs (e.g. fork sequence, etc.). Just as our approach it is according to [1] assigned to the late modeling concept. However, the composition is left to the user and is restricted afterwards by conditions. Also conditions related to external environment are not considered.

Flexibility as a service is offered by the WFMS YAWL [16,8,9]. The Worklet approach [8] offers a set of self-contained sub-processes. Selection rules (Ripple Down Rules) are used to pick up a Worklet. However, dynamics are restricted to flexible selection of ready-made sub-processes which corresponds to the concept of late binding introduced in [1]. DECLARE [9] avoids the disadvantages of Worklets by using declarative models describing loosely-structured processes. The approach also has drawbacks with data integration. Constraints are only defined between tasks and task parameters. In addition, process models are very complex, if many rules have to be used to describe the execution in detail.

We present a new approach to support flexible workflows in the clinical environment. Therefore, our flexible workflows will be adapted in dependency of the current state of data generated by various clinical systems.

# 3 Flexible Data Aware Workflows

## 3.1 Dynamic Process Specification

Within the PERIKLES project, HL7 messages, generated by various clinical systems, will be persisted as XML type documents in a XML Data Base. Our processes will be adapted in dependency of the current state of theses HL7 messages and other XML type data sources during runtime using a *dynamic dispatch* of activities. Therefore, our approach observes messages and data which are broadcasted via different channels and specifies where corresponding changes in the process should take effect, i.e. where dynamically generated sub-process are executed. We use a notation of a core process which is extended with special *observer* and *generator* tasks. In order to achieve flexibility within the perioperative process the full specification of the process model is completed at runtime. To illustrate our approach Fig. 3 outlines the newly introduced concepts.

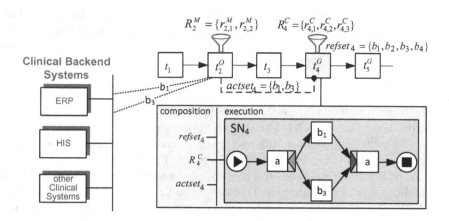

**Fig. 3.** Dynamic process specification

**Bricklets.** $b_i$ are the building blocks for re-using specific activities which are bundled into sub-processes. They are not directly part of the process specification but will be executed at well defined points. The bricklets are a mean for separating the application specific process from data specific parts which rely on up-to-date data.

**Definition 1 (Bricklet).** *Let* $B = \{b_1, b_2, \cdots, b_i\}$ *with* $i \in N$ *be the set of bricklets. A bricklet* $b_i$ *is a valid process model, which contains at least one task definition. Bricklets will be assembled into subnets* $SN_i$.

**Observer Tasks.** $t_i^O$ define points within the workflow where the actual broadcasted messages and data will be investigated. Usually, observer tasks are inserted after activities which expected to cause major changes of the data. The task $t_2^O$ in Fig. 3 denotes an observer task which makes use of the *matching rule set* $(R_2^M)$. The rules $(r_{2,1}^M, r_{2,2}^M)$ specify which activities should be added or removed from the process if there are certain parts in the HL7 message or if they are absent.

Whether a HL7 message fragment exists or not is determined using the path expression $pexpr_j$ and the function $match(pexpr_j)$. If the expression gets evaluated true corresponding bricklets are added to or removed from the construction set $actset_4$ of *generator tasks* $t_4^G$. Furthermore, the selected fragments are returned as $pfrag_j$.

**Definition 2 (Observer Task).** *Let* $T^O$ *denote the set of* observer tasks $t_i^O = (R_i^M, match)$ *with* $i \in N$. *Then:*

- $R_i^M = \{r_{i,1}^M, r_{i,2}^M, \cdots, r_{i,j}^M\}$ *with* $j \in N$ *is a set of matching rules.*
- $r_{i,j}^M : match(pexpr_j) \mapsto (op, t_m^G, B_j, pfrag_j)$ *is a matching rule.*
- $pexpr_j$ *is used to specify data parts expected within the data. It is basically a XPath expression.*
- $op = \{add, delete, merge, undo\}$ *is the set of change operations.*

- $t_m^G \in T^G$ is a generator task.
- $B_j \subseteq refset_m$ is a set of predefined bricklets.
- $pfrag_j$ contains the resulting XPath 1.0 nodeset using $pexpr_j$.

**Matching Rules.** $R_i^M$ associate parts of a message (based on content and/or structure) with a set of bricklets (activities) and define points in the control flow where the activities should be scheduled. So, XPath expression will describe the parts within message instances which should (not) match and trigger activities in the subsequent workflow. Sometimes the existence or absence of a message will not only add but remove also scheduled activities depending whatever the default behavior may be, e.g. if the patient withdraw the prior informed consent (PIC) several treatment activities will most likely be cancelled immediately.

Each $pexpr_j$ within a matching rule $r_{i,j}$ is closely associated with an operation $op$. Where an operation $op$ may only use bricklets from set $refset_i$.

**Definition 3 (Change Operation).** *Let* $op = \{add, delete, merge, undo\}$ *denotes the set of possible operations to manipulate the construction set* $actset_i$ *(hereinafter actset) of generator tasks* $t_i^G$. *Then:*

- *The* add *operation appends the set of activated bricklets* $B_j$ *to the activation set actset.b. For each activated bricklet also the corresponding number* $count(pfrag_j)$ *is stored in* $actset.f(b_k)$.
  $add(t_m^G, B_j, pfrag_j) \mapsto \forall\, b_k \in B_j : \{actset.b = actset.b \cup b_k$
  $\wedge\; actset.f(b_k) = count(pfrag_j)\}$
- *The* merge *operation appends a set of predefined bricklets* $B_j$ *only into actset.b if they are not member of it. Virtual, this operation updates* $actset.f(b_k)$
  $merge(t_m^G, B_j, pfrag_j) \mapsto \forall\, b_k \in (B_j \cap actset.b) : actset.f(b_k) = count(pfrag_j)$
- *The* delete *operation removes bricklets from actset.*
  $delete(t_m^G, B_j, pfrag_j) \forall b_k \in B_j : \{(actset.b = actset.b \setminus \{b_k\})$
  $\wedge delete(actset.f(b_k))\}$
- *Let* $B_j^{-1}$ *be the compensation of* $B_j$ *then the* undo *operation appends a set of compensating bricklets* $B_j^{-1}$ *to the activation set actset to rollback operations* $B_j$ *after a data fragment was removed from the document.*
  $undo(t_m^G, B_j) \mapsto \forall\, b_k \in B_j : \{actset.b = actset.b \cup b_k\}$

**Generator Tasks.**[2] $t_i^G$ specify points within the flow of control where bricklets are combined at run-time to build up a subnet of activities, e.g. $SN_4$ in Fig. 3. The resulting subnet is then deployed and executed. Essentially, the generator tasks are responsible for dynamic dispatching the activities/bricklets like selecting and executing method calls in object-oriented systems. For building up the subnets a set of composition rules ($R_i^C$) and set of scheduled activities ($actset_4$) is used. The scheduled activities must belong to a set of allowed activities ($refset_4$) per distinct generator task. If a generator task is executed within

---

[2] It resembles the idea of *pockets of flexibility* introduced in [11].

the process, it has to compose a valid execution order for the activated bricklets. The generator tasks is the anchor point for providing flexibility at the process instances level.

**Definition 4 (Generator Task).** *Let $T^G$ be the set of* generator tasks $t_i^G$ : $(R_i^C, actset_i, refset_i) \mapsto SN_i$ with $i \in N$. Then:

- $SN_i$ is a valid subnet executed if $t_i^G$ is processed within the control flow.
- $R_i^C = \{r_{i,1}^C, r_{i,2}^C, \cdots, r_{i,j}^C\}$ with $j \in N$ defines a set of construction rules which are used for the generation of a valid $SN_i$.
- $actset_i$ is a set of active bricklets $(b_k)$ and corresponding number of data fragments $(f(b_k))$ chosen by different observer tasks $t_m^O$.
- $refset_i$ defines all bricklets allowed for $t_i^G$.

**Construction Rules.** $R_i^C$ define relationships between bricklets and how they are combined into a resulting control flow. If a bricklet is a pre-requisite for another, a sub-sequent order can be specified. Further, a bricklet can be executed sequential or parallel n-times. If not stated otherwise, bricklets can be executed arbitrarily and in parallel. The construction rules are used to generate a valid subnet $SN_i$ during runtime, which have to be instantiated for $t_i^G$ at runtime.

**Definition 5 (Construction Rules).** *Let $R_i^C$ be the set of construction rules* $r_{i,j}^C$. A construction rule $r_{i,j}^C \in \{b_k \prec b_l, b_k \overset{n}{\prec}, b_k \overset{n}{||}\}$ defines how a bricklet $b_k$ is inserted into the subnet $SN_i$ iff $b_k \in actset_i$.

- $b_k \prec b_l$: Iff bricklet $b_l \in actset_i$, $b_l$ is immediately executed after $b_k$.
- $b_k \overset{n}{\prec}$: The bricklet $b_k$ will be inserted sequentially n times.
- $b_k \overset{n}{||}$: The bricklet $b_k$ will be inserted n times in parallel.

By using these concepts, we avoid complex process structures. The primary process specification is a model of the application's point of view. Wherever message specific activities have to be carried out, they are hidden by generator tasks and descriptive matching and composition rules. These rules determine the dynamic execution of a re-usable set of message specific activities.

## 3.2 Composing Sub-processes

After the activation of bricklets, which is done by the observer tasks, the construction of a valid sub-process has to be controlled by the generator task. Therefore, we provide an algorithm for combining bricklets $b_k$ into a valid subnet using the construction rule set $R_i^C$. The composition is done during runtime to offer a flexible generation of subnets.

Since $actset_i$ changes during runtime, $SN_i$ has to be generated only when $t_i^G$ is activated. This is a two-step procedure. First a directed acyclic graph is created with all activated bricklets $b_n \in actset_i$. In the second step we transform the graph into a valid sub-process (YAWL subnet).

**Definition 6.** *Let $G_i^C = (V, E)$ be a digraph. $V$ is the set of vertices and $E$ is the set of directed edges. The graph $G_i^C$ contains only one starting vertex "start" $\in V$ and one ending vertex "end" $\in V$.*

**Definition 7.** *The indegree $deg^-(b_k)$ is the number of head endpoints for bricklet $b_k$. The outdegree $deg^+(b_k)$ is the number of tail endpoints for $b_k$.*

Listing 1 shows a simple algorithm to calculate $SN_i$. Since the subnet is composed during runtime no deferred choice is needed and no composition rule is mapped to OR-splits, too. We avoid cycles in the constructed subnet graph by enforcing acyclicity of the construction rule set $R_i^C$ at modeling time[3].

**Listing 1.** Algorithm to calculate subnets

```
 1 initialize G with G.V = {start, end} ∪ actset_i and G.E = {}
 2 foreach r_{i,j}^C ∈ R_i^C {
 3    if r_{i,j}^C equals b_k ≺ b_l and {b_k, b_l} ⊆ actset_i {
 4       add directed edge (b_k, b_l) }}
 5 foreach r_{i,j}^C ∈ R_i^C {
 6    //expand replaces b_k by n nodes b_{k.m} of type b_k ∧ m ∈ {1,...,n}
 7    if r_{i,j}^C equals b_k ⊀ⁿ and b_k ∈ actset_i {
 8       n = actset_i.f(b_k); expand(b_k, n);
 9       add directed edge between successive b_{k.m} }
10    if r_{i,j}^C equals b_k ||ⁿ and b_k ∈ actset_i {
11       n = actset_i.f(b_k); expand(b_k, n)
12       if ∃r_{i,m}^C ∈ R_i^C ∧ r_{i,m} equals b_k ≺ b_l {
13          foreach b_{k.o} ∈ {b_{k.1},...,b_{k.n}} { add directed edge (b_{k.o}, b_l) }}
14       if ∃r_{i,m}^C ∈ R_i^C ∧ r_{i,m} equals b_l ≺ b_k {
15          foreach b_{k.o} ∈ {b_{k.1},...,b_{k.n}} { add directed edge (b_l, b_{k.o}) }}}}
16 foreach b_k ∈ G.V {
17    if deg^-(b_k) = 0 { add directed edge (start, b_k) }
18    if deg^+(b_k) = 0 { add directed edge (b_k, end) }}
```

## 4   Implementation Using Yawl and Component Services

The approach presented above was exemplified using YAWL [17] and the corresponding WFMS YAWL. Two YAWL *Custom Component Services* for the observer and generator task types were implemented. We have extended the YAWL editor to describe the matching and construction rule sets. This allows for modeling everything within the standard YAWL environment. The bricklets are implemented as YAWL nets which contain always a start and end condition.

After constructing a digraph for subnet $SN_i$ within generator task $t_i^G$, the graph is tansformed into a valid YAWL net. This YAWL net then gets executed by the WFMS. The transformation is based on rules $R_{1...6}$ shown in Fig. 4. In the resulting net each bricklet is represented by a composite task. This tasks in turn is a container for the bricklet process.

---

[3] This can be done by applying $R_i^C$ on $refset_i$.

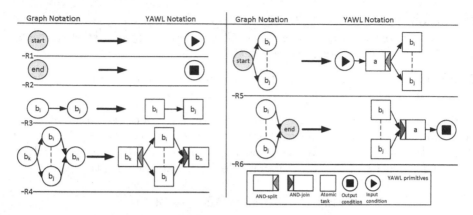

**Fig. 4.** Graph to YAWL mapping rules

$R_1$ maps the *start* node to a YAWL *Input Condition* where the process starts.

$R_2$ maps the *end* note to a *Output Condition* where the process ends.

$R_3$ maps a sequential path from node $b_i$ and $b_j$ to corresponding tasks $b_i$, $b_j$.

$R_4$ maps the split of node $b_k$ to a *And-Split task* $b_k$. Nodes $b_i$, $b_j$ are mapped to corresponding tasks $b_i$, $b_j$. Node $b_n$ is mapped to a *And-Join task* $b_n$.

$R_5$ is for circumstances where the start node *start* is part of a parallel execution. *start* is mapped to a *Input Condition* together with a *And-Split task a. a* is a dummy task. Nodes $b_i$, $b_j$ are mapped to corresponding tasks $b_i$, $b_j$.

$R_6$ is for the same situation as $R_5$, if the end node *end* is part of a parallel execution. *end* is mapped to a *Output Condition* together with a dummy *And-Join task a*. Nodes $b_i$, $b_j$ are mapped to corresponding tasks $b_i$, $b_j$.

## 5    Implementing the Sample Scenario

In Fig. 5 (a) the process from Fig. 2 is realized using our approach. Task *request statement* ($t_1$) is modeled as an observer task which controls the dynamic dispatch of activities in generator task *planning* $t_2$. Task $t_2$ provides the set of selectable bricklets $refset_2 = \{b_1, b_2, b_3, b_4, b_5\}$, which are correspond to the tasks in Fig. 2. The observer task $t_1$ uses a set of matching rules $R_1^M = \{r_{1,1}^M, r_{1,2}^M, r_{1,3}^M\}$ with $r_{1,1}^M = add(t_2, b_2, "//OBR[../PID/PID.3/CX.1='123'][OBR.4/CWE.1='X-ray']")$ and $r_{1,2}^M = add(t_2, \{b_1, b_4\}, "//OBR[../PID/PID.3/CX.1='123'][OBR.4/CWE.1='haemogram']")$[4]. For the sub-process construction in $t_2$, the rule set $R_1^C = \{b_1 \prec b_4, b_1 \overset{2}{\prec}, b_2 \overset{2}{\|}\}$ is used. They reflect the order of the activities in Fig. 2. Due to matching rules $r_{1,1}^M$, $r_{1,2}^M$ the observer task $t_1$ activates the bricklets in $actset_2 = \{b_1, b_2, b_4\}$, which is a subset of $refset_2 = \{b_1, b_2, b_3, b_4, b_5\}$. Fig. 5 (b)–(d) depict the construction of digraph $G$. First, all activated bricklets ($b_1, b_2, b_4$) will be inserted into $G.V$ (Fig. 5 (b)). The application of rules $b_1 \prec b_4$ (edge from $b_1$ to $b_4$), $b_1 \overset{2}{\prec}$ (edge from first

---

[4] The XPath queries on the HL7 messages match for the patient 123 and if they contain a X-ray or a haemogram.

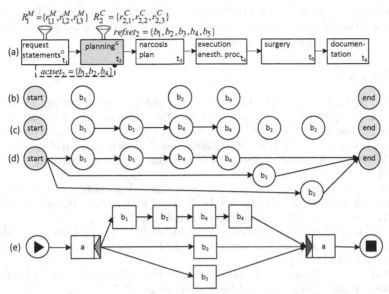

b₁: X-ray analysis  b₂: haemogram analysis  b₃: angiography analysis  b₄: analysis of r statement  b₅: analysis of i statement

**Fig. 5.** Digraph construction and transformation into a YAWL subnet

$b_1$ to second $b_1$) and $b_2 \parallel$ ($b_2$ is duplicated) is shown in (c). We assume that $count(pfrag_j)$ returns always 2. The final step (d) connects all vertices with $deg^-(b_i) = 0$ or $deg^+(b_i) = 0$ with the "start" and "end" nodes. The YAWL subnet (e) results from transforming digraph $G$ into YAWL. This subnet gets deployed and executed at run-time by generator task $t_2$.

## 6  Conclusion and Future Work

Process support in the perioperative process is a field that bears much practical relevance. We provided an approach for a flexible perioperative process. With respect to other approaches, we achieve flexibility by monitoring data changes and specifying where corresponding changes should take effect. This is done by extending the WFMS YAWL with observer tasks which monitor these changes. Generator tasks allow for flexible execution of process instances. Our technique presented here can be described best as a late modeling, descriptive approach using under-specification [1].

The added value of our approach is that both context conditions on external data and the resulting changes of the process instances are described within one process model. Additionally, all components of our approach will be provided and executed within an extension of the WFMS YAWL. A prototype that implements the approach will finally allow a detailed case study and evaluation.

In future research we will extent relationships between data operations and rule sets for process constructions to provide more freedom in combining bricklets (process fragments) into sub-processes. One of the challenges concerns the automatic generation of construction rules. Also data dependencies between bricklets have to be considered in more detail.

# References

1. Weber, B., Sadiq, S., Reichert, M.: Beyond rigidity — dynamic process lifecycle support. Computer Science — Research and Development 23, 47–65 (2009)
2. Kühn, R., Bandt, M., Dittmar, A., Meyer, H., Forbrig, P.: Hops: modeling flexible, clinical processes as the basis of workflow-based assistance system (german). In: USEWARE 2010. Number 2099 in VDI-Berichte/VDI-Tagungsbände, pp. 77–86 (2010)
3. Kühn, R., Dittmar, A., Forbrig, P.: Alternative Representations of Workflow Control-Flow Patterns Using HOPS. In: Forbrig, P., Günther, H. (eds.) BIR 2010. LNBIP, vol. 64, pp. 115–129. Springer, Heidelberg (2010)
4. Ouyang, C., Wynn, M.T., Fidge, C., ter Hofstede, A.H.M., Kuhr, J.C., Becker, T.: Workflow support for scheduling in surgical care processes. Accepted paper at ECIS 2011 (2011)
5. Sandberg, W.S., Ganous, T.J., Steiner, C.: Setting a Research Agenda for Perioperative Systems Design. Surgical Innovation 10(2), 57–70 (2003)
6. Bandt, M., Kühn, R., Schick, S., Meyer, H.: Beyond flexibility - workflows in the perioperative sector of the healthcare domain. ECEASST 37 (2011)
7. van der Aalst, W.M.P., ter Hofstede, A.: Yawl: Yet another workflow language. Information Systems 30(4), 245–275 (2005)
8. Adams, M., ter Hofstede, A.H.M., Edmond, D., van der Aalst, W.M.P.: Worklets: A Service-Oriented Implementation of Dynamic Flexibility in Workflows. In: Meersman, R., Tari, Z. (eds.) OTM 2006, Part I. LNCS, vol. 4275, pp. 291–308. Springer, Heidelberg (2006)
9. Pesic, M., Schonenberg, H., van der Aalst, W.M.P.: Declare: Full support for loosely-structured processes. In: EDOC, pp. 287–300 (2007)
10. Reichert, M., Dadam, P.: ADEPT$_{flex}$ — Supporting Dynamic Changes of Workflows Without Losing Control. J. Intell. Inf. Syst. 10(2), 93–129 (1998)
11. Sadiq, S.W., Orlowska, M.E., Sadiq, W.: Specification and validation of process constraints for flexible workflows. Inf. Syst. 30(5), 349–378 (2005)
12. Reijers, H.A., Russell, N., van der Geer, S., Krekels, G.A.M.: Workflow for Healthcare: A Methodology for Realizing Flexible Medical Treatment Processes. In: Rinderle-Ma, S., Sadiq, S., Leymann, F. (eds.) BPM 2009. LNBIP, vol. 43, pp. 593–604. Springer, Heidelberg (2010)
13. Müller, R., Greiner, U., Rahm, E.: Agentwork: A workflow system supporting rule-based workflow adaptation. Data and Knowledge Engineering 51(2), 223–256 (2004)
14. Mans, R.S., Russell, N.C., van der Aalst, W.M.P., Bakker, P.J.M., Moleman, A.J., Jaspers, M.W.M.: Proclets in healthcare. Journal of Biomedical Informatics 43(4), 632–649 (2010)
15. Hallerbach, A., Bauer, T., Reichert, M.: Capturing variability in business process models: the provop approach. Journal of Software Maintenance 22(6-7), 519–546 (2010)
16. van der Aalst, W.M.P., Adams, M., ter Hofstede, A.H.M., Pesic, M., Schonenberg, H.: Flexibility as a Service. In: Chen, L., Liu, C., Liu, Q., Deng, K. (eds.) DASFAA 2009. LNCS, vol. 5667, pp. 319–333. Springer, Heidelberg (2009)
17. van der Aalst, W.M.P., ter Hofstede, A.H.M.: Yawl: yet another workflow language. Information Systems 30(4), 245–275 (2005)

# Developing a Process Quality Improvement Questionnaire – A Case Study on Writing Discharge Letters

Robert Heinrich[1], Barbara Paech[1], Antje Brandner[2],
Ulrike Kutscha[2], and Björn Bergh[2]

[1] University of Heidelberg, Institute of Computer Science,
Im Neuenheimer Feld 326, Germany-69120 Heidelberg
{heinrich,paech}@informatik.uni-heidelberg.de
[2] University Hospital Heidelberg, Center of Information Technology and Medical Engineering,
Speyerer Straße 4, Germany-69115 Heidelberg
{Antje.Brandner,Ulrike.Kutscha,
Bjoern.Bergh}@med.uni-heidelberg.de

**Abstract.** Business process quality assessment plays an important role in business process management. Business process quality is often assessed by identifying potentials for improvement. In practice, a questionnaire is a commonly used means. However, creating a questionnaire requires a high expertise because systematic approaches are missing. Moreover, questionnaires for process improvement often focus on single quality aspects. In this paper, we describe a systematic approach to create a questionnaire to identify business process quality problems. The approach is based on a comprehensive business process quality model. We applied the approach in a case study at a German university hospital and present results of the preliminary evaluation phase.

**Keywords:** Business Process Quality, Business Process Quality Improvement, Quality Model, Health Care Process, Case Study.

## 1 Introduction

Business process quality is a central aspect of business process management. However, it is not easy to capture quality adequately. One means to capture quality is benchmarking [2]. Benchmarking assesses quality in an abstract way, for example by comparing Key Performance Indicators between organizations or classifying processes in a maturity model like COBIT [12] or the BPMM [15]. However, benchmarking does not provide insights in specific quality problems. To capture details on quality problems several techniques are available such as analyzing the process output, monitoring errors of involved IT systems or asking for the actor's opinion. In this paper, we focus on the identification of process quality problems from the actor's view. Therefore, a questionnaire is an effective means. However, developing such a detailed questionnaire to identify business process quality problems is a non-trivial task. It requires a lot of a priori knowledge, for example, of the domain, the process to be assessed or typical problems. Often, this task is not performed in a systematic way.

F. Daniel et al. (Eds.): BPM 2011 Workshops, Part II, LNBIP 100, pp. 261–272, 2012.

Moreover, questionnaires for business process improvement often focus on single quality aspects. For example, [5] mainly focuses on time and cost aspects of a process. [4] considers effectiveness and resource utilization. Both do not consider e.g. safety, analyzability or maturity of the process. One reason for this may be that there is no common quality model for business processes. In contrast, software product quality is standardized in the ISO/IEC 9126 quality model [9]. We developed a comprehensive quality model for business processes [7], [8] which is based on software product quality standards and allocated quality aspects from business process management literature. The model aims at providing a common view on business process quality. It serves as a basis for business process quality improvement, business process quality simulation, support for management decision and quality requirements elicitation.

In this paper, we describe one possible application of our model in practice. We show how to develop a questionnaire to identify quality problems from the actors' view. Thereby, the quality model serves as a checklist. To evaluate the approach we are conducting a case study in cooperation with the University Hospital Heidelberg. The case study is conducted in the hospital context as especially in the medical domain business process quality plays an important role [4]. In this paper, we present our experience gained in the preliminary evaluation phase.

The paper is structured as follows: In Section 2, as a background, we present our research on a comprehensive and practically relevant quality model for business processes. Section 3 discusses related work. Section 4 describes our approach to identify quality problems. Section 5 presents the case study and describes the results of a preliminary evaluation. Section 6 concludes the paper and presents future work.

## 2    Background

Process quality is in the focus of research and practice since some decades in the quality initiative domain and there are many high level and expert based techniques like TQM, Kaizen or Six Sigma. [17] gives a good overview of quality initiatives. However, a comprehensive and detailed view on the – in particular non-financial – quality aspects of a business process is still missing.

Therefore, we developed the comprehensive Business Process Quality Reference-Model (BPQRM) [7], [8] using characteristics we transferred from software product quality standards. To the characteristics we allocated a broad range of detailed quality aspects from business process management and business process assessment literature. We use a hierarchical structure of quality aspects defined as follows. A *business process quality characteristic* is a category of business process quality attributes, for example the maturity of an activity. A *business process quality attribute* is an inherent property of a business process that can be distinguished quantitatively or qualitatively, for example the error density of an activity. A *business process quality measure* is a variable to which a value is assigned as the result of measurement. Measures can be defined as *base measures* or *derived measures*. A base measure is a measure for which the value is directly applicable to the process, e.g. the number of errors or the number of (sub) activities. A derived measure is a measure that is defined as a function of two or more values of base measures, e.g. the number of errors per activity size.

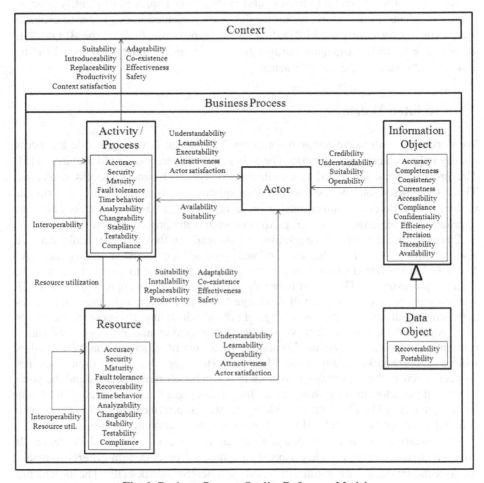

**Fig. 1.** Business Process Quality Reference-Model

Business process quality refers to the components of a business process. Components are the activities of the process, the actors performing these activities, the objects handled and created by the process as well as the resources necessary for execution. As an activity can be subdivided into sub activities, we consider a process itself as an activity. In the BPQRM we associated a set of quality characteristics to each component of a business process. We took the ISO/IEC 9126 software product quality characteristics for resources and also adapted them for activities. For information objects we took the ISO/IEC 25012 [11] data quality characteristics. The actor characteristics we developed based on quality aspects from practice. Figure 1 shows the BPQRM (characteristic level). The nodes correspond to the components and the characteristics are listed either within the node or on an edge between nodes. If the assessment of a characteristic depends on information of another component, we located it on the edge.

The focus of this paper is to present and evaluate our approach to identify process quality problems. Furthermore, we utilize the study presented in this paper to evaluate the practical applicability of the BPQRM, as our approach is built on the BPQRM. If we are able to derive a meaningful questionnaire from the model, we consider the involved attributes as relevant in practice.

# 3    Related Work

We conducted a literature research for general advice on how to generate a process quality improvement questionnaire. The only relevant source we could identify is [5]. The process check list in [5] is a collection of typical business process problems. Thus, it is based on the assumption that quality is often threatened by similar problems in different organizations or projects. The creation of a process checklist requires a high expertise, however, there is no systematic procedure described.

To ensure the relevance of the resulting questionnaire to the domain of health care we also identified several health care related process improvement approaches. As mentioned in the introduction, benchmarking [2] is often used to assess the quality of business processes and IT-support in health care practice. For example, [3] monitors IT systems that support the creation of discharge letters and therefore focuses on time-to-completion of discharge letters and usage of patient scheduling. [6] presents the results of a systematic search to identify evidence-based quality and efficiency indicators relevant to hospitals or physicians' practices. Indicators of structural quality as well as indicators of process quality were identified. However, this publication does not sufficiently cover the complexity of quality issues in health care processes and the point of view of the actor. In prior work one author of this paper presented quality indicators for the actor view [1]. Our current work can be seen as a refinement as it is based on a comprehensive quality model and further describes the creation of a questionnaire.

[4] presents a screening instrument to identify problems of hospital processes. It uses a matrix that relates quality aspects of a hospital process with criteria to assess the aspects. Problems are identified based on selected matrix cells. The instrument utilizes different methods for the evaluation of the criteria. One of that is a questionnaire. However, the selection of the matrix cells and the creation of the questions are not described in detail. Moreover, the quality aspects used in this instrument are a subset of the BPQRM.

# 4    Approach to Identify Quality Problems

In this section we describe how to create a questionnaire for an interview study. A questionnaire is an effective means to identify process quality problems from the actor's view. However, the selection of the questions is crucial to the success of the study. To support this selection we propose the BPQRM as a checklist. Figure 2 gives an overview of the four phases of our approach.

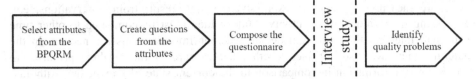

**Fig. 2.** Deriving a Questionnaire to Identify Quality Problems

**Phase 1, Select Attributes:** In [8] we collected example attributes and measures for each characteristic in Figure 1. Note that in the following we abbreviate base measure by using the term measure. Because of the large number of attributes, we first have to choose a subset which is suitable to identify problems of a specific process. We developed a set of selection criteria to select attributes from the BPQRM. The selection criteria are presented in Table 1. Note that these criteria can be used to select attributes for an arbitrary assessment method. In this publication we focus on assessment by interview, so we only select attributes whose measures can be captured in an interview. The selection criteria are inspired by literature on the selection of requirements engineering tools [16] and criteria for selecting measures in ISO/IEC 15539 [10]. We adapted the idea to define different views on the attributes from [16]. The criteria domain, expressiveness, effort and method are adapted from [10].

**Table 1.** Criteria for Attribute Selection

| View | Criterion | Description |
|------|-----------|-------------|
| Domain View | Domain | Is the attribute suitable and relevant for the domain? |
| Outcome View | Expressiveness | How high is the expressiveness of the attribute's measures? |
| | Knowledge added | Does the attribute promise to provide new information? |
| Operational View | Effort | How high is the effort to capture the attribute's measures? |
| Method View | Method | Are the attribute's measures able to be captured using the available method? |
| Customer View | Importance | How high is the attribute's importance for the customer? |
| | Constraints | Are there any constraints from the customer regarding the attribute? |

In the following, we give a more detailed description of the views and criteria. An attribute may be highly relevant in one domain whereas it is less relevant in another domain. For example, precision or security has a higher relevance in the medical context than in a general office context, where it may be neglected for cost reasons. Therefore, we consider the suitability and relevance of an attribute to a specific domain in the domain view. In the outcome view we consider the expressiveness of the attribute's measures with respect to the ability to derive improvements. There are measures with high expressiveness which directly provide information about problems in the process, e.g. measures capturing inadequate IT support. Furthermore, there are measures with lower expressiveness that result from observations, e.g. processing time values of an activity. Time values must be compared to other time values to interpret the value and decide whether improvements are needed. In the outcome view we also consider whether the capture of the attribute promises to provide new information in comparison to the current state of knowledge. Although an attribute is relevant, expressive and provides new information, there may be high effort required to capture the attribute's measures. For example, diagrams or other auxiliary means have to be created in case of an interview. Thus, we consider effort in the operational view. The method view is concerned with the methods available to capture the attribute's measures. Examples of methods are monitoring, data analysis or interview. For the attribute selection one must consider that the attribute's measures can be captured by the available method. For example, consistency of a data object can be determined easier using the method data analysis than using an interview. As in this approach we want to create a questionnaire for an interview study, we focus on the method interview. The customer's opinion should be considered, too. The customer is the organization whose business processes are analyzed. In the customer view we consider the importance of an attribute to the customer. Moreover, constraints from the customer should also be considered, for example the assessment of employees of the customer may be problematic. Each attribute in [8] is analyzed using the selection criteria. To support the reproduction of the analysis each criterion must be justified. We propose to use a matrix form with the selection criteria on one axis and the attributes on the other axis to document the justification. In addition to attributes in [8], domain specific knowledge such as standards, guidelines and policies should be considered as a source of attributes, too.

**Phase 2, Create Questions:** After the selection of the attributes the questions have to be created. As questions created ad-hoc from the attributes may be relatively abstract, we relate questions to a specific business process model. Thus, before creating the questions, the process to be evaluated should be captured in a process model, e.g. by using one of the commonly used business process modeling notations like BPMN [14]. The process model helps the interviewees to understand the questions by visualizing the activities they perform, the objects they handle, the IT systems they use (in some modeling tools) as well as the interfaces between the process components. Before starting the interview the process model is explained to the interviewee. Then, the interviewee has to mark the activities s/he performs in the process model. Section B1.1 in Table 2 presents an example.

To create questions for the attributes one should consider how to measure the attributes. As a measure per definition (see Section 2) is used to measure the related attribute, it gives a good idea of what to ask for. However, further adaptations are necessary to create concrete and useful questions for an interview situation.

Based on the attributes two types of questions can be derived: qualitative and quantitative questions. A qualitative question for example is "what is the problem?". A quantitative question for example is "how many problems are there?" or "how much time does it take?". The answers to qualitative questions directly describe quality problems, but are not presented in a measureable manner. The answers to quantitative questions are measureable. They can be used to compare one process to another or process components with each other and thereby identify problems. Note that there is no relation to the expressiveness of the attribute's measures. For each attribute qualitative questions as well as quantitative questions are possible. As answers to quantitative questions are hard to estimate by the interviewees, we recommend avoiding them, where possible, and instead asking a qualitative question from which a quantitative statement can be derived. In other words, one should avoid asking for the number of process components (e.g. activities) that have a specific property. Instead, one should better ask the interviewee to name process components which have a specific property. Thus, the number is provided implicitly. For example, the attribute *attractiveness* of the process may be determined by the measures *number of activities which are considered as attractive by the actors* and *total number of activities*. Thus, we ask the interviewees for the activities they like to perform. In Table 2, the first question in section B1.2 is a qualitative question, however, one can derive a quantitative statement from it. The total number of activities can be determined from the process model. The second question in B1.2 is a qualitative question which leads to a qualitative statement. Here, the interviewee describes the problems with the activities.

**Table 2.** Example of a Questionnaire

| B1 | Questions on activities | |
|---|---|---|
| Now, present the process model to the interviewee. | | |
| | General questions on activities | |
| 1 | Which activities in the process do you perform? (Please mark your activities in the process model) | |
| | Are there any activities you perform in the process that are not contained in the process model? If yes, please add these activities to the model. | |
| | Questions on actor satisfaction and attractiveness of the process | |
| 2 | Attractiveness | Which of your activities in the process do you like to perform? |
| | | What bothers you about the activities you do not like to perform? |

For estimations a good granularity of the metric (e.g. output per day/week/month) is important to help the interviewee to give a meaningful answer. Therefore, typical frequencies of execution, error rates and amounts of objects in the process should be considered. This information should be captured before creating the questionnaire.

**Phase 3, Compose Questionnaire:** The questionnaire is composed by arranging the questions in a meaningful manner. Guidelines for this can be found in literature from psychology and social sciences such as [13]. An example of a questionnaire structure is presented in Section 5.1.

**Phase 4, Identify Quality Problems:** As described above (phase 2), potentials for improvement either directly arise out of the interviewee's answers (in case of a qualitative statement) or are derived by comparison (in case of a quantitative statement). In case of questions on errors (deviation from the specified behavior), we also recommend to ask for the frequency and the severity of the errors in order to prioritize the errors.

Our approach provides a systematic way to select attributes from the BPQRM. For the derivation of the questions from the attributes we provide heuristic support as this includes context-specific adaptations. The results of the interviews of course depend on the interviewer and the interviewees. Expertise is still required in all the phases. It is not the goal of our approach to enable a non-expert to create a meaningful questionnaire. However, we aim to provide a methodical support that can be used by experts.

# 5    Case Study

We conducted a case study to evaluate our approach. We study the process of writing discharge letters at a German university hospital. A discharge letter is a summary of the performed patient treatment and is used for communication between physicians for follow-up treatments. The process of writing discharge letters is chosen because all the process components of the BPQRM are contained in the process and there are a large number of quality aspects to be captured. In the study the people are interviewed separately. We do not conduct group interviews.

At the beginning of the case study we captured the current state of the process in a BPMN process model. Therefore, the authors of the Institute of Computer Science cooperated with the authors of the Center of Information Technology and Medical Engineering (ZIM) of the hospital. The process model is created based on documents provided by the hospital and on interviews with our health care expert co-authors. It consists of 15 activities, 5 information objects, 4 actors and 1 IT system (hospital information system, HIS). Due to the limited space we cannot display the process model here. As described in phase 2 in Section 4, this process model is used as a basis for the interviews.

We evaluate our approach by assessing the effort to create a questionnaire (see Section 5.1) and the adequacy of the questions to identify problems in a preliminary evaluation (see Section 5.2). Thus, we use the following research questions (RQ).

- RQ1: How much effort is necessary to develop a questionnaire based on the BPQRM? The effort is measured in person hours.
- RQ2: Are the questions adequate to identify business process quality problems?

As we have not yet conducted a full interview study we report the results of a preliminary interview study with 3 interviewees.

## 5.1    Effort to Develop a Questionnaire

In this section, we describe how we developed the questionnaire for the case study from the BPQRM and present the effort required. Out of more than 200 attributes in [8] we finally selected 20 attributes which fit best the selection criteria shown in

Table 1. There are further relevant attributes in [8]. However, because of a time restriction of a maximum of one hour for the interview, we have to limit ourselves to 20 attributes. Table 3 presents the selected characteristics and attributes per component of the business process. The characteristics are presented in bold and the attributes are listed below. See [8] for more information on the characteristics and attributes.

Table 3. Selected Characteristics and Attributes

|  | | | |
|---|---|---|---|
| **Activity** | **Maturity**: Error density, Callbacks | **Time behavior:** Transport time efficiency | **Interoperability**: Freedom of collision |
| | **Attractiveness:** Attractiveness | **Resource utilization:** Adequate resource usage, Capacity of the resource | **Actor satisfaction**: Problems of the actors, Challenging work |
| | **Suitability**: Significance | **Understandability:** Understandable purpose | |
| **Res.** | **Maturity**: Error density | **Interoperability:** Freedom of collision | **Attractiveness:** Ergonomics |
| | **Understandability:** Understandable purpose | **Learnability:** Correct Execution | |
| **IO** | **Availability**: Availability | **Operability:** Ease of manipulation | **Currentness**: Currency |
| | **Compliance**: Conformity | | |

In the medical domain, attributes of characteristics such as security, precision or maturity are highly relevant. We considered this in the domain view. In the outcome view we excluded attributes whose measures are not sufficiently expressive. For example, we did not ask for help accessibility to assess learnability as we consider this as less expressive than the frequency of faulty operations (correct execution). Moreover, we excluded attributes which do not promise to bring additional knowledge. For example, we did not ask for actor documentation as we already knew that there is no documentation available. In the operational view we focused on attributes which can be captured without additional auxiliary means. Therefore and as we considered time values as hard to estimate by the interviewees (method view), we excluded questions on time (transport time efficiency focuses on transport means and routes). However, the questionnaire contains a general question whether the entire process takes too long. This is the only question on quality which is not directly related to an attribute. Our health care expert co-authors put high emphasis on characteristics like maturity and actor satisfaction and less emphasis on characteristics like changeability or adaptability of the process. We considered this in the customer view. Moreover, on request of the hospital, we excluded attributes which directly or indirectly allow the assessment of the quality or capability of the process actors. For example, we did not ask for the precision of the discharge letter as this may assess the capability of its author.

After selecting the attributes for the case study we created questions for the interview based on the selected attribute's measures. We created qualitative as well as quantitative questions. Altogether, we created 43 questions on quality for the study. The row IO in Table 3 presents the selected attributes related to information objects. Due to the time restriction we decided to ask only for availability for all the objects within the process. The other attributes are asked solely for the discharge letter.

The questionnaire consists of 2 parts (A and B) and 5 Sections. Section A asks for personal details of the interviewee such as her/his role in the process or contact details for possible further queries. Section B contains the questions to assess the quality of the process and consists of 4 sub sections. Section B1, B2, B3, and B4 contain questions respectively on the actor satisfaction and the attractiveness of the process, on the quality of the supporting IT system, on the quality of the information objects used in the process and on errors within activities, the IT and the discharge letter.

The attribute selection lasted about 20 person hours. The creation of the questions required about 8 person hours. The final arrangement of the questionnaire required further 2 person hours. The effort to create a questionnaire for the example process from the BPQRM is therefore about 30 person hours. Additionally, the composition of the process model required about 6 person hours. All the steps involved several iterations with our health care expert co-authors. In the opinion of the experts this is an adequate effort.

## 5.2    Adequacy of the Questions

To evaluate the adequacy of the derived questions to identify quality problems we conducted a preliminary study. The goal of the preliminary evaluation is to validate the developed questionnaire in practice before starting a comprehensive interview study. We consider the questions as adequate if the identified problems are assessed as useful by our health care expert co-authors. The preliminary evaluation was conducted with 3 employees of the ZIM who in the past were involved as actors in the process of writing discharge letters, but who were not involved in creating the questionnaire. Although these employees of the ZIM currently are not involved in the process, they can provide meaningful answers as they were involved in the past and they have good knowledge of the current process and the supporting IT system.

For the preliminary study we only analyze those questions of our questionnaire, which lead to qualitative statements (30 of the 43 questions), as we want to identify problems directly, not to compare the discharge process to another one. The questions were answered by the interviewees and the answers directly lead to the bullet points in the list below.

Note that the results of the preliminary study are not representative because of the small number of interviewees and the fact that the interviewees were not involved in the process of writing discharge letters at the time the study was conducted. Nevertheless, we identified major weaknesses of the process and the supporting IT system in the interviews. Altogether, we identified 12 quality problems. Due to the limited space we present an excerpt in the following.

- The entire process of writing discharge letters is considered as boring and annoying by the physicians. It is considered as additional bureaucratic effort which does not contribute to their core activities. More automation of the process is required by the interviewees. We identified this by asking for attractiveness of the activities (attribute *attractiveness*).
- The entire process is considered as too time-consuming. This was the answer to the general question on time as mentioned in Section 5.1.

- The step *documentation of diagnosis* is performed twice in the activity *create discharge letter*. Once for clinical purpose and again for billing. The purpose of the repetition is not understood by the interviewees. We identified this by asking for activities whose purpose is not understood by the actors (attribute *understandable purpose*).
- The HIS used for writing discharge letters provides a Microsoft Word integration as a so called Word container. Data can be moved from the HIS to the Word container, however, there is no integration in the other direction. Data once contained in the Word container cannot be moved back to the HIS in a structured way. Thus, the actors often have to use copy and paste to transfer information between discharge letters. Moreover, data contained in the Word container cannot be updated. We identified this by asking for activities not adequately supported by the HIS (attribute *adequate resource usage*).
- Our questions for learnability and ergonomics of the HIS showed that the HIS is complex and hard to handle (attributes *correct execution* and *ergonomics*). The actors often do faulty operations or there are navigation problems, because there is no consistent menu guidance. Especially diagnostic findings are hard to access as the actors have to switch between single parts of the findings. An overview of the findings is missing in the HIS.
- The actor has to set a status to forward the discharge letter in the system. However, the interviewees prefer to send the letter directly to a person or a group of persons. Thus, setting the status is not used. We identified this by asking for activities not adequately supported by the HIS (attribute *adequate resource usage*).
- Our question on availability showed that after 9 months the access to findings is locked. However, the interviewees stated that sometimes they require old information (attribute *availability*).

We received positive feedback from our health care expert co-authors. The findings of the preliminary evaluation are assessed as useful input for process quality improvement. Our health care expert co-authors consider the derived questions as an adequate means to identify quality problems of the example process. However, further evaluations will be made before the questionnaire is applied in a comprehensive study.

Although the effort for the conduction of the interviews was already restricted to a maximum of one hour, it is still considered as relatively high by the interviewees. Therefore, we plan to reduce the number of questions in a full study.

# 6    Conclusion and Future Work

In this paper, we presented a systematic approach to identify business process quality problems. Based on a comprehensive quality model a questionnaire for an interview study was derived. As an example process we used the process of writing discharge letters at a German university hospital. We presented the results of a preliminary evaluation of the approach. The results showed that the questions can be derived with reasonable effort and that they are an adequate means to identify quality problems.

The results of the preliminary evaluation convinced us to conduct a comprehensive and representative case study using our approach in the future. We want to apply our approach to further business processes of several domains to achieve a more comprehensive evaluation. Moreover, we plan to examine further application areas of our quality model.

# References

1. Ammenwerth, E., Breu, R., Paech, B.: User-Oriented Quality Assessment of IT-Supported Healthcare Processes – A Position Paper. In: Rinderle-Ma, S., Sadiq, S., Leymann, F. (eds.) BPM 2009. LNBIP, vol. 43, pp. 617–622. Springer, Heidelberg (2010)
2. Camp, R.C.: Benchmarking - The Search for Industry Best Practices that Lead to Superior Performance. ASQC Quality Press (1989)
3. Dugas, M., Eckholt, M., Bunzemeier, H.: Benchmarking of hospital information systems: Monitoring of discharge letters and scheduling can reveal heterogeneities and time trends. BMC Medical Informatics and Decision Making 8(15) (2008)
4. Ehlers, F., Ammenwerth, E., Haux, R.: Process Potential Screening - An Instrument to Improve Business Processes in Hospitals. Methods of Information in Medicine 45(5), 506–514 (2006)
5. Fischermanns, G.: Praxishandbuch Prozessmanagement, Verlag Dr. Götz Schmidt, 7th revised edn. (2009) (in German)
6. Gandjour, A., Kleinschmit, F., Littmann, V., Lauterbach, K.W.: An evidence-based evaluation of quality and efficiency indicators. Quality Management in Health Care 10(4), 41–52 (2002)
7. Heinrich, R., Paech, B.: Defining the Quality of Business Processes. In: Engels, G., Karagiannis, D., Mayr, H.C. (eds.) Modellierung 2010. LNI, vol. P-161, pp. 133–148 (2010)
8. Heinrich, R., Paech, B.: Business Process Quality - A Technical Report, University of Heidelberg, Institute for Computer Science, Technical Report (2010)
9. ISO/IEC 9126-1: Software engineering — Product quality — Part 1: Quality model, 1st edn. (2001)
10. ISO/IEC 15939: Systems and software engineering — Measurement process, 2nd edn. (2007)
11. ISO/IEC 25012: Software engineering — Software product Quality Requirements and Evaluation (SQuaRE) — Data quality model, 1st edn. (2008)
12. ITGI: Control Objectives for Information and Related Technologies (COBIT), Version 4.1, IT Governance Institute (2007)
13. Oppenheim, A. N.: Questionnaire design, interviewing and attitude measurement. Continuum International Publishing Group Ltd. (2000)
14. OMG: Business Process Model and Notation (BPMN), Version 2.0 (2011)
15. OMG: Business Process Maturity Model (BPMM), Version 1.0 (2008)
16. Pohl, K., Rupp, C.: Requirements Engineering Fundamentals. Rocky Nook (2011)
17. Raisinghani, M.S., Ette, H., Pierce, R., Cannon, G., Daripaly, P.: Six Sigma: concepts, tools, and applications. Industrial Management & Data Systems 105(4), 491–505 (2005)

# A Personalized Access Control Framework for Workflow-Based Health Care Information

Nazia Leyla and Wendy MacCaull

Centre for Logic and Information
St. Francis Xavier University
Antigonish, Canada
{x2009gte,wmaccaul}@stfx.ca

**Abstract.** Access control is one of the key features of any health care organization. Without a strong access control mechanism, there is a risk of inappropriate use of personal health information. Here we focus on Personalized Access Control (PAC) [1] where the patient decides who can access his/her health record. We enhance the PAC model of [1] by proposing a prototypical framework, which incorporates a workflow into the PAC model to express the context of health care processes, and by providing a mechanism to capture a patient's consent to enforce the PAC policy. We enforce the "need to know" principle by associating roles with each task in a workflow and handle problems with delegation. We present a case study outlining the present working procedures of the Seniors' Wellness Program in our local health authority, using NOVA Workflow for workflow modeling and Ponder2 for representing and enforcing policy.

**Keywords:** personalized access control, workflow, health care information system, EHR.

## 1   Introduction

The world-wide use of information systems, allowing us to store, organize, gather, extract, and investigate an array of services, is increasing rapidly and with it, there is a growing need for security. Access control is one of the most important security aspects for protecting information from unauthorized use. Access control is particularly important in the health care information systems. As more and more patient information is recorded electronically, it becomes essential to protect that information from unauthorized access and, therefore, misuse. Currently, Electronic Health Record (EHR) systems are becoming increasingly common for storing health information [2]. These EHRs contain a great deal of health data, including sensitive information, such as fertility status and abortion history, emotional problems, HIV status, physical abuse, and so on. Without a strong access control mechanism, there is a risk of breach of security resulting in an inappropriate access to personal health information, which can not only adversely affect the patient but also lead to complaints, allegation of negligence and possible liability for the organization. Protecting information from abuse, thus, ensuring people's right to privacy is, therefore, a major concern in the management, design, and development of health care infrastructure [3].

F. Daniel et al. (Eds.): BPM 2011 Workshops, Part II, LNBIP 100, pp. 273–284, 2012.
© Springer-Verlag Berlin Heidelberg 2012

The vast majority of articles, dealing with the development and implementation of generic access control polices, models, and mechanisms (38 in 52 articles) [4], use the Role Based Access Control (RBAC) model in order to develop their access control systems. The RBAC [5] is the most common method used in health care organizations and acts as a basis for other methods. RBAC associates permissions to groups of users according to their roles within the organization. However, health related data is owned by the patient, and it should be disclosed only when permission is obtained from the patient [6]. In [1], the authors provide a model for a Personalized Access Control (PAC) framework where the patient is the administrator of his/her health record. PAC is about making sure information is accessible only to authorized users, which allows the patient to grant a person read and/or write access to his/her health record and to revoke this when they choose.

In a health care organization, it is also necessary to ensure that works are performed in a planned way meeting health care requirements. A Workflow Management System (WfMS) enables health care organizations to automate their health care process, in order to enhance efficiency and effectiveness. To ensure that only authorized users execute workflow tasks, appropriate authorization mechanisms must be in place, so that authorization is granted only when the task starts and is revoked as soon as the task finishes [7]. Getting patients' permissions for the disclosure of their health records can be represented as a task in a health care workflow.

In this paper, we enhance the PAC model [1] and propose a prototypical framework, which incorporates a workflow into the PAC model, and provides a mechanism of capturing a patient's permissions and enforcing the PAC policy. We focused on three problems of an access control mechanism: the incorporation of a patient's permissions with the access control mechanism, the "need to know" principle, and delegation. We collected information about the present working procedures of a Seniors' Wellness Program and constructed a workflow model using the NOVA Workflow [8] modeling tool. We identified the access control requirements of this program, converted them into policies, represented by Ponder [9] policy language, integrated the Ponder2 policy interpreter with NOVA Workflow to enforce those policies, and conducted a case study validating the proposed framework.

The paper is organized as follows: in Section 2, we analyze the PAC requirements and describe a high-level design of our PAC framework. Section 3 presents a patient scenario for the Seniors' Wellness Program. Section 4 presents the implementation and the validation of our framework. In Section 5, we conclude the paper and give a discussion of related and future work.

## 2    A Personalized Access Control Framework

Based on the literature [1,10,11], discussions with different health care providers (HCP) from the local health care authority - the Guysborough Antigonish Strait Health Authority (GASHA) - and the existing GASHA forms for the Seniors' Wellness Program, we articulated the following requirements for our PAC framework:

- The patient decides what permissions to assign to whom.
- Two policy sets: Common access policy, determined by the hospital (or other institution) where the patient is being treated; and Personalized access policy, determined by the patient to protect the privacy of the information stored in the EHR must be detailed.
- The patient is not allowed to update or delete the Common policies.
- The patient is allowed to update or delete any of his/her Personalized access policies at any time.
- Who may give consent if the patient is unable to give consent must be known.
- A specific relationship must be established between the patient and the required HCP before a health service is started. There are two kinds of situations in which a HCP offers a health care service:
  - The patient and the HCP have not established a specific relationship yet, e.g., a new patient and/or an outpatient. In this case, an authorization setup must be established before service can be given to the patient.
  - The patient and HCP have already established a specific relationship, e.g., an inpatient and/or a follow-up patient.
- HCP can conduct appropriate operations on a patient's EHR. Read and write are two common types of operations.
- Whenever a new HCP is added to a patient's care team, the patient is notified immediately via an e-mail, phone, fax, or any other communication service, so that he/she can give/deny consent for that HCP.

We propose a PAC framework addressing these requirements, which is illustrated by Fig. 1. The framework begins by a subject (we use subject and HCP interchangeably) executing a task (1). The Role Management service authenticates the subject with the information stored in the Database (e.g., MySQL) (2). While executing the task the engine generates an access request on behalf of the task (3) and sends this request to the Ponder Policy Interpreter (4). The Interpreter executes the access request and sends back the patient's personal decision to the subject (5). The main components of the framework are: the NOVA Workflow Management System, a Role Management Module, a Policy Interpreter, and an EHR. We discuss each below.

**NOVA Workflow Management System.** The WfMS we use in our framework is NOVA Workflow [8], an innovative workflow management system developed by our research group. It provides a workflow execution engine, and a graphical editor for workflow specifications. We integrated our policy interpreter with NOVA Workflow using service classes, which are generated automatically for each task in the workflow. In our framework, a workflow represents a process of a health care organization as a set of well-defined tasks which are executed according to the health care organization's policies to achieve certain objectives. We develop workflow models using NOVA Workflow editor and the workflow is executed by the workflow engine. There are some tasks in the workflow that need access to an EHR for their successful execution. While executing a task, the workflow engine may generate an access request. This access request includes

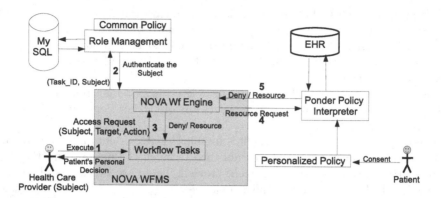

**Fig. 1.** Workflow-based PAC Framework

the following information related to this task: who wants to access the patient records (the subject), what the information is that the subject wants to access (the target), the type of operation (e.g., read, write, etc.), and on which instance the task is performed (the patient). A task in the workflow contains the information necessary to generate an access request.

**The Role Management (RM) Module.** After the representations of the tasks into NOVA Workflow, the allocation of roles to tasks must be made. We developed a module for NOVA Workflow to support role management. In our framework, the roles associated with each task are stored for authentication. Assigning a role to each task guarantees that at runtime, work items for each of these tasks are offered only to participants that perform that role. Unlike Personalized policies which are enforced on the individual subject while accessing a patient's record, the RM module enforces Common policies on the subjects based on their roles (with or without some constraints, such as time, location, etc. E.g., the policy may not allow a HCP to execute a task after 5 P.M., even if the HCP has the patient's consent). This ensures the "need to know" principle.

**The Ponder2 Policy Interpreter.** Another important component is the Ponder Policy Interpreter, which uses the policy framework Ponder2 [9]. To protect resources from unauthorized access, Ponder2 provides Authorization policy, which is a set of (subject, target, action)-tuples, which defines the activities that a member of the subject domain can perform on the set of objects in the target domain. We specify policies using the Ponder2 policy language and the interpreter organizes the subjects and the targets based upon which policies operate in hierarchical domains of Managed Objects (MO), which are an abstract representations of subjects and targets specified in a workflow. Each MO has methods for operations of those workflow tasks that need access to the patient's record. The execution of a task in the workflow corresponds to the execution of a method in the corresponding MO. When the method is executed the operation will be performed; the corresponding authorization policy is activated dynamically when the corresponding workflow task is executed. Hence there is a direct mapping between access policies and workflow tasks, which ensures the HCP can only perform the operations they are allowed to do.

We assign access rights directly to the HCP who needs access to a record. These rights define what actions can be performed on a health record by the subject executing the task. The policy interpreter derives the access rights from the patients's Personalized policies and enforces them. The interpreter allows the insertion and activation of new authorization policies at run time. This feature allows us to dynamically adapt the access rights of a subject to the actual needs expressed in the task that is executing.

**Electronic Health Record (EHR).** The EHRs act as the resources in our work. Suppose an EHR is already established by the health care organization for which we are specifying the workflow. Workflow generates a request on behalf of a subject to access the records of this EHR. The subject may wish to perform several operations, like reading, writing, or updating a patient's data on this EHR. Patients have control over their own EHR by giving/denying the subject permission for each of the operations.

## 3   Case Study

This work is a part of a research and development project in collaboration with GASHA and a technology industry partner; the goal is to develop a next generation careflow management system for information, communication and process management and pilot it in several programs in GASHA. GASHA has established a service area for Seniors' Health, called the Seniors' Wellness Program, in response to an aging population and ongoing pressures on the Acute Care system created by the increasing number of individuals in hospital medical beds waiting for nursing home placement. The program strives to enhance coordination and continuity along the continuum of care, including Outpatient, Inpatient, Continuing Care, Adult Day Program, Seniors Health Services, Geriatric Assessment Clinic (GAC), Community Rehabilitation Services (CRS), and Volunteers.

Here we consider two aspects of this Program: the GAC, which focuses on the prevention and treatment of diseases and disabilities in older adults, and decreases the effects of aging on the body; and the CRS, which is a short-term outpatient program specializing in intensive rehabilitation.

We interviewed different HCPs in the GAC and analyzed the recorded interviews, the paper-based forms (for assessment and other purposes) and other documents, and built the GAC workflow model. We finalized the model with the Project Manager of the Program in three iterations. Fig. 2 shows the high-level model of the GAC consisting of composite tasks. Each of the composite task has a subnet workflow. Here we outline a representative set of tasks of the workflow involving the GAC and the CRS for describing our proposed framework. Before executing the tasks, HCPs (Secretary1, Nurse1, Nurse2, Doctor1) must be registered in the system and authorized to execute tasks appropriate for their role.

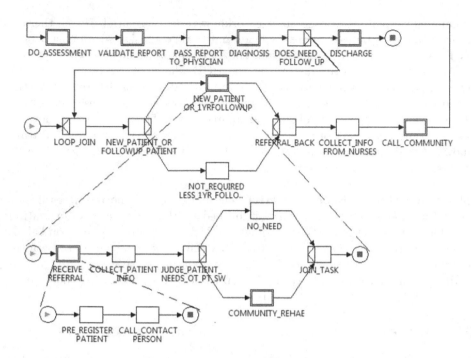

**Fig. 2.** Workflow Model for the GAC of the Seniors' Wellness Program

*Task 1 (PRE_REGISTER_PATIENT).* Secretary1 receives the referral of a patient, say Adam, and pre-registers the patient. At this point, Adam's demographic information is taken including a designated contact person.

*Task 2 (CALL_CONTACT_PERSON).* Once Secretary1 assigns Adam a suggested care team (from those authorized HCP in the GAC) she contacts Adam or his designated contact person to get their consent (or Secretary1 can build an initial care team by consulting with Adam, if he is available at that time). Then Adam explicitly assigns with whom he wants to share his record.

*Task 3 (COLLECT_PATIENT_INFO).* Nurse1 needs to see Adam's record to collect background information and to identify the relevant parts of the information from the consultations that are done by other HCPs.

*Task 4 (JUDGE_PATIENT_NEEDS_OT_PT_SW).* Nurse1 makes a decision about whether Adam needs any Occupational Therapy (OT) or Physiotherapy (PT) and makes a referral to the CRS.

*Task 5 (COLLECT_INFO_FROM_NURSES).* Secretary1 collects information from the nurses, e.g., which home care the patient uses, previous PT, OT etc.

*Task 6 (CALL_COMMUNITY).* Secretary1 contacts the CRS and asks for copies of their reports, the home care for the services they have, and the family physician for other doctors' consultation information. This information is sent to Secretary1.

*Task 7 (DO_ASSESSMENT).* Nurse2 does assessments and different tests.

*Task 8 (VALIDATE_REPORT).* After gathering all the test results, Nurse2 talks with family members to validate the information.

*Task 9 (PASS_REPORT_TO_PHYSICIAN).* Nurse1 and Nurse2 put all results, past histories, etc. into the system.

*Task 10 (DIAGNOSIS).* Doctor1 accesses the information for Adam's diagnosis.

*Task 11 (DISCHARGE).* Adam is discharged from the clinic.

Suppose in Task 7, Nurse2 delegates her responsibility to another nurse, say Nurse4, to carry out Task 7. Nurse4 does assessments and different tests on behalf of Nurse2. An authorization setup and a relationship with Adam is needed here for Nurse4 as well. To execute Task 7, Nurse4 needs to be registered first. Then she is authorized to do the task, after that Secretary1 takes Adam's consent for Nurse4 for accessing his health record. Therefore, a delegation is same as adding a new HCP into the care team.

In some situations a patient does not want to be notified each time a new person is added to his domain. After the initial selection of the care team there will be an option of whether he/she wants to be notified each time a HCP is added to his/her care team.

Table 1 shows HCPs and their roles, tasks, and task-related access rights.

**Table 1.** Access Rights Need for the Health Care Providers

| HCP | Role | Task # | Access Rights |
|-----|------|--------|---------------|
| Secretary1 | Secretary | Task 1 & Task 2 | Needs No Access |
| Nurse1 | Nurse | Task 3 & Task 4 | Needs Read Access |
| Secretary1 | Secretary | Task 5 & Task 6 | Needs Read Access |
| Nurse2 | Nurse | Task 7 & Task 8 | Needs Read and Write Access |
| Nurse1 & Nurse2 | Nurse | Task 9 | Need Read and Write Access |
| Doctor1 | Doctor | Task 10 | Needs Read and Write Access |

# 4   Implementation and Validation of the PAC Framework

## 4.1   Implementation

**Implementing the Role Management Module.** In our framework, the Role Management Module provides two services: mapping the tasks to the roles in the workflow and generating an identification for each HCP. The task mapping function is defined as a (Task_ID, Role)-tuple, where Task_ID is the identification of a task in the workflow and Role is the job position held by the HCP in the health care domain. At design time a set of roles are mapped and associated with each Task_ID. Here we assume that an employee has a uniquely identified Role. A HCP must login with her authentication credentials and let the system authenticate her. Based on her credentials the system identifies her Role and determines if it corresponds to a (Task_ID, Role)-tuple. Common policy is applied to her in this way.

**Implementing the Ponder Access Control Module.** In order to provide access rights to a patient's record during the workflow execution, Personalized access policies are associated directly with those HCPs who execute the tasks. The implementation of the module consists of three steps:

**I. Create and instantiate Managed Objects (MOs).** Represent all the subjects and targets associated in the workflow as MOs and assign them to the appropriate place in the domain hierarchy for use in the policy specification.

To start the execution of the tasks in the workflow, it is required to instantiate the MOs corresponding to the subjects who execute the tasks. Fig. 3 illustrates how a task starts after the instantiation of the MO. The subject is registered in

the system (1). The MO Initialization file for that subject will be created (2.1) along with a credential, which is stored for the authentication (2.2). The credential is provided to the subject (3). For executing the task the subject gives his/her credential (4). The authentication service then validates the given credential (5). The given credential for the subject then instantiates the MO and thus loads the workflow task (6).

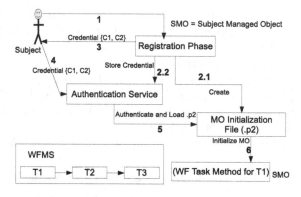

Fig. 3. Instantiating a MO and Loading the Workflow Task

**II. Create and update the authorization policies from the consents given by the patients.** An authorization policy is defined on a (subject, action, target)-triple; in the policy specification we use the domain path for specifying the subject and the target. Here the subject is the MO we have created for the HCP, the target is the patient's MO (the EHR is accessed through the patient's MO), and the action is the operation of a workflow task that the subject's MO needs to do on the Patient's MO. To specify authorization policies, the subjects executing the actions as depicted in Fig. 4 must be identified to the patient, who gives or withholds consent for each.

**III. Integrate NOVA Workflow with the Ponder2 Access Control Module.** To integrate NOVA Workflow with our system we extended the service classes and implemented our actual work. When a task invokes a method in the service class, the method collects the task information (subject, target, type of operation). Based on the subject and the target, Ponder2 loads the MOs and enforces the authorization policy. Ponder2 can be

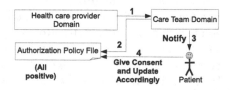

Fig. 4. Process of Creating Authorization Policy

run as either a stand-alone application or can be started within a Java Virtual Machine (JVM); we use the latter.

## 4.2   Validation of the PAC Framework

We use the case study from Section 4 to show how patient consent is obtained and validate that the authorization policy is enforced on the tasks.

During the phase of a HCP registration, according to our case study Secretary1, Nurse1, Nurse2, and Doctor1 are registered in the system. Only the hospital administrator can register new subjects with the system. A Secretary needs to be authorized in the system first to receive the referral for the patient and to process the referral. When Secretary1 is registered into the system two things happen: (1) An e-mail goes to the registered Secretary along with her login e-mail_ID/Password. Her e-mail will be her login e-mail_ID and the password is generated randomly; and (2) A Secretary MO Initialization file is generated, which includes the domain path for the Secretary along with the specification of the Secretary to create an instance through the Secretary MO. The registration process is the same for all the other subjects.

After the registration process, Secretary1 gets her credentials (login e-mail_ID/Password). When Secretary1 provides the credentials to the system, the authentication service then matches her role with the stored {Task_ID, Role}-tuple and gives permission to execute the task, as the Role *secretary* is associated with the Task_ID *Receive_Referral*. Thus while a task is executing, the access control mechanism checks the access right of a task against the current needs of the HCP executing the task and the Common policy is applied. Therefore, the workflow allows us to enforce the "need to know" principle.

In the getting consent phase,

- the four subjects, Secretary1, Nurse1, Nurse2, and Doctor1 are assigned to Adam's care team, i.e., an authorization policy file is created for Adam that contains a segment of an authorization policy for each of the assigned subjects. The default authorization policy for all the subjects is initially positive, meaning that all actions are authorized unless a negative authorization policy is specified.
- an e-mail is sent to Adam, which includes a web service link for each of the subjects along with a link for giving consent to each subject. Note that, the patient/designated contact person can be notified for giving consents by means other than an e-mail, such as phone, fax, etc.

Suppose that Adam had some bad experiences with Nurse1, and does not want to share his record with Nurse1; he, therefore, gives a negative consent. Then a negative authorization policy is assigned to Nurse1.

When Nurse1 executes Task 3 (see Section 4) the authorization policy for Nurse1 is dynamically loaded. When a new task is activated in the workflow (here Task 3), its corresponding service classes start executing and thus the WfMS can identify the task, and enable the corresponding authorization policy. As we know from the previous section, the execution of a task in the workflow may correspond to the execution of a specific method of the subject's MO. Therefore, here the execution of Task 3 depends on the execution of a corresponding method in the Nurse MO that executes the access request for Nurse1. Task 3 shows that

Nurse1 needs to read Adam's therapy history. Nurse1 proceeds to execute Task 3 after giving the credentials. The workflow engine identifies the task and its associated role and associated authorization policy. At this point, the Common policy is applied and Nurse1 gets permission to execute the task. When Nurse1, via her Nurse MO, performs the action of reading Adam's therapy history for the Patient MO, the access control mechanism captures such an action and enforces the authorization policy, which is Adam's Personalized policy. Because the negative authorization policy for that action is already in place, the action of reading the therapy history cannot be authorized. This means the access request to Adam's health record is denied and the following alternative action takes place: the Secretary is notified that Nurse1 is not allowed to access Adam's EHR, the Secretary then removes Nurse1 from Adam's care team and assigns a new subject (a Nurse) to his care domain, and the process of taking Adam's consent begins again.

The newly assigned nurse is Nurse3 and we assume Adam does not have any problem with her, so he gives her permission to get his record. After the enforcement of the Common policy as above, when Nurse3 requests a read action on Adam's therapy history, she gets access to Adam's EHR as she has been given the read access right, and gets the record of previous OT and/or PT history. The tasks are designed in such a way that Nurse3 can get information about Adam's Therapy only at this point of Task 3 and thus we can ensure that the required part of the record is accessible precisely when it is needed. After this task, the WfMS engine invalidates the corresponding authorization policy. All policies related to tasks in Table 1 are enforced the same way as the above so the tasks' corresponding operations may be performed.

## 5    Discussion and Conclusion

Atluri et al. in [7] introduced the Workflow Authorization Model where authorization constraints for data and resources were synchronized with the execution of the workflows. In [12] an access control matrix was used for regulating access control of data in the execution of a workflow task. Russello et al. [13] presented a workflow-based access control mechanism that adapts the access rights of subjects to the actual tasks that they have to fulfill. Although in these three methods, access rights were provided on the basis of the workflow tasks, they did not consider getting patients' consents before accessing patients' health records. The authors in [6] described a framework for enforcing patients' consents based on YAWL WfMS, which did not show how to enforce Common policy. In addition, their approach to getting patient's consent was different as they considered different types of policies called consent meta policies. In [14] the authors proposed a decentralized approach to handle access control in a workflow, which modeled security policies jointly with the workflow specification; their approach was not task-based, and they neither considered of getting patients' consents nor how to handle delegation.

There are issues that were outside the scope of this work, but are important to mention. Here we use the PAC for protecting patients' information, but it is not an absolute solution for securing a system. To improve security it could be coupled with auditing. Auditing requires the recording of all user requests and activities for later analysis. Research incorporating auditing into the access control system may be found in [15]. Our approach is not suitable for emergency situations; there may be emergency situations when waiting to get patient permissions could cause the death of the patient. The Privacy Legislation Act for urgent or emergency health care in [16], lists several situations where a HCP may provide health care to an adult without the adult's consent. In such emergency cases, a break-the-glass (BTG) [17] procedure should be applied in an ad-hoc manner, which would permit HCPs to override the existing access control rules and access what they need for continuing a patient's treatment. Our approach is suitable for long term health care processes where patient care spans over a long duration, e.g., Palliative care and Senior care. In our work, a single HCP is responsible for a task but in real life some tasks may require a team of HCPs; dealing with a team remains future work for us. For large and complex systems, the explicit description of the domain hierarchy will be a cumbersome process. However these complex relationships can be expressed precisely using an ontology. Research directions for supporting the access control model using an ontology can be found in [18,19].

In this paper, we described a PAC framework for a health care information system incorporating a workflow system, and validated it for a real world health care application. The main drawback of current access control mechanisms is that the granting of access rights requires statically binding a subject to a resource, where the subject and the resource must be known in advance. By using a workflow, however, we guarantee that access rights are dynamically adjusted to the actual needs of the subject. It is anticipated that the PAC framework can be integrated with other WfMS. More details including a formalism for our framework and some performance issues showing how the system scales may be found in [20]. We could also consider the hierarchical context of the workflow tasks by recognizing the composite task and its subnet workflows using the same variable. In the future, we will incorporate a mechanism for handling emergency health care situations, develop an audit-trail system for monitoring, and incorporate an ontology to structure the access control policies.

# References

1. Rostad, L., Nytro, O.: Personalized access control for a personally controlled health record. In: CSAW 2008: Proceedings of the 2nd ACM Workshop on Computer Security Architectures, pp. 9–16. ACM, New York (2008)
2. Rostad, L.: Access control in healthcare applications. In: NOKOBIT 2005, pp. 241–253 (2005)
3. Jacobsson, A.: Privacy and Security in Internet-Based Information Systems. PhD thesis, Blekinge Institute of Technology (2008)
4. Ferreira, A., Chadwick, D., Antunes, L.: Modelling access control for healthcare information systems. In: Doctoral Consortium at the 9th International Conference on Enterprise Information Systems, ICEIS (2007)

5. Sandhu, R.S., Coyne, E.J., Feinstein, H.L., Youman, C.E.: Role based access control models. IEEE Computer 29(2), 38–47 (1996)
6. Russello, G., Dong, C., Dulay, N.: Consent-based workflows for healthcare management. In: Proceedings of the 2008 IEEE Workshop on Policies for Distributed Systems and Networks, pp. 153–161. IEEE Computer Society, Washington, DC, USA (2008)
7. Atluri, V., Huang, W.: An Authorization Model for Workflows. In: Martella, G., Kurth, H., Montolivo, E., Hwang, J. (eds.) ESORICS 1996. LNCS, vol. 1146, pp. 44–64. Springer, Heidelberg (1996)
8. Rabbi, F.: Design, development and verification of a compensable workflow modeling language. M.Sc., St. Francis Xavier University (expected 2011) Preliminary version, http://logic.stfx.ca/~software/DDVCWML.pdf
9. Twidle, K., Lupu, E., Dulay, N., Sloman, M.: Ponder2 - a policy environment for autonomous pervasive systems. In: POLICY 2008: Proceedings of the 2008 IEEE Workshop on Policies for Distributed Systems and Networks, pp. 245–246. IEEE Computer Society, Washington, DC, USA (2008)
10. Wei, D.: Privacy protection reference model for shared electronic health record, M.Sc. Thesis, Dalhousie University (2005)
11. Personal Information Protection and Electronic Documents Act, C.I.O.H.R.C, http://www.cihi.ca/CIHI-ext-portal/pdf/internet/protection_qa_EN (last accessed March 2011)
12. Knorr, K.: Dynamic access control through petrinet workflows. In: Proceedings of the 16th Annual Computer Security Applications Conference, pp. 159–167. IEEE Computer Society, New Orleans (2000)
13. Russello, G., Dong, C., Dulay, N.: A workflow-based access control framework for e-health applications. In: International Conference on Advanced Information Networking and Applications Workshops, pp. 111–120. IEEE Computer Society, Los Alamitos (2008)
14. Samiha, A., Cuppens-Boulahia, N., Cuppens, F.: Deploying access control in distributed workflow. In: Proceedings of the Sixth Australasian Conference on Information Security, AISC 2008, vol. 81, pp. 9–17. Australian Computer Society, Inc., Darlinghurst (2008)
15. Fernández-Medina, E., Trujillo, J., Villarroel, R., Piattini, M.: Access control and audit model for the multidimensional modeling of data warehouses. Decision Support Systems 42, 1270–1289 (2006)
16. (Consent), H.C., 181, C.F.A.A.R.C., http://www.bclaws.ca/EPLibraries/bclaws_new/document/ID/freeside/00_96181_01 (last accessed March 2011)
17. Ferreira, A., Chadwick, D., Farinha, P., Correia, R.C., Zhao, G., Chilro, R., Antunes, L.: How to securely break into RBAC: The BTG-RBAC model. In: Proceedings of the 25th Annual Computer Security Applications Conference (ACSAC), pp. 23–31. ACM press (2009)
18. Lymberopoulos, L., Lupu, E., Sloman, M.: Ponder policy implementation and validation in a cim and differentiated services framework. In: Proceedings of IFIP / IEEE Network Operations and Management Symposium, Seoul, South Korea, pp. 31–44 (2004)
19. Finin, T., Joshi, A., Kagal, L., Niu, J., Sandhu, R., Winsborough, W., Thuraisingham, B.: ROWLBAC - Representing Role Based Access Control in OWL. In: Proceedings of the 13th Symposium on Access control Models and Technologies. ACM Press, Estes Park (2008)
20. Leyla, N.: A personalized access control framework for workflow-based healthcare information. M.Sc. Thesis, St. Francis Xavier University (2011)

# Three Challenges for Process Model Reuse

Jan Mendling

Wirtschaftsuniversität Wien, Augasse 2-6, 1090 Vienna, Austria
jan.mendling@wu.ac.at

**Abstract.** This paper discusses three specific challenges for process model reuse. Models are intrinsically biased towards a particular purpose. For reuse this bias needs to be neutralized. We focus on research that can ultimately contribute to a canonical representation of behavior, a canonical formulation of labels, and canonical terminology. Each of these three challenges is sketched and pointers to technical papers are provided.

**Keywords:** Business Process Modeling, Reuse, Matching, Similarity, Semantics.

## 1 Introduction

Reuse is considered to be beneficial for creating new business process models [1,2,3], in particular in a setting where an ERP system is customized along with its accompanying process models. While the sheer amount of existing reference models provides some evidence for their benefits, the actual act of reuse is often not that easy. Several approaches have been defined towards offering a business analyst a more usable tool for adapting and reusing process models. One example is the work on configurable process models [4,5], which is complemented with techniques to guarantee correctness in the reuse phase [6]. Still, configurable languages do not cover the full spectrum of potential reuse options.

The general reuse problem is partial incorporated in the idea of modeling itself. A process model is a mapping of a business process that is simplifying and serving a specific purpose. An implication of this definition is that a model is biased towards particular application scenario and towards the representational preferences of the modeler. When a model is meant to be reused, we have to neutralize these bias as much as possible. This paper discusses three specific challenges for reuse, namely how a canonical representation of behavior, a canonical style of labels, and a canonical terminology can be defined. The underlying problems share some characteristics with heterogeneity as being researched for database schema matching [7,8].

The idea of this paper is to sketch concepts for addressing each of the three challenges. Each section provides pointers to relevant technical papers. Section 2 discusses fine-granular representations of behaviour with a focus on behavioural profiles. Section 3 summarizes works on labeling styles and label refactoring. Section 4 points to problems of terminology and granularity. Section 5 concludes the paper with a brief summary and outlook on future research.

F. Daniel et al. (Eds.): BPM 2011 Workshops, Part II, LNBIP 100, pp. 285–288, 2012.
© Springer-Verlag Berlin Heidelberg 2012

## 2  Representation of Behaviour

The behaviour of a process can be defined in different ways on different levels. There is a plethora of modeling languages available with partially overlapping constructs [9,10,11]. The modeler has also several choices for defining behaviour in a specific process model. Two process models can be trace equivalent or bisimilar, but still have different structure. This insight has been utilized for refactoring of process models, in particular structuring [12,13]. Therefore, a process model might not be in the right modeling language and not be defined using an appropriate structure when it is available for reuse.

A way to overcome this heterogeneity of behavioural representation is to identify fine-granular constraints on the behaviour of the process. A similar idea has been used in the database community for harmonization and integration of database schemas [8,14]. Different relations can be used to characterize the behaviour of a process, for instance the alpha relations [15], transition adjacency [16] or behavioural profiles [17,18]. Behavioural profiles can be calculated from a free choice process model in cubic time. They describe each pair of activities in terms of being exclusive, ordered or interleaving (concurrent or repeatable). Behavioural profiles can be used for the identification of so-called action patterns [19]. Action patterns describe often co-occurring activities in terms of their behaviour. This provides a fine-granular representation of behaviour that can be used for giving recommendations to the modeler while modeling.

## 3  Labeling Styles

The activity labels in a process model can be formulated in various ways. Different styles of labeling have been found in process models from practice [20,21]. The so-called verb-object style is often recommended as it offers little risk of linguistic ambiguity. A verb-object label is for instance *process order*. But many labels in process models are also stated following different types of action-noun styles. Examples would be *processing of order*, *order processing*, or *processing order*. These examples also highlight that the identification of the verb and the corresponding business object is often complicated by the fact that single words can be both verbs and nouns, as for instance *to* process and *the* process.

This heterogeneity of formulation can be tackled using tools from natural language processing. A corresponding approach has to take into account and recognize the different style of activity labeling, parse each label accordingly, provide the action and the business object, such that it can be composed into a verb-object activity label [22]. In this way, labels can be refactored and harmonized. Our experiments with process models from practice show that such a refactoring approach works quite accurately even for linguistically ambiguous labels. In this way, it becomes easier for matching approaches to find activities and process fragments that might be relevant for a particular case of reuse.

# 4  Terminology

Even if the labeling style chosen for a process model is homogenous, there are still various leeways in selecting the terms for defining the activities. The problem of homonyms (same word, different meanings) and synonyms (different words, same meaning) is well understood and extensively covered by tools such as Word-Net [23]. More difficult are challenges in terms of meronyms and hyponyms. A meronym like *activity node* is in a part-of relationship with a holonym like *process model*. A hyponym like *XOR-gateway* is in a more-specific relationship with a hypernym *routing element*.

The terms and the corresponding activities being used in a process model might not be on the right level of abstraction or granularity for a specific reuse case. If they are too coarse-granular or too unspecific, there is hardly any way to fill in the missing detail automatically. In case the model is too specific, there are semantic abstraction techniques available. A set of activities or a whole process model can be collapsed using the naming technique defined in [24]. It uses different naming strategies identified in process models from practice for deriving name proposals linguistically. An alternative is the semantical abstraction approach defined in [25]. In this way, a given process model can be generalized to the abstraction level which is appropriate for the reuse case.

# 5  Conclusion

In this paper, we have discussed the challenges of neutralizing the representational bias of modeling language and structure, of labeling styles, and of terminology. Many of the covered techniques have been developed to tackle a singular problem of reuse. In future research, it is desirable to integrate the available techniques towards a holistic approach to process model reuse. Further challenges need to be addressed as well, such as for instance psychological barriers of eliminating irrelevant model elements [26].

# References

1. Curran, T., Keller, G., Ladd, A.: SAP R/3 Business Blueprint: Understanding the Business Process Reference Model. Enterprise Resource Planning Series. Prientice Hall PTR, Upper Saddle River (1997)
2. Rosemann, M.: Using reference models within the enterprise resource planning lifecycle. Australian Accounting Review 10(3), 19–30 (2000)
3. Fettke, P., Loos, P.: Classification of reference models - a methodology and its application. Information Systems and e-Business Management 1(1), 35–53 (2003)
4. Rosemann, M., van der Aalst, W.M.P.: A Configurable Reference Modelling Language. Information Systems 32, 1–23 (2007)
5. La Rosa, M., Dumas, M., ter Hofstede, A.H.M., Mendling, J.: Configurable multi-perspective business process models. Inf. Syst. 36(2), 313–340 (2011)
6. van der Aalst, W.M.P., Dumas, M., Gottschalk, F., ter Hofstede, A.H.M., La Rosa, M., Mendling, J.: Preserving correctness during business process model configuration. Formal Asp. Comput. 22(3-4), 459–482 (2010)

7. Kim, W., Seo, J.: Classifying schematic and data heterogeneity in multidatabase systems. IEEE Computer 24(12), 12–18 (1991)
8. Spaccapietra, S., Parent, C., Dupont, Y.: Model Independent Assertions for Integration of Heterogeneous Schemas. VLDB Journal (1), 81–126 (1992)
9. van der Aalst, W.M.P., ter Hofstede, A., Kiepuszewski, B., Barros, A.: Workflow Patterns. Distributed and Parallel Databases 14(1), 5–51 (2003)
10. Mendling, J.: Metrics for Process Models: Empirical Foundations of Verification, Error Prediction, and Guidelines for Correctness. LNBIP, vol. 6. Springer, Heidelberg (2008)
11. La Rosa, M., Reijers, H.A., van der Aalst, W.M.P., Dijkman, R.M., Mendling, J., Dumas, M., García-Bañuelos, L.: Apromore: An advanced process model repository. Expert Syst. Appl. 38(6), 7029–7040 (2011)
12. Polyvyanyy, A., García-Bañuelos, L., Dumas, M.: Structuring Acyclic Process Models. In: Hull, R., Mendling, J., Tai, S. (eds.) BPM 2010. LNCS, vol. 6336, pp. 276–293. Springer, Heidelberg (2010)
13. Weber, B., Reichert, M., Mendling, J., Reijers, H.A.: Refactoring large process model repositories. Comp. Industry 62(5), 467–486 (2011)
14. Schmitt, I., Saake, G.: A comprehensive database schema integration method based on the theory of formal concepts. Acta Informatica 41(7-8), 475–524 (2005)
15. van der Aalst, W.M.P., Weijters, A., Maruster, L.: Workflow Mining: Discovering Process Models from Event Logs. IEEE Transactions on Knowledge and Data Engineering 16(9), 1128–1142 (2004)
16. Zha, H., Wang, J., Wen, L., Wang, C., Sun, J.: A workflow net similarity measure based on transition adjacency relations. Comp. Industry 61(5), 463–471 (2010)
17. Weidlich, M., Polyvyanyy, A., Mendling, J., Weske, M.: Efficient Computation of Causal Behavioural Profiles Using Structural Decomposition. In: Lilius, J., Penczek, W. (eds.) PETRI NETS 2010. LNCS, vol. 6128, pp. 63–83. Springer, Heidelberg (2010)
18. Weidlich, M., Mendling, J., Weske, M.: Efficient consistency measurement based on behavioral profiles of process models. IEEE Trans. Software Eng. 37(3), 410–429 (2011)
19. Smirnov, S., Weidlich, M., Mendling, J., Weske, M.: Action Patterns in Business Process Models. In: Baresi, L., Chi, C.-H., Suzuki, J. (eds.) ICSOC-ServiceWave 2009. LNCS, vol. 5900, pp. 115–129. Springer, Heidelberg (2009)
20. Mendling, J., Reijers, H.A., Recker, J.: Activity labeling in process modeling: Empirical insights and recommendations. Inf. Syst. 35(4), 467–482 (2010)
21. Leopold, H., Smirnov, S., Mendling, J.: Recognising activity labeling styles in business process models. Enterpr. Mod. Inf. Sys. Architectures 6(1), 16–29 (2011)
22. Leopold, H., Smirnov, S., Mendling, J.: Refactoring of Process Model Activity Labels. In: Hopfe, C.J., Rezgui, Y., Métais, E., Preece, A., Li, H. (eds.) NLDB 2010. LNCS, vol. 6177, pp. 268–276. Springer, Heidelberg (2010)
23. Miller, G.: Wordnet: A lexical database for english. Comm. ACM 38(11), 39–41 (1995)
24. Leopold, H., Mendling, J., Reijers, H.A.: On the Automatic Labeling of Process Models. In: Mouratidis, H., Rolland, C. (eds.) CAiSE 2011. LNCS, vol. 6741, pp. 512–520. Springer, Heidelberg (2011)
25. Smirnov, S., Reijers, H.A., Weske, M.: A Semantic Approach for Business Process Model Abstraction. In: Mouratidis, H., Rolland, C. (eds.) CAiSE 2011. LNCS, vol. 6741, pp. 497–511. Springer, Heidelberg (2011)
26. Holschke, O.: Impact of Granularity on Adjustment Behavior in Adaptive Reuse of Business Process Models. In: Hull, R., Mendling, J., Tai, S. (eds.) BPM 2010. LNCS, vol. 6336, pp. 112–127. Springer, Heidelberg (2010)

# A Modular Approach to Build Workflow Engines

Mario Sánchez, Diana Puentes, and Jorge Villalobos

Universidad de los Andes
Bogotá, Colombia
{mar-san1,dm.puentes64,jvillalo}@uniandes.edu.co

**Abstract.** To provide BPM and workflow solutions with the dynamism to support frequent changes in the corporate environment, it is necessary to adopt novel strategies to efficiently develop and adapt workflow engines. One such strategy is to build new engines by reusing as much as possible from existing components. This requires two things: firstly, the mechanisms and technologies to build a library of reusable, extensible and adaptable workflow components; secondly, a platform to integrate those components into full applications. In this paper we show that Cumbia, being a platform for the development of workflow engines based on the modularization of workflows according to concerns, suits this task. This is illustrated with YOC, a Cumbia based implementation of YAWL.

**Keywords:** Modularity, Reuse, Workflow Engine, YAWL, Cumbia.

## 1 Introduction

The efforts to reuse existing assets in workflow environments are frequently studied only from the point of view of the designers of the workflows. However, doing so from the perspective of the developers of workflow languages and engines opens up interesting opportunities. Currently, building new workflow engines, or modifying existing ones to support new requirements, is expensive [6]. This is in part because engines' implementations are tightly coupled to a single language, and in part because they are not developed with flexibility and extensibility in mind.

This paper shows how the Cumbia platform offers an effective alternative for designing and developing workflow engines by reusing as much as possible from existing ones. This approach uses the platform as the common base for many different workflow engines. Also, it proposes the creation of a library of reusable *concern specific workflow languages*, which are implemented as Cumbia *metamodels*, and can be assembled in multiple ways to support different requirements. Therefore, Cumbia can be considered the base of a product line of workflow engines. This paper also shows that using Cumbia results in engines that are extensible and adaptable to new business requirements.

The main features of Cumbia that make the above things possible are the following. Cumbia is a model driven platform based on executable modeling

F. Daniel et al. (Eds.): BPM 2011 Workshops, Part II, LNBIP 100, pp. 289–300, 2012.
© Springer-Verlag Berlin Heidelberg 2012

[11,13], where each *workflow specification language* is represented with a meta-model. Correspondingly, a *workflow specification* is represented in Cumbia by a model definition, and it is executed by a component called *Cumbia Kernel*. To enable this execution, a metamodel specification includes both structure and behavior: this is achieved by describing elements in the metamodel using an abstraction that we have called *open objects*, which is based on plain objects and on reified state machines that coordinate their execution.

Another feature of Cumbia is the modularization of *concerns* [12]: for each concern that is relevant for a workflow application, a *concern specific metamodel* is built thus defining a *concern specific language*. This strategy results in smaller, composable languages, and brings advantages such as ease of use, development, maintenance, and flexibility [14]. Concern specific metamodels are used to describe concern specific models, which are woven together at run time. This requires the specification of relations between the models, which involves three additional elements of Cumbia: M2CL, M1CL, and CCL (see section 3 and [7,8]). As it is extensively discussed in [10], there have been other works around the topic of workflow modularization (e.g. AMFIBIA, AO4BPEL), but they have limitations that have been solved in Cumbia.

This paper uses YAWL to illustrate the advantages that Cumbia brings to the construction of workflow engines. YAWL is a workflow language well known in the academic community, whose design was mostly guided by the structure of the control flow. Since other aspects where introduced as complements, their constructs are not as powerful as those for describing the control flow. However, if we were to modify YAWL to improve one of those aspects, we would encounter serious problems because neither the language nor its engine were designed with language flexibility in mind. Hence, introducing changes would require a lot of effort, or even a complete reimplementation of the engine.

The rest of the paper is structured as follows. Section 2 describes the implementation of YOC, an engine for YAWL built on top of Cumbia. The focus of this description is the implementation and extension of the control concern. Section 3 then shows how Cumbia enables improvements to YOC, including the incorporation of new concerns or the replacement of old ones. Finally, the paper is concluded in section 4.

## 2   A Cumbia-Based Engine for YAWL

YAWL (Yet Another Workflow Language) [3] is a well known workflow language which originated in the academic community but has also been used in commercial applications. Its notation and semantics are common place, and it subsumes the core elements found in most workflow languages. From the point of view of the control-flow, YAWL is very expressive. It supports most workflow patterns [9] and it has been frequently used as a case study in workflow research.

Unlike languages where the semantics is informally defined, such as BPMN, YAWL's semantics is formally specified using Extended Workflow Nets (EWF-Nets). EWF-Nets are an extension to Petri nets, which are also defined in terms of Petri nets. Because of this formality, implementing the language does not require a subjective interpretation of its specification.

Typically, there five dimensions are involved in a YAWL process:

*Control.* It is the core of YAWL and defines the tasks in a process and their order of execution.

*Application.* This dimension defines the actual tasks to realize in a process. For example, specifying whether an activity must be automatic or must be performed by a human belongs in this dimension, as well as specifying bindings and bridges to concrete external applications (e.g. *services*). In spite of its importance, this dimension is only represented in YAWL by one element, `Decomposition`, which determines the specific behavior of `Tasks`.

*Data.* This dimension describes the data produced and consumed in a process, and its relation to tasks. YAWL's engine uses XSD schemas to define the structure of data, and uses XPath and XQuery to define what data each task consumes, and how the data produced by each task is transformed and stored.

*Time.* This dimension describes timeouts and expiration dates for tasks. In YAWL's engine these are also defined using low level XML expressions.

*Resources.* This dimension describes who participates in a process and the policies to assign participants to tasks. In YAWL, this involves a complex procedure that offers the tasks to qualified participants which may accept or refuse the offer, and then assigns the task to one of the willing. The mechanisms to define which participants are qualified to perform the tasks range from very simple (e.g. "Anyone can do the task", or "User X must do the task"), to very complex (e.g. "Users with characteristics Y and Z, and which have not participated yet in this case"). At run time, the assignment procedure can be modified or bypassed by the administrator of the process.

## 2.1  YOC: YAWL on Cumbia

The first step to implement YOC was to identify the concerns to support: we started from the five dimensions; then, we assimilated the control and application dimensions because it is not likely that they will evolve independently, and we do not expect to have control models reused independently from application models, and vice-versa. The next step was to design and develop a metamodel for each concern. Figure 1 shows the relations between these metamodels: the one for control can be considered the central one, since the metamodels for time and resources have dependencies towards it. The initial version of YOC did not include a metamodel for the data concern.

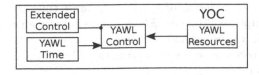

**Fig. 1.** Concern specific metamodels in YOC

Most of the effort went into the development of the control metamodel because the control concern is the most complex and the best documented aspect of YAWL. Figure 2 shows the structure of the control metamodel in YOC, which includes the assimilated application dimension, i.e. Decomposition is included in this metamodel.

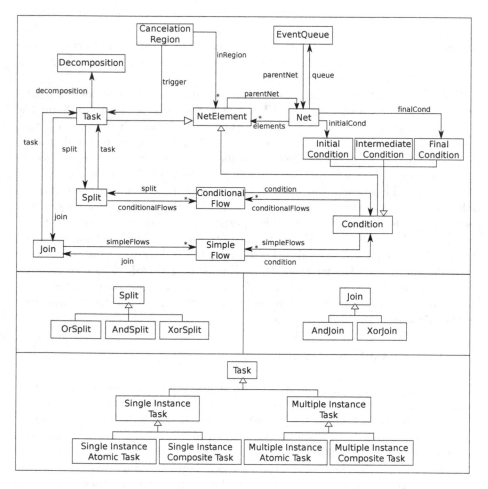

**Fig. 2.** Structure of the control metamodel for YOC (in parts for readability)

The semantics of the elements that YAWL provides to model the control dimension are defined in terms of EWF-Nets, and thus they depend on the transfer and consumption of tokens: *Flows* define how tokens can be transferred between elements in a process, and elements are only executed when tokens are available for them to consume (as in Petri nets). There are four main categories of elements in YAWL.

*Nets*, which enclose structured sets of elements. However, unlike processes in BPMN, nets cannot be directly nested.

*Tasks*, the units of work in a net. Tasks can be *atomic*, and represent something that has to be performed once. They can also be *multiple*, and represent the same action that has to be performed multiple times, in parallel. Tasks are *composite* when they represent sub-nets. Each Task has a *split behavior* and a *join behavior* that determine the interaction of a Task with other elements in the Net. This fulfills a role similar to that of Gateways in BPMN.

*Conditions* are elements that can contain one or more tokens, without consuming them. They are analogous to places in Petri nets, and they create some of the most complex synchronization problems from the viewpoint of implementation. Conditions are so named because they contain a token when a certain condition holds in the net.

*Cancellation regions* group tasks and conditions which should be *cancelled* when a certain task (located outside the cancellation region) is executed. The cancellation operation removes all the tokens in the region, and aborts the execution of every task in it. Cancellation regions are not easily modeled with Petri nets, and they are one of the main reasons to define YAWL's semantics using EWF-nets.

To implement this metamodel we made four important decisions. Firstly, we left out *OR-Joins*. The reason for this is that supporting the semantics associated to this construct requires a strong algorithmic effort (as shown in YAWL's own implementation [15]), which is not valuable to illustrate the expressive power of the Cumbia platform. Solutions to the *OR-Join* problem [2] are largely independent of the underlying implementation artifacts.

Secondly, we assumed AND-Join and AND-Split behaviors for every task where these behaviors are not explicitly defined. This does not change the semantics of processes because in YAWL it is mandatory to specify a join behavior for all tasks with more than one incoming flow, and to specify a split behavior for all tasks with more than one outgoing flow. The official YAWL editor assumes the same behaviors that we do, and our implementation only makes this explicit.

Thirdly, we introduced a condition in each flow connecting two tasks. This does not change the semantics of the language either, as we are only reversing YAWL's designers' decision of hiding these conditions to simplify the layout of diagrams. In terms of Petri nets, our decision is equivalent to forcing *flows* to connect *places* and *transitions*, and disallowing *flows* connecting two *transitions*.

Finally, we had to select a strategy to implement YAWL's coordination model, which calls for atomic updates. Since Cumbia is mostly based on concurrent execution and asynchronous interactions, it was not straightforward to support the synchronization requirements. This is analogous to the known problem of implementing Petri nets-based workflows. To solve this, we evaluated the three solution strategies proposed in [5], and then implemented a centralized control system, without *locksets*. The centralized queue (EventQueue) is local to each process instance and registers which tasks are enabled and can be executed at

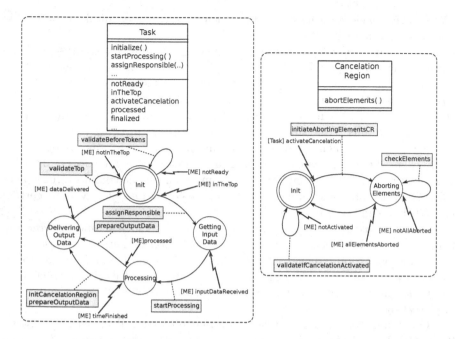

**Fig. 3.** The open objects that model a `Task` and a `Cancelation Region`

any given moment. `Tasks` are removed from the queue when they are no longer enabled, and this guarantees that *i*) no deadlocks are caused by tokens assigned to tasks that never execute; *ii*) and guarantees that no inconsistencies happen because of `tasks` that execute without having the required tokens. From the point of view of EWF-nets and Petri nets' semantics, this strategy results in a correct implementation: at most one transition can be activated at any given time; and the consumption and production of tokens happen in different times, but no other actions can occur before the whole procedure is completed.

For reasons of space we are going to detail only two elements of this meta-model, namely `Task` and `Cancelation Region`. Every element in a Cumbia metamodel is represented with an *open object*, which means that every element has a class (which in Cumbia is called the *entity*) and an associated state machine. Figure 3 depicts the open object that models `Tasks` in YOC. On the upper part there is the entity, which holds the internal state of a `task` and implements its behavior. The entity also generates events, and these are listed on the lower part of the box.

On the bottom part of the figure, there is the state machine, which reifies the life cycle of a `task`. This state machine is composed by four states connected by transitions triggered by events. In this case, all the events are generated by the `task` itself (they have the mark [ME]) but they can also be generated by other elements in the metamodel (see the state machine of `Cancelation Region`). Finally, some of the transitions have actions associated: when those transitions are triggered, the corresponding actions are executed.

Cancelation Regions are also modeled with an open object in the YOC control metamodel. Figure 3 depicts such open object. We can see, from the structure of its state machine, that a Cancelation Region interacts with other elements in a net. On the one hand, each Cancelation Region has a *trigger task* which activates it by generating the event **activateCancelation**. When that event is received, the Cancelation Region can go from the state *Init* to the state *Aborting Elements*.

On the other hand, the Cancelation Region also interacts with the elements that it groups: when the transition from *Init* to *Aborting Elements* is triggered, the action *initiateAbortingElementsCR* is executed. That action invokes the method abortElements() in the entity, which locates all the elements in the region and removes the tokens that they currently hold. If one of the elements is a Task that is currently being executed, its execution is aborted.

These two examples illustrate important aspects of the implementation of metamodels in Cumbia: the reification of state machines, the interaction between elements based on actions and method invocations, the interaction based on events, the relevance of the state machines for the coordination of the execution, and the implementation of elements' behavior in the methods of the classes. In [1] there are more details about this metamodel and its state machines.

## 2.2    Extend the Control Flow - Support Ad Hoc Subprocesses

According to the specification of the language, the documentation of the official engine, and several papers, YAWL has some inherent flexibility, which is represented by decompositions and worklets. The mechanism of decompositions serves to differentiate the concrete tasks in a process: for each task added to a net, a decomposition is selected and it determines the concrete actions that must happen during the execution of the task. However, decompositions are static: at design time, process designers have to choose the concrete actions to be executed in each task. To counter this limitation, YAWL's designers introduced *worklets* [4], which are dynamically selected YAWL processes that act as subnets. Using worklets, a dynamic element is introduced into YAWL specifications.

However, these flexibility mechanisms are not enough for every new requirement that may appear as they are limited to tasks. It is possible to encounter requirements in YAWL-based applications that are difficult to model with the standard language, and would be better supported with modifications to the language. In this respect, the main advantage of Cumbia is offering a platform where modifications to the languages can be introduced with relative ease.

To illustrate this, we modified the control metamodel of YOC and introduced a new construct to represent *Ad Hoc Subprocess*[1]. To support them, we extended the control flow metamodel and added two new elements, namely

---

[1] In workflow languages such as BPMN, an Ad Hoc Subprocess is a kind of unstructured process, which groups activities but does not specify their order of execution. Typically, this order is defined at run time and it is necessary to execute once, and only once, every activity in the Ad Hoc Subprocess.

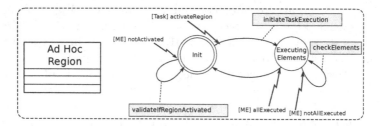

**Fig. 4.** The state machine of `Ad Hoc Region`

`Ad Hoc Region` and `Ad Hoc Task`. The former was based on the old element `Cancelation Region`, while the latter was based on `Task`. An `Ad Hoc Region` has a similar structure to a `Cancelation Region`, but different behavior (see figure 4). When an `Ad Hoc Region` is activated, the tasks contained in it become ready to be executed. However, these cannot be normal task, as they are not related to other elements and do not share flows. Therefore, they are special `Ad Hoc Tasks`. The differences between these and the basic `Tasks`, are mostly relegated to the actions of the state machine. In particular the code in the action `Start processing` is different from the original `Task`, because the order of execution of Tasks is defined at run time.

We cannot present one example for every kind of metamodel extension that is possible in Cumbia. However, this experiment evidences important aspects of the support for extensions offered in the platform: we added a new element into an existing metamodel, and we related this new element with old elements. These relations were not only structural, but they also implied interactions between new and old elements. Finally, the new elements are seamlessly blended with the old ones, and can be used indistinctively.

## 3    Beyond a Basic Cumbia-Based Engine

This section shows two reuse scenarios where Cumbia-based engines are built or adapted with existing components. The final result is shown in figure 5: `YAWL Time` was replaced with a metamodel called `XTM`; and a metamodel for the auditing concern, `LOG`, was introduced to work with the control and the resources concerns.

For the scenarios described in this section, the critical features of Cumbia are the decomposition of concerns, the management of multiple metamodels, and the run-time weaving process. The following are the four elements of the approach that support this:

- The *coordination mechanisms* offered by the open objects. They not only serve between elements found in the same model, but they can also be used between elements in two different model instances. As a result, coordinating multiple models is not a lot different from coordinating a single one.

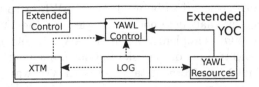

**Fig. 5.** Metamodels in the extended YOC

- *M2CL*, the language to describe the possible relations between elements of two or more *metamodels* [7,8]. M2CL specifications are external to the metamodels and thus they maintain their independence.
- *M1CL*, the language to describe the relations between specific elements of two or more *models* [7,8]. These relations must be instances of the relations described in an M2CL specification, and they are kept in a specification that is external to the model descriptions.
- *CCL*, the low level language to describe how to alter the open objects and coordinate their execution [7,8]. While M2CL specifications are written by experts in the metamodels involved, and M1CL specifications are written by the same domain experts that write the models, CCL specifications are automatically generated from those other specifications.

### 3.1   Replace a Metamodel - Handle Complex Time Restrictions

In Cumbia, the modularization of concerns and of metamodels makes it possible to have concern-level flexibility. This means that the metamodel selected for a concern can be replaced with another one if it does not support all the requirements. This section illustrates this in a concrete scenario: starting from the basic implementation of YOC that was described, we introduced changes into the applications that were localized in a single concern, without affecting the other ones.

YAWL provides a few elements to describe time restrictions, but they are not very expressive and they are basically limited to timeouts. However, in many contexts the time restrictions associated to workflows can be quite more complex than timeouts. Therefore, it is reasonable to improve YOC by giving it more powerful capabilities to express time restrictions. Luckily, time is such an important concern for workflows that we already had XTM, a very expressive metamodel to describe advanced time restrictions in workflows. XTM is independent of the control flow metamodel, and we have used it before with BPMN and BPEL, among others.

With respect to describing time restrictions, XTM is much more expressive than YAWL. This means that many things that can be said with XTM cannot be expressed in YAWL, or can only be expressed in very complicated ways. This is evident from the number of types of time restrictions supported in XTM (17) which go from very simple (e.g. restrict the duration of a task) to very complex (e.g. make the duration of a task depend on the time elapsed between a series of events). In [1] there is a longer description of the metamodel of XTM and the time restriction patterns that it supports.

Since XTM was not developed to be used with YAWL or to be used in YOC, there are no elements in that metamodel that tie it to the YOC control meta-model. Furthermore, YOC's implementation of YAWL's control concern is obliv-ious of the time concern and of the metamodel implementing it. Therefore, replacing the original YAWL Time metamodel with XTM was done without an impact on the other concerns. Besides integrating XTM into YOC's architecture, which was simple thanks to its modular design, the only change required in-volved the definition of a new M2CL specification. This spec relates the control metamodel and XTM and it is completely external to the metamodels involved. As a result, there are no hard dependencies between them and they can be replaced with relative ease.

This scenario shows the value in Cumbia of a library of composable languages or metamodels, which can be reused in different applications. In the example presented, XTM was an existing metamodel in this library, and it was possible to integrate it with YOC because it did not have any explicit dependency towards another metamodel.

### 3.2   Introduce a New Concern - Auditing Workflows

Not every workflow engine involves the same concerns. While control, time and resources are the most common, others (e.g. auditing, billing, or security – au-thorization) are equally important in particular contexts. Therefore, workflow engine developers should be able to select and integrate as many concerns as they require in each case.

This section illustrates this by introducing into YOC functionalities that do not fit in any of the previously included concerns. These functionalities are to support the logging of information about workflows's execution, such as the duration of each task, or their intermediate results, or the names of the people assigned to perform them. For this, a new concern has to be introduced, the *auditing concern*, and a metamodel has to be designed and implemented for it.

The metamodel developed to support this concern is very simple (see figure 6), but it is enough to support the requirements described. Also, it can be ex-tended and made more powerful using the mechanisms described in the previous sections. Finally, it is desirable for metamodels to be as small as possible: smaller languages are easier to adapt, extend, and maintain [14], and thus are more likely to be reused.

**Fig. 6.** Metamodel for the Logging concern

There are two open objects in the LOG metamodel, namely **Logged Event Receiver** and **Logger**. The former receives and processes the events produced in the other concerns. The latter registers those events in a log file. Models built with this metamodel are then woven to models describing the control, resources, and time concern. This means that elements in logging models react to the execution of elements in the other models by either capturing events or by receiving method invocations from actions. Since the LOG metamodel is not tied to any other particular metamodel, we can use it to register what occurs in *any* of the other concerns. For example, we can create log files with the time of execution of each task and the sizes of input data used in each task execution (control concern), and a detailed registry of tasks distribution among employees (resources concern).

Considering that every concern in Cumbia is developed using open objects, and given that the weaving mechanisms are independent of the metamodels, we can add new concerns in any moment, as they become necessary. To do this, we only need to develop the corresponding metamodel, and create the necessary M2CL specifications.

Another characteristic to highlight of this approach, is that the applications created by adding new metamodels maintain the properties of the base applications. Therefore, we can keep on adding, modifying or replacing concerns indefinitely. Also, if a certain concern is no longer necessary in an application, we can remove it in the same way as it was added.

## 4    Conclusion

In this paper, we have addressed the issue of building workflow engines by reusing previously developed modular elements. The solution proposed is based on Cumbia, a platform for the development of engines which supports the modularization of languages and workflows based on concerns. This, together with powerful composition mechanisms that focus both on structure and behavior, has made possible the construction of a library of Cumbia-based concern specific workflow engines.

The ultimate goal of this work is to establish a product line where new workflow engines are built mostly by assembling components developed for previous ones. This paper has illustrated the means proposed to achieve this with an example based on YAWL. It should be noted that the level of reuse achieved is made possible not only by the composition mechanisms offered by Cumbia, but also by its mechanisms for adaptation and extension.

Building various engines on top of the same platform has further advantages. Complementary tools, such as monitoring applications, can be language agnostic and be reused with several workflow languages. Also, engines are built on top of an existing and tested platform. This reduces the implementation effort and allows more focus on the language itself. Finally, improvements to the platform are made once but they benefit a large number of applications.

We are currently advancing this research in two directions. We are working on more case studies to improve our metamodel library which already comprises engines for BPMN, BPEL, IMS-LD (a language for the description of workflows in the e-learning domain), PaperXpress (a collaborative workflow-based tool to support writing efforts), and other domain specific workflow languages. On the other hand, we are working on the design of composable editors that should complement at the graphical / design level, what is already done at the behavior / run-time level.

# References

1. Cumbia, http://cumbia.uniandes.edu.co
2. van der Aalst, W.M.P., Desel, J., Kindler, E.: On the semantics of EPCs: A vicious circle. In: Nüttgens, M., Rump, F.J. (eds.) Business Process Management using EPCs (EPK 2002), pp. 71–79 (2002)
3. van der Aalst, W., ter Hofstede, A.: YAWL: Yet Another Workflow Language (Revised Version). Tech. rep., Queensland University of Technology, Brisbane, QUT Technical report, FIT-TR-2003-04 (2006)
4. Adams, M., ter Hofstede, A.H.M., Edmond, D., van der Aalst, W.M.P.: Worklets: A Service-Oriented Implementation of Dynamic Flexibility in Workflows. In: Meersman, R., Tari, Z. (eds.) OTM 2006, Part I. LNCS, vol. 4275, pp. 291–308. Springer, Heidelberg (2006)
5. Barril, P.: Net Execution. In: Girault, C., Valk, R. (eds.) Petri Nets for Systems Engineering, ch.20, pp. 417–431. Springer, Heidelberg (2002)
6. Nutt, G.J.: The evolution towards flexible workflow systems. Distributed System Engineering 3, 276–294 (1996)
7. Rodríguez, C., Sánchez, M., Villalobos, J.: Executable model composition - A multilevel approach. In: ACM Symposium on Applied Computing (SAC 2011). ACM, NY (2011)
8. Rodríguez, C., Sánchez, M., Villalobos, J.: Metamodel Dependencies for Executable Models. In: Bishop, J., Vallecillo, A. (eds.) TOOLS 2011. LNCS, vol. 6705, pp. 83–98. Springer, Heidelberg (2011)
9. Russell, N., ter Hofstede, A.H.M., van der Aalst, W.M.P., Mulyar, N.: Workflow Control-Flow Patterns: A Revised View. Tech. Rep. BPM-06-22, BPMcenter.org (2006)
10. Sánchez, M.: Executable Models for Extensible Workflow Engines, chap. 2.3 Workflow Modularization. Ediciones Uniandes (2011)
11. Sánchez, M., Jiménez, C., Villalobos, J., Deridder, D.: Extensibility in Model-Based Business Process Engines. In: Oriol, M., Meyer, B. (eds.) TOOLS EUROPE 2009. LNBIP, vol. 33, pp. 157–174. Springer, Heidelberg (2009)
12. Sánchez, M., Villalobos, J.: A flexible architecture to build workflows using aspect-oriented concepts. In: AOSD Workshop on Aspect-oriented Modeling (AOM 2008), pp. 25–30. ACM, NY (2008)
13. Sánchez, M., Villalobos, J., Romero, D.: A State Machine Based Coordination Model applied to Workflow Applications. Avances en Sistemas e Informática 6(1), 35–44 (2009)
14. Warmer, J.B., Kleppe, A.G.: Building a Flexible Software Factory Using Partial Domain Specific Models. In: 6th OOPSLA Workshop on Domain-Specific Modeling (DSM 2006), pp. 15–22. University of Jyvaskyla (2006)
15. Wynn, M.T., Edmond, D., van der Aalst, W.M.P., ter Hofstede, A.H.M.: Achieving a General, Formal and Decidable Approach to the OR-Join in Workflow Using Reset Nets. In: Ciardo, G., Darondeau, P. (eds.) ICATPN 2005. LNCS, vol. 3536, pp. 423–443. Springer, Heidelberg (2005)

# A Component Abstraction for Business Processes

Souvik Barat and Vinay Kulkarni

Tata Consultancy Services, 54-B Industrial Estate, Hadapsar, Pune, India
{souvik.barat,vinay.vkulkarni}@tcs.com

**Abstract.** With continued increase in business dynamics, it is becoming increasingly harder to deliver purpose-specific business system in the ever-shrinking window of opportunity. As business systems for the same intent tend to be similar but never the same, they have considerable overlap with well-defined differences. Software product line engineering techniques attempt to address this problem for software artifacts. Separation of business process concerns from application functionality, as advocated in process centric application development, demands solution on similar lines for business processes too. To this effect, we propose an abstraction for business processes that addresses composition, variability and resolution in a unified manner. We present the abstraction, its model-based realization, and illustration with an example.

**Keywords:** Business process component, business process family, business process reuse.

## 1 Introduction

We are in the business of developing business-critical software systems, typically for large enterprises. Our experience is that no two systems, even for the same business intent such as straight-through-processing of trade orders, back-office automation of a bank, or automation of insurance policies administration are identical. Though there exists a significant overlap across functional requirements for a given business intent, the variations are manifold too. We have witnessed that such systems tend to vary along three dimensions, namely, Business process, Functionality, and Solution architecture. Service orientation enables separation of business process concerns from application services. The concerns along Functionality and Solution architecture dimension get addressed through application service implementation. Similar business applications tend to have considerable overlap of application services. To leverage this commonality, we have developed a component abstraction that enables decomposition of application services into common and variable parts, identification of places where variations occur, a type-safe mechanism for plugging in variable parts at these placeholders, and a resolution mechanism to ensure that appropriate variable parts get plugged into the appropriate placeholders. Thus, the component abstraction addresses composition, variability and resolution in a unified manner with locality. We have realized this abstraction using model-based techniques to support a family of business applications [11].

In this paper, we build upon the same principles to address composition, variability and resolution of business processes. We propose a model-based realization of the

F. Daniel et al. (Eds.): BPM 2011 Workshops, Part II, LNBIP 100, pp. 301–313, 2012.
© Springer-Verlag Berlin Heidelberg 2012

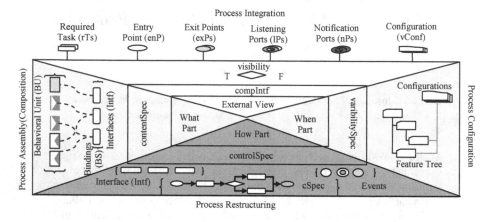

**Fig. 1.** Visualization of Process Component Abstraction

abstraction and illustrate the key concepts with the help of a non-trivial example. The paper is organized as follows – section 2 describes the process component abstraction, section 3 presents an illustrative example and the process component metamodel is presented in section 4. We discuss the related work in section 5 and conclude with a short summary.

## 2     Process Component Abstraction

We propose process component abstraction to specify a behavioral unit for representing a business process or its parts in a modular, hierarchically composable, extensible and configurable manner. The abstraction enables i) *composition* to realize larger process components from existing process components ad infinitum, ii) *configuration* to adapt a process component for pre-defined situations, and iii) *extension* to adapt a process component for unknowable situations apriori. In addition, the abstraction makes clear separation of interface from implementation with *compIntf*, describing the interface of a process component, and *compImpl* describing the implementation in terms of three parts namely *controlSpec*, *contentSpec* and *variabilitySpec* as shown in Fig. 1. The four parts are fairly independent from each other thus supporting independent evolution and have predetermined correlations that ensure overall consistency.

**Component Interface:** It specifies an external view of the process component by describing explicit interaction points with the environment. It provides restricted visibility to its internal structure ranging from zero visibility (i.e. black box component) to partial introspection (i.e. gray-box component) with contentSpec and variabilitySpec being visible.

We introduce the concept of interface port, iPort, and a basic form of interface, task interface, to formalize a process component interface. Formally, an interface port is defined as a tuple iPort = <name, portType, DT > where

-   portType describes the interaction role, i.e. Input or Output;
-   DT is a set of data types from a type system T.

A task interface is defined as tuple Intf = <enP, exPs, lPs, nPs > where

- enP: An input interaction point of a process component, which describes the entry point of a behavioral unit, i.e. either task or process component. It is similar to start event of a traditional business process model.
- exPs: Set of output interaction points that specify exit points of a behavioral unit, for instance, successful completion, process abandoned, and process cancelled. It is similar to the end event of traditional business process model.
- lPs: Set of input interaction points for sensing environmental events of interest. IPs are relevant for a process component representing long running and context (environment) aware business process.
- nPs: Set of output interaction points for notifying significant intermediate milestones to the environment. nPs are similar to the intermediate events of long running business processes.

Component interface, compIntf, is a refinement of the task interface abstraction and is formally defined as compIntf = <enP, exPs, lPs, nPs , rTs, visibility, vConf>, where

- visibility is a Boolean flag e.g. black-box or gray-box.
- rTs is the set of required tasks of a process component. A process component expects these set of tasks to be performed by external components to achieve the overall objective of a process component. Each of these required tasks is specified using task interface abstraction, i.e. Intf.
- vConf is the set of configurations where each configuration identifies consistent resolution of process component variability.

**Control Specification:** The control specification specifies the flow definition of a process component. We decouple the control aspect of the process component from other aspects by representing the set of process steps of a process component as task interfaces, i.e. Intf. Formally a controlSpec is defined as a 3-tuples <PSIntf, Events, cSpecSet> where

- PSIntf is the set of interfaces, intf, representing the process steps,
- Events are the set of events used in flow definitions, and
- cSpecSet is a set of control definitions, where each control definition, cSpec $\in$ cSpecSet, is the flow definition defined using (subset of) PSIntf and Events.

The formalism supports multiple control definitions of a process component to allow variability in control flow, i.e. a same set of process steps can be performed in a slightly different order to achieve the same mission objective. We mandate that each cSpec of cSpecSet must have distinguished start node and set of end nodes.

The conformance criteria of a controlSpec = <PSIntf, Events, cSpecSet> with respect to compIntf = <enP, exPs, lPs, nPs , rTs, visibility, vConf> are defined as follows:

- The entry point of component interface must be compatible with the entry port of start node of all cSpec $\in$ cSpecSet. The compatibility criterion is defined in terms of interaction role (i.e. input and output port type) and data types of consumed and produced data.
- All exit points of the component interface must be compatible with the exit points of end nodes of cSepcSet.

- All notification ports must be either triggered by an event ∈ Events or produced from any of the process steps, i.e. task interface.
- All listening ports should be either mapped to intermediate event ∈ Events or mapped to listening port of a process step, i.e. task interface.

We assume one-to-one mapping between elements of compIntf.nPs and Event, but one could notify a meaningful event by inferring occurrences of several basic events using existing CEP based approaches such as [2]. Similar mechanism can be used for listening events of interest. We consider the integration of existing CEP approaches to produce or consume meaningful event as our future work.

**Content Specification:** Content specification describes the possible realization(s) of the process steps by defining the bindings between task interface and behavioral unit. This behavioral unit could be one of the following elements – (sub) process component with smaller objective (SC), atomic task like service (S) exposed by enterprise application and human task (H), or required task (RT) of a process component, i.e. compIntf.rTs.

Formally, a contentSpec of a process component PC is defined as 3-tuples <PSIntf, BU, BS> where,

- PSIntf is a set of task interfaces defined in controlSpec, i.e. controlSpec.PSIntf;
- BU is the set of behavioral units, i.e. collection of SC, S, H and RT; and
- BS is a set of bindings. A binding, bind(srcIntf, destIntf) is between two interfaces, i.e. source interface and destination interface. We term a binding as internal binding when srcIntf ∈ PSIntf and destIntf is the interface of one of the elements from BU. We verify the consistency of a binding by validating the conformance between srcIntf and destIntf, where interface conformance is defined with respect to entry point, exit points, listening ports and notification ports.

Content specification allows more than one binding for a task interface. This opens up the scope for defining variability and configuring them to serve purpose specific behaviors.

**Variability Specification:** The variability specification of a process component specifies the existence of behavioral variability and its resolution in a declarative form. Formally, a variability specification is a 6-tuple <FT, Const, VP, Var, FBind, Conf>, where

- FT is a feature tree of a set of features, where each feature (F) describes the variability of a process component in an abstract manner. An FT is similar to the feature tree described in [4]. Primarily, we categorize a feature into two kinds – Leaf Feature and Group Feature. Leaf feature is a label that describes a possible choice, and group feature is a label for organizing feature structure and representing choice point.
- Const is a set of constraints defined with respect to F to describe inclusion and exclusion relationships of features.

- VP is the set of variation points, where each variation point represents the location where the behavioral variation exists of a process component. Typically, process component and task interface are the candidate variation points as a process component can expose several valid configurations through component interface and it can contain different control definitions in controlSpec; similarly a task interface can associate with more than one binding in contentSpec.
- Var is the set of variants where each variant represents a fragment of process component. Typically, bindings and control specifications can be seen as candidates for variants, i.e. element of Var.
- FBind is the feature binding. A feature binding is a binding of a group feature and variation point or a leaf feature and element of Var.
- Conf is the set of configurations, where each configuration selects a valid and consistent (with respect to Const) set of leaf features. We define a configuration as consistent if the configuration, conf ∈ Conf, selects a set of leaf features such that one and only one element of var ∈ Var exists for each variation point, vp ∈ VP. The (sub) set of configurations, Conf, are exposed though component interface as compIntf.vConf.

## 2.1 Process Component Classifications

A process component that cannot be decomposed into smaller process components is termed as elementary process component. An elementary process component does not bind to any other process components and instead binds to atomic task(s), i.e. services (S) human tasks (H). In the similar run, we term a process component as composite process component if it contains at least one process component through internal binding. A composite process component can introspect the contentSpec and variabilitySpec of a sub process component if visibility flag of sub process component interface is true. Thus it can use the variabilitySpec of sup process components while defining the variability, otherwise composite process component can only use the vConf of the sub process components to define its variability. We term a process component as configurable process component if more than one bindings exist for at least one task interface of a process component or more than one control definitions exist for a process component. Otherwise, it is termed as non-configurable process component.

A process component is defined as integrable process component if it has at least one required task. A process component integrates with other process component through a binding, we term as external binding. An external binding binds a required task of a process component with a compIntf of outer process component.

## 2.2 Process Component Operators

We propose a set of operators to assemble, integrate, configure and extend a process component. Assembly operator assembles a set of process components together to form a larger process unit, i.e. a composite process component. A composite process component, compProc = <compCompIntf, compContentSpec, compControlSpec, compVSpec>, can be defined by assembling a set of process components PC, where compControlSpec captures the glue specification of the assembly, compContentSpec

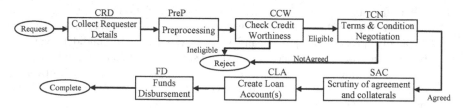

**Fig. 2.** A sample loan origination business process

specifies the internal bindings between task interface used in glue specification and elements of PCs, and compVSpec describes variability of compProc in terms of the variability of PCs. Integrate operator integrates a set of process components using external bindings. Configure operator resolves behavioral variability of a process component, i.e. selects appropriate choice for each variation point such that no constraint is violated. Extension operator extends the behavior of a process component by:

i)   Adding new binding for an Intf. We term this kind of extension as content extension. The content extension leads to adding new behavioral variability of a process component, i.e. either new variation point (element of VP) along with choices (element of Var) or new choice (element of Var) in existing variation point, and

ii)  Adding new control specification, i.e. cSpec in cSpecSet, we term this kind of extension as control extension. The control extension leads to adding new behavioral variability of a process component, i.e. new choice (element of Var),

iii) Adding new configuration by selecting new set of choices. We term this as configurability extension, which may leads to a new entry in vConf of a process component interface.

## 3     Illustrative Example

We consider a simplified version of a loan origination process as an illustrative example for demonstrating the concepts presented so far. A loan origination process, typically, is about providing loan to the eligible applicant(s) after validating them for credit worthiness. The process starts with a request from applicant(s) containing specific loan product, reasons for requesting the loan and the desired amount as input data, and ends either by rejecting the request or by dispatching the approved loan amount (may not be same as the requested amount) to the applicant. The various process steps of loan origination process are shown in Fig. 2. Each process step has its mission objectives. The mission objectives of each of these process steps are as follows: Collect Requester Details (CRD) collects information from the applicant, Preprocessing (PreP) process step validates the collected information and orders Credit reports, Appraisal reports, etc for checking credit worthiness. Check Credit Worthiness (CCW) is an underwriting process step which analyzes collected data and reports, assigns conditions, and determines the sanctioned amount against applied loan amount. Terms & Condition Negotiation (TCN) process step is for discussing the terms and conditions with the applicant(s) and prepares the loan agreement if

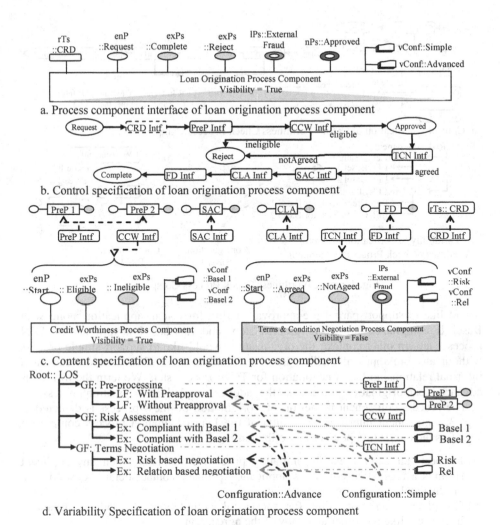

a. Process component interface of loan origination process component

b. Control specification of loan origination process component

c. Content specification of loan origination process component

d. Variability Specification of loan origination process component

**Fig. 3.** Loan origination process component

applicant agrees to defined terms and conditions. Rest of the process steps, namely Scrutiny of Agreement and Collateral (SAC), Create Loan Account (CLA) and Fund Disbursement (FD) are respectively for scrutinizing signed agreement and submitted collateral documents, creating loan account in the enterprise system, and finally closing and disbursing the loan amount to applicant. For illustration purpose, we consider the process step CRD is outsourced to external agency with the remaining process steps being managed internally by the loan origination department (LOD). Underwriting department, a sub-unit of LOD, manages *Check Credit Worthiness* (CCW) process step by decomposing into finer process steps such as Credit Risk Analysis (CR), Operational Risk Analysis (OR), Market Risk Analysis (MR) and Supervisory Review (SR). We consider this process as being used in two contexts having somewhat different behavioral requirements. In one context, the enterprise

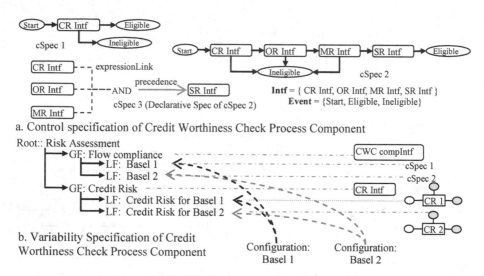

a. Control specification of Credit Worthiness Check Process Component

b. Variability Specification of Credit
Worthiness Check Process Component

**Fig. 4.** Credit Worthiness Check Process Component

would like to support partial pre-approval facility for a loan application along with Basel II compliance for CCW process step, and risk-based negotiation in TCN process step. In other context, the organization would like to support simple process without any pre-approval facility, Basel I compliance for CCW process step, and informal relationship-based negotiation for TCN process step. We term the former as advanced loan origination process and the latter as simple loan origination process.

The process component model of loan origination business process is depicted in Fig. 3. Component interface (compIntf) of the loan origination process component specifies the interaction points as described in Fig 3.a,

a) Request- an entry point for initiating process component when any applicant submits a request; it consumes applicant's primary contact details, desired loan product and loan amount as input data,
b) Complete – an exit point for successful completion; it produces financial instrument like pay order and copy of the agreement
c) Reject – an exit point for rejection notification; it produces rejection notification,
d) External Fraud – a listening port to consume the news about external fraud happening in the environment (this information is an additional factor while negotiating with applicant in TCN process step) and
e) Approved - a notification port for notifying the approval notification once CCW process step is completed.

The component interface also describes two valid configurations, Simple and Advanced, of the loan origination process. Fig. 3.b describes the control flow specification of the loan origination process component. It describes the flow of process steps using interface (Intf) abstractions.   Fig. 3.c describes the content specification in terms of bindings between task interfaces and component interface of process component.   CRD interface binds with required task, i.e. rTs::CRD, of component interface, which is not shown in the figure.  Multiple bindings for a single

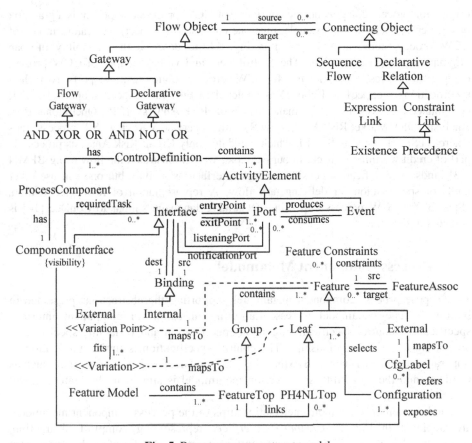

**Fig. 5.** Process component metamodel

process step denote variability. PreP1 process component supports preprocessing with pre-approval facility and PreP2 without it. Thus variations in PreP process step are achieved by mapping two non-configurable process components whereas the variability of CCW and TCN process steps are achieved by binding with configurable process components. Fig. 3.d describes the variability specification of the loan origination process component in terms of,

a) Abstract representation of variability as a feature tree,
b) Mappings between Group Feature to Variation Points, e.g. {Pre-processing → PreP Component Interface}, and Leaf Features to Process Component Interface, e.g. {With PreApproval → PreP1}, and Leaf Feature to the configuration of lower level process component, i.e. {Compliant with Basel 1 → Basel 1}, and
c) Set of configurations describing the selections, e.g. Advanced = {With PreApproval, Compliant with Based 2, Risk based negotiation}.

In this example, available configurations, i.e. the configuration exposed by compIntf.vConf, of CCW and TCN are used to describe the variability of loan origination process component. We consider that CCW process component is a gray-box process component in this example, thus one can use (introspect) the feature model of CCW process component described in Fig. 4.b to describe the variability of loan origination process component. The controlSpec, and variabilitySpec of CCW process component is described in Fig. 4. CCW process component supports two flow specifications – cSpec1 and cSpec2 as depicted in Fig. 4.a. CSpec2 supports Basel II compliance process flow, which mandates Credit Risk Analysis (CR), Operational Risk Analysis (OR), Market Risk Analysis (MR) with Supervisory Review (SR) process steps whereas cSpec1 supports Basel I, which mandates only Credit Risk Analysis process as part of credit worthiness check. In our example, we demonstrated the flow using BPMN [13] kinds of specification considering task interface as activity but one can use other kinds of specification for defining task flow. A representation of flow specification, cSpec 3, for CCW process step using declarative language similar to ConDec [14] is depicted in Fig. 4.a.

## 4    Process Component Metamodel

We propose process component metamodel supporting the abstractions presented in section 2. The metamodel is, essentially, a unification of component interface specification, control specification, content specification and variability specification describing their interrelationships. The control specification is further unification of imperative languages such as BPMN, EPC [23], and declarative specifications such as ConDec, and the variability specification metamodel is similar to the feature model described in [4].

The key elements and their interrelationships of the process component metamodel are depicted in Fig. 5. *ComponentInterface*, representing compIntf abstraction, specializes *Interface* which represents Intf abstraction. An Interface has one entry point, at least one exit point, and optional listening and notification ports. In addition, ComponentInterface may have a set of required tasks and may expose a set of internally consistent configurations. An Interface has *Bindings* of two kinds, namely, Internal and External. Internal Binding is the binding between a task interface and one of the three options i) component interface of a process component, ii) an interface that represents a service or human task or iii) interface which is exposed through component interface as required task that describes contentSpec. External binding is the binding between required task and component interface of outer process component that describes integration specification of process components. A process component can contain many *ControlDefinitions* as controlSpec. ControlDefinition is essentially flow description defined using *Activity Elements* (and its sub elements). We use a generalized metamodel, combining the constructs of imperative and declarative specifications. However, one can use a BPMN compliant metamodel, such as [10], by constraining a task interface into single entry and single exit point to visualize it as an activity. Alternatively a set of interaction ports can be used along with events to describe control specification, or one can map all interaction ports to events and specify the control flow in terms Events and Gateways. The variability specification is described using feature hierarchy, featureAssoc and mappings from feature to variation points or variations. Feature hierarchy structure depicted in figure extend feature tree described in abstraction section, where RootFeature, derives from Group Feature, represents the root of a feature tree, and external feature, kind of leaf feature, represents the configuration of lower level process component. FeatureAssoc is used for describing feature relationships, i.e. dependency, inclusion, exclusion. One can define complex constraints using FeatureConstrains. We use External Feature and PH4NLTop to address the composability of variability specification of (sub) process components in a composite process component. We use PH4NLTop to map a feature model of sub process component to support the introspection of feature tree of gray box sub process component. On the other hand all valid configurations of black-box sub process components can be mapped though External Features to represent choices of group features of process component.

## 5    Related Work

Several approaches [5, 19, and 16] allow visualization of a business process as a set of process fragments or building blocks. The key motivation here is to improve the flexibility and reuse [of parts] in an effective manner. A component abstraction, Eva component, to visualize business process as encapsulated behavioral unit is presented in [20]. An Eva component consists of an *Exporter Interface* describing the provided part, an *Importer Interface* describing the required part, and a body containing the realization expressed in terms of Feva-nets. These approaches support adaptation and evolution of business process by providing different implementations for a process fragment/component. Though identical in philosophy, our approach is based on the concept of fractal [3]. It is a richer component abstraction that supports multi-dimensional separation of concerns such as interface, content and control, and enables independent adaptation and evolution of each of these concerns. Van der Aalst et al also argued in [22] that the need for flexibility and adaptability along multiple dimensions; and proposed an approach supporting hierarchical decomposition and behavioral variability by combining YAWL [21], Worklets [1] and Declare [15]. The approach achieves the behavioral variability by enabling the selection of appropriate worklets for a process step at runtime (similar to selecting appropriate internal binding in our approach). In contrast, we support design time variability along content and control specifications, and provide an intuitive feature model based mechanism to select appropriate and consistent set of variants. The approaches presented in [17, 18, 6, 7, 8, 12] support behaviour variability of a flattened out business process, whereas we support variability for business processes that can be specified as hierarchical composition of process components. Moreover, the use of model-driven approach in our approach, as advocated in [9], supports seamless interoperability between different aspects of a process component and achieves other advantages pertaining to model-driven approach. For instance, it enables model-based transformation for using existing process execution engine and existing approaches.

# 6    Conclusion

We proposed a process component abstraction to represent business process fragments with a richer component abstraction such that each unit is encapsulated with well-defined interface and amenable for composition, extension and configuration. The proposed approach supports clear separation of control, content and variation concerns while specifying a process component and enables independent evolution along each of these dimensions with assured consistency as a whole. We also illustrated how different paradigms, like event-based or activity-based paradigm, and different types of specification languages, i.e. imperative or declarative, can be used to specify control flow of process component. Testing large monolithic business processes is hard. Specifying variability on a flattened out process flow structure [10] is hard to use in practice. To overcome these problems, we proposed an abstraction that addresses composition, variability and resolution in a unified manner with locality. We demonstrated how variability management can be handled in localized context and propagated to the larger unit in a systematic manner. Use of the proposed abstraction to address testing and richer analyses is left for future work. We believe model-based nature of our approach will help target multiple process execution platforms, lead to use of richer analyses techniques and testing mechanisms by applying suitable model-to-model transformations.

# References

1. Adams, M., ter Hofstede, A.H.M., Edmond, D., van der Aalst, W.M.P.: Worklets: A Service-Oriented Implementation of Dynamic Flexibility in Workflows. In: Meersman, R., Tari, Z. (eds.) OTM 2006, Part I. LNCS, vol. 4275, pp. 291–308. Springer, Heidelberg (2006)
2. Barros, A., Decker, G., Grosskopf, A.: Complex Events in Business Processes. In: Abramowicz, W. (ed.) BIS 2007. LNCS, vol. 4439, pp. 29–40. Springer, Heidelberg (2007)
3. Bruneton, E., Coupaye, T., Leclercq, M., Quéma, V., Stefani, J.: The FRACTAL component model and its support in Java. Softw., Pract. Exper. 36(11-12), 1257–1284 (2006)
4. Busch, C., Helsen, S., Eisenecker, U.: Staged Configuration Using Feature Models. In: Nord, R.L. (ed.) SPLC 2004. LNCS, vol. 3154, pp. 266–283. Springer, Heidelberg (2004)
5. Eberle, H., Unger, T., Leymann, F.: Process Fragments. In: Meersman, R., Dillon, T., Herrero, P. (eds.) OTM 2009, Part I. LNCS, vol. 5870, pp. 398–405. Springer, Heidelberg (2009)
6. Fantinato, M., Toledo, M.B.F., Gimenes, I.M.S.: Ws-Contract Establishment with QoS: an Approach Based on Feature Modelling. Int. J. Cooperative Inf. Syst. 17(3), 373–407 (2008)
7. Gottschalk, F., van der Aalst, W.M.P., Jansen-Vullers, M.H., la Rosa, M.: Configurable Workflow Models. Int'l. J. of Coop Inf. Systems (IJCIS) 17(2), 177–221 (2007)
8. Hallerbach, A., Bauer, T., Reichert, M.: Managing Process Variants in the Process Lifecycle. In: 10th Int'l Conf. on Enterprise Information Systems (ICEIS 2008), pp. 154–161 (2008)

9. Kindler, E., Axenath, B., Rubin, V.: AMFIBIA: A Meta-Model for the Integration of Business Process Modelling Aspects. The Role of Business Processes in Service Oriented Architectures (2006)

10. Kulkarni, V., Barat, S.: Business Process Families Using Model-Driven Techniques. In: zur Muehlen, M., Su, J. (eds.) BPM 2010 Workshops. LNBIP, vol. 66, pp. 314–325. Springer, Heidelberg (2011)

11. Kulkarni, V.: Raising family is a good practice. In: FOSD 2010, pp. 72–79 (2010)

12. La Rosa, M., Dumas, M., ter Hofstede, A.H.M., Mendling, J.: Configurable multi-perspective business process models. Inf. Syst. 36(2), 313–340 (2011)

13. OMG (2010): BPMN 2.0, OMG document - dtc/10-06-04, http://www.bpmn.org

14. Pesic, M., van der Aalst, W.M.P.: A Declarative Approach for Flexible Business Processes Management. In: Eder, J., Dustdar, S. (eds.) BPM Workshops 2006. LNCS, vol. 4103, pp. 169–180. Springer, Heidelberg (2006)

15. Pesic, M., Schonenberg, H., Aalst, W.M.P.: DECLARE: Full Support for Loosely-Structured Processes. In: EDOC 2007, pp. 287–300 (2007)

16. Polyvyanyy, A., Smirnov, S., Weske, M.: The Triconnected Abstraction of Process Models. In: Dayal, U., Eder, J., Koehler, J., Reijers, H.A. (eds.) BPM 2009. LNCS, vol. 5701, pp. 229–244. Springer, Heidelberg (2009)

17. Rosemann, M., van der Aalst, W.M.P.: A configurable reference modelling language. Inf. Syst. 32(1), 1–23 (2007)

18. Schnieders, A., Puhlmann, F.: Variability Mechanisms in E-Business Process Families. In: Abramowicz, W., Mayr, H. (eds.) 9th International Conference on Business Information Systems (BIS 2006). LNI, vol. P-85, pp. 583–601 (2006)

19. Schumm, D., Karastoyanova, D., Kopp, O., Leymann, F., Sonntag, M., Strauch, S.: Process Fragment Libraries for Easier and Faster Development of Process-based Applications. Journal of Systems Integration 2(1) (2011)

20. Sünbül, A., Weber, H., Padberg, J.: Evolutionary Development Of Business Process Centered Architectures Using Component Technologies. Journal of Integrated Design & Process Science 5(3), 13–24 (2001)

21. Van der Aalst, W.M.P., ter Hofstede, A.H.M.: YAWL: yet another workflow language. Inf. Syst. 30(4), 245–275 (2005)

22. van der Aalst, W.M.P., Adams, M., ter Hofstede, A.H.M., Pesic, M., Schonenberg, H.: Flexibility as a Service. In: Chen, L., Liu, C., Liu, Q., Deng, K. (eds.) DASFAA 2009. LNCS, vol. 5667, pp. 319–333. Springer, Heidelberg (2009)

23. Van der Aalst, W.M.P.: Formalization and verification of event-driven process chains. Information & Software Technology 41(10), 639–650 (1999)

# Ontology-Based Discovery
# of Workflow Activity Patterns

Diogo R. Ferreira[1], Susana Alves[1], and Lucinéia H. Thom[2]

[1] IST – Technical University of Lisbon, Portugal
{diogo.ferreira,susana.alves}@ist.utl.pt
[2] Université Joseph Fourier, France / Institute of Informatics, UFRGS, Brazil
lucineia@inf.ufrgs.br

**Abstract.** Workflow activity patterns represent a set of recurrent behaviors that can be found in a wide range of business processes. In this
paper we address the problem of determining the presence of these patterns in process models. This is usually done manually by the analyst,
and it requires interpreting the process in terms of the semantics of those
patterns. We describe an ontology-based approach to perform this discovery in an automated way. The approach makes use of an ontology, and
a mapping between the elements in the given process and the classes in
the ontology. A reasoner is then used to discover the patterns, and a
SPARQL query is used to retrieve them. The approach is illustrated for
a business process in a travel booking scenario.

**Keywords:** Business Process Modeling, Workflow Activity Patterns,
Ontology Engineering, Semantic Reasoning.

## 1 Introduction

Business processes can be seen as being composed of a number of different patterns, which have already been thoroughly studied in the literature [1,2]. There
have been also attempts at explaining business processes by means of a single
pattern, such action-workflow [3] or a basic transaction pattern [4]. In general,
these patterns fulfill a double role of facilitating the understanding of processes
on one hand, and on the other hand providing the building blocks from which
new processes can be designed. Most of the previous work has therefore focused
on identifying these building blocks and deciding which of them are most appropriate to capture the common structures of business processes.

Here we take a different viewpoint of assuming that these patterns have been
already defined, and instead we focus on the problem of determining whether a
given set of patterns is present in a given business process. In particular, we are
interested in recognizing the presence of patterns by making use of the semantics
of the business process, i.e. we are looking not only at the structural behavior of
business processes, but especially at the *meaning* of the activities contained in a
process. For example, if we know that a certain activity can be interpreted as an
approval step, then it is possible that the process contains an approval pattern,
which occurs very often in business processes.

F. Daniel et al. (Eds.): BPM 2011 Workshops, Part II, LNBIP 100, pp. 314–325, 2012.
© Springer-Verlag Berlin Heidelberg 2012

We are dealing with so-called *workflow activity patterns* [5] which represent business functions that typically occur in every business process, such as *activity execution, decision making, notification, approval*, etc. These business functions cannot be identified solely by looking at the structure of a process; it is necessary to understand the purpose of each activity in order to decide whether it corresponds to a known business function. In addition, we cannot say that the process contains an approval pattern just because it has an approval step; all the required elements of the approval pattern should be present in order to consider that the process contains such pattern. Section 2 provides a summary of these patterns.

Discovering workflow activity patterns in business processes is typically done manually by the process analyst, and it is not a trivial task since the purpose and use of any given activity can be given different interpretations. Also, if such pattern analysis must be conducted over a large repository of process models, it can become a tedious and error-prone task. Our goal is to provide an automated means which can significantly accelerate the discovery of patterns in process models and relieve the analyst from having to do an exhaustive manual search. Since, to a large extent, such discovery is based on semantics, we turn to an ontology- and reasoning-based approach, as described in Section 3.

Throughout the paper we use the example of a travel booking process introduced in [5]. The experimental evaluation of the proposed approach in more realistic and complicated process models faces a number of additional challenges that we are unable to address here. However, by describing the principles and implementation of the approach, the reader will hopefully get a sense for the potential of using ontologies and automated reasoning to address challenging problems in the area of Business Process Management, especially those which, like the problem addressed here, must rely on semantics to a large extent.

## 2  Workflow Activity Patterns

Workflow activity patterns (WAPs) [5] are common structures that can be found in a variety of business processes. These structures involve control-flow constructs as well as interactions between participants and also the semantics of the activities being performed. Our starting point will be the seven WAPs as defined in [5]. These comprise the following behaviors:

1. *Approval*: An object (e.g. a document) has to be approved by some organizational role. A requestor sends the approval request to a reviewer, who performs the approval and returns a result.
2. *Question-Answer*: When performing a process, an actor might have a question before working on the process or on a particular activity. This pattern allows to formulate such question, to identify an organizational role who is able to answer it, to send the question to the respective actor filling this role, and to wait for response.

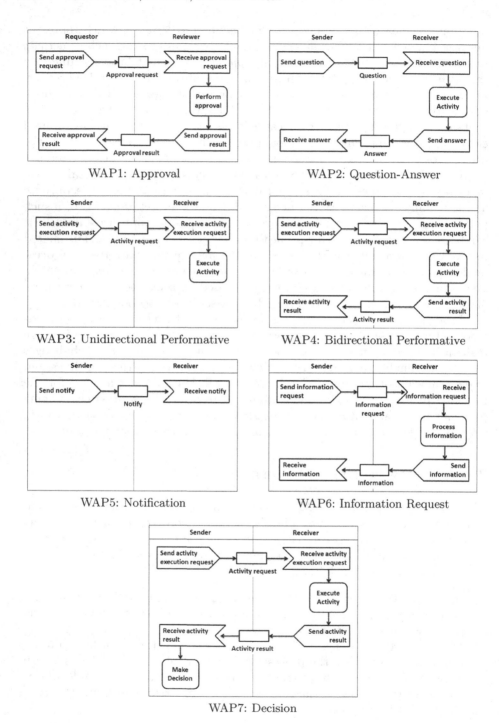

**Fig. 1.** Simplified versions of the seven WAPs defined in [5]

3. *Unidirectional Performative*: A sender requests the execution of a particular activity from a receiver (e.g., a human or a software agent) involved in the process. The sender continues execution of his part of the process immediately after having sent the request.
4. *Bidirectional Performative*: A sender requests the execution of a particular activity from another role (e.g., a human or a software agent) involved in the process. The sender waits until the receiver notifies him that the requested activity has been performed.
5. *Notification*: The status or result of an activity execution is communicated to one or more process participants.
6. *Information Request*: An actor requests certain information from a process participant. He continues process execution after having received the desired information.
7. *Decision*: During process enactment, the performance an activity is requested. Depending on the result of the requested activity, the process continues execution with one or several branches. This pattern allows to include a decision activity with connectors to different subsequent execution branches (each of them associated with a specific transition condition). Exactly those branches are selected for execution whose transition condition evaluates to true.

Figure 1 provides a summary of these workflow activity patterns in graphical form. The patterns are composed of certain elements, namely *signals* (send and receive), *activities* (e.g. "Perform approval") and *messages* (e.g. "Approval request"). For example, WAP1 begins by a send signal with an approval request message; then there is a receive signal for that same message; then an activity to perform the approval; and finally the exchange of the approval result by another pair of send and receive signals.

For simplicity, we have deliberately omitted some elements from these patterns. For example, WAP2 as originally defined in [5] contains additional activities before "Send question", namely an activity "Describe question" and another activity "Identify role habilities". These are elements that could be used, in effect, to distinguish WAP2 from other patterns. By omitting some elements, the patterns become very similar in terms of structure, as can be seen in Figure 1. However, there are some clear differences in purpose and semantics between them, and it is precisely these semantics, rather than structure, that we will use to discover them in business process models.

## 3   Ontology-Based Approach

Figure 2 shows an example of a travel booking process that has been modeled using the same kind of elements that were used to define the seven workflow activity patterns. However, the process makes use of its own vocabulary that is specific to this application domain. Our goal is to understand the semantics of each activity and to reason about these elements in order to determine which patterns are present in this process. Note that Figure 2 already includes an indication of the patterns that were found manually by an analyst. Our goal is to discover these patterns automatically and compare the results.

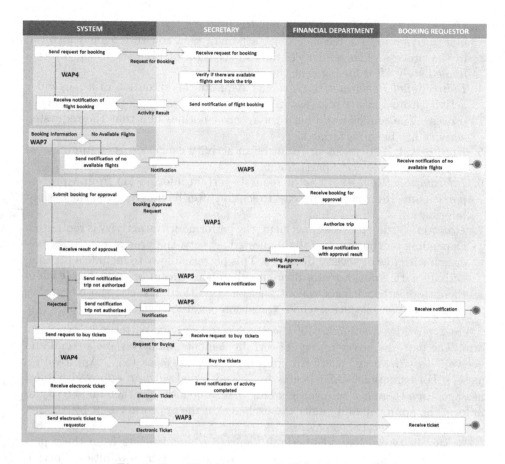

**Fig. 2.** Travel booking example (adapted from [5])

## 3.1 Defining the WAP Ontology

In order to reason about concrete examples such as the one depicted in Figure 2, we need an *ontology* that provides a description of the patterns to be discovered, and we need a *mapping* of the elements in the given process to the concepts defined in that ontology. For example, one should understand that the shape "Send request for booking" in Figure 2 is in effect a send signal with an activity request message as in WAP4; one should also realize that "Authorize trip" corresponds to a "Perform approval" activity as in WAP1; and so on. In order to do this, one needs to have an ontology that specifies these pattern elements.

Figure 3 shows the class hierarchy for the WAP ontology that has been developed in this work, as it appears in Protégé[1]. Basically, there are two top-level classes, Element and Pattern, with Element being the superclass for the various pattern elements, and Pattern being the superclass for the definitions of the several

---

[1] Protégé is available at: http://protege.stanford.edu

**Fig. 3.** Class hierarchy for the WAP ontology

workflow activity patterns. The rationale for this ontology can be summarized as follows:

- Each Pattern is defined as containing certain elements of the classes Signal and Activity. For this purpose we define the object property hasElement with domain Pattern and range Element. Example: PatternApproval hasElement ActivityPerformApproval.
- Each Signal has a certain kind of Message and for this purpose we define the object property hasMessage with domain Signal and range Message. Example: PatternApproval hasElement (SignalSend and (hasMessage MessageApprovalRequest)).

Each subclass of Pattern is defined by an equivalent class expression that specifies all the elements that the pattern contains. The complete definition for WAP1 is as follows:

PatternApproval ≡ Pattern
              and (hasElement some (SignalSend
                           and (hasMessage
                                  some MessageApprovalRequest)))
              and (hasElement some (SignalReceive
                           and (hasMessage
                                  some MessageApprovalRequest)))
              and (hasElement some ActivityPerformApproval)
              and (hasElement some (SignalSend
                           and (hasMessage
                                  some MessageApprovalResult)))

and (hasElement some (SignalReceive
and (hasMessage
some MessageApprovalResult)))

In general, a process may contain many elements, with only some of them matching a given pattern. Therefore, we make use of the keyword some, meaning that it is necessary for a pattern/signal to have at least one element/message of that kind, but possibly more. The definitions for the remaining patterns are analogous, and they are omitted for brevity; those definitions are similar to the one above, but make use of different elements. In particular, the definitions for WAP3 and WAP5 are shorter, while WAP7 has an additional activity.

On a final note about the ontology, we should mention that this is not the first time that an ontology for workflow activity patterns has been defined. In [6] the authors make use of a WAP ontology for the purpose of supporting process modeling; in this case the ontology describes the patterns and the relationships between them in order to produce recommendations about the possible use of other patterns in the same model; ultimately, it is the user who decides whether a given pattern should be inserted in the model. Here, we have built a different WAP ontology for the specific purpose of being able to infer which patterns are present in a given process model; we have therefore focused more on specifying the building blocks (elements) of these patterns, and on how these patterns are defined in terms of the elements they contain.

### 3.2 Mapping of Model Elements to Ontology Classes

While the ontology above defines the classes, the process model contains the elements that will be mapped as *individuals* of those classes. For example, the first shape "Send request for booking" in Figure 2 corresponds to two elements: a signal and a message. The signal is an individual of SignalSend and the message is an individual of MessageActivityRequest. We have therefore:

Element1 : SignalSend
Element2 : MessageActivityRequest
Element1 hasMessage Element2

As another example, the shape "Authorize trip" is an individual of ActivityPerformApproval, so we could have:

Element3 : ActivityPerformApproval

Now, the whole process is represented as an individual of Pattern so that from the above we would have:

Process1 : Pattern
Process1 hasElement Element1
Process1 hasElement Element3

Note that there is no need to assert Process1 hasElement Element2 since Element2 is a message and it is associated with Element1 via the hasElement property.

Once the mapping between the shapes in the model and the classes in the ontology is known, creating these individuals is straightforward and can be done automatically. Then a reasoner can be invoked to infer the patterns that the process contains.

However, the critical point is precisely in creating the mapping, e.g. knowing that "Send request for booking" corresponds to two classes (SignalSend and MessageActivityRequest) and "Authorize trip" corresponds to ActivityPerformApproval. This mapping must be done manually by the analyst, and it is equivalent to annotating the model shapes with classes from the ontology. This can be achieved in a similar way to other approaches that involve semantic annotation of business processes [7,8,9]. Still, creating such mapping is made difficult by the fact that the shapes in a process model use a domain-specific vocabulary and are often labeled in different ways. To facilitate this task, it would be desirable to have the shapes in a process model labeled in a consistent way, such as using *verb-object* style as proposed in [10].

For the process in Figure 2 we have the following mapping:

Send request for booking :: SignalSend MessageActivityRequest
Receive request for booking :: SignalReceive MessageActivityRequest
Verify if there are available flights and book the trip :: ActivityExecute
Send notification of flight booking :: SignalSend MessageActivityResult
Receive notification of flight booking :: SignalReceive MessageActivityResult
Send notification of no available flights :: SignalSend MessageNotify
Receive notification of no available flights :: SignalReceive MessageNotify
Submit booking for approval :: SignalSend MessageApprovalRequest
Receive booking for approval :: SignalReceive MessageApprovalRequest
Authorize trip :: ActivityPerformApproval
Send notification with approval result :: SignalSend MessageApprovalResult
Receive result of approval :: SignalReceive MessageApprovalResult
Send notification trip not authorized :: SignalSend MessageNotify
Receive notification :: SignalReceive MessageNotify
Send request to buy tickets :: SignalSend MessageActivityRequest
Receive request to buy tickets :: SignalReceive MessageActivityRequest
Buy the tickets :: ActivityExecute
Send notification of activity completed :: SignalSend MessageActivityResult
Receive electronic ticket :: SignalReceive MessageActivityResult
Send electronic ticket to requestor :: SignalSend MessageNotify
Receive ticket :: SignalReceive MessageNotify

Provided with this mapping, the individuals and their properties are generated automatically. For each class in the mapping, a new individual is created from that class. If the first class is a Signal and the second class is a Message, we add the property hasMessage which relates those two individuals. Finally, we create an individual of Pattern to represent the whole process, and we associate all signals and activities to the process via the property hasElement.

## 3.3    Pattern Discovery through Reasoning

Through the use of reasoning, it is possible to obtain additional statements that can be inferred from the available classes and individuals. The type of inference we will be most interested in is class membership. As explained above, each WAP is defined by an equivalent class expression that specifies the elements that the pattern contains. If a process has all the elements that satisfy a given pattern expression, then the process will become a member of that class (a subclass of Pattern). In general, a process may end up as a member of several classes, meaning that one can find in the process all the elements required by those patterns.

As an example, let us consider the following excerpt of the travel booking process:

Submit booking for approval :: SignalSend MessageApprovalRequest
Receive booking for approval :: SignalReceive MessageApprovalRequest
Authorize trip :: ActivityPerformApproval
Send notification with approval result :: SignalSend MessageApprovalResult
Receive result of approval :: SignalReceive MessageApprovalResult

These will result in the following individuals being created:

Element1 : SignalSend
Element2 : MessageApprovalRequest
Element1 hasMessage Element2
Element3 : SignalReceive
Element4 : MessageApprovalRequest
Element3 hasMessage Element4
Element5 : ActivityPerformApproval
Element6 : SignalSend
Element7 : MessageApprovalResult
Element6 hasMessage Element7
Element8 : SignalReceive
Element9 : MessageApprovalResult
Element8 hasMessage Element9
Process1 : Pattern
Process1 hasElement Element1
Process1 hasElement Element3
Process1 hasElement Element5
Process1 hasElement Element6
Process1 hasElement Element8

A semantic reasoner is then able to infer the following statements:

Process1 rdf:type Thing
Process1 rdf:type PatternApproval

The process is a member of Thing since it is a Pattern and a Pattern is a subclass of Thing. The reasoner is also able to infer that the process is a member of PatternApproval since, by the elements it contains, it satisfies the expression for that class.

It should be noted that even before the individuals are created, invoking a reasoner on the WAP ontology produces the following statements:

PatternBidirectionalPerformative rdfs:subClassOf PatternUnidirectionalPerformative
PatternDecision rdfs:subClassOf PatternBidirectionalPerformative

This can be easily understood by inspection of Figure 1. In fact, WAP4 contains all the elements of WAP3 and therefore WAP4 satisfies the definition of WAP3. The same happens with WAP7 and WAP4; WAP7 extends WAP4 and therefore it fits the definition of WAP4. This means that any process that contains WAP4 will also be listed as containing WAP3, and any process containing WAP7 will contain WAP4, and therefore WAP3 as well.

### 3.4   Retrieving the Patterns with SPARQL

From the WAP ontology and the individuals created from a given process, the reasoner is able to produce a large number of statements. Not all of these statements will be equally interesting. For example, knowing that a process is a Thing is trivial; also, if a process contains both WAP3 and WAP4, the most interesting statement is that it contains WAP4, since we know that any process that contains WAP4 also contains WAP3. In general, we are interested in class memberships that are closer to the leafs of the class hierarchy, as this represents more specific knowledge about the process and the patterns it contains.

In order to retrieve the patterns that a process contains, we use the following SPARQL query:

```
1: PREFIX wap: ...
2: PREFIX rdf: ...
3: PREFIX rdfs: ...
4: SELECT ?pattern WHERE { wap:Process1 rdf:type ?pattern .
5:                         ?pattern rdfs:subClassOf wap:Pattern .
6:                         FILTER (?pattern != wap:Pattern) .
7:                         OPTIONAL { ?pattern2 rdfs:subClassOf ?pattern .
8:                                    wap:Process1 rdf:type ?pattern2 }
9:                         FILTER (!bound(?pattern2)) }
```

The query determines all class memberships of Process1 (line 4) where the class must be a subclass of Pattern (line 5). According to the OWL standard, a class is by definition a subclass of itself, so Pattern will also appear in the results; we exclude this case with the filter expression in line 6. In lines 7-9 we exclude the case when the result indicates that the process contains both a pattern and a subclass of that pattern (as in WAP3 and WAP4). Lines 7-8 check if there is a subclass (e.g. WAP4) of the pattern (e.g. WAP3) that the process also contains. If so, then we are interested in the subclass (WAP4) rather than in the original class (WAP3). Line 9 excludes the result when there is such case.

Running this query on the travel booking example produces the following results: PatternApproval, PatternBidirectionalPerformative, and PatternNotification. Note that PatternUnidirectionalPerformative is excluded by lines 7-9 since PatternBidirectionalPerformative is a subclass of PatternUnidirectionalPerformative.

These results indicate that the process contains enough elements to satisfy the definition of three different patterns: WAP1, WAP4 and WAP5. However, when comparing these results with Figure 2, we note the absence of WAP7 and WAP3. This can be explained as follows:

- With regard to WAP7, this pattern is not detected since the process does not include an ActivityMakeDecision. The analyst considered that such activity is implicit in the diamond shape, but the element is absent from the mapping.
- With regard to WAP3, that part of the process is inferred as an instance of WAP5 rather than WAP3. This is because the message has been classified as MessageNotify in the mapping. However, it appears that the analyst originally thought that it was a MessageActivityRequest.

### 3.5   Implementation

The WAP ontology was developed and tested in Protégé 4.1 together with the Pellet Reasoner Plug-in[2]. We load the ontology and create the individuals in Java with the Jena framework[3] version 2.6.3. The Pellet reasoner[4] version 2.2.2 is invoked through Jena to perform reasoning over the ontology together with the individuals. The SPARQL query is also executed through Jena.

Basically, using Jena we load the ontology file created with Protégé into an ontology model (OntModel). Then we read a text file containing the mapping. For each class in the mapping we retrieve a class reference (OntClass) from the model, and then create an individual from that class using OntClass.createIndividual(). If the element is a signal then we also create and associate a message individual via the hasMessage property. Using the Pellet reasoner, we create an inference model (InfModel) and then run the SPARQL query over this new model. Iterating through the results provides the subclasses of Pattern contained in the process.

## 4   Conclusion

In this paper we have described an approach to automate the discovery of workflow activity patterns in process models by means of reasoning over an ontology. In this ontology, the classes define the elements that each pattern contains, and the individuals represent the elements of a given process. Once the mapping between the process elements and the ontology elements is established, it is possible to invoke a semantic reasoner to determine which patterns are present in the process. This is done mainly by checking whether the process contains the necessary elements to fulfill the definition of each pattern.

---

[2] http://clarkparsia.com/pellet/protege/

[3] http://jena.sourceforge.net/

[4] http://clarkparsia.com/pellet/

In future work, we intend to develop the approach further in order to check that the elements are not only present, but that they also comply with the sequential behavior of workflow activity patterns. Meanwhile, we believe that the current approach can be useful to show the potential of using ontologies and automated reasoning to address challenging problems in the area of Business Process Management, especially those which, like the problem addressed here, rely on semantics to a large extent.

# References

1. van der Aalst, W., ter Hofstede, A., Kiepuszewski, B., Barros, A.: Workflow patterns. Distributed and Parallel Databases 14(1), 5–51 (2003)
2. Dietz, J.L.G.: Generic Recurrent Patterns in Business Processes. In: van der Aalst, W.M.P., ter Hofstede, A.H.M., Weske, M. (eds.) BPM 2003. LNCS, vol. 2678, pp. 200–215. Springer, Heidelberg (2003)
3. Medina-Mora, R., Winograd, T., Flores, R., Flores, F.: The action workflow approach to workflow management technology. In: Proceedings of the 1992 ACM Conference on Computer-Supported Cooperative Work, CSCW 1992, pp. 281–288. ACM (1992)
4. Dietz, J.L.: The deep structure of business processes. Communications of the ACM 49, 58–64 (2006)
5. Thom, L.H., Reichert, M., Iochpe, C.: Activity patterns in process-aware information systems: basic concepts and empirical evidence. International Journal of Business Process Integration and Management 4(2), 93–110 (2009)
6. Thom, L.H., Reichert, M., Chiao, C.M., Iochpe, C., Hess, G.N.: Inventing Less, Reusing More, and Adding Intelligence to Business Process Modeling. In: Bhowmick, S.S., Küng, J., Wagner, R. (eds.) DEXA 2008. LNCS, vol. 5181, pp. 837–850. Springer, Heidelberg (2008)
7. Born, M., Dörr, F., Weber, I.: User-Friendly Semantic Annotation in Business Process Modeling. In: Weske, M., Hacid, M.-S., Godart, C. (eds.) WISE Workshops 2007. LNCS, vol. 4832, pp. 260–271. Springer, Heidelberg (2007)
8. Zouggar, N., Vallespir, B., Chen, D.: Semantic enrichment of enterprise models by ontologies-based semantic annotations. In: Proceedings of the 12th International EDOC Conference Workshops, pp. 216–223. IEEE Computer Society (2008)
9. Filipowska, A., Kaczmarek, M., Stein, S.: Semantically Annotated EPC within Semantic Business Process Management. In: Ardagna, D., Mecella, M., Yang, J. (eds.) BPM 2008 Workshops. LNBIP, vol. 17, pp. 486–497. Springer, Heidelberg (2009)
10. Mendling, J., Reijers, H., Recker, J.: Activity labeling in process modeling: Empirical insights and recommendations. Information Systems 35(4), 467–482 (2010)

# Staged Configuration of Multi-perspectives Variants Based on a Generic Data Model

## Regular Paper

Stephanie Meerkamm

Chair for Applied Computer Science, University of Bayreuth, Universitätsstr. 30,
95447 Bayreuth, Germany
{stephanie.meerkamm}@uni-bayreuth.de

**Abstract.** Usually, for a particular business process different variants exist in order to fulfill the individual requirements of the different users. The management of the process variability is an important aspect mainly during modeling which serves for the purpose of documentation. One common way to deal with variability is configuration. This paper presents a generic *concept of a configurator* which captures the characteristics of the process domain, inter alia the multi-perspectives of processes. One of the main contributions of this paper is intended to be a *staged configuration process*. The sequence of the partial decisions concerning the selection of a variant can be determined individually. In order to capture the process variability we developed a *generic data model* which empowers the derivation of variants based on a process model which integrates all possible variants.

**Keywords:** process variants, staged process configuration, multi-perspectives, generic data model.

## 1 Introduction

Usually, for a particular business process different variants exist. This is contrary to the increased need of adaption of business process according to the individual requirements of customers and the different contexts or domains to which the processes are applied [1].

*Variants* are defined as artifacts with a *similar function* and which have a large part in common with similar process elements [2]. However, *they differ significantly* with regard to multiple aspects. In the context of processes this means that there are, for example, variations in the process steps, in the tool which is necessary to execute a certain process step, or the organizational unit assigned to a step. Comparing different variants, process elements may be missing, be there additionally, or be simply placed at another position in a process model [3-5].

Fig. 1 illustrates an extract of the process model generated in one of the projects of our chair which integrates two variants of the "check-in" procedure of a hospital into a single process model (Another partial process model for the "emergency check in"

F. Daniel et al. (Eds.): BPM 2011 Workshops, Part II, LNBIP 100, pp. 326–337, 2012.

also exist, however, this is not illustrated here). Three so called *variation points*, the variable positions (they are indicated by numbers), and the appropriate *variant options*, which can be selected (they are indicated by characters), can be identified. They affect the organizational, functional, and data oriented aspects respectively. Although simplified, the example illustrates that already a small process can have several variation points, each carrying multiple variant options, affecting the different perspectives [6-9] that characterize a process in a particular domain.

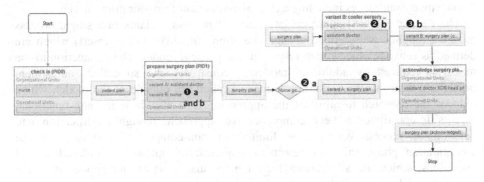

**Fig. 1.** Integrated process model "check in"

One common way to deal with variability management is configuration [3, 4, 10, 11]. It aims at designing an artifact (here the process) assembled from a set of predefined components (here the different perspectives) [12]. As a basic paradigm a *configurable and generic (process) model* is useful or rather necessary; a possible approach will be presented. The model has to integrate all possible variants into one single model. From this basic process model variants can be derived. With this the model also provides a basis for the reuse of process models and process elements [4, 11, 13, 14].

The number of variation points within a process model can become very high. This causes users to be easily overwhelmed by the large number of decisions they have to take concerning the variation points. It is especially difficult to oversee all of this when dependencies between these variant related decisions are taken into account. Therefore a *staged configuration process* is useful in which the user does not need to take all decisions at once but is led step by step through a configuration process [15, 16]. In the staged configuration process, which will be presented in this paper, each stage resolves one or more variation points. The grouping can be determined individually, without consideration of the sequence of the variation points along the control flow. Besides, the different priorities the individual users give to the offered variant options can be taken into account. Proceeding this way, step by step, the initial huge set of possible variants is reduced which finally results in the desired variant. Furthermore, dependencies between variant options belonging to different variation points are nicely coped with.

The paper is structured as follows: Section 2 gives an overview of existing variability management approaches in the context of process management. In Section 3 the concept of the process configurator is presented. In Section 4 we go into detail regarding the generic data model for capturing the variability. The prototype of a modeling tool is presented in Section 5 and Section 6 concludes the paper.

## 2    Related Work

In this Section we want to give a short overview of existing process variant management approaches including a critical assessment from our point of view.

The *Provop* [17, 18] approach integrates all process variants in a single process model. It applies well-defined change operations (modify, delete, insert) which are defined as separate objects with respect to the process model. The connection to the model is realized by additional modeling constructs, the so called "adjustment points". In doing so the variability is made explicit but outside of the model, which reduces the comprehensibility of the approach. As it also includes non-functional aspects it constitutes a very comprehensive approach, though modification and deletion of process elements is limited to non-composite processes. In the configuration phase the user selects a sequence of options (= ordered list of operations, which are all relevant for an individual variant) and applies it to the process model. Thus, all variation points are resolved in one single step. Such an approach is only useful in a case where all variant relevant characteristics of a process can be defined at one point of time. However, with the dynamic nature of business today it cannot always be guaranteed that all information is available at one point of time. For dynamic changes, selecting a variant or switching from one variant to another during runtime is planned to be allowed for, but so far this has not been realized. However, a complete switch implicates many organizational changes and the repetition of process steps which have already been done.

Another single model approach is possible by means of configurable event process chains (*C-iEPC*) [4, 19-21]. Initially, a whole processes family has to be generated. In doing so the variable elements (functions, connectors, roles and objects [21]) are marked individually as variation points. As EPCs in general are rather difficult to understand, especially for the end-user with a non-technical background, the user of the process model is integrated into the configuration process by means of questionnaires. This abstracts away from the modeling notation as the answers on the questionnaires are directly linked to the variation points of the process models. With a questionnaire the user can individually determine the variant's relevant characteristics. The questionnaire guides the configuration process, so that the user knows in which order he has to resolve the variation points. Although it is a very comprehensive approach, no staged configuration is possible so far.

An approach, which explicitly defines a staged configuration process, is presented in [22, 23] by *Becker et al.*. At the outset an integrated multi-perspective process model, called reference model, is generated. Logical terms and attributes are linked to the process elements in order to highlight which elements can be removed in the context of a certain scenario. The configuration is done in three stages: enterprise level, user group level and finally the user level. The concept of stages is motivated by the fact, that the designer of the initial reference is not able to anticipate the specifics which are relevant for the final user. We absolutely support this idea, but unfortunately, the number of stages cannot be determined individually according to the actual circumstance and the level of abstraction level cannot be changed. We would like to focus it mainly at the user group level.

Each of these approaches optimizes the management of process variants on one or more special aspects. None of these approaches suggests methods which completely satisfy our main requirements in one approach: The support of staged, multi-perspective configuration which can individually determined by the user. In the following Section we shall report on the developed concept of a process configurator.

## 3    Concept of the Process Configurator

The requirements for the process configurator have been analyzed initially in [24]; we not want to focus them again. Fig. 2 gives an overview on the concept of the process configurator. The staged configuration process has been motivated by [15, 16]; our main contribution is the individual regrouping of the variation points.

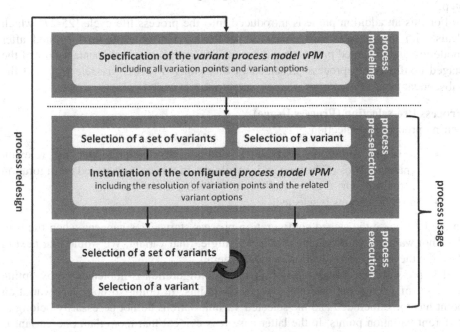

**Fig. 2.** Concept of the process configurator and the staged configuration

**Process Modeling**
The whole procedure starts from the top of Fig. 2 during modeling time. First of all a general *process model PM* has to be defined [25-27]. In the context of this approach, the POPM (Perspective Oriented Process Modeling) concept [28] is used for modeling process model PM. POPM as a graphical modeling language covers all

aspects of a process in a modularized manner. The five main perspectives of POPM are: functional perspective in order to identify the activities, which is strongly related to the behavioral perspective defining the order of the process steps; the data perspective to define the input and output of the process step, and finally, the organization and operational perspective in order to identify by whom, and by means of which tools or systems, the activities are executed.

Based on this, the *variant process model vPM* is defined. Such a variant process model integrates all possible variants into one single model. In order to get this, each single variant has to be identified in the initial PM which has to be done manually. For this the explicit definition of *variation points vp,* the variable positions in a process model, and *variant options vo,* the selectable process elements for a variant, has to be done.

## Process Usage

From the resulting variant process model vPM the individual *process variants v* are derived by configuration. As, due to the amount of variation points and their dependencies, the decision to select one single variant from the integrated process model is a complex one, it should be possible to approach the final solution step by step.

For this an addition phase is introduced into the process life cycle [25-27] which deals with the overall management of processes. The new phase is located after modeling and is named *process pre-selection*. This phase is an elementary part of the staged configuration process presented in this paper. *Process pre-selection* and the subsequent *process execution* are regrouped to the so called *process usage*.

### Process Pre-selection (Process Usage)

During process pre-selection

- a single variant is selected, if enough information about the relevant characteristics of the process is available. In this case no staged configuration is realized. Or
- a set of variants is selected.

In the latter case the staged configuration process starts. This happens when the user does not want or is not yet able to select a single, final variant. We would like next to describe the staged configuration in greater detail.

The pre-selection in the sense of a staged configuration is implemented by opting for a set of variant options of the variation points. In doing so not every variation point has to be included and the selected variant options do not necessarily belong to different variation points. In the latter case it is evident that more than one variant is selected. In this regard we should make clear that, in contrast to the small example in Fig. 1, a single variant option can be relevant for one or more different variants. Configuring a medical check-in process, for example, all check-in processes normally include the closing of a contract concerning the treatment; for the emergency case this step is an obligation. The decision on which variation points are resolved, and at which stage of the configuration process, should be determined individually by the person who configures the process. The order of the variation points along the control flow is irrelevant in this context. The variation points with the dedicated variant options need to be presented accordingly in order to give the user the possibility to select these ones he wants to or is able to resolve at this stage.

The relevant part of the initial process model is then *instantiated viz. configured.*

(1) Variant options viz. process elements, which are no longer essential and relevant, are deleted at each variation point

(2) In case only one variant option of a variation point remains the latter one is replaced by the selected variant option.

(3) Dependencies between variant options which belong to different variation points have to be considered. This leads to the deletion of variant options which belong to other variation points, which can also result in resolving a variation point completely

(4) The remaining process elements have to be reconnected for a valid process model

The result for the first stage of the configuration process is a *partial variant process model vPM'* derived from the initial variant process model vPM. The new process model still carries variation points. For the time being this is possible or rather allowed. But before a process is completely executed all variation points have to be resolved, viz. the number has to be reduced to zero, as variants are mutually exclusive during execution.

After each configuration step a *validation* concerning the correctness of the resulting process model has to be done [29-31]. For example it has to be ensured that all arcs connect the right elements i.e., a control flow starts at an atomic or rather a composite process and ends at another one. An automatic solution would be preferable as doing it manually is more time-consuming and error-prone.

**Process Execution (Process Usage)**
With the partial variant process model vPM', the process owner can start the execution. As variants are mutually exclusive during execution, at one point of time all variation points have to be resolved. Only then is the valid execution of the process guaranteed. Thus, at the least, when the process owner is directly confronted with an unresolved variation point during execution he has to select one of the offered variant options. The final result is a *process variant v* or rather a *process model PM'*. This is a partial process model from the initial vPM.

The maximum number of possible stages is limited by the number of variation points. This is the case when each of them is resolved at a separate stage. The number of stages is automatically reduced by the dependencies between variant options of different variation points. Because of such dependencies some variation points are resolved at the same time. Furthermore, the number of stages can be reduced by explicitly regrouping the resolution of several variation points for one stage.

As during pre-selection, the decision which and how many variation points are relevant for a single stage of the configuration process, should be determined individually. For every single run of the configuration process this can be carried out anew according to the actual circumstances. The *validation* concerning the correctness of the resulting process model has to be done likewise.

**Process Redesign**

Changes concerning the process and their variants can now be integrated and mistakes can be eliminated. With the redesign, the whole configuration process starts again and with this a continuous flow of process improvement.

# 4    Configurable, Generic Data Model

From the example in Fig. 1, it is clear that a user can easily be overwhelmed by to the number of variation points, the variant options and their dependencies. This is so mainly in cases where a process is much more complex than in Fig. 1. In order to capture the variability and to implement the requirements from [24] there is a need for a special model, called a *generic data model*. With nodes and edges as basic elements, it is independent from any process modeling language; it is supposed be mapped to a model generated with languages as BPMN or EPC, which focus less functionality concerning variability but usability. The requirements dictate the necessity of a visual approach for the generic data model. This is supposed to be a graphical notation of a part-whole-relationship, a tree based on generalization hierarchies. Trees are extremely expressive means of representing configurable objects. They are commonly used for the logical representation of hierarchical structures including the presentation of a high number of variants because of the high level of abstraction, compactness and clarity that they provide.

Our approach is inspired by works such as [32], [33] or [34] which use trees to describe configurable products and/or services. Our goal is to transfer this idea into the domain of process modeling and process variants. We now want to process the generic data model as it is actually conceptualized. Based on [24], it integrates the experiences and findings from an evaluation presented in [35]. The presentation is illustrated by using the example from Fig. 1.

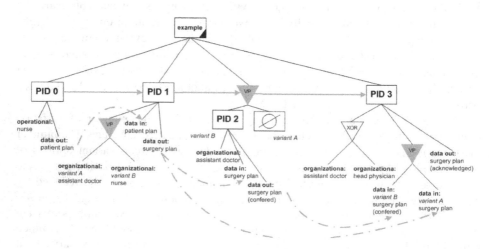

**Fig. 3.** Generic data model

Processes are symbolized as nodes. Composite processes demonstrate that several processes are composed into a higher level. The composition can be done repeatedly resulting in several hierarchical levels within the tree. The root of the tree always has to be a composite process. Elementary processes are not further decomposable (Fig. 3, process steps 0-3). We further define a *control flow* between the processes, which is demonstrated by the grey dashed arrow between the elementary processes in Fig. 3.

*Alternatives (OR) and exclusive alternatives (XOR)*, modeled as nodes, aggregate several processes. In order to distinguish between optional and mandatory alternatives an "Empty Element" is introduced, illustrated by the crossed circle within a process. *Conjunctions (AND)* symbolize the parallel execution of the attached processes. In our example none of these are used.

The concept presented so far leads to a functional structure of the configuration concept, which is a common method to handle the complexity of configurable objects [10, 12, 20]. Furthermore it fits well into the process-oriented application context.

We want to further enlarge the concept with *aspect oriented nodes*. The processes, be it elementary or complex, can be connected with this additional type of nodes or rather, in order to be more precise, leaves. The most common aspects are the organizational, operational and data oriented aspects [7, 9, 28]. A concrete example is "nurse" for the organizational aspect for process 0. In the style of process, the aspect oriented nodes or rather elements can also be defined as composite or rather hierarchical. OR and XOR are used as logical connectors in terms of the aspect oriented nodes, as it can be seen at process 3 in Fig. 3 for the organizational aspect.

The data-oriented nodes distinguish between input and output data for a process step. In order to know exactly which output data is consumed by the next process step as input data an explicit *data flow* is defined. This is illustrated in Fig. 3 by the grey dashed and pointed arrow between output data element "patient plan" of process step 0 and input data element "patient plan" of process step 1.

In order to restrict the domain of possible process specified by (exclusive) alternatives, to support the clarity of the model and to ensure that the process finally realizes its function during execution so called *implications* are necessary. Implications specify dependencies between and within process elements. They are supposed to be modeled by using a thin black arrow. For the process model in Fig. 3 implications are not necessary.

Last but not least we would like to introduce the modeling element *variation point*, the colored triangle with the labeling "VP" in our example, which implements the configurability. The attached nodes or rather process elements are the *variant options*. They must belong to the same aspect concerning a single variation point. With this the variation points can clearly be separated from a normal XOR which is part of the behavioral aspect of the process model, thus only functional nodes can be attached to. The variation points themselves can be defined for every arbitrary aspect as it can be seen in Fig. 3. Furthermore, the variation points can be set up hierarchically, which results in the definition of 'a variant within a variant'. This is useful mainly in very comprehensive processes as it results in an additional structure for the data model.

In order to restrict the domain of possible variants and to ensure that the configured variant finally realizes its function, it is necessary to display to which variant(s) a variant option belongs. As can be seen in Fig. 3, this is realized by adding an additional text field (attribute) to a variant option indicating the relevant variant(s).

It should be mentioned that, in contrast to the example in this article, particularly in comprehensive process models, a variant option can belong to several variants. The concept is functionally comparable to the implications in conjunction with alternatives, also introduced in this Section.

With all this the generic model captures the configurable aspects of the processes and the dependencies in a compact, comprehensive und structured way. This empowers the derivation of variants and the reuse of process elements. Additional aspects of a special domain can easily be added. However, the model bears limitations: Existing process models have to be mapped to the tree. The manual execution of this task is both time-consuming and error-prone, thus it is recommended that the transformation is automated.

## 5     Tool Support with OMME

The developed modeling concept for the configurable process models is on the way to be implemented in a modeling environment. For this the first prototype of the so called *Open Meta Modeling Environment (OMME)* [36, 37] is used. The architecture is on the orthogonal classification approach of Atkinson and Kühne [38]. The main advantage of this modeling environment is that it finally allows the definition and storage of arbitrary modeling languages and (meta) models; these can be linked to each other. A textual and a graphical entering of the models are possible.

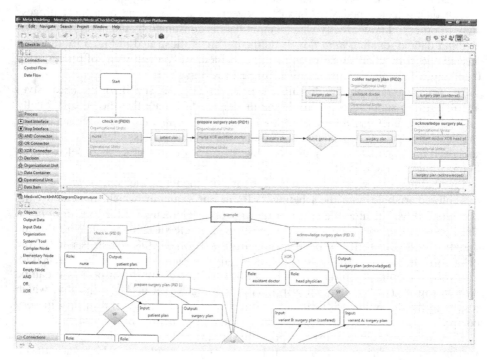

**Fig. 4.** Screenshoot OMME

As a first use case the Perspective Oriented Process Modeling (POPM) framework [28] is integrated. An example of a process model can be seen in Fig. 4 below. It is also possible to integrate other process modeling languages, but for the time being they are not considered. Furthermore, a first version of the generic data model concept from Section 4 is implemented. An example which directly corresponds to the POPM model can be seen in Fig. 4 top above.

However, both the POPM model and the generic data model are stored on the same repository, but so far they cannot be automatically linked to each other; this is only possible using the textual notation of OMME. Besides, the implementation of the graphical editor turned out to be difficult [36]. Due to this, for example, the layout of the variation point had to be adapted. Case studies are running in order to test the actual version of OMME. Afterwards it is planned to implement a new version.

# 6    Conclusion and Outlook

This paper introduces the *concept of a process configurator* with *a staged configuration process*. The advantage is that the user must not be restricted to taking one single decision to select a variant, but can approach to the solution by resolving the variation points in several steps. In addition, the user can determine the order of the resolved variation points individually and with this select the most essential variant options at the beginning of the configuration process; variant options the user is not sure about can be postponed as far as possible to the end of the configuration process, which can be continued up to the time of execution. This aims at a better adaption of the processes to actual circumstances. The variability of the processes with all their different aspects and the configuration mechanism is captured in a special *generic data model*. It aims at hiding the complexity from the user and addresses a shortcoming of many existing process modeling languages; it is independent from any process modeling language.

Whereas an evaluation of the configurable modeling concept has already been done, the implementation in a modeling tool just started. As it is still a prototype the integration of the concept and the future development will be done in parallel as far as possible. Further research for the process configurator involves the implementation of the configuration component including an interface for the user.

# References

1. Mutschler, B., Reichert, M., Bumiller, J.: Unleashing the effectiveness of process-oriented information systems: Problem analysis, critical success factors and implications. IEEE Transaction on Systems, Man and Cybernetics (Part C) 38, 208–291 (2008)
2. DIN: Begriffe für Stücklisten und das Stücklistenwesen (DIN 199-2) (2002)
3. Gottschalk, F., van der Aalst, W.M.P., Jansen-Vuller, M.H., La Rosa, M.: Configurable Workflow Models. International Journal of Cooperative Information Systems 17, 223–255 (2008)
4. LaRosa, M.: Managing variability in process-aware information systems. PhD. Queensland University of Technology, Brisbane (2008)

5. Schäppi, B., Andreasen, M., Kirchgeorg, M., Radermacher, F.J.: Handbuch Produktentwicklung. Carl Hanser Verlag, München (2005)
6. Bobrik, R., Reichert, M., Bauer, T.: Requirements for visualization of system-spanning business process. In: DEXA, pp. 948–954 (2005)
7. Curtis, B., Kellner, M.I., Over, J.: Process Modeling. Communications of the ACM 35, 138–146 (1992)
8. Davenport, T.H.: The Coming Commoditization of Processes. Havard Business Review 83, 100–108 (2005)
9. Scheer, A.-W.: ARIS - Business Process Modeling. Springer, Berlin (2000)
10. Riitahuhta, A.: Views and Experiences of Configuration Management. In: Riitahuhta, A., Pulkinen, A. (eds.) Design for Configuration. Springer, Berlin (2001)
11. Tiihonen, J., Soininen, T.: Product Configurators - Information System Support for Configurable Products. Increasing Sales Productivity through the Use of Information Technology during the Sales Visit. A Survey of the European Market. Hewson Consulting Group (1997)
12. Mittal, S., Fraymann, F.: Towards a Generic Framework of Configuration Task. In: 11th International Conference Artifical Intelligence (IJCAI 1989), San Francisco, USA (1989)
13. Sabin, D., Weigel, R.: Product Configuration Frameworks-A Survey. IEEE Intelligent Systems 13, 42–49 (1997)
14. Becker, J., Delfmann, P., Dreiling, A., Knackstedt, R., Kuropka, D.: Configurative Process Modeling – Outlining an Approach to increased Business Process Model Usability. In: 15th IRMA International Conference. Gabler, New Orleans (2004)
15. Czarnecki, K., Helsen, S., Eisenecker, U.: Staged Configuration Using Feature Models. In: Nord, R.L. (ed.) SPLC 2004. LNCS, vol. 3154, pp. 266–283. Springer, Heidelberg (2004)
16. Czarnecki, K., Helsen, S., Eisenecker, U.: Staged Configuration Through Specialization and Multi-Level Configuration of Feature Models. Software Process: Improvement and Practice 10 (2005)
17. Hallerbach, A., Bauer, T., Reichert, M.: Capturing Variability in Business Process Models: The Provop Approach. Journal of Software Maintenance and Evolution: Research and Practice 22, 519–546 (2009)
18. Hallerbach, A., Bauer, T., Reichert, M.: Managing Process Variants in the Process Life Cycle. In: 10th Int'l. Conf. on Enterprise Information Systems (ICEIS 2008), Barcelona Spain (2008)
19. La Rosa, M., Lux, J., Seidel, S., Dumas, M., ter Hofstede, A.H.M.: Questionnaire Driven Configuration of References Models. In: Krogstie, J., Opdahl, A.L., Sindre, G. (eds.) CAiSE 2007. LNCS, vol. 4495, pp. 424–438. Springer, Heidelberg (2007)
20. Rosemann, M., van der Aalst, W.M.P.: A Configurable Reference Modeling Language. Information Systems 32, 1–23 (2007)
21. La Rosa, M., Dumas, M., ter Hofstede, A., Mendling, J.: Configurable Multi-Perspective Business Process Models. Information Systems 36, 313–340 (2011)
22. Becker, J., Delfmann, P., Knackstedt, R.: Adaptive Reference Modeling: Integrating Configurative and Generic Adaption Techniques for Information Models. In: Becker, J., Delfmann, P. (eds.) Reference Modeling, pp. 27–58. Springer, Berlin (2007)
23. Becker, J., Knackstedt, R., Kuropka, D., Delfmann, P.: Subjektivitätsmanagement für die Referenzmodellierung: Vorgehensmodell und Werkzeugkonzept. KnowTech, Dresden (2001)
24. Meerkamm, S.: Configuration of Multi-perspectives Variants. In: zur Muehlen, M., Su, J. (eds.) BPM 2010 Workshop. LNBIP, vol. 66, pp. 277–288. Springer, Heidelberg (2011)
25. Becker, J., Kugler, M., Rosemann, M.: Processmanagement. Springer, Heidelberg (2003)

26. Allweyer, T.: Geschäftsprozessmanagement – Strategie, Entwurf, Implementierung, Controlling. W3L-Verlag, Herdecke (2005)
27. Weske, M.: Business Process Management - Concepts, Languages, Architectures. Springer, Heidelberg (2007)
28. Jablonski, S., Bussler, C.: Workflow Management – Modeling Concepts, Architecture and Implementation. International Thomson Computer Press, London (1996)
29. Lauesen, S., Vinter, O.: Preventing Requirement Defects: An Experiement in Process Improvement. Requirements Engineering 6, 37–50 (2001)
30. Lindland, O.I., Sindre, G., Sølvberg, A.: Understanding Quality in Conceptual Modeling. IEEE Software 11, 42–49 (1994)
31. van der Aalst, W.M.P., Dumas, M., Gottschalk, F., ter Hofstede, A., La Rosa, M., Mendling, J.: Preserving Correctness During Business Process Model Configuration. Formal Aspects of Computing 22, 459–482 (2010)
32. Gairola, A.: Montagegerechtes Konstruieren - Ein Beitrag zur Konstruktionsmethodik. Fachbereich Nachrichtentechnik. Doctoral thesis. Technische Hochschule Darmstadt, Darmstadt (1981)
33. Hümmer, W., Meiler, C., Müller, S., Dietrich, A.: Data Model and Personalized Configuration Systems for Mass Customization - A Two Step Approach for Integrating Technical and Organizational Issues. In: International Conference on Economic, Technical and Organizational Aspects of Product Configuration Systems, Kopenhagen, Denmark (2004)
34. Rosemann, B., Meerkamm, H., Trautner, S., Feldmann, K.: Design for Recycling, Recycling Data Management and Optimal End-of-Life Planning based on Recycling Graphs. In: International Conference on Engineering Design (ICED 1999), Munich, Germany (1999)
35. Meerkamm, S., Jablonski, S.: Configurable Process Models: Experiences From A Medical And An Administrative Case Study. In: 19th European Conference on Information Systems - ICT and Sustainable Service Development (ECIS 2011), Helsinki, Finland (2011)
36. Volz, B., Jablonski, S.: OMME - A Flexible Modeling Environment. In: Workshop on Flexible Modeling Tools (FlexiTools@SPLASH 2010), Reno/Tahoe, Nevada, USA (2010)
37. Volz, B., Jablonski, S.: Towards an Open Meta Modeling Environment. In: 10th Workshop on Domain-Specific Modeling (DSM 2010) Reno/Tahoe, Nevada, USA (2010)
38. Atkinson, C., Kühne, T.: Concepts for Comparing Modeling Tool Architectures. In: Briand, L.C., Williams, C. (eds.) MoDELS 2005. LNCS, vol. 3713, pp. 398–413. Springer, Heidelberg (2005)

# An Infrastructure Oriented for Cataloging Services and Reuse of Analysis Patterns

Lucas Francisco da Matta Vegi, Douglas Alves Peixoto, Liziane Santos Soares, Jugurta Lisboa-Filho, and Alcione de Paiva Oliveira

Departamento de Informática, Universidade Federal de Viçosa
Viçosa-MG, Brazil, 36570-000
{lucasvegi,douglasalves.ufv}@gmail.com, {liziane.soares,jugurta}@ufv.br,
alcione@dpi.ufv.br

**Abstract.** Patterns have been employed as a mechanism for reuse in several phases of software development. Analysis patterns consist of artifacts for reuse during the requirements analysis and conceptual modeling. However, they are generally, documented in a textual manner which is not precise to be treated by a computer, thus limiting the dissemination and a wider reuse. Within the geo-processing area, Spatial Data Infrastructures (SDI) has been used quite effectively as an instrument for the reuse of geospatial data and services. Based on the development of SDIs, this article proposes an Analysis Patterns Reuse Infrastructure (APRI) comprising web services and a metadata representation for the specification of analysis patterns, in order to support the cataloging and reusing of analysis patterns.

**Keywords:** Analysis Patterns, Reuse, Dublin Core, SOA, Spatial Data Infrastructure.

## 1 Introduction

Spatial Data Infrastructure (SDI) is a relevant base collection of technologies, policies and institutional arrangements that facilitate the availability of and access to spatial data. The SDI provides a basis for spatial data discovery, evaluation, and application for users and providers within all levels of government, the commercial sector, the non-profit sector, academia and by citizens in general [1]. Currently, most of SDI are based on Service-Oriented Architecture (SOA), allowing to create shared environments, distributed and interoperable based on Web Services [2].

The use of SDI allow the availability of spatial databases resulting from different providers, bringing facilities to the user to acquire new datasets, without the need to build them or convert them, generating duplicity and overcharging his work [3].

Appropriate documentation of data and services is a very important point in the development of an SDI. This documentation is produced through defined metadata from a standard metadata specification, for instance, Dublin Core [4].

F. Daniel et al. (Eds.): BPM 2011 Workshops, Part II, LNBIP 100, pp. 338–343, 2012.

Fowler [5] describes analysis patterns as an idea that has proven to be useful in a given practical context and that can be useful in other contexts. This category of patterns is focused on the reuse of artifacts generated during the requirements analysis and conceptual modeling phases.

Analysis patterns were a well-researched topic in the past, resulting in publications in various domains. However, recently the number of publications in this subject decreased. The work of Blaimer, Bortfeldt and Pankratz [6] places the theme back in focus, wherein the authors present a detailed review of the literature about analysis patterns and propose new research challenges in this subject.

Documentation of analysis patterns is important to describe the context in which they can be reused and make possible the sharing of knowledge among designers [7]. Describing a pattern improperly can generate redundant patterns or patterns in an inadequate context, thus compromising their reuse by other designers [8].

In the field of Geographic Information Systems (GIS), SDI has been used very efficiently as a tool for reusing services and geospatial data. In a way analogous to how geospatial data are documented and recovered in an SDI, the documentation of analysis patterns by means of metadata and its recovery made through Web services can contribute to the dissemination and increase of reuse of these patterns.

Thus, the aim of this paper is to propose a service-oriented infrastructure to support the cataloging and reuse of analysis patterns.

The rest of the paper is organized as follows: Section 2 describes related work with metadata standards and ways of specifying analysis patterns. Section 3 describes the architecture of a service-oriented infrastructure for reuse of analysis patterns. Section 4 presents some concluding remarks.

## 2   Related Works

### 2.1   Metadata Standards

Metadata consists of data about data. Metadata standards are used to standardize the set of elements of the data description. For example, a standard for geospatial metadata may contain the title, a general description, authors, the spatial limits of the data, quality aspects, and other elements, thus facilitating the search, retrieval and reuse data appropriately [4].

The structure of a data description, given by metadata, can vary according to the domain of the described data. Considering this situation, many standards have been created in order to establish structures of metadata for specific areas and thus enable a common understanding for a community of users.

The standard CSDGM (Content Standard for Digital Geospatial Metadata) is the most used standard worldwide to describe spatial data. It was created by the FGDC (Federal Geographic Data Committee) in 1994 to support construction of U.S. SDI (NSDI - National Spatial Data Infrastructure) [9]. This standard is composed by 469 elements.

The ISO 19115 standard [10] was proposed in 2003 with the aim of becoming the main standard in the field of spatial data and services. This metadata standard is very wide and rich in detail, consisting of 509 elements.

There are also generic standards metadata that can be used more widely, for example, the Dublin Core Metadata Initiative (DCMI) [11]. The Dublin Core standard is only composed of 15 elements, and usually all of these elements are present in any broader metadata standard. No element of the Dublin Core is mandatory and all of them can be repeated many times during a data description. Its simplicity brings benefits such as lower costs of implementation and promotion of interoperability between data from different domains, however, the small number of elements that make up the standard does not provide sufficient semantic descriptions of data to describe complex domains [12].

Although the Dublin Core standard is generic and very simple, it can be used as a basis for creating profiles for specific domains from the addition of new elements, specification of rules for the occurrence of the elements and definition of types of values for each element [4].

### 2.2 Templates for Analysis Patterns Specification

Analysis patterns can be specified from predefined templates and outlines. The usability of an analysis pattern is reduced if the author does not use a template or uses an incomplete one to specify the pattern [6].

So far, there is no widely accepted template for specifying analysis patterns, therefore, different methodologies are used for specification. Quite often they are derived from templates geared to specify design patterns and does not fully meet the specificities of analysis patterns [6].

Considering the shortcomings in the templates oriented to specification of analysis patterns, Pantoquilho, Raminhos and Araújo propose in [13] a specific template for analysis patterns documentation. This template contains the elements of the previous approaches used to describe patterns, as well as several additional elements for a more complete description of the analysis patterns.

## 3  A Web Services Infrastructure for Reuse of Analysis Patterns

Based on the infrastructure for the reuse of geospatial data, this paper proposes an Analysis Patterns Reuse Infrastructure (APRI), composed of Web services, thereby featuring architecture of SOA (Service-Oriented Architecture) [14].

The scenario offered by SOA has providers, integrators and service users as actors, and users can be human or client softwares. Thus, data and services of the APRI can be accessed by human users and software clients.

The APRI (Figure.1) consists of the following components:

– *Pattern Portal:* contains a set of Web sites focused on obtaining the analysis patterns and tools and services that provide discovery, cataloging and reuse of them.

- *Metadata Repository:* are repositories that contain metadata in XML (eXtensible Markup Language) for the specification of analysis patterns and services contained in the APRI. The template used for the specification of analysis patterns is a customization of the 15 elements of the Dublin Core standard with the items of the template proposed by Pantoquilho, Raminhos and Araújo [13].
- *Analysis Pattern Repository:* are repositories that contain the analysis patterns in the XMI format (XML Metadata Interchange), allowing their use for visualization and collaboration services.
- *Portrayal Service:* are services that support the visualization of the analysis patterns of APRI.
- *Catalog Service:* these services enable the discovery and use of analysis patterns and services of APRI, based on their metadata.
- *Access Service:* these services allow to access and download the analysis patterns.
- *Collaboration Service:* these services allow the experienced designer to contribute improving the analysis patterns.

The definition of this services infrastructure for reuse of analysis patterns is based on components proposed by Béjar [15], for creating SDI.

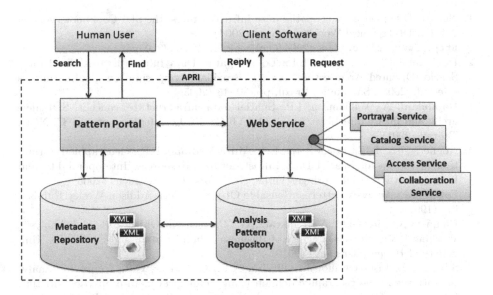

**Fig. 1.** Analysis Patterns Reuse Infrastructure (APRI)

## 4   Final Considerations

The architecture proposed in this paper allows the development of a service-oriented infrastructure for the cataloging and reusing of analysis patterns. This proposal seeks to solve a problem in the reuse of analysis patterns, related to the manner through which patterns are documented. With a more suitable documentation, analysis patterns can be more easily discovered, studied and reused.

The Dublin Core standard has being widely used for items documentation such as work of art, museum pieces, maps, websites, etc. One of the advantages of this standard is that the metadata can be easily found by Web search engines, as they are structured by tags, making easy the semantic contextualization. Thus, the Dublin Core can also be adapted to document analysis patterns.

The use of Web services allows as much the reuse of analysis patterns by human designers as the automatic reuse done with CASE tools support. A APRI prototype is being developed by the information systems research group of *Departamento de Informática* at *Universidade Federal de Viçosa*.

As future work, we can mention the studies on the use of the Dublin Core as a metadata standard for documenting other computational artifacts.

**Acknowledgements.** This project is partially financed by Brazilian funding agencies: FAPEMIG, CNPq and CAPES. The authors also acknowledge the financial support of the company Sydle.

# References

1. Nebert, D.D.: Developing spatial data infrastructures: the SDI Cookbook, version 2.0. (GSDI-Technical Working Group) (2004),
   http://www.gsdi.org/docs2004/Cookbook/cookbookV2.0.pdf
2. Davis Júnior, C.A., Alves, L.L.: Local Spatial Data Infrastructures based on a Service-Oriented Architecture. In: 8th Brazilian Symposium on GeoInformatics (GeoInfo 2005), São Paulo, Brazil, pp. 30–45 (2005)
3. Rajabifard, A., Williamson, I.P.: Spatial data infrastructure, concept, SDI hierarchy and future directions. In: GEOMATICS 1980 Conference, pp. 28–37. NCC, Tehran (2001)
4. Nogueras-Iso, J., Zarazaga-Soria, F.J., Muro-Medrano, P.R.: Geographic Information Metadata for Spatial Data Infrastructures: Resources, Interoperability and Information Retrieval. Springer-Verlag New York, Inc., Secaucus (2005)
5. Fowler, M.: Analysis Patterns: Reusable Object Models. Addison-Wesley Publishing (1997)
6. Blaimer, N., Bortfeldt, A., Pankratz, G.: Patterns in Object-Oriented Analysis, Working Paper No. 451, Faculty of Business Administration and Economics, University of Hagen (Germany) (2010)
7. Silva, E.O., Lisboa Filho, J., Oliveira, A.P., Gonçalves, G.S.: Improving analysis patterns in the geographic domain using ontological meta-properties. In: 10th International Conference On Enterprise Information Systems (ICEIS), Barcelona, Espanha, pp. 256–261 (2008)
8. Hamza, H.S.: Improving analysis patterns reuse: An ontological approach. In: Proc. of Ontologies as Software Engineering Artifacts Workshop, OOPSLA 2004 (2004)
9. FGDC.: Content Standard for Digital Geospatial Metadata Workbook version 2.0. Federal Geographic Data Committee, Metadata Ad Hoc Working Group (2000)
10. ISO.: Geographic information - Metadata. ISO 19115:2003, International Organization for Standardization (2003)

11. Dublin Core Metadata Initiative (DCMI), http://www.dublincore.org
12. National Information Standards Organization - NISO (U.S.).: The Dublin Core Metadata Element Set: an American national standard. NISO Press, Bethesda, MD, USA (2001)
13. Pantoquilho, M., Raminhos, R., Araújo, J.: Analysis Patterns Specifications: Filling the Gaps. In: II VIKING PLOP, Bergen, Norway (2003)
14. Doyle, A., Reed, C.: Introduction to OGC Web Services (2001)
15. Béjar, R., Latre, M.Á., Nogueras-Iso, J., Muro-Medrano, P.R., Zarazaga-Soria, F.J.: An architectural style for spatial data infrastructures. International Journal of Geographical Information Science 23(3), 271–294 (2009)

# Towards an Integration of GRC and BPM – Requirements Changes for Compliance Management Caused by Externally Induced Complexity Drivers

Thomas Schäfer, Peter Fettke, and Peter Loos

Institute for Information Systems (IWi) at the German Research Center for Artificial Intelligence (DFKI), Campus,
Building D3₂, D-66123 Saarbrücken, Germany
`{thomas.schaefer,peter.fettke,peter.loos}@iwi.dfki.de`

**Abstract.** The paper discusses a selection of business challenges faced by organizations in context of integration between governance, risk, compliance and business process management. The focus is set on three complexity drivers for compliance, which are externally imposed on organizations by a business environment which itself is characterized by recent supervision system failures leading to major market crises as well as ongoing globalization. The examined complexity drivers are 1. heightened complexity of business processes with an increased number of process interfaces, 2. rising frequency of process changes and 3. a continuously growing amount of compliance regulations. A selection of fundamental research works is discussed to assess the visibility of the three complexity drivers, i.e. whether the authors show awareness of the selected complexity drivers implicitly or explicitly. The paper highlights a combined view on those three complexity drivers and, in consequence, derives requirements changes originating thereof for compliance management and modeling.

**Keywords:** Business Process Management, Governance, Risk, Compliance, Business Process Compliance, Complexity Drivers, Requirements Changes.

## 1    Introduction

The integrated view on Governance, Risk and Compliance (GRC) as an important concept to support the sustainability of modern organizations is gaining more and more attention in scientific research as well as business practice in recent years. A significant range of legislation has been established in this area, e.g. Sarbanes-Oxley, MiFID, Basel II, HIPAA and more. Current developments like extended financial market regulations through Basel III in the aftermath of the financial markets crisis and linked discussions in the media portend, that this trend will continue in the future.

The recent crisis revealed dramatic failures of supervisory and control functions as they are implemented today. Organizations nowadays face the challenge, that GRC efforts steadily become more complex and expensive across numerous industries.

F. Daniel et al. (Eds.): BPM 2011 Workshops, Part II, LNBIP 100, pp. 344–355, 2012.
© Springer-Verlag Berlin Heidelberg 2012

The complexity of organizations and their business processes is continuously growing, for example due to extended cooperation with external parties, dissolution of organizational boundaries or outsourcing initiatives. Concurrently we perceive a significantly increased amount and diversity of laws, policies and regulations, which have to be adhered to by various kinds of organizations. Examples like the current case of the U.S. company Cignet Health demonstrate the potentially serious impact of non-compliance. Cignet was fined 4.3 million USD because they did not provide requested information to their customers in time and thus were failing HIPAA compliance requirements [1]. Due to these environmental changes, the requirements profile for the corporate GRC function has been altered in a way, which makes it necessary to support the existing compliance and risk management functions with new methods and solutions.

Within the current paper a selection of current business challenges is discussed, which organizations face in the context of integration between GRC and BPM. The focus is set on compliance aspects of the before mentioned integration, specifically on three complexity drivers which are externally imposed on organizations by a business environment as characterized above. For this purpose, the remainder of the paper is structured as follows: Subsequent to this introduction, the domain specific concepts and terminology as they are used for the paper are laid out in section 2. The authors identify a selection of significant complexity drivers for compliance management in section 3 and derive major gaps as well as challenges resulting from these. Building upon this a selection of fundamental research works in the field of compliance management and business process management integration is examined in section 4 to assess whether the three complexity drivers are considered in these papers. The visibility of the three complexity drivers is explored, i.e. whether the authors show awareness of the selected complexity drivers implicitly or explicitly, by mentioning them or by offering solutions to manage the respective complexities. An evaluation is performed to which extent a combined view on these complexity drivers for compliance management including resulting business challenges has already been explicitly discussed in the community so far and the results are put together in an overview. Based on their findings the authors present an outlook and potential for future research in this field in section 5.

## 2    Terminology

### 2.1    Governance, Risk and Compliance

As noted before, the term "Compliance" is often referred to as part of the triple "Governance, Risk and Compliance" (GRC) in recent discussion. Hereafter follows a condensed definition of these terms and further relevant concepts as they are understood in this paper. While the authors focus on compliance as one of the core concepts of GRC, it is considered useful to clarify the distinction between each of those terms as well as the links and dependencies between them.

According to Becht et al. the term "Corporate Governance" is derived from an analogy between the government of states and the governance of corporations [2].

It describes a way of (good) responsible corporate management following all applicable legislation and generally accepted standards of diligent organizational management. Generally it can be described as a framework of policies and rules, which is applied to steer and manage an organization. Shleifer and Vishny emphasize on the shareholder perspective by observing that Coporate Governance "deals with the ways in which suppliers of finance to corporations assure themselves of getting a return on their investment."[3]

The term "risk" has been subject to comprehensive research in economic sciences. In their standard ISO 31000 (2009) the *International Organization for Standardization* defines risk as the "effect of uncertainty on objectives", where uncertainties include the potential occurrence of events and uncertainties caused by a lack of information or ambiguity. It has to be pointed out, that this definition includes both negative and positive impacts. Hence, for the current paper risk shall be interpreted as a potential deviation from a target, which was defined in a situation of incomplete information availability. Extending this, risk management shall be defined as structured process with the aim of achieving a unified and anticipating handling of risk in an organization [3]. This encompasses in the shape of an iterative risk management process specifically an assessment of risks as well as the implementation of detective, preventative and compensating controls for identified risks. During this process all identifiable risks should be reduced to a level which is consistent with the organizations individual risk appetite. In this case the result is considered economically efficient and the residual risks are accepted by responsible management.

Compliance is defined by Sadiq and Governatori  as "ensuring that business processes, operations and practice are in accordance with a prescribed and/or agreed set of norms" [4]. As such it encompasses laws and regulatory requirements, organizational policies, internal codices and guidelines as well as ethical norms in all kinds of organizations. It is important to distinguish precisely between this meaning and the usage of the term "Compliance" in a medical/psychological context, where it refers to cooperative behavior of patients and adherence to therapy. This ambiguous usage of the term requires special attention and diligence in every related literature review. Compliance management (CM) in general denotes a process for enforcing compliance by taking suitable provisions. CM strives to ensure that an organization adheres to all relevant laws and policies. Its ultimate aim is to effectively and efficiently fulfill all external and internal regulations applicable in an organizations individual business context. Responsibility for this is generally assigned to senior management.

The three individual subjects "Governance", "Risk (Management)" and "Compliance" are often merged into an integrated concept "GRC" in recent literature. In their frame of research Racz and Weippl derive a comprehensive definition based on a literature review and an online expert survey:

*"GRC is an integrated, holistic approach to organisation-wide governance, risk and compliance ensuring that an organisation acts ethically correct and in accordance with its risk appetite, internal policies and external regulations through the alignment of strategy, processes, technology and people, thereby improving efficiency and effectiveness."* [5]

## 2.2 Business Process Management

According to a recent literature review on business process management performed by Houy et al. [6], a business process can be understood as a chronological sequence of activities to fulfill a business task during which a value is delivered by transformation of materials or information. Highlighting the element of client demand in accordance with Hammer and Champy [7], business processes can be defined as sequences of intra-organizational activities which are performed to satisfy the needs of customers. Business process management (BPM) denotes the corresponding management discipline comprising a set of methods, techniques and software tools to support the design, implementation, monitoring and analysis of operational business processes in order to facilitate an optimized value creation [8]. BPM can be applied by organizations as an instrument to retain or gain competitive advantages [9]. Current research activities support an evolutionary view, where BPM itself is conducted as an iterative process following a lifecycle model to facilitate continuous improvement of business processes [10].

## 2.3 Business Process Compliance (BPC)

Conceptually, business process compliance (BPC) denotes the execution of business processes in adherence to applicable internal and external regulations and as such represents an integrated view on business process management and compliance. Figure 1 illustrates the evolution of BPM and GRC integration towards BPC in recent years.

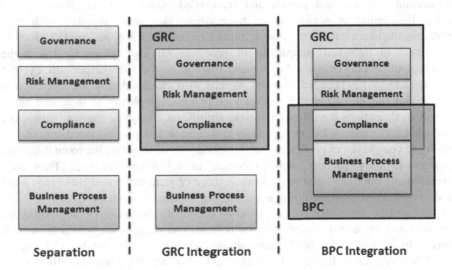

**Fig. 1.** Evolution of BPM and GRC Integration

A classification given by Kharbili et al. [11] distinguishes between three general validation mechanisms for BPC: While the "design-time" approach utilizes validation of process models during the modeling phase to identify compliance conflicts, the "runtime" approach inspects via process monitoring individual process instances during execution in order to highlight potential discrepancies towards a predefined set of rules. "Backward" validation as the third concept follows a retrospective approach and uses data and process analysis methods to extract potential compliance violations ex post.

# 3     Requirement Changes for Compliance Management

Recent experiences revealed significant weaknesses in established systems for business supervision and control. Organizations face the challenge, that GRC efforts steadily become more complex and expensive. As this can be observed specifically in the area of compliance management, the following analysis will focus on this part. We will identify three significant changes to be observed in today's business and market environments, which lead to an unprecedented level of complexity for compliance management. It is important to note that while various other sources of complexity, e.g. ambiguous business language and regulation specifications, stem from compliance management inherently, the highlighted complexity drivers are externally imposed on compliance managers and need to be treated. Two of those are related to general changes in business processes, the third one is specifically linked to one of the core matters of compliance, i.e. regulations. First of all, the complexity of organizations and their business processes in general is continuously growing with advancing globalization being one major driver for this development [12]. Extended cooperation with external parties and intensified outsourcing initiatives entail a further dissolution of organizational boundaries. This trend together with other developments like a long-term growing rate of mergers and acquisitions [13] does not only result in tightened complexity of processes, it also brings forth a higher frequency of process changes. In financial institutions the average periodic cycle of process changes has dropped from 84 months to 6 months during the last 20 years [14]. Taking this into account, beside general process complexity an increased rate of process modifications constitutes a second significant change in the way business is conducted and needs to be appropriately reflected in compliance management. The higher the complexity of processes and the more volatile they are, the more difficult it becomes to fully capture such processes in a formal structure. Thus these developments implicitly lead to a growing share of semi-structured processes which have to be adequately treated from a compliance management perspective.

Concurrently with this rising process complexity we observe a significantly increased amount and diversity of laws, policies and regulations, which have to be adhered to by various kinds of organizations. To name a few notable examples of established regulation frameworks, Sarbanes-Oxley, MiFID, Basel II, HIPAA, and MaRisk can be mentioned and the trend continues with current developments addressing extended financial market regulation, e.g. Basel III. From the authors perspective this growing plethora of legislation and internal guidelines marks a third significant source of additional complexity for compliance management in the future.

We recapitulate the three complexity drivers outlined before:

1.  Growing complexity of business processes
2.  Increased rate of business process changes
3.  Plethora of laws, regulations and policies

These developments give an indication that the requirements profile for the corporate GRC function has changed in a way, which makes it necessary to bolster existing compliance and risk management functions with new methods and solutions.

To meet the changed requirements compliance management needs to become more efficient in practice. BPM methods and specifically process modeling could potentially be utilized to support this in various ways. Past experience in the rigorously regulated financial sector and discussions with practitioners confirm that in many companies those business units responsible for compliance and those responsible for business process management are traditionally separated from an organizational perspective. A loose coupling between these functions is often implemented in the context of new process setup and process modifications by requiring compliance department input or formal sign-offs for selected items. Furthermore there is a need to transfer knowledge about new compliance requirements from compliance specialists to those organizational units who ultimately are subject to the new requirements in an efficient way. In order to assess to which extent existing research and approaches to support compliance management with business process management methods already address the issues stated above, we analyze in the following chapter a selection of well-respected publications in this area. We will inspect whether the authors explicitly refer to changed requirements in compliance management and specifically to one or more of the three complexity drivers outlined before. If so, we will point out how those are treated in the respective publication.

# 4     Consideration of Requirements Changes in Related Work

## 4.1    Selected Research Publications

A keyword search in three major citation databases (Thomson Reuters Web of Knowledge, EBSCOhost, DBLP) for combinations of "business process management", "compliance", "risk management" and "governance" was performed. Based on the results a selection of fundamental research works in the field of compliance management and business process management integration (see table 1) has been examined to assess whether the three requirements changes emphasized on in chapter 3 are taken into account in these papers. For the evaluation (see table 1), visibility of the researchers awareness of the three selected complexity drivers constitutes the central criteria. A distinction is made between "explicit" discussion of one or more of the selected complexity drivers and statements that are implicitly linked to a complexity driver. Explicit references are considered to demonstrate a stronger awareness of a complexity driver compared to implicitly supportive statements. The main focus is set on evaluating the authors awareness of the selected complexity drivers without the necessity to offer sophisticated solutions at this stage.

We will investigate how complexity drivers and changed requirements for compliance management as laid out in section 3 are reflected and take a closer look on the implications suggested by the authors where applicable. Only such research work was selected, which was regularly referred to by other authors in the given domain, generally in the sections explaining theoretical foundations and notable research in the area of business process management and compliance. A focus was set on recent papers for those authors with various research contributions in the investigated field.

## 4.2     Awareness of Complexity Drivers and Changed Requirements

Governatori and Rotolo present in [15] a formal language to express regulatory constraints with the capability to model chains of reparational obligations. While the authors illustrate selected complexity drivers they encountered during their research they focus on aspects directly linked to formal modeling. The three externally induced requirements changed under review in this paper are not discussed.

In their work [16] Schumm et al. introduce the concept of "Compliance Fragments", denoting such parts of business processes, which serve to support compliance. They develop a rule language and utilize sub-graph matching techniques to extract and highlight or hide compliance relevant activities, e.g. validation and control steps. This method enables the authors to automatically generate process models with various grades of detail, denoted "Process Views". Schumm et al. consider Process Views an apt technique to tackle the increasing size of business processes. This supports our first statement of changed requirements due to risen process complexity. References to a quickening pace for process changes or a higher amount of applicable regulations are not stated in the latter contribution.

Ly et al. present in [17] with their SeaFlows Toolset a framework for compliance verification of process models. The authors enrich process models with a layer for compliance rules expressed in a graph-based specification language. Process structures are then validated against these rules implementing design-time compliance checking. Furthermore a data-aware compliance checking component is introduced to support validation of process instances at runtime. Ly et al. focus on the implementation of the SeaFlows prototype and the related requirements for (semi-) automated compliance verification. In this context they identify growing complexity of process models, which implicitly links to a growing complexity of processes themselves, as one of the main drivers for their efforts stating that increasing process model complexity necessitates automated compliance verification. They discuss the probability of process modifications over time briefly and argue in this context that solutions need to be developed, which allow for a swift assertion of compliance during and after process changes. The latter claim implicitly supports our second complexity driver ("Change Frequency"), as a higher rate of process changes implies more efficient ways of validating processes against all relevant regulation frameworks. Still, none of the three examined complexity drivers is explicitly discussed by Ly et al. in the selected publication.

Already in 2007 Lu et al. [18] presented first concepts towards a quantitative approach for measuring compliance of business processes against a given set of control objectives. They point out that for the time being compliance is often considered a burden rather than an opportunity by companies and discuss the advantages of compliance-by-design concepts versus established retrospective reporting approaches as a potential way to alleviate this burden. The authors refer to a new set of challenges due to corporate scandals and new regulations, which implicitly aims towards the direction of requirements change no. 3 (regulation degree), but they do not further elaborate on this issue. Later Lu et al. describe the lack of sustainability as most serious drawback of established retrospective compliance approaches and highlight difficulties in adopting established compliance monitoring systems to changing legislatures. This statement supports the increasing relevance of business process change frequencies as a complexity driver. It can be stated, that the authors implicitly support two of the three changed requirements examined here, but none of these are covered explicitly in detail.

Kharbili et al. [11] performed a review on the state-of-the-art of business process compliance checking in 2008. They give an overview on approaches for design-time and run-time compliance checking - both subsumed as "forward compliance checking" due their preventive nature – as well as retrospective approaches denoted as "backward compliance checking". Although they acknowledge the relevance of formal modeling as proposed by many existing approaches, Kharbili et al. view the complexity of current solutions and prior knowledge necessary for users as a significant adoption barrier. While the authors do not elaborate explicitly on the three changed requirements examined here, they confirm a need to keep compliance costs reasonable while adapting to the complexity of ambiguous and continuously changing regulations combined with evolving business processes.

Zur Muehlen et al. [19] aim at a more strategic approach to compliance management and provide an analysis of the expressive power and representational capabilities of selected process and rule languages as well as combinations thereof. While increased process complexity or change frequencies are not covered the authors state in conformance with our changed requirement no. 3, that the pressure to adhere to a growing amount of regulations is a core driver for business demands directed towards advanced compliance management solutions.

In their *Methodical Framework for Aligning Business Processes and Regulatory Compliance* [4] Sadiq and Governatori emphasize on the challenge arising from continuously increasing obligations and regulatory requirements for organizations. This corresponds with changed requirement no. 3 concerning degree of regulation.

In a research report of the IBM Research Laboratory Liu et al. [20] present a static compliance checking framework for business process models. They propose an approach where in a first step business processes as well as compliance rules are modeled separately in a high-level language (BPEL and BSPL respectively). After this an automated transformation to lower-level formal specifications performed. The authors utilize Pi calculus and Finite State Machines for processes as well as Linear Temporal Logic for compliance rules. According to the authors the process specifications can then be verified against defined compliance rules, allowing for efficient compliance checking of large process model repositories. In this context Liu et al. refer to growing process complexity and especially highlight a growing amount of regulations to be adhered to by organizations, which correlates to two of the changed requirements under review in this paper.

Becker et al. [21] present a design-time model checking approach to support business process compliance explicitly focusing on the financial sector. In their paper they refer to all of our three identified complexity drivers. The authors acknowledge a growing complexity of business processes. They point out a high frequency of business rule changes in the examined domain as one of the most prominent complexity drivers. For the financial sector as industry subject to their review the authors observe a high level of regulation with a trend to further growth in the future.

**Table 1.** Awareness of Complexity Drivers in Selected Literature

| Publication | Year | Complexity Driver 1 "Process Complexity" | Complexity Driver 2 "Change Frequency" | Complexity Driver 3 "Degree of Regulation" | Overall Complexity Driver Awareness* |
|---|---|---|---|---|---|
| Governatori et al. [15] | 2010 | ○ | ○ | ○ | |
| Schumm et al. [16] | 2010 | ◐ | ○ | ○ | ◐ |
| Ly et al. [17] | 2010 | ◐ | ◐ | ○ | ◐◐ |
| Lu et al. [18] | 2007 | ○ | ◐ | ◐ | ◐◐ |
| Kharbili et al. [11] | 2009 | ○ | ◐ | ◐ | ◐◐ |
| Zur Muehlen / Indulska [19] | 2007 | ○ | ○ | ● | ● |
| Sadiq / Governatori [4] | 2009 | ○ | ○ | ● | ● |
| Liu et al. [20] | 2007 | ◐ | ○ | ● | ●◐ |
| Becker et. al. [21] | 2011 | ● | ● | ● | ●●● |

*Complexity Driver Awareness:*    ● - yes    ◐ - implicit    ○ - no

As demonstrated above all of the three selected complexity drivers concerning integration of business process management and compliance are supported by leading authors in this field of research. Still, the analysis revealed that although the reviewed publications in many cases implicitly support the complexity drivers and resulting requirements changes stated here, a distinct awareness for them has rarely been articulated. An explicit consideration of all three changes together and hence an overall perspective on arising consequences could only be observed in the most recent 2011 publication by Becker et al.

These findings could trigger a broader discussion on the state of requirements engineering concerning the modeling of compliance obligations in context of business process management. After certain fundamental research has been performed in recent years on how compliance obligations can be modeled, one of the future challenges will be the question of economic efficiency of existing approaches, i.e. does the benefit derived from modeling compliance and following a certain approach overcompensate its costs. For this calculation not only setup costs (training, modeling etc.) but also operational costs (adjustments, maintenance etc.) must be taken into account and potential alternatives up to ultimately not implementing measures for certain compliance regulations should be considered.

## 5    Conclusion and Outlook

In the given paper current challenges for GRC were laid out with a focus on aspects of compliance management. A need for enhancement of available solutions as well as development of new tools to cope with the continuously growing requirements concerning GRC in business practice was pinpointed. Three externally induced complexity drivers for business processes - namely growing complexity of business processes, frequent process changes and an increasing level of regulation – were examined in detail in a context of their implications on requirements changes for compliance management. A selection of leading publications in the area was reviewed in order to assess to which extent the mentioned external complexity drivers are reflected in current research. Though a partial, implicit coverage in certain publications could be elucidated a lack of distinct, express consideration of all three complexity drivers was perceived.

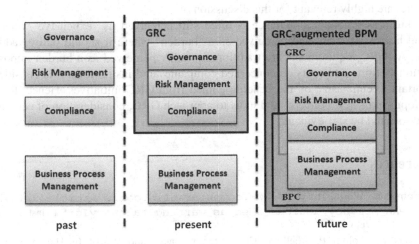

**Fig. 2.** GRC-augmented BPM

Yet the combination of these complexity drivers implies changes in the requirements for compliance management and the approaches supporting it. They shift attention towards economic aspects and questions on how to implement compliance management efficiently. The prevalent concepts for modeling compliance have to be validated against these requirements. A tighter integration between GRC and BPM might offer potential for future progress in this area. While in the past both fields were treated separately by experts focusing on their individual disciplines we perceive a process of integration today. With BPC as execution of processes in adherence to applicable regulations an important integration step is on its way. Still, integration should not stop at this point, it might go further and cover the whole GRC domain. A potential outcome could be a "GRC-augmented BPM" (see figure 2), where the individual building blocks mutually profit from each other. While in BPC processes are enhanced with compliance knowledge, established BPM concepts could be applied to improve compliance management vice versa. One might think of organizational aspects or the before mentioned considerations of economic efficiency here. Similar to the "time-to-market" concept for new products, a "time-to-user" concept could be established for new compliance obligations. There is a need for efficient methods to transfer knowledge about new compliance requirements from compliance specialists to those organizational units who ultimately are subject to the new requirements. We face the threat that if modeling compliance obligations is perceived as tedious and too expensive, organizations might opt for not modeling them any further past common textual representations which are not bidirectionally linked to relevant business processes. Currently it is still unclear in which cases the benefit of modeling compliance requirements outweighs the costs of time and resources spent for modeling and maintenance of these, i.e. under which conditions modeling compliance is economically efficient. Further research will be necessary in this area to develop suitable concepts and metrics to assess these economic aspects. Here again aspects of corporate governance as well as of risk management (e.g. risk appetite) are highly relevant for this discussion.

In business practice compliance is often still perceived as "expensive" where it should be cost-efficient and perceived as a "burden" where it should deliver added-value. As GRC requirements are traditionally rather perceived as a burden imposing additional efforts and costs on concerned companies and institutions, it is considered important to emphasize on the benefits gained from GRC initiatives. Hence, for the development of new concepts and tools to approach GRC, consideration of economic aspects should be self-evident.

# References

1. Computer World, http://www.computerworld.com/s/article/9211359/ HIPAA_privacy_actions_seen_as_warning?taxonomyId=84 (last accessed May 13, 2011)
2. Becht, M., Bolton, P., Röell, A.: Corporate governance and control. In: Handbook of the Economics of Finance, vol. 1, pp. 1–109 (2003)
3. Shleifer, A., Vishny, R.W.: A survey of Corporate Governance. The Journal of Finance LII, 737–783 (1997)
4. Sadiq, S., Governatori, G.: A Methodical Framework for Aligning Business Processes and Regulatory Compliance. In: Brocke, J., Rosemann, M. (eds.) Handbook of Business Process Management. Springer, Heidelberg (2009)
5. Racz, N., Weippl, E., Seufert, A.: A Frame of Reference for Research of Integrated Governance, Risk and Compliance (GRC). In: De Decker, B., Schaumüller-Bichl, I. (eds.) CMS 2010. LNCS, vol. 6109, pp. 106–117. Springer, Heidelberg (2010)
6. Houy, C., Fettke, P., Loos, P.: Empirical research in business process management – analysis of an emerging field of research. Business Process Management Journal 16, 619–661 (2010)
7. Hammer, M., Champy, J.: Reengineering the corporation: a manifesto for business revolution. HarperBusiness, New York (1993)

8. van der Aalst, W.M.P., ter Hofstede, A.H.M., Weske, M.: Business Process Management: A Survey. In: van der Aalst, W.M.P., ter Hofstede, A.H.M., Weske, M. (eds.) BPM 2003. LNCS, vol. 2678, pp. 1–12. Springer, Heidelberg (2003)
9. Hung, R.Y.: Business Process Management as Competitive Advantage: a Review and Empirical Study. Total Quality Management & Business Excellence 17, 21–40 (2006)
10. Scheer, A.-W., Bräbänder, E.: The Process of Business Process Management. In: vom Brocke, J., Rosemann, M. (eds.) Handbook on Business Process Management 2 - Strategic Alignment, Governance, People and Culture, pp. 239–265. Springer, Berlin (2010)
11. El Kharbili, M., de Medeiros, A.K.A., Stein, S., van der Aalst, W.M.P.: Business Process Compliance Checking: Current State and Future Challenges. In: Loos, P., Nüttgens, M., Turowski, K., Werth, D. (eds.) MobIS, vol. 141, pp. 107–113. GI, Saarbrücken (2008)
12. Schwandt, A.: Measuring organizational complexity and its impact on organizational performance – A comprehensive conceptual model and empirical study, p. 274. Technical University of Berlin, Berlin (2009)
13. Gaughan, P.A.: Mergers, acquisitions, and corporate restructurings. Wiley (2010)
14. Ammon, R., Gebauer, B., Jobst, D.: Business Rule Engines within Enterprise Platforms. In: Conference Business Rule Engines within Enterprise Platforms (2005)
15. Governatori, G., Rotolo, A.: A Conceptually Rich Model of Business Process Compliance. In: 7th Asia-Pacific Conference on Conceptual Modelling (APCCM 2010), vol. 110, pp. 3–12. ACS (2010)
16. Schumm, D., Leymann, F., Streule, A.: Process Views to Support Compliance Management in Business Processes. In: Buccafurri, F., Semeraro, G. (eds.) EC-Web 2010. LNBIP, vol. 61, pp. 131–142. Springer, Heidelberg (2010)
17. Ly, L.T., Knuplesch, D., Rinderle-Ma, S., Göser, K., Pfeifer, H., Reichert, M., Dadam, P.: SeaFlows Toolset – Compliance Verification Made Easy for Process-Aware Information Systems. In: Soffer, P., Proper, E. (eds.) CAiSE Forum 2010. LNBIP, vol. 72, pp. 76–91. Springer, Heidelberg (2011)
18. Lu, R., Sadiq, S., Governatori, G.: Compliance Aware Business Process Design. In: ter Hofstede, A.H.M., Benatallah, B., Paik, H.-Y. (eds.) BPM Workshops 2007. LNCS, vol. 4928, pp. 120–131. Springer, Heidelberg (2008)
19. zur Muehlen, M., Indulska, M., Kamp, G.: Business Process and Business Rule Modeling Languages for Compliance Management: A Representational Analysis. In: International Conference on Conceptual Modeling, pp. 127–132. Australian Computer Society (2007)
20. Liu, Y., Müller, S., Xu, K.: A static compliance-checking framework for business process models. IBM Systems Journal 46, 335–361 (2007)
21. Becker, J., Philipp, B., Delfmann, P., Eggert, M., Weiss, B.: Supporting Business Process Compliance in Financial Institutions - A Model-Driven Approach. In: Wirtschaftsinformatik 2011, Zurich, pp. 355–364 (2011)

# Designing an Automated Audit Tool for the Targeted Risk Exposure Reduction

Yurdaer Doganata and Francisco Curbera

IBM T J Watson Research Center, 19 Skyline Drive, Hawthorne NY 10532
{yurdaer,curbera}@us.ibm.com

**Abstract.** The risk exposure of an organization is the cost of being non-compliant for all process instances that are subject to auditing and it can be reduced by auditing internal controls for every process instance, detecting and eliminating the cause of non-compliance. This paper discusses the design consideration for an automated auditing tool to achieve the desired level of risk exposure reduction. A method is provided to measure the effectiveness and the limits of such tools and adjust their performance for various risk exposure levels.

**Keywords:** continuous assurance, risk management, risk exposure, automated auditing, internal controls.

## 1 Introduction

Detecting compliance failures help organizations better control their operations and remain competitive. The quality of product and services can not be ensured in a business if the processes do not conform to design goals and comply with the rules and regulations. Moreover, organizations may be subject to serious financial penalty as well as civil and penal consequences if they fail to comply with established guidelines, rules and regulations. Hence, non-compliance may have severe consequences and needs to be managed either by correcting violations or reducing the associated risk. Companies invest significantly on detecting compliance failures to ensure governance and manage risk. The cost of reducing the risk of being non-compliant could run into millions of dollars [1]. AMR Research survey reveals that the spending of companies on governance and risk management and compliance expected to grow to $29.8 billion in 2010, up nearly %4 over the $28.7 billion spent in 2009 [2].

Internal controls can provide a reasonable assurance that the goal of an organization is met and for some organizations they are required by law. In order to manage the risk associated with compliance failures and for the continuous assurance of business goals, organizations use Enterprise Risk Management framework such as COSO ERM [3]-[5]. ERM framework provides for a systematic way of creating internal control points as part of audit and compliance activities.

In completely managed processes the compliance against internal controls can be checked by using process automation software. In the absence of process automation

F. Daniel et al. (Eds.): BPM 2011 Workshops, Part II, LNBIP 100, pp. 356–369, 2012.

software that can control and record who did what and when, the compliance check is a costly and time consuming task performed manually by auditors [6]. Automated continuous auditing systems, on the other hand, can provide for an almost cost-free auditing opportunity if the initial cost of building such a system is excluded. Such a system can run continuously and performs evaluation for all process instances without adding to the cost of auditing. While continuous auditing systems eliminate or reduce the dependency on audit professionals, they are not infallible. The tools that are built to realize automated continuous auditing rely on information extraction from process events, data and documents, including e-mail transactions between the people within the organizations. The information about the processes extracted from these sources can contain errors and, due to these errors, the audit results may be faulty. Moreover, testing certain compliance conditions requires a level of text analysis that is not yet available in automated systems. Hence, the automated systems can perform fast and extensive auditing of the internal control points at the cost of making mistakes. As a result, some compliance failures may be missed while some other cases that are compliant may be declared non-compliant.

The focus of this paper is to discuss the factors that impact the effectiveness of continuous assurance with automated audit tools. The subject is important for organizations which need to determine how much they should invest to remain compliant. This paper aims to help understanding the characteristics of the operational environment that affect the efficiency of automated tools, and in particular the conditions that necessitate hiring experts for manual auditing to avoid compliance failures. Ultimately, the companies expect to reduce the risk exposure at least as much as they spend for compliance assurance. Therefore, they need to know how they can optimize the return on their investment.

Another aspect of the research presented here is to provide for a mathematical foundation of designing automated audit tools that reduces the risk of being non-compliant to the targeted level. The performance of an automated audit tool depends on various parameters that determine its ability to differentiate compliant from non-compliant process instances. Hence, the design considerations include how to select the parameters to affect the performance of the tool to achieve the desired level of risk exposure reduction.

The paper is organized as follows. After the related work, in section 3 the risk exposure in an organization for running potentially non-compliant processes is defined. In section 4, the method of using automated auditing tools along with limited auditor intervention to reduce the risk exposure is described. The effectiveness measure of such tools are also introduced and calculated in this section. Section 5 mainly focuses on designing an auditing tool with the desired effectiveness.

## 2     Related Work

The effect of using automated auditing tools on detecting compliance failures is investigated in [7] and a methodology is proposed to measure the effectiveness. The approach is based on evaluating all process instances by using the automated audit machine and asking experts randomly re-evaluate some of the instances marked as compliant and non-compliant by the automated machine. As a result, it is shown that the average number of non-compliant instances detected can be increased by a factor if the automated auditing tool is utilized. The improvement factor which is the effectiveness measure is found as a function of sensitivity and specificity of the tool. In [8], the risk of being non-compliant is measured and the cost of reducing the risk by performing internal audits with the help of automated audit tools is calculated.

This paper expands the results of [7][8] in two areas. Firstly, the feasibility analysis of building an automated auditing tool to achieve the desired reduction in risk exposure in an environment where the prevalence of non- compliance is known is presented. Secondly, a method to design an automated auditing tool to achieve the targeted performance is introduced and the design considerations are discussed.

The problem of using automated audit machines to determine the compliance failures is equivalent to determining the prevalence of a medical condition through screening the population by using a medical diagnostic test which is not a gold standard [9] [10]. The statistical methods used in epidemiology are also applicable in detecting compliance failures and building continuous assurance systems.

## 3    The Risk of Being Non-compliant

As mentioned in the introduction section, there is a cost associated with non-compliant process instances. The cost of being non-compliant is determined by the amount of penalties that the company will pay for not complying with the rules and regulations as well as the cost of not being able to ensure quality and remain competitive. If the processes are executed with the potential to violate the compliance rules, the organization that executes these processes takes a risk. Compliance officers are responsible to determine the amount of risk exposure for being non-compliant and find ways to minimize this risk.

Risk exposure of an organization can be defined as the cost of being non-compliant for all process instances that are subject to auditing. It is proportional with the number of process instances and the penalty paid for every non-compliant case. The risk of running potentially non-compliant processes can be reduced by auditing internal controls for every process instance, detecting and eliminating the cause of non-compliance. While risk exposure can be completely eliminated by auditing every process instance, this may not be a cost effective solution, since manual auditing incurs a significant cost.

The risk exposure in an organization for running potentially non-compliant processes is expressed as:

$$\Re = Np\,\omega r$$

where $\omega$ is the ratio of the process instances externally audited, $N$ is the total size of the process instances, $p$ is the prevalence of non-compliance for the population and $r$ is the penalty to be paid per non-compliant instance. Assuming early detection and intervention to correct failures on some or all the non-compliant process instances, the prevalence of non-compliance is improved since thee overall number of non-compliant instances is reduced. If $\lambda$ is the ratio of the process instances that can be audited manually, then the average number of non-compliant instances that can be fixed is found as $\lambda.N.p$. Hence, the new prevalence of non-compliance after manual auditing is reduced to $p(1-\lambda)$ where $0 \leq \lambda \leq 1$.

One of the challenges of reducing the risk exposure is to decide how much budget should be allocated for auditing. Budget allocation must be sufficient enough to justify the investment by reducing the cost associated with risk exposure. In order for the investment to make financial sense, the return of investment must be at least positive. In this case, the return is defined as the amount by which the risk exposure is reduced. A company is expected to reduce the risk exposure at least as much as it spends for compliance assurance.

## 4    Effectiveness of an Automated Audit Tool to Ensure Compliance

In order to measure the effectiveness of an automated audit tool, we consider a methodology that enables detecting the largest number of non-compliant instances within a budget constraint. The methodology is based on evaluating all process instances by using the automated audit machine and asking experts to randomly re-evaluate some of the instances marked as compliant and non-compliant by the automated machine. We assume that the budget permits the expert evaluation of only $M = M_1 + M_2$ cases. Here $M_1$ is the number of cases marked as non-compliant and $M_2$ is the number of cases marked as compliant by the audit machine. This way the sample space that the experts operate is reduced. The effectiveness of the proposed methodology can be measured by comparing the expected number of non-compliant process instances detected. If the number is higher than what experts would have determined under budget constraint without using the methodology, then we can conclude that the methodology improves the auditing process in general.

The analysis of this methodology is detailed in [7] and it is shown that using automated auditing tools and the methodology described above improves the detection of non-compliance instances by a factor of $\chi$ as below:

$$\chi = \frac{1}{p(1-\psi)+\psi} \tag{1}$$

where

$$\psi = (1-\theta)/\eta \tag{2}$$

and $\theta$ is the specificity and $\eta$ is the sensitivity of the tool and $p$ is the prevalence of non-compliance instance in the population. Equation (1) reveals that if the sum of the sensitivity and the specificity of the tool is 1, then $\psi = 1$ and there is no improvement. A tool with $\psi = 1$ may not help detecting all non-compliant process instances since the improvement factor is $\chi = 1$. On the other hand, for $\psi < 1$, the improvement factor $\chi > 1$, hence the detection of non-compliance instances can be improved by a factor, $\chi$, using auditing tools and limited manual auditing, as expressed in equation (1).

Note that the improvement factor depends on the prevalence of non-compliance, sensitivity and the specificity of the auditing tool. This is an improvement over what can be done manually on limited set of process instances. Due to budget constraints, the set is usually much less than the total number of process instances. Hence, by using the methodology described in the previous section and the automated audit tool, the prevalence of non-compliance can be reduced by a factor of $\lambda.\chi.p$ where $0 \le \lambda \le 1$ is the ratio of the process instances that can be audited manually within the budget constraint.

By detecting and fixing some of non-compliant cases within the set of all process instances, the prevalence of non-compliance is improved since there is less number of non-compliant instances after the detected non-compliant instances are fixed. As a result, the new prevalence of non-compliance is found as follows:

$$p' = p(1-\lambda\chi) = p(1-\frac{\lambda}{p(1-\psi)+\psi}) \quad for \quad \lambda\chi \le 1 \tag{3}$$

Since the risk exposure is proportional to the prevalence, then the percent of reduction in risk exposure, $\Phi$, can be found as $100\lambda\chi$.

$$\Phi = 100(\frac{\lambda}{p(1-\psi)+\psi}) \quad for \quad \lambda \le p(1-\psi)+\psi \tag{4}$$

In other words, if the risk exposure has to be reduced by $\Phi\%$ then (4) has to be satisfied. Equation (4) has some practical implications. Desired reduction percentage may not be achieved due to the constraint on $\lambda$, the ratio of the process instances that can be audited manually within the budget constraint and $\psi$, the performance measure of the tool for a given prevalence of non-compliance, $p$. This means that for a given $p$, it may not be possible to build a tool that could reduce the risk at a desired level. Fig. 1 shows the risk exposure reduction percentage as a function of the performance of the audit tool, $\psi$. Hence, in order to reduce the risk exposure to the desired level for a given prevalence $p$, $\lambda$ and $\psi$ values should be selected as plotted in Fig. 1 based on equation (4). The values of $\lambda$ and $\psi$ determine the operating point where $\lambda$ is controlled by the number of manually audited process instances and $\psi$ is related to the performance measure of the tool which is tunable. Fig. 1 shows that risk exposure is reduced more with higher $\lambda$ values and lower $\psi$ values. As an example, when the prevalence of non-compliance is, $p=0.3$, then the risk exposure can be reduced 20% provided that the operating point is $\lambda=0.1$ and $\psi=0.3$. Since $\lambda$ is the ratio of the process instances that can be audited manually within the budget constraint, it is directly proportional with the cost of hiring auditors for manual auditing. $\psi$, on the other hand, is related to the sensitivity and the specificity of the automated audit tool and there is a cost associated with building tools with desired performance measures. Hence, the reduction in risk exposure must be large enough to cover the cost of hiring experts and tuning automated auditing tool for the desired performance.

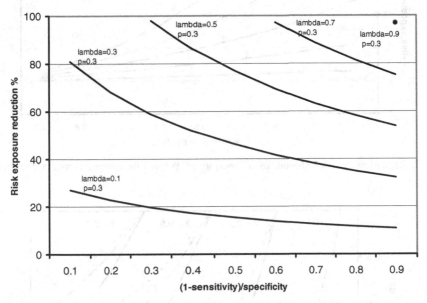

**Fig. 1.** Reduction of risk exposure as a function of $\psi$ for different $\lambda$ values when prevalence is 0.3

Figure 1 shows that risk exposure is reduced most with higher values of $\lambda$. This is expected since $\lambda$ is related to the number of process instances manually audited by experts that are labeled as non-compliant by the auditing tool. As $\lambda$ increases, the number of actually non-compliant process instances in the system is reduced along with the risk. In the example depicted by Fig. 1, when $\lambda = 0.9$, i.e., 90% of all process instances labeled non-compliant examined by experts, and the *(1-sensitivity)/specificity* of the audit tool is 0.9, the risk exposure is almost completely eliminated. This is the case when either the sensitivity or the specificity of the tool is very high, hence almost all the process instances labeled non-compliant are actually non-compliant and they are all detected and eliminated by experts.

Fig. 2, on the other hand, shows the effect of prevalence of non-compliance on the risk exposure reduction when $\lambda$ is constant. The designers of risk management systems need to know how the sensitivity and the specificity values of the automated tool should be tuned to reduce the exposure to the desired amount when the prevalence of non-compliance is constant.

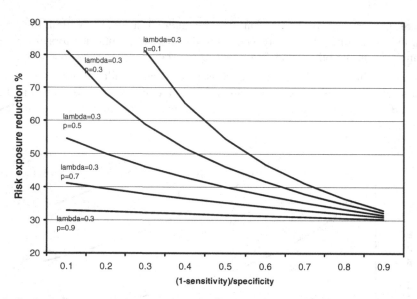

**Fig. 2.** Reduction in risk exposure as a function of $\psi$ for different prevalence values when $\lambda = 0.3$

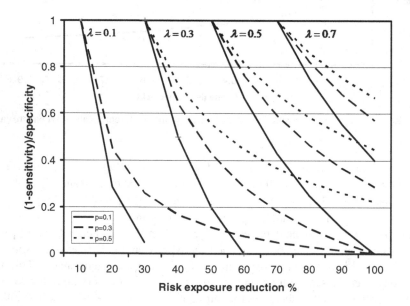

**Fig. 3.** $\psi = (1\text{-sensitivity})/\text{specificity}$ as a function of desired level of risk exposure reduction

Achieving the desired risk exposure reduction for a given prevalence of non-compliance may not be possible with an automated audit tool, if the sensitivity and the specificity measures of the tool cannot be tuned. Fig. 3 demonstrates this fact for different $\lambda$ and prevalence, $p$, values. As an example for $\lambda = 0.3$ and $p=0.1$, represented as the solid line in the second group of curves, the risk exposure reduction cannot be more than 60% no matter how good the auditing tool is. On the other hand, if $p=0.1$, reduction in risk exposure can be increased to 70% by adjusting the $\psi$ level to 0.2. This means that even if the sensitivity of the tool is 1, i.e., the tool is capable of identifying all actual non-compliant cases, the specificity of the tool, i.e., the proportions of negatives (compliant cases) which are correctly identified must be larger than 0.8. Since $\psi \leq 0.2$ can only be satisfied when specificity is greater than 0.8 if sensitivity is 1.

# 5    Designing an Auditing Tool for the Desired Exposure Reduction

Fig. 3 shows the relationship between the performance of the auditing tool and the desired level of risk exposure reduction. This can be used as a guideline in designing auditing tools. The sensitivity and the specificity measures of such a tool can directly be computed using the relationship depicted in Fig. 3. As an example, in an environment where the prevalence of non-compliance is 0.1 and the ratio of the manually audited processes is 0.2, by using equation (3) which is plotted in Figure 9, the $\psi$ value is found as a function of risk exposure reduction factor , $\Phi$, as

$$\psi = (\frac{200 - \Phi}{9\Phi}) \qquad (5)$$

Therefore, for $\Phi = 50\%$ risk exposure reduction, $\psi$ is found as 150/450 = 1/3 or $\eta = 3(1 - \theta)$. Hence, if an auditing tool is designed with the right specificity and sensitivity, then the risk exposure can be reduced by 50%. The question of how to design an automated audit tool with the right specificity and the sensitivity ratios is addressed in this section.

As defined in the previous section, sensitivity is the proportion of actual positives that are correctly identified and specificity is the proportion of actual negatives that are correctly identified. Therefore, the sensitivity and the specificity of the automated tool are expressed as follows:

$$\eta : Sensitivity = TP / (TP + FN) = \Pr(F = 1 / I = 1) \qquad (6)$$

$$\theta : Specificity = TN / (TN + FP) = \Pr(F = 0 / I = 0) \qquad (7)$$

where $F$ indicates what the tool observes and $I$ indicates what the actual state is. So, when ($F=1$, $I=1$), the tool observes a positive when the sample is actually positive. Similarly, ($F=0$, $I=1$) indicates that the tool observes a negative while the actual sample is positive.

Designing an auditing tool with the desired sensitivity and specificity levels requires the understanding of how the sensitivity and specificity measures are controlled. This depends on the definition of internal controls and the methodology used by the tool to detect compliance failures. This is explained further with an example below.

The internal control points of firewall rule revalidation process (FWRR) can be used to understand how to design an automated audit tool with the desired level of performance measures [7][14]. The FWRR process is developed particularly for e-business hosting companies who manage customer machines and make sue that they are not hacked. The purpose is to ensure that proper firewall rules are implemented and the customer is informed. FWRR ensures both the e-hosting account representatives and the customers understand what rules exist in the customer environment and ensure customer is aware of existing deviations from best practices defined by the e-hosting security policy. If not executed properly, customers are at risk for or not being made aware of what protocols are in place and required for the support of their environment. As a result, the e-hosting company may be held liable for insecure activities, if the customers is not informed of and signs off on the risk involved.

In FWRR process, the information security advisor reviews the firewall rulesets and modifies as needed before he sends the ruleset to the account team representative. The ruleset is then sent to the customer for validation. One of the internal controls is to check if the account team has sent the firewall ruleset to the customer within five days after the account team received it from the information security advisor. The account team sends the rulesets to the customers as an e-mail attachment. The auditing tools checks all the e-mails sent within 5 days after the ruleset is created and determine if a member of the account team send an e-mail to the customer for the purpose of revalidating the firewall rulesets.   The decision is based on extracting some features of the e-mail and using these features to calculate the likelihood of one of the following hypotheses:

$H_0$: The email is from Account team to customer

$H_1$: The email is NOT from account team to customer

Here $H_0$ is the null hypothesis and $H_1$ is the alternative hypothesis. A true positive, $TP$, is rejecting $H_0$ when $H_1$ is valid. Similarly a false negative, $FN$, is accepting $H_0$ when $H_1$ is valid. Hence the sensitivity $\eta$ and the specificity $\theta$ of the auditing tool is expressed as:

$$\eta = \Pr(reject \ H_0 | H_1 \ is \ valid) \tag{8}$$

$$\theta = \Pr(accept \ H_0 | H_0 \ is \ valid) \tag{9}$$

In order to decide if an e-mail is from the account team to the customer regarding annual Firewall rule revalidation, all the e-mail that are sent from Account Team within 5 days after the ruleset is created to the customer is analyzed. The decision is based on the text analysis of the body and the subject of the e-mail, the content of the "To:' and "From:" fields. The body, subject, from and to fields constitute the salient features of an e-mail. As a result of analyzing these salient features, the e-mail is rated by assigning a number based on the features that are found in the e-mail. The selected features should help differentiating between a null hypothesis and an alternative one.

The rate of an e-mail, $T$, depends on the weights assigned to each observed feature and can be expressed as:

$$T = \sum_{i=1}^{N} c_{i1}F_i + c_{i0}(1-F_i) \qquad c_i \in \Re, \quad F_i \in \{0 , 1\} \tag{10}$$

Here $F_i$ is binary variable which is equal to "1" if the $i^{th}$ feature exists and can be extracted from the e-mail, "0" otherwise and $c_i$ is the associated weight of the feature. Hence, if a salient feature is observed, the rate of the e-mail increased by the associated weight $c_{i0}$. If the salient feature does not exist, on the other hand, then the rating is reduced by $c_{i1}$. As an example, the features of the e-mail that is sent from a member of the account team to the customer may contain the features listed in Table 1. Each feature has a certain weight in determining the type of the e-mail. The weights of the features associated with the e-mail sent to the customer are shown below:

**Table 1.** The salient features of the e-mail used in hypotheses testing

| $i$ | Features of the e-mail | $c_{i1}$ | $c_{i0}$ |
|---|---|---|---|
| 1 | The e-mail address in the FROM: field belongs to a member of account team | 10 | -10 |
| 2 | The e-mail address in the TO: field belongs to the customer | 20 | -20 |
| 3 | Subject contains the following key words: "Annual", "rule", "revalidation" | 10 (for each keyword) | -10 (for each keyword) |
| 4 | The body contains the following key words: "eBH security policy", "rulesets", "validate" | 10(for each keyword) | -10(for each keyword) |
| 5 | The body has an attachment | 10 | -50 |

In this example, the value of $T$ is distributed between 90 and -130. If an e-mail contains all the features listed in Table 1, it is rated as 90. If none of the features are observed, then it is rated as -130. The rate variable $T$ can be assumed to have beta distribution $Beta(\alpha, \beta)$ without lack of generality because $Beta(\alpha, \beta)$ is a flexible family of distribution and a wide range of density shapes can be derived by changing the associated parameters of a beta distribution [13]. Hence, the distribution of $T$ is assumed to be $Beta_{H_0}(\alpha_0, \beta_0)$ for null hypothesis and $Beta_{H_1}(\alpha_1, \beta_1)$ for the alternative hypothesis where the $(\alpha, \beta)$ values depend on weights $c_i$ of selected feature. Hence, achieving the auditing tool performance depends on selecting the feature weights appropriately.

The audit tool calculates the value of $T$ for every e-mail and classifies them based on the null hypothesis $H_0$ or alternative hypothesis $H_1$. The decision regions for the tool to classify an e-mail as the one sent by the account team to the customer is defined by the following probabilities:

$$\Pr(reject \ H_0) = \Pr(T \leq T_0) \quad and \quad \Pr(accept \ H_0) = \Pr(T > T_0) \tag{11}$$

where $T_0$ is the decision threshold. The probability of accepting or rejecting the null hypothesis can be found by using the cumulative density function of $T$:

$$\Pr(T \leq T_0 \mid H_0 \ \ is \ \ valid) = I_{T_0}(\alpha_0, \beta_0) = \frac{Beta(T_0; \alpha_0, \beta_0)}{Beta(\alpha_0, \beta_0)} = \frac{\displaystyle\int_{T_{min}}^{T_0} t^{(\alpha_0-1)}(1-t)^{(\beta_0-1)}dt}{\displaystyle\int_{T_{min}}^{T_{max}} t^{(\alpha_0-1)}(1-t)^{(\beta_0-1)}dt} \tag{12}$$

where the cumulative density function $I_{T_0}(\alpha_1, \beta_1)$ is called the regularized incomplete beta function and clearly for $T = T_{max}$, $I_{T_{mac}}(\alpha_1, \beta_1) = 1$. In Figure 4, the probabilities that the threshold is less than $T^*$ under null and alternative hypothesis are shown as $I_{T^*}(\alpha_0, \beta_0)$ and $I_{T^*}(\alpha_1, \beta_1)$ respectively.

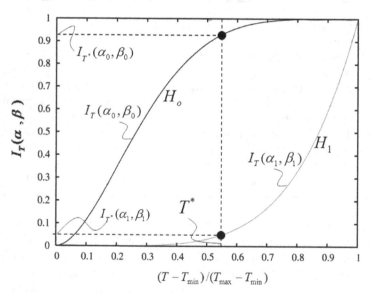

**Fig. 4.** The regularized incomplete beta function under null and alternative hypothesis

The sensitivity and the specificity of the tool can now be expressed in terms of the cumulative density function for the selected threshold $T^*$ as

$$\eta = \Pr(reject \ H_0 \mid H_1 \ \ is \ \ valid) = 1 - I_{T^*}(\alpha_1, \beta_1) \tag{13}$$

$$\theta = \Pr(accept \ H_0 \mid H_0 \ \ is \ \ valid) = I_{T^*}(\alpha_0, \beta_0) \tag{14}$$

Hence the equation for $\psi$ to achieve the targted level of risk reduction is found in terms of $\alpha_0, \alpha_1, \beta_0, \beta_1$ and $T^*$ as:

$$\psi = (1-\theta)/\eta = (1-I_{T^*}(\alpha_0, \beta_0))/(1-I_{T^*}(\alpha_1, \beta_1)) \tag{15}$$

Using equation **(10)** and the fact that the distribution of $T$ is *beta*, the first and the second moments of $T$ are expressed as:

$$\bar{T} = E(T) = \frac{\alpha}{\alpha + \beta} = \sum_i (c_{i0} p_{i0} + c_{i1} p_{i1}) \tag{16}$$

$$\bar{S}^2 = Var(T) = \frac{\alpha\beta}{(\alpha + \beta)^2 (\alpha + \beta + 1)} = \sum_i (c_{i0}^2 p_{i0} + c_{i1}^2 p_{i1}) + \bar{T}^2 \tag{17}$$

where $p_{i0}$ denotes the probability that $i^{th}$ feature $F_i$ does not exist and the $p_{i1}$ denotes that $F_i$ exists in the sample. Hence, the parameters of the beta distribution are estimated by using the mean $\bar{T}$ and the variance $\bar{S}$ of $\bar{T}$ as follows:

$$\alpha = \bar{T}(\frac{\bar{T}(1-\bar{T})}{\bar{S}^2} - 1), \quad \beta = (1-\bar{T})(\frac{\bar{T}(1-\bar{T})}{\bar{S}^2} - 1) \tag{18}$$

Equation **(18)** shows that $\alpha$, $\beta$ can be expressed as a function of feature coefficients by using **(16)** and **(17)**. Hence:

$$\alpha = f_\alpha(\overline{C}_0, \overline{C}_1), \quad \beta = f_\beta(\overline{C}_0, \overline{C}_1) \tag{19}$$

where $\overline{C}_0 = [c_{00} c_{01} \ \cdots \ c_{0N}]$, $\overline{C}_1 = [c_{10} c_{11} \ \cdots \ c_{1N}]$ and $c_{0i}$, $c_{1i}$ are the feature wights. Similarly, the desired level of risk reduction can also be expressed as function of feature coefficients from **(15)** and **(19)**.

$$\psi = f_\psi(\overline{C}_0, \overline{C}_1, T^*) \tag{20}$$

Note that distribution of the features $F_i$ can be estimated by using the labeled e-mail samples for the null $H_0$ and the alternative $H_1$ hypotheses. As an example, if there are 100 e-mails labeled as AT2CUST "From account team to customer" and 95 of these e-mails have attachments, then $p_{5,1} = 0.95$. Similarly, if only 20 e-mails out of 100 that are labeled otherwise, $p_{5,0} = 0.2$ is found. If the statistics of $T$ under null hypothesis $H_0$ is used, then equation **(18)** yields $(\alpha_0, \beta_0)$, otherwise, it yields $(\alpha_1, \beta_1)$.

  Once the performance indicator of the tool $\psi$ is expressed in terms of the feature weights, designing the optimal auditing tool is reduced to solving the following non-linear optimization problem:

$$\max_{c_0, c_1 \in \Re} \{\psi\} = f_\psi(\overline{C}_0, \overline{C}_1, T^*) \tag{21}$$

subject to

$$\alpha_0 = f_{\alpha_0}(C_0, C_1) > 0 \tag{22}$$

$$\alpha_1 = f_{\alpha_1}(C_0, C_1) > 0 \tag{23}$$

$$\beta_0 = f_{\beta_0}(C_0, C_1) > 0 \tag{24}$$

$$\beta_1 = f_{\beta_1}(C_0, C_1) > 0 \tag{25}$$

$$I_{T^*}(\alpha_1, \beta_1) < T_{FN} \tag{26}$$

$$1 - I_{T^*}(\alpha_0, \beta_o) < T_{FP} \tag{27}$$

where $T_{FN}$ is the threshold for false negative and $T_{FP}$ is the threshold for false positive.

If the maximum value of $\psi$ found as a solution of (21) is less than the value that satisfies the desired level of risk exposure reduction $\Phi$ found in (3), then there exists no solution. This means that an automated auditing tool with the targeted performance cannot be built. Otherwise, the solution of (21) yields a set of coefficients $c_i$ that would help achieving the targeted risk exposure reduction if applied in rating each e-mail as described in equation (10). In addition, a decision threshold for classifying the e-mail is found as the solution of (26) and (27).

# 6    Concluding Remarks

The mathematical foundation described in this paper can be used to determine the effectiveness of an auditing tool to detect the compliance status of internal controls. The effectiveness depends on the prevalence of non-compliance and the budget constraints that limits the use of expert auditors. Hence, before the effectiveness is calculated, statistically significant number of process instances should be labeled to estimate prevalence of non-compliance. The effectiveness of the tool is measured by the increase in the number of non-compliant instances detected by the experts after the tool eliminates the instances that are compliant. Hence, the auditing tool helps the experts to detect more non-compliant instances with less effort. This improves compliance without increasing the budget for expert auditing.

In addition to measuring the effectiveness of automated auditing tools, it is also important to understand the limitations of the tool and the factors to be considered for designing a tool with the desired performance. The design parameters depend on the features of the control point and the extraction of these features often non-deterministic. When there is no certainty about the observed features of business artifacts, a decision about the compliance is made by using statistical hypothesis testing. Hence, the design of the automated audit tool requires selecting the right features around the key control points and estimating their statistical properties.

In this paper, the problem of finding the optimum weights for the features of the business artifacts that are related to the internal controls is reduced to a non-linear optimization problem. This work is focusing on selecting the optimal weights of the features. Hence, features are assumed to be known. The problem of selecting the features related the internal control optimally is left as a future work.

# References

1. Greengard, S.: Compliance Software's Bonus Benefits. Business Finance Magazine (February 2004)
2. Gartner: Simplifying Compliance: Best Practices and Technology, French Caldwell, Business Process Management Summit (2005)
3. Enterprise Risk Management Integrated Framework, Committee of Sponsoring Organizations of the Treadway Commission (COSO), Jersey City, NJ (2004)
4. COSO (2009) Guidance on monitoring internal control systems. American Institute of Certified Public Accountants
5. COSO – Committee of sponsoring organizations of the treadway commission, http://www.coso.org
6. AMR Research: The Governance, Risk Management, and Compliance Spending Report (2010)
7. Doganata, Y., Curbera, F.: Effect of Using Automated Auditing Tools on Detecting Compliance Failures in Unmanaged Processes. In: Dayal, U., Eder, J., Koehler, J., Reijers, H.A. (eds.) BPM 2009. LNCS, vol. 5701, pp. 310–326. Springer, Heidelberg (2009)
8. Doganata Y., Curbera F.: A method of calculating the cost of reducing the risk exposure of non-compliant process instances. In: Proceedings of 1st ACM Workshop on Information Security Governance, WISG 2009, pp. 7–9 (2009)
9. Joseph, L., Gyorkos, T.W., Coupal, L.: Bayesian estimation of disease prevalence and the parameters of diagnostic tests in the absence of a gold standard. American Journal of Epidemiology 141, 263–271 (1995)
10. Enøe, C., Georgiadis, M.B., Wesley, O.J.: Estimation of sensitivity and specificity of diagnostic tests and disease prevalence when the true disease state is unknown. Preventive Veterinary Medicine 45, 61–81 (2000)
11. Hagerty, J., Hackbush, J., Gaughan, D., Jacaobson, S.: The Governance, Risk Management, and Compliance Spending Report, 2008-2009. AMR Research Report (March 25, 2008)
12. Corfield, B.: Managing the cost of compliance, http://justin-taylor.net/webdocs/tip_of_the_iceberg.pdf
13. Katsis, A.: Sample size determination of binomial data with the presence of misclassification. Metrika 63, 323–329 (2005)
14. Mukhi, N.K.: Approaches towards Dealing with Complex Systems Configuration. In: Meersman, R., Dillon, T., Herrero, P. (eds.) OTM 2010. LNCS, vol. 6428, pp. 35–37. Springer, Heidelberg (2010)

# A Noisy 10GB Provenance Database

You-Wei Cheah[1], Beth Plale[1], Joey Kendall-Morwick[1], David Leake[1],
and Lavanya Ramakrishnan[2]

[1] School of Informatics and Computing, Indiana University, Bloomington IN
[2] Lawrence Berkeley National Lab, Berkeley, CA
{yocheah,plale,jmorwick,leake}@cs.indiana.edu,
lramakrishnan@lbl.gov

**Abstract.** Provenance of scientific data is a key piece of the metadata record for the data's ongoing discovery and reuse. Provenance collection systems capture provenance on the fly, however, the protocol between application and provenance tool may not be reliable. Consequently, the provenance record can be partial, partitioned, and simply inaccurate. We use a workflow emulator that models faults to construct a large 10GB database of provenance that we know is noisy (that is, has errors). We discuss the process of generating the provenance database, and show early results on the kinds of provenance analysis enabled by the large provenance.

**Keywords:** Data provenance, scientific workflows, provenance quality, case-based reasoning.

## 1  Introduction

Data provenance provides the lineage or history of how data is generated. Provenance information is valuable in scientific datasets because it may be the only source of comprehensive information about how an e-Science data product was arrived at. Because the scientific workflow development process involves scientists refining their workflows repeatedly over time, provenance can also help scientists track their decisions and enhance the process of finding the optimum workflow. Moreover, provenance supports experiment reproducibility and reuse of scientific data and can contribute to assessments of the quality of a data set [19]. With the increase in awareness of the importance of preserving society's investment in data driven research, the need for useful data provenance has become increasingly critical.

Research on provenance in scientific workflows has focused on provenance capture and management, resulting in systems such as Karma [18] and provenance support in workflow tools such as Kepler [11] and Pegasus [7]. In order to capture provenance, workflow engines must be instrumented or logs mined. Provenance traces are stored and managed using an internal provenance data model, often with interoperability support using the Open Provenance Model (OPM) [13].

Provenance is often not complete. The protocol between application and the provenance storage can be unreliable [4]. Additionally, the entire category of semi-structured workflows assumes there are gaps in the provenance record. Semi-structured

F. Daniel et al. (Eds.): BPM 2011 Workshops, Part II, LNBIP 100, pp. 370–381, 2012.

workflows in e-Science encompass automated and non-automate components where the specification is not known in advance.

In order to study scalable analysis techniques that are resilient to errors in provenance data, we built a 10GB database of provenance data with known failure patterns. In this paper, we define the methodology behind the database's construction. The database is populated from a workload of workflows that are modeled based on real workflows. The workflows making up the workload originate in a number of scientific domains. We emulate different workflow execution scenarios by controlled injection of failures and message drops during workflow execution. We examine the resulting distribution and include performance evaluations for the generation process of the database. As the larger research goal guiding this effort is analysis techniques for provenance use that run at scale and are resilient to failures, we discuss early work on two analysis approaches, one a graph analysis approach to detecting inferior workflow runs, and one that uses reasoning techniques to repair provenance graphs.

The remainder of this paper is organized as follows. Section 2 discusses related work and Section 3 identifies requirements for generating the gigabyte provenance database. Section 4 discusses the system components used to generate the database; Section 5 details the workflow workload. In Section 6, we discuss our methodology. Section 7 evaluates the performance, and Section 8 discusses provenance analysis enabled by the research. Section 9 concludes the paper and discusses future work.

## 2    Related Work

Provenance research falls primarily into main categories: 1.) business provenance, 2.) provenance capture that is tightly coupled to a workflow system, 3.) database provenance, and 4.) provenance capture in semi-structured e-Science environments. Over the years, multiple surveys [4, 20] have been conducted and have mapped out provenance systems in these categories. An example of business provenance involves lineage tracing in data warehousing systems [3]. For the other three categories in provenance research, a few example systems are Kepler [11] and Pegasus [7] (Category 2), Trio [22] (Category 3), and ES3 [5] (Category 4). Systems such as Karma [18] involve provenance research in two categories (Category 2 and 4). These systems provide a source for realistic provenance data; however, these systems do not provide a controlled provenance generation environment and do not necessarily contain provenance with failures. This is the missing gap that this paper addresses.

Many synthetic workloads have been developed and used over the years, several in the area of distributed systems [2, 12, 21]. Similarly, a number of workloads [1, 14] have been generated and used in networks research. These workloads were developed for performance evaluations, and for benchmarking purposes in their respective areas. However, none of these workloads attempt to model failures. To the best of our knowledge, no workloads have been developed specifically for the purpose of provenance research. With the creation of a noisy 10GB provenance database that models failures of provenance notifications, we present a synthetic database that reflects the needs of provenance research.

# 3     Provenance Database Requirements

For a provenance database to be useful for study, several requirements must be met:

**Large Scale.** The database should consist of a significant number of provenance records to allow research to be done at scale.

**Diversity.** The provenance in the database should be drawn from workflows that are varied, such as those originating from different scientific domains and which have different characteristics in terms of size, breadth, and length.

**Realism.** The composition of workflows used to generate the provenance should have different availability and failure characteristics that are reflective of workflows that occur in the real world.

Using the WORKEM [16] workflow emulator to generate provenance, the six major workflows developed as part of the emulator, and the failure model built into WORKEM, we have achieved scale, diversity, and realism in the 10GB provenance database.

# 4     System Components

The two components used in the creation of the provenance database are WORKEM and Karma version 3.0. Figure 1 gives an overview of the system framework used to populate the workload gigabyte provenance database.

**WORKEM** is an emulation framework that emulates workflow execution [16]. It consists of an application service emulation layer that is built on top of a workflow engine, Apache ODE, and a task state model. Workflows are coded as BPEL

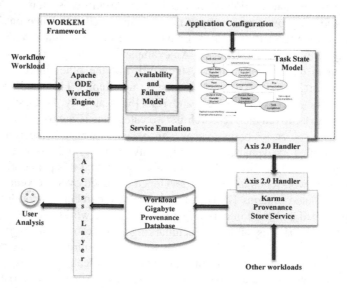

**Fig. 1.** Workload Gigabyte Provenance Database generation framework

workflow scripts and workflow notifications are generated through a generic service that models task execution as a finite state machine. An availability and failure model is built into WORKEM enabling the modeling of different workflow scenarios. This model allows the user to configure the probability of dropping messages or failure for any node in WORKEMs task state model.

The current implementation of WORKEM is deployed with a suite of workflows based on a workflows survey [15]. The workflows are modeled using Xbaya [17]. We use the existing suite of workflows in the population of the database. These workflows will be further described in Section 5.

In Figure 1, workflow scripts are loaded into the Apache ODE workflow engine. The workflow is orchestrated by ODE, which instead of calling out to a real task, calls an emulated task that has been configured to have the black-box behavior of a real workflow node. Prior to the workflows execution, it passes through a failure model to see if the node should be "executed" at all, or if it should send erroneous information. The workflow task sends provenance notifications to Karma through Axis 2. Upon receipt the provenance notifications are integrated into the database.

**Karma** version 3.0 [18] is a provenance collection and management system. In this study, it is used to consolidate and store notifications generated by WORKEM. Karma is a versatile provenance system in that it accepts provenance in a number of ways. Karma is able to listen on a message bus or receive messages directly through a web service interface. Asynchronous threads process provenance notifications to extract provenance information and store the information to a relational Karma database that is OPM compatible. We have instrumented WORKEM with an Axis 2.0 handler to facilitate a direct transfer of notifications from WORKEM to Karma.

For each state in the WORKEM task state model, a message containing activity information is passed to Karma and translated into Karma's information model. Karma in turn populates the workload gigabyte provenance database using translated raw workflow notifications. Messages are represented using service invocations, data transfers, response status messages and computational messages.

The access layer shown in Figure 1, is an access interface to the provenance store. Currently, Karma supports a number of query API calls to ease the retrieval of provenance information. However, multiple access layers may be implemented to serve different purposes.

## 5    Workflow Workload

The provenance database is generated from the following six workflows, namely:

    i.    LEAD North American Mesoscale (NAM) initialized forecast workflow
    ii.   SCOOP ADCIRC Workflow
    iii.  NCFS Workflow
    iv.  Gene2Life Workflow
    v.   Animation Workflow
    vi.  MotifNetwork Workflow

These workflows are pseudo-realistic, in the sense that they are modeled after real life workflows [15] using WORKEMs task state model. The LEAD NAM, SCOOP and NCFS are weather and ocean modeling workflows, Gene2Life and MOTIF are bioinformatics and biomedical workflows, and the Animation workflow carries out computer animation rendering. Some of the workflows are small, having few nodes and edges, while others like Motif have a few hundred nodes and edges. The characteristics are summarized in Table 1.

**Table 1.** Overview of Workflow Structure

| Workflow Name | Number of Nodes (Tasks) | Number of Edges | Maximum Width |
|:---:|:---:|:---:|:---:|
| LEAD NAM | 6 | 11 | 3 |
| NCFS | 7 | 19 | 2 |
| SCOOP | 6 | 10 | 5 |
| Gene2Life | 8 | 15 | 2 |
| Animation | 22 | 42 | 20 |
| Motif | 138 | 275 | 135 |

## 6    Methodology

We model failures in two specific ways a) task failures where a node in a workflow does not complete successfully b) a task completes but the notification is not successfully transmitted. These failure rates are modeled using uniform distributions in the emulator to determine if a particular invocation must fail or drop a notification. To generate the database, each of the six workflow types is run 2000 times per failure mode, with the failure modes as follows:

i.    No failures and dropped notifications (success case)
ii.   1% failure rate
iii.  1% dropped notification rate
iv.   1% failure rate and 1% dropped notification rate

Specifically, WORKEM generates notifications based on a task state model using workflows coded as BPEL workflow scripts. A total of 9 states are present within the task state model. These states represent different workflow execution states and can be categorized into status notifications; computation notifications and data transfer notifications. The failure and dropped notification rates were configured for all states in WORKEMs task state model. These 4 population cases were determined based on preliminary testing, which displayed a good number of workflows with different characteristics. Using these configurations, we were able to achieve a wide variety of workflow execution traces by using the above configurations.

For each population case, we configured WORKEM to generate workflows using 10 threads in parallel, with each thread responsible for generating 200 workflows for a total of 2000 workflows. This process was repeated across a total of 6 workflow types with a goal of generating a total of 48,000 workflows.

WORKEM generated roughly 48,000 workflows with various failures and dropped messages. The total number of workflows differs slightly from the intended number for a few reasons. For the SCOOP workflow, we encountered a single failure in Apache ODE during generation through WORKEM. For the Animation workflows,

50 workflows were removed from the database due to an error during configuration. The causes of the 36 missing Motif workflows remain unknown.

As shown in Figure 2, the distribution is surprisingly dissimilar. Even though the generation settings for WORKEM were identical across workflows, we observe that WORKEMs failure model does not result in the same uniform distribution across different workflows since the configuration for failure rates are per task in the workflow. This is evident through the Animation and Motif workflows. As seen in the success category of Figure 2, only 2000 Motif workflows result without any failures. All of these workflows originate from the workflow run that was configured without any failures. Comparatively, for the failed case, we observe a total of 2430 workflows. Similarly, Animation workflows only have 2197 workflows without failures, whereas it has 2907 workflows with dropped and failed characteristics. Both Animation and Motif workflows that do not have failures or dropped messages are approximately half of what the smaller workflows exhibit, that confirms that the larger a workflow, the higher the failure rate and dropped messages rate.

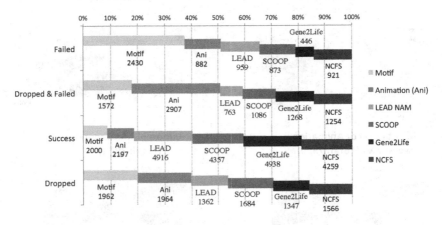

**Fig. 2.** Distribution of workflows by population cases

The smaller workflows appear to have the same distribution amongst each other. As seen in Figure 3, about 55-60% of these workflows have no failures and dropped messages, while workflows with dropped messages are approximately 20% and workflows with failures or dropped messages accounting for the remaining 20-25%. The larger Motif and Animation workflows have a different distribution. Approximately 50% of these workflows generated appear to be failed workflows, while the other half is split between workflows that have dropped messages and successful workflows.

# 7    Performance Evaluation

We examined performance of the provenance database generation process to better understand the complexities involved in generation. We use as our testbed a Dell PowerEdge 6950, quad dual-core AMD Opteron 2.4GHz with 16GB of RAM running Red Hat Enterprise Linux version 2.6.9-89.29.1.ELsmp. Both WORKEM and Karma were run on this machine. MySQL server v5.0.41 is the database system and it uses the machine's local disk. As populating the database took considerable time, it was carried out while other work was going on the server.

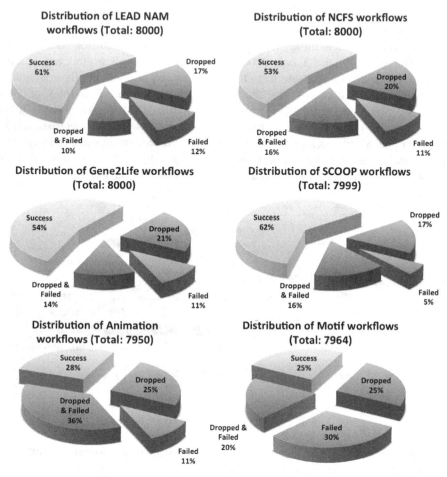

**Fig. 3.** Distribution of workflows by workflow types

**Analysis.** The average population time per workflow for the different population cases discussed in Section 6 is presented in Table 2. We note a number of interesting observations. For all workflows, the average population time per workflow is the largest for the population case with dropped notifications. The LEAD NAM workflow is the sole workflow that does not exhibit this, but even then the average population time per workflow is fairly close to that of the case without failures or dropped messages. We also observe that the population case without failures or dropped notifications is significantly faster when compared to the population case with dropped notifications.

The larger the workflows, the longer the average population time per workflow for all population cases. This is evident in larger workflows such as Motif and Animation. In these workflows, population cases that involve failures have the lowest average population time, indicating that most of these failures occur earlier in the workflow. This is especially evident in the Motif workflows. For Gene2Life and NCFS workflows, we observe that the population case with no failures or dropped notifications has a substantially lower average time than the population cases with failure rates or dropped notification rates.

**Table 2.** Average population time per workflow organized based on population cases

| Workflow Types \ Workflow Runs | Success case (sec.) | 1% failure rate (sec.) | 1% dropped notification rate (sec.) | 1% failure rate & 1% dropped notification rate (sec.) |
|---|---|---|---|---|
| Animation | 28.2 | 17.3 | 35.3 | 21.3 |
| Gene2Life | 7.4 | 21.8 | 26.9 | 20.8 |
| LEAD NAM | 8.6 | 6.5 | 8.5 | 6.3 |
| Motif | 198.9 | 29.8 | 216.4 | 41.4 |
| NCFS | 7.2 | 21.7 | 23.1 | 16.8 |
| SCOOP | 19.1 | 21.4 | 24.0 | 23.2 |

**Workflow Population Characteristics.** We further examine characteristics of population time for the various workloads. We plot population times of each workflow run (y-axis) based on the start time for each workflow (x-axis). Figure 4 shows the database being populated with workflow provenance in a well-behaved manner. A couple of the workflows (NCFS and Gene2Life) showed a sudden decrease in population time by 75% around half way through the population cycle. We do not show this graph as it is likely due to background activity on the machine. The largest workflow, Motif, shows a partitioning in population time for the failure cases that reflects completion times shown in Table 2 for Motif (Figure 5). The 1% dropped notification rate averages 216 seconds while the 1% failure rate combined with the failure+dropped case (rightmost column of Table 2), averages 35 seconds.

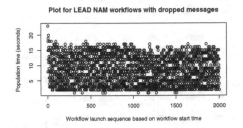

**Fig. 4.** Plot of workflows with uniform distributions in population timings

**Fig. 5.** Partitioning in population timings for Motif workflows that involve failures

**Size of Database.** The total size of the workload gigabyte provenance database dump using Karma version 3.0 is 10.64 Gigabytes. This is a sizable database that takes approximately an hour and 5 minutes on average to import into MySQL on our experimental quad dual-core server.

# 8      Towards Large-Scale Provenance Analysis

The 10GB provenance database was developed to serve as a test platform for research into analysis algorithms that run at scale and are resilient to failures. Here we discuss two ongoing efforts.

**Provenance Quality Assessment.** Provenance, as we have already pointed out, can be messy. Provenance messages may be dropped, messages can be incomplete, which could occur when the application scope at a point of notification generation is more restricted than anticipated, or execution of the application (or workflow) can simply fail. We are examining fast statistical approaches that operate over large volumes of data to zero in on suspicious provenance records. Provenance goodness is determined by constructing the best possible provenance graph for an execution based on the captured provenance record, then assessing the goodness of the resulting graph by looking at the partitions in a provenance graph. A provenance graph can be modeled as $P_G = \{V, E\}$, where V is a collection of vertices that are linked by one or more directed edges, E.

The approach we use is to construct a provenance graph from nothing (no guiding workflow template) based only on the captured provenance. A current assumption of the approach is that all notifications contain the correct ID for the workflow execution instance to which they belong. WORKEM supports this assumption. While simplifying the problem, this approach still may yield disconnected components. The query of a graph using a workflow ID searches over the database tables for entities (processes) that have matching IDs. If there are dropped messages, the queried graph may have missing edges or missing vertices. The only guarantee for the retrieved graphs is that the components of the graph are linked through that workflow ID.

In early results, we ran the algorithm against the 10GB provenance database and show the results in Figure 6 for the LEAD NAM workflow preliminary, observing the

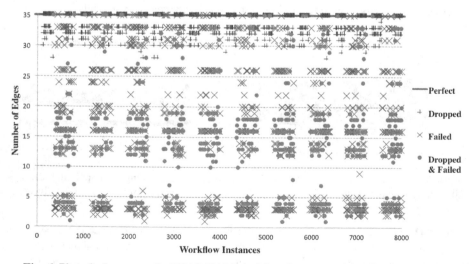

**Fig. 6.** Plot of edge counts for LEAD NAM workflow instances with different statuses

number of edge counts for each workflow instance. The plot points are classified based on the statuses of each workflow. As one would expect, the perfect workflows have the complete 35 edges. We observe that workflows with dropped messages cluster towards the upper end of Figure 6. This implies that dropped messages for successful workflows are few. In comparison, workflows that involve failures typically result in more missing notifications, resulting in lesser number of edges in their provenance graphs. We also note that approximately 30% of imperfect workflows possess the full 35 edges. This is due to Karma not taking into account some of WORKEM's notifications, such as computation start and stop notifications and response status notifications. Though these workflows experience missing notifications when generated through WORKEM, the provenance graphs extracted from Karma, which construct graphs based on the objects and edges defined in the Open Provenance Model, appear to be perfect.

**Automatic Provenance Repair.** We are investigating the use of artificial intelligence methods to repair faults in provenance traces. We have developed a system, Phala [8] that uses case-based reasoning [10] from similar known workflows and additional methods to predict the missing steps in a partial workflow. Case-based reasoning systems reason from specific prior examples, solving new problems by retrieving records of prior problem-solving and adapting their solutions to fit new circumstances. Given an incomplete provenance trace, Phala retrieves prior traces involving similar steps, and predicts the missing steps by analogy to the provenance information in the prior traces. Phala's approach is strongly data-driven, relying on the database of previously-observed provenance rather than on knowledge-intensive analysis. As the pool of relevant prior provenance traces grows through provenance capture, so does the system's ability to suggest suitable repairs. Even incomplete stored provenance traces may be useful if they are, locally, more complete than the target trace. Note that the provenance database Phala uses need not be restricted to a single domain; its retrieval/similarity assessment criteria select relevant cases.

For large databases of cases, controlling retrieval/similarity assessment cost is a key issue. This is particularly important for structured cases such as workflows, in which similarity calculations must take into account structural similarity of the workflow graphs. To avoid the expense of full graph matching over the stored data, Phala uses a two-step retrieval process. The first phase uses coarse-grained criteria to retrieve a set of initial candidates from the full database, restricting structural considerations to small independent sub-structures over which cases are indexed; the second phase considers the complete structure of each case retrieved from the first phase and re-ranks cases accordingly. To improve accuracy and robustness to noise, Phala uses multiple reasoning techniques to generate predictions and reconciles divergent predictions through a confidence-weighted voting scheme [9].

Phala's approach has been tested for aiding users at incrementally extending a workflow during initial workflow construction (see [8] for results of an evaluation of accuracy and scalability). Provenance repair is a natural application for the system, but the size of provenance databases far exceeds that of datasets to which case-based reasoning has previously been applied. The 10GB provenance database provides a challenging testbed for future study and refinement of Phala's methods for handling large-scale provenance sources.

# 9     Conclusions and Future Work

In this paper, we present our methodology behind building a 10GB noisy provenance database, and the reasons why its existence is important. This sizable database consists of a varied distribution of realistic workflows. We provide details of our methodology for populating the database and provide evaluations of this workload database in terms of its distribution and performance. This provenance database is now made available at: http://pti.iu.edu/d2i/provenance_gigabyte_database.

We are now using the provenance database to study provenance quality assessment. Our current graph analysis algorithm for this task makes simplifying assumptions about the existence of a workflow ID that ties together all notifications belonging to a provenance record. We plan to explore loosening this restriction. In addition, in order to determine how close a provenance record comes to a perfect record, one needs some sense of what is expected. This can be done by requiring a workflow template, which is realistic in some provenance capture settings but not others, or will require learning algorithms that can build a sense over time of a good provenance record. Finally, we are exploring using the graph structure to propagate node and edge quality metrics through the provenance graph.

**Acknowledgements.** We thank Karma team members Yiming Sun, Mehmet Aktas and Girish Subramanian. This work funded in part by National Science Foundation NSF-OCI-6721674 and by a grant from the Data to Insight Center of Indiana University. This work was supported by the Director, Office of Science, of the U.S. Department of Energy under Contract No. DE-AC02-05CH11231.

# References

1. Antonatos, S., Anagnostakis, K., Markatos, E.: Generating realistic workloads for network intrusion detection systems. In: ACM Workshop on Software and Performance, Redwood Shores, CA, USA (2004)
2. Bodnarchuk, R.R., Bunt, R.B.: A synthetic workload model for a distributed systems file server. In: Proceedings of the SIGMETRICS International Conference on Measurement and Modeling of Computer Systems, pp. 50–59 (1991)
3. Cui, Y., Widom, J.: Lineage tracing for general data warehouse transformations. VLDB Journal 12, 41–58 (2003)
4. Freire, J., Koop, D., Santos, E., Silva, C.T.: Provenance for Computational Tasks: A Survey. Computing in Science and Engineering 10(3), 11–21 (2008)
5. Frew, J., Metzger, D., Slaughter, P.: Automatic capture and reconstruction of computational provenance. Concurrency and Computation: Practice and Experience 20(5), 485–496 (2008)
6. Groth, P., Moreau, L.: Recording Process Documentation for Provenance. IEEE Transactionson Parallel and Distributed Systems 20(9), 1246–1259 (2009)
7. Kim, J., Deelman, E., Gil, Y., Mehta, G., Ratnakar, V.: Provenance Trails in the Wings/Pegasus System. Concurrency and Computation: Practice and Experience 20(5), 587–597 (2008)

8. Leake, D.B., Kendall-Morwick, J.: Towards Case-Based Support for e-Science Workflow Generation by Mining Provenance. In: Althoff, K.-D., Bergmann, R., Minor, M., Hanft, A. (eds.) ECCBR 2008. LNCS (LNAI), vol. 5239, pp. 269–283. Springer, Heidelberg (2008)
9. Leake, D., Kendall-Morwick, J.: Four Heads are Better than One: Combining Suggestions for Case Adaptation. In: McGinty, L., Wilson, D.C. (eds.) ICCBR 2009. LNCS, vol. 5650, pp. 165–179. Springer, Heidelberg (2009)
10. Lopez de Mantaras, R., McSherry, D., Leake, D., Smyth, B., Craw, S., Faltings, B., Maher, M.L., Cox, M., Forbus, K., Keane, M., Aamodt, A., Watson, I.: Retrieval, Revision, and Retention in CBR. Knowledge Engineering Review 20(3), 215–240 (2006)
11. Ludäscher, B., Altintas, I., Berkley, C., Higgins, D., Jaeger-Frank, E., Jones, M., Lee, E., Tao, J., Zhao, Y.: Scientific Workflow Management and the Kepler System. Concurrency and Computation: Practice & Experience, Special Issue on Scientific Workflows (2005)
12. Mehra, P., Wah, B.: Synthetic Workload Generation for Load-balancing Experiments. IEEE Parallel and Distributed Technology 3(3), 4–19 (1995)
13. Moreau, L., Plale, B., Miles, S., Goble, C., Missier, P., Barga, R., Simmhan, Y., Futrelle, J., McGrath, R., Myers, J., Paulson, P., Bowers, S., Ludaescher, B., Kwasnikowska, N., Van den Bussche, J., Ellkvist, T., Freire, J., Groth, P.: The Open Provenance Model. Technical report, Electronics and Computer Science, University of Southampton, (2008)
14. Noble, B.D., Satyanarayanan, M., Nguyen, G.T., Katz, R.H.: Trace-Based Mobile Network Emulation. In: Proceedings of SIGCOMM 1997, Cannes, France, pp. 51–61 (September 1997)
15. Ramakrishnan, L., Plale, B.: A Multi-Dimensional Classification Model for Workflow Characteristics. In: Workflow Approaches to New Data-centric Science, with ACM SIGMOD 2010, Indianapolis, IN (2010)
16. Ramakrishnan, L., Plale, B., Gannon, D.: WORKEM: Representing and Emulating Distributed Scientific Workflow Execution State. In: Proceedings of the 10th IEEE/ACM Int'l. Symposium on Cluster, Cloud and Grid Computing, Melbourne, Australia (2010)
17. Shirasuna, S.: A Dynamic Scientific Workflow System for the Web Services Architecture. PhD thesis, Indiana University (September 2007)
18. Simmhan, Y., Plale, B., Gannon, D.: Karma2: Provenance Management for Data Driven Workflows. International Journal of Web Services Research 5(2) (2008)
19. Simmhan, Y., Plale, B., Gannon, D.: Towards a Quality Model for Effective Data Selection in Collaboratories. In: IEEE Workshop on Workflow and Data Flow for Scientific Applications, held in conjunction with ICDE, Atlanta, GA (2006)
20. Simmhan, Y., Plale, B., Gannon, D.: A survey of data provenance in e-science. SIGMOD Record 34(3), 31–36 (2005)
21. Sreenivasan, K., Kleinman, A.J.: On the construction of a representative synthetic workload. Communications of the ACM, 127–133 (1974)
22. Widom, J.: Trio: A System for Integrated Management of Data, Accuracy, and Lineage. In: CIDR, Pacific Grove, California (January 2005)

# An Architecture for a Blended Workflow Engine

## Integrating an Activity-Based Perspective with a Goal-Based Perspective

Bernardo Oliveira Pinto and António Rito Silva

INESC-ID/Instituto Superior Técnico
{bernardo.pinto,rito.silva}@ist.utl.pt

**Abstract.** Semi-structured workflow approaches are essential to support collaboration whenever unanticipated events occur in dynamic environments. These approaches promote ad-hoc work. However, semi-structured workflows need to balance the support of unexpected situations with guidance for the situations where a standard behaviour is wanted. The blended workflow approach proposes an integration of two different workflow perspectives, the activity-based perspective, which precisely defines how to coordinate work for expected situations, and a goal-based perspective, which allows people to accomplish the business process goals without constraining their behaviour. The existing workflow engines do not provide support for an approach that fuse activity-based and goal-based perspectives. Therefore, this paper goal is to describe how both perspectives can be integrated. We describe an architecture for a blended workflow engine which combines activity and goal-based perspectives and supports the integrated execution of both specifications while keeping them consistent.

**Keywords:** Activity-based, Goal-based, Workflow Architecture, Workflow Reference Model.

## 1 Introduction

Most industrial workflow systems are activity-based. The work is specified by defining activities and on how they can be coordinated using control-flow primitives, as sequential and parallel execution, to achieve the business process goals [1]. Activity-based workflows prescribe the activities execution order and lack flexibility to handle unexpected situations for which they were not codified.

In a different trend, closely related to knowledge work, both researchers and industry are proposing new workflow approaches that foster users collaboration to deal with unexpected situations. These workflows support ad-hoc behaviour and delegate to end users the responsibility to guarantee that the business process goals are achieved. However, they lack the guidance provided by activity-based workflows.

The blended workflow approach [2] is a new approach which intends to bridge the gap between completely structured workflows and ad-hoc workflows.

F. Daniel et al. (Eds.): BPM 2011 Workshops, Part II, LNBIP 100, pp. 382–393, 2012.

The idea behind the blended workflow approach is that a workflow management system should allow users to deviate from the structured execution whenever it is necessary, but may allow them to regain the guidance provided by structured workflows once the unexpected situation is dealt with. To do so, blended workflow proposes the consistent coexistence of two workflow models, a prescriptive activity-based model and a descriptive goal-based model.

Current workflow engines either support prescriptive workflows [3] or descriptive ones [4], but, as far as we know, there is no proposal for a workflow engine that integrates both. The challenges that such engine has to face are on how to support the consistent execution of both models, such that during execution users can move back and forth between these two perspectives.

In this paper we will describe a solution to the implementation of this approach, i.e. how can we join activities and goals in a workflow management system, in such a manner that the system behaves as described in the blended workflow approach [2]. Actually, a third model, an object model, is defined to integrate the execution of the goal and activity models.

In the next section we describe the architecture of the solution driven by its relevant aspects, and section 3 uses an example to show how the workflow prototype can be used. The current prototype is described in section 4 and we drive some conclusions of our work, in section 5.

## 2   Blended Workflow System Architecture

The architecture of the blended workflow system follows the Workflow Reference Model [5]. A central service of the Workflow Reference Model is the Workflow Enactment Service, which is responsible for interpreting the process specification and for executing process instances.

The Workflow Enactment Service of the blended workflow system architecture is composed by two Workflow Engines, depicted in figure 1. The *Activity Workflow Engine* is responsible for activity management whereas the *Goal Workflow Engine* is responsible for goal management. These two engines provide the end user with two independent perspectives of the workflow instance. Although each end user action is applied to only one of the engines, both perspectives are updated to give consistent views of the workflow instance.

The end user interaction through the *Activity Engine* is structured, in the sense that the order by which the user interacts with the engine, i.e. the order by which the user performs operations is completely specified. On the other hand, the *Goal Engine* allows a semi-structured interaction, so that the end user does not have to follow a specific order to achieve the process goals.

Although proving independent modes of interactions, the engines are synchronised through a shared *Data Repository*. This repository contains the data that is used by both engines and ensures that they always access the most up-to-date data. Therefore, a notification mechanism is used to inform engines about changes. Both engines are always notified because the changes in the data model may impact on more activities and/or goals than the one manipulated by the end user action, as it will be explained below.

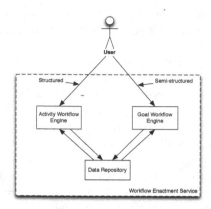

**Fig. 1.** The general architecture of the blended workflow system

A detailed description of the system architecture, depicted in Figure 2, shows the internal structure of each one of the modules and the dependencies among modules.

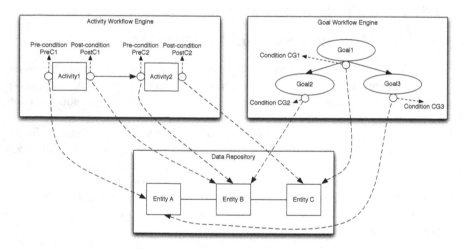

**Fig. 2.** A more detailed view of the system's architecture

The *Activity Workflow Engine* comprises the activities, illustrated by *Activity1* and *Activity2*, and the control-flow between them, illustrated by the arrow connecting the two activities. In addition, the engine execution extends a traditional activity-based workflow engine by including specific pre- and post- conditions, illustrated by *PreC1*, *PreC2*, *PostC1* and *PostC2*. To enable an activity for execution, its pre-condition must hold true, and an activity is considered executed if its post-condition holds true. The activity engine of a blended workflow integrates the traditional control-flow with an additional data-flow, given by the pre- and post-conditions. The activities pre- and post-conditions are used by the activity engine to evaluate the shared state, represented by the dashed arrows from conditions to the shared state, and conclude about which activities can be enabled or are completed.

The *Goal Workflow Engine* is constituted by goals, illustrated by *Goal1*, *Goal2* and *Goal3*, and goal decomposition relationships, illustrated by the solid arrows. Goals are specified by a condition, illustrated by *GC1*, *GC2* and *GC3*, over the data in the *Data Repository*, illustrated by the dashed arrows. End users interactions with the goal engine result in changes in shared state that fulfil goals, i.e. their conditions hold true.

A blended workflow instance has to execute according to both activity-based and goal-based specifications. This means that any successful execution following the activity-based specification must fulfil the goal specification, and in particular the top goal. The goal conditions and the activities pre- and post- conditions constitute the blended workflow specification for goal achievement, whereas the activities control-flow specify a particular behaviour, the standard behaviour, on how to achieve the goals. Therefore, the activity-based specification is an over-specification of the goal specification and the conditions over the *Data Repository* is where both specifications overlap.

The *Data Repository* contains the data entities, illustrated by *Entity A*, *Entity B* and *Entity C*, their attributes, and the relationships among them, represented by the solid edges. During execution of a blended workflow instance, both engines change the shared state and the execution completes when the shared state makes the goal conditions hold true.

End users interact with workflow instances through both interfaces, structured and semi-structured, respectively activity and goal operations. In addition to the execute activity and fulfil goal operations, three other operations provide further execution flexibility: skip activity, skip goal and create goal. Skip activity operations allow end users to leave out an activity in the execution of a workflow instance, because there was a change in the conditions that permit its execution, for instance the actor cannot perform the work. Similarly, skip goal operations allow end users to disregard the execution of a goal, possibly because of an unexpected situation the goal became nonessential for the workflow instance. Finally, operation create goal empower end users to define new goals for a workflow instance.

Considering Figure 2 as an example, we describe how the blended workflow system architecture supports operations: activity execution, skip activity, goal achievement, skip goal, and create goal.

**Activity Execution.** For a user to execute an activity it has to be enabled by control-flow and its pre-condition must hold true, e.g. for *Activity1* to be executed, *PreC1* must hold true, which means that *Entity A* must be in a state that satisfies *PreC1*. After *Activity1* execution, *PostC1* holds true, which means that *Entity B* is in a state that satisfies this condition, the control-flow enables *Activity2* and *Activity2* is activated if *PreC2* also holds true. However, there may be the case where *PreC2* does not hold true, because it refers data is neither produced be *Activity 1* nor by any other previous activity (see below how pre-activities can be generated to deal with this situation). When there are changes in the shared state, the conditions that depend on the updated data are re-evaluated, for instance, after *Activity1* is executed *GC2* and *PreC2* are re-evaluated and the state of *Goal2* and *Activity2* may also change.

**Skip Activity.** When an activity is skipped, the state of the data referred by the activity post-condition is changed to *skipped* and the control flow proceeds as if the activity has been executed, yet its post-condition is not fulfilled. Similarly to activity execution, the change in the data state triggers the conditions that depend on the changed data. Considering the figure, if the user skips *Activity1*, *Entity B* state will be changed to *skipped* and *Activity2* is enabled by control-flow, but since *PreC2* does not hold true, *Activity2* will not be activated and pre-activities need to be generated. Also, as *Goal2* refers *Entity B*, it will be skipped.

**Goal Achievement.** When a goal is achieved, the blended workflow evaluates which activities may have complete. Considering the figure, if the user explicitly achieves *Goal2*, *PostC1* and *PreC2* will be re-evaluated and if *Entity B*'s state satisfies these conditions, *Activity1* will be considered as completed and *Activity2* enabled for execution.

**Skip Goal.** When a goal is skipped, all its sub-goals, that were not achieved yet, are also skipped and the state of the data referred by these goals' definition is also changed to *skipped*. The activity engine re-evaluates the post condition of all the activities enabled by control-flow and if the result of the evaluation is *skipped*, the activities are skipped. Afterwards, the blended workflow analyses the pre-conditions of the activities which are enabled by control flow, and depend on the skipped data, and generate pre-activities for them. Considering the Figure 2, if a user skips *Goal2*, *Entity B* will also be skipped and, consequently, *Activity1* will be skipped.

**Create Goal.** Users can create a new goal for a particular workflow instance. By creating a new goal, they also have to specify the condition that defines it. Additionally, the user needs to create new entities and/or add new attributes to existing entities, which the condition refers. A new goal achievement does not have any impact on the activity-based specification. Considering the figure, the user can create a new goal, *Goal4*. She can also create a new entity *Entity D*, that has a relation with *Entity B*. Finally, the end user specifies how *Goal4*'s condition depend on *Entity D*.

For the sake of simplicity, in the all the above cases, when a goal or activity is skipped, the state of data they refer to becomes skipped. However, as we will explain in the implementation section, this only occurs for the atomic data elements which have an empty value. On the other hand, in the examples we considered all entities as atomic data elements, they contain a single attribute.

Pre-activities are generated when there is a need to enable for execution an activity that is enabled by control-flow but its pre-condition does not hold true.

This happens when the user skips a previous activity or a goal. The system generates pre-activities that empower the end user provide the missing data and enable the activity for execution.

## 3   Application Example

Figure 3 presents the user interface of the blended workflow prototype. The user interface comprises an activity view (the view on the left), a goal view (the view on the right) and a workspace (the space on the bottom). It is through the workspace that the end user interacts with the blended workflow. During interaction the workspace is on either activity mode or goal mode.

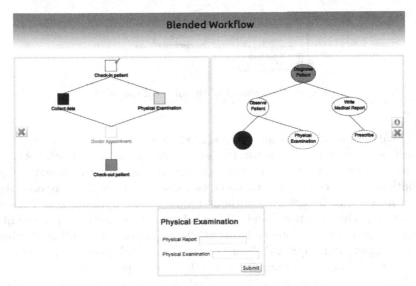

**Fig. 3.** A screenshot of the prototype when the user is executing a blended workflow instance

Each box in the activity view represents an activity and each ellipse in the goal view represents a goal. Dashed ellipses represent optional goals. Table 1 describes the graphical notation used in the prototype.

To illustrate the blended workflow approach consider an example of a medical episode. The activity-based specification of medical episode comprises the activities *Check-in Patient, Collect Data, Physical Examination, Doctor Appointment* and *Check-out Patient*. The goal specification defines a set of goals: *Diagnose Patient, Observe Patient, Write Medical Report, Collect Data, Physical Examination* and *Prescribe*.

These two specifications use the data specification that is presented in Figure 4.

As examples of the conditions implemented in the activity and goal specification, consider the *Medical Report* entity. The condition of the *Write Medical*

**Table 1.** Activity/Goal colours and their meaning

| Color | Description |
|---|---|
| Blue | Selected (currently active) activity/goal |
| Grey | Activity/Goal cannot be executed |
| Black | Activity/Goal is skipped |
| White | Activity/Goal is available for execution |
| White with a corner tick | Activity/Goal is already executed |
| Transparent | Activity/Goal condition refers data that was skipped |

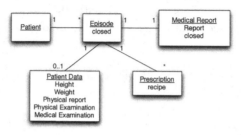

**Fig. 4.** Data model of the medical episode

*Report* goal requires the creation of a `Medical Report` object containing a written diagnosis written by the doctor. In the activity-based view, *Doctor Appointment* post-condition also requires the creation of the `Medical Report` object and, optionally, a `Prescription` object can also be created. Therefore, *Write Medical Report* can be achieved without requiring the optional goal *Prescribe* to be fulfilled. On the other hand, *Doctor Appointment* activity pre-condition requires the existence of object `Patient Data`, holding values for attributes `Height`, `Weight`, and `Physical Examination`, on which post-conditions of activities *Collect Data* and *Physical Examination* are dependent.

To illustrate the flexibility of the blended workflow approach we describe an unexpected situation, an administrative strike.

In the case of an administrative strike, the activities performed by the administrative staff cannot be executed. There are two ways of executing the workflow in this case:

**Skipping Activities and Executing Pre-activities.** In this case, the nurses have to skip activity *Check-in Patient*.

Next, they will also have to skip activity *Collect data* and execute a pre-activity to enable *Physical Examination* activity. This pre-activity consists in defining *Patient* and *Episode* objects, which are required by *Physical Examination* pre-condition. Once *Physical Examination* activity is executed, both the activity and the goal are, respectively, executed and accomplished.

Finally, the physician has to execute a pre-activity to set the `Height` and `Weight` attributes and thus, enable the *Doctor Appointment* activity. After executing this pre-activity, the goal *Collect Data* is fulfilled and the the activity

*Doctor Appointment* becomes executable again. After the physician executes *Doctor Appointment* activity the goal *Diagnose Patient* is fulfilled.

**Skipping Activities and Achieving Goals.** To do this deviation from the "usual" execution, the physician only needs to achieve the top goal. To do so, he has to skip the first three activities (*Check-in Patient*, *Collect Data* and *Physical Examination*), and then, he can achieve the *Diagnose Patient* goal by achieving its mandatory subgoals, *Observe Patient* and *Write Medical Report*. In this case, only the *Doctor Appointment* activity will be considered as completed, since its post-condition is satisfied by *Write Medical Report* achievement.

# 4   System Implementation

The system implementation addresses the issue of how to keep the activity and goal views consistent, so when an activity is executed or a goal achieved the changes made in the data model are automatically reflected in both views. Before we describe the implementation of activities and goals, we first address the implementation of the data and conditions, because views consistency is built on top of them.

## 4.1   Data Implementation

The data model describes which are the entities, the attributes within each entity and the relations between entities. Moreover, it also specifies which are the key attributes/entities necessary for an entity to exist. This means that an entity is only defined when all its key attributes/entities are defined. The class diagram in UML of the data implementation is depicted in Figure 5. It follows a meta-model approach to allow the dynamic definition of new data entities, relations and attributes, which may be necessary when a new goal is created.

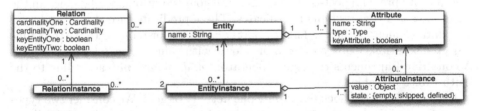

**Fig. 5.** Class diagram in UML of the data model

The `Entity` class represents an entity type in the data model specification. This class has a list of `Attribute` and a list of `Relation` it is part of. Relations are binary and have cardinalities. Class `EntityInstance` represents the instance of the entity and has a list of `AttributeInstance` and a list of `RelationInstance`. When an attribute instance is created its state is set to *empty*. An entity is in state *empty* when at least one of its key attributes is in state *empty* or one of its key relations refer to an empty entity. After an attribute instance value is set, its state is updated to *defined*.

When a blended workflow specification is loaded, instances of `Entity`, `Attribute` and `Relation` are created, and for each new workflow instance the shared space is populated with the minimal set of instances of `EntityInstance`, `AttributeInstance` and `RelationInstance` required to achieve the workflow goals. Afterwards, during the workflow execution, the values of the attribute instances are set and, eventually, the goals will be achieved.

Since the blended workflow allows the definition of a new goal during workflow execution, new objects of `Entity`, `Attribute` and `Relation` can be created for a particular workflow instance. In this case, these objects are private for the particular workflow instance.

Considering the medical episode example and its data model, depicted in figure 4, when the process is defined, one instance of the `Entity` class is created for each one of the entities in the data model: *Patient, Episode, Patient Data, Prescription* and *Medical Report*. Instances of `Attribute` are also created for each attribute, e.g. along with the entity *Medical Report*, an instance of the `Attribute` is created for the *Report* attribute and another for the *Closed* attribute. Being the *Report* the *Medical Report*'s key attribute, its `keyAttribute` attribute is set to *true*. Along with the entity and attribute creation, the system also creates an instance of the `Relation` class, for each relation between entities.

During the workflow execution it may be the case that the physician creates more than one *Prescription*. In this situation the system creates another instance of the `EntityInstance` associated to the *Prescription* object, along with the necessary `AttributeInstance` objects, and one `RelationInstance` object, which relates the existing `EntityInstance` of the *EpisodeInstance* and the new *PrescriptionInstance*.

## 4.2   Conditions Implementation

The activity pre- and post-conditions and the goal condition are all defined in the same way: as a composition of predicates. These predicates are atomic and refer to a data element, either an `EntityInstance` object or an `AttributeInstance` object. Conditions follow a three-valued logic with values: *true, false* and *skipped*. A condition implements the logical operators *and, or* and *not*, according to the truth tables in Table 2.

Each predicate is associated to only one activity or goal. We consider two types of atomic predicates: the `Exists(data)` predicate and a relational predicate `Relational(data, value)` predicate, which compares `data` with `value`. The return values for these predicates are presented in Table 3.

To implement these conditions, we used the declarative style described in [6]. The relation among conditions, activities and goals, and the structure of the conditions' implementation is depicted in figure 6.

These operators allow one to aggregate the predicates mentioned before and to specify a composition of predicates that are optional. Hence, considering, for example, the post-condition of the *Collect data* activity, it is

**Table 2.** The values that the condition returns when applying the specified logical operators

(a) Not

|  | True | False | Skipped |
|---|---|---|---|
| **NOT** | False | True | Skipped |

(b) And

| **AND** | **True** | **False** | **Skipped** |
|---|---|---|---|
| **True** | True | False | Skipped |
| **False** | False | False | Skipped |
| **Skipped** | Skipped | Skipped | Skipped |

(c) Or

| **OR** | **True** | **False** | **Skipped** |
|---|---|---|---|
| **True** | True | True | True |
| **False** | True | False | False |
| **Skipped** | True | False | Skipped |

**Table 3.** The values that the predicates return

(a) Exists

| **State** | **Defined** | **Empty** | **Skipped** |
|---|---|---|---|
| **Eval.** | True | False | Skipped |

(b) Relational ($==, >, <, ...$)

| **State** | **Defined** | **Empty** | **Skipped** |
|---|---|---|---|
| **Eval.** | True/False | False | Skipped |

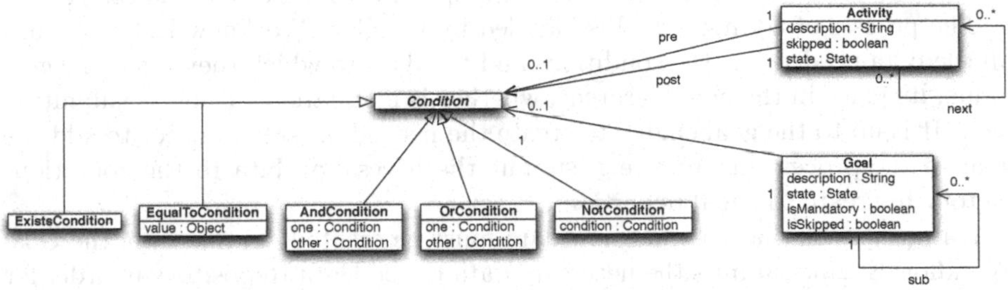

**Fig. 6.** Class diagram in UML of the conditions implementation and their relation with activities and goals

specified as `Exists(Patient Data.height).and(Exists(Patient Data.weight))` and the goal *Physical Examination* definition is specified as `Exists(Patient Data.Physical Report).and(Exists(Patient Data.Physical Examination))`. These conditions correspond to the composition of two `ExistsCondition` objects in the context of an `AndCondition` object.

## 4.3 Activities and Goals Implementation

As described in Section 2 when a data value is changed both views are notified. The elements in the data model and the conditions implement the Observer pattern [7], where the "observers" are the conditions and the "observables" are the entity and attribute instances of the data model. This way, when there are changes in the data model, i.e. some entity or attribute is defined, skipped or created, only the state of the activities and goals that include the conditions which refer the updated data are re-evaluated. Figure 7 represents how the observer pattern is implemented. Class `Condition` inherits from `DataObserver` and classes `EntityInstance` and `AttributeInstance` extend `DataObservable`.

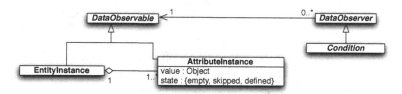

**Fig. 7.** Implementation of the observer pattern in blended workflow

Skip operation differs from the activity execution and goal achievement operations in the way the shared space is changed. When an activity or a goal is skipped, all the `AttributeInstance` objects referred by the, respectively, activity post-condition and goal condition, which state is *empty*, are updated to state *skipped*. Afterwards, when conditions are re-evaluated, using the truth tables in Table 2, activities and goals can become skipped if they evaluate as *skipped*.

The process of adding a goal is handled by the Goal Workflow Engine. Thus, all the data needed, i.e. the conditions and the data to which they refer, the goal name, its place in the goal hierarchy, whether is mandatory or not, is submitted to it. It is up to the goal engine to create the needed objects in order to add the goal to the process instance, e.g. submit the necessary data to the conditions factory to create the goal definition.

It may also be the case that new data must be created. In this case, the Goal Workflow Engine submits the necessary data to the Data Repository in order for it to create the entities/attributes, integrate them in the data model and create the empty instances. This has to be done before creating the conditions for the goal definition, because the specific object references of the entity/attribute instances are needed for the condition creation.

## 5   Conclusions

This work describes the implementation of the blended workflow approach, a semi-structured approach that combines two perspectives to describe a workflow: an activity perspective, which describes the workflow in a completely structured manner, and a goal perspective, which describes the workflow in a declarative manner.

Blended Workflow allows users to perform various operations during the process execution: *activity execution, skip activity execution, goal fulfilment, skip goal fulfilment, create new goal.* With these operations the user can easily deviate from the structured execution whenever it is necessary. Moreover, the system keeps both models consistent, through a Data Repository, which receives the data up-dates (through the various operations the system allows) and propagates them. This way, the user is capable of regaining the guidance provided by structured workflow once the unexpected situation is dealt with.

**Acknowledgements.** This work was supported by FCT (INESC-ID multi-annual funding) through the PIDDAC Program funds.

# References

1. OMG: Business process modelling notation (October 2009), http://www.bpmn.org/
2. Silva, A.R.: A blended workflow approach. In: 7th International Workshop on Business Process Design, Clermont-Ferrand, France (August 2011)
3. Russell, N., ter Hofstede, A., van der Aalst, W.: Newyawl: Designing a workflow system using coloured petri nets. In: Proceedings of the International Workshop on Petri Nets and Distributed Systems (PNDS 2008) (2008)
4. Eindhoven University of Technology: DECLARE Manual (2008)
5. Hollingsworth, D.: The workflow reference model version 1.1. Workflow Management Coalition (1995)
6. Evans, E.: Domain-driven design: tackling complexity in the heart of software. Addison Wesley (2004)
7. Gamma, E., Helm, R., Johnson, R., Vlissides, J.: Design patterns: elements of reusable object-oriented software. Addison-Wesley Longman Publishing Co., Inc., Boston (1995)

# Process Mining in Auditing: From Current Limitations to Future Challenges

Mieke J. Jans

Hasselt University, Faculty of Business Economics
3590 Diepenbeek, Belgium
mieke.jans@uhasselt.be

In the first book on process mining[1], Wil van de Aalst densely defines the goal of process mining "to use event data to extract process-related information", like automatically discovering a process model by observing events that are recorded by some information system. This definition is broad, since it addresses the mining of all processes that are supported by an information system, revealing the wide range of possible applications of process mining. With the growing of the digital universe, the recording of events reaches new heights all the time. Given this omnipresence of recorded events and hence the large amount of possibilities to apply process mining, a well-defined focus on an application field is essential. Auditing is such a field. The auditor functions as an independent examiner of financial statements to give reasonable assurance on the accuracy of these statements. That way, the auditor provides 'trust' to shareholders and other third parties related to the audited organization. This trust is a crucial element of the economic system.

The profession of auditing is overseen by international and national nonprofit organizations. The two largest oversight bodies are the Public Company Accounting Oversight Board (PCAOB) in the US and the International Auditing and Assurance Standards Board (IAASB). Auditing standards like the ones issued by the PCAOB and the IAASB place an important emphasis of auditing on understanding the processes that precede financial reporting. In order to understand the likely sources of misstatement, the auditor has to understand the flow of transactions and to identify the controls that management has implemented to address potential misstatements or to prevent unauthorized acquisition, use, or disposition of a company's assets (AS No. 5, paragraph 34). To achieve these objectives, the standards present the use of walkthroughs as the most effective means. Walkthroughs are performed by following a transaction from origination through a process, including information systems, until it is reflected in the company's financial records. This approach, currently used in the auditing profession, can be drastically ameliorated by employing the techniques of process mining in order to achieve abovementioned objectives. The technique of the walkthroughs can, by applying process mining, (1) be automated, and (2) extended to the full population instead of a sample, resulting in a transparent overview of the

---

[1] Wil M. P. van der Aalst: *Process Mining: Discovery, Conformance and Enhancement of Business Processes..* Springer, 2011.

F. Daniel et al. (Eds.): BPM 2011 Workshops, Part II, LNBIP 100, pp. 394–397, 2012.

process. However, in order to fully replace the technique of manual walkthroughs by process mining, several current limitations need to be addressed.

An important aspect of an audit that holds a current limitation for process mining in auditing, is that it should provide reasonable assurance about whether the financial statements are free of material misstatement. A fact is defined as 'material' if there is "a substantial likelihood that the fact would have been viewed by the reasonable investor as having significantly altered the 'total mix' of information made available." (AS No. 11, paragraph 2) This dimension of materiality requires a delicate assessment of the auditor, taking into account all information and all possible misstatements in order to state whether a level of materiality is reached or not. Hence this is not easy to convert into exact rules. Therefore, a conciliation between the definition of materiality and a process mining approach should be found.

In the search for a fit between materiality and process executions, it is important to keep in mind the different dimension a process represents when compared to an account. A process execution, or pattern, is a path that can be followed and that ends in crediting or debiting an account. A process execution at itself cannot give insight into materiality. To this end, extra information needs to be added to the pattern, like how many transactions followed this path, which value was created by following this path, how many persons were involved, does the path cover more than one financial booking period? As such, questions that need to be answered in the pursuit of a translation of processes to materiality, are amongst other: "When is a certain deviating process execution warranting further examination to exclude a material misstatement?"; "How can a process deviation be quantified in terms of risk?"; "Is there a certain threshold of cases that follow a certain process execution to consider it as material, or a threshold on the affected amount of money?" The materiality issue is an important issue in auditing and given its delicate assessment, this probably will not be answered very easily. Probably this issue will in a process mining approach, just like in the current approach, require expertise of the auditor and cannot be fully replaced by algorithms. This however should not refrain us from searching for indicators to help the auditor in his task.

To supersede the entire range of the manual walkthroughs, it is important that the process under examination is completely embedded in an information system. The start transaction, all following transactions, and the final financial reporting transaction need to be captured by the information system. If not, the automated process mining will not be able to mine the whole process, but only the part that is supported by an information system. This restriction demands a certain level of maturity of the organization, before process mining can be applied in an auditing context. If only part of a process can be mined, no assurance can be provided on the process and its reporting outcome. The consequence of this limitation is that a full integration for all audits cannot be reached. However, since the digitalization of the world continues, more and more organizations and processes will be suited for process mining. If this trend continues, as assumed, the application possibilities of process mining will grow each day. By the time the process mining field is fully adopted to audit requirements, most audits will take place in an information system environment and can be complemented and improved by process mining techniques. However, the official auditing standards will always have to make a distinction between processes or organizations that are suited for process mining (and hence are subjected to more thorough examinations) and those that are not. If not framed correctly, this distinction may turn into a breeding ground for discussions and/or abuse. The different examination depths may even lead to different costs of capital. This issue has to be thought over seriously when inserting process mining into standards.

In order to apply process mining techniques, some conditions concerning the data structure must be met. These conditions form a current limitation on experiencing the full advantage of today's process mining capabilities. The main issue is that advanced ERP systems are based on a relational database structure. Process mining on the other hand starts from a flat file: reality is flattened into an event log. An example makes this clear. The information concerning an invoice might be captured in two tables of an ERP system: a table containing header information and a table containing item line details. Events that relate to this invoice my affect the header table or the item detail table. For example the approval of the invoice will occur at header level, while the booking of this invoice will take place on line item level. These two levels make it difficult to assign process activities to one process instance. If an invoice -as a whole- is selected as process instance to follow throughout the process and its subsequent activities, it is not possible to accurately link the activities on item level -like booking the separate item lines- to the process instance. On the other hand, if the item level detail were chosen as process instance, the activities on header level -like approval- are not correctly matched. One activity on header level would be presented multiple times in all related item level process instances. It still is possible to mine the process with these limitations, but it creates extra manual examination of the output, exactly what process mining aims to reduce. Ongoing research into 3-D process models may hold an answer to this challenge.

In case process mining in auditing is naturalized, evidentially speaking qualitative tools for both event log building and process mining analysis are needed. There are already some providers of commercial process mining tools and one provider of an event log building tool. However, more work needs to be done, not the least in adapting these general tools to specific audit requirements. The IT capabilities of the end user, the auditor, has to be taken into account; the typical audit related questions and interests; the type of desired output; and the related responsibilities. Also securing the extracted data out of the information system is an important issue and needs to be dealt with. One option is to secure the data like in some Generalized Audit Software where no alterations are possible once the data is imported into the tool.

Another point of interest are the identified outliers. In case an auditor identifies outliers -in accounts, transactions or processes-, the auditor needs to clear these outliers of containing a risk of material misstatements. The positive identification of outliers in process executions are true positives, as opposed to some data mining algorithms that might also output false positives. However, the current, existing process discovery algorithms in the domain of process mining are not yet adapted to auditing purposes, since the discovered patterns do not report in a comprehensive way on loops. This might give the impression that hundreds of different process executions exist, while in reality it can be a combination of loops. New visualizations that output 'main'-patterns along with the identification of 'sub'-patterns that are possibly repeated within one pattern need to be created.

As a last item, it is important to point out that process mining increases the insights in the examined process and there is a possibility that an auditor will experience this as an increasing work factor. It is important to counter this perceptions. The better insights that are gained should be perceived as a leap forward in the assurance that the auditor, both internal and external, can provide on an organizations financial statements. Today's audit will not only be automated, but will be drastically re-engineered. The efforts to adapt the current domain of process mining to audit requirements and possibly also vice versa are truly necessary for an adoption success. But this would be in a later stadium, after the adaptation of the process mining field to the auditing profession.

As an overall conclusion we can say auditing is an interesting field that can benefit from what process mining has to offer. The needs of auditing are complement to the aims of process mining: clarifying processes with the intent of providing assurance. This complement aspect should encourage both researchers and practitioners to seek for solutions on the current limitations. The limitations require further fundamental research on algorithms and applied research on practical process mining implementations to learn from. In the end, the standard setting bodies need these inputs to present a process mining approach as part of the auditing examination.

# Data-Privacy Assessments for Application Landscapes: A Methodology

Klaus Haller

Swisscom IT Services Finance
Testing & QA
Pflanzschulstr. 7, CH-8004 Zürich, Switzerland
klaus.haller@swisscom.com

**Abstract.** Data privacy is a major issue for companies today. Risks can come from external attacks or from internal users disclosing sensitive data to the public. In the latter case, restricting user access to data mitigates the risk. Thanks to role-based access models, users see only the data that they need for their work. This paper presents a methodology for assessing how effective such restrictions are. It is based on classifying data, analyzing access paths, and understanding the impact of design principles. Its special contribution is its end-to-end view. It is applicable directly to complex IT landscapes being the norm today.

**Keywords:** Information Systems, Privacy, Testing.

## 1 Introduction

Data leaks are a major threat for companies in all business sectors. They can ruin the reputation and cause high costs [1]. Data leaks emerge as military spy plots, such as the Los Alamos National Lab case [2]. They can be low-key, such as non-medical person having access to patients' records [3]. Then, there are stories about bank data thefts [4,5]. But even "non-sensitive" sectors are at risk when handling customer data. Involuntary examples exist in various sectors, e.g. the airline sector (Lufthansa's leak regarding the use of frequent flyer data of German politicians [6]) or online gaming (Sony's PlayStation Network case [7]).

Outsiders can break into IT systems (Sony case). Also, internal users might disclose data (banking examples). To address the last threat, companies restrict the data access for users. They can see only the data needed for their work. The technical bases are role-based access models [8]. But they work only if set up correctly. This paper presents a methodology to assess this. It is part of a broader initiative on testing and quality assurance for database applications and information system (IS) landscapes [9,10,11]. The focus of this paper is to systemize the data privacy aspect. Various consulting projects have proved its importance. Thus, the aim of the paper is to foster discussions between consulting and academia about this topic.

The paper illustrates the methodology, using a fictive credit-rating application *CreditPlus*. It calculates how likely small and medium-sized enterprises (SME) do not pay back loans. Input data is balance sheets. CreditPlus stores them and calculates the credit rating. A bank with branches in the US, the UK, and Switzerland (CH) uses the

F. Daniel et al. (Eds.): BPM 2011 Workshops, Part II, LNBIP 100, pp. 398–410, 2012.

software. CreditPlus is adapted for each country. This reflects varying accounting standards. Besides the US, UK, and CH users, there is an auditing and risk team in Germany. It enforces the bank's risk policy and processes in all countries. Also, it calculates the distribution of the risk exposure (e.g. 5% of the loans in the retail sector, 11% in hotels etc.). The software developers work in Romania, and the testers in Singapore. This scenario covers two practical sourcing scenarios:

- Global software development and testing
- Global sourcing of business activities

W.l.o.g., the paper narrows down the data privacy aspect on whether customer-identifying data crosses borders. The set-up involves just three branches, one auditing and risk team, a software development team, and a testing team. Still, six countries are involved. This has a severe impact on the data flow (Figure 1):

- Developers in Romania and testers in Singapore need test data. The closer the data to the "real world", the more efficient the software development, the testing, and the bug fixing. This implies copying (some kind of) US, UK, and CH customer data to Romania and Singapore from time to time.[1]
- The auditing and risk team in Germany calculates the risk exposure. It checks whether the branches stick to the bank's policies. The team needs continuous online access to the US, UK, and CH data.

Many companies have faced such challenges for many years. They have solutions put in place, either in ad-hoc style or based on a comprehensive approach. But one gap remains: assessing whether a concrete solution really works. This is the focus of the paper. It starts first with a formal data privacy model (Section 2). Section 3 introduces the methodology for assessing data privacy compliance. The two following sections enhance this core finding. Section 4 looks at the challenge of software for which only limited know-how exists. Section 5 looks at how data sanitization impacts assessments. The paper concludes with a discussion of related work (Section 6) and a short summary (Section 7).

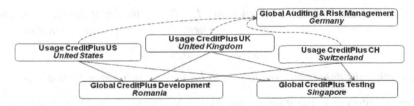

**Fig. 1.** Sample set up for global sourcing and cross-border data flows
(continues line: on-request copy, dashed line: online access)

## 2    Data Privacy Model (DPM)

This section presents the data privacy model (DPM). It is a formal model for reasoning about the data privacy of IS landscapes. It has four key concepts: the usage vector, the data

---

[1] There are other options for test data, too. However, they are often less helpful for complex environments. See [10] for a detailed discussion.

criticalness function, the data access diagram, and the privacy compliance correctness criterion (Figure 2 compiles them and acts as a guides through this paper). The usage vector comprises (some of) the factors influencing whether a user can see data items:

- The *roles* a concrete user has: A credit officer has to know the name of his customer, not necessarily a compliance officer. Also, software developers working on future releases do not need access to customer data.
- The *responsibility segment* - UK credit officers are not allowed to see all customer data. They focus on a segment, e.g. UK corporations with starting letters A-L.
- The *country* the user *works*: UK credit officers are only allowed to see UK customers.
- The user's *current country*. A UK credit officer is allowed to see UK customers if he is accessing the system from the UK. He might not be allowed to access the data when abroad.

Certainly, one can model more components depending on the circumstances.

**Definition 1 (Usage vector).** *A usage vector û is a 4-tuple $<R, c_w, c_c, S>$ with R being the roles of the user, $c_w$ the country he usually works in, $c_c$ the country where he currently is, and S the segment he is responsible for. U denotes all possible usage vectors.*

W.l.o.g., this paper focuses on the country of work as the only component of the usage vector. This allows for a more focused discussion.

The **data criticalness function** models how sensitive data items are. It is obvious for many that they are sensitive - for example, customer names or IBAN account numbers. A data item might also be known to be non-sensitive. Account balances (without link to any customer) are an example. Then, there are data items for which it is not known (potentially sensitive data items). The DPM sums up the sensitive and potentially sensitive data items to *red* data items. The non-sensitive data items are *green* data items. Whether a data item is red or green is not a global property. It depends on the context, i.e., the usage vector (Figure 2, left).

**Definition 2 (Data Criticalness Function).** *Let $D_{IS}$ be the set of data items in the IS landscape, $U_{IS}$ the set of all usage vectors. Then, the data criticalness function*

$$C: D_{IS} \times U_{IS} \rightarrow \{red, green\}$$

*states whether the data items are allowed to be seen for this usage context.*

The second concept is the **data access diagram** (Figure 2, middle). A data access diagram has three layers for describing *who* can access *which data items* using which *application features*. The usage vectors $U_{IS}$ form the top layer, and the data items $D_{IS}$ the lower layer. Features form the middle layer. They represent the application logic with a focus on data privacy. A feature links a usage vector (e.g. London-based UK credit officers for A-L customers) with data items (e.g. all corporations in London with starting letters A-L). Arrows in Figure 2 illustrate such links.

**Definition 3 (Feature).** *A feature $f_i$ is a pair $<U_i, D_i>$ with $U_i$ being a set of usage vectors getting access to a set of data items $D_i$ by using feature $f_i$. $F_{IS}$ is the set of all features in the IS landscape.*

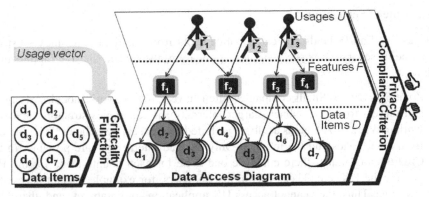

**Fig. 2.** The Data Privacy Model (DPM)

This allows formalizing the concept of data access diagrams:

**Definition 4 (Data Access Diagram).** *A data access diagram $A_{IS}$ is a triple $< U_{IS}, D_{IS}, F_{IS} >$ with $U_{IS}$ being the set of all usage vectors, $D_{IS}$ the set of all data items, and $F_{IS}$ the set of all features $f_i$ of the IS landscape. Obviously, $U_{IS} \supseteq \{U_i | \exists \langle U', D' \rangle \in F_{IS} : U' = U_i\}$ and $U_{IS} \supseteq \{D_i | \exists \langle U', D' \rangle \in D_{IS} : D' = D_i\}$ holds.*

The fourth DPM concept is the correctness criterion **data privacy compliance**. It is a formal way to say that the IS landscape respects all data privacy demands. It is based on the data access diagram. The data access diagram is data privacy compliant, if *all* usage vectors are only linked to green data items. There must be no single link to red data items.

**Definition 5 (Data Privacy Compliance).** *Let $A_{IS} =< U_{IS}, D_{IS}, F_{IS} >$ be the data access diagram. C is the data criticalness function. The IS landscape is data privacy compliant, iff $\forall <U', D'> \in F_{IS}, u \in U', d \in D' : C(d,u) = green.$*

## 3    Data Privacy Assessment

A data privacy assessment must state whether the IS landscape is data privacy compliant (Definition 5). A "non-compliant" alone does not help. It must come with a list of identified leaks and risks. Then, managers can decide which risks should be addressed and how. A data privacy assessment has three areas (Figure 3): classifying the data (with preparatory steps for identifying privacy rules), understanding the line of separation, and analyzing the data access paths.

**Fig. 3.** Data Privacy Assessment for IS Landscapes

## 3.1    Line of Separation

Four layers of an IS landscape can separate users from the data items they must not see ("line of separation"): the zone, the application, the tenant, and the (application) feature.

- *Zone Separation.* Small companies often have a flat network model. All clients and servers form one subnet. Larger international companies structure their network into zones. A zone is a subnet with dedicated security policies. It is shielded from other zones and the internet. Only defined interactions are possible. In the CreditPlus example, there could be one zone for each country: one for the US, one for the UK, etc. Then, CreditPlus US users, for example, cannot access the UK zone. Thus, they cannot access UK applications or databases, and, therefore, no UK data items.

- *Application Separation.* Users of various countries work in the same subnet or zone. The separation takes place on the application level. Each application "belongs" to a country. CreditPlus UK, CreditPlus CH, and CreditPlus US are separate applications. Users can only log into the CreditPlus application of their country.

- *Tenant Separation.* Multi-tenant applications [12] have been on the rise for some years. They enable separating users of various countries by means of tenants: one tenant per country. Users see only the data of the tenant they belong to. So there is one CreditPlus application with three tenants (UK, US, and CH). Each user is tagged with her country of residence, e.g. CH. If she uses CreditPlus, she sees only CH data items, but no UK or US ones.
One remark regarding local authorities: Normally, one database in one country stores the data for *all* tenants. The application blocks users (e.g. UK users) from data of other tenants (e.g. the US tenant). The application cannot prevent local authorities from enforcing access on the database level. Then, the local authorities see the data items of all tenants.

- *(Application) Feature Separation.* Here, all users of all countries work with one application. They have different access rights, e.g. depending on their country. This ensures that they see only customers of their country. So, there is one CreditPlus application. It has three wizards for finding customers: "Find customer (UK)", "Find customer (US)", and "Find customer (CH)". The UK users, for example, could access only the "Find customers (UK)" wizard. They could not access the two others. Again, the aspect of local authorities enforcing data access on the database level must be considered.

## 3.2    Classifying Data

In the world of theory, classifying data means applying the data criticalness function $C$ to all data items for all usage vectors. In practice, this is not possible. First, the number of usage vectors is too high. One must choose a subset of the most relevant ones. One could look only at the country aspect as this paper does in the running example. The second challenge is that the data criticalness function $C$ is normally not known. Moreover, it is (nearly) impossible to formalize the system in such a way.

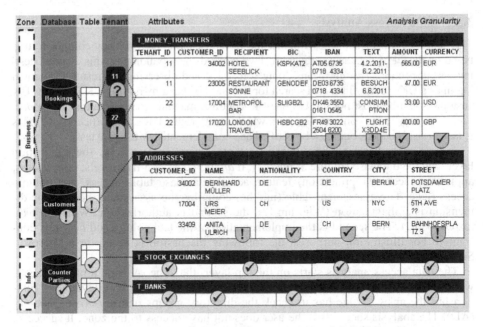

**Fig. 4.** Example for Data Classification ("!" means red, "✓" green)

Thus, classifying data is an intellectual task. It might also need input from the legal and compliance department. Two subtasks are important:

- Collecting all laws, regulations, and company internal rules (e.g. how to protect data of politically exposed customers).
- Analyzing the organization: users and roles, business processes, and the tasks of the users. This results in a list of users needing access to which data items.

The outcome is *privacy rules*, e.g. in form of a text document They are a kind of informal function C.

Testers use them to classify all data items of the IS landscape. They are classified as red when they identify concrete customers. The classification starts on the column level.[2] As Figure 4 illustrates, the customer ID in table T_MONEY_TRANSFERS is red. So are the recipient's name, her IBAN, and the booking text. Amount, currency, the recipient's BIC and the customer's tenant ID are uncritical (green). For table T_ADRESSES, again, the customer ID is red. So are name and street. City, country, and nationality are green (this depends often on the concrete context). The tables T_STOCK_EXCHANGE and T_BANKS do not contain red columns.

The column classification can be aggregated. Tables without any red column are green. Databases without any red table are green. Zones without any red database are green. Such aggregations ease the analysis of data access paths in the next subsection. But a last remark on multi-tenancy: users must not see data items of other tenants. If the user belongs to tenant 11, all data of other tenants (e.g. 22) is red.

---

[2] For ease of presentation, the paper abstracts from the multi-column aspect. Columns on their own might not identify a customer, a combination of them might. An example is two columns, business sector and balance sheet sum. One column alone is not enough to identify a company. The combination of two can make it quite easy.

## 3.3    Data Access Analysis

The data access analysis states whether the IS landscape is data privacy compliant. It is based on the DPM data access diagram. Two methods help building up this diagram, testing and inspection. *Testing* means doing something and observing the result. One could log in as a UK credit officer and search for US and UK customers. It is OK if he sees UK customers, but he must not see US ones. In contrast, manual or (semi-)automatic *inspection*s look only at the configuration, e.g. which access rights UK credit officers have. This is faster (i.e., cheaper), but must be verified and complemented with some tests.

Access control can be *established* on three layers: the network, the application layer, and the database (Figure 5, middle). It *affects* access on five levels: zone access, application access, (application) feature access, database table access, and column access (left). The assessment table (middle) compiles the assessment needs. One dimension is authentication (Who am I?), the second is authorization (What am I allowed to do?). The second is the implementation of the technology and how it is configured. For illustration purposes, the following discussion is based on a Microsoft Server network layer combined with an Oracle database.

The data access analysis starts on the top layer, the zone. A **zone analysis** checks whether a user can login into the zone (authentication). The network layer configuration has the answer. One has to check the directory groups of the Active Directory (AD). The analysis succeeds if the user does not have access to the zone. It succeeds, too, if the user has access *and* the zone is "green". In other words, the zone must not contain red data items (see Section 3.2). If the user has access and the zone is red, an application level analysis must follow. Standard software (e.g. Microsoft Server) is the norm on the network level. It can be assumed to be implemented correctly. There is no need to assess the implementation itself (Figure 5).

An **application analysis** looks at which applications a user can access and which databases such applications connect to. First, the user must be able to start the application. This is the authorization on the network level stored in the AD. Secondly, the user must be allowed to log into the application (if requested by the application).

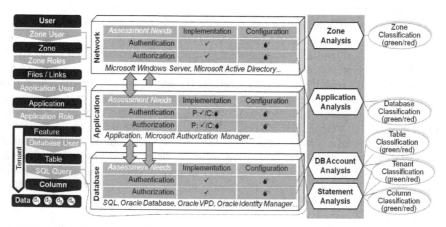

**Fig. 5.** Enriched Data Access Model: access levels (left), access control levels (middle), and assessment needs (right)

◆*/✓ assessment needed/not needed, P/C: packaged/custom software

This is the authentication on the application layer. The application can implement its own authentication service. It can also use the Windows Authorization Server [13]. In both cases, an assessment looks at the configuration. In the latter case, the AD is the place to look at, otherwise, the application-specific configuration. In the case of custom software, one might check the correctness of the implementation, i.e. whether the authorization works. This is an issue for legacy code from times when data privacy was not taken as seriously as today.

If the user can log into the application, the assessment continues with gathering all the databases that the application connects to. Sources can be the documentation, long-term application managers, or an own analysis. If there is a connection to at least one red database, a database (db) account analysis must follow.

A **db account analysis** checks if the application can access red tables and columns.[3] The starting point is a list with all the db accounts that the application uses. Again, the list can come from the documentation, from talking with long-term staff, or from own experiments. The db accounts have db roles. Db roles represent access rights to tables. SQL databases store them in the database catalogue. Looking this up is the second step. The third step is matching access rights with the red and green classification of tables and columns. If there are no access rights for red tables and columns, the assessment is successful. If not, a statement analysis must follow. Again, there is no need for checking the correctness of the implemented authentication and authorization mechanisms on the database layer. Commercial databases can be assumed as correct.

If a multi-tenant system relies on the database for tenant separation, the db account analysis also covers this aspect.[4] Up to now, the section focussed on the columns dimension. This is whether certain users can see, e.g. the customer names of T_BALANCES in Figure 6. Multi-tenant systems have a second dimension: the tenants. Table T_BALANCES stores data for three tenants: US, UK, and CH. The tenant separation is based on Oracle's virtual private database (VPD) [14]. VPD demands that tables with tenant-specific data have a tenant ID column. Oracle extends SQL statement (select, insert, update, delete) for such tables transparently. It adds a "WHERE tenant id=XX" clause. Configuring a database for VPD has two aspects. First, the table must be under a VPD policy. Secondly, database users must be associated with a tenant ID. A tenant level analysis must check this.

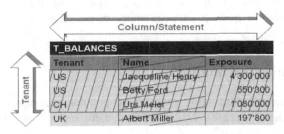

**Fig. 6.** Tenant Level and Statement Level Analysis

---

[3] The idea is to look at the application and not the application user. This speeds up the analysis. A more detailed analysis is only done for a statement analysis.

[4] Using mature technologies, such as VPD, simplifies the assessment. They can be assumed to be correct. Otherwise, one must test the tenant separation implementation as part of the application analysis.

Finally, if all previous analysis methods did not prove data privacy compliance, the only option left is a **statement analysis**. It looks at all SQL statements, such as those submitted using JDBC. All statements must retrieve only green columns and green tenants. Thus, an application can be assessed as green (even if accessing red tables or columns) if the application "voluntarily" reads only green data items. Such an analysis is costly. It implies inspecting the complete source code. Thus, in practice, it is unpractical. An access path reconstruction (Section 4) might be preferable.

To conclude: There are various levels for checking if users (or usage vectors) access red data items. One starts at the top and steps only down if necessary. Certainly, one can stop at any level and assume that the IS landscape is not data privacy compliant.

## 4     Access Path Reconstruction

A statement level analysis requires the source code, and is expensive. This makes reconstructing the access path without looking at the implementation an option. The reconstruction treats the IS landscape as a black box. It primarily analyzes the GUI, and tries to build the data access diagram.

The first step is to list all GUIs and group them into GUIs for presenting data ("Customer Overview" in Figure 7) and GUIs for searching for data ("Customer Search" in Figure 7). The presentation GUIs are analyzed for their objects, such as customer static data and exposure, and their attributes, such as name, country, and limit. All attributes must be green (1a). The second step (1b) looks at the object instances (respectively rows) that a user can find. The "Customer Search" GUI, for example, should allow UK users only to search for UK customers.

The two initial steps 1a and 1b allow for an assessment whether a user might see red data items or not. It reflects the tenant and responsibilities (e.g. for the segment retail banking UK). If there is a need for more details, one can also match GUIs to database tables (2). The documentation or the application management team might help. This allows validating the search GUI analysis. One can compare the data items that one has found using the GUI (e.g. UK and US tenant data) with the data stored in the table (e.g. UK, US, and CH data). Thus, one can find overseen data items.

To conclude: An access path reconstruction sounds hard and expensive (and it is). Nevertheless, it allows making an assessment based on GUIs when all other approaches fail.

## 5     Sanitization Techniques

Sanitization makes red data items green. Two popular techniques are vertical and horizontal greening (Figure 8). Understanding them means understanding the data privacy risks they come with.

*Vertical greening* transforms or masks data on its way from the database up to the GUI. Figure 8 (left) provides an example. The attribute of the GUI mask "Customer overview" shows all attributes. One is red ("name"). So, it is masked. Vertical greening is an "on-the-fly" greening approach. It becomes active when data is retrieved from the database and shown on the GUI. It supports both sourcing scenarios, global software development and testing and global sourcing of business activities.

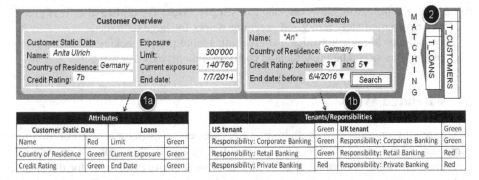

| Attributes | | | | Tenants/Reponsibilities | | | |
|---|---|---|---|---|---|---|---|
| Customer Static Data | | Loans | | US tenant | Green | UK tenant | Green |
| Name | Red | Limit | Green | Responsibility: Corporate Banking | Green | Responsibility: Corporate Banking | Green |
| Country of Residence | Green | Current Exposure | Green | Responsibility: Retail Banking | Green | Responsibility: Retail Banking | Red |
| Credit Rating | Green | End Date | Green | Responsibility: Private Banking | Red | Responsibility: Private Banking | Red |

**Fig. 7.** Access Path Reconstruction for CreditPlus sample masks

*Horizontal greening* replicates the data (e.g. the complete database). Then, the replica is "greened". One can drop red columns or tables, delete all data in red columns, shuffle the values, or replace them with synthetic values. Figure 8 (right) illustrates this. The data item "Anita Ulrich" becomes "Miller AG" in the replicated database. The rest of the application, i.e. the way from the database to the GUI, can remain unchanged.

Horizontal greening is a batch activity. It can be used for the global software development and testing scenario. It is suitable for the global sourcing of business activities scenario for OLAP-style applications only. OLAP-style application do not write data to the database. Combining horizontal greening and OLTP-style applications requires addressing the replication problem (and being able to understand what rows are a replica of which other rows).

Assessing the effectiveness of greening addresses completeness and greenness. *Completeness* demands finding *all* red data items. *Greenness* demands that the greened data really become uncritical. It must not happen that customer names are masked, so that they can be reconstructed (easily).

Assessing the completeness requires finding the links between the red columns of database tables and GUIs. Then, one has to check whether there is a greening mechanism in place. It can be either (a) directly on the way between the database and the GUI (vertical greening) or (b) the data item is derived as a copy from another database and during or after the copy the data item is greened.

The second aspect to be checked is greenness. Horizontal and vertical greening require different approaches. Vertical greening can only be checked by inspecting the online masking algorithm or running many tests. Both options are feasible for

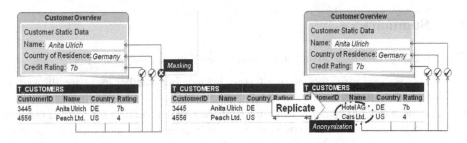

**Fig. 8.** Greening Techniques (left: vertical greening, right: horizontal greening)

horizontal greening, too. However, one can simply assess the replica after it is greened. One sees immediately how good greening works for large data sets.

To conclude: Many companies use greening techniques. Checking their completeness and greenness can be implemented easily in data privacy assessments.

# 6    Related Work

When looking on related work, there is, first, pioneering work on access control concepts such as role-based access control [8] (also a base for this paper). Concrete implementations such as Bertino, et al. [15], elaborate security challenges for databases, and how systems overcome them. Similar work on the operating system layer looks on how to enforce usage control for X windows systems [16].

The logical next step is to check whether applications implement access control correctly. The work of Pretschner, et al. [17] on model-based tests for access control policies falls into this category. They discuss how to generate test cases efficiently for testing policies and which input they need. Le Traon and Baudry [18] focus on the relationship between functional tests and security policy tests and how they overlap. Besides work on testing, there are also approaches for formalizing the systems and reasoning about them, for example, whether business processes have data leaks (Accorsi and Wonnemann [19]). Stoller et al. [20] and Schaad and Moffett [21] are interested in whether a (given complex) formal access policy is compliant. This complements this paper, which provides a methodology for *extracting* a simple yet meaningful policy model from a real system. The compliance decision itself is trivial.

A different research direction focuses on the usage of data. Stufflebeam, et al. [20], for example, compare P3P and EPAL. They are newer policy specification techniques for formalizing the purpose for storing data. The manifesto for Hippocratic Databases (Agrawal, et al. [21]) demands a privacy-aware database management system. Whereas this work is more on the requirements level, later work of Byun and Li [22] discusses how to implement such a database. They associate data stored in a database with reasons why it is stored (e.g. for marketing, for research, etc.). Queries also have a purpose and return only the data stored for this purpose.

Finally, there are approaches to actively test the security of systems. Internal engineers or external consultants try to break into the IT landscape. They attack actively to identify security leaks (see Palmer [23] about "ethical hacking").

# 7    Summary

This paper provides data privacy assessments based on four key concepts:

- The *usage vector* for formalizing factors influencing whether users are allowed to see certain data.
- The more theoretical *data criticalness function* which decides for a usage context if a data item is allowed to be seen. It is complemented on the practical side with privacy rules and a guideline for *classifying data* complements.

- The theoretical concept of *data access diagrams* linking usage vectors, data items and application features to see who can access which data. The practical counterpart is a *data access analysis* with the concrete examples of a zone, application, database account, and statement analysis.
- A formal *data privacy compliance correctness* criterion.

The paper also discussed briefly data access based only on GUIs, for example, for legacy applications and the impact of sanitization. In one sentence: The methodology provides a quick "health-check" for IT managers stating whether users can access only the data that they are supposed to see.

**Acknowledgments.** The author would like to thank Hans-Joachim Lotzer for the valuable discussions.

# References

1. Five Countries: Cost of Data Breach. Ponemon Institute (2010)
2. Breach at Los Alamos: A special report. The New York Times, March 6 (1999)
3. 100,000 non-clinical NHS staff have access to confidential records. The Telegraph, March 25 (2010)
4. The Liechtenstein Connection. Spiegel Online International, February 16 (2008)
5. International Tax Evasion Scandal Spreads. Spiegel Online International, March 3 (2008)
6. Up and away: A dogfight over frequent-flyer miles is distracting Germany's politicians. The Economist, August 8 (2002)
7. U.S. Officials Quiz Sony on Data Theft. The Wall Street Journal, April 30 (2011)
8. Ferraiolo, D., et al.: Proposed NIST Standard for Role-Based Access Control. ACM Transactions on Information System Security 4(3), 224–274 (2001)
9. Haller, K.: White-box testing for database-driven applications: a requirements analysis. In: 2nd Int. Workshop on Testing Database Systems, DBTest 2009, Providence, RI, June 29 (2009)
10. Haller, K.: The test data challenge for database-driven applications. In: 3rd Int. Workshop on Testing Database Systems, DBTest 2010, Indianapolis, IN, June 7 (2010)
11. Haller, K.: On the implementation and correctness of information system upgrades. In: IEEE Int. Conference on Software Maintenance (ICSM), Timisoara, Romania, September 12-18 (2010)
12. Haller, K.: Web services from a service provider perspective: tenant management services for multitenant information systems. ACM SIGSOFT Software Engineering Notes 36(1), 1–4
13. Windows Authorization Manager. MSDN, http://msdn.microsoft.com/ (retrieved May 22, 2011)
14. Browder, K., Davidson, K.A.: The virtual private database in Oracle9iR2, White Paper, Oracle (January 2002)
15. Bertino, E., et al.: Database security: research and practice. Information Systems 20(7), 537–556 (1995)
16. Pretschner, A., et al.: Usage Control Enforcement with Data Flow Tracking for X11. In: 5th Intl. Workshop on Security and Trust Management (STM), Saint Malo, France, September 24-25 (2009)

17. Pretschner, A., et al.: Model-Based Tests for Access Control Policies. In: Int. Conference on Software, Testing and Validation, Lillehammer, Norway, April 9-11 (2008)
18. Le Traon, Y., Baudry, B.: Testing security policies: going beyond functional testing. In: Int. Symposium on Software Reliability (ISSRE 2007), Sweden, November 5-9 (2007)
19. Accorsi, R., Wonnemann, C.: InDico: Information Flow Analysis of Business Processes for Confidentiality Requirements. In: ERCIM Workshop on Security and Trust Management, Athens, Greece, September 23-24 (2011)
20. Stoller, S., et al.: Efficient Policy Analysis for Administrative Role Based Access Control. In: 14th Conf. on Computer and Communications Security (CCS), Alexandria, VA (2007)
21. Schaad, A., Moffett, J.: A lightweight approach to specification and analysis of role-based access control extensions. In: SACMAT, Monterey, CA (2002)
22. Stufflebeam, W., et al.: Specifying Privacy Policies with P3P and EPAL: Lessons Learned. In: Workshop on Privacy in the Electronic Society, WPES, Washington, DC, October 28 (2004)
23. Agrawal, R., et al.: Hippocratic Databases. In: 28th Int. Conference on Very Large Data Bases (VLDB 2002), Hong Kong, China, August 20-23 (2002)
24. Byun, J.-W., Li, N.: Purpose based access control for privacy protection in relational database systems. VLDB Journal 17(4), 603–619 (2008)
25. Palmer, C.: Ethical hacking. IBM Systems Journal 40(3) (2001)

# Flexible Scoping of Authorization Constraints on Business Processes with Loops and Parallelism

Samuel J. Burri and Günter Karjoth

IBM Research – Zurich
{sbu,gka}@zurich.ibm.com

**Abstract.** Real-life business process specifications include situations where work may be repeated due to exceptions such as the lack of resources or failed approvals. However, most authorization constraint models for business processes describe them as partially ordered sets of tasks. This abstraction simplifies the analysis of constraints greatly but prevents their use in real systems because control flows with loops are not supported. To overcome this limitation, we scope authorization constraints to task instances using the concept of release, which removes associations between users and their previously executed tasks. We define a model applying releases to cardinality and interval constraints, such as Separation of Duty (SoD). The latter is based on the notion of intervals defined by pairs of tasks and imposing conditions on the users executing them. We extend BPMN to visualize our constraints, bridging the gap between IT and business people as well as to auditors.

## 1 Introduction

Business process modeling is increasingly used not only to improve organizational efficiency and quality but also to enforce internal controls in order to fight fraud and to comply with regulatory requirements. Most security requirements for business processes are concerned with human activities. Separation of Duties (SoD) for example is a well-known class of constraints that prevent a single user from executing all critical tasks. Various frameworks have been developed for specifying and analyzing authorization constraints for business processes. However, they are limited in the kinds of constraints they can handle and make over-simplistic abstractions of a business process' control flow, rendering them inapplicable to real systems.

We model business process as *workflows* and observe that business process modeling languages, such as BPMN [4], allow workflows with loops. In the loop-back pattern [5] for example, an exclusive gateway or boundary event loops back to a previous step in the control flow, typically used for rework in the case of exceptions. Thus successfully terminated workflow instances may contain an arbitrary number of instances of a task. But most authorization constraint models are defined only on workflows with a partial order on tasks [2]. This restriction simplifies the analysis of constraints greatly but prevents their use. First attempts to overcome this limitation were made by Crampton *et al.* covering loops

F. Daniel et al. (Eds.): BPM 2011 Workshops, Part II, LNBIP 100, pp. 411–422, 2012.
© Springer-Verlag Berlin Heidelberg 2012

over single tasks [7] and Solworth allowing constraints in the presence of loops but only if the first task is executed by the same person [6]. Basin *et al.* were the first who scoped constraints to subsets of task instances, using their new concept of release [1].

Assume that the compliance of a business process is independent of the number of attempts to execute critical activities until successful completion. Then a SoD constraint might be satisfied if only the users differ who executed these tasks last. A *release* [1] admits to repeal the association of users and their previously executed tasks in a controlled manner and is therefore well suited to model such cases. In this paper, we extend above authorization constraints with conditions over users, called interval constraints and defined over subwords of workflow instances. Furthermore, by not requiring that SoD constraints are defined over disjoint sets of tasks, we increase expressivity. We also add cardinality constraints setting a lower limit on the number of users executing a set of tasks. To model these constraints graphically, we extend a few BPMN artifacts [4]. Examples illustrate the expressivity of the defined constraint language.

## 2   Model

Let $\mathcal{T}$ be a set of *tasks* and $\mathcal{U}$ be a set of *users*. For a task $t$ and a user $u$, the tuple $(t, u)$ models the execution of $t$ by $u$, called a *task instance (of $t$)*. We use the shorthand notation $t.u$ for $(t, u)$. To simplify the correspondence between our formal model of business processes and BPMN models, we introduce a set of *events* $\mathcal{E}$ to model BPMN events. Let $\Sigma = (\mathcal{T} \times \mathcal{U}) \cup \mathcal{E}$ be the set of all task instances and all events. A *workflow* is a labelled transition system $(Q, \Sigma, \delta, q^0)$, where $Q$ is a set of states, the ternary relation $\delta \subseteq Q \times \Sigma \times Q$ is a nondeterministic state transition function, and $q^0 \in Q$ is a start state.

A sequence of task instances $L = \langle \sigma_1, \ldots, \sigma_n \rangle \in \Sigma^*$ is a *workflow instance* of a workflow $(Q, \Sigma, \delta, q^0)$ if there exists a set of states $\{q_1, \ldots, q_{n-1}\}$ such that $(q_{k-1}, \sigma_k, q_k) \in \delta$ for all $k \in \{1, \ldots, n\}$. A sequence $S = \langle \sigma_k, \sigma_{k+1}, \ldots, \sigma_{k+l} \rangle$, for $k \in \{1, \ldots, n\}$ and $l \in \{0, \ldots, n-k\}$, is a *subword* of $L$. E.g. $\langle \sigma_2, \sigma_3 \rangle$ is a subword of $L = \langle \sigma_1, \sigma_2, \sigma_3, \sigma_4 \rangle$ but $\langle \sigma_1, \sigma_3 \rangle$ is not. Furthermore, a sequence $S = \langle \sigma_{i_1}, \sigma_{i_2}, \ldots, \sigma_{i_m} \rangle$, for $m \in \{1, \ldots, n\}$ and $i_1 < i_2 < \ldots < i_m$, is a *subsequence* of $L$. E.g., $\langle \sigma_1, \sigma_3 \rangle$ is a subsequence of the above $L$ but $\langle \sigma_3, \sigma_1 \rangle$ is not.

We will later use events to scope authorization constraints. For this reason, we introduce a few auxiliary definitions to characterize specific subwords of a workflow instance. For a subset of events $E \subseteq \mathcal{E}$, we denote by $[E]_L$ the set of maximal subwords in $L$ that do not contain an event in $E$.

Let $[t, t']_L$ denote the set of subwords $\langle \sigma_i, \ldots, \sigma_j \rangle$ of $L$, for $i < j$, starting with a task instance of $t$ and ending with a task instance of $t'$, *i.e.* $\sigma_i = t.u$ and $\sigma_j = t'.u'$ for two users $u$ and $u'$. Furthermore, let $[\![t, t']\!]_L$ denote the set of all subwords in $L$ that either start with $t$ and end with $t'$ or start with $t'$ and end with $t$, *i.e.* $[\![t, t']\!]_L = [t, t']_L \cup [t', t]_L$. We call an element of $[\![t, t']\!]_L$ an *interval* defined by $t$ and $t'$. Note that we do not require $t$ and $t'$ to be different. However, because $i < j$, an interval is at least of length 2.

Given a workflow instance $L$ and a set of tasks $T$, $L \upharpoonright T$ is the subsequence $\langle \sigma_{i_1}, \ldots, \sigma_{i_m} \rangle$ of $L$ that contains only the task instances of tasks in $T$. E.g., $\langle t_1.u_1, t_2.u_2, t_3.u_3 \rangle \upharpoonright \{t_1, t_3\} = \langle t_1.u_1, t_3.u_3 \rangle$. Furthermore, the auxiliary function users returns the set of users who have executed the task instances in $L$. We now introduce a running example to illustrate all these definitions.

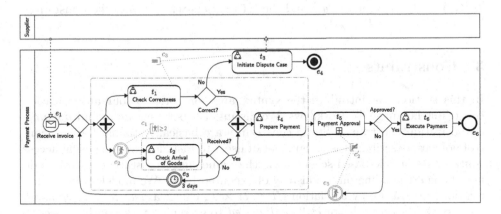

**Fig. 1.** Payment workflow augmented with constraints

*Example 1.* Figure 1 shows a BPMN model of a *payment process* that is based on the invoice lifecycle proposed by the European Expert Group on e-Invoicing [3]. We model this process by a workflow over the set of tasks $\mathcal{T} = \{t_1, \ldots, t_6\}$, where $t_1$ corresponds to Check Correctness, $t_2$ to Check Arrival of Goods, etc, and $\mathcal{E} = \{e_1, \ldots, e_6\}$, where $e_1$ corresponds to the start event, $e_3$ to the internal timer event, etc. Ignore the grey BPMN elements for the moment. Furthermore, we assume the set of users $\mathcal{U} = \{u_1, u_2, u_3\}$.

The process is started when the customer receives an invoice from the supplier. He then checks in parallel whether the invoice is correct ($t_1$) and whether the goods have arrived ($t_2$). The supplier initiates a dispute case ($t_3$) and aborts the process if the invoice is not correct. If the goods have not arrived yet, then the customer waits for 3 days and then checks again. If both checks finally succeed, the payment is prepared ($t_4$) and if approved ($t_5$) also executed ($t_6$). The process loops back to the start if the payment is not approved.

For space reasons we omit a formal definition of the workflow that corresponds to the payment process. However, it is straightforward to see that the following workflow instance corresponds to a successful execution of the process:

$$L = \langle \; e_1, \; e_2, \; t_2.u_1, \; t_1.u_2, \; e_3, \; t_2.u_1, \; t_4.u_2, \; t_5.u_2, \; e_5,$$
$$e_2, \; t_1.u_1, \; t_2.u_2, \; t_4.u_2, \; t_5.u_3, \; t_6.u_1, \; e_6 \; \rangle$$

Omitting the users for readability, the set of maximal subwords of $L$ not containing $e_2$ is then

$$[\{e_2\}]_L = \{\langle e_1 \rangle, \; \langle t_2, \; t_1, \; e_3, \; t_2, \; t_4, \; t_5, \; e_5 \rangle, \; \langle t_1, \; t_2, \; t_4, \; t_5, \; t_6, \; e_6 \rangle\}$$

and the set of intervals defined by $t_1$ and $t_5$ is

$$[\![t_1, t_5]\!]_L = \{\langle t_1, e_3, t_2, t_4, t_5 \rangle, \ \langle t_1, e_3, t_2, t_4, t_5, e_5, e_2, t_1, t_2, t_4, t_5 \rangle,$$
$$\langle t_5, e_5, e_2, t_1 \rangle, \ \langle t_1, t_2, t_4, t_5 \rangle\}.$$

Reducing $L$ to the workflow instance containing only task instances of $t_2$ is $L \restriction \{t_2\} = \langle t_2.u_1, \ t_2.u_1, \ t_2.u_2 \rangle$ and the set of users who execute these instances is $\mathsf{users}(L \restriction \{t_2\}) = \{u_1, u_2\}$.

## 3    Constraints

In this section, we introduce the syntax and semantics of our authorization constraint language for workflows. We distinguish between *static* and *dynamic* authorization constraints. Static constraints are basically standard access control policies, describing the assignment of users to task, for example using access control lists or role-based schemas. As the name suggests, static constraints do not change depending on the history of executed tasks. We model static authorizations abstractly by a relation $UT \subseteq \mathcal{U} \times \mathcal{T}$, called a *user-task assignment*, and say that a user $u$ is *statically authorized* to execute a task $t$ with respect to $UT$ if $(u, t) \in UT$. Static SoD and static Binding of Duty (BoD) is subsumed by this definition.

In the following, we focus on dynamic authorization constraints defining authorizations that depend on who has previously executed tasks in a workflow instance. We distinguish between *cardinality constraints* that impose restrictions on the number of different users executing a set of tasks and *interval constraints* that impose relations between the users who execute pairs of task instances.

### 3.1    Cardinality Constraints

We start with a formal definition of cardinality constraints.

**Definition 1.** *A cardinality constraint is a triple* $(T, k, E)$*, where* $T \subseteq \mathcal{T}$ *is a set of tasks,* $k > 1$ *an integer, and* $E \subseteq \mathcal{E}$ *a set of events. A workflow instance* $L$ *satisfies a cardinality constraint* $(T, k, E)$ *if for all* $S \in [E]_L$, $|\mathsf{users}(S \restriction T)| \geq \min\{k, |S \restriction T|\}$.

We use the set of events $E$ to split $L$ into subwords $S$. For each of them the cardinality constraint requires that at least a threshold of $k$ users must execute the instances of the tasks $T$. This kind of constraint is also known as *relaxed SoD* [7] or *k-out-of-n* constraint for $|T| = n$. The minimum between $k$ and $|S \restriction T|$ ensures that a constraint is also well-defined if a subword $S$ contains less than $k$ instances of tasks in $T$. We omit the set notation in case of singleton sets and also the set $E$ if empty.

*Example 2.* Consider task $t_2$ (Check Arrival of Goods) of the payment process. Due to the inner loop passing through the internal timer event $e_3$, $t_2$ may be executed multiple times before the payment is approved. The cardinality constraint $c_1 = (t_2, 2, e_3)$ requires that at least two different users must execute $t_2$ if $t_2$ is executed more than once. This ensures that if the goods are supposedly not received, a second user must have a look at the situation, thereby reducing the risk of fraud.

Recall workflow instance $L$ from Example 1. The first and third subword in $[e_2]_L$, $S_1 = \langle e_1 \rangle$ and $S_3 = \langle t_1.u_1, t_2.u_2, t_4.u_2, t_5.u_3, t_6.u_1, e_6 \rangle$, satisfy $c_1$. However, subword $S_2 = \langle t_2.u_1, t_1.u_2, e_3, t_2.u_1, t_4.u_2, t_5.u_2, e_5 \rangle$ does not satisfy $c_1$ because $t_2$ is executed more than once but only by user $u_1$. Thus $L$ does not satisfy $c_1$.

Example 2 raises an interesting question about the enforcement of cardinality constraints. Consider $S_4 = \langle t_2.u_1, t_1.u_1, e_3, t_2.u_1, e_3, \mathbf{t_2.u_2}, t_4.u_1, t_5.u_1, e_5 \rangle$, which satisfies $c_1$. The two workflow instances $S_2$ and $S_4$ have the same prefix $\langle t_2.u_1, t_1.u_1, e_3, t_2.u_1 \rangle$ which does not satisfy $c_1$. An enforcement mechanism for $c_1$ cannot know whether the execution of the payment process will extend this prefix to a workflow instance like $S_2$ that does not satisfy $c_1$ or to one like $S_4$ that satisfies $c_1$. A *pessimistic* enforcement mechanism would require the first $k$ instances of tasks in $T$ to be executed by different users and thereby ensure that every prefix of a workflow instance satisfies $c_1$. An *optimistic* enforcement mechanism would tolerate prefixes that do not satisfy $c_1$ "hoping" that the final workflow instance does satisfy $c_1$.

Our definition of $[E]_L$ to contain only the maximal subwords of $L$ between events in $E$ allows a pessimistic or an optimistic enforcement. If we defined $[E]_L$ to contain all prefixes of maximal subwords in $L$ between events in $E$, then only a pessimistic enforcement would be possible.

### 3.2   Interval Constraints

Interval constraints impose relations between the users who execute pairs of task instances.

**Definition 2.** *An (atomic) interval constraint is a triple $((t, t'), \rho, E)$, for a pair of tasks $(t, t') \in \mathcal{T} \times \mathcal{T}$, a relation on users $\rho \subseteq \mathcal{U} \times \mathcal{U}$, and a set of events $E \subseteq \mathcal{E}$. A workflow instance $L$ satisfies an interval constraint $((t, t'), \rho, E)$ if for all $S \in [E]_L$ and $\langle t_i.u_i, \ldots, t_j.u_j \rangle \in [\![t, t']\!]_S$, $(u_i, u_j) \in \rho$.*

We use again (release) events to scope interval constraints. The set of events $E$ splits $L$ into subwords $S$. For each interval constraint contained in a subword $S$, $\langle t_i.u_i, \ldots, t_j.u_j \rangle \in [\![t, t']\!]_S$, it must hold that the user who executes the first task $t_i$ is related to the one who executes the last task $t_j$ as specified by $\rho$. For example, we may choose $\rho$ to be the inequality relation $\neq$ for expressing SoD or the equality relation $=$ for expressing BoD. We can also apply interval constraints to single tasks. For example, the constraint $((t, t), \neq)$ requires that each instance of $t$ must be executed by a different user and the constraint $((t, t), =)$ requires that all instances of $t$ are executed by the same user. The interval constraint $((t, t), manager\text{-}of)$ requires that the task $t$ can only be executed again if the user is the manager of the user who executed the previous instance of $t$.

Consider an interval constraint $((t, t'), \rho, E)$ and a workflow instance $L$. Furthermore, assume $S = \langle t_i.u_i, \ldots, t_j.u_j \rangle \in [\![t, t']\!]_L$ and that no $e \in E$ is contained in $S$. We say the task instance $t_i.u_i$ *allocates* user $u_i$ to relation $\rho$. The task instance $t_j.u_j$ is called *restricted* because the choice of $u_j$ depends on the user who was previously allocated when $t_i$ was executed. Note that a task in the scope of a loop may be a restricted as well as an allocating task. We now proceed with our running example.

*Example 3.* Consider task $t_1$ (Check Correctness) and $t_5$ (Payment Approval) of the payment process. The interval constraint $c_2 = ((t_1, t_5), \neq, e_5)$ requires that within one (outer) loop of the payment process task instances of $t_1$ must be executed by different users than instances of $t_5$, thereby separating the duties between the checking of invoices and the approval of payments.

Consider again Example 1. The release event $e_5$ splits the work flow instance $L$ into two maximal subwords, $S_1 = \langle e_1, e_2, t_1.u_2, e_3, t_2.u_1, t_4.u_2, t_5.u_2 \rangle$ and $S_2 = \langle e_2, t_1.u_1, t_2.u_2, t_4.u_2, t_5.u_3, t_6.u_1, e_6 \rangle$. The subword $\langle t_1.u_2, e_3, t_2.u_1, t_4.u_2, t_5.u_2 \rangle$ in $[\![t_1, t_5]\!]_{S_1}$ does not satisfy $c_2$ because the instances of $t_1$ and $t_5$ are executed by the same user, *i.e.* $(u_2, u_2)$ is not an element of the relation $\neq$, whereas the subword $\langle t_1.u_1, t_2.u_2, t_4.u_2, t_5.u_3 \rangle$ in $[\![t_1, t_5]\!]_{S_2}$ satisfies $c_2$ because $t_1$ is executed by $u_1$ and $t_5$ by $u_3$, *i.e.* $(u_1, u_3) \in \neq$. As a result, the workflow instance $L$ does not satisfy the interval constraint $c_2$.

For two sets of tasks $T, T' \subseteq \mathcal{T}$, we generalize atomic interval constraints to *(compound) interval constraints* of the form $((T, T'), \rho, E) = \{((t, t'), \rho, E) \mid t \in T$ and $t' \in T'\}$. Note that $T$ and $T'$ must not necessarily be disjoint. In fact, we write $(T, \rho, E)$ for $((T, T), \rho, E)$. A workflow instance $L$ satisfies a compound interval constraint if it satisfies all the respective atomic interval constraints.

### 3.3   Constrained Workflows

By splitting a workflow instance $L$ into subwords using a set of events $E$, we enable a scoping of cardinality and interval constraints to subsets of task instances in $L$. When the control flow passes through an event $e \in E$ the history of who has executed previous task instances is rendered irrelevant with respect to future task executions. Therefore, we call them *release events*. Finally, we combine authorization constraints and workflows.

**Definition 3.** *A* constrained workflow *is a triple* $(W, UT, C)$, *where $W$ is a* workflow, *$UT$ a user-task assignment, and $C$ a set of cardinality and interval constraints. A workflow instance $L$ satisfies a constrained workflow* $(W, UT, C)$ *if*

- *$L$ is an instance of $W$,*
- *for every task instance $t.u \in L$, $(u, t) \in UT$, and*
- *$L$ satisfies every constraint in $C$.*

*Example 4.* Let $W$ be the workflow corresponding to the payment process from Example 1 and assume $UT = \mathcal{U} \times \mathcal{T}$; *i.e.* every user is statically authorized to execute every task. Furthermore, let $C = \{c_1, c_2', c_3\}$ where $c_1 = (t_2, 2, e_3)$ is the cardinality constraint from Example 2, $c_2' = ((\{t_1, t_2, t_4\}, t_5), \neq, e_5)$, and $c_3 = ((t_1, t_2), =)$. Note that the interval constraint $c_2$ from Example 3 is contained in $c_2'$. Consider once more workflow instance $L$ from Example 1. Although $L$ is an instance of $W$ and for all task instances $t.u$ in $L$, $(u, t) \in UT$, $L$ does not satisfy the constrained workflow $(W, UT, C)$ because $L$ does not satisfy $c_1$ and $c_2$ as explained in the previous examples.

## 4    Graphical Notation

In this section, we describe our extension of BPMN to visually model cardinality and interval constraints and affects of the placement of a release events, with respect to a workflow's control flow, on the semantics of our constraints.

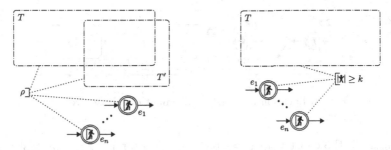

**Fig. 2.** Visualization of interval and cardinality constraints in BPMN

### 4.1    BPMN Extension

BPMN 2.0 [4] provides a few artifacts to describe human involvement in business processes. A task with an icon in the upper left corner depicting a person, as illustrated in Figure 1, is called a *user task*. They are meant to be executed by humans, as opposed to tasks that are executed by machines. Some modelers understand process lanes as synonyms for roles and the placement of a task in a lane as its assignment to the respective role.

BPMN comes also with a number of artifacts for annotations. For example, a dash-dotted box, called *group artifact*, is used to group tasks. We use them to define sets of tasks. A dotted line ending with a half-open box containing text is called a *text annotation*. We generalize them to link sets of tasks and release points. Furthermore, we introduce a new class of internal BPMN events, illustrated with a person leaving a door, for modeling release events.

Figure 2 illustrates how we extend and combine these artifacts to visualize cardinality and interval constraints. An interval constraint $((T, T'), \rho, E)$ is illustrated by two group artifacts that define the sets of users $T$ and $T'$ and a text annotation stating $\rho$ that links $T$, $T'$, and the release events $e_1$ to $e_n$ in $E$. Similarly, a cardinality constraint $(T, k, E)$ is illustrated by a group artifact defining $T$ and a text annotation depicting a stylized set of users combined with $\geq k$ that links $T$ and the release events $e_1$ to $e_n$ in $E$.

*Example 5.* In the payment process from Example 1, the grey elements in Figure 1 visualize the constraints $c_1$, $c_2'$, and $c_3$ from Example 4.

## 4.2 Placement of Release Events

We have modelled releases as (BPMN) events, which release previously allocated users when executed; i.e., their allocation is not considered for the associated constraint. But it is far from obvious where to place release events with respect to a workflow's control flow. In fact, depending on the location within the given workflow, the effect of the release event may differ.

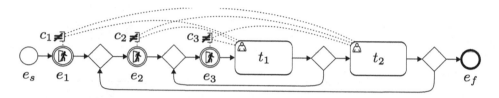

**Fig. 3.** Location matters – placement of release events

In Figure 3, the constraints $c_i = ((t_1, t_2), \neq, e_i)$ for $1 \leq i \leq 3$ on tasks $t_1$ and $t_2$ only differ in the placement of the release event. Whenever release event $e_2$ is passed then release event $e_3$ is passed as well. Thus, when a workflow instance satisfies constraint $c_3$ then it satisfies constraint $c_2$ as well. Therefore constraint $c_2$ and $c_3$ are superfluous because of $c_1$. It also becomes obvious that release event $e_1$ has no effect because it will only be passed at the begin of the workflow instance where the constraint history is still empty. In general, release events on a transition from (to) the initial (final) state can be safely ignored.

Let us look again at the interval constraint $c_2' = (((\{t_1, t_2, t_4\}, t_5), \neq, e_5)$ from Example 3 and the payment process from Example 1. Tasks $t_1$ and $t_2$ are restricted with respect to task $t_5$ whenever the outer loop is executed. Constraint $c_2'$ is only reset when control goes from task $t_5$ to task $t_1$ and to task $t_2$ respectively. We note that it is sufficient to consider only the task before the release event. Thus, release event $e_5$ can also be defined as the two task tuples $\{(t_5, t_1), (t_5, t_2)\}$ representing the transitions, which trigger the reset of the execution history.

Similarly, when translating the (graphical) location of release events $e_1$, $e_2$, and $e_3$ in Figure 3 to task tuples, we notice that these release events are strictly ordered with respect to set inclusion:

$$e_1 = \{(e_s, t_1)\}, \ e_2 = e_1 \cup \{(t_2, t_1)\}, \ e_3 = e_2 \cup \{(t_1, t_1)\}.$$

It is future work to extend this representation to control flows with parallelism, as shown below.

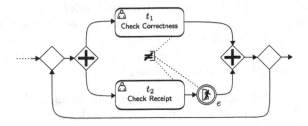

**Fig. 4.** A constraint over parallel tasks

The interval constraint in Figure 4 illustrates the behavior of a release event within the parallel execution of tasks and why we have made the convention to coincide the execution of a release events with the preceding task. It says that the second task must be executed by a different user but only if task $t_1$ was executed first.

Consider the workflow instance $\langle t_1.u_1, t_2.u_2, e, t_2.u_3, e, t_1.u_4 \rangle$. The constraint $((t_1, t_2), \neq, e)$ defines four intervals of which only the most left does not include a release event and thus requires users $u_1$ and $u_2$ to be different. Note further that on workflow instance $\langle t_2.u_1, e, t_1.u_2, t_1.u_3, t_2.u_4 \rangle$ user $u_4$ cannot be user $u_2$ or $u_3$.

## 5    Constraint Properties and Composability

In this section, we elaborate on cases where unnecessary details in constraint specifications can be safely removed and on the effect of composing constraints.

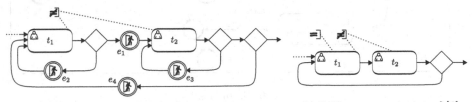

a) Different placements of release events        b) Self-same constraint of [6]

**Fig. 5.**

Assume that the two tasks in the workflow in Figure 5a) are constrained. We compare four possible placements of a release event, which results in interval constraints $c_i = ((t_1, t_2), \neq, e_i)$ for $1 \leq i \leq 4$:

1. Release $e_1$ located between the two conflicting tasks makes task $t_2$ an allocating task for task $t_1$ because the execution history is always cleared before task $t_2$ is executed.
2. Workflow instance $\langle t_1.u_1, t_1.u_2, t_2.u_1 \rangle$ satisfies interval constraint $c_2$ whereas workflow instance $\langle t_1.u_1, t_1.u_2, t_2.u_2 \rangle$ does not. However, both instances satisfy the cardinality constraint $((t_1, t_2), 2)$ illustrating that cardinality and interval constraints differ in their expressivity.

3. Release $e_3$ demands that the user who executed task $t_2$ for the first time must not have executed task $t_1$ before. Furthermore, in case of complete repetition, the user who executed task $t_2$ last cannot execute task $t_1$ afterwards.
4. Release $e_4$ ensures that after a complete repetition of the two tasks no old dependencies must be considered anymore.

Solworth [6] introduced SoD constraints where allocating tasks are limited to a single person ("self-same"); see Figure 5b) for a definition in our constraint language.

We state without proof two basic properties of interval constraints. First, adding more release events weakens a constraint. On the contrary, removing tasks from interval definitions weakens a constraint.

– If $L$ satisfies $((T_1, T_2), \rho, E_1)$ and $E_1 \subseteq E_2$ then $L$ satisfies $((T_1, T_2), \rho, E_2)$.
– If $L$ satisfies $((T_1, T), \rho, E)$ and $T_2 \subseteq T_1$ then $L$ satisfies $((T_2, T), \rho, E)$.

These two opposing properties are a result of the way interval constraints are defined. More tasks increases the number of intervals whereas more events reduces the number of relevant intervals.

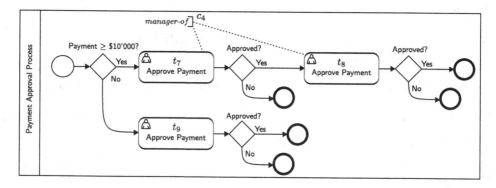

**Fig. 6.** Refinement

The subprocess in Figure 6 is a refinement of task $t_5$ (Payment Approval) in our running example. It opens the question how to relate constraints from different levels of abstraction. Expanding refined tasks to the highest level would preserve the history of constraint $c_4$ over multiple runs of the outer loop. A release at the end of the subprocess, however, scopes the constraint to the subprocess and enables a transparant treatment at the higher levels.

## 6   Related Work

To capture integrity requirements at the enterprise level, Thomas and Sandhu introduced task-based authorization to define the authorization functions associated with business activities [8]. In their seminal work [2], Bertino, Ferrari, and Atluri were the first to check the consistency of constraints defined over sequences of individual workflow tasks.

Little prior work exists about constraints in the presence of loops or parallelism. Requiring a partial order on tasks, Crampton *et al.* only permit single tasks to be executed more than once (self loop) [7]. Solworth allows SoD constraints in the presence of loops if the first allocating task is always executed by the same person [6]. Thus, except for the constraint given in Figure 5b), none of the other constraints can be expressed in their models. Having no restriction on the execution order of tasks in our model, we can generalize the specification of constraints to apply on sets of tasks.

Wolter and Schaad define a task authorization constraint to be applicable on set of tasks and beyond simple task sequences. Over a set of conflicting tasks it states the minimal number $n$ of different users that have to execute these tasks and a maximal number $m$ of task executions a single user can perform [10]. However, it is not very intuitive to understand the restriction given by these two numbers. In fact, as $n$ is only a lower bound, it fails to describe binding of duty constraints as there is always the possibility to add more users without violating the threshold. Relations over users, as introduced by Crampton and integrated into our language, cannot be specified.

Solworth gave the first graphical annotation for SoD constraints by connecting the conflicting tasks by a red line. Wolter and Schaad extended BPMN to express their authorization constraints graphically [10]. Multiple instance tasks and looped tasks are considered as a group with exactly one task but an arbitrary number of task instances. Authorization constraints can be assigned to a single task (in case of loops and multiple instances), a group, or a lane in form of a text annotation. In case of a lane, the overall constraint on its tasks is determined by the combination of constraints associated with the lane and the lanes, groups and tasks embedded in the lane. In [9], Wolter and Meinel elaborate further on this graphical notation.

Basin *et al.*, who introduced the concept of release, gave an operational semantics in terms of CSP processes [1]. Constraints were only defined over pairs of disjunct tasks and task sets respectively and did not include user relations and cardinality requirements. But they defined and proved algorithms to determine obstruction-freeness. It is future work to carry over the applicability of those algorithms onto our language.

## 7   Conclusions

The concept of release allows flexible scoping of authorization constraints on workflows with loops and parallelism. We formally defined a constraint language that models authorization policies at the granularity of task instances, imposing requirements on the number of users executing a set of tasks and requirements on the users executing conflicting task pairs. A key feature and strength of our approach is that it naturally extends the intuition and visual approach of graphical languages for business process modeling.

A denotational semantics is given, and examples of equivalent constraints are shown. This is a first step towards an algebra for interval constraints to simplify and combine constraints. As interval constraints can also be defined over pairs of same tasks, the algorithms of [1] have to be adopted to achieve obstruction-free workflow execution in order not to unjustifiably deny the execution of a business process.

**Acknowledgments.** We thank the anonymous reviewers for their helpful comments. This work was partially funded by the European Commission under the Seventh Framework Project "PoSecCo" (IST 257129).

# References

1. Basin, D., Burri, S.J., Karjoth, G.: Obstruction-free authorization enforcement: Aligning security and business objectives. In: 24th IEEE Computer Security Foundations Symposium, pp. 99–113. IEEE Computer Society Press (2011)
2. Bertino, E., Ferrari, E., Atluri, V.: The specification and enforcement of authorization constraints in workflow management systems. ACM Transactions on Information and System Security 2(1), 65–104 (1999)
3. Expert Group on e-Invoicing. Final Report of the Expert Group on e-Invoicing (2009), http://bit.ly/bwlgEF
4. Business Process Model and Notation (BPMN), Version 2.0. OMG Standard (January 2011), http://www.omg.org/spec/BPMN/2.0/PDF
5. Silver, B.: BPMN Method and Style. Cody-Cassidy Press (2009)
6. Solworth, J.A.: Approvability. In: ACM Symposium on Information, Computer and Communications Security (AsiaCCS 2006), pp. 231–242. ACM Press (2006)
7. Tan, K., Crampton, J., Gunter, C.: The consistency of task-based authorization constraints in workflow systems. In: 17th IEEE Computer Security Foundations Workshop, pp. 155–169. IEEE Computer Society Press (2004)
8. Thomas, R., Sandhu, R.: Conceptual foundations for a model of task-based authorizations. In: 7th IEEE Computer Security Foundations Workshop, pp. 66–79. IEEE Computer Society Press (1994)
9. Wolter, C., Meinel, C.: An approach to capture authorisation requirements in business processes. Requirements Engineering 15, 359–373 (2010)
10. Wolter, C., Schaad, A.: Modeling of Task-Based Authorization Constraints in BPMN. In: Alonso, G., Dadam, P., Rosemann, M. (eds.) BPM 2007. LNCS, vol. 4714, pp. 64–79. Springer, Heidelberg (2007)

# On the Modeling and Verification of Security-Aware and Process-Aware Information Systems

Jason Crampton[1] and Michael Huth[2]

[1] Information Security Group, Royal Holloway
University of London
jason.crampton@rhul.ac.uk
[2] Department of Computing
Imperial College London
m.huth@imperial.ac.uk

**Abstract.** Many business processes are modeled as workflows, which often need to comply with business rules, legal requirements, and authorization policies. *Workflow satisfiability* is the problem of determining whether there exists a workflow instance that realizes the workflow specification while simultaneously complying with such constraints. Although this problem has been studied by the computer security community in the past, existing solutions are tailored for particular workflow models, so their applicability to other models or richer forms of analysis is questionable. We here investigate whether the satisfiability of formulas in an NP-complete fragment of linear-time temporal logic can serve as a more expressive and versatile tool for deciding the satisfiability of workflows. We also show that this fragment can solve this problem for a standard model from the literature.

## 1  Introduction

Informally, a workflow is a set of logically related tasks that are performed in some sequence in order to achieve some business objective. A *workflow schema* is an abstract specification of the workflow tasks, indicating the order in which the tasks in every workflow instance of that schema should be performed. For each task in the schema, we identify a set of authorized users. (A "user" may well be, or be represented by, a software agent within an IT system, often known as a subject in the access control literature.) Each workflow task in a workflow instance is assigned to an authorized user, who is responsible for *performing* or *executing* the task.

In addition, a workflow schema may have constraints on the users that may be assigned to particular pairs of tasks in any instance of the workflow. Such constraints may be imposed for varying reasons: audit requirements, access control, business logic, etc. Two examples of such constraints are *separation of duty* (also known as the *two-man rule*) and *binding of duty* (where a user is required to perform one task if she has performed some earlier task in the workflow instance).

*Example 1.* An illustrative example of a constrained workflow for purchase order processing is shown in Figure 1. The purchase order is created and approved (and then dispatched to the supplier). The supplier will present an invoice, which is processed by

F. Daniel et al. (Eds.): BPM 2011 Workshops, Part II, LNBIP 100, pp. 423–434, 2012.

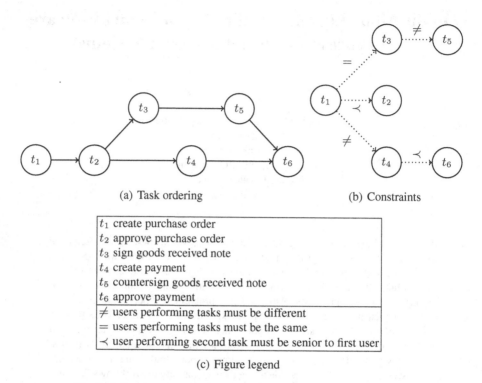

(a) Task ordering                    (b) Constraints

| $t_1$ create purchase order |
| $t_2$ approve purchase order |
| $t_3$ sign goods received note |
| $t_4$ create payment |
| $t_5$ countersign goods received note |
| $t_6$ approve payment |
| $\neq$ users performing tasks must be different |
| $=$ users performing tasks must be the same |
| $\prec$ user performing second task must be senior to first user |

(c) Figure legend

**Fig. 1.** A simple constrained workflow for purchase order processing

the create payment task. When the supplier delivers the ordered goods, a goods received note must be signed and countersigned. Only then may the payment be approved. Note that a workflow specification need not be linear: the processing of the goods received note and of the invoice can occur in parallel.

In addition to constraining the order in which tasks are to be performed, some business rules are specified to prevent fraudulent use of the purchase order processing system. These rules take the form of constraints on users that can perform pairs of tasks in the workflow: e.g. the same user may not sign and countersign the goods received note.

It is readily apparent that the imposition of constraints and the limited number of authorized users for particular tasks may result in a workflow schema being *unsatisfiable*, meaning that there would be no way of selecting an authorized user for each task in such a way that all the constraints are satisfied. A workflow can therefore only be realized if it is satisfiable. It is therefore important to be able to decide workflow satisfiability, both *statically* (realizability under full control over user-task assignment) and *dynamically* (realizability when some tasks were already executed by authorized users).

The problems of user-task assignment and workflow satisfiability have been studied by researchers in the security community using a variety of *bespoke* methods and algorithms [1,2,3]. The bespoke nature of these methods makes it hard to assess whether they adapt easily to other, more expressive workflow models or to more sophisticated analyses (e.g. those that cross workflow instances).

The extant work in the literature does, however, tell us about the computational complexity of these problems for specific types of models. Wang and Li [3], for example, show that workflow satisfiability is NP-hard for many types of models, by exhibiting a simple reduction from graph-colorability to workflow satisfiability.

In this paper we therefore explore whether tried and tested techniques and tools from the formal methods community can provide a more robust, more expressive, and more adaptable foundation for authorized workflow systems. We will particularly assess the approaches of model checking for linear-time temporal logic (LTL) and its automata-theoretic extensions [4], and of temporal logic satisfiability [5]. The use of LTL for the verification of process-aware information systems has already been suggested in [6].

We argue that the use of these techniques in that problem space has good to great potential. In particular, we demonstrate how an NP-complete fragment of linear-time temporal logic is a natural target language for several analyses of an important workflow model studied in the literature.

*Outline of paper.* We first provide technical background from temporal-logic model checking and from workflow authorization schemes. Then we study workflow satisfiability for one such authorization scheme and show that it reduces to satisfiability in an NP-complete fragment of propositional linear-time temporal logic. Next we look at workflow satisfiability in practice to assess the nature and scope of needs for solutions. In particular, we demonstrate that the aforementioned logic can express richer types of analyses. We then conclude the paper and point out future work.

## 2   Technical Background

First we recall the definition of a representative authorization scheme for workflow systems, and the definition of its workflow satisfiability [2]. Then we define the propositional linear-time temporal logic LTL(F) [5] that allows us to reduce the workflow satisfiability problem for that scheme to one of the satisfiability of a formula in LTL(F). Throughout, we write $<$ for the strict version of a partial order $\leq$.

### 2.1   Constrained Workflow Authorization Schemas

**Definition 1.** *A* constrained workflow authorization schema *is a triple* $(T, A, C)$ *where*

- $(T, \leq)$ *is a finite partial order of* tasks, *where* $t < t'$ *means that task* $t$ *has to be completed before task* $t'$;
- $A \subseteq T \times U$, *where* $U$ *is a finite set of users and* $(t, u) \in A$ *is the* authorization relation;
- $C$ *is a set of* entailment constraints, *tuples of form* $(D, t \rightarrow t', \rho)$ *where* $D \subseteq U$, $t, t' \in T$ *and* $\rho \subseteq U \times U$.

The partial order $(T, \leq)$ expresses constraints on the order in which tasks may be executed: any topological sort of $T$ consistent with $\leq$ renders such a legal execution sequence, which we call a *linearization*. Relation $t < t'$ therefore specifies that task $t$

must occur prior to task $t'$. Additionally, the partial order expresses which tasks (those incomparable with respect to $\leq$) may be executed independently from each other, e.g. concurrently.

Relation $A$ specifies the authorization policy for the workflow. The informal interpretation of $A$ is that $u$ is authorized to perform task $t$ if and only if $(t, u) \in A$. Note that this relation abstracts away the particularities of the underlying access-control model but that is ensures that constraints are expressed at the level of users.

A constraint $(D, t \rightarrow t', \rho)$ encodes a business rule or other forms of constraints by encoding restrictions on the users that can perform certain pairs of tasks. The constraint $(D, t \rightarrow t', \rho)$ requires that if $u \in D$ and $u' \in U$ are assigned to tasks $t$ and $t'$, respectively, then $(u, u') \in \rho$. Relation $\rho$ and set $D$ can vary with each element of $C$.

**Definition 2.** *Let $(T, A, C)$ be a constrained workflow authorization schema.*

1. *An* authorized plan *for $(T, A, C)$ is a pair $(L, \alpha)$, where*
   - *$\alpha\colon T \rightarrow U$ is a total function that assigns tasks to users such that $(t, \alpha(t)) \in A$ for all $t \in T$;*
   - *$L$ is a linearization of $T$; and*
   - *for all $(D, t \rightarrow t', \rho) \in C$, we have that if $\alpha(t) \in D$ then $(\alpha(t), \alpha(t')) \in \rho$.*
2. *We say that $(T, A, C)$ is* satisfiable *if and only if it has an authorized plan.*

Authorized plans are implementable realizations of a constrained workflow authorization schema: they assign all tasks only to authorized users such that all entailment constraints are met, and they provide a linearization of all tasks as a task scheduler.

Let us return to our purchase order example and suppose that the underlying access control mechanism is role-based. There are two roles, FinAdm and FinClrk (corresponding to the jobs of financial administrator and financial clerk, respectively), with FinClrk < FinAdm in the role hierarchy. The FinAdm role is authorized to perform tasks $t_2$ and $t_6$, (corresponding to purchase order approval and payment approval, respectively). The FinClrk role is authorized to perform the remaining tasks. Suppose, finally, that there are only two users Alice and Bob, where Alice is assigned to the FinAdm role and Bob is assigned to the FinClrk role (with the consequence that Alice is assumed to be more senior than Bob).

Now, if Alice executes $t_1$ (as she is authorized to do by role inheritance), then the workflow instance becomes unsatisfiable, because the constraint on tasks $t_1$ and $t_2$ requires that $t_2$ be executed by a user more senior than Alice. However, if Bob executes $t_1$, then the constraint on tasks $t_1$ and $t_4$ requires that Alice performs $t_4$, with the consequence that there is no authorized user to perform $t_6$ (since it must be performed by a user more senior than the user that performed $t_4$). In other words, the workflow schema is unsatisfiable, given the current user population and authorization policy. If we were to add a third user Carol and assign her to the FinClrk role, then the schema is satisfiable: one possible authorized plan is

$$[(t_1, \text{Bob}), (t_2, \text{Alice}), (t_4, \text{Carol}), (t_3, \text{Bob}), (t_5, \text{Carol}), (t_6, \text{Alice})].$$

Note that if we added the constraint that $t_2$ (approve purchase order) and $t_6$ (approve payment) are performed by different users, which is not unreasonable, then the workflow schema becomes unsatisfiable because there is a single user assigned to FinAdm.

Crampton [2] introduced the notion of a *well-formed* workflow schema, and showed that if $(L, \alpha)$ is an authorized plan of $\mathcal{AS} = (T, A, C)$, then $(L', \alpha)$, where $L'$ is any other linearization of $T$, is also an authorized plan of $\mathcal{AS}$. Well-formedness is a restriction on the constraints that may be specified on tasks that are not comparable to each other (with respect to $\leq$); such tasks may appear in either order in a linearization of $T$. Informally, well-formedness requires that constraints on such tasks are mutually consistent in some appropriate sense.

In Figure 1, every constraint is defined between a pair of tasks that belong to the partial ordering. Well-formedness would require that if we introduced a constraint on $t_3$ and $t_4$ with constraint relation $\rho$, then there should also be a constraint on $t_4$ and $t_3$ with constraint relation $\bar{\rho}$, where $\bar{\rho}$ denotes the converse of $\rho$. The most natural type of relation to use in this situation would be one that is symmetric (whence $\rho = \bar{\rho}$); both $\neq$ and $=$ are symmetric, for example.

We would expect that workflow schemata will be well-formed in many application domains. For such schemata, the results in [2] mean that we can fix a particular linearization of $L$ before considering the problem of identifying a suitable $\alpha$. And this problem decomposition may be exploited in solutions to the planning problem.

Nevertheless, there will be business processes that cannot be represented using a well-formed workflow schema. In the purchase order example illustrated in Figure 1, for example, it would be quite reasonable to impose constraints on $t_3$ and $t_4$ that would mean the resulting workflow schema was not well-formed: for example, $(U, t_3 \rightarrow t_4, \prec)$ and $(U, t_4 \rightarrow t_3, \neq)$ require that if the sign goods received note (GRN) task is performed before the create payment task, then the user that creates the payment must be more senior that the user that signs the GRN, whereas if the tasks are performed in the reverse order, we only require the users to be different (since the more commercially sensitive task has been performed first in this case).

## 2.2 Linear-Time Temporal Logic LTL(F)

We now show that the satisfiability problem for this workflow model can be expressed as a satisfiability problem in a fragment of propositional linear-time temporal logic that has NP-complete satisfiability checks [5].

Given a finite set AP of atomic propositions, the propositional temporal logic LTL(F) is generated by the following grammar:

$$\phi ::= p \mid \neg\phi \mid \phi \wedge \phi \mid \mathsf{F}\phi$$

where $p$ is from AP and F is the temporal connective "Future" such that $\mathsf{F}\,p$ states that $p$ will be true at some point in the future.

A *model* of a formula $\phi$ is an infinite sequence of states $\pi = s_0 s_1 \ldots$, where each $s_i$ is a subset of AP. We write $\pi \models \phi$ if $\pi$ is a model for $\phi$. We say that a formula $\phi$ is *satisfiable* if and only if it has a model. We write $\pi^i$ to denote the infinite suffix $s_i s_{i+1} \ldots$ of $\pi$. The formal semantics of formulas is then given in Figure 2.

We use the usual abbreviations for disjunction ($\vee$), implication ($\rightarrow$), logical equivalence ($\leftrightarrow$) and the "Global" temporal connective $\mathsf{G}\,\phi$, which stands for $\neg\mathsf{F}\neg\phi$.

$$\pi \models p \quad \text{iff} \quad p \in s_0$$

$$\pi \models \neg\phi \quad \text{iff} \quad \text{not } \pi \models \phi$$

$$\pi \models \phi_1 \wedge \phi_2 \quad \text{iff} \quad (\pi \models \phi_1 \text{ and } \pi \models \phi_2)$$

$$\pi \models \mathsf{F}\,\phi \quad \text{iff} \quad \text{there is some } i \geq 0 \text{ such that } \pi^i \models \phi$$

**Fig. 2.** Formal semantics of temporal logic LTL(F) over infinite sequences of states $\pi$

## 3  Expressing Workflow Satisfiability in LTL(F)

In this section, we show how to construct an LTL(F) formula $\phi_{\mathcal{AS}}$ from a constrained workflow authorization schema $\mathcal{AS} = (T, A, C)$ – be it well-formed or not – such that $\phi_{\mathcal{AS}}$ is satisfiable (as a formula of LTL(F)) if and only if $\mathcal{AS}$ is satisfiable (in the sense given in Definition 2). This correspondence is constructive in that the respective models translate directly and in a meaningful way.

We first define the set of atomic propositions AP to be $\mathsf{AP} = U \cup T \cup \{\checkmark\}$, where we assume that sets $U$, $T$ and $\{\checkmark\}$ are mutually disjoint. The atomic proposition $\checkmark$ models the fact that each task in $T$ has been assigned a user.

Formula $\phi_{\mathcal{AS}}$ is a conjunction of formulas as depicted in Figure 3. The conjuncts of $\phi_{\mathcal{AS}}$ together guarantee that infinite sequences $\pi$ with $\pi \models \phi_{\mathcal{AS}}$ correspond to authorized plans of $\mathcal{AS}$; and conversely, that authorized plans of $\mathcal{AS}$ give rise to infinite sequences $\pi$ with $\pi \models \phi_{\mathcal{AS}}$. We will prove this formally in Theorem 1 below. The intuition for this encoding of $\mathcal{AS}$ is that

- $t \in s_i$ means that task $t$ is scheduled in state $s_i$
- $u \in s_i$ means that user $u$ is assigned to any task scheduled at state $s_i$
- $\checkmark \in s_i$ means that state $s_i$ does not schedule any tasks from $T$.

By abuse of language, we will speak below of states scheduling tasks and assigning users in accordance with the above intuition.

We now discuss the intended meaning of each formula specified in Figure 3. Let $\pi$ be any infinite sequence of states such that $\pi \models \phi_{\mathcal{AS}}$, keeping in mind that no such $\pi$ exists if $\phi_{\mathcal{AS}}$ is unsatisfiable.

(1) Formula $\phi_{\mathsf{F}T}$ states that all tasks, including "task" $\checkmark$ are eventually scheduled in $\pi$.
(2) Formula $\phi_{\mathsf{G}T}$ states that all states of $\pi$ assign some task from $T$ or assign task $\checkmark$.
(3) Formula $\phi_{seT}$ is a kind of single-event condition. It specifies that whenever a state in $\pi$ schedules any task $t$ from $T$, then that state cannot schedule any other task, not even the $\checkmark$ task.
(4) Formula $\phi_{\mathsf{G}U}$ states that all states of $\pi$ either schedule task $\checkmark$ or assign some user.
(5) Formula $\phi_{seU}$ also captures a kind of single-event condition. It specifies that, for all users $u$ and at all states of $\pi$, if a state assigns user $u$ and does not schedule task $\checkmark$, then that state does not assign any other users.

$$\phi_{FT} = \bigwedge_{t \in T \cup \{\checkmark\}} F\,t \tag{1}$$

$$\phi_{GT} = G\left(\checkmark \vee \bigvee_{t \in T} t\right) \tag{2}$$

$$\phi_{seT} = \bigwedge_{t \in T} G\left(t \rightarrow \bigwedge_{t' \in T \cup \{\checkmark\} \setminus \{t\}} \neg t'\right) \tag{3}$$

$$\phi_{GU} = G\left(\checkmark \vee \bigvee_{u \in U} u\right) \tag{4}$$

$$\phi_{seU} = \bigwedge_{u \in U} G\left(u \wedge \neg\checkmark \rightarrow \bigwedge_{u' \in U \setminus \{u\}} \neg u'\right) \tag{5}$$

$$\phi_{\leq} = \bigwedge_{t \in T} G\left(t \rightarrow G(\checkmark \vee \bigwedge_{t' < t} \neg t')\right) \tag{6}$$

$$\phi_{\checkmark} = G\left(\checkmark \rightarrow G\,\checkmark\right) \tag{7}$$

$$\phi_A = \bigwedge_{t \in T} G\left(t \rightarrow \bigvee_{(t,u) \in A} u\right) \tag{8}$$

$$\phi_C = \bigwedge_{(D,t \rightarrow t',\rho) \in C} \phi_{(D,t \rightarrow t',\rho)} \tag{9}$$

$$\phi_{(D,t \rightarrow t',\rho)} = \bigwedge_{u \in D} \left(F\,(t \wedge u)\right) \rightarrow G\left(t' \rightarrow \bigvee_{(u,u') \in \rho} u'\right) \tag{10}$$

$$\phi_{AS} = \phi_{FT} \wedge \phi_{GT} \wedge \phi_{seT} \wedge \phi_{GU} \wedge \phi_{seU} \wedge \phi_{\leq} \wedge \phi_{\checkmark} \wedge \phi_A \wedge \phi_C \tag{11}$$

**Fig. 3.** Defining $\phi_{AS}$ in LTL(F) for schema $\mathcal{AS} = (T, A, C)$

(6) Formula $\phi_{\leq}$ specifies, for each task $t$ from $T$, that whenever $t$ is scheduled at a state in $\pi$, then all future states can only schedule task $\checkmark$ or a task $t'$ such that $t' \not\leq t$.

(7) Formula $\phi_{\checkmark}$ states that $\checkmark$ models the completion of authorized plans: whenever a state of $\pi$ schedules $\checkmark$, then all subsequent states in $\pi$ schedule only $\checkmark$ as well.

(8) Formula $\phi_A$ encodes the authorization schema $A$. It specifies that for all tasks $t \in T$ and states $s_i$ of $\pi$, if $s_i$ schedules $t$, then $s_i$ assigns some user $u$ with $(t, u) \in A$.

(9) Formula $\phi_C$ encodes the entailment constraints in $C$. It is a conjunction of formulas $\phi_{(D,t \rightarrow t',\rho)}$, one for each element of $C$.

(10) Formula $\phi_{(D,t \rightarrow t',\rho)}$ encodes an entailment constraint $(D, t \rightarrow t', \rho)$ of $C$. It is a conjunction with one conjunct for each user $u$ from $D$. For each such user $u$, that conjunct specifies that if there is a state of $\pi$ that schedules task $t$ and assigns user $u$, then all states of $\pi$ that schedule task $t'$ are such that they assign at least one user $u'$ such that $(u, u')$ is in $\rho$.

It should be clear that most of these formulas over-approximate intended behavior of a constrained workflow authorization schema. For example, $\phi_{(D,t \rightarrow t',\rho)}$ ensures that there is some assignment of users that satisfies the entailment constraint. It does not prevent the assignment of users that violate these constraints. But it is the interaction of all conjuncts in $\phi_{AS}$ that gives these approximations the desired precision.

**Theorem 1.** *Let* $AS = (T, A, C)$ *be a constrained workflow authorization schema and* $\phi_{AS}$ *its encoding in* LTL(F). *Then* $\phi_{AS}$ *is satisfiable if and only if* $AS$ *is satisfiable.*

The proof of this result can be found in the appendix. It is easy to show that our encoding is sound (that is, that $\phi_{AS}$ is satisfiable if $AS$ is): the encoding $\phi_{AS}$ just has to specify things that are true of an authorized plan of $AS$. The crucial result is the completeness of our encoding. In its proof we use all formulas in Figure 3, except for $\phi_{\checkmark}$. That formula (and indeed the use of the atomic proposition $\checkmark$) is therefore not needed to prove Theorem 1. However, $\phi_{\checkmark}$ should be useful as it indicates in some analysis result $\pi$ that a specific finite prefix of $\pi$ already contains an authorized plan.

The translation from $AS$ to $\phi_{AS}$ is also linear in the size of $AS$, rendering a reduction of workflow satisfiability to temporal logic satisfiability within NP.

## 4   Workflow Satisfiability in Practice

Having demonstrated that we can express satisfiability of the workflow schema from [2] in LTL(F), we now explore the shortcomings of these models and the limitations of LTL(F) as a tool for reasoning about workflow satisfiability. Specifically, we identify several situations of practical interest that cannot be represented using existing workflow models for which satisfiability results are known.

### 4.1   Workflow Patterns

The study of authorization constraints as a mechanism to enforce business rules such as separation of duty in workflow systems has assumed rather simplistic workflow specifications: Bertino *et al.* assume that the set of tasks is a list [1]; this has been extended to the analysis to workflows in which the set of tasks is partially ordered and a task may be executed several times [2]. However, these workflow models are not able to encode the richer workflow patterns that both occur in practice and have been studied in the workflow modeling community, notably in the work of van der Aalst and ter Hofstede [7]. In other words, research on workflow satisfiability needs to be extended to account for these richer workflow control patterns. Suppose, for example, that different items in a purchase order may be delivered separately. Then the tasks $t_3$ and $t_5$ in our purchase order example may be executed multiple times in pairs. The resulting workflow specification is shown in Figure 4.

Moreover, existing approaches on workflow satisfiability assume that the number of tasks is fixed and that all tasks are executed, although there may be some flexibility in the order in which tasks are performed. However, as we have seen in the example in Figure 4 the number of tasks that is executed in a workflow instance may vary. Other common workflow patterns where the number of tasks is not pre-determined include OR-forks and OR-joins: in the former the execution of a task causes more than one task to enter the ready state, but only one of those tasks is required to be executed; in contrast, an OR-join only requires one of several preceding tasks to be executed for the next task to enter the ready state.

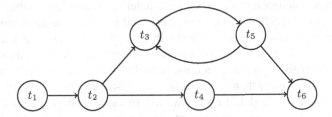

**Fig. 4.** A workflow specification with cycles

To model OR-forks, we may generalize the form of formula $\phi_{FT}$ such that it is in disjunctive normal form where "atomic" propositions are of form $F\,t$ with $t$ from $T$. This allows us to model alternative workflows, where each term of the DNF represents a possible workflow and where only one of these workflows needs to be executed or synthesized. Since LTL(F) has NP-complete satisfiability checks, this more general problem stays within NP. It is straightforward to extend this modeling of *initial* OR-forks to those occurring at any point of the work flow, by making use of the G modality.

In contrast, OR-joins seem to require reasoning about the past. It is therefore not immediately clear whether this can be accommodated in LTL(F) as the encoding of past tense operators in LTL uses Untils.

All this suggests that foundations for workflow models need to be fairly expressive. In particular, LTL(F) cannot reason about the past and, more generally, temporal logics with support for past tense may still not suffice due to their inability to "count". The automata-theoretic extensions of temporal logics in [4] may give us sufficient counting abilities but the acceptance notions of automata cannot cope well with the presence of constraints such as those found within workflow specifications.

### 4.2 Workflow Execution Models

A workflow specification is instantiated by the workflow management system (WFMS) to create a *workflow instance*. Note that at any stage in the execution of a workflow instance, the (finite) set of tasks that have been completed is an order ideal in $T$.[1] The set of tasks that remain to be performed is, by definition, an order filter in $T$. Given an order ideal $I \subseteq T$, the set of *next* or *ready* tasks is defined to be the set of minimal elements in the order filter $T \setminus I$.

Two different modes of task selection and assignment are known for WFMSs:

- A *static* execution model assigns an (authorized) user to each task in a workflow when a workflow instance is created by the WFMS. (It is this execution model that has been assumed up to now in this paper.)
- A *dynamic* execution model assigns users to ready tasks during the execution of a workflow instance.

---

[1] An order ideal $I \subseteq X$ in a partially ordered set $(X, \leqslant)$ has the property that if $x \in I$ and $y \leq x$, then $y \in I$. A set $F \subseteq X$ is an order filter if its complement $X \setminus F$ is an order ideal.

Any WFMS that employs a static execution model is in complete control of the allocation of tasks in a workflow instance to users, and performs the allocation when the workflow schema is instantiated. A WFMS that employs a dynamic execution model may also allocate tasks to users but in an incremental way and based on dynamic needs. However, an alternative dynamic execution model is to maintain and advertise a list of ready tasks and allow users themselves to select (self-assign) tasks from that list.

In a static execution model, the satisfiability of the workflow specification is performed once and the task-user assignment list is a model for the workflow specification. In a dynamic execution model, the satisfiability of the workflow instance has to be checked when each task is assigned. A WFMS can perform this check by considering the satisfiability of a modified authorization schema.

More formally, let $\mathcal{AS} = (T, A, C)$ be a workflow authorization schema and let $I \subseteq T$ be an order ideal representing a set of completed tasks in a workflow instance $W$. Let $\alpha(t)$ represent the user that performed task $t \in I$. Then $\mathcal{AS} \rhd I$, defined as $(T, A', C)$ where $A' = A \cap \{(t, \alpha(t)) : t \in I\}$ is also a workflow authorization schema (one in which there is a single authorized user for each task in $I$). Now suppose that tasks in $I$ have been completed and $u$ wishes to perform the ready task $t$. Then it suffices to compute the satisfiability of the workflow authorization schema $\mathcal{AS} \rhd (I \cup \{t\})$. We can decide this by deciding the satisfiability of $\phi_\Gamma \wedge \phi_{\mathcal{AS}}$ in LTL(F), where

$$\phi_\Gamma = \mathsf{G}\,(t \leftrightarrow u) \wedge \bigwedge_{t' \in I} \mathsf{G}\,(t' \leftrightarrow \alpha(t'))$$

Even when a static execution model is used, there may be situations in which we wish to assign particular tasks to particular users. One obvious reason is to ensure that user workloads are fair. Checking that a workflow remains satisfiable when a particular subset of tasks are assigned to particular users is no different from checking satisfiability at task selection time in a dynamic execution model. Formally, let $\Gamma'$ be a context that assigns task $t_i$ to user $u_i$ for $i = 1, 2, \ldots, k$. In order to determine whether $\mathcal{AS}$ is satisfiable under these additional assumptions, we simply check for the satisfiability of $\phi_{\Gamma'} \wedge \phi_{\mathcal{AS}}$ in LTL(F) where we set

$$\phi_{\Gamma'} = \bigwedge_{i=1}^{k} \mathsf{G}\,(t_i \leftrightarrow u_i)$$

## 4.3  Richer Workflow Constraints

Existing approaches on workflow satisfiability assume that constraints are defined on pairs of tasks. In practice, we may wish to define threshold constraints. Such a constraint specifies a set of tasks $T' \subseteq T$ and an integer $k \leqslant |T'|$, which we denote by the pair $(T', k)$. We suggest two possible and relevant definitions of satisfaction for $(T', k)$:

– $(T', k)$ is satisfied if the assignment of users to tasks $T'$ involves at least $k$ users.
– $(T', k)$ is satisfied provided no user performs $k$ or more of the tasks.

With both interpretations, separation of duty can be modeled by letting $T'$ have two elements and by setting $k = 2$. Although such constraints are, in principle, expressible in

LTL(F) in a manner similar to the encoding of constraints in $\phi_C$ above, such encodings will grow exponentially in that parameter $k$.

Most existing research on workflow satisfiability assumes that the scope of a constraint is a workflow instance. This is clearly limiting for general needs in security, audit, and control. For example, we may require that different users execute the same task in different instances of a workflow schema. To the best of our knowledge, the only research in this area is the work of Warner and Atluri [8]. However, this work considers rather artificial constraints and does not account for control flow constraints.

LTL(F) is able to reason about relationships between instances of workflows. For example, suppose that we want to compute two plans, one for the first instance of the workflow and then another one for a second instance. The idea would be to copy each atomic proposition $a$ in a primed version $a'$. Then $\phi'_{AS}$ is the formula $\phi_{AS}$ except that each atom is written in its primed version. Synthesis of authorized plans for both instances under additional constraints reduces to satisfiability of LTL(F) formulas, e.g.

$$\phi_{AS} \wedge \phi'_{AS} \wedge \bigwedge_{u \in U} (F\,(t \wedge u) \to G(t' \to \neg u))$$

gives us plans for the unprimed and the primed instance of the workflow for $AS$, and it also ensures that designated task $t$ is assigned a different user in the second instance.

# 5  Conclusions and Future Work

We studied current approaches to modeling and synthesizing workflows in the presence of authorization specifications. We observed that extant work develops algorithmic techniques that are customized to particular models and target specific analysis or synthesis needs. These approaches are therefore bespoke, brittle under change of model or analysis, and lack expressive features needed for workflow specifications in practice.

We then pointed out that formal methods offers expressive specification formalisms with generic analysis capabilities. Model checking of an NP-complete fragment of linear-time temporal logic, for example, covers a range of analysis needs for satisfiability of authorized workflows. We now discuss directions for future work.

*Richer workflows and* LTL(F). We want to study whether LTL(F) is expressive enough to deal with workflows in which tasks are not given by a partial order but as an expression in a declarative language in which tasks are composed sequentially, where sets of tasks may be chosen non-deterministically (OR/AND-joins and OR/AND-forks, for example), and where workflows may be repeated.

*Parameterized analyses.* Our use of temporal logic LTL(F) demonstrated the benefits of having a formalism in which many different analyses can be expressed (here as formulas in LTL(F)) and where the analysis algorithm is generic and then instantiated with parameter instances (here a satisfiability solver for LTL(F)). We feel this is essential in order to make analysis capabilities less brittle under change of specifications.

*Pattern-based modeling and verification* The identification of *patterns* for workflow systems [7,9] needs to be extended to patterns for security, audit, and control. Declarative languages for workflows then ought to be able to express these additional patterns, and programs written in such languages have to be analyzable for pattern compliance and consistency. We already suggested that temporal logic and its automata-theoretic extensions alone will be inadequate for supporting these analysis capabilities.

*Workflows and collaboration in the cloud.* As software and platform alike increasingly become services hosted in the cloud, workflows and their management systems need to be realizable in clouds as well. Related to that, workflows from different organizations will have to be composed so that the composition meets the constraints of each organization. How to do such compositions is a challenging problem since organizations may not share all their constraints with each other, suggesting a workflow satisfiability problem under *imperfect information* and for *multiple agents*. Here, we think that methods from algorithmic game theory may be of use.

*Need for empirical comparison of methods.* We also think it is important to critically evaluate modeling and verification methods for workflow satisfiability in terms of their expressiveness and scalability. For example, while LTL(F) has NP-complete satisfiability checks, the problem's complexity becomes PSPACE-complete as soon as we add, say, a temporal operator for "Next State". But empirical data are needed in order to determine whether these worst-case complexities have any bearing on deciding the satisfiability of workflows as they arise in practice.

# References

1. Bertino, E., Ferrari, E., Atluri, V.: The specification and enforcement of authorization constraints in workflow management systems. ACM Transactions on Information and System Security 2(1), 65–104 (1999)
2. Crampton, J.: A reference monitor for workflow systems with constrained task execution. In: Proceedings of the 10th ACM Symposium on Access Control Models and Technologies, pp. 38–47 (2005)
3. Wang, Q., Li, N.: Satisfiability and Resiliency in Workflow Systems. In: Biskup, J., López, J. (eds.) ESORICS 2007. LNCS, vol. 4734, pp. 90–105. Springer, Heidelberg (2007)
4. Vardi, M.Y., Wolper, P.: Reasoning about infinite computations. Information and Computation 115, 1–37 (1994)
5. Sistla, A.P., Clarke, E.M.: The complexity of propositional linear temporal logics. Journal of the ACM 32, 733–749 (1985)
6. van der Aalst, W.M.P., Pesic, M., Schonenberg, H.: Declarative workflows: Balancing between flexibility and support. Computer Science - R&D 23(2), 99–113 (2009)
7. van der Aalst, W.M.P., ter Hofstede, A., Kiepuszewski, B., Barros, A.: Workflow patterns. Distributed and Parallel Databases 14(1), 5–51 (2003)
8. Warner, J., Atluri, V.: Inter-instance authorization constraints for secure workflow management. In: Proceedings of the 11th ACM Symposium on Access Control Models and Technologies, pp. 190–199 (2006)
9. Russell, N.C.: Foundations of Process-Aware Information Systems. PhD thesis, Faculty of Information Technology, Queensland University of Technology (December 2007)

# Conformance Checking of RBAC Policies in Process-Aware Information Systems

Anne Baumgrass[1], Thomas Baier[2], Jan Mendling[2], and Mark Strembeck[1]

[1] Institute of Information Systems and New Media
Vienna University of Economics and Business (WU Vienna), Vienna, Austria
`firstname.lastname@wu.ac.at`
[2] Institute of Information Systems
Humboldt-Universität zu Berlin, Germany
`firstname.lastname@wiwi.hu-berlin.de`

**Abstract.** A process-aware information system (PAIS) is a software system that supports the definition, execution, and analysis of business processes. The execution of process instances is typically recorded in so called event logs. In this paper, we present an approach to automatically generate LTL (Linear Temporal Logic) statements from process-related RBAC (Role-based Access Control) models. These LTL statements are used to check if process executions that are recorded via event logs conform to the access control policies defined via a corresponding RBAC model. To demonstrate our approach, we implemented a RBAC-to-LTL component, and used the ProM tool to test the resulting LTL statements with event logs created from process simulations in CPN tools.

**Keywords:** Process-Aware Information Systems, Conformance Checking, LTL, Security, Role-Based Access Control.

## 1 Introduction

Process-aware information systems (PAIS) support the execution of business processes [6]. In this context, access control policies define which users are allowed to perform certain tasks (see, e.g., [14,16]). In recent years, role-based access control (RBAC) [8,13] has developed into a de facto standard for access control in both, research and industry. In RBAC, roles model different work profiles. They are equipped with the exact number of permissions that is needed to perform their tasks. These roles are then assigned to human users according to their respective work profile (see [15]). To check if the process instances that are executed via a PAIS adhere to the access control policies which are defined in the corresponding RBAC model, one can use the event logs that have been recorded by the information system during process execution (see, e.g., [7]). The analysis of event data has been intensively studied in the area of process mining [1,19]. Often, Linear Temporal Logic (LTL) is used as formal language to check conformance of models and logs (see, e.g., [2]). However, most existing conformance checking approaches focuses on the control flow perspective (see, e.g., [11,12]), and do not provide operators to check access control policies.

F. Daniel et al. (Eds.): BPM 2011 Workshops, Part II, LNBIP 100, pp. 435–446, 2012.

In this paper, we present an approach to check if the data recorded in the event logs of a PAIS conforms to the corresponding process-related RBAC model including binding and mutual exclusion constraints. In particular, we automatically transform process-related RBAC models to corresponding LTL rules. These LTL rules are then used to check the event logs for violations of the policies that are defined via the RBAC model. The results of this conformance check can serve as basis for security and domain experts to detect violations that could result from misconfigurations or implementation errors and thereby help to increase the security of the respective PAIS. The LTL rules that are generated by our approach can be used in any kind of log analysis tool that is based on LTL. To demonstrate our approach we implemented a RBAC-to-LTL component that transforms the XML representation of process-related RBAC models to corresponding LTL rules. Subsequently, we use tools such as ProM [18,21] to check these LTL rules.

The remainder of this paper is structured as follows. Section 2 gives an overview of RBAC and LTL. Next, Section 3 describes our approach of transforming process-related RBAC models to LTL. In Section 4, we demonstrate our approach using event logs created from process simulations in CPN tools. After discussing related work in Section 5, Section 6 concludes the paper.

## 2    Background

### 2.1    Process-Related RBAC Models

In order to transform RBAC policies to LTL rules, we need a corresponding metamodel which defines the semantics of process-related RBAC models. In our approach, we use the formal metamodel for process-related RBAC models defined in [16]. However, due to the page restrictions, we cannot repeat the corresponding definitions in this paper. Therefore, we use the BusinessActivities UML extension defined in [16] to introduce the corresponding concepts via a small example model.

The BusinessActivities extension enables the definition of process-related RBAC models via extended UML activity models. In addition to roles and role-hierarchies, it allows for the specification of static and dynamic mutual exclusion constraints, as well as binding constraints on the tasks of a business process. Figure 1a depicts an example of a BusinessActivity that models a simple credit application process. This process includes five actions, three of which are so-called Business Actions ("Negotiate contract", "Approve contract", and "Check credit worthiness") which include binding or mutual exclusion constraints.

Figure 1b shows the roles for the credit application process. In this example, we have a role BankManager and a corresponding junior-role BankClerk. The role-to-role assignment relation is modeled via a dashed arrow. The arrowhead is a triangle including a "J" to indicate the end of the relation that points to the junior-role. Such a role-hierarchy is defined as a mapping $rh$. The mapping $rh^*$ defines the inheritance in the role-hierarchy. It includes all direct and transitive junior-roles that the senior-role inherits from (for details see [16]).

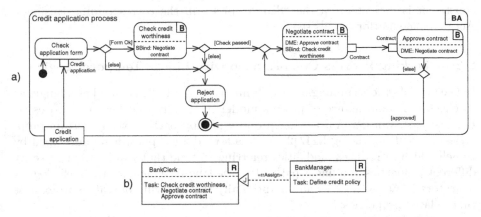

**Fig. 1.** A credit application process modeled as a BusinessActivity [16]

The task-to-role assignment *tra* defines which task types are assigned to a particular role. In a role-hierarchy the senior-role inherits the permissions from its (direct and transitive) junior-roles. Thus, in our example the BankManager inherits the permission to execute the tasks "Check credit worthiness", "Negotiate contract", and the "Approve contract" from the BankClerk role (see Figure 1b). The task-to-role assignment implies a mapping task ownership (*town*) which allows to determine all tasks that are assigned to a particular role. In turn, the mapping $town^{-1}$ returns all roles a task is assigned to. The role-to-subject assignment *rsa* defines which roles are assigned to a particular subject. Similar to the task-to-role assignment relation, *rsa* implies a mapping role-ownership *rown*, which allows to determine all roles that are assigned to a particular subject. Again, a mapping $rown^{-1}$ exists which returns all subjects assigned to a role (for details see [16]).

Mutual exclusive tasks result from the division of powerful rights or responsibilities to prevent fraud and abuse. Mutual exclusion constraints can be subdivided in static and dynamic mutual exclusion. In essence, a static mutual exclusion (SME) constraint defines that two mutual exclusive tasks must never be assigned to the same subject. In turn, a dynamic mutual exclusion constraint defines that two mutual exclusive tasks must never be performed by the same subject in the *same process instance*. Figure 1a depicts a DME constraint between the Business Actions "Negotiate contract" and "Approve contract". In the graphical representation, this DME constraint is indicated via the "DME" prefix in the corresponding BusinessAction elements. In contrast to mutual exclusion constraints, binding constraints define that bound tasks must be executed by the same subject (or role). In particular, a subject-binding (SB) constraint defines that two bound tasks must be performed by the same individual. In turn, a role-binding (RB) constraint defines that bound tasks must be performed by members of the same role, but not necessarily by the same individual. The example from Figure 1a shows a subject binding constraint between the "Check credit worthiness" and the "Negotiate contract" tasks. This subject-binding constraint is indicated via the "SBind" prefix in the corresponding Business-Action elements (for details see [16]).

## 2.2  Checking Process Conformance with Linear Temporal Logic

In the area of process mining, Linear Temporal Logic (LTL) is used as a language to check the conformance of process models with executed business processes. For instance, van der Aalst et al. propose an approach to verify certain properties in event logs using LTL [2]. LTL is a modal temporal logic developed by Pnueli which introduces modalities referring to time that can be used to verify different properties in a linear path [10]. The language includes the basic logical operators $(\wedge, \vee, \Rightarrow, \Leftrightarrow, \exists, \forall)$ and additionally the following operators to express time-related properties:

**Nexttime** ($\bigcirc A$) specifies that a property A holds in the next state of the path.
**Eventually** ($\Diamond A$) specifies that a property A evaluates to true at least at one point in the path.
**Always** ($\Box A$) specifies that a property A has to hold in every state of the path.
**Until** ($A \cup B$) specifies that a property A has to hold until property B holds.

Van der Aalst et al. [2] extended the language to exploit the structure of event logs. In particular, they introduce operands to access the different properties contained in an event log, such as attributes of the process instance and the audit trail entries. Furthermore, they provide tool support by introducing the LTL Checker in the ProM framework [4]. The LTL Checker provides a set of predefined formulas that can be used out of the box and can be easily extended. In our approach, we rely on LTL since it has proven to be a valuable means to check conformance of event logs. Further, LTL gives us the flexibility to extend our approach to enable the checking of a process's control flow with respect to the corresponding process-related RBAC model.

## 3  Transformation of RBAC Models to LTL Statements

In this section, we present our approach to check if business process executions comply with a corresponding process-related RBAC model. Figure 2 depicts the main concepts of our approach and their interrelations.

At first, we transform a particular process-related RBAC model that is modeled via the BusinessActivities extension (see Section 2.1) to corresponding LTL statements (see Section 2.2). Below, we describe this automated transformation in detail. The resulting LTL statements then represent the properties of the RBAC model that need to hold for each process execution. Subsequently, we use the automatically derived LTL rules to assess event logs using the LTL checker plug-in of the process mining workbench ProM (see also [2]). In this way, we check if a process instance conforms to the RBAC model and reveal violations in case a particular process execution (resp. the corresponding event log) is not consistent with the respective RBAC model.

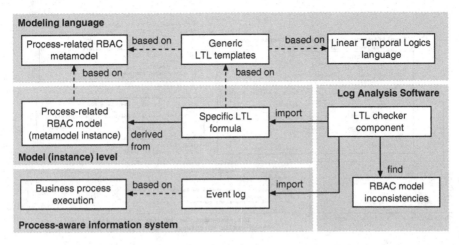

**Fig. 2.** Conformance checking for process-related RBAC models

In order to support the automated transformation of process-related RBAC models (modeled via the BusinessActivities extension), we developed a corresponding RBAC-to-LTL component. Figure 3 shows the conceptual structure of this component. In particular, we first generate the XML representation of a particular process-related RBAC model. Subsequently, we parse this XML representation to create a corresponding in-memory object model. This in-memory object model is then used to derive specific LTL rules. To generate the LTL rules we use special purpose LTL templates. In essence, these LTL templates define patterns for the different properties of a RBAC model, including static and dynamic mutual exclusion, subject-binding and role-binding, as well as task-to-role assignment relations (see also Section 2.1).

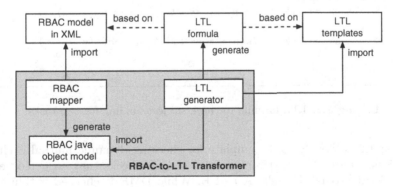

**Fig. 3.** Transformation of RBAC models in XML representation to LTL formulas

Figure 4 shows an actual example for the transformation of a subject-binding constraint to a corresponding LTL statement. In particular, the upper right corner shows an excerpt from the XML representation of the respective RBAC

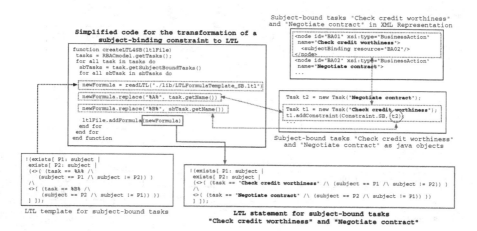

**Fig. 4.** Example transformation of a subject-binding in XML representation to LTL

model. The source code excerpt beneath shows the creation of corresponding Java objects from XML representation. The subsequent generation of the corresponding LTL statement via a respective LTL template is shown in the source code excerpt on the left-hand side. The LTL template for checking subject-binding constraints between two tasks is also shown in Listing 1.1. In particular, we check that in a certain process instance two subject-bound tasks are executed by the same individual. In LTL we achieve this by testing if no two persons P1 and P2 exist who executed task A and task B respectively (see Listing 1.1).

```
1    !(exists[ P1: subject |
2      exists[ P2: subject |
3      (<>( (task == %A% /\ (subject == P1 /\ subject != P2)) )
4      /\
5      <>( (task == %B% /\ (subject == P2 /\ subject != P1)) ))
6      ]
7    ]);
```

**Listing 1.1.** LTL formula to check subject-binding for two tasks

Listing 1.2 shows the LTL template for checking dynamic mutual exclusion constraints. The DME constraint defined in LTL checks that no person exists who executes two DME tasks A and B. While DME is checked within single process instances, SME requires two tasks to be mutual exclusive over all process instances (PI) (see [16]). However, using the LTL checker we can only assess constraints within individual process instances. In order to check SME with the LTL formula shown in Listing 1.2, we can, for example, combine all process instances of a certain event log into a single PI.

```
1   !(exists[ P: subject |
2   (<>( (subject == P /\ task == %A%) )
3   /\
4   <>( (subject == P /\ task == %B%) ))
5   ]);
```

**Listing 1.2.** LTL formula to check mutual exclusion for two tasks

```
1   (
2   <>((task == %A% /\
3   (subject == P1 \/ (... \/ (subject == P_N-1 \/ subject == P_N ...)))))
4   \/ !( <>( task == %A% ) )
5   );
```

**Listing 1.3.** LTL formula to check task-to-role assignment (excerpt)

From the perspective of event logs, constraints involving roles – such as role-binding (RB) and task-to-role assignment – are more complex. This is due to the fact that normally role information is not included in event logs. Therefore, we indirectly check if a certain rule for task-to-role assignments holds in the event log by checking the subjects who perform the corresponding task. At first, we retrieve the roles a task is assigned to ($town^{-1}$, see also Section 2.1). Next, we check if one of the subjects assigned to theses roles ($rown^{-1}$) performed the respective task instance. Listing 1.3 shows the form of a corresponding check in LTL. In particular, we check if for a role R that owns a task A one of the subjects assigned to R (or to one of R's senior-roles) actually executed task A.

Checking a role-binding constraint in LTL is similar to checking task-to-role assignments. Because typically role information is not included in the event logs, we have to use the executing subjects in order to check if two role-bound tasks have been executed by the same role. Thus, we build subformulas for each role R and check if two role-bound tasks A and B have been executed by a subject assigned to this role R. Algorithm 1 shows how such a LTL formula is build. An excerpt of a LTL formula created with this algorithm is shown in Listing 1.4. It checks if two tasks A and B (assigned to role R1 and R2) were executed by subjects either owning role R1 or R2. We use placeholders and replacements in order to dynamically derive the correct structure of brackets in the LTL formula[1].

## 4   Consistency Checking of an Example Process

We test our approach using an event log created with CPN Tools (see [5]). In particular, we modeled the credit application process from Figure 1 in the CPN

---

[1] Constructs in LTL have to be structured similar to binary trees. Thus, we cannot write $(A \lor B \lor C)$, but must use $(A \lor (B \lor C))$ or $((A \lor B) \lor C)$.

```
1   (
2     ((<>((task == %A%) /\ (subject == S1_R1 \/ (subject == S2_R1 \/ ...)))
3       /\
4        <>((task == %B%) /\ (subject == S1_R1 \/ (subject == S2_R1 \/ ...)))))
5     \/
6     (<>((task == %A%) /\ (subject == S1_R2 \/ (subject == S2_R2 \/ ...)))
7       /\
8        <>((task == %B%) /\ (subject == S1_R2 \/ (subject == S2_R2 \/ ...)))))))
9     \/ !( ( <>( task == %A% ) /\ <>( task == %B% ) ) )
10  );
```

**Listing 1.4.** LTL formula to check role-binding of two tasks (excerpt)

---

**Algorithm 1.** Generation of role-binding formulas

1: **function** GETLTL4RBIND(task1, task2, roles)
2:     $formula$ = '%RF%'
3:     **for all** $role \in roles$ **do**
4:         $formulaR$ = '(%TF% $\vee$ !(($\Diamond$(task == "$task1$.getName()")
5:                                   $\wedge$ $\Diamond$(task == "task2.getName()")))'
6:         $formulaT1$ = '$\Diamond$((task == "$task1$.getName()" $\wedge$ %SF%))'
7:         $formulaT1$ = '$\Diamond$((task == "$task2$.getName()" $\wedge$ %SF%))'
8:         $subFormula$ = "
9:         $subjects$ = $role$.getSubjects()
10:        **for all** $subject \in subjects$ **do**
11:            $subFormula$ = 'subject == "$subject$.getName()"'
12:            **if** !**isLastSubject()** **then**
13:                $subFormula$ = '( $subFormula$ $\vee$ %SF% )'
14:            **end if**
15:            $formulaT1$ = $formulaT1$.replace('%SF%', subFormula)
16:            $formulaT2$ = $formulaT2$.replace('%SF%', subFormula)
17:        **end for**
18:        $formulaR$ = $formulaR$.replace('%TF%', '( $formulaT1$ $\wedge$ $formulaT2$ )')
19:        **if** !**isLastRole()** **then**
20:            $formulaR$ = '( $formulaR$ $\vee$ %RF% )'
21:        **end if**
22:        $formula$ = $formula$.replace('%RF%', formulaR)
23:        **return** $formula$
24:    **end for**
25: **end function**

---

Tools environment and generated corresponding event logs in MXML format [20]. We use the CPN Tools event log simulation to determine the structure and content of the event log for our conformance check. This also allows us to integrate all kinds of violations of the access control policies in a controlled manner. For example, we can manipulate the event log and include tasks and performers that do not conform to the corresponding RBAC model. In this way, we can check event logs that include all kinds of inconsistencies. In Listing 1.5 we show an excerpt of an event log created with CPN Tools.

```
1  ...
2  <AuditTrailEntry>
3   <WorkflowModelElement>Check credit worthiness</WorkflowModelElement>
4   <Originator>Bob</Originator>
5   ...
6  </AuditTrailEntry>
7  <AuditTrailEntry>
8   <WorkflowModelElement>Negotiate contract</WorkflowModelElement>
9   <Originator>Bob</Originator>
10  ...
11 </AuditTrailEntry>
```

**Listing 1.5.** Excerpt of a simulated event log for a credit application process

```
1  ...
2  <node id="BA01" xsi:type="BusinessAction" name="Check credit worthiness">
3   <subjectBinding resource="BA02"/>
4  </node>
5  <node id="BA02" xsi:type="BusinessAction" name="Negotiate contract">
6   <dynamicExclusion resource="BA03"/>
7   <subjectBinding resource="BA01"/>
8  </node>
9  ...
```

**Listing 1.6.** Excerpt of the process-related RBAC model instance in XML representation

Manually checking an event log for inconsistencies is error-prone and time-consuming. Therefore, our approach supports the automated definition of LTL statements from the XML representation of process-related RBAC models (see Section 3). For this purpose, we converted the graphical model from Figure 1 into its corresponding XML representation. Listing 1.6 shows an excerpt of a corresponding XML document including the two subject-bound tasks "Check credit worthiness" and "Negotiate contract".

Now we use our RBAC-to-LTL component (see Section 3) to parse the XML document and derive LTL statements for all properties defined in the RBAC model. Listing 1.7 shows the generated LTL construct for subject-binding of the tasks "Check credit worthiness" and "Negotiate contract".

Subsequently, the automatically generated LTL statements can be imported in a software such as ProM to analyze the corresponding event logs and to reveal violations of the policies defined via the respective process-related RBAC model. Figure 5 shows the result of a corresponding analysis in ProM for our event log of the credit application process. In general, we have two different views in ProM: the rule perspective and the instance perspective. Both perspectives are composed similarly. As shown in Figure 5, the rule perspective has a tab for satisfied rules and a tab for unsatisfied rules. For each of the unsatisfied

```
1   formula SB_task_check_credit_worthiness_and_negotiate_contract () :=
2   {
3       <p>Task "Check credit worthiness" and task "Negotiate contract"
4           must be executed by the same person.</p>
5   }
6   SB_task_A_and_B( "Check credit worthiness", "Negotiate contract" );
```

**Listing 1.7.** LTL formula to check the subject-bound tasks "Check credit worthiness" and "Negotiate contract"

rules it shows which process instances (cases) in the event log satisfy this rule and which do not. To directly see the respective violation we can select the case and inspect its event log entries. For example, Figure 5 shows a violated subject-binding constraint in case 15 for the subject-bound tasks "Check credit worthiness and "Negotiate contract". In the rightmost view from Figure 5 we can see the event logs entries for this process instance. Furthermore, we see which two subjects executed these subject-bound tasks as well as the date and time of this execution event. In this case, two users named Lea and Bob have been executing these subject-bound tasks.

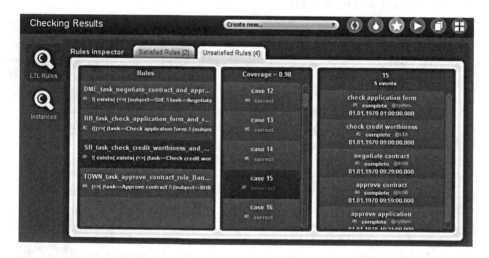

**Fig. 5.** LTL Checker results for the simulated credit application process

## 5   Related Work

In [9], Hansen and Oleshchuk introduce an approach to check the implementation of RBAC constraints using the Spin[2] model checker. They formally express the given RBAC properties via LTL. To check the conformance in Spin, Hansen

---
[2] http://spinroot.com/

and Oleshchuk use the RBAC implementation in PROMELA, the internal specification language of Spin. In contrast to our approach, however, they do not
assess the compliance of actual process executions with a corresponding RBAC
model. A similar approach was presented by Ahmed and Tripathi [3], who specify and statically verify security requirements for CSCW (Computer Supported
Cooperative Work) systems with Spin.

Moreover, the work on business process compliance checking from the area of
process mining is directly related to the work presented in this paper. Van der
Aalst et al. [2] presented a general approach to verify different properties in event
logs. Furthermore, in [17] van der Aalst and de Medeiros apply process mining
to address security issues. They analyze event logs to discover security violations
in process execution. In particular, they check if new events in a certain process
execution comply with a process model that defines acceptable behavior. In
addition, they introduce an approach to check whether new audit trails conform
to the predefined ordering relation of tasks. Another approach in this area has
been introduced by Rozinat and van der Aalst [12], where the stream of events
is replayed from a log in order to reveal inconsistencies. However, the focus
of these approaches is on analyzing the process flow perspective. Thereby, our
work supplements these approaches with a perspective on process-related RBAC
models.

# 6   Conclusion and Outlook

In this paper, we presented an approach to automatically generate LTL statements from process-related RBAC models (see Sections 2.1 and 3). The LTL
statements generated by our RBAC-to-LTL software component can be applied
to check the event logs of business process instances for violations of the corresponding RBAC policies. For example, these checks help to find misconfigurations or implementation errors in PAIS. Thus, the results of such an event log
analysis can give a first insight into the modifications of the corresponding PAIS
or its configuration which are necessary to comply with a tailored RBAC model.
To test our approach, we used the ProM tool to import the LTL statements that
are generated by our RBAC-to-LTL component and checked the event logs of
a credit application process. In our future work, we plan to integrate our work
with related approaches for analyzing the control flow.

# References

1. van der Aalst, W.M.P., Weijters, A.J.M.M.: Process mining: a research agenda.
   Computers in Industry 53 (April 2004)
2. van der Aalst, W.M.P., de Beer, H., van Dongen, B.: Process Mining and Verification of Properties: An Approach based on Temporal Logic. In: Meersman, R., Tari,
   Z. (eds.) OTM 2005, Part I. LNCS, vol. 3760, pp. 130–147. Springer, Heidelberg
   (2005)

3. Ahmed, T., Tripathi, A.R.: Static verification of security requirements in role based CSCW systems. In: Proceedings of the 8th ACM Symposium on Access Control Models and Technologies (SACMAT) (2003)
4. de Beer, H.: The LTL Checker Plugins: A Reference Manual. Eindhoven University of Technology, Eindhoven (2004)
5. de Medeiros, A., Günther, C.W.: Process Mining: Using CPN Tools to Create Test Logs for Mining Algorithms. In: Proceedings of the Sixth Workshop and Tutorial on Practical Use of Coloured Petri Nets and the CPN Tools, pp. 177–190 (2005)
6. Dumas, M., van der Aalst, W.M.P., ter Hofstede, A.: Process-Aware Information Systems. John Wiley & Sons, Inc. (2005)
7. El Kharbili, M., Alves de Medeiros, A., Stein, S., van der Aalst, W.: Business Process Compliance Checking: Current State and Future Challenges. In: MobIS, pp. 107–113 (2008)
8. Ferraiolo, D., Kuhn, D., Chandramouli, R.: Role-Based Access Control, 2nd edn. Artech House (2007)
9. Hansen, F., Oleshchuk, V.: Conformance Checking of RBAC Policy and its Implementation. In: Deng, R.H., Bao, F., Pang, H., Zhou, J. (eds.) ISPEC 2005. LNCS, vol. 3439, pp. 144–155. Springer, Heidelberg (2005)
10. Pnueli, A.: The Temporal Logic of Programs. In: Foundations of Computer Science, pp. 46–57 (1977)
11. Rozinat, A., van der Aalst, W.M.P.: Conformance Testing: Measuring the Fit and Appropriateness of Event Logs and Process Models. In: Bussler, C.J., Haller, A. (eds.) BPM 2005. LNCS, vol. 3812, pp. 163–176. Springer, Heidelberg (2006)
12. Rozinat, A., van der Aalst, W.: Conformance checking of processes based on monitoring real behavior. Information Systems 33(1), 64–95 (2008)
13. Sandhu, R., Coyne, E., Feinstein, H., Youman, C.: Role-Based Access Control Models. IEEE Computer 29(2) (February 1996)
14. Sandhu, R., Samarati, P.: Access Control: Principles and Practice. IEEE Communications 32(9) (September 1994)
15. Strembeck, M.: Scenario-Driven Role Engineering. IEEE Security & Privacy 8(1) (January/February 2010)
16. Strembeck, M., Mendling, J.: Modeling process-related RBAC models with extended UML activity models. Information and Software Technology 53(5), 456–483 (2011)
17. van der Aalst, W., de Medeiros, A.: Process Mining and Security: Detecting Anomalous Process Executions and Checking Process Conformance. Electronic Notes in Theoretical Computer Science 121, 3–21 (2005)
18. van der Aalst, W., van Dongen, B.F., Günther, C.W., Rozinat, A., Verbeek, H.M.W., Weijters, A.J.M.M.: ProM: The Process Mining Toolkit. In: Proceedings of the BPM 2009 Demonstration Track, vol. 489. CEUR-WS.org (September 2009)
19. van der Aalst, W., van Dongen, B., Herbst, J., Maruster, L., Schimm, G., Weijters, A.J.M.M.: Workflow mining: A survey of issues and approaches. Data & Knowledge Engineering 47(2) (2003)
20. van Dongen, B., van der Aalst, W.: A Meta Model for Process Mining Data. In: Proceedings of the Open Interop Workshop on Enterprise Modelling and Ontologies for Interoperability (2005)
21. Verbeek, H.M.W., Buijs, J., van Dongen, B., van der Aalst, W.: ProM 6: The Process Mining Toolkit. In: Proceedings of BPM 2010 Demonstration Track, vol. 615, pp. 34–39. CEUR-WS.org (September 2010)

# Modeling Business Rules for Supervisory Control of Process-Aware Information Systems

Eduardo A.P. Santos, Rosemary Francisco, Agnelo D. Vieira,
Eduardo de F.R. Loures, and Marco A. Busetti

Industrial Engineering, Pontifical Catholic University of Parana
Imaculada Conceicao 1155, Curitiba, Brazil
eduardo.portela@pucpr.br
http://www.pucpr.br

**Abstract.** Companies are demanding more flexibility from their Process Aware Information Systems (PAIS). However, regulations and standards that impose limits to process executions are becoming increasingly important for business process management. The need for a compliance agenda and the security requisites for PAIS are pushing companies to search and to acquire new systems and technics for control and audit business processes. The aim is to avoid process execution that violates some business rules. In order to build an approach that support companies in auditing and controlling their business processes, there is a need for a formal and systematic modeling of business rules. In the present paper we have two objectives. The first one is to propose a set of business rules related to the ordering of tasks and to the involvement of a role or agent in cases. The second one is to build a supervisory control of PAIS that ensures compliance of business rules. To evaluate the correctness of our approach we applied it in two different business processes.

**Keywords:** Process-Aware Information System, business rules, supervisory control, compliance, security.

## 1 Introduction

Companies are developing and executing business processes to reach their goals. According to [1], Process-Aware Information Systems offer promising perspectives in executing business processes, and a growing interest in aligning information systems in a process-oriented way can be observed. A *Process-Aware Information System* (PAIS) is a software system that manages and executes operational processes involving people, applications, and/or information sources on the basis of process models. Business process design is primarily driven by process improvement objectives. However, according to [2], the role of control objectives stemming from regulations and standards is becoming increasingly important for businesses.

[3] states that business process need to be executed within certain boundaries. Moreover, the authors state that these boundaries are defined by business rules

F. Daniel et al. (Eds.): BPM 2011 Workshops, Part II, LNBIP 100, pp. 447–458, 2012.

coming from different sources. Business rules may stem from legislature and regulatory bodies (e.g. Sarbanes-Oxley, Basel II, GAAP, HIPAA), standards and codes of practice (e.g. SCOR, ISO9000) and also business partner contracts and shareholders.

The implementation of business rules in PAIS is a topic that has received a lot of attention in the last years. As organizations struggle to meet compliance agendas, there is an urgent need to provide systematic approaches that assure the execution of tasks without violate business rules. As PAIS work autonomously or in cooperation with people, in many situations to manage and to control the whole set of activities can become a very complex task. In fact, the process manager has to check whether the business rules are being followed on a continuous basis, to assess the operating effectiveness of their business rules, and must monitor the execution of the business processes closely [3]. In this context many works propose implement some kind of system or technic to support administration on business process compliance and auditing [3] [2].

Our proposal may be divided in two parts. First we propose a set of business rules related to the ordering of tasks and to the involvement of resources (a role or agent) in cases. We use automata to represent these business rules. The whole set of automata models is used in the second part of our proposal. Here we build a controller that monitors and supervises a PAIS. The controller is synthesized according to Supervisory Control Theory [4]. Such controller is a separate system that prevent the occurrence of some events of the PAIS. The conceptual model of SCS presented here is similar of that presented in [5]. The controller works as following. The process engine of PAIS generates a set of information elements which is completely observed and processed by the controller. This set is formed by a partial trace of events, a list of enabled tasks and a case identifier. According to the business rules established in controller, a list of disabled tasks is sent to PAIS. Thus, the controller provides a "map" or "guide" to users, informing them which tasks can be executed and which tasks cannot. Restricting these options based on control rules can ensure correctness and support efficiency. At the same time, as the controller engine can easily and systematically be modified (if control rules change), this approach is declarative making it very flexible and customizable.

The remainder of this paper is structured as follows. In Section 2 the business rules models are presented. Two examples of business processes are shown in Section 3. We identify and model the business rules related to these processes. In Section 4 we describe the synthesis procedure and the implementation of the supervisory control. Finally, in section 5 we discuss and provide conclusions.

## 2   Modeling Activities and Business Rules

We consider that a PAIS is constituted of a set of tasks. In our approach each task is assigned to an automaton representing its behavior. The task life-cycle as stated in [6] is considered as basis to represent such behavior. Figure 1(a) illustrates the life-cycle for a task instance or work item as they are often known in a workflow context. The diagram indicates the states through which a work item passes during execution and it characterize the way in which work is distributed to the resources. Figure 1(b) shows the automaton corresponding to the task life-cycle. This automaton does not include some states of task life-cycle diagram. This automaton models relevant aspects that will be considered for supervisory control: the distribution of resources just after a case has been created; the beginning and ending of a task; the suspension and resuming of a task; and the possibility to re-start a task. Figure 1(c) shows the semantics of events of the task life-cycle automaton.

Once a task is triggered, a work item is created. This state is represented as initial state (state C) in automaton shown in Figure 1(b). Thus, at state C, there are two possibilities: a task may be allocated to a single resource (from now we refer to $agent$) $A = agent_1, agent_2, ..., agent_p$ or to agents assigned to roles and groups ($R = role_1, role_2, ..., role_r$ and $G = group_1, group_2, ..., group_g$). As the task life-cycle shown in Figure 1(a), the automaton shown in Figure 1(b) is work item based, i.e. it represents the behavior of a task related to a specific work item. Notice that the tasks considered in a PAIS are indexed by $ti$ ($t = t1, t2, ..., ti$).

The fundamental idea of our approach is that the execution of tasks in PAIS is restrained by business rules. In this section we show automata models to represent such business rules. Thus, we use these models in the context of supervisory control, as the SCT uses this formalism in the synthesis procedure of controller. In addition, we are building a repository of business rules that may be used in other projects.

Since it is in principle impossible to list all possible business rules, we only present groups of them that occur frequently in workflow systems. According to [3], in general business rules concern the following aspects: ordering based, i.e. about the execution order of tasks in cases; agent based, i.e. about the involvement of a role or agent in cases and processes; value based, i.e. in forms belonging to a task. In our work we consider two groups: ordering based rules and the involvement of a role or agent in cases and processes. In order to apply the Supervisory Control Theory in the context of PAIS, is necessary to model the business rules using automata.

1. *Ordering based rules*: express constraints concerning the ordering of events and activities in processes.
   - *Rule 1*: A task $t1$ should always be performed before task $t2$ in any case of process.
   - *Rule 2*: Tasks $t1$ e $t2$ should not be performed in parallel.
   - *Rule 3*: In any case of process task $ti$ can not be executed more than $n$ times.
   - *Rule 4*: In the case both tasks $t1$ and $t2$ are suspended, task $t1$ has priority of resume over task $t2$.
   - *Rule 5*: A specific substring is considered illegal in the case some tasks are being executed in parallel. It is possible to build an automaton that represent this business rule using the algorithm described in [7].

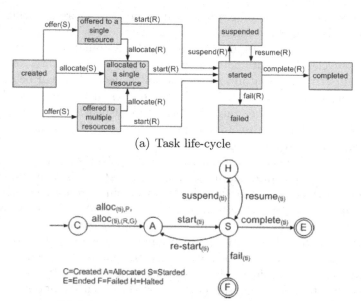

(a) Task life-cycle

(b) Automaton representing the task life-cycle

| $alloc_{(ti),P}$ | a case is allocated for an agent P |
|---|---|
| $alloc_{(ti),(R,G)}$ | a case is allocated for agents with a specific Role (R) and Group (G) |
| $start_{(ti)}$ | a task $ti$ is initiated |
| $re\text{-}start_{(ti)}$ | a task $ti$ is re-initiated |
| $complete_{(ti)}$ | a task $ti$ is completed |
| $suspend_{(ti)}$ | a task $ti$ is temporarily suspended |
| $resume_{(ti)}$ | a task $ti$ is resumed |
| $fail_{(ti)}$ | a task $ti$ fails |

(c) Events and its semantics

**Fig. 1.** Task life cycle representation - resource perspective

2. *Agent based rules*

– *Rule 6 (4-eyes principle)*: two tasks *t1* and *t2* in the same case should always be executed by different agents. The model that represents this rule is shown in Figure 3(b). Initially, each rule can be assigned to each agent, as shown in Figure 3(a). The models *E1* and *E2* represent a constraint on the agents *P1* and *P2*, respectively. The business rule is then obtained by synchronous product of the models *E1* and *E2*, as shown in Figure 3(b). Thus, if *n* agents are associated with the process, the business rule model is achieved through synchronous product specifications between *E1*, *E2*, ..., *En*.

– *Rule 7 (Mutually exclusive agents)*: Two agents should never appear together in a case. The model that represents this rule is shown in Figure 3(c). Notice that tasks *t1* and *t2* can be allocated to the agent *P1* and agent *P2*

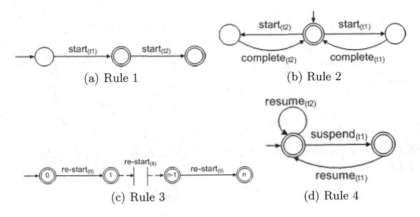

**Fig. 2.** Ordering based rules

in the initial state. After an agent is allocated to a task, the other agent can not be allocated anymore (if it happens the automaton will block because an unmarked state is reached).

– *Rule 8 (Task limit on an agent)*: an agent cannot do more than $n$ tasks in any case of a process. The model that represents this rule is shown in Figure 3(d).

## 3 Example

As an example to illustrate our approach, we use the same process treated in [3]. This is the *Administer Account Transfer* process as shown in Figure 4. According to [3], the organization has the following agents: Joe, Sue, Eric and Beth. These agents fulfill the roles within the organization. We consider the same business rules defined in [3]. Agent-Joe and agent-Sue are not allowed to work together in any case (Rule 7). Agent-Eric is not allowed to execute more than 4 tasks (Rule 8), and agent-Beth cannot do more than one task (Rule 8). Last, tasks *t7* and *t8a* in a case may not be executed by the same agents (Rule 6), and this also applies to tasks *t7* and *t8b*, and for tasks *t10a* and *t10b*.

A second example is a process corresponding to a conformance checking of products in the context of a manufacturing industry. Figure 5 shows the conformance checking process model. In this case we only consider ordering based rules. Also, these rules are related to a specific part of process named *Non-Conformance Causes Identification Sub-Process*. The employees can decide in which order to execute these tasks. Ideally, the employees finish these as soon as possible. All tasks have a fixed duration, however, tasks *t2 - B* and *t3 - C* use the same database application and if *t2* is directly followed by *t3*, then the combined duration of the tasks is much shorter, since there is no closing time for *t2 - B* and not set-up time for *t3 - C*, moreover *t3 - C* can use the data provided by *t2 - B*, without data re-entry (Rule 1). Tasks *t1 - A* and *t5 - E*, during their execution, can unexpectedly suspend. In case both tasks suspend

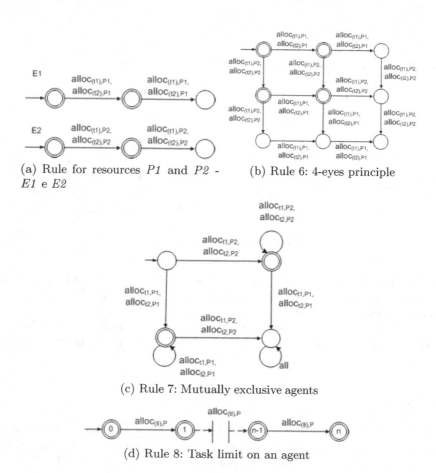

(a) Rule for resources *P1* and *P2* - *E1* e *E2*

(b) Rule 6: 4-eyes principle

(c) Rule 7: Mutually exclusive agents

(d) Rule 8: Task limit on an agent

**Fig. 3.** Agent based rules

simultaneously, the resume of *t1* - *A* has priority over the *t5* - *E* (Rule 4). Also, for security reasons, tasks *t2* - *B* and *t4* - *D* should not be executed at the same time (Rule 2). It is necessary a mutual exclusion between them.

## 4    Implementing the Control Structure

[4] consider a very general control paradigm for how the supervisor (or the controller) interacts with the plant (or uncontrolled system). In this paradigm, the supervisor sees (or observes) some, possibly all, of the events that plant executes. Then, the supervisor tells which events in the current active event set of the plant are allowed next. More precisely, the supervisor has the capability of disabling some, but not necessarily all, feasible events of the plant. The decision about which events to disable will be allowed to change whenever the supervisor observes the execution of a new event by the plant. In this manner, the supervisor exerts dynamic feedback control on the plant.

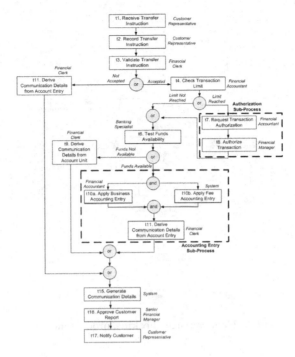

**Fig. 4.** Administer account transfer

For supervisor synthesis we use the Local Modular Control (LMC) approach as proposed in [8]. Using LMC approach as procedure, instead of synthesizing a single global supervisor that satisfies the entire set of business rules, a local supervisor is synthesized in order to satisfy each business rule. Thus, each local supervisor only restricts a subset of tasks of the PAIS to be controlled. This subset of tasks forms a *local plant*. A local plant is obtained by performing the synchronous product of the tasks automata which share events with the considered business rule. The synthesis of a local supervisor is performed considering the corresponding business rule and its local plant (using the same procedure as stated in Supervisory Control Theory).

The first step to synthesize local supervisors is to obtain the local plant to each specification. It is presented here how we obtained two local supervisors, one for each process presented in Section 3. The first one is related to the business rule 7 (mutually exclusive agents) - Agent-Joe and agent-Sue are not allowed to work together in any case - of Administer Account Transfer process. The automaton that models this rule is Figure 6(c) (based on the model shown in Figure 3(c). To save space, we show the synthesis procedure considering only two tasks: *t1* and *t2*. We begin calculating the local plant associated to the mentioned business. In this case, the local plant is obtained by the synchronous product of automata that model *t1* and *t2*. The models of these two tasks are shown in Figures 6(a) and 6(b) (the general automaton that models a task is shown in Figure 1(b)). The synthesis of a local supervisor is performed considering the corresponding

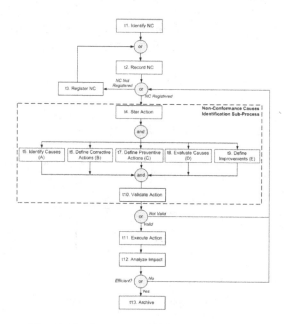

**Fig. 5.** Conformance checking process model

business rule its local plant. As a final step before implementation, reduction of supervisor is taken into account. The reduction in the number of states of a supervisor can represent memory economy and clarify the control logic. The reduced supervisor has a smaller number of states and the same control action that the corresponding supervisor has. We use the reduction algorithm proposed by [9]. The reduced local supervisor is shown in Figure 6(d). The box attached to each state represents the set of disabled events (the control action of local supervisor).

The second example of local supervisor synthesis is shown in Figure 7. Considering that in the conformance checking process there are no business rules related to agents allocation, we exclude the corresponding events (and initial state) from the automaton shown in Figure 1(b). Thus, we use the automata as shown in Figures 7(a) and 7(b). Considering the business rule as shown in Figure 7(c) (task B should always be performed before task C in any case of process), the local modular approach and reduction algorithm we find the local reduced supervisor as shown in Figure 7(d). Notice that each local supervisor shown in Figures 6(d) and 7(d) disable some events in some of its states. This control action restrain the execution of tasks as certain events will not be allowed to occur. In this way business rules are not violated.

In order to implement the control logic of local supervisors, we consider the supervisory control as a separate system coupled to the process engine of PAIS. The supervisory control independently checks if the tasks are being performed according to pre-established control action. Our purpose is to implement the supervisory control using the Process Mining Framework ProM [10]. The first

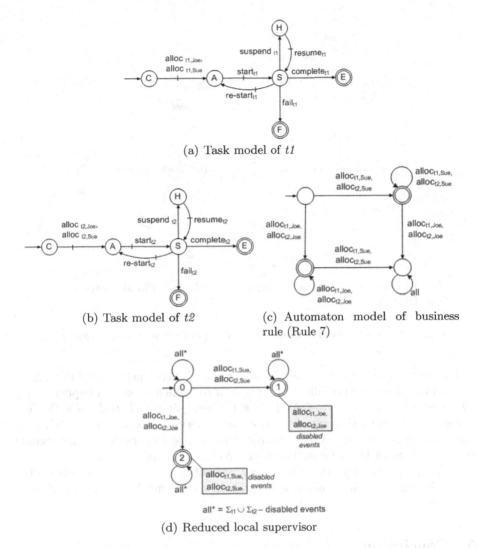

(a) Task model of *t1*

(b) Task model of *t2*

(c) Automaton model of business rule (Rule 7)

(d) Reduced local supervisor

**Fig. 6.** Models involved in synthesis local supervisor procedure - example 1

implementation of supervisory control in ProM is described in [5]. The controller has been implemented in ProM and the YAWL environment was chosen as the implementation platform to simulate the conformance checking process. YAWL provides a very powerful and expressive workflow language based on the workflow patterns identified in [11] [12]. It also provides a workflow enactment engine, and an editor for process model creation, that support the control flow, data and (basic) resource perspectives. The YAWL environment is open-source and has a service-oriented architecture, allowing the supervisory control to be developed as a service independent to the engine.

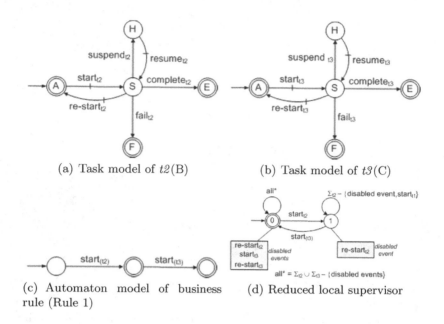

(a) Task model of $t2$(B)

(b) Task model of $t3$(C)

(c) Automaton model of business rule (Rule 1)

(d) Reduced local supervisor

**Fig. 7.** Models involved in synthesis local supervisor procedure - example 2

During the execution of tasks, the supervisory control has to inform to YAWL which tasks users are not allowed to perform (or which tasks can happen next). The control action sent to YAWL is a list assigning each task to a Boolean value. When a task is assigned to false, the supervisory control is disabling the event that corresponds to the beginning of such task. Otherwise, the supervisory control allows tasks to be executed in YAWL. As long as an event occurs in YAWL, the program in the supervisory control is updated and a new control action is sent. The implementation details in ProM and YAWL is out of scope of this work.

## 5   Conclusion

Many approaches has proposed to add control to the business processes and to avoid incorrect or undesirable executions of the activities. In [13] and [14] a constraint-based WFMS called DECLARE is presented. Declare is a framework that implements various declarative languages. In DECLARE the possible ordering of activities are determined by constrains. Thus, any order of execution sequence can be possible as long as constraints are not violated. Everything that does not violate the constraints is allowed. A stream of research proposes using rule-based or constraint-based modeling languages. [15] uses process grammars for definition of rules involving activities and documents. The Freeflow prototype [16] uses constraints for building declarative process models. [17] presents a constraint-based language that uses rules involving preconditions (that must hold before an activity can be executed), postconditions (that must hold after an activity is executed).

The business rules as proposed in the presented paper are identified and modeled as a part of the supervisory control synthesis. Each business rule is translated into an automaton and we may use them in different projects. We intent to use the whole set of automata business rules to check violations after execution (model checking), as a complement of our work. The supervisory control has been implemented by extending ProM and the experiment that has been performed to show its feasibility. The computational infra-structure already implemented in ProM allows communication with external applications and allows the controller to be integrated with PAIS that records events. In this paper we point out that the supervisory control in ProM can cooperate with the YAWL system. Future work will aim at extending the application and implementation of supervisory control in large-scale business processes. Through a large number of case studies we intent to make supervisory control a tool for keep PAIS within certain boundaries. Moreover, we plan to incorporate other control approaches and investigate the suitability of the approaches in particular settings.

# References

1. Weber, B., Reichert, M., Rinderle-Ma, S.: Change patterns and change support features–enhancing flexibility in process-aware information systems. Data & Knowledge Engineering 66, 438–466 (2008)
2. Sadiq, S., Governatori, G., Namiri, K.: Modeling Control Objectives for Business Process Compliance. In: Alonso, G., Dadam, P., Rosemann, M. (eds.) BPM 2007. LNCS, vol. 4714, pp. 149–164. Springer, Heidelberg (2007)
3. van der Aalst, W., van Hee, K., van der Werf, J.M., Kumar, A., Verdonk, M.: Conceptual model for on line auditing. Decision Support Systems 50, 636–647 (2011)
4. Ramadge, P.J.G., Wonham, W.M.: The control of discrete event systems. Proceedings of the IEEE 77, 81–98 (1989)
5. Santos, E.A.P., Francisco, R., Pesic, M., van der Aalst, W.: Supervisory Control Service-A control approach supporting flexible processes. Technical report, BPM Center Report, BPMcenter. org (2010)
6. ter Hofstede, A.H.M., van der Aalst, W.M.P., Adams, M., Russell, N.: Modern Business Process Automation: YAWL and its Support Environment. Springer-Verlag New York Inc. (2010)
7. Cassandras, C.G., Lafortune, S.: Introduction to discrete event systems. Springer, Heidelberg (2008)
8. De Queiroz, M.H., Cury, J.E.R.: Modular supervisory control of large scale discrete event systems. Discrete Event Systems: Analysis and Control, 103–110 (2000)
9. Su, R., Wonham, W.M.: Supervisor reduction for discrete-event systems. Discrete Event Dynamic Systems 14, 31–53 (2004)
10. van Dongen, B.F., de Medeiros, A.K.A., Verbeek, H.M.W., Weijters, A.J.M.M., van der Aalst, W.M.P.: The ProM Framework: A New Era in Process Mining Tool Support. In: Ciardo, G., Darondeau, P. (eds.) ICATPN 2005. LNCS, vol. 3536, pp. 444–454. Springer, Heidelberg (2005)

11. van der Aalst, W.M.P., ter Hofstede, A.H.M., Kiepuszewski, B., Barros, A.P.: Workflow patterns. Distributed and Parallel Databases 14, 5–51 (2003)
12. van der Aalst, W.M.P., ter Hofstede, A.H.M.: YAWL: yet another workflow language. Information Systems 30, 245–275 (2005)
13. van der Aalst, W., Pesic, M., Schonenberg, H.: Declarative workflows: Balancing between flexibility and support. Computer Science-Research and Development 23, 99–113 (2009)
14. Pesic, M., Schonenberg, M., Sidorova, N., van der Aalst, W.: Constraint-Based Workflow Models: Change Made Easy. In: Meersman, R. (ed.) OTM 2007, Part I. LNCS, vol. 4803, pp. 77–94. Springer, Heidelberg (2007)
15. Glance, N., Pagani, D., Pareschi, R.: Generalized process structure grammars GPSG for flexible representations of work. In: 1996 ACM Conference on Computer Supported Cooperative Work, pp. 180–189 (1996)
16. Dourish, P., Holmes, J., MacLean, A., Marqvardsen, P., Zbyslaw, A.: Freeflow: mediating between representation and action in workflow systems. In: 1996 ACM Conference on Computer Supported Cooperative Work, pp. 190–198 (1996)
17. Wainer, J., de Lima Bezerra, F.: Constraint-Based Flexible Workflows. In: Favela, J., Decouchant, D. (eds.) CRIWG 2003. LNCS, vol. 2806, pp. 151–158. Springer, Heidelberg (2003)

# Separating Compliance Management and Business Process Management

Elham Ramezani[1], Dirk Fahland[2,*], Jan Martijn van der Werf[2,**], and Peter Mattheis[1]

[1] Hochschule Furtwangen, Germany
{ramezani,Peter.Mattheis}@hs-furtwangen.de
[2] Eindhoven University of Technology, The Netherlands
{j.m.e.m.v.d.werf,d.fahland}@tue.nl

**Abstract.** The ever growing set of regulations and laws organizations have to comply to, introduces many new challenges. Current approaches that check for compliance by implementing controls in an existing information system (IS) decrease the maintainability of both the set of compliance rules and the IS. In this position paper, we advocate the separation of the compliance process from the organization's business processes. We introduce a life cycle for the management of compliance rules. A separate compliance engine is used to define and check compliance rules independent from the existing IS within an organization.

**Keywords:** compliance management life cycle, compliance requirements, compliance rule, compliance checking.

## 1  Introduction

Organizations are confronted with more and more regulations and laws to comply to. At a first glance, this seems rather as a burden for organizations. However, organizations see this as an opportunity to streamline their business and operations [10].

Compliance management (CM) within an organization comprises the design, implementation, maintenance, verification and reporting of compliance requirements originating in regulations and law enforcements. CM is closely related to risk management. Violating a compliance requirement introduces potential risks like consequences on management level, lost contracts with customers, service level agreements not been made, or non-identified security flaws [9,13]. Therefore CM requires constant monitoring within organizations.

In the ideal situation, we would have a continuous auditing process that gives us real time insights into violation of business rules. Clearly this cannot be done manually. Therefore we need better techniques and software tools that make it possible to check arbitrary business rules automatically and in real time. Information systems (IS) play

* Supported by the European Community's Seventh Framework Programme FP7/2007- 2013 under grant agreement no 257593 (ACSI).
** Supported by the PoSecCo project (project no. 257129), partially co-funded by the European Union under the Information and Communication Technologies (ICT) theme of the 7th Framework Programme for R&D (FP7).

F. Daniel et al. (Eds.): BPM 2011 Workshops, Part II, LNBIP 100, pp. 459–464, 2012.
© Springer-Verlag Berlin Heidelberg 2012

a major role in executing business processes either in cooperation with employees or autonomously. One of the approaches to enforce compliance in business operation is to embed *controls* in information systems, i.e., integration of compliance with BPM [3,8]. However, implementing controls as tasks within an existing IS decreases the maintainability of both the IS as well as the set of compliance rules.

In this paper, we advocate to adapt the business process management (BPM) life cycle to manage compliance in a similar way. We propose to use a common business vocabulary based on BPM to specify compliance rules, and to separate the business operation from the process of compliance checking. Rather than inserting controls in the business process directly, we propose a specialized engine for CM that communicates with existing IS.

In the remainder of this position paper, we introduce the idea and the main concepts of a compliance management life cycle in Sect. 2 and discuss various aspects and open challenges in Sect. 3.

## 2 Compliance Management

The challenges posed by the need to implement compliance requirements in an organization call for a structured methodology. In this section, we make a step towards Compliance Management (CM), that is, a methodology to elicit, specify and formalize, implement, check and analyze, and optimize compliance requirements in organizations. We suppose the management of compliance requirements to follow a life cycle as sketched in Fig. 1.

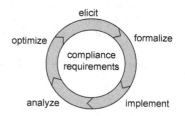

**Fig. 1.** Compliance Management Life Cycle

An initial life cycle for compliance has been proposed in [8]. In this paper, we take this idea one step further and *separate* CM from BPM. The key idea for separation is to introduce a separate *compliance engine* that is coupled with an existing information system (IS) to check its compliance, as sketched in Fig. 2.

In the following, we discuss each of the phases and at the same time introduce:

1. a business vocabulary for compliance rules similar to the basic notions of business process models in BPM,
2. a generic architecture of a compliance engine to implement compliance rules for checking compliance at a given IS, and
3. discuss techniques to check compliance.

**Eliciting Compliance Requirements.** In a rapidly evolving regulatory and compliance environment organizations are exposed constantly to different compliance sources [12]. The elicitation phase of the CM life cycle identifies the *compliance requirements* relevant for an organization by analyzing the profile of the organization including information such as company size, industry, region, and products or services.

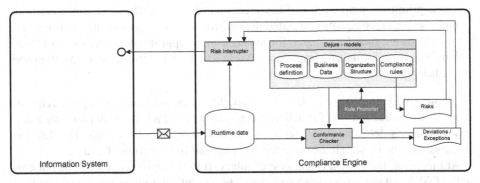

**Fig. 2.** Architecture of Compliance Engine

**Specifying and Formalizing Compliance Rules.** The compliance requirements selected in the elicitation phase often originate in legal texts and have a very informal and abstract character. In order to be able to have tool support for compliance checking, these requirements should be represented in a formal and structured notation called *compliance rules*. The rules should focus on the business aspects of the requirements, rather than the technical aspects of the IS.

To guide this step and for maintainability, we propose to capture each aspect of a compliance requirement in a separate compliance rule based on a *business vocabulary*. This vocabulary builds on an abstract conceptual model of processes [3] which contains all primitive notions of business processes that are required to formulate compliance rules for processes in a precise manner. These primitives will then form the base vocabulary for writing compliance rules. Compliance requires distinguishing at least the following four primitives.

**Process definition.** A possibly hierarchical process consists of a set of *tasks* and subprocesses, which are usually *ordered* in some way.
**Business data definition.** Process data is represented by a *data model* consisting of a set of *entity types* and *relationships* between these entity types; each entity type defines a number of *attributes*. The actual data of the process is given by a number of *entities* for each type. Each entity assigns a *value* to its attributes, and is *associated* to other entities according to the relationships. Tasks are associated with entity types defining which attributes the task is allowed to read, write, or update.
**Organizational definition.** Each task is associated to a set of *roles*, e.g. a clerk or a manager, restricting who is allowed to execute that task. Roles may be ordered in a hierarchy. *Agents*, e.g., users or other systems, have a role assigned, which determines the tasks they are allowed to execute.
**Runtime.** A process is run by creating a new *case* (process instance); agents then execute tasks for a particular case. To execute a task in a case, an agent first gets assigned a role and a *permission* to execute the task, if permitted by its role. When the permission is granted, executing the task creates an *event* that records for which task and case the event was raised and by whom. Furthermore, it records which entities have been created or updated. The events are ordered by the moment in time they occurred.

These primitives pinpoint to the key elements of process definition and execution. Compliance rules are usually first stated in semi-formal sentences over these primitives; the sentences are then formalized, for instance in an appropriate logic, like in [8], in which the authors formalize compliance rules in a temporal object logic, or, as proposed in [3], using predicate logic.

**Implementing Compliance Rules.** To ensure that an IS complies with a given requirement, its formalization (the formalized compliance rules) has to be implemented in a way that allows detecting if an execution violates some compliance rule. For this, the executions of the IS have to be observed and checked for violation of a rule.

At this point, the chosen business vocabulary of the compliance rules turns out crucial to CM. Each term in a compliance rule refers to information in the IS that needs to be observed and checked. The aforementioned business vocabulary allows for a generic architecture of a *compliance engine* that *extends* a given IS for checking compliance. For this, we propose to adapt the idea of an *online auditing tool* (OLAT) and a corresponding architecture [3] as shown in Fig. 2 to CM. In this way, the formalized compliance rules can be checked independently of the IS.

The engine assumes a *De Jure model* to be given, consisting of process models, data models, organizational models, and compliance rules, all formulated in the business vocabulary. The existing IS should send a message for every action it performs. This message is then recorded by the compliance engine in its *runtime data*. Hence, the runtime data comprises all information on process executions, that is, the current status and the history of the runtime primitives presented above. For instance, the events that have occurred, their order and duration, the values that were written by a particular event, the authorizations to access data granted to specific roles, or the role assignments given to specific agents.

In the *external* compliance checking setting, where the engine is separated from the IS, a *compliance checker* compares the De Jure models to the observed executions, i.e., the runtime data, and signals deviations or exceptions.

In the *internal* compliance checking setting, the engine is additionally allowed to control the IS by a *risk interrupter*. The risk interrupter takes as input the discovered deviations and assesses based on its information how severe the violation of the compliance rule would turn out in the future. In case of a severe risk, it can interrupt the process execution in the IS.

**Checking and Analyzing Compliance Rules.** Having implemented compliance requirements as formalized compliance rules in a compliance engine allows checking compliance in an automated way. Thereby neither the proposed CM method, nor our architecture is tied to a particular compliance checker or a particular formalization of compliance rules (which are fed to the checker). For external compliance checking existing techniques like replay [4], temporal logic checking [2], or general database queries [3] can be used. In case of internal compliance checking operational support [11,14] can be used to prevent compliance violations, for instance by revoking or granting data access, or by blocking or enforcing tasks.

Other techniques check compliance by incorporating the compliance rules already in the design [5,6,15], or the model is checked after design [7,10]. However, in these cases runtime monitoring and automatic detection [5,1] is essential, as a correct model does not necessarily imply a correct execution.

**Optimization.** Each of the compliance checkers indicates if an execution of the IS violated a compliance rule. Depending on the setting, different steps for improving compliance then can be taken.

As mentioned above, internal compliance checking allows to prevent or mitigate compliance violations using operational support [11,14]. If a violation cannot be prevented, particulary in case of external compliance checking, two cases may arise. (1) Either the deviation indicates a problem in the De Jure model, e.g., a wrong compliance rule. In this case, a *rule promoter* can be used to update the De Jure model to eliminate false positives in the future, see Fig. 2. (2) Or the IS or the business process are non-compliant and the process designer has to plan how to *optimize* IS and process to achieve compliance. The violated rule precisely tells which aspect of the process (e.g., which task and role) was non-compliant and where the process has to be improved.

# 3 Conclusions and Future Work

In this position paper we advocate the idea of managing compliance separated from BPM. In order to support this idea we introduce an engine that allows for the formal definition and auditing of compliance rules. The engine supports both detective and preventive approaches to check compliance rules. For external auditing, only the detective approach is allowed. However, the engine can be used to interrupt a business process if the next action would lead to a violation.

The crucial aspect of this approach is to identify a business vocabulary that allows to express all compliance requirements in the basic notions of business processes. By instrumenting the IS to report to the compliance engine all state changes of the primitives in the business vocabulary, compliance of the processes can be checked in a generic way and separately from the IS implementation itself. This approach requires to synchronize CM and BPM only in their formalization phases (to create consistent process models and compliance rules) and their optimization phases (to plan changes to models and rules). In all other phases, CM and BPM are separated, allowing to develop dedicated techniques particulary for CM.

Our proposed approach still faces many challenges. The elicitation phase in the life cycle still requires intense human work and knowledge for interpreting compliance sources and defining compliance requirements and compliance rules. However, tool support may assist in identifying affected processes and eliciting compliance requirements and rules. Moreover, laws usually require organizations to document how regulatory goals are achieved [13]. In particular, a compliance solution has to allow to explicitly trace the enforcement of compliance requirements in business operation. While this is not addressed in this paper, we believe that our structured approach supports traceability of compliance.

Finally, the proposed CM life cycle and our architecture address the technical side of compliance in organizations. It is meant to complement and facilitate governance programmes, such as the Unified Governance Framework [13], which define legal strategies and their enforcement on all organizational layers.

Each of the mentioned challenges is subject to further research. However the most urgent activity is experimentation of the separated compliance engine with a prototype which covers the CM life cycle.

# References

1. A Methodological Framework for Aligning Business Processes and Regulatory Compliance
2. van der Aalst, W.M.P., de Beer, H.T., van Dongen, B.F.: Process Mining and Verification of Properties: An Approach Based on Temporal Logic. In: Meersman, R. (ed.) OTM 2005. LNCS, vol. 3760, pp. 130–147. Springer, Heidelberg (2005)
3. van der Aalst, W.M.P., van Hee, K.M., van der Werf, J.M.E.M., Kumar, A., Verdonk, M.: Conceptual Model for Online Auditing. Decision Support Systems 50(3), 636–647 (2011)
4. Adriansyah, A., Sidorova, N., van Dongen, B.F.: Cost-based Fitness in Conformance Checking. In: ACSD 2011. IEEE (2011)
5. El Kharbili, M., de Medeiros, A.K.A., Stein, S., van der Aalst, W.M.P.: Business Process Compliance Checking: Current State and Future Challenges. In: Modellierung betrieblicher Informationssysteme (MobIS). LNI, pp. 107–113 (2008)
6. Fötsch, D., Pulvermüller, E., Rossak, W.: Modeling and Verifying Workflow-based Regulations. In: Regulations Modelling and their Validation/ Verification, pp. 825–830 (2006)
7. Ghose, A., Koliadis, G.: Auditing Business Process Compliance. In: Krämer, B.J., Lin, K.-J., Narasimhan, P. (eds.) ICSOC 2007. LNCS, vol. 4749, pp. 169–180. Springer, Heidelberg (2007)
8. Giblin, C., Liu, A.Y., Müller, S., Pfitzmann, B., Zhou, X.: Regulations Expressed As Logical Models (REALM). JURIX, 37–48 (2005)
9. Kharbili, M., Stein, S., Markovic, I., Pulvermüller, E.: Towards a Framework for Semantic Business Process Compliance Management. In: GRCIS. CEUR Workshop Proceedings, vol. 339, pp. 1–15 (2008)
10. Lu, R., Sadiq, S., Governatori, G.: Compliance Aware Business Process Design. In: ter Hofstede, A.H.M., Benatallah, B., Paik, H.-Y. (eds.) BPM Workshops 2007. LNCS, vol. 4928, pp. 120–131. Springer, Heidelberg (2008)
11. Maggi, F.M., Montali, M., Westergaard, M., van der Aalst, W.M.P.: Monitoring Business Constraints with Linear Temporal Logic: An Approach Based on Colored Automata. In: Rinderle-Ma, S., Toumani, F., Wolf, K. (eds.) BPM 2011. LNCS, LNBIP, vol. 6896, pp. 132–147. Springer, Heidelberg (2011)
12. Menzies, C.: Sarbanes-Oxley und Corporate Compliance: Nachhaltigkeit, Optimierung, Integration. Schäffer Poeschel, Stuttgart (2006)
13. Waidner, M., Pfitzmann, B., Powers, C.: IBM's Unified Governance Framework (UGF). Technical report, IBM Research Division, Zurich, IBM Research Report RZ 3699 (99709) (December 10, 2007)
14. Rozinat, A., Wynn, M.T., van der Aalst, W.M.P., ter Hofstede, A.H.M., Fridge, C.J.: Workflow Simulation for Operational Decision Support. Data & Knowledge Engineering 68, 834–850 (2009)
15. Sadiq, S., Governatori, G., Namiri, K.: Modeling Control Objectives for Business Process Compliance. In: Alonso, G., Dadam, P., Rosemann, M. (eds.) BPM 2007. LNCS, vol. 4714, pp. 149–164. Springer, Heidelberg (2007)

# Checking Satisfiability Aspects of Binding Constraints in a Business Process Context

Sigrid Schefer[1], Mark Strembeck[1], and Jan Mendling[2]

[1] Institute for Information Systems, New Media Lab,
Vienna University of Economics and Business (WU Vienna), Austria
firstname.lastname@wu.ac.at
[2] Institute of Information Systems,
Humboldt-Universität zu Berlin, Germany
jan.mendling@wiwi.hu-berlin.de

**Abstract.** Binding of Duty (BOD) constraints define that the same subject (or role) who performed a certain task $t_1$ must also perform a corresponding bound task $t_2$. In this paper, we describe algorithms for checking the *satisfiability of binding constraints* in a business process context. In particular, these algorithms check the configuration of a process-related RBAC model to find satisfiability conflicts. Furthermore, we discuss options to resolve satisfiability conflicts.

**Keywords:** access control, binding of duty, business processes.

## 1 Introduction

*Separation of duty (SOD)* and *Binding of Duty (BOD)* constraints specify rules to control task allocation and execution in workflows (see, e.g., [2,3,5,6,7,8,9]). They constrain task authorizations by defining that two (or more) tasks must be performed by different individuals (SOD) or by the same individual (BOD). In a business process context, SOD constraints enforce conflict of interest policies. Conflict of interest arises as a result of the simultaneous assignment of two mutually exclusive tasks to the same subject. Thus, mutually exclusive tasks result from the division of powerful rights to prevent fraud and abuse.

BOD can be subdivided into subject-based and role-based constraints (see, e.g., [5,6]). A *subject-based BOD constraint* defines that the same individual who performed the first task must also perform the bound task(s). In contrast, a *role-based BOD constraint* defines that bound tasks must be performed by members of the same role, but not necessarily by the same individual. Throughout the paper, we will use the terms *subject-binding* and *role-binding* as synonyms for subject-based and role-based BOD constraints respectively. *Satisfiability* of a business process requires that a set of authorized subjects is able to perform all tasks in the workflow (see, e.g., [4,7]). However, process verification typically focuses on pure control flow aspects such as soundness [1]. In this paper, we look at workflow verification with a focus on workflow satisfiability aspects of process-related binding constraints.

F. Daniel et al. (Eds.): BPM 2011 Workshops, Part II, LNBIP 100, pp. 465–470, 2012.
© Springer-Verlag Berlin Heidelberg 2012

## 2  Satisfiability of Binding Constraints

In [5], we presented a set of algorithms to ensure the consistency of process-related RBAC models. However, a RBAC model can be consistent while at the same time the corresponding processes may still not be satisfiable. The algorithms defined below detect satisfiability conflicts of workflows that include binding constraints. Note that the checks in the if-clauses of our algorithms complement each other. Thus, checks of prior if-clauses do not have to be repeated in subsequent if-clauses. The algorithms' runtime complexity is in the worst-case scenario $\mathcal{O}(n^2)$. The worst case memory consumption for the sets of elements is $\mathcal{O}(n)$, for relations among these elements it amounts to $\mathcal{O}(n^3)$. The underlying formal definitions and consistency requirements are specified in [5,6].

To ensure the satisfiability of a *subject-binding* (SB) constraint, subject-bound tasks must be assigned to the same subject, either directly or transitively via the role-hierarchy. Algorithm 1 checks if a SB constraint specified on two task types $t_1$ and $t_2$ is satisfiable. If a satisfiability conflict is detected, the algorithm returns the name of the respective conflict. In Algorithm 1, line 1 first checks if a SB constraint is defined on two task types $t_1$ and $t_2$. Only if a SB constraint is specified, the algorithm proceeds with the subsequent satisfiability checks.

**Algorithm 1.** *Check if a SB constraint on two task types is satisfiable.*

*Name:* $isSBconstraintSatisfiable(t_1, t_2)$

*Input:* $t_1, t_2 \in T_T$

1:  *if* $t_1 \notin sb(t_2)$ *then return* **true**

2:  *if* $\nexists s \in S, r_1, r_2 \in R \mid r_1 \in rown(s) \ \wedge \ r_2 \in rown(s) \ \wedge$

3:      $t_1 \in town(r_1) \ \wedge \ t_2 \in town(r_2)$

4:      *then return* $SubjectAssignmentConflict$

5:  *if* $t_1 \in dme(t_x)$ *then* (

6:      *if* $\nexists s_1, s_x \in S, r_1, r_x \in R \mid s_1 \neq s_x \ \wedge \ r_1 \in rown(s_1) \ \wedge$

7:          $r_x \in rown(s_x) \ \wedge \ t_1 \in town(r_1) \ \wedge \ t_x \in town(r_x)$

8:          *then return* $TransitiveDMEConflict$ )

9:  *if* $t_2 \in dme(t_x)$ *then* (

10:     *if* $\nexists s_2, s_x \in S, r_2, r_x \in R \mid s_2 \neq s_x \ \wedge \ r_2 \in rown(s_2) \ \wedge$

11:         $r_x \in rown(s_x) \ \wedge \ t_2 \in town(r_2) \ \wedge \ t_x \in town(r_x)$

12:         *then return* $TransitiveDMEConflict$ )

13: *return* **true**

**Subject-Assignment Conflict:** Algorithm 1, lines 2-4 check if at least one subject is assigned to a role which owns the subject-bound tasks (see [5,6]). Otherwise, a subject-assignment conflict occurs. In Figure 1a, two subject-bound task types $t_1$ and $t_2$ are assigned to $r_1$, but no subject is assigned to $r_1$ which causes an unsatisfiable SB constraint. Moreover, if subject-bound tasks are assigned to different roles, at least one subject must be assigned to all roles that own the subject-bound tasks. This type of subject-assignment conflict is shown in Figure 1d where two subject-bound task types $t_1$ and $t_2$ are assigned to different roles and different subjects.

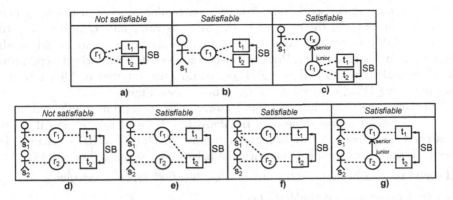

**Fig. 1.** Subject-assignment conflicts affecting the satisfiability of SB constraints

**Resolutions to Subject-Assignment Conflict:** Figures 1b and 1c show two options to resolve a subject-assignment conflict. The SB constraint is satisfiable if at least one subject is authorized to perform both task types. To resolve the satisfiability conflict in Figure 1d the following resolutions are applicable. Firstly, $t_1$ and $t_2$ can be assigned to the same subject $s_1$ by assigning both tasks to $r_1$ (Figure 1e). Secondly, $s_1$ can be assigned to the role $r_2$ which owns $t_2$ (Figure 1f). Alternatively, $r_1$ can be defined as senior role of $r_2$ (Figure 1g). Subsequently, $s_1$ can perform $t_1$ and the inherited task $t_2$.

**Transitive DME-Conflict:** The simultaneous definition of SB and dynamic mutual exclusion (DME) constraints on tasks is not possible as they cannot be satisfied at the same time (see [5,6]). Yet, a DME constraint can be defined on one of the subject-bound tasks and a third task.

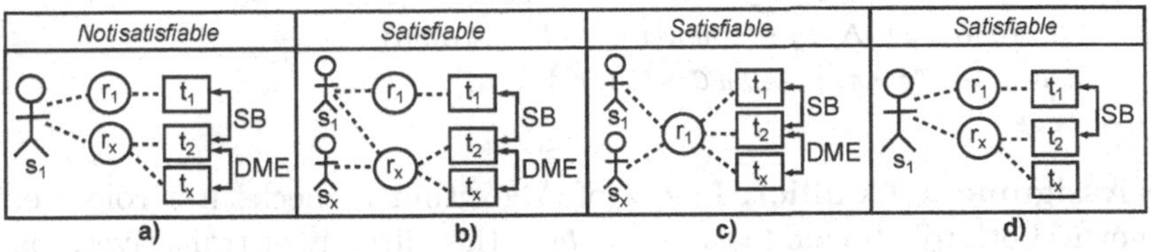

**Fig. 2.** Transitive DME-conflicts affecting the satisfiability of SB constraints

Algorithm 1, lines 5-12 check the satisfiability of a SB constraint on two tasks $t_1$ and $t_2$ if a DME constraint is defined on $t_1$ or $t_2$ and some other task type $t_x$. This configuration is not satisfiable if only a single subject $s_1$ is authorized to perform these tasks (see Figure 2a). Due to the DME constraint, instances of $t_2$ and $t_x$ cannot be performed by the same subject in the same process instance. Therefore, we need at least two subjects to perform the three tasks. Consequently, either the SB or the DME constraint is not satisfiable in Figure 2a.

**Resolutions to Transitive DME-Conflict:** Figure 2 illustrates three options to resolve this satisfiability conflict. Firstly, another subject $s_x$ can be assigned to the role owning $t_x$ (see Figure 2b). In a particular process instance, $s_1$ can perform $t_1$ and $t_2$ and thereby satisfy the SB constraint and $s_x$ performs $t_x$ to satisfy the DME constraint. A similar resolution is shown in Figure 2c, where all three tasks are assigned to $r_1$. However, as two subjects are authorized to perform the three tasks, the SB and the DME constraints are satisfiable. Alternatively, the conflicting DME constraint can be removed (see Figure 2d).

To ensure the satisfiability of a *role-binding (RB)* constraint, role-bound tasks must be assigned to the same role. In Algorithm 2, line 1 first checks if a RB constraint is defined on two task types $t_1$ and $t_2$. Only if a RB constraint is specified, the algorithm proceeds with the subsequent satisfiability checks.

**Algorithm 2.** *Check if a RB constraint on two task types is satisfiable.*

Name: $isRBConstraintSatisfiable(t_1, t_2)$
Input: $t_1, t_2 \in T_T$
1: if $t_1 \notin rb(t_2)$ then return true
2: if $\nexists r \in R \mid t_1 \in town(r) \ \wedge \ t_2 \in town(r)$
3:     then return $RoleAssignmentConflict$
4: if $\nexists s \in S, r \in R \mid r \in rown(s) \ \wedge \ t_1 \in town(r) \ \wedge \ t_2 \in town(r)$
5:     then return $SubjectAssignmentConflict$
6: if $t_1 \in dme(t_2)$ then (
7:     if $\nexists s_1, s_2 \in S, r \in R \mid s_1 \neq s_2 \ \wedge \ r \in rown(s_1) \ \wedge$
8:       $r \in rown(s_2) \ \wedge \ t_1 \in town(r) \ \wedge \ t_2 \in town(r)$
9:         then return $DirectDMEConflict$ )
10: if $t_1 \in dme(t_x)$ then (
11:     if $\nexists s_1, s_x \in S, r \in R \mid s_1 \neq s_x \ \wedge \ r \in rown(s_1) \ \wedge$
12:       $r \in rown(s_x) \ \wedge \ t_1 \in town(r) \ \wedge \ t_x \in town(r)$
13:         then return $TransitiveDMEConflict$ )
14: if $t_2 \in dme(t_x)$ then (
15:     if $\nexists s_2, s_x \in S, r \in R \mid s_2 \neq s_x \ \wedge \ r \in rown(s_2) \ \wedge$
16:       $r \in rown(s_x) \ \wedge \ t_2 \in town(r) \ \wedge \ t_x \in town(r)$
17:         then return $TransitiveDMEConflict$ )
18: return true

**Role-Assignment Conflict:** Line 2 of Algorithm 2 checks if a role $r$ exists which owns both role-bound tasks $t_1$ and $t_2$, either directly or transitively via the role-hierarchy. Otherwise, Algorithm 2, line 3 returns a role-assignment conflict. Figure 3a shows an example where the current task-to-role assignments defined for $t_1$ and $t_2$ result in an unsatisfiable RB constraint.

**Resolutions to Role-Assignment Conflict:** Figure 3 illustrates two options to resolve a role-assignment conflict. Firstly, both tasks can be assigned to the same role (see Figure 3b). Secondly, $t_1$ and $t_2$ can be assigned to two roles where one of the roles, e.g., $r_1$ is a senior role of the second role, e.g., $r_2$ (see Figure 3c). As a result, members of $r_1$ can perform $t_1$ and the inherited task $t_2$.

**Subject-Assignment Conflict:** Algorithm 2, line 4 checks if there is at least one subject assigned to a role owning two role-bound tasks. Otherwise, Algorithm 2, line 5 returns a subject-assignment conflict.

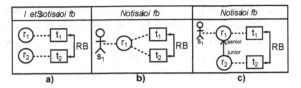

**Fig. 3.** Role-assignment conflict affecting the satisfiability of RB constraints

**Resolutions to Subject-Assignment Conflict:** The RB constraint in Figure 3b is satisfiable if at least one subject is assigned to $r_1$. Alternatively, each subject owning a senior-role of $r_1$ can perform $t_1$ and $t_2$ (see Figure 3c).

**Direct DME-Conflict:** A DME constraint can be defined on role-bound tasks or on one of the role-bound tasks and a third task. Figures 4a and 4d show corresponding example configurations. Usually, DME constraints and RB constraints do not conflict (see [5,6]). However, in case only a single subject is assigned to a role owning role-bound and DME tasks, either the DME or the RB constraint cannot be satisfied.

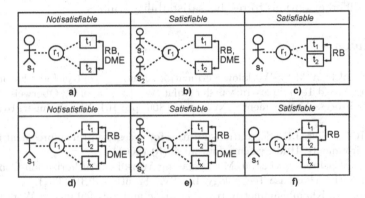

**Fig. 4.** DME-conflicts affecting the satisfiability of RB constraints

Algorithm 2, lines 6-9 check the satisfiability of a RB constraint on two task types $t_1$ and $t_2$ if a DME constraint is defined on $t_1$ and $t_2$ at the same time. This configuration is shown in Figure 4a. In order to fulfill both constraints, at least two subjects need to be assigned to $r_1$.

**Resolutions to Direct DME-Conflict:** Figure 4 shows two options for resolving this conflict. A second subject $s_2$ can be assigned to $r_1$ (see Figure 4b). Then, each of the two subjects can perform one of the two role-bound and DME tasks. Thus, the RB as well as the DME constraint are satisfiable, because $t_1$ and $t_2$ can be performed by two different subjects. Alternatively, the RB constraint is satisfiable if the conflicting DME constraint is removed (see Figure 4c).

**Transitive DME-Conflict:** Algorithm 2, lines 10-17 check the satisfiability of a RB constraint on two task types $t_1$ and $t_2$ if a DME constraint is defined on either

$t_1$ or $t_2$ and some other task type $t_x$. This configuration is shown in Figure 4d. Due to the DME constraint, instances of $t_2$ and $t_x$ cannot be performed by a single individual in the same process instance (see [5,6]). Thus, we need at least two subjects to execute instances of these three tasks. Consequently, either the RB or the DME constraint is not satisfiable if only a single subject $s_1$ is assigned to $r_1$.

**Resolutions to Transitive DME-Conflict:** Figure 4 illustrates two options to resolve this satisfiability conflict. Firstly, a second subject $s_x$ can be assigned to $r_1$ (see Figure 4e). Alternatively, the RB constraint is satisfiable if the conflicting DME constraint is removed (see Figure 4f).

# 3    Conclusion

Satisfiability of a workflow guarantees that there is always a set of authorized subjects that allows a process to proceed. In this paper, we addressed satisfiability aspects of workflows that include subject-binding and/or role-binding constraints in a process-related RBAC context. For this purpose, we provided algorithms to check if a given binding constraint is satisfiable. In addition, we discussed different options to resolve satisfiability conflicts.

# References

1. van der Aalst, W.M.P.: Workflow Verification: Finding Control-Flow Errors Using Petri-Net-Based Techniques. In: van der Aalst, W.M.P., Desel, J., Oberweis, A. (eds.) Business Process Management. LNCS, vol. 1806, pp. 161–183. Springer, Heidelberg (2000)
2. Botha, R.A., Eloff, J.H.: Separation of duties for access control enforcement in workflow environments. IBM Systems Journal 40(3) (2001)
3. Casati, F., Castano, S., Fugini, M.: Managing Workflow Authorization Constraints through Active Database Technology. Inf. Sys. Frontiers 3(3) (2001)
4. Crampton, J., Khambhammettu, H.: Delegation and Satisfiability in Workflow Systems. In: Proceedings of ACM SACMAT (2008)
5. Strembeck, M., Mendling, J.: Generic Algorithms for Consistency Checking of Mutual-Exclusion and Binding Constraints in a Business Process Context. In: Meersman, R., Dillon, T.S., Herrero, P. (eds.) OTM 2010. LNCS, vol. 6426, pp. 204–221. Springer, Heidelberg (2010)
6. Strembeck, M., Mendling, J.: Modeling Process-related RBAC Models with Extended UML Activity Models. Inf. Software Techn. 53(5) (2011)
7. Tan, K., Crampton, J., Gunter, C.A.: The Consistency of Task-Based Authorization Constraints in Workflow Systems. In: Proceedings of the 17th IEEE Workshop on Computer Security Foundations (June 2004)
8. Wainer, J., Barthelmess, P., Kumar, A.: W-RBAC - A Workflow Security Model Incorporating Controlled Overriding of Constraints. International Journal of Cooperative Information Systems 12(4) (2003)
9. Warner, J., Atluri, V.: Inter-instance authorization constraints for secure workflow management. In: Proc. of ACM SACMAT (2006)

# Time-Based Trace Clustering
# for Evolution-Aware Security Audits

Thomas Stocker

Albert-Ludwigs-Universität Freiburg, Germany
stocker@iig.uni-freiburg.de

**Abstract.** This paper proposes a novel trace clustering approach for workflow mining to allow for security audits that regard the evolution of process models along time. Specifically, the trace-clustering method allows auditors to distinguish between different "active" process variants within a timeframe, thereby allowing the visualization of the process evolution. Separately analyzing subsequent process variants allows auditors to localize time-frames and corresponding models for identified vulnerabilities and thus more sophisticated security audits.

## 1 Introduction

The deployment of configurable workflows "as-a-service" [1] that may evolve along time [20] allows enterprises to work more efficient and react more flexibly on changing requirements, such as customer demands or changes in the technological, business or legal context. Although workflows are extensively employed in mission-critical activities demanding strong security and privacy guarantees [4], there is today a lack of audit methods to assert their compliance with security properties [13]. Computer assisted auditing techniques (CAAT) are missing that cope with the *security analysis* of *evolving* workflows [15]. As a consequence, a significant number of exploited process vulnerabilities and data leaks [12] goes undetected.

Workflow mining as a method for extracting a process from a set of executions [16] can help auditors to reconstruct process usage and behavior. Traditionally, workflow mining extracts a single, representative model that consolidates all the different executions happening in the log file. Trace clustering techniques have been proposed as a preprocessing step for workflow mining [8,9,14]. They group traces according to different characteristics and, subsequently, apply workflow mining to a particular set of clusters. Current clustering approaches group traces according to their structural similarity, thereby neglecting the time aspect; they fail to mine the process' "history" (i.e. *evolution provenance*) of business processes, identifying time points of process changes.

Tackling this shortcoming, this paper proposes an approach for time-based log clustering that is able to consider the evolution of process tenancies within a specified timeframe. The idea is to cluster traces according to the time point where a workflow tenancy is first run. In doing so, a chronological ordering of

F. Daniel et al. (Eds.): BPM 2011 Workshops, Part II, LNBIP 100, pp. 471–476, 2012.

workflow tenancies is obtained. Conducting security audits separately for every tenancy allows an auditor to localize identified vulnerabilities more precisely and to detect correlations to the modifications that have been made on the original workflow.

Structure: Section 2 reviews the related work. Section 3.2 presents the initial proposal of the time-based trace clustering technique and Section 4 reports on ongoing work.

## 2 Related Work

Trace clustering approaches either iteratively check the appropriateness of mined models to decide on further clustering [9,18,19] or focus on trace similarity which is mostly measured by distances of feature vectors (i.e. the number of activities of a trace) [5,14]. Obtained models reflect different process characteristics but are loosely coupled with each other, hence failing to show the change of process models along time.

Recent mining approaches consider change in workflows [10]. In [11] Lakshmanan et al. utilize spectral graph analysis to compute the difference of cluster-graphs to identify changes. However by using fixed cluster sizes, this approach is rather imprecise. Workflow dynamics in the sense of context changes can be characterized as *concept drift*, which is a well-studied paradigm in the data mining area. Bose et al. [6] provide methods to handle concept drift in process mining by showing that workflow changes are indirectly reflected in workflow logs and change point detection is feasible by examining activity relations.

In contrast to [6], this approach does not consider ordering relations (follows/precedes) but variations on the distance of activity pairs within a trace (the number of intermediate activities) as structural property. Sequentially processing traces according to time, traces whose structure differs from the typical trace structure so far are treated as indicators for new clusters. Proceeding this way ensures that a log file is partitioned into chronologically subsequent clusters, whose sizes depend on the frequency of changes in process structure. However, change operations that caused a new model (set of add/remove operations) are not identified. The main focus of the paper is on the identification of time points of permanent process changes.

## 3 Time-Based Clustering Method

In order to detect workflow adjustments, expected workflow behavior is determined on the basis of trace structure. Model adjustments are defined as operations that change the way a process can be executed in the sense of adding or removing transitions and/or activities. Structural changes influence the relation of workflow activities and affect the structure of log traces, specifically the distance between activities.

The clustering approach consists of two steps. In the first step, distances of activity pairs are extracted for every log-trace. The second step partitions a given log into clusters of subsequent traces having a similar structure. Identified clusters can then serve as input for arbitrary mining algorithms to construct process models for further analysis (e.g., information flow analysis using the InDico-approach [2]).

## 3.1 Workflow Logs and Activity Distances

A basic assumption is that log entries have a timestamp and are chronologically ordered. Fig. 1 shows a workflow net with a corresponding log-file. Including the dashed edges leads to another version of this workflow with the two additional activities E and F. Traces related to the new workflow structure appear in the log below the dashed line. Equally named activities or loops in process models can cause activity names to occur several times within the same trace. At this point these possibilities are neglected and pairwise inequality of trace activity names is assumed.x

The distance between any two workflow activities within a trace is defined as the number of intermediate activities. Considering the first trace of the log in Fig. 1, the distance between A and D is 2. If two activities are aligned in a sequence within a workflow their distance remains constant over time and ranges in fixed boundaries conditioned by a minimum and maximum distance in any other case.

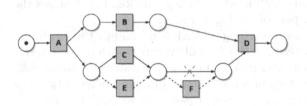

| Trace | Activities |
|-------|------------|
| 1 | A B C D |
| 2 | A C B D |
| 3 | A C B D |
| 4 | A B C D |
| 5 | A B C F D |
| 6 | A E F B D |
| 7 | A B E F D |

Fig. 1. Workflow net and corresponding log

Workflow adjustments cause interval variations for activity-pair distances. Considering the workflow change in Fig. 1, the distance interval of $(B, D)$ extended from $[0, 1]$ to $[0, 2]$. Depending on the number and position of inserted or removed workflow activities and links between them, distance intervals are enlarged, reduced or moved (same value range, but different starting point, i.e. $[1, 3] \rightarrow [2, 4]$).

## 3.2 Clustering Log Traces

The distance matrix stores the distances of activity-pairs extracted from the workflow log. For every pair of subsequent activities this matrix contains the

| Trace | Activities | Distances | | | | | | |
|---|---|---|---|---|---|---|---|---|
| | | (A,B) | (A,C) | (A,D), | (B,C) | (B,D) | (C,B) | (C,D) |
| 1 | A B C D | 0 | 1 | 2 | 0 | 1 | - | 0 |
| 2 | A C B D | 1 | 0 | 2 | - | 0 | 0 | 1 |
| 3 | A C B D | 1 | 0 | 2 | - | 0 | 0 | 1 |
| 4 | A B C D | 0 | 1 | 2 | 0 | 1 | - | 0 |
| | intervals | [0;1] | [0;1] | 2 | 0 | 1 | 0 | [0;1] |

**Fig. 2.** Distance matrix for the upper part of the log in Fig. 1

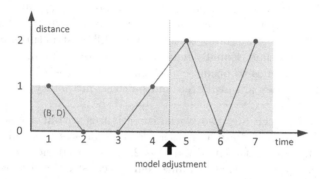

**Fig. 3.** Distance graph of the activity pair (B,D)

distance between these activities within every trace of the log. Fig. 2 shows the distance matrix for the upper part of the log in Fig. 1.

Sequentially processing traces according to their timestamp, the clustering algorithm uses samples to determine the typical workflow behavior in terms of boundaries for the minimum and maximum observed value of activity-pair distances. Such a behavior is determined on the basis of a parameter $w$ (window size) that defines the minimum number of traces used as "training" data (sample size) and the minimum number of traces grouped as a cluster.

Considering a cluster that holds all traces accumulated so far, for every activity-pair of the next trace two cases have to be distinguished. Either their actual distance *outruns* their typical distance interval within the sample or it *remains inside* the typical interval. While the first case definitely introduces a new cluster, as old boundaries do not hold anymore, in the second case further checks must determine if the actual trace is a candidate of a new cluster or not. If it belongs to a new cluster with a smaller distance interval, the next $w$ distances reflect these new boundaries. The algorithm uses a $w$-size lookahead to check this property. As long as the activity-pair distances of observed traces do not introduce new distance intervals, they are put in the same cluster. Once a new interval is detected, the typical behavior is calculated again by choosing a new sample on the basis of the next $w$ traces.

This approach allows the identification of modifications and the time point from which they hold, thereby allowing time-based clustering. Fig. 3 shows the distance progress for the activity pair $(B, D)$ of the workflow in Fig. 1. Within the first four traces the distance remains inside the interval $[0, 1]$, but with trace 5 this interval is enlarged to $[0, 2]$. With a windows size of 4, the algorithm would recognize this event as a change in the process structure.

## 4 Summary

This paper proposed a novel trace-clustering approach that allows for the reconstruction of the process history, so that auditors can also appreciate the different ways in which a process evolves over time. This information can be used to find interesting and/or critical starting points for analysis (security relevant process variants, e.g. those appearing as exceptions or models with low incidence) and to localize identified vulnerabilities.

A key aspect of the proposed trace clustering method is the window size parameter $w$ to determine its precision in detecting changes on the process structure. In general, the larger the window, the coarse the obtained models; vice-versa, the smaller $w$ is, the richer the detection of tenancies. Current work investigates ways to determine an adequate window size that does not depend on the characteristics of a particular log.

## References

1. Accorsi, R.: Business process as a service: Chances for remote auditing. In: IEEE Computer Software and Applications Conference (to appear, 2011)
2. Accorsi, R., Wonnemann, C.: Strong non-leak guarantees for workflow models. In: ACM Symposium on Applied Computing (SAC), pp. 308–314 (2011)
3. Adam, N., Atluri, V., Huang, W.: Modeling and analysis of workflows using petri nets. Journal of Intelligent Information Systems 10(2), 131–158 (1998)
4. Atluri, V., Warner, J.: Security for workflow systems. In: Handbook of Database Security, pp. 213–230. Springer, Heidelberg (2008)
5. Jagadeesh Chandra Bose, R.P., van der Aalst, W.: Trace Alignment in Process Mining: Opportunities for Process Diagnostics. In: Hull, R., Mendling, J., Tai, S. (eds.) BPM 2010. LNCS, vol. 6336, pp. 227–242. Springer, Heidelberg (2010)
6. Jagadeesh Chandra Bose, R.P., van der Aalst, W.M.P., Žliobaitė, I., Pechenizkiy, M.: Handling Concept Drift in Process Mining. In: Mouratidis, H., Rolland, C. (eds.) CAiSE 2011. LNCS, vol. 6741, pp. 391–405. Springer, Heidelberg (2011)
7. Cummins, F.: BPM meets SOA. In: Handbook on Business Process Management 1, pp. 461–479 (2010)
8. de Medeiros, A.K.A., Guzzo, A., Greco, G., van der Aalst, W.M.P., Weijters, A.J.M.M., van Dongen, B.F., Saccà, D.: Process Mining Based on Clustering: A Quest for Precision. In: ter Hofstede, A.H.M., Benatallah, B., Paik, H.-Y. (eds.) BPM Workshops 2007. LNCS, vol. 4928, pp. 17–29. Springer, Heidelberg (2008)
9. Greco, G., Guzzo, A., Pontieri, L., Saccà, D.: Discovering expressive process models by clustering log traces. IEEE Transactions on Knowledge and Data Engineering 18(8), 1010–1027 (2006)
10. Günther, C., Rinderle-Ma, S., Reichert, M., van der Aalst, W.M.P., Recker, J.: Using process mining to learn from process changes in evolutionary systems. Business Process Integration and Management 1, 111 (2007)

11. Lakshmanan, G., Keyser, P., Duan, S.: Detecting changes in a semi-structured business process through spectral graph analysis. In: IEEE Conference of Data Engineering Workshops, pp. 255–260 (2011)
12. Lowis, L., Accorsi, R.: Finding vulnerabilities in SOA-based business processes. IEEE Transactions on Service Computing (to appear, 2011)
13. Sayana, A.: Using CAATs to support IS audit. Information Systems Control Journal (2003)
14. Song, M., Günther, C.W., van der Aalst, W.M.P.: Trace Clustering in Process Mining. In: Ardagna, D., Mecella, M., Yang, J. (eds.) BPM 2008 Workshops. LNBIP, vol. 17, pp. 109–120. Springer, Heidelberg (2009)
15. Teeter, R., Alles, M., Vasarhelyi, M.: Remote Audit: A research framework. Journal of Emerging Technology in Accounting (to appear)
16. van der Aalst, W.M.P., Weijters, T., Maruster, L.: Workflow mining: Discovering process models from event logs. IEEE Trans. Knowl. Data Eng. 16(9), 1128–1142 (2004)
17. van der Aalst, W.M.P., ter Hofstede, A.H.M., Weske, M.: Business Process Management: A Survey. In: van der Aalst, W.M.P., ter Hofstede, A.H.M., Weske, M. (eds.) BPM 2003. LNCS, vol. 2678, pp. 1–12. Springer, Heidelberg (2003)
18. van Dongen, B.F., van der Aalst, W.M.P.: Multi-phase process mining: Aggregating instance graphs into EPCs and Petri nets. In: PNCWB Workshop, pp. 35–58 (2005)
19. van Dongen, B.F., van der Aalst, W.M.P.: Multi-phase Process Mining: Building Instance Graphs. In: Atzeni, P., Chu, W., Lu, H., Zhou, S., Ling, T.-W. (eds.) ER 2004. LNCS, vol. 3288, pp. 362–376. Springer, Heidelberg (2004)
20. Wei, Y., Blake, M.B.: Service-oriented computing and cloud computing: Challenges and opportunities. IEEE Internet Computing 14, 72–75 (2010)

# Author Index